REFORMATION THEOLOGY

REFORMATION THEOLOGY
A READER OF PRIMARY SOURCES
WITH INTRODUCTIONS

Edited by Bradford Littlejohn with Jonathan Roberts

ISBN-10: 0692970606

ISBN-13: 978-0692970607

Front cover image taken from Hermann Wislicenus, *Luther vor Karl V. auf dem Reichstag zu Worms 1521* (1880; Imperial Palace of Goslar)

Cover design by Rachel Rosales, Orange Peal Design

Dedicated to the memory of the 16th-century martyrs who gave their lives for truth and the glory of God

TABLE OF CONTENTS

GENERAL INTRODUCTION

A Story Worth Retelling

AS THIS book goes to press, the crescendo of Reformation 500 commemorations throughout the Western world is reaching its highest pitch, with innumerable conferences, publications, symposia, blog series, festivals, and more. Protestants are by and large celebrating, while Catholics are mostly trying to remind us how much damage the Reformation did and ecumenists are somberly nodding their heads in agreement. Ordinary educated folks, however, might be forgiven for getting a bit sick of it all. Was the Reformation really quite that big of a deal? We live in a society in which hype is the *lingua franca* of public communication, and cynics might ask whether Reformation 500 is just another instance of it.

And yet, when all the dust of anniversary commemorations settles, the fact will remain that few episodes in Western history have so shaped our world as the Protestant Reformation and the counter-Reformations which accompanied it. From a purely secular standpoint, the political and cultural ramifications were incalculable. Before the Reformation, however many squabbles there may have been between king and pope, society in western Europe was a seamless garment, Christendom, in which every power and authority, and every duty and loyalty could at least theoretically be coordinated in relation to the pole provided by the Church's teaching. After the Reformation, this garment was torn first in two, as the laity and civil authority claimed their own status independent from the clergy and papal authority, and then into more and more pieces as nations and confessions defined themselves against one another.

The tearing garment metaphor, however, has a rather negative ring to it; more positively, we might characterize the Reformation as a firestorm tearing through an old, stagnant, and dying forest, sowing the seeds for a burst of new and newly diverse life, or as an unchaining, which set the various strata of society and faculties of humanity free to develop under their own power, instead of laboring in obedience to an oppressive hierarchy. It is difficult to deny that the Reformation helped set in motion political reforms, cultural and artistic revitalizations, economic developments, and spiritual renewals that profoundly enriched the life of western Europe and indeed through it the whole world. Even those most inclined to lament the divisions in the church and the putative disenchantment and desacralization of the cosmos initiated by Luther's reforms would hardly wish to return to the superstition, heteronomy, and corruption of the late Middle Ages from which the Reformation announced a deliverance.

Of course, when framing such large narratives, we can hardly claim that it all started in 1517. Many of the trends which burst forth in the Reformation were already well underway from as much as two centuries earlier, as the texts in this book attest, and the religious reforms initiated by Luther took place alongside political and educational reforms, some of which may have happened, or were already happening, anyway. It would be impossible—even if it were desirable—to try to disentangle the various contributions of the Protestant Reformation and Renaissance humanism, so thoroughly were the two phenomena intertwined in nearly every part of Europe that the Reformation touched.

Given the immense range of cultural, political, and educational—not to mention socio-economic—factors contributing to the Reformation, it may seem transgressively old-fashioned to compile a book consisting strictly of theological texts. The nearest equivalent to this volume currently on the market, *A Reformation*

Reader, edited by Denis Janz,[1] does contain numerous small excerpts from theological writings, but fills its pages largely with letters, narratives, and Reformation-era writings on topics as diverse as "The Status of Women" and "Eating, Sleeping, and Dying." There is no doubt that, for understanding the full lived experience and motivations of the Reformation's myriad actors, such broad reading is essential. Indeed, the fact that our reader takes a different tack is not so much a dismissal of the approach taken by Janz, but rather a recognition that there is no need to reinvent that particular wheel. However, there *is* still a need in our 21st-century context, which has replaced ideas with identity or economics, to return to the importance of theology, of doctrines taught, confessed, and bled and died for, as the beating heart of the Reformation.

Even for secular readers for whom *all* these doctrines are frivolous myths and superstitions, the fact remains that for the men and women at the time, they were matters of truth or falsehood, life or death, heaven or hell. To understand why the Reformation unfolded as it did, we must understand the ideas that were so forcefully articulated, opposed, and debated by Protestants and Catholics. For Protestant or Catholic believers in this forgetful age, the need to understand these disputed doctrines is all the more imperative. And since ideas do not exist in isolation from one another, but have a logic and coherence that links them together, we can and indeed must identify the ideas that were central and foundational, the core principles which, once articulated or challenged, had downstream consequences in the alteration of many other doctrines and religious practices. That is what this volume seeks to offer.

This does not mean, of course, that we should stick to some notion of purely theological concepts like the five *solas* of the Reformation and leave aside all ideas of a practical and political character. On the contrary, the central theological ideas of the

---

[1] Denis R. Janz, ed., *A Reformation Reader: Primary Texts with Introductions* (Minneapolis: Fortress, 2008).

Reformation were irreducibly ecclesiological and thus, given the seamless garment of late medieval society, irreducibly political. We have sought to highlight this fact with the selection of texts in this book, particularly in the lead-up to the Reformation. The relative authority of king and pope, and the nature of the church as either a clerocracy or a community of the faithful, were issues just as central to the Reformation as Luther's discovery of salvation by faith alone—indeed, the latter doctrine would have been incoherent had it not been accompanied with a profound rethinking of the nature of the church.

Principles of Selection

The need to produce a Reader of some manageable size and yet to offer a reasonably comprehensive overview of what the Reformation was all about posed some daunting challenges when it came to selecting appropriate texts. Our first principle was to eschew the approach of Janz (who includes no less than 122 texts, averaging just a couple of pages each) and include excerpts long enough to give the reader a good grasp of the larger argument and issues at stake. We aimed to make nearly every excerpt long enough to spend some time wrestling with, but short enough to read in a sitting. This principle determined the number of texts we could include as being roughly thirty. So, which thirty texts?

Our next principle was to be sure to offer both sides of the argument, Protestant and Catholic. We make no claims to false objectivity; this edition has been prepared by Protestants chiefly for the education and edification of Protestants, although we hope that Catholics and non-religious readers may profit richly from it as well. The majority of texts selected come from the pens of Protestant writers, but pre-Reformation reforming Catholics and fierce opponents of the Reformation are represented as well. In particular, we thought it essential to include the chief formal repudiations of the Reformation by the Roman Church—Leo X's bull of excommunication, and key sessions of the Council of Trent—as well as critiques penned by Rome's most capable 16th-century polemicists: Thomas Cajetan, Thomas More, and Robert Bellarmine. We also thought it essential to include an example of the Counter-Reformation spirituality that proved so successful in winning many souls back to the obedience of Rome—Ignatius of Loyola's *Spiritual Exercises*.

Our third principle was to be sure to present the Reformation not as some bolt from the blue, but as the culmination of late medieval conflicts and reforming efforts. These took many different forms, from largely political conflicts (though with massive ecclesiological implications) between prince and pope, to scholastic debates over transubstantiation, to humanist critiques of the moral corruption of the church and the papacy. It seemed appropriate to reach more than two centuries back to the high-water mark of papal arrogance, the pontificate of Benedict VIII, and the first rumblings of dissent that his claims provoked. Marsilius of Padua's radical ecclesiological ideas were an obvious forerunner of the Reformation, as were the controversial reforming efforts of Wycliffe in Oxford and Hus in Prague. Finally, Erasmus's scathing satire *Julius Exclusus* offers a clear picture of why, by 1517, so many were ready to hear Luther's assault on the corruption of the papacy.

Our fourth principle was to be sure to present selections from all those Protestant Reformers recognized at the time as the most brilliant and influential, or at least as many of them as possible. Accordingly, Martin Luther and Philipp Melanchthon, the chief architects of the Lutheran tradition, John Calvin, Heinrich Bullinger, and Peter Martyr Vermigli, the leading spokesmen for continental Reformed theology, and Thomas Cranmer and Richard Hooker, the chief theologians of the early Church of England, are all featured here. Unfortunately omitted for the sake of space (given the necessity of particularly spotlighting the crucial works of Luther) are Ulrich Zwingli and Martin Bucer, who played crucial roles in beginning the reformations at Zurich and Strasbourg, respectively.

Fifth, although our chief purpose was to present the theology of the magisterial Reformation, we wanted to also give at least some indication of the internal conflicts generated by the Protestant movement, in the emergence of radical movements like those of the Anabaptists in Switzerland and the Puritans in England. Both movements combined an extreme form of the Protestant commitment to *sola Scriptura* with a powerful zeal to purge the church of lukewarm believers and remaining papal corruptions. For the Anabaptist *Schleitheim Confession*, this meant a stark separation of church from world and political authority. For the Puritan *Admonition to Parliament*, it meant a stark contrast between pure church and corrupt church and a demand that political authorities complete the unfinished business of reformation.

Sixth, although wanting to center readers' attention on the crucial events and texts of the early decades of the Reformation, we did not want to give the impression that the Reformation was somehow finished by the time its leading architects died in the 1540s-1560s. On the contrary, many historians have seen the Reformation (or the Reformations, plural) as an ongoing process that continued at least until the Peace of Westphalia in 1648, or perhaps beyond. We have not sought to extend our reader that far, but we have attempted to give some sense of the continuing refinement of Protestant theology in the course of conflict against internal dissent and external critiques from the 1570s up through the crucial Synod of Dordt in 1618.

Seventh and finally, given the need to include such a wide range of texts, we faced the challenge of how to maintain at least some coherence and sense of common threads through the volume. Accordingly, we abandoned any pretensions toward providing examples of the full array of theological and liturgical debates that proliferated in the Reformation period. Luther's original narrow protest against indulgences soon opened up into a broad theological war fought on many fronts, with individual salvation, the sacraments, the authority of church ministers, the role of political authority, the authority and interpretation of Scripture, the role of

Mary and the saints, the value of church festivals and ceremonies, the role of philosophy in theology, and much more becoming sharply contested terrain. In an effort to render this Reader manageable, we have deliberately chosen to highlight only certain doctrinal flashpoints, those which we believe to have stood near the very heart of Reformation conflicts. Chief among these are the doctrine of the church, and its relation to the state (highlighted in the readings from Boniface, Marsilius, Hus, the Council of Constance, Luther's *Letter to the German Nobility*, the Schleitheim Articles, Bullinger, and Chemnitz), the doctrine of the Eucharist, and transubstantiation in particular (highlighted in the readings from Wycliffe, Luther's *Babylonian Captivity,* Cajetan, the Council of Trent's 13th Session, Vermigli, and the Book of Common Prayer), the doctrine of justification *sola fide* and related issues (highlighted in Luther's *Freedom of a Christian*, Melanchthon, the Council of Trent's 6th Session, Ignatius of Loyola, Ursinus, and the Canons of Dordt), and the meaning of the Protestant commitment to *sola Scriptura* (highlighted in the readings from More, the *Admonition to Parliament*, Hooker, Bellarmine, and Whitaker). Indeed, the only readings that do not neatly fit with these four themes amply justify their inclusion on other grounds: Erasmus's *Julius Exclusus* highlights the moral corruption of the Renaissance Papacy, the *Ninety-Five Theses* and the bull *Exsurge Domine* focus attention on the controversy over indulgences that originally kicked off the Reformation, the excerpt from Calvin's *Institutes* spotlights an oftneglected and misrepresented aspect of Protestant theology, showing that neither total depravity nor *sola Scriptura* were meant to deny the reality of God's self-revelation through nature, and the excerpt from *Foxe's Book of Martyrs* reminds us of the high drama and life-or-death stakes of the Reformation for many of its leading actors.

Editorial Objectives

So much for our principles of selection with these texts. Beyond choosing the most appropriate and accessible excerpts, we have tried to keep our editorial intrusion as minimal as possible. In his memorable essay, "On Reading Old Books," C.S. Lewis remarks that:

> The student is half afraid to meet one of the great philosophers face to face. He feels himself inadequate and thinks he will not understand him. But if he only knew, the great man, just because of his greatness, is much more intelligible than his modern commentator. The simplest student will be able to understand, if not all, yet a very great deal of what Plato said; but hardly anyone can understand some modern books on Platonism. It has always therefore been one of my main endeavours as a teacher to persuade the young that firsthand knowledge is not only more worth acquiring than secondhand knowledge, but is usually much easier and more delightful to acquire.[2]

The same goes, we are convinced, for the great Reformers. There are, to be sure, plenty of arcane debates, abstruse distinctions, and tedious polemics to be found in the vast outpouring of theological literature in the 16th century. However, the chief points of debate are by no means as difficult to understand as most imagine, and they speak to perennial questions of church organization and religious experience that are still very much with us today. Accordingly, in this edition of our Reformation Reader, aimed chiefly at an undergraduate (or equivalent) audience, we have sought to allow the voices from the past to speak, as much as possible, without interruption or unnecessary interpretation. There will be, to be sure, citations and allusions that are lost on the modern reader, or difficult theological terms or contextual clues that escape his understanding, but in none of these texts, we believe, are these so widespread or crucial as to significantly impair understanding. We have thus adopted a policy of largely refraining from adding anno-

---

[2] C.S. Lewis, "On the Reading of Old Books," in *God in the Dock* (Grand Rapids: Eerdmans, 1970), 200.

tations in most cases, with two chief exceptions: first, we have filled in and filled out Scripture references where they were lacking; second, chiefly in the early English texts, we have supplied glosses of unfamiliar terms in the footnotes (in the format: [2] *hap:* chance or fortune). Besides these and the initial footnote at the beginning of each selection specifying the source, other annotations, whether in footnotes or in brackets, are taken over from our source editions unless specified otherwise, and are generally pretty minimal.

Once the reader embarks on his journey through any one of these primary sources, we wanted him to be distracted as little as possible, grappling instead face-to-face with the thoughts of the great minds of the past. The main thing the contemporary reader needs, we are convinced, is simple historical contextualization, a broad narrative tapestry on which to see the particular men, moments, and conflicts that gave rise to these texts. It is this that the introductions to each text chiefly aim to supply. Indeed, though these introductions are certainly no substitute for a good Reformation history,[3] alongside which this volume should ideally be read, we have sought to construct these introductions in such a way that, strung together, they do provide at least something of a coherent story of the Reformation. In them you will find brief biographies of the key actors on this tempestuous historical stage, but more importantly, biographies of the concepts and convictions around which they struggled, and which drove them to extraordinary, heroic, and sometimes terrible deeds. At the end of each, you will also find a short list of recommended texts for further reading on the history and the topic.

As you immerse yourself in this story five centuries on, we hope that you will not merely grow in understanding of what drove these men to do the things they did, but that you too will be inspired to extraordinary deeds on behalf of the church of our day, a church desperately in need of fresh reformation.

---

[3] The best, for all its flaws, probably being Diarmaid MacCulloch's *The Reformation: A History* (New York: Penguin, 2005).

ABOUT THIS EDITION

THE STORY behind this particular volume is something of an odd one. My friend Jonathan Roberts, back before he was really my friend and when he was just some guy on the internet who bombarded me with messages about things that the Davenant Institute (then the Davenant Trust) ought to do, sent me an email out of the blue declaring that we needed to put together and publish a Reformation Reader in time for the Reformation 500 anniversary. It sounded like a worthy but exhausting undertaking, and so I dutifully put it on my list of Future Projects to Consider, and over the next year and a half or so put Jonathan off with vague excuses or reassurances (depending on my mood) whenever he mentioned it again.

Then in January of this year, 2017, my friend Daniel Foucachon approached me about editing the fourth volume of the Old Western Culture reader series that his curriculum company, Roman Roads Media, was producing. Entitled *The Reformation*, it was slated to include a selection of key theological writings from the period leading up to and encompassing the Reformation, though as a Great Books reader, it also included extended selections from Chaucer and Spenser. We agreed that I would identify selections and write introductions for his volume if Davenant could subsequently reproduce this material, subtracting the Chaucer and Spenser, and adding a number of additional texts, for the Reformation Reader that Jonathan had so long lobbied.

I worked closely with Daniel and his assistant Andrea Pliego in identifying nineteen texts (twenty-one if you count the two Boniface VIII and Council of Constance excerpts separately) that together provided a good representative survey of the key theological conflicts that led to and played out in the Protestant Reformation. We chopped them down to manageable 10-30 page excerpts (in most cases), and I researched and wrote short historical and thematic introductions for each of them. Subsequently, Jonathan and I undertook to find roughly ten more authors and texts that would fill out the Davenant edition of the reader with more theological breadth, historical depth, and a fuller representation of Catholic opponents of the Reformation particularly. I researched and wrote the introductions for most of the new material, while Jonathan covered his two favorites, Whitaker and Bellarmine. My assistant Brian Marr put in countless and invaluable hours in scanning, formatting, and editing, and somehow or other we have squeezed the thing out just in time for the 500th anniversary, October 31, 2017. Note that there will be a few subtle differences between our edition and the Roman Roads edition even where the content overlaps, as we made a few emendations later in the editorial process.

Given our tight timeline and limited resources, we make no pretensions to have produced the best possible reader of Reformation theology. We limited ourselves to texts already available in English translation, for one thing, which left many true gems of Reformation and counter-Reformation literature off the table. To be sure, most of the most significant works have already been translated, but we do cherish aspirations of a future edition of this textbook that might include a few excerpts never before translated into English. We also recognize that in many cases, existing translations leave much room for improvement. For the present edition, we have accepted them as they are, aside from cleaning up formatting and where necessary silently correcting obvious typographical errors, but again this is something that might be revisited in subsequent editions. Most of the selections we use are taken from older editions now in the public domain, though where there were strong reasons to use a more recent text, we procured the necessary permissions or else kept our excerpts within the bounds of Fair Use standards.

We also recognize that for readers interested in digging deeper, there are some important bells and whistles lacking in the present edition, such as annotations providing citations of sources referenced in the texts. If the present Student Edition be well-received, our aim is to produce within a year or so a Scholars' Edition that includes such additional features.

Given our desire to build on what we have begun here and to make this work as truthful, faithful, and useful as possible, we invite corrections and suggested improvements from all our readers (be they as small as a typo or as large as suggesting a different text selection that might profitably be substituted). If you desire to submit such a suggestion or correction, please email it to secretary@davenantinstitute.org and we will take it under consideration for inclusion in the next revised edition. In the meantime, may this volume be a rich blessing to the church!

Bradford Littlejohn, editor

INTRODUCTION TO BONIFACE VIII'S *CLERICOS LAICOS* AND *UNAM SANCTAM*

THE simultaneously tragic and comic saga of conflicts between princes and popes that dominated the later Middle Ages reached its climax—and its low point—in the ugly high-stakes brawl between Pope Boniface VIII (r. 1294-1303) and King Philip IV of France (r. 1285-1314) from 1296-1303. The episode reflected badly on all parties, and ended ignominiously for Pope Boniface himself, but not before producing an enduring statement of some of the most extreme pretensions of the medieval Catholic Church.

There was, of course, no neat distinction between church and state in the Middle Ages in the modern sense—after all, every member of Western European society was in theory a Christian. But there was a sharp distinction between clergy and laity, and with it, a series of escalating conflicts about just how much power each party had. On the one hand, the Church had succeeded in establishing the clergy as a virtually autonomous state-within-a-state in each of Western Europe's kingdoms: they were immune from taxes, from civil courts, and from many laws, ultimately answerable to the Pope alone. As rising royal powers sought to contest this autonomy (after all, the Church's estates were often fabulously rich, and their tax immunity took a huge bite out of royal revenues), the popes for their part often went even further, claiming not merely sole authority over the clergy, but an indirect authority over lay rulers as well. Christ had given Peter "two swords" (Lk. 22:38) which referred to the sword of spiritual authority *and* that of tem-

1

poral authority. To be sure, the Pope normally delegated the latter to kings and princes, but he could in principle intervene directly in civil affairs or even depose rulers when he saw fit. If he had seen fit only for holy and spiritual reasons, things might not have been so bad, but many popes of this period were as worldly and ambitious as their royal rivals.

Boniface VIII, although apparently sincere in his commitment to the theological principles which undergirded his sometimes extraordinary claims, was not a particularly likable character. Scholar Brian Tierney describes him as "an arrogant, very able ruler, impatient of opposition, given to hot outbursts of rage" and his rival, Philip IV, as "a man of cold ambition." [1] Their particular dispute, though rooted in the long-simmering conflicts described above, emerged out of one of France's regular wars with England. Both parties, desperate to fund their "just war" against one another, resorted to taxing the clergy within their realms, in violation of papal decrees. Although neither party responded particularly well when Boniface tried to bring them to heel, Philip proved more brazenly defiant than his English counterpart, Edward Longshanks.

When Boniface issued the bull *Clericis Laicos* in 1296, threatening Philip and his courtiers with excommunication if they continued to tax the Church, Philip duly forbade the export of any currency from France. Since the Papacy itself had no compunction about levying a heavy tax on French churchmen to finance its own expenditures, Philip had deftly succeeded in driving Boniface to the brink of bankruptcy. Boniface soon capitulated, issuing another bull which, while not retracting *Clericis Laicos* directly, sullenly conceded that if a king deemed there to be a national emergency, he could tax the clergy without consulting the Pope.

Gaining confidence after this easy victory, Philip provoked another round of conflict in 1301 by arresting and trying a French bishop for heresy and blasphemy. Clergy, of course, were only

---

[1] Brian Tierney, *The Crisis of Church and State, 1050–1300* (Toronto: University of Toronto Press, 1988), 172.

supposed to be tried by other clergy, so Boniface summoned his advisors and released another bull, *Ausculta Fili*, which condescendingly reprimanded Philip and reminded him that he was subject to Boniface's authority. Boniface did not say in exactly what sense he meant this, but Philip and his advisors took it as the Pope's claim to be feudal overlord over the kingdom of France. They had little difficulty in rallying most of the nation, including even many French clergy, against the Pope.

In response, Boniface issued the justly famous bull *Unam Sanctam*, which is widely considered the starkest and strongest official statement of papal authority ever produced. In it, Boniface put forth two sets of claims, insisting on a plenitude of power in all spiritual matters and temporal matters alike. Under the former heading, he declared that "it is absolutely necessary for salvation that every human creature be subject to the Roman Pontiff." Under the latter, he confidently asserted the "two swords" theory in which the material sword was administered "by the hands of kings and soldiers, but at the will and sufferance of the priest," so that "temporal authority [is] subjected to spiritual power." None of the arguments that he cobbled together for the purpose were new as such, but nowhere else had they all been brought together in one place for the purpose of making such sweeping claims (nowhere, at least, except in the treatise *On Ecclesiastical Power*, penned a few months earlier by *Unam Sanctam's* ghost-writer, Giles of Rome).

Philip responded by raiding the papal palace, having Boniface beaten by thugs, and then, when he died soon afterward, posthumously condemned in a mock trial convened by a puppet pope, his successor, Clement V (r. 1305-1314). Thus, the full temporal claims of the document were soon rendered a dead letter, but they have never been retracted by the Catholic Church, and the spiritual claims continued to be broadly accepted in the centuries that follow. The document thus remains an eloquent statement of the highly institutional and authoritarian ecclesiology that the Protestant Reformers set out to repair.

Further Reading

For further reading, see Stephen K. Ozment, *The Age of Reform* (New Haven: Yale University Press, 1980), chapter 4; Brian Tierney, *The Crisis of Church and State, 1050–1300* (Toronto: University of Toronto Press, 1988).

BONIFACE VIII,
CLERICOS LAICOS (1296)[1]

BISHOP Boniface, servant of the servants of God, in perpetual memory of this matter. Antiquity teaches us that laymen are in a high degree hostile to the clergy, a fact which is also made clear by the experiences of the present times; in as much as, not content within their own bounds, they strive after what is forbidden and loose the reins in pursuit of what is unlawful. Nor have they the prudence to consider that all jurisdiction is denied to them over the clergy—over both the persons and goods of ecclesiastics. On the prelates of the churches and on ecclesiastical persons, monastic and secular, they impose heavy burdens, tax them and declare levies upon them. They exact and extort from them the half, the tenth or twentieth or some other portion or quota of their revenues or of their goods; and they attempt in many ways to subject them to slavery and reduce them to their goods; and they attempt in many ways to subject them to slavery and reduce them to their sway. And with grief do we mention it, some prelates of the churches and ecclesiastical persons, fearing where they ought not to fear, seeking a transitory peace, dreading more to offend the temporal than the eternal majesty, without obtaining the authority or permission of the Apostolic chair, do acquiesce, not so much rashly as improvidently, in the abuses of such persons. We, therefore, wishing to put

---

[1] From Rymer's *Foedera*, Vol. 1,. Pt. II, ed. A. Clarke and F. Holbrooke (London: G. Eyre and A. Strahan, 1816), 836. Translated in Ernest F. Henderson, *Select Historical Documents of the Middle Ages* (London: George Bell, 1910), 432–34.

a stop to such iniquitous acts, by the counsel of our brothers, of the apostolic authority, have decreed: that whatever prelates, or ecclesiastical persons, monastic or secular, of whatever grade, condition or standing, shall pay, or promise, or agree to pay as levies or talliages to laymen the tenth, twentieth or hundredth part of their own and their churches' revenues or goods—or any other quantity, portion or quota of those same revenues or goods, of their estimated or of their real value—under the name of an aid, loan, subvention, subsidy or gift, or under any other name, manner or clever pretense, without the authority of that same chair [shall incur the sentence of excommunication][2].

Likewise emperors, kings, or princes, dukes, counts or barons, podestas, captains or officials or rectors—by whatever name they are called, whether of cities, castles, or any places whatever, wherever situated; and any other persons, of whatever pre-eminence, condition or standing who shall impose, exact or receive such payments, or shall any where arrest, seize or presume to take possession of the belongings of churches or ecclesiastical persons which are deposited in the sacred buildings, or shall order them to be arrested, seized or taken possession of, or shall receive them when taken possession of, seized or arrested—also all who shall knowingly give aid, counsel or favour in the aforesaid things, whether publicly or secretly—shall incur, by the act itself, the sentence of excommunication. Corporations, moreover, which shall be guilty in these matters, we place under the ecclesiastical interdict.

The prelates and above-mentioned ecclesiastical persons we strictly command, by virtue of their obedience and under penalty of deposition, that they by no means acquiesce in such demands, without express permission of the aforesaid chair; and that they pay nothing under pretext of any obligation, promise and confession made hitherto, or to be made hereafter before such constitution, notice or decree shall come to their notice; nor shall the aforesaid

---

[2] Here we have added brackets to clarify an ambiguity in the source text.—Davenant eds.

secular persons in any way receive anything. And if they shall pay, or if the aforesaid persons shall receive, they shall be, by the act itself, under sentence of excommunication. From the aforesaid sentences of excommunication and interdict, moreover, no one shall be able to be absolved, except in the throes of death, without the authority and special permission of the apostolic chair; since it is our intention by no means to pass over with dissimulation so horrid an abuse of the secular powers. Notwithstanding any privileges whatever—under whatever tenor, form, or manner or conception of words that have been granted to emperors, kings, and other persons mentioned above; as to which privileges we will that, against what we have here laid down, they in no wise avail any person or persons. Let no man at all, then, infringe this page of our constitution, prohibition or decree, or, with rash daring, act counter to it; but if any one shall presume to act, he shall know that he is about to incur the indignation of Almighty God and of His blessed apostles Peter and Paul.

Given at Rome at St. Peter's on the sixth day before the Calends of March (Feb 25), in the second year of our pontificate.

BONIFACE VIII,
UNAM SANCTAM (1302)[1]

URGED by faith, we are obliged to believe and to maintain that the Church is one, holy, catholic, and also apostolic. We believe in her firmly and we confess with simplicity that outside of her there is neither salvation nor the remission of sins, as the Spouse in the Canticles [Sgs. 6:8] proclaims: "One is my dove, my perfect one. She is the only one, the chosen of her who bore her," and she represents one sole mystical body whose Head is Christ and the head of Christ is God [1 Cor. 11:3]. In her then is one Lord, one faith, one baptism [Eph. 4:5]. There had been at the time of the deluge only one ark of Noah, prefiguring the one Church, which ark, having been finished to a single cubit, had only one pilot and guide, i.e., Noah, and we read that, outside of this ark, all that subsisted on the earth was destroyed.

We venerate this Church as one, the Lord having said by the mouth of the prophet: "Deliver, O God, my soul from the sword and my only one from the hand of the dog" [Ps. 21:20]. He has prayed for his soul, that is for himself, heart and body; and this body, that is to say, the Church, He has called one because of the unity of the Spouse, of the faith, of the sacraments, and of the charity of the Church. This is the tunic of the Lord, the seamless tunic, which was not rent but which was cast by lot [Jn. 19:23–24]. Therefore, of the one and only Church there is one body and one

---

[1] Translated by Mary Mildred Curley in "The Conflict Between Pope Boniface VIII and Philip IV, the Fair" (PhD diss., Catholic University of America, 1927).

head, not two heads like a monster; that is, Christ and the Vicar of Christ, Peter and the successor of Peter, since the Lord speaking to Peter Himself said: "Feed my sheep" [Jn. 21:17], meaning, my sheep in general, not these, nor those in particular, whence we understand that He entrusted all to him [Peter]. Therefore, if the Greeks or others should say that they are not confided to Peter and to his successors, they must confess not being the sheep of Christ, since Our Lord says in John "there is one sheepfold and one shepherd." We are informed by the texts of the gospels that in this Church and in its power are two swords; namely, the spiritual and the temporal. For when the Apostles say: "Behold, here are two swords" [Lk. 22:38] that is to say, in the Church, since the Apostles were speaking, the Lord did not reply that there were too many, but sufficient. Certainly, the one who denies that the temporal sword is in the power of Peter has not listened well to the word of the Lord commanding: "Put up thy sword into thy scabbard" [Mt. 26:52]. Both, therefore, are in the power of the Church, that is to say, the spiritual and the material sword, but the former is to be administered for the Church but the latter by the Church; the former in the hands of the priest; the latter by the hands of kings and soldiers, but at the will and sufferance of the priest.

However, one sword ought to be subordinated to the other and temporal authority, subjected to spiritual power. For since the Apostle said: "There is no power except from God and the things that are, are ordained of God" [Rom. 13:1–2], but they would not be ordained if one sword were not subordinated to the other and if the inferior one, as it were, were not led upwards by the other.

For, according to the Blessed Dionysius, it is a law of the divinity that the lowest things reach the highest place by intermediaries. Then, according to the order of the universe, all things are not led back to order equally and immediately, but the lowest by the intermediary, and the inferior by the superior. Hence we must recognize the more clearly that spiritual power surpasses in dignity and in nobility any temporal power whatever, as spiritual things surpass the temporal. This we see very clearly also by the payment, benediction, and consecration of the tithes, but the acceptance of power itself and by the government even of things. For with truth as our witness, it belongs to spiritual power to establish the terrestrial power and to pass judgement if it has not been good. Thus is accomplished the prophecy of Jeremias concerning the Church and the ecclesiastical power: "Behold today I have placed you over nations, and over kingdoms" and the rest [Jer. 1:10]. Therefore, if the terrestrial power err, it will be judged by the spiritual power; but if a minor spiritual power err, it will be judged by a superior spiritual power; but if the highest power of all err, it can be judged only by God, and not by man, according to the testimony of the Apostle: "The spiritual man judgeth of all things and he himself is judged by no man" [1 Cor. 2:15]. This authority, however, (though it has been given to man and is exercised by man), is not human but rather divine, granted to Peter by a divine word and reaffirmed to him [Peter] and his successors by the One Whom Peter confessed, the Lord saying to Peter himself, "Whatsoever you shall bind on earth, shall be bound also in Heaven" etc., [Mt. 16:19]. Therefore, whoever resists this power thus ordained by God, resists the ordinance of God [Rom. 13:2], unless he invent like Manicheus two beginnings, which is false and judged by us heretical, since according to the testimony of Moses, it is not in the beginnings but in the beginning that God created heaven and earth [Gen. 1:1]. Furthermore, we declare, we proclaim, we define that it is absolutely necessary for salvation that every human creature be subject to the Roman Pontiff.

INTRODUCTION TO MARSILIUS OF PADUA'S *DEFENDER OF THE PEACE*

HOWEVER much we may like to label great landmarks in the history of human thought as "revolutionary" and "ahead of their time," few books really deserve such clichéd epithets. Every writer is a product of his time and can hardly be expected to say something that is nowhere to be found in his contemporaries. One of the very rare exceptions to this rule is Marsilius of Padua (c. 1275-c. 1342); his 1324 *Defensor Pacis* was a work so revolutionary and sweeping in its condemnation of the prevailing medieval understanding of the church and state that Marsilius was forced to flee even the anti-papal stronghold of Paris and take refuge with the German prince Ludwig of Bavaria. The book was anathematized in 1327 and a few years later Pope Clement VI was to write, "We are bold to say that we have almost never read a worse heretic than that Marsilius. For we have extracted from the mandate of Benedict our predecessor on a certain book of his [the *Defensor*] more than 240 heretical articles."[1]

Two hundred years later, many architects of the Protestant Reformation, especially in England, were to hail the *Defensor* as a great articulation of their own ecclesiological and political principles, and to republish the text widely. Still later, historians and political theorists identified Marsilius's work as a truly startling anticipation of modern political ideas, with its focus on national sover-

---

[1] Quoted in Carlo Pincin, *Marsilio* (Turin: Giappichelli, 1967), 233. Translated in Annabel Brett, ed. and trans., *Marsilius: Defender of the Peace*, Cambridge Texts in the History of Political Thought (Cambridge: CUP, 2005).

eignty, representation as the foundation of legislative authority, and the thoroughly secular character of political life. Alexander Passerin d'Entreves says that, according to the "unanimous judgment of modern historians" the *Defensor* is "a landmark not only in the development of medieval political theory but in the history of political thought as a whole."[2]

The context of Marsilius's great work was one we are already familiar with from the previous reading: the tussle between pope and prince over the rightful boundaries of ecclesiastical and civil authority within Western Christendom. Indeed, Marsilius's work can be considered in some ways the equal and opposite reaction to Boniface's extraordinary claims in *Unam Sanctam*. Rather than supreme earthly authority belonging to the Pope, with the civil government little more than a department of the Church, Marsilius sketches a model in which supreme authority belongs to the civil magistrate, with the church little more than a department of state. Indeed, beginning his treatise by sketching peace as the goal of every human society, Marsilius openly blames papal ambition and tyranny as the main cause for the war and discord in western Europe. In this, Marsilius draws extensively on the revival of Aristotle and his *Politics* that had fueled many anti-papal political writings of previous decades, though he is much more thoroughgoing in his use of Aristotle to outline a basically self-sufficient civil order dedicated to the pursuit of earthly goods.

To understand what Marsilius is up to in the *Defensor*, however, one other key piece of context is necessary: the Franciscan poverty controversy. St. Francis of Assisi had a century before established a mendicant order of monks dedicated to the ideal of apostolic poverty—that is, the monks must claim no worldly possessions of their own, but only make use of the necessary goods made available to them by Christian patrons. Although the Franciscans

---

[2] Alexander Passerin d'Entreves, *The Medieval Contribution to Political Thought: Thomas Aquinas, Marsilius of Padua, Richard Hooker* (Oxford: OUP, 1939), 44.

applied this principle only to their own order, not to the entire church, the argument made the defenders of clerical wealth and power quite nervous—with good cause, as it turned out. Marsilius took up the arguments of the Franciscans and applied them to *all* clergy. The church, he argued, was not to be in the business of piling up its own wealth; indeed, it could claim no earthly power over possessions at all, but must make humble use of what lay Christians provided.

Marsilius extended the argument further, however, to claim that properly speaking, the church could not claim earthly power over people either—this was the fundamental confusion that had caused all the unnecessary conflicts. To be sure, the church had the duty to preach the evangelical law of Christ, but this law did not, within history at least, function as law in the full and proper sense, which for Marsilius included coercive force. Christ himself would at the end of history act to enforce the consequences of his law, but until that time, ministers of his gospel proclaimed it only with a teaching authority. Accordingly, within history, the only properly *political* authority was the civil magistrate, who was responsible even for the external administration of the church (church buildings, tithes, and offices, the punishment of heresy, etc.).

The feature of Marsilius's project that was to prove most attractive to later thinkers, though, was his emphasis on *the people* as the foundation of both church and state. The "authority of making laws belongs," he declares, "to the whole body of citizens, or its better part which represents the whole." The qualification at the end tells us that Marsilius does not envision pure democracy, but he did put great emphasis on the whole community as the basis and agent of political authority. Likewise, he was to define the church not as an institution or the body of the clergy, but as "the whole body of the faithful who believe in and invoke the name of Christ," and he was to defend the authority of councils over against that of the Pope. These ideas were shocking at the time but were to gain greater influence in the conciliar movement of the 15th century and even more so in the Protestant Reformation.

Further Reading

For further reading, see Alexander Passerin d'Entreves, *The Medieval Contribution to Political Thought: Thomas Aquinas, Marsilius of Padua, Richard Hooker* (Oxford: OUP, 1939); Annabel S. Brett, "Introduction" to *Marsilius of Padua: Defender of the Peace*, Cambridge Texts in the History of Political Thought (Cambridge: Cambridge University Press, 2005); Oliver O'Donovan and Joan Lockwood O'Donovan, *From Irenaeus to Grotius: A Sourcebook in Christian Political Thought* (Grand Rapids: Eerdmans, 1999), 423-52.

MARSILIUS OF PADUA,
DEFENDER OF THE PEACE (1324)[1]

NOW WE declare according to the truth and on the authority of
Aristotle that the law-making power or the first and real effective
source of law is the people or the body of citizens or the prevailing
part of the people according to its election or its will expressed in
general convention by vote, commanding or deciding that something be done or omitted in regard to human civil acts under penalty or temporal punishment; by the prevailing part of the people I
mean that part of the community by whom the law is made,
whether the whole body of citizens or the main part do this or
commit it to some person or persons to be done; these last are not
nor can be the real law-making power, but can only act according
to instructions as to subject-matter and time, and by the authority
of the primal law-making power.

On the authority of Aristotle by a citizen I mean him who
has a part in the civil community, either in the government, or the
council, or the judiciary, according to his position. By this definition boys, slaves, foreigners, and women are excluded, though according to different limitations. Having thus defined citizen and the
prevailing section of the citizens, let us return to the object proposed, namely to demonstrate that the human authority of making

---

[1] From Oliver J. Thatcher, ed., *The Library of Original Sources* (Milwaukee:
University Research Extension Co., 1907), Vol. V: *The Early Medieval
World*, 423–30.

laws belongs only to the whole body of citizens as the prevailing part of it. [...]

For the primal human authority of making laws belongs to that body by whom the best laws can be made. This, however, is the whole body of citizens or its better part which represents the whole. I now prove the second proposition, namely that the best law will result from the deliberation and decision of the whole body. [...] That this can be done best by the citizens as a whole or the better part of them, I demonstrate thus, since the truth of anything will be judged more accurately, and its common advantage be studied more diligently, if the whole body of citizens discuss it with intelligence and feeling [...]. So the reality of a general law will be best attended to by the whole people, because no one consciously injures himself.

On the other side we desire to adduce in witness the truths of the holy Scripture, teaching and counselling expressly, both in the literal sense and in the mystical, according to the interpretation of the saints and the exposition of other authorized teachers of the Christian faith, that neither the Roman bishop, called the pope, nor any other bishop, presbyter, or deacon, ought to have the ruling or judgment or coercive jurisdiction of any priest, prince, community, society or single person of any rank whatsoever [...]. For the present purposes, it suffices to show, and I will first show, that Christ Himself did not come into the world to rule men, or to judge them by civil judgment, nor to govern in a temporal sense, but rather to subject Himself to the state and condition of this world; that indeed from such judgment and rule He wished to exclude and did exclude Himself and His apostles and disciples, and that He excluded their successors, the bishops and presbyters, by His example, and word and counsel and command from all governing and worldly, that is, coercive rule. I will also show that the apostles were true imitators of Christ in this, and that they taught their successors to be so. I will further demonstrate that Christ and His apostles desired to be subject and were subject continually to the coercive jurisdiction of the princes of the world in reality and in person, and that they taught and commanded all others to whom they gave the law of truth by word or letter, to do the same thing, under penalty of eternal condemnation. Then I will give a section to considering the power or authority of the keys, given by Christ to the apostles and to their successors in offices, the bishops and presbyters, in order that we may see the real character of that power, both of the Roman bishop and of the others. [...]

We wish, therefore, first to demonstrate that Christ wished to exclude and did exclude both Himself and His apostles from the office of ruler. This appears in John, 18. For when Christ was accused before Pontius Pilate, vicar of the Roman emperor in Judea, for saying that he was king of the Jews, and Pilate asked Him if He had said that, or if He had called Himself a king, He replied to the question of Pilate: "My kingdom is not of this world;" [v. 36] that is, I am come not to reign by temporal rule and dominion, as the kings of the world reign. It remains to show that Christ not only refused the rule of this world and coercive jurisdiction on earth, whereby He gave an example for action to His apostles and disciples and their successors, but that He also taught by word and showed by example that all, whether priests or not, should be subject in reality and in person to the coercive judgment of the princes of this world. By His word and example Christ demonstrated this first in physical things, in the incident contained in Matthew 22, when to the Jews asking Him: "Tell us, therefore, what thinkest Thou; is it lawful to give tribute unto Caesar or not?" looking at the penny and its superscription, he replied: "Render, therefore, unto Caesar the things which are Caesar's, and unto God the things which are God's." [vv. 17, 21 ...]

Further not only in physical things did Christ show that He was subject to the coercive jurisdiction of a prince of the world, but He showed it also in Himself [...] for it plainly appears that He permitted Himself to be taken and led to the court of Pilate, vicar of the Roman emperor, and endured that He be condemned and handed over by the same judge to the extreme punishment.

Following upon this, it remains to demonstrate what power, authority and judgment Christ wished to give to the apostles and their successors, and did in fact give according to the words of the holy Scripture. Among other things which seem to have direct reference to this are the words which Christ spoke to Peter, Matt. 16: "I will give unto thee the keys of the kingdom of heaven;" [v. 19] also those spoken by Him to all the apostles, when He said: "Whatsoever ye shall bind on earth shall be bound in heaven, and whatsoever ye shall loose on earth shall be loosed in heaven." On these words especially is based the claim and title to the plenitude of power, which the Roman bishop ascribes to himself. [...]

By the sacrament of baptism, which Christ commanded to be administered by the apostles, He caused them to understand also the administration of the other sacraments instituted for the eternal salvation of mankind; one of these is the sacrament of repentance by which the actual guilt of the human soul, both mortal and venial, is destroyed, and the soul, corrupt in itself through guilt, is restored by the grace of God, without any human effort, God ordaining that meritorious works should not win eternal life. Hence it is written in Romans 6[:23]: "The gift of God is eternal life." The ministers of this sacrament, as of the others, are the priests and presbyters, as successors of the apostles of Christ, to all of whom it is shown by the aforesaid words of Scripture the power of the keys was given, that is, the power of conferring the sacrament of repentance, in other words, the power of loosing and binding men in regard to their sins [...]. It will appear later how it is possible for priests to receive into or exclude from the kingdom; and from this also the character and extent of the power of those keys, given by Christ to Peter and the other apostles. [...] By his guilt the sinner is under the bond of eternal condemnation for the future life, and if he persists in his guilt, he is cast off from the association of the faithful in this world, by a kind of punishment resting with the believers of Christ, called excommunication. [...] And on the other hand we should notice that the sinner receives a three-fold benefit through his sorrow for sin and open confession to the priests, to which acts, both singly and taken together, the name repentance is given. The first benefit is that he is cleansed from his inner guilt and restored to himself by the grace of God; the second, that he is freed from the bond of eternal damnation, to which he was bound by his guilt; and the third, that he is reconciled to the church, that is, he is reunited or ought to be reunited to the body of believers. [...]

From these words of the saints [...] it clearly appears that God alone remits to the truly penitent sinner his guilt and his debt of eternal condemnation, and that without any office of the priest preceding or intervening, as has been demonstrated above. [...] For it is God alone who cannot err as to whose sin should be remitted or retained. For He alone is not moved by unfair feeling nor judges unjustly. Not of such character is the church or the priest whoever he may be, even the Roman bishop [...]. The anathema of the church inflicts upon those who are justly expelled, this punishment: that the grace and protection of God is withdrawn from them and is abandoned by them themselves, so that they are free to rush into the destruction of sin, and greater power of destroying them is given to the devil. [...]

[St.] Ambrose says that "the word of God remits sins; the priest performs his service but has no right of authority. But we may say that the priest is as it were the turnkey of the heavenly judge, so that he frees the sinner in the same sense that the turnkey of an earthly judge frees a prisoner. For just as the guilty man is condemned to or released from guilt and civil penalty by the word or sentence of a judge of this world, so by the divine word anyone is either to be freed from or condemned to guilt and the debt of damnation and the punishment of the future life. And just as no one is freed from guilt and penalty or condemned by the action of the turnkey of a worldly judge, and yet by his action in closing or opening the prison the guilty one is shown to be freed or condemned, so no one is freed from or bound to guilt and the debt of eternal condemnation by the action of the priest, but it is demonstrated before the eyes of the church who is held bound or freed by

God, when he receives the benediction of the priest, or is admitted to the communion of the sacraments." […] Therefore just as the turnkey of an earthly judge fulfills his office in opening and closing the prison, but exercises no right of judicial authority of condemning or pardoning, since even if he actually opened the prison for a criminal not pardoned by the judge and announced to the people with his own voice that the man was free, the guilty man would not on this account be freed from his guilt and the civil penalty, or on the other hand if he refused to open the prison and declared with his own words that he whom the judge had freed by his sentence was not pardoned but condemned, that man would not on this account be held subject to the guilt and penalty; so likewise the priest, the turnkey of the heavenly judge, performs his duty by the verbal pronunciation of the absolution or malediction. But if those who ought to be condemned by the divine judge or are already condemned, the priest should pronounce as not worthy to be condemned or as not condemned, or vice versa, through ignorance or deceit or both, not on this account would the former be dissolved or the latter damned, because the priest had not handled the key or keys with discretion according to the merits of the accused.

Proceeding from what has been demonstrated, we will show here first that no one of the apostles was given pre-eminence over the other in essential dignity by Christ […]. For Christ, giving to the apostles the authority over the sacrament of the Eucharist, said to them: "This is My Body which is given for you, this do in remembrance of Me." [Lk. 22:19; …] And he did not say these words more to Peter than to the others. For Christ did not say: "Do thou this, and give the right of doing it to the other apostles," but He said, "Do" in the plural, and to all without distinction. And later Christ said to the apostles: "'As My Father has sent Me, even so send I you.' He breathed on them and saith unto them, 'Receive ye the Holy Ghost, whosoever sins ye remit, they are remitted unto them, and whosoever sins ye retain, they are retained'" [Jn. 20:21–23.] Now Christ said: "I send you as My Father sent Me;" He did not say to Peter or to any other apostle in the singular, "I send thee as the Father, etc., do thou send the others." Nor again did Christ breathe upon him, but upon them, not upon one through another. Nor did Christ say to Peter: 'Receive the Holy Ghost, and afterwards give it to the others," but he said, "Receive," in the plural and speaking to all indifferently […].

It likewise appears that neither St. Peter nor any one of the apostles had pre-eminence over the others in the right of distributing the temporal offerings of the primitive church; whence it is written in Acts 4[:34-35]: "For as many as were possessors of lands or houses sold them, and laid them at the apostles' feet, and distribution was made unto every man according as he had need." Behold, the distribution of the temporal offerings of the church was made by the apostles in general, not by Peter alone; for it is not said: they laid them at the feet of Peter, but of the apostles. Nor it is said that "Peter distributed them," but that "distribution was made." […]

But if Peter has been called the prince of the apostles by some of the saints, the term is used broadly and by a misuse of the word prince; otherwise it would be plainly opposed to the opinion and oracle of Christ, where He said: "The princes of the Gentiles exercise dominion over them, but it shall not be so among you" [Lk. 22:25]. And it must be said that the saints spoke thus not because of any power given to him by Christ over the other apostles, but because perchance he was older than the others: or because he was the first to confess that Christ was the true consubstantial Son of God, or perhaps because he was more fervent and constant in faith, or because he was intimate with Christ and was more frequently called by Him into His counsel and secrets. […]

Moreover, he did not have coercive jurisdiction over the rest of the apostles more than they over him, neither consequently have his successors. For Christ forbade this to them directly, as in Matt. 20[:24-26], Luke 22[:24-26]: "And there was also a strife among them, which of them should be counted the greatest. And He said unto them: The kings and princes of the Gentiles exercise dominion over them, and they that are great exercise authority upon them, but it shall not be so among you;" Christ could not have denied this more plainly. Why then should anyone in regard to this believe more in human tradition, than in the most evident word of Christ? [...]

Further, the Roman bishop is not, nor should he be called the successor of St. Peter by the laying on of hands, for there has been a Roman bishop upon whom St. Peter has not laid his hand either directly or indirectly; nor again because of the seat or the determination of the place, first because no one of the apostles was appointed to any people or any place by divine law; for he said to all: "Go ye therefore and teach all nations;" and in the second place, St. Peter is said to have been at Antioch before he was at Rome.

The aforesaid plenitude of power the bishops of Rome have used continually up to the present and are now using for the worse, especially against the Roman prince and principality. For they are able to exercise against him this their wickedness, that is, the subjection of the empire to themselves, because of the division among the inhabitants of the empire, and are able by their so-called pastors and most holy fathers to stir up and nourish the discord already incited. For they further believe that, the empire once subdued, the way lies open for them to subject the rest of the kingdoms, although they are especially and peculiarly under obligation to the emperor and empire of the Romans, by reason of benefits received, as is known to all. But, to speak only of what is known to everyone and needs no word from us, smitten with cupidity and avarice, with pride and ambition, made even worse by ingratitude, they are seeking in every way to prevent the creation of a Roman emperor, and are striving either to break up the empire, or to transfer it in another form to their own control, lest the excesses which they have committed should be corrected by the power of the aforesaid princes and they should be subject to well-merited discipline. But although with the purpose which we have mentioned they are placing obstructions in the way of the prince on every side, yet craftily hiding their object they say they are doing this to defend the rights of the spouse of Christ, that is, the church, though such pious sophistry is ridiculous. For temporal power and greed, and lust of authority and rule is not the spouse of Christ, nor has He wedded such a spirit, but has expressly repudiated it, as has been shown from the divine Scriptures. […] Nor is this the heritage of the apostles which they left to their true, not fictitious, successors. […]

And so, by their striving for worldly things, the spouse of Christ is not truly defended. The recent Roman popes do not defend her who is the spouse of Christ, that is, the Catholic faith and the multitude of the believers, but offend her; they do not preserve her beauty, that is, the unity of the faith, but defile it, since by sowing tares and schisms they are tearing her limb from limb, and since they do not receive the true companions of Christ, poverty and humility, but shut them out entirely, they show themselves not servants but enemies of the husband.

INTRODUCTION TO JOHN WYCLIFFE'S
TRIALOGUS

IF MARSILIUS of Padua shocks us by his uncanny anticipations of Reformation ecclesiology and certain modern political ideas, John Wycliffe (c. 1320-1384) is sure to do so just as emphatically. Writing some 150 years before Luther, the seemingly inexhaustible torrent of his pen poured out invectives against the papacy (which Wycliffe did not hesitate to name as Antichrist, as the Protestant Reformers were later to do), the idleness and corruption of monastic life, the worship of relics, the idolatry of images, the theology and practice of indulgences, and much more. Theologically, he denied the temporal power of the church and outlined a distinction of the visible and invisible churches, forthrightly attacked the theology of transubstantiation, and exalted Scripture as the only final norm of Christian faith, using it as the basis for brazenly rejected centuries of unbiblical traditions that had come to dominate the church. Perhaps his most lasting legacy was his insistence that the Bible be translated into the vernacular language so that it could be read by ordinary people, a project likewise at the heart of Luther's later reform. To be sure, it would be anachronistic to call Wycliffe a Protestant before Protestantism—most importantly, he shows little sign of anticipating Luther's doctrine of justification *sola fide*, even if he did emphasize the importance of individual faith. But the degree to which he bundled together so many of the same calls for reform that were to appear after 1517 shows that there was nothing random about the set of issues which were later to comprise the basic Protestant program.

Like Luther, Wycliffe's journey to reform did not take place all at once, although it was fairly rapid once it began. Born in the mid-1320s, Wycliffe had spent many years establishing a formidable academic reputation at the University of Oxford as a philosopher and theologian before he began to be drawn into public controversies in the 1370s. Called upon to participate in negotiations between the English crown and the papacy regarding the latter's numerous claims to a share of the wealth of the English church, Wycliffe, like many other sober-minded observers of the late medieval church, was sickened by the greed and worldliness of the papacy and much of the church that it oversaw. Wycliffe began to attack the papal claims of temporal power and Petrine succession. He also developed a distinctive political theory according to which godly civil magistrates had the right to expropriate the material resources of a corrupt church and put them to better use, leaving the church impoverished but better able to focus on its central task of preaching the Word of God. Even more radically (at least from a theological standpoint) he turned his attention to the medieval church's all-important power of excommunication, arguing that priests have no authority to bind or loose souls beyond what the law of Christ declares. The combination of boundless temporal greed with the claim of boundless spiritual authority, Wycliffe recognized, was a recipe for every kind of oppression of the Christian people and distortion of the truth.

If he had stopped there, Wycliffe might have succeeded in leading a sustained reform movement with considerable political and academic backing. However, around 1380, he set his sights on two new issues: the translation of Scripture into the vernacular and the doctrine of transubstantiation—which, he realized, was the source of much of the church's power over ignorant ordinary believers. Both provoked strong opposition, but as was to be the case a century and a half later, it was transubstantiation where the battle raged most fiercely. Many of Wycliffe's former supporters abandoned him at his apparent heresy on this point, and a synod in London in 1382 condemned twenty-four of his teachings as heretical or erroneous. Wycliffe himself escaped direct persecution, perhaps on account of remaining friends in high places, and continued writing feverishly and vociferously, with no sign of backing down, until his death by stroke in 1384.

At Oxford, many of Wycliffe's supporters were rooted out or bullied into recanting his most objectionable doctrines, but the project he had begun of translating the Bible into English was carried forward by friends to completion in 1395. This text, and the ongoing activities of Wycliffite preachers called Lollards, preserved a small underground movement all the way up until the time of the English Reformation. However, there is little indication that their teachings had much direct influence on the 16th-century English Reformers, and indeed Luther seems to have been ignorant of Wycliffe.

The extract from Wycliffe's voluminous writings chosen here comes from his *Trialogus*, one of his later works that covers a dizzying array of subjects with an often equally dizzying display of scholastic erudition and precision. It is constructed as a "tria-logue" between *Alithia* (Truth), *Pseudis* (Falsehood), and *Phronesis* (Wisdom), who represents the voice of Wycliffe himself, coming to the defense of *Alithia*. In this excerpt (in which *Pseudis* does not speak), Wycliffe develops his attack on the theory of transubstantiation, which he strongly rejected on both biblical and philosophical grounds, and goes so far to dismiss it as "heresy" (somewhat cheekily, inasmuch as this was the charge lodged at him). This theory, in the mature scholastic form which it had taken on over the past couple centuries, held that, once consecrated, the bread and wine in the Eucharist are replaced by Christ's body and blood; that is, the consecrated elements cease to be truly bread and wine, but simply maintain the "accidents," or physical appearance and qualities, of bread and wine, without the underlying substance. This claim was in direct contravention of the received Aristotelian metaphysics, which quite reasonably maintained that the accidents of a given thing could not exist without its substance, and of the words of Christ, who, argues Wycliffe, clearly refers to the bread as bread.

Wycliffe is far from denying any kind of real presence of Christ in the Eucharist, but he does insist that this presence be understood symbolically and spiritually. In this, he followed Augustine closely, and although he hardly worked out a complete theory of what he thought *did* happen in the Eucharist before his untimely death, his insights here clearly anticipate closely those of the later Protestants, and perhaps especially the Reformed doctrine of the Eucharist.

Further Reading

For further reading, see Robert Vaughan, ed., *Tracts and Treatises of John de Wycliffe* (London: Blackburn and Pardon, 1845) (available at http://oll.libertyfund.org/titles/wyclife-tracts-and-treatises-of-john-de-wycliffe); G.R. Evans, *John Wyclif: Myth and Reality* (Downers Grove, IL: IVP Academic, 2006).

JOHN WYCLIFFE,
TRIALOGUS (1384)[1]

II: What is Denoted by the Pronoun "This" in the Words of the Consecration

Alithia:

I AM DELIGHTED, brother, with your clear statement in regard to the faith of the church, which has been only too long hidden. I see not how the friars, or others, can escape your reasoning, without either inventing a sense for this passage of Scripture, or actually refusing to believe it.

Phronesis:

Neither we ourselves, nor any one besides, can deny the force of this reasoning, and the good catholic should cherish it with care, as very dear to him. But heretics have assigned various significations to this Scripture. In the first place, they say, that the pronoun *"this,"* in the proposition of the sacrament, *"this is my body,"* denotes simply the body of our Lord, and not the bread, for otherwise, according to them, the proposition would be false. As to what John, "On God," and other illiterate heretics maintain, that the pronoun denotes nothing, I pass it over, as not worthy to be mentioned, and proceed to bring argument in full against the first heresy. The former of these pronouns denotes the bread which Christ took in his hands, and the pronoun following it the same thing which was be-

---

[1] Robert Vaughan, trans., *Tracts and Treatises of John de Wycliffe* (London: Blackburn and Pardon, Hatton Garden, 1845).

fore denoted by the other. The subject, therefore, of the sacramental proposition, refers to this same *bread*. How is the believer to
comprehend that Christ took bread in his hands, blessed, brake it,
and gave it his disciples to eat, unless he understands by the former
pronoun, "*bread?*" For the sacramental words had not yet been uttered, that it should cease to be bread. Our opinion is confirmed by
Matt. 16, where Christ bids all his apostles drink of that cup, which
they did. Also Mark 14[:23]: "And he took the cup, and when he
had given thanks, he gave it to them, and they all drank of it," and
in the same way, concerning the bread, whence the apostle's words,
in 1 Cor. 11[:26] are "For as often as ye eat this bread," &c.; and
from all this it appears either that the Author of Scripture gives us a
false representation, or that the apostles ate of the bread offered
them by Christ. From the same source it is also plain that the second pronoun denotes the same bread which is made the subject
of the sacramental proposition, "this is my body," for otherwise
the causal would be in every view absurd, and besides, Christ
would have been deluding his church.

This reasoning, founded on the object denoted by the pronoun, ought to give the faithful abundant confidence. The words
of Christ point out the object of which the apostles took cogni-
zance, but it is inconsistent to make them denote the mere body of
Christ in its proper nature. Our Lord's words, then, must denote
something else, and nothing can they denote pertinently more than
the bread which Christ had held out to them in his hand. If the
mere natural body of our Lord is meant, then the signification of
these words of Christ would be, "This my body is my body." But
with this the apostles were acquainted before, and it would be out
of place, in connection with the injunction that they should each
eat of the bread.

Again, if the reference of the pronoun to bread be out of
place in this connection, how can it consistently be taught that the
transubstantiation of the bread, by virtue of the words pronounced
at the sacrament, is an accident without a subject and an innovation
of Christ's body in place of the sacramental bread? This fictitious

reference, which they ascribe to these pronouns, does away with the entire meaning of the sacrament.

Again, in the second sacramental clause concerning the wine, that wine in the cup is meant; therefore, by the connection from a sufficient resemblance between this clause about the wine, and the former one in which the bread is consecrated, it appears plainly that this same bread must be referred to, because no catholic would deny that the *contents* of the cup are meant, by metonymy, for Christ, in Mark 14[:24] speaks thus: "This is my blood of the new testament." There is no catholic in existence who believes that cup of metal to be, sacramentally, the blood of Christ, but understands the term as referring to the wine contained in it. Further, to lay bare the wily turnings of this sophistry, the Holy Spirit ordained that it should be written in the masculine gender, *Hic est sanguis meus* (this is my blood), wherefore, among the many significations of scriptural passages, concerning which we are certain, this is one of the most certain, that in this, the proposition of the sacrament, bread, or wine, is meant.

This being admitted, the catholic must pass over to the complex signification of the sacramental proposition, "this is my body," abandoning, as the height of heresy, the opinion that the Gospel, especially the words of Christ, can contain anything impossible or inappropriate. But since every word of Christ's is true, and, in the highest sense of the term, catholic, and Christ has said that this bread is his body, it follows manifestly that this is true. It is about this point, however, that heretics maintain their struggle; they cannot deny that the pronoun denotes bread, and so they assign an extremely heretical compound, threefold signification. They say, first, that this, namely, the bread, is not the body of Christ, but that by virtue of the sacramental words it will be *in a certain way* the body of Christ. The second method appears more heretical still, for the opinion that the bread will afterward become the body of Christ is as inadmissible as the heretic's own error, for according to his showing, that bread would then be turned into or identified with the body of Christ, and consequently it would end in transubstantiation, and hence be the veritable body of Christ. Thus, in the second interpretation, we correct the first, that this bread will become, in a certain manner, the body of Christ. The third course again (it being evident that nothing of that bread will remain in the body of Christ) consists in denying any prior sense at all, saying that the Author of Scripture means that this accident *per se* without any subject is the sacramental sign of the body of Christ. And this is the signification of the proposition, "This is my body." The heretic sees that neither the matter, nor the form of bread, is transmuted into the body of Christ. In fact, the things themselves do not agree in subject; accordingly, he regards it as evident that the catholic should not admit that out of this bread will be made the body of Christ, as a statue is made out of bronze or day is made out of night, (for they are both incongruous in subject) but because these accidents *per se* without a subject are sacramentally the figures of the body of Christ. Oh how abominable is that figment which would make it appear that it is not bread which is denoted by that pronoun—as is shown above!

An impossibility, according to our modern doctors, is incomprehensible, and according to Augustine and other saints it cannot be included even in the Divine Omnipotence, and so concerning the whole affair these men are at a loss to express the genus of the accident to which this venerable sacrament should be referred. They speak falsely, therefore, when they say that it might be meaner than horse-food or than anything that may be named. So then, as these heretics, subsequent to the time of the loosing of Satan, have had no more understanding of this term than magpies, and as they falsely assert that neither Christ nor his apostles understood it, and so of course none of the fathers who came after them, we need not directly refute this error, for believers well know how constantly the body of Christ is made anew by an idiotic and unworthy priest, and it is not until these sacramental words have been duly uttered that the accident without a subject is created, so that the demonstrative pronoun of the sacramental proposition may remain for ever without denoting an accident without a subject, so long as the bread continues bread.

It is this doctrine of the saints that whosoever imposes upon Scripture a sense foreign to it, such as the Holy Spirit requireth not, such a man must be a heretic. This sense given to the above terms, by the persons alluded to, neither Scripture, revelation, nor reason can establish. No one of the saints, prior to the loosing of Satan, was acquainted with it. Jerome, Augustine, and other saints, and a vigorous reason all totally contradict it. The doctrine, then, must be wholly abandoned as one of special falsehood. These men must amend Holy Writ and make it say, not that the accident without a subject, which they cannot comprehend, is the body of Christ, but that it is the sign of the body of Christ. But how then, by virtue of this sentence, comes transubstantiation, or the accident without a subject? Since this accident without a subject may equally signify the body of Christ, these heretics cannot state at what instant transubstantiation, or the accident without a subject, really takes place.

Thus, then, is this three-fold doctrine annihilated, a doctrine contemptible and erroneous, after the manner of all other heresies which affect to be the doctrine of Christ. We must abide, then, by the opinion of the learned and acute Jerome, who says that the bread, by virtue of Christ's word, is sacramentally the body of our Savior. Of what sort that bread is, and of what it is in its own nature, the true theologian can see by observation of other hosts, not consecrated.

III: Showing that the Bread Remains Bread After Consecration

Alithia:
I am delighted with your stringent and lucid replies to the heretics in this matter, and the more so, because so great a multitude of friars, and others, who call themselves Christians, exclaim against your doctrine, and plot in various ways against your life. According to your former statements, these men are, of necessity, manifest

heretics, and, consequently, should be expelled from the church, or, at least, excluded from every grade of ecclesiastical dignity, and so from all holding of temporalities and receiving of alms. I pray you, now, to explain how it is that the bread remains bread after consecration, for many declare that if they had believed thus, they would never have observed the ceremony as they have done.

Phronesis:
On a subject of this nature, we must attend to the words of Scripture and give them absolute credence. And the words of Scripture tell us that this sacrament *is* the body of Christ, not that it *will* be, or that it is sacramentally a *figure* of the body of Christ. Accordingly, we must on this authority admit without reserve that the bread, which is this sacrament, is veritably the body of Christ. But the simplest layman will see that it follows that, inasmuch as this bread is the body of Christ, it is therefore bread, and remains bread, and is at once both bread and the body of Christ. Again, the point may be illustrated by examples of the most palpable description. It is not necessary, but, on the contrary, repugnant to truth, that a man, when raised to the dignity of lordship or prelacy, should cease to be the same person. The man, or the same substance, would remain in all respects, though in a certain degree elevated. So we must believe that this bread, by virtue of the sacramental words, becomes by the consecration of the priest veritably the body of Christ, and no more ceases to be bread than humanity ceases, in the instance before supposed; for the nature of bread is not destroyed by this, but is exalted to a substance more honored. Do we believe that John the Baptist, who was made by the word of Christ to be Elijah (Matt. 11[:14]) ceased to be John, or ceased to be anything which he was substantially before? In the same manner, accordingly, though the bread becometh the body of Christ by virtue of his words, it need not cease to be bread. For it is bread substantially, after it has begun to be sacramentally the body of Christ. For thus saith Christ, "This is my body," and in consequence of these words, this must be admitted, like the assertion in the eleventh

chapter of the gospel of Matthew, about the Baptist: "And if ye will receive it, this is Elijah." And Christ doth not, to avoid equivocation, contradict the Baptist, when he declares, "I am not Elijah" [Jn. 1:21]. The one meaning that he was Elijah *figuratively,* the other, that he was not Elijah *personally.* And in the same manner it is merely a double meaning, and not a contradiction, in those who admit that this sacrament is *not* naturally the body of Christ, but that this same sacrament *is* Christ's body figuratively.

Concerning the assertion made by some hardened heretics that they would never have celebrated the ordinance had they believed this, it would indeed have been well for the church and have contributed much to the honor of God if such apostates had never consecrated their *accident,* for in so doing they blaspheme God in many ways and make Him the author of falsehood. For the world God created they straightway destroy, inasmuch as they destroy what God ordained should be perpetual—primary matter—and introduce nothing new into the world, save the mendacious assertion that it pertains to them to perform unheard of miracles, in which God himself certainly may have no share. In fact, according to their representations, they make a new world. What loss would it have been, then, if heretics, so foolish, had never celebrated an ordinance, the proper terms of which they so little understand and who are so ignorant of the quiddity of the sacrament they observe and worship?

With regard to the points touching the truth of the belief, that this sacrament is bread, let heretics be on the watch and summon up all their powers; for He who is called Truth teaches us (Matt. 6) to pray that he would give us our daily, or supersubstantial, bread. And according to Augustine, on this passage in our Lord's sermon on the mount, by daily bread Christ intends, among other happy significations, this venerable sacrament. Are we not, then, to believe what would follow, viz. that if the sacrament for which we pray is our daily bread, then in the sacrament there must be bread? In the same manner the apostles recognized Christ with breaking of bread, as we are told in Luke 24[:35]. And Augustine, with the papal enactment, De Con. Dist. III. *non omnes,* tells us that this bread is this venerable sacrament. Or are we to doubt its following that the apostles having known Christ in the breaking of this bread, therefore that seeming bread must have been bread? Our apostle, likewise, who takes his meaning from our Lord, calls this sacrament the bread which we break, as is manifest in 1 Cor. 10[:16], and often again in the following chapter. Who then would venture to blaspheme God by maintaining that so chosen a vessel could apply erroneous terms to the chief of the sacraments— especially with the foreknowledge that heresies would take their rise from that very subject? It is impossible to believe that Paul would have been so careless of the church, the spouse of Christ, as so frequently to have called this sacrament bread, and not by its real name, had he known that it was not bread, but an accident without a subject, and when he was besides aware by the gift of prophecy of all the future heresies which men would entertain on the matter. Let these idiot heretics say and bring sufficient reason to prove their statements, what this sacrament, which their falsehoods desecrate, really is, if not the holy bread. As was said above, Christ, who is the first Truth, saith, according to the testimonies of the four evangelists that this bread is his body. What heretic ought not to blush, then, to deny that it is bread?

We are thus shut up, either to destroy the verity of Scripture, or to go along with the senses and the judgment of mankind and admit that it is bread. Mice and other creatures are aware of this fact; for according to philosophers, they have the power of discerning what is good for them to eat. Oh, if believers in the Lord will look on and see Antichrist and his accomplices so strong as to have power to condemn and persecute even unto death those sons of the church who thus yield their belief to the Gospel, yet certain I am that, though the truth of the Gospel may for a time be cast down in the streets and be kept under in a measure by the threats of Antichrist, yet extinguished it cannot be, since he who is the Truth has said that "heaven and earth shall pass away, but that his words shall not pass away!" [Matt. 24:35; Mk. 13:31; Lk. 21:33]. Let the believer, then, rouse himself and demand strictly from our heretics what the nature of this venerable sacrament is, if it be not bread, since the language of the Gospel, the evidence of our senses, and arguments that have in their favor every probability, say that so it is. For I am certain that even heathens who make their own gods are perfectly aware of what they are in their own proper nature, though they pretend that a portion of divinity is bestowed upon them supernaturally by the highest God of all. The believer, therefore, hesitates not to affirm that these heretics are more ignorant, not only than mice and other animals, but than pagans themselves; while on the other hand, our aforementioned conclusion that this venerable sacrament is in its own nature veritable bread, and sacramentally Christ's body, is shown to be the true one.

IV: The Preceding Statements Confirmed by Argument

Alithia:

I am pleased to find that a man must be shut up, as it seems, to one of two courses—denying the evangelist, as an arch-heretic, or admitting what you require concerning this sacrament. Will you now add a few arguments to the authorities you have brought forward, for we all admit that God can do nothing without good reason, that he cannot destroy a guiltless existence or put confusion on that intelligence which he has implanted in our nature, unless some greater good, or better reason shall induce him?

Phronesis:

I am pleased with your manner of expressing confidence in God. We must, in order to the end now proposed, proceed in the way which the arguments on this topic require, that the truth of our faith may the more clearly appear. Let us lay it down, then, that of all the external senses which God has bestowed upon man, touch and taste are least liable to error in the judgments they give. But this heresy would overturn the evidence of those senses without cause, and the sacrament which does that must be a sacrament of Antichrist. With regard to the evidence of touch in the sacrament, the certainty of experiment, which the heretic will not deny, shows us that this consecrated bread, when but newly baked, differs in its manner of breaking, in the degree of brittleness, and the sort of sound produced in breaking it, from bread that is stale, and which is of greatest toughness in damp weather. Now accidents of this sort, hardness, softness, brittleness, toughness, cannot exist *per se*; nor can they be the subjects of other accidents: it remains, therefore, that there must be some subject, as bread, or some thing by which they are made subjects. For since this sacrament, which is always the same, is found at one time hard, at another soft; at one time brittle, at another tough; the philosopher plainly sees that there must be a subject of some sort besides, as the seat of qualities, which undergoes these respective changes (for otherwise all distinction between such accidents must be denied), or else in such a transmutation a new sacrament is continually created. But if the first be granted, then no accident is distinguished from a material substance, and since those accidents remain, they would then become the material substance, as in the first instance.

In the same way in the sacrament of the cup, the same applies to the sense of taste, since it may happen that the wine, though retaining at first its taste and sweetness, might, by remaining in the vessel a day, lose its taste and become sour. Now according to the judgment of our taste and our reason, we must supply a subject of some sort, whose qualities are thus changed. For quantity, such as length, breadth, and thickness does not admit of the predication of qualities of this sort concerning them. We must therefore admit a subject besides quantity, which is changed by qualities of this sort, since the quantity must always be existing whenever the substance is rarified or condensed.

But I have argued at length on this point elsewhere, and brought against this error the testimony of Augustine in many places. I proceed, therefore, to remark, in the third place, on the great perplexity consequent on the delusion to which our internal faculties are subject, since when the knowledge obtained by our external senses is insufficient, the inward senses must be subject to delusion, and no heretic of this sort will affirm in the terms of the schools that he is acquainted with the quiddity or the differentia of sensible substances. On the contrary, he will admit with ignorant philosophers that of such sensible existences he knows nothing, so that, it being admitted that many hosts consecrated and unconsecrated may be mingled together by men who are not aware of it, then the heretic cannot distinguish his accident from bread, just as we cannot distinguish between consecrated and unconsecrated hosts, inasmuch as the effect of consecration is not sensible, but beyond the perception of the senses. Mice, however, have an innate knowledge of the fact, that the substance of bread is retained, as at first, but these unbelievers have no such knowledge, since they know not what bread or what wine are consecrated, except as they have seen the act of consecration performed. That which is consecrated does not admit of a second consecration, because, if so, an accident, *per se,* without bread or wine, may be consecrated. It is plain, accordingly, that they must ever be in doubt as to whether they do truly consecrate. What, I ask, could move our Lord Jesus Christ thus to take away the power of judgment from his worshippers? In no way doth it redound to their good, nor can it be established by reason or Scripture that it is necessary for men to be so deceived; for bread and wine, retaining their old form, would be a fitter representation of the body and blood of Christ than an accident without a subject, and the body and blood of Christ can be as well in any part whatever of such a body as in any particle of such a most monstrous accident, and then would Scripture faith be preserved, the advantage on all sides more, and the reverence for God greater. In like manner, such blasphemers convict the prelates, beyond escape, of a culpable negligence as regards the duties of the grammarian. For the schoolmaster teaches the translation of the aforesaid Latin words, according to the common understanding of them, but to avoid the danger of heresy it should be enjoined upon such persons to teach their boys to translate them in accordance with that blasphemous absurdity. The apostles knew the Lord in the breaking of bread, *i.e.,* in the breaking of an accident without a subject; for otherwise a boy of capacity might imagine that the bread had been substantially broken by God—a most perilous notion according to these heretics. The schoolmaster would be culpable who did not explain such an equivocation as—*the dog shines in the sky,* but were to teach, according to the ordinary meaning of the word, that a barking animal and not a star shone there. Much more culpable would he be, then, if he should fail to explain an equivocal expression in a matter involving such an injury to the faith. But blessed be the Lord of goodness, that he hath so confounded the wisdom of these heretics, that to this very day they know not how to construe the aforesaid words of the Gospel so as to make them yield the sense they affix to them. For neither in construing nor in preaching do they themselves understand their own words, when they say that the apostles knew Christ in the breaking of bread, *i.e.,* of an accident without a subject. And so Antichrist, in this heresy, overturns grammar, logic, and natural science, and, what is more lamentable, destroys the meaning of the Gospel. But God, as he always preserveth a natural understanding among the laity, so he hath always kept the catholic sense among some of the clergy, as in Greece, or elsewhere, according to his pleasure. Oh who can excuse the friars and other apostates, in that they know not how, or do not dare, or through jealousy do not wish to instruct the people on these points, from whom, to say nothing of their obligation to love the brethren, they receive so great emolument? Verily the natural understanding of man would condemn false brethren of this sort, for like foes at home, they would do more than idolaters abroad, to perplex the simple populace. What greater blasphemy than to assert that Christ, who is God, and the Lord of truth, hath given special authority to errors of this sort among his people? Without a doubt the chief cause is a departure from the commandments of the Gospel. Thus these false followers of Antichrist show themselves more ignorant than brutes or pagans.

V: How and From What Cause the Heresy Concerning the Sacrament of the Eucharist Hath Grown Up

Alithia:

I am pleased to hear you express yourself so boldly in behalf of evangelical truths, and that you have so far unfolded them by argument. But I would fain know how and from what cause it was that this heresy took its rise, even supposing it to have been introduced by Satan and his followers into the church.

Phronesis:

I should be worse than an infidel were I not to defend unto the death the law of Christ, and certain I am that all the heretics and disciples of Antichrist can never impugn this evangelical doctrine. On the contrary, I trust, through our Lord's mercy, to be superabundantly rewarded by him after this short and miserable life for this lawful contention which I wage. I know from the Gospel, that Antichrist, with all his devices, can only kill the body, but Christ, in whose cause I contend, can cast both soul and body into hell-fire. Certain I am that he will not suffer his servants to be destitute of what is needful, since he freely exposed himself to a dreadful death, and has ordained that all his more beloved disciples shall undergo severe suffering with a view to their profiting.

The reason why men fall into this heresy is that they disbelieve the Gospel and embrace in preference the papal laws and apocryphal sayings. And of all the kinds of infidelity that ever grew up in the church of God, this draws men down deeper and more imperceptibly into the vortices of error and causes more to apostatize from our Lord Jesus Christ. And be it granted that Innocent III was led away by this madness, though the friars take upon themselves to say that it is not my place to discuss this point, yet I am sure from the faith of Christ, that whatever Innocent III has laid down in this matter should not be received by believers, except in as far as it is founded on the commandments of the Gospel; for the same faith of Christ makes me confident that all truth is contained therein, and especially all truth relating to faith, and most in harmony with its design. Since these things are not from Christ or his law, but, on the contrary, it is contained in his law, as is plain from what is said before, that this sacrament is the body of Christ and bread, every believer ought accordingly to obey his Lord herein. But herein it is manifestly inferred that the sacrament is not an accident without a subject, since it cannot be shown that God has raised an accident to be his body. Accordingly, adhering to the faith, I will deny this as the greatest heresy, and with this view I have elsewhere sent the satraps the following conclusions thereupon, with a protest agreeably thereto. The first is: if by virtue of these sacramental words an accident is matter without a subject in the sacrament of the altar, that accident is itself the sacrament. It is plain from this that the said sacrament, according to the concurrent acknowledgment of these heretics, is not a substance, so that the sacramental words leave nothing remaining in the sacrament save this sort of accident. The second conclusion is that of all the heresies that have ever grown up in the holy church of God, none is more abominable than that which makes this venerable sacrament an accident without a subject, it being plain that by this heresy the very words of Christ are made to be heretical, so far as in it lies, and heresy is introduced over the greater part of the church. The third conclusion is that this sacrament is, on the testimony of the Gospel, true bread naturally, and the body of Christ veritably and sacramentally, as the above-mentioned passages from the Gospels show.

With regard to your second question, it appears to me that Christ, who is head over all devils, teaches us figuratively by this how the kingdom of the evil one is divided against itself, and must finally be made desolate, showing that its principal supporters in their very blessing are divided against themselves—as in the matter of the sect of the friars, so that each one of them is opposed to all the rest, and no one can efficiently maintain its own sentiments. And inasmuch as their prelates presume to bless, for the payment of money, those whom the Lord hath cursed, so they often curse those whom the Lord hath blessed; accordingly the Lord signifies to us, in that passage of Malachi, that their benediction after their own pleasure should often be called the malediction of God. For they say that in the consecration of their host they bless the bread and wine so that it becomes nothing, since according to their doctrine no part of it remains in the body of Christ, or in his sacrament, but taking annihilation in its proper sense, it is annihilated and turned into nothing. But Christ, though he was called an austere man by the slothful servant, never cursed anything whatever with a severity like this, for when he cursed the fig-tree (Mark 11) the substance of the tree remained, since Christ destroyeth not utterly his creatures on account of sin, or the appearance of sin, and since no creature can do anything unless without the previous act of God. Hence it is plain that, though they may bless the bread (as they falsely say) so as to cause it to become nothing, yet Christ, since it is his own workmanship, preserves it. Nor must we pass over what is said by John, in his treatise "On God," that the bread remains bread, but that where it is unknown, since believers are well assured that the bread, by virtue of the blessing of Christ, is turned into a something better, because it is turned into the body of our Lord, and remains bread because the body itself remains sacramentally; and if they say it is transubstantiated by virtue of the sacramental words, it is enough for me, since that substance cannot pass into another which has no existence in the passage. Let us praise Jesus Christ, then, in that the author of this lie is not He who spake and it was done, but rather that liar who spake and it was not done, who commanded and it was brought to naught. But if you reply that it follows from this that the pope and his cardinals have many times erred from the faith, and often deceive both themselves and their churches, the conclusion is true, though lamentable. Whether, however, they died penitent for such heresy or remained heretics after death, it is not for us rashly to decide. Yet God who knoweth things secret knoweth the truth in this matter, as do those to whom it is his pleasure himself to reveal it. For we are not bound to proclaim or believe that any pope, as such, is a father in the greatest blessedness after death, as his greedy flatterers during his lifetime clamorously assert, but the more he departed in life, even to the last, from the pattern of Christ, the more deep will be his condemnation in hell. But I believe many have been led into this heresy who finally repented, as was the case, in my opinion, with the Bishop of Lincoln and others, who have left behind them in their writings the opinion that an accident cannot exist without its subject, and yet the aforesaid Bishop of Lincoln, in his "Glossa de Divinis Nominibus," thus writes: "An accident may perhaps exist without a subject." I believe this subtle doctor to have meant that such an accident in the sacrament must exist in the act of our mind, since we have sensation actually to admonish us. But the consideration of the quiddity of its substance must be put in abeyance, and our consideration of the created substance must be employed about that which is signified by it—as a man entering a church does not set himself to consider the quiddity of the wood of the image, or the cross, but worshippeth it in respect of that of which it is the sign. So it is in the matter of the consecrated host, and because this is sometimes the case and sometimes not, I repeat what the Bishop of Lincoln says, "there may perhaps be an accident without a subject." It is in this way that those philosophers speak who hold that time has its existence in the mind, and that it is rendered sensible by the act of attention. For the existence of time is known to us because it is the measure of sensible motion, by the actual consideration of the mind, just as that which is perceptible to the senses has this passive power reduced to act during the time that it is actually being perceived. I think it very probable that great philosophers have been secretly of this opinion on the matter. But it would be useless to inquire into the intention of the author of this error. So I leave the discussion and contention with regard to this gloss to be carried on by theologians, being certain always of the faith of the Gospel, whereupon I rest without the smallest fear.

VI: In What Way the Bread is the Body of Our Lord, and Not the Identical Body Itself

Alithia:

I am pleased again with the acute and lucid explanation of your sentiments, and in my opinion, the truth of Scripture is of infinitely greater authority than that of any person now living, or of any community that could be named, so that if there had been a hundred popes, and all the friars had been turned into cardinals, no concession ought to have been made to their opinion in a matter of faith, save in so far as they rest upon Scripture. I see farther that you do not condemn the pope, or anyone, on account of this error, because you are ignorant in what way they died, but it is far more likely in your eyes that doctors have erred from the faith, or been slothfully silent, than that a single word of the Gospel may possibly be false.

But there is one thing I would fain know, and that is, in what sense the bread is the body of the Lord, and yet not identically the very body.

Phronesis:

I see that you discern the truth on many points, and as to the mode in which that bread is the body of our Lord, such it surely is— believe this firmly, for Christ, who cannot lie, hath so said. Now you know there are three methods of predication: the formal, the essential, and the figurative. Passing by the two former, let us here attend to the third. It is according to the third mode that Christ, as I have before observed to you, calls John the Baptist Elijah (Matt. 11[:14]). The apostle says of Christ (2 Cor. 10[:4], when deducing a moral from the acts of the old law) that he was a rock. And in Gen. 12, the Scripture asserts that seven ears of corn, and seven fat kine are the seven years of fertility. And as Augustine observes, the Scripture does not say—are the *signs* of those years, but that they are the years themselves. And you will meet with such modes of expression constantly in Scripture. And in these expressions, without a doubt, the predication is made figuratively, and is not the predication essential, or the predication formal. Now all such expressions show that the thing of the subject is ordained by God to be the figure of the thing of the predicate. So again it is said that the sacramental bread is, after that mode, specially the body of the Lord, since Christ has so declared authoritatively. Yet I am ready to believe in a more subtle meaning, should I be taught it, either by Scripture or by reason. But of this meaning I am confident, nor have heretics who would oppose me, any means of resistance on this point, since according to appearance, this accident without a subject, as they teach, which is the sacrament is the body of Christ, that is, sacramentally the sign and figure of the body itself. Then there is a greater relation between bread and the body of Christ (as Augustine shows) than between it and an accident of this sort, wherefore it is no mere coloring to say that the bread is figuratively the body of Christ. For, as Augustine teaches in what he says on John, corn is collected of a multitude of grain and ground; secondly, water is poured on it, and it is kneaded; and thirdly, it is taken as the food of the body for nourishment. In a similar way believers receive the sacramental bread in fragments; it is afterwards watered by evangelical faith and kneaded in the heart; and when baked by the fire of charity, is spiritually eaten. Accordingly, Augustine says on John, "Believe with a faith molded by charity, and thou hast eaten," and this must be understood of eating spiritually.

Furthermore, those heretics are not to be listened to who endeavor to do away with the meaning thus assigned by the false objection that such a figurative mode of expression is not used on any other occasion in the Gospel. For in Luke 22[:19] it is immediately subjoined, "Do this in remembrance of me," as if it had been said, This sacramental bread should be taken as an efficient memorial of me. Paul (1 Cor. 11) speaks in a similar manner—"this cup," &c., where there can be no doubt of its being a figurative expression, since in Mark 14[:24] Christ saith, "This is my blood," &c., where the words show the same thing, for the mind of the Catholic cannot comprehend that the bread is the body of Christ, except by a figurative understanding of these words, inasmuch as to identify these two things is impossible. Beyond all doubt, then, the expression "this is my body," is figurative, as are those in the Gospel of John: "unless ye eat the flesh of the Son of man," with many like them, which Christ spake in another sense [Jn. 6:53]. Nevertheless, there are some expressions in Scripture which must be understood plainly and without figure, as we grant in the matter of the incarnation, that our Jesus is God and man, which is plain from collated passages, as John 1, Eph. 1, and Heb. 1, whence it is thought that the cunning of the fiend hath long been busy about this fallacy, to lead the church into that heresy. And the cause of it is that the church prelates are not preferred according to Christ's ordaining, nor does the law of Antichrist suffer them to be zealous for the law of the Lord. As if the devil had been devising to this effect, saying, "If I can, by my vicar Antichrist, so far seduce the believers of the church as to bring them to deny that this sacrament is bread, and to believe it a most abominable accident, I may in the same manner lead them, after that, to believe whatever I shall have a mind, inasmuch as Scripture language and the senses of men plainly teach the opposite of that dogma, and doubtless after a space by the same means these simple-hearted believers may be brought to say that however a prelate shall live, be he effeminate, a homicide, a simonist, or stained with any other vice, this must never be believed concerning him by the obedient people."

Nevertheless, from motives of gain, such exemption must not be suffered to extend to the inferior clergy. And of the pope, it must be believed, as though it were a matter of faith, that he falls into no error, especially in regard to the faith of the church, but that he is a most blessed father, because he sins not. Thus it would appear, that the passage explained above, in Matt. 24[:15], "When ye shall see the abomination of desolation," refers to this heresy about the host.

INTRODUCTION TO *SACROSANCTA* AND *FREQUENS*

POPE BONIFACE VIII's ill-advised attempt in 1302 to assert the plenitude of papal authority over Christendom did not merely fail in the face of King Philip IV's determined opposition; it backfired rather spectacularly. Determined to prevent future popes from interfering in French affairs, Philip ensured that Boniface's successor, Clement V, was a Frenchman. Additionally, to make extra sure that he would not get too independent-minded, Philip pressured Clement to move the papal court to Avignon, in southeastern France, rather than Rome.

The notion of the Bishop of Rome ruling from somewhere that patently was not Rome shocked many Christians of the time; however, such was the power and wealth of the French church that there was no successful opposition until 1378, when Pope Urban VI was consecrated in Rome. Thus ended what came to be known as the Babylonian Captivity of the Church (so-called because it lasted around seventy years). But the cure proved to be worse than the disease. The French cardinals disavowed Urban and elected an anti-pope, Clement VII, who maintained the papal court at Avignon. The two popes duly excommunicated one another, France and its political allies promptly lined up behind Clement, and its enemies promptly lined up behind Urban.

This unseemly spectacle, known as the Great Schism, did not merely diminish the authority of the papacy, but shook Western Christendom to its core. After all, for centuries the Church had elaborated a theory in which all power flowed downward from God through the Pope and thence to kings, bishops, and the rest.

47

If one could not even be sure who was rightfully pope, the whole legitimacy structure of European society was thrown into question.

Theologians from across Europe busied themselves with the question of how to make sense of the chaos and how to resolve it, foremost among them the great nominalist theologians at the University of Paris, Pierre d'Ailly (1351-1420) and Jean Gerson (1363-1429). D'Ailly and Gerson laid the intellectual foundations of the movement known as conciliarism, which rethought the whole top-down conception of authority that had come to dominate the Church and proposed a more bottom-up approach. In this understanding, although the Pope retained a preeminent role, he was not above earthly accountability, for Christ had granted his authority to the whole body of the church—although by this they meant the whole body of the clergy. This was by no means radical as the ideas of Marsilius, and indeed most of the conciliarists were relatively conservative thinkers—as indeed their later execution of John Hus attests. While they admitted that normally only the Pope has authority to call and preside over a council, they insisted that this rule had not envisioned a crisis such as the Great Schism, when both popes were undermining the good and health of the church.

By 1409, the movement had gained enough traction to convene a Council at Pisa without papal support, but rather than ending the schism, it succeeded only in establishing a *third* rival pope, Alexander V. This new phase of crisis, along with the alarming support that the Hus was then gaining for his "heresies," was sufficient to goad leading churchmen, including two of the three rival popes, to convene a new council at Constance in 1414, with Gerson its lead theologian.

The 1415 decree *Sacrosancta* outlined the Council's self-understanding, asserting that it

> has its power immediately from Christ, and every one, whatever his state or position, even if it be the Papal dignity itself, is bound to obey it in all those things which pertain to the faith and the healing of the said schism, and to the general

reformation of the Church of God, in head and members.

This was not quite so radical a statement as it might first appear, since this conciliar authority was only envisioned as taking precedence in a time of great crisis and a vacuum of papal leadership. However, the conciliarists did envision church councils as playing an ongoing role in limiting papal authority, reforming abuses, and preventing any future schisms. Accordingly, in their 1417 decree *Frequens*, the Council provided for subsequent councils in 1423, 1431, and thereafter every ten years, and also issued several bold decrees restricting common abuses of papal power.

Although Constance did succeed in ending the Great Schism, with only one pope, Martin V, by the end of 1417, the larger success of the conciliar movement proved abortive. The Council of Basel which convened in 1431 became bolder in its assertion of conciliar authority, and clashed repeatedly with Pope Eugenius IV, who shrewdly outmaneuvered and undermined it until the movement petered out in 1450. However, with the shocking proliferation of papal abuses in the subsequent decades, the Protestant Reformers and their more conservative sympathizers would appeal to the conciliarist legacy, calling for a renewal of church councils to reform abuses and restrain the authority of the Pope.

Further Reading

For further reading, see Stephen K. Ozment, *The Age of Reform* (New Haven: Yale University Press, 1980), chapter 4; Francis Oakley, *The Conciliarist Tradition: Constitutionalism in the Catholic Church, 1300–1870* (Oxford: Oxford University Press, 2003), ch. 4; Philip H. Stump, *Reforms of the Council of Constance (1414–1418)* (Leiden: Brill, 1994).

THE COUNCIL OF CONSTANCE, *SACROSANCTA* (1414)[1]

IN THE NAME of the Holy and indivisible Trinity; of the Father, Son, and Holy Ghost. Amen. This holy synod of Constance, forming a general council for the extirpation of the present schism and the union and reformation, in head and members, of the Church of God, legitimately assembled in the Holy Ghost, to the praise of Omnipotent God, in order that it may the more easily, safely, effectively and freely bring about the union and reformation of the church of God, hereby determines, decrees, ordains and declares what follows: It first declares that this same council, legitimately assembled in the Holy Ghost, forming a general council and representing the Catholic Church militant, has its power immediately from Christ, and every one, whatever his state or position, even if it be the Papal dignity itself, is bound to obey it in all those things which pertain to the faith and the healing of the said schism, and to the general reformation of the Church of God, in head and members. It further declares that any one, whatever his condition, station or rank, even if it be the Papal, who shall contumaciously refuse to obey the mandates, decrees, ordinances or instructions which have been, or shall be issued by this holy council, or by any other general council, legitimately summoned, which concern, or in any way relate to the above mentioned objects, shall, unless he repudiate his conduct, be subject to condign penance and be suitably

---

[1] Translated by J. H. Robinson in *Translations and Reprints from the Original Sources of European History*, Series I, Vol. III (Philadelphia: University of Pennsylvania Press, 1912), 31-32.

punished, having recourse, if necessary, to the other resources of the law. [...]

THE COUNCIL OF CONSTANCE, *FREQUENS* (1417)[1]

On general councils

THE FREQUENT holding of general councils is a pre-eminent means of cultivating the Lord's patrimony. It roots out the briars, thorns and thistles of heresies, errors and schisms, corrects deviations, reforms what is deformed and produces a richly fertile crop for the Lord's vineyard. Neglect of councils, on the other hand, spreads and fosters the aforesaid evils. This conclusion is brought before our eyes by the memory of past times and reflection on the present situation. For this reason we establish, enact, decree and ordain, by a perpetual edict, that general councils shall be held henceforth in the following way. The first shall follow in five years immediately after the end of this council, the second in seven years immediately after the end of the next council, and thereafter they are to be held every ten years for ever. They are to be held in places which the supreme pontiff is bound to nominate and assign within a month before the end of each preceding council, with the approval and consent of the council, or which, in his default, the council itself is bound to nominate. Thus, by a certain continuity, there will always be either a council in existence or one expected within a given time. If perchance emergencies arise, the time may be shortened by the supreme pontiff, acting on the advice of his brothers, the cardinals of the Roman church, but it may never be

---

[1] Taken from Ernest F. Henderson's translation in *Decrees of the Ecumeical Councils*, ed. Norman P. Tanner (London: Sheed & Ward, 1990).

prolonged. Moreover, he may not change the place assigned for the next council without evident necessity. If an emergency arises whereby it seems necessary to change the place—for example in the case of a siege, war, disease or the like—then the supreme pontiff may, with the consent and written endorsement of his aforesaid brothers or of two-thirds of them, substitute another place which is suitable and fairly near to the place previously assigned. It must, however, be within the same nation unless the same or a similar impediment exists throughout the nation. In the latter case, he may summon the council to another suitable place which is nearby but within another nation, and the prelates and other persons who are customarily summoned to a council will be obliged to come to it as if it had been the place originally assigned. The supreme pontiff is bound to announce and publish the change of place or the shortening of time in a legal and solemn form within a year before the date assigned, so that the aforesaid persons may be able to meet and hold the council at the appointed time.

Provision to guard against future schisms

If it happens—though may it not!—that a schism arises in the future in such a way that two or more persons claim to be supreme pontiffs, then the date of the council, if it is more than a year off, is to be brought forward to one year ahead; calculating this from the day on which two or more of them publicly assumed the insignia of their pontificates or on which they began to govern. All prelates and others who are bound to attend a council shall assemble at the council without the need for any summons, under pain of the law's sanctions and of other penalties which may be imposed by the council, and let the emperor and other kings and princes attend either in person or through official deputies, as if they had been besought, through the bowels of the mercy of our lord Jesus Christ, to put out a common fire. Each of those claiming to be the Roman pontiff is bound to announce and proclaim the council as taking place at the end of the year, as mentioned, in the previously assigned place; he is bound to do this within a month after the day on which he came to know that one or more other persons had assumed the insignia of the papacy or was administering the papacy; and this is under pain of eternal damnation, of the automatic loss of any rights that he had acquired in the papacy, and of being disqualified both actively and passively from all dignities. He is also bound to make the council known by letter to his rival claimant or claimants, challenging him or them to a judicial process, as well as to all prelates and princes, insofar as this is possible. He shall go in person to the place of the council at the appointed time, under pain of the aforesaid penalties, and shall not depart until the question of the schism has been fully settled by the council. None of the contenders for the papacy, moreover shall preside as pope at the council. Indeed, in order that the church may rejoice more freely and quickly in one undisputed pastor, all the contenders for the papacy are suspended by law as soon as the council has begun, on the authority of this holy synod, from all administration; and let not obedience be given in any way by anyone to them, or to any one of them until the question has been settled by the council.

If it happens in the future that the election of a Roman pontiff is brought about through fear, which would weigh upon even a steadfast man, or through pressure, then we declare that it is of no effect or moment and cannot be ratified or approved by subsequent consent even if the state of fear ceases. The cardinals, however, may not proceed to another election until a council has reached a decision about the election, unless the person elected resigns or dies. If they do proceed to this second election, then it is null by law and both those making the second election and the person elected, if he embarks upon his reign as pope, are deprived by law of every dignity, honour and rank—even cardinalatial or pontifical—and are thereafter ineligible for the same, even the papacy itself; and nobody may in any way obey as pope the second person elected, under pain of being a fosterer of schism. In such a case the council is to provide for the election of a pope. It is lawful, however, and indeed all the electors are bound, or at least the greater part of them, to move to a safe locality and to make a statement about the said fear. The statement is to be made in a prominent place before public notaries and important persons as well as before a multitude of the people. They are to do this as quickly as they can without danger to their persons, even if there is a threat of danger to all their goods. They shall state in their allegation the nature and extent of the fear and shall solemnly swear that the allegation is true that they believe they can prove it and that they are not making it out of malice or calumny. Such an allegation of fear cannot be delayed in any way until after the next council.

After they have moved and have alleged the fear in the above form, they are bound to summon the person elected to a council. If a council is not due for more than a year after their summons, then its date shall be brought forward by the law itself to only a year ahead, in the way explained above. The elected person is bound under pain of the aforesaid penalties, and the cardinals under pain of automatically losing the cardinalate and all their benefices, to announce and proclaim the council within a month after the summons, in the way mentioned above, and to make it known as soon as possible. The cardinals and other electors are bound to come in person to the place of the council, at a suitable time, and to remain there until the end of the affair.

The other prelates are bound to answer the cardinals' summons, as mentioned above, if the person elected fails to issue a summons. The latter will not preside at the council since he will have been suspended by law from all government of the papacy from the time the council begins, and he is not to be obeyed by anyone in any matter under pain of the offender becoming a promoter of schism. If the aforesaid emergencies arise within a year before the beginning of a council-namely that more than one person claim to be pope or that someone has been elected through fear or pressure—then those who claim to be pope, or the one elected through fear or pressure, as well as the cardinals, are deemed by law as having been summoned to the council. They are bound, moreover, to appear in person at the council, to explain their case and to await the council's judgment. But if some emergency happens during the above occurrences whereby it is necessary to change the place of the council—for example a siege or war or disease or some such—then nevertheless all the aforesaid persons, as well as all prelates and others who are obliged to attend a council, are bound to assemble at a neighbouring place suitable for the council, as has been said above. Moreover, the greater part of the prelates who have moved to a particular place within a month may specify it as the place of the council to which they and others are bound to come, just as if it had been the place first assigned. The council, after it has thus been summoned and has assembled and become acquainted with the cause of the schism, shall bring a suit of contumacy against the electors or those claiming to be pope or the cardinals, if perchance they fail to come. It shall then pronounce judgment and shall punish, even beyond the aforesaid penalties and in such a way that the fierceness of the punishment acts as an example to others, those who are to blame—no matter of what state or rank or pre-eminence, whether ecclesiastical or secular, they may be—in starting or fostering the schism, in their administering or obeying, in their supporting those who governed or in making an election against the aforesaid prohibition, or who lied in their allegations of fear.

The disturbance caused by fear or pressure at a papal election corrodes and divides, in a lamentable way, the whole of Christianity. In order that it may be assiduously avoided, we have decided to decree, in addition to what has been said above, that if anyone brings to bear or causes, or procures to be brought about, fear or pressure or violence of this kind upon the electors in a papal election, or upon any one of them, or has the matter ratified after it has been done, or advises or acts in support of it, or knowingly receives or defends someone who has done this, or is negligent in enforcing the penalties mentioned below—no matter of what state or rank or pre-eminence the offender may be, even if it be imperial or regal or pontifical, or any other ecclesiastical or secular dignity he may hold—then he automatically incurs the penalties contained in pope Boniface VIII's constitution which begins Felicis, and he shall be effectively punished by them.

Any city—even if it be Rome itself, though may it not be!—or any other corporation that gives aid, counsel or support to someone who does these things, or that does not have such an offender punished within a month, insofar as the enormity of the crime demands and there exists the possibility of inflicting the punishment, shall automatically be subject to ecclesiastical interdict. Furthermore, the city, apart from the one mentioned above, shall be deprived of the episcopal dignity, notwithstanding any privileges to the contrary. We wish, moreover, that this decree be solemnly published at the end of every general council and that it be read out and publicly announced before the start of a conclave, wherever and whenever the election of a Roman pontiff is about to take place.

On the profession to be made by the pope

Since the Roman pontiff exercises such great power among mortals, it is right that he be bound all the more by the incontrovertible bonds of the faith and by the rites that are to be observed regarding the church's sacraments. We therefore decree and ordain, in order that the fullness of the faith may shine in a future Roman pontiff with singular splendour from the earliest moments of his becoming pope, that henceforth whoever is to be elected Roman pontiff shall make the following confession and profession in public, in front of his electors, before his election is published.

In the name of the holy and undivided Trinity, Father and Son and Holy Spirit. Amen. In the year of our Lord's nativity one thousand etc., I, N., elected pope, with both heart and mouth confess and profess to almighty God, whose church I undertake with his assistance to govern, and to blessed Peter, prince of the apostles, that as long as I am in this fragile life I will firmly believe and hold the catholic faith, according to the traditions of the apostles, of the general councils and of other holy fathers, especially of the eight holy universal councils—namely the first at Nicaea, the second at Constantinople, the third at Ephesus, the fourth at Chalcedon, the fifth and sixth at Constantinople, the seventh at Nicaea and the eighth at Constantinople—as well as of the general councils at the Lateran, Lyons and Vienne, and I will preserve this faith unchanged to the last dot and will confirm, defend and preach it to the point of death and the shedding of my blood, and likewise I will follow and observe in every way the rite handed down of the ecclesiastical sacraments of the Catholic church. This my profession and confession, written at my orders by a notary of the holy Roman church, I have signed below with my own hand. I sincerely offer it on this altar to you, almighty God, with a pure mind and a devout conscience, in the presence of the following. Made etc.

That prelates may not be translated without their consent

When prelates are translated, there is commonly both spiritual and temporal loss and damage of a grave nature for the churches from which they are transferred. The prelates, moreover, sometimes do not maintain the rights and liberties of their churches as carefully as they otherwise might, out of fear of being translated. The importunity of certain people who seek their own good, not that of Jesus Christ, may mean that the Roman pontiff is deceived in such a matter, as one ignorant of the facts, and so is easily led astray. We therefore determine and ordain, by this present decree, that henceforth bishops and superiors ought not to be translated unwillingly without a grave and reasonable cause which, after the person in question has been summoned, is to be inquired into and decided upon with the advice of the cardinals of the holy Roman church, or the greater part of them, and with their written endorsement. Lesser prelates, such as abbots and others with perpetual benefices, ought not to be changed, moved or deposed without a just and reasonable cause that has been inquired into.

We add, moreover, that for abbots to be changed the written endorsement of the cardinals is necessary—just as it is necessary for bishops, as has been said—saving, however, the constitutions and privileges of any churches, monasteries and orders.

On spoils and procurations

Papal reservations as well as the exacting and receiving of procurations which are due to ordinaries and other lesser prelates, by reason of a visitation, and of spoils on deceased prelates and other clerics, are seriously detrimental to churches, monasteries and other benefices and to churchmen. We therefore declare, by this present edict, that it is reasonable and in the public interest that reservations made by the pope, as well as exactions and collections of this kind made by collectors and others appointed or to be appointed by apostolic authority, are henceforth in no way to occur or to be attempted. Indeed, procurations of this kind, as well as spoils and the goods of any prelates found at their deaths, even if they are cardinals or members of the papal household or officials or any other clerics whatsoever, in the Roman curia or outside it, no matter where or when they die, are to belong to and to be received by, fully and freely, those persons to whom they would and ought to belong with the ending of the aforesaid reservations, mandates and exactions. We forbid the exaction of such spoils on prelates even inferior ones and others, which are outside and contrary to the form of common law. However, the constitution of pope Boniface VIII of happy memory, beginning Praesenti, which was published with this specially in mind, is to remain in force.

INTRODUCTION TO JOHN HUS'S
ON THE CHURCH

IF JOHN Wycliffe anticipated many of Luther's reforms from a purely theological perspective, it was left to his Czech disciple John (or Jan, in Czech spelling) Hus (c. 1369-1415) to provoke the political and ecclesiastical showdown which illustrated just how difficult meaningful church reform would be. Whereas Wycliffe died in his bed in his sixties, Hus was to die a martyr's death in his early forties, consigned to the flames by the Council of Constance in 1415. The irony of his fate is that Hus was not nearly so theologically radical as Wycliffe; indeed, interpreters have long sharply debated just how much a disciple of Wycliffe he was or wasn't, with some arguing for complete dependence and others insisting that he was careful to distance himself from Wycliffe's errors and was simply misunderstood by a paranoid church bureaucracy. The truth, as it usually does, seems to lie somewhere between these extremes.

Hus was concerned, as Wycliffe was, for the practical reform of the church, riddled as it was with greed and superstition, and for the preaching of the Scriptures (and indeed, he played a part in producing a Czech translation of the Bible). He did not, though, follow Wycliffe in his more radical positions, such as his denunciation of the Pope as Antichrist or, most significantly, his rejection of transubstantiation. Still, and crucially, he did come to oppose the sale of indulgences, and like Wycliffe, the whole ecclesiology that lay behind them. But before examining his ecclesiology and his treatise *De Ecclesia*, it may be good to explain how the theology of Wycliffe ended up in far-off Bohemia (as the modern-day Czech

Republic was then called), as well as the series of events that brought Hus to prominence and then to the stake.

Wycliffe's influence in Bohemia was the unintended by-product of the marriage between King Richard II of England and Anne of Bohemia in 1382, after which a steady stream of Bohemian scholars was brought over to study at Oxford, where the influence of Wycliffe's disciples and writings remained strong until the end of the century. Initially, it was only Wycliffe's philosophical writings that made it to the University of Prague, where they made a strong impression and gained for Wycliffe a loyal following, apparently unaware of (or unconcerned about) the "heresy" of his other works. John Hus, who had begun teaching in the University toward the end of the 1390s, was one of these early followers. By 1403, it appears, many of Wycliffe's theological writings, including some that had been denounced in England as heretical, had made their appearance in Prague, provoking a condemnation by the Archbishop of forty-five supposedly heretical Wycliffite teachings. Despite this condemnation, several members of the University, including Hus (by then a prominent preacher in the city) defended some of the teachings, recognizing in them themes that resonated with those of recent Bohemian reform movements. Still, few sought to endorse the whole of Wycliffe's reforming program.

The slow-simmering quarrel between defenders and opponents of Wycliffe might never have gone much further except for a series of events set in motion in 1409. That year, the Council of Pisa convened to try to end the Great Schism, deposing the two rival claimants to the papacy, Benedict XIII and Gregory XII, and electing in their place Alexander V (soon succeeded by John XXIII). As neither of the former claimants stepped down, there were now *three* rival popes, each supported by some rulers in Christendom. At the University of Prague, conflict raged between the Bohemian faculty, who followed the lead of their King Vaclav IV (r. 1363-1419) in endorsing Alexander V, whereas the Germans and Poles at the University supported Gregory. Vaclav responded by re-organizing the University to give the Bohemian faculty three votes and the other nations only one, to which the latter responded by leaving en masse. For the new, now exclusively Czech university, Vaclav appointed John Hus as rector. Thus thrown into prominence, Hus found his Wycliffite leanings the objects of intense scrutiny and suspicion, and his opponents on the faculty made common cause with Archbishop Zbynek against him. By 1411, Hus had been excommunicated, although Vaclav vigorously opposed what he saw as the meddling of the church authorities, and pressured the Archbishop into backing down. When Zbynek suddenly died in late 1411 and was replaced with a weak and ineffective successor, it looked like Hus might be left alone after all. That year, however, Pope John XXIII, Alexander's successor, authorized the preaching of indulgences to raise funds for a "holy crusade" against King Ladislaus of Naples, a supporter of his arch-rival, Pope Gregory XII. Hus and many in Prague were appalled at this shameless exploitation of the spiritual state of the common people to fund an unholy war between the popes, and fiercely opposed the indulgence preachers.

When Hus took up his pen to denounce the indulgences, he sealed his fate. In 1412, not only was Hus excommunicated anew, but all of Prague was placed under interdict (a suspension of all the sacraments on which salvation depended) until they handed him over. His fate was delayed for three years by the weakness and internal division of the ecclesiastical forces arrayed against him and the fitful support of King Vaclav IV and other powerful allies. But in 1415 he was summoned to answer for his heresies at the Council of Constance, which, having deposed all three rival popes, was now the supreme ecclesiastical authority. Despite a promise of safe-conduct, he was tried for heresy, quickly condemned, and burned at the stake.

It is devilishly difficult to sort out which "heresies" Hus might actually have been guilty of and which were false accusations, but much of the Council's ire was directed against the arguments so forcefully summarized in Hus's *De Ecclesia*, composed in the midst of controversy in 1413. Drawing heavily on the writings of

St. Augustine and on Wycliffe's book by the same name (not to mention extensive and careful arguments from Scripture), Hus's *On the Church* was a revolutionary document and, perhaps more than even he realized, a frontal assault on the late medieval Roman Catholic system. In it, he argued that, properly speaking, the church is not an institutional organization or the body of the clergy, but the whole body of the elect united to Christ their mystical head. As such, the true church is invisible, and the church that we see in history is a mixed multitude, consisting of true followers of Christ and those destined for perdition. This redefinition of the church along spiritual lines meant that not only were the papacy and the priesthood demoted to secondary importance, but their authority was in fact radically challenged. There was no guarantee that a priest or even a pope was among the elect, and in fact, if the pope acted wickedly or commanded against the law of God, he probably was not. In such cases, his claims to authority were null and void, and indeed believers were obliged to disobey. Only insofar as the priest or pope commanded in line with the truth of Christ did he truly represent the authority of Christ. Thus, as Hus says in his masterful treatment of the power of the keys, excerpted below, "it is clear that no man may be loosed from sin or receive the remission of sins, unless God have loosed him or given him remission," no matter what the priest says. By assigning the highest power claimed by the Church—the power over sins and salvation—to Christ alone, Hus challenged the entire ecclesiastical edifice down to its foundations, though it would be another century before it began to crack.

Further Reading

For further reading, see David S. Schaff, *John Huss: His Life, Teachings, and Death, After Five Hundred Years* (New York: Charles Scribner's Sons, 1915); Thomas A. Fudge, *Jan Hus: Religious Reform and Social Revolution in Bohemia* (New York: I.B. Tauris, 2010); František Šmahel and Ota Pavlíček, eds., *A Companion to Jan Hus* (Leiden: Brill, 2015.

JOHN HUS,
ON THE CHURCH (1413)[1]

Chapter 1: On the Unity of the Church

AS EVERY earthly pilgrim ought faithfully to believe the holy
catholic church just as he ought to love Jesus Christ, the Lord, the
bridegroom of that church, and also the church herself, his bride;
but as he does not love this, his spiritual mother, except he also
know her by faith, therefore ought he to learn to know her by faith,
and thus to honor her as his chief mother.

Therefore, in order to reach a proper knowledge of her, it is
to be noted (1) that the church signifies the house of God, constituted for the very purpose that in it the people may worship its
God, as it is written: "Have ye not houses to eat and to drink in?"
(1 Cor. 2:22). Or, to speak with Augustine: "Do you despise the
church of God, the house of prayer?" (2) The church signifies the
ministers belonging to the house of God. Thus the clerics belonging to one material church call themselves the church. But according to the Greeks, a church is a congregation held to gather under
one rule, as Aristotle teaches when he says: "All have part in the
church" (*Politics* 2:7). In view of this meaning, therefore, the congregation of all men is called the church. This appears in Matt.
25:31-33, which says: "When the Son of Man shall come in his glory and all his angels with him, then shall he sit upon the throne of
his glory and before him shall be congregated all nations." What a

---

[1] Taken from David Schaff, trans., *De Ecclesia: The Church by John Huss*
(New York: Charles Scribner's Sons, 1915).

great congregation of all men under the rule of Christ the king that will be! Because, however, the whole of that congregation is not the holy church it is added, "and he will separate them, the one from the other, as a shepherd separates the sheep from the goats."

From this it is evident that there is one church of the sheep and another of the goats, one church of the righteous and another of the reprobate. Likewise, the church of the righteous is on the one hand catholic, that is, universal, which is not a part of anything else. Of this I am now treating. On the other hand, it is particular, a part with other parts, as the Savior said: "Where two or three are congregated together in my name, there am I in the midst of them" (Matt. 18:20). From this it follows that two righteous persons congregated together in Christ's name constitute, with Christ as the head, a particular holy church, and likewise three or four and so on to the whole number of the predestinate without admixture. In this sense the term church is often used in Scripture, as when the apostle says: "To the church which is in Corinth, to the sanctified in Jesus Christ" (1 Cor. 1:1). Likewise Acts 20:28: "Take heed to yourselves and to the whole flock in which the Holy Spirit hath made you bishops, to feed the church which he hath purchased with his own blood." And in this sense, all the righteous now living under Christ's rule in the city of Prague, and more particularly the predestinate, are the holy church of Prague, and the same is true of other particular churches of saints of which Ecclesiasticus 24:2, speaks: "In the congregations of the Most High shall [wisdom] open her mouth," and also 31:11: "All the congregation of the saints shall declare his alms."

But the holy catholic—that is, universal—church is the totality of the predestinate or all the predestinate present, past, and future. This definition follows St. Augustine on John, who shows how it is that one and the same church of the predestinate, starting at the beginning of the world, runs on to the apostles, and thence to the day of judgment. For Augustine says: "The church which brought forth Abel, Enoch, Noah and Abraham, also brought forth Moses, and at a later time the prophets before the Lord's advent and she, which brought forth these, also brought forth the apostles and our martyrs and all good Christians. For she has brought forth all who have been born and lived at different periods, but they have all been comprised in a company of one people. And the citizens of this city have experienced the toils of this pilgrimage. Some are experiencing them now, and some will be experiencing them, even to the end of the world" (*C. Recur.* 32:4). How clearly that holy man shows what the holy catholic church is! And, in the same place and in a similar way, he speaks of the church of the wicked. This, he says, "brought forth Cain, Ham, Ishmael, and Esau, and also Dathan and other like persons of that people. And she, which brought forth these, also brought forth Judas, the false apostles, Simon Magus, and other pseudo-Christians, down to these days—all obstinately hardened in fleshly lusts, whether they are mixed together in a union or are clearly distinguished the one from the other." So much, Augustine.

From this statement it appears that the holy universal church is one, the church which is the totality of the predestinate, including all, from the first righteous man to the last one to be saved in the future. And it includes all who are to be saved who make up the number, in respect to the filling up of which number all the saints slain under the altar had the divine assurance that they should wait for a time until the number should be filled up of their fellow servants and brethren (Rev. 6:9-11). For the omniscient God, who has given to all things their weight, measure, and number, has predetermined how many shall ultimately be saved. Therefore, the universal church is also Christ's bride about whom the Canticles speak, and about whom Isaiah 61:10 [speaks]: "As a bridegroom decked with a crown, and as a bride adorned with jewels." She is the one dove of which Christ said: "My dove is one, my excellent one" (Song of Songs 6:9). She is also the strong woman whose maidens are clothed with double garments (Prov. 21:2). She is the queen, of whom the Psalmist says: "The queen stands at thy right hand in vestments of gold" (Psalm 45:9). This is Jerusalem, our mother, the temple of the Lord, the kingdom of heaven and the city of the Great King; and this whole church, as Augustine says, "is to be understood not only of that part which sojourns here, praising God from the rising to the setting of the sun, and which, after its old captivity, is singing the new song, but also of that part in heaven which, continuing true to the purpose for which it was constituted, has always been loyal to God, and has never felt misery from any fall. This part among the holy angels remains blessed and, as it behooves it to do, helps the part sojourning upon the earth, because she who is to be one by the companionship of eternity is now also one by the bond of love. And this whole church was constituted to worship God. Therefore, neither the whole nor any part of it wishes to be worshipped as God" (*Enchiridion*, 41). So far, Augustine.

This is the holy catholic church which Christians profess immediately after professing their faith in the Holy Spirit. First, because, as Augustine says, she is the highest creature, therefore she is placed immediately after the Trinity, which is uncreated, and second, because she is bound to Christ in a never-ending matrimony, and by the love of the Holy Spirit. And third, because, the Trinity being once acknowledged, it is proper that it should have her as a temple in which to dwell. Therefore Augustine, as above [*Enchiridion*, 41] concludes: "That God dwells in his temple—not only the Holy Spirit, but the Father likewise, and also the Son. And of his body—by virtue of which he is made head of the church of God which is among men, in order that in all things he might have the pre-eminence—the Son said: 'Destroy this temple and in three days I will build it up again'" (John 2:21). From these words of Augustine we deduce (1) that the universal church is one, praising God from the beginning of the world to the end; (2) that the holy angels are a part of the holy catholic church; (3) that the part of the church called pilgrim or militant is helped by the church triumphant; (4) that the church triumphant and the church militant are bound together by the bond of love; (5) that the whole church and every part of it are to worship God, and that neither she nor any part of it wishes to be worshipped as God.

From all this the conclusion follows that the faithful ought not to believe in the church, for she is not God, but the house of God, as Augustine in his *Exposition of the Creed* says, but they should believe that the catholic church is the bride of the Lord Jesus Christ—bride, I say, chaste, incorrupt, and never capable of being corrupted. For St. Cyprian, the bishop and glorious martyr, says: "The church is one, which is spread abroad far and wide by the increase of her fruitfulness" (24:1, *C. Loquitur*). And he adds: "Nevertheless the head is one, the origin is one, and one is the copious mother of fruitfulness. The bride of Christ cannot be defiled. She is incorrupt and chaste. She knows one house and guards with chaste modesty the sanctity of one couch." The holy church is also the husbandman's vineyard, of which Gregory in his Homilies says: "Our Maker has a vineyard, namely the universal church, which starts from righteous Abel and goes down to the last elect person who shall be born in the end of the world, which bears as many saints as the vineyard sends forth branches." Of the church St. Remigius also says in his *Homily Quadragesima* on the text: "'The men of Nineveh shall rise up in judgment with this generation and condemn it.' The holy church is made up of two parts, those who have not sinned and those who have ceased to sin." St. Isidore also, in speaking of the church, says: "The holy church is called catholic for the reason that it is universally distributed over all the world" (*de Summo Bono,* 14). Augustine and Ambrose likewise in their canticle, *Praising God,* say: "The holy church throughout all the world doth acknowledge Thee." And Ambrose speaks thus of her: "What house is more worthy of the entrance of apostolic preaching than is the holy church? Or who else is to be preferred above all others than Christ, who was accustomed to wash the feet of his guests and did not suffer any whom he received into his house to dwell there with soiled steps, that is, works?" (24:1). And, speaking of this church, Pope Pelagius cites Augustine as saying, "There cannot be two churches," and then adds: "Truly, as it has often been said, there can be only one church, the church which is Christ's body, which cannot be divided into two or more bodies" (24:1, *C. Schis-*

ma). Jerome also says of the church: "The church of Christ has no spot or wrinkle or anything of that sort, but he who is a sinner or is soiled with any filth cannot be said to be of Christ's church" (*de Pan., Dist. 1: C. Eccl*). This holy universal church is Christ's mystical body, as the apostle says, Eph. 1:22: "He gave himself to be the head over all the church, which is his body." Again he said, "He is the head of the body, which is the church" (Col. 1:18) and again, "For his body's sake, which is the church" (Col. 1:24) and "Christ is the head of the church and himself is the Savior of his body" (Eph. 5:23) and further on: "Christ loved the church and gave himself for it that he might sanctify it, washing it with the washing of water in the word of life that he might present it to himself a glorious church, not having spot or wrinkle or anything of that kind, but that it should be holy and without spot" (Eph. 5:25-27.)

Upon this text the holy doctors lean, as when Augustine says, "Christ is the head of the church, which is his body destined in the future to be with him in his kingdom and unending glory" (*de doctrina Christi*). Gregory says, "Because Christ and the church are one, the head and the body are one person" (*Moralia,* 35:9). And on Ezekiel, *homily 15*, he says: "The church is one substance with Christ, its head." And Bernard on the Canticles, *homily 12*: "The church is Christ's body, more dear than the body he gave over to death." And Pas Paschasius says: "Even as it is found in the Scriptures—the church of Christ, or the bride of God, is truly called Christ's body, truly because the general church of Christ is his body and Christ is called the head and all the elect are called members. From these members the one body of the church is brought unto a perfect man and the measure of the fulness of Christ. But the body of Christ, that is, the bride of God, is called in law the church. This is according to the apostle's words: 'And they twain shall be one flesh.' This, he says, is a great sacrament in Christ and the church. For, if Christ and the church are one flesh, then certainly there is one body, one head, one bridegroom, but different elect persons, members the one of the other" (*de sacra, corporis Christi*). So far, Paschasius.

These quotations from the saints show that the holy catholic church is the number of all the predestinate and Christ's mystical body—Christ being himself the head—and the bride of Christ, whom he of his great love redeemed with his blood that he might at last possess her as glorious, not having wrinkle of mortal sin or spot of venial sin, or anything else defiling her, but that she might be holy and without spot, perpetually embracing Christ, the bridegroom.

Chapter II: One Universal Church Divided into Three Parts

It having been said what the holy universal church is—that she is only one just as the number of all the predestinate is one, and also that she is distributed in her members throughout all the world—it must be known that this holy universal church is tripartite, that is, divided into the church triumphant, militant, and dormient.

The church militant is the number of the predestinate now on its pilgrimage to the heavenly country, and is called militant because it wages Christ's warfare against the flesh, the world and the devil.

The church dormient is the number of the predestinate suffering in purgatory. It is called dormient because being there she does not enjoy the blessedness which in the present life through God's prevenient and assisting grace she merited that she might get her reward in the heavenly country after the satisfaction made in purgatory.

The church triumphant consists of the blessed at rest in the heavenly country who kept up Christ's warfare against Satan and have finally triumphed. There will, however, be one great church on the day of judgment, made up of all these. And as a symbol of these three parts the doctors say the sacrament of the Eucharist is broken into three parts. The first part, the part immersed in the liquid sacrament, they say, signifies the church triumphant which is absorbed and inebriate with the dipping of the divine essence, as says the head of the church, making merry with his friends and companions: "Let us be drunken, my beloved" (Song of Songs 5:1). But the two other parts in the hand of the Lord and to be purged through the merit of the church are set forth by those two parts which the priest holds in his hands, the greater, being laid down, signifies the militant church and the lesser, resting upon it, signifies the church waiting in purgatory. For this church in purgatory depends upon the suffrages of the church militant. And for these two parts we pour out our double prayers to the Lamb, who is the head of the church, that he may have mercy upon us. But as for the third part, to whose dwelling-place and rest we look forward, we pray that the same Lamb of the threefold nature may at last give us peace. For this reason, Christ in his state of humiliation visited three places of the church, (1) the navel of our habitable world, dwelling thirty-three years in Judea and Jerusalem; (2) the limbus, in which the Fathers were purified, by bringing out a fragment of his church in the spirit; and (3) ascending to heaven he led captivity captive, which, after his triumph, he crowned by placing it at God's right hand. This, therefore, is the threefold division of this one universal or catholic church, although, however, there are particular churches.

But this universal church is a virgin, the bride of Christ—who is a virgin—from whom as from a true mother we are spiritually born. A virgin, I say, all beautiful and in whom there is no spot (Song of Songs 4:7), "having neither spot nor wrinkle" (Eph. 5:27), holy and immaculate, and so most chaste even as she is in the heavenly country. Nevertheless, by fornicating with the adulterant devil and with many of his children she is partially corrupt by wrong-doing. However, she is never received as the bride to be embraced, beatifically at the right hand and in the bed of the bridegroom, until she has become a pure virgin, altogether without wrinkle. For Christ is the bridegroom of virginity, who, as he lives forever, cannot allow the bride to desert him and fornicate spiritually. Thus it is said of the multitude of the heavenly denizens that they are virgins and follow the Lamb wheresoever he goeth (Rev.

14:4). But in the very first moment of the world Christ was predestinated to be the bridegroom of the church, and by establishing the angels [in glory] he gave a dowry to one part of the bride. And so also by establishing righteous Abel and other saints, up to the time of the incarnation, the church remained continually in her espousals. At the incarnation he made his second marriage by creating to be a queen a part of the whole church, which by a certain fitness is called the Christian church. For then our leader and legislator familiarly addressed his bride, as the apostle says (Heb. 1). By assuming human nature he put on our armor and as a giant overcame the enemies of the church and taught how a part of the church, as a jealous bride, ought to follow him.

Therefore, the whole of Christian doctrine is involved in that prayer of the church in which we pray the bridegroom, by his coming into the flesh, that he may teach us to despise earthly things and love heavenly things—to despise, that is, to subordinate terrestrial things in our affections and to love Christ the bridegroom above all things.

Hence, it is evident that the universal holy church is Christ's one and only bride, the virgin to be in the end most chaste, whom the Son of God bound to himself in matrimony out of eternal love and by the grace of adoption, and the church we firmly believe, saying with the Creed, "I believe one holy catholic church," and about which the word is added in the second Creed, "and apostolic [church]." It is called apostolic for the reason that the apostles are full participants of this same mother church, which is fully purified in the Spirit, and which they themselves planted with the teaching and blood of Christ; and by whose teaching (i.e., of the apostles) and authority their vicars now rule the young bride, who seeks only the bridegroom of the church. So runs the Decretal 24 where pope Leo says: "Peter's authority has its seat wherever its just sentence is carried." For Peter himself dwells in heaven, seeing and looking after what God binds and looses. Hence Boniface VIII says: "We are bound with living faith to believe and hold that the holy catholic and apostolic church is one" (*Extravagante*).

The unity of the catholic church consists in the unity of predestination, inasmuch as her separate members are one by predestination and in the unity of blessedness, and inasmuch as her separate sons are finally united in bliss. For, in the present time, her unity consists in the unity of faith and the Christian virtues and in the unity of love, even as Augustine draws forth in expounding John 17:21, "that they all may be one," and in his letter to Dardanus, where he expounds the text "it is expedient that one man die for the people" (John 18:14). "Caiaphas," Augustine says: "prophesied that God would gather together in one his children" (John 11:52), that is, not in one material locality, "but he has gathered them together into one spirit and one body, whose only head is Christ." To this unity the apostle refers: "endeavoring to keep the unity of the Spirit in the bond of peace. There is one body, one Spirit, one Lord, one faith, one baptism, one God and Father of all" (Eph. 4:3). Nor is it to be doubted that without this union, as indicated before, is there any salvation.

Chapter III: All Christians are not Members of the Church

Against what has already been said the objection is raised (1) that if the treatment is correct then no reprobate would be a part of our holy mother, the universal church. But the consequence is false, for every Christian is a part of that church, as appears from the parable: "The kingdom of heaven is like unto a net cast into the sea which gathered in all manner of fish" (Matt. 13:47). On this St. Gregory in his *Homilies* says: "The holy church is compared to a net cast into the sea because she is committed to fishers and because every one is drawn up through her from the waves of this present world to the eternal kingdom lest they sink in the depths of eternal death." (2) The falsehood of the treatment is confirmed by Matt. 22:2: "The kingdom of heaven is likened to a king, who made a marriage feast for his son and sent forth his servants to call them that were bidden to the marriage feast." Going out, they gathered in all whom they found, both good and bad, and the marriage feast was full of guests. Here Gregory says: "By the very quality of the guests it is evident that by this royal marriage the present church is meant, in which the bad meet with the good, a mixed church made up of a diversity of children." (3) It is confirmed by what is said, "The Son of man shall send forth his angels and gather together out of his kingdom all things that offend and them that do iniquity" (Matt. 13:41); and (4) by Matt. 5:20: "Whoso shall break one of the least of these commandments and teach men so, shall be least in the kingdom of heaven." Commenting on both these passages, Gregory says: "The kingdom of heaven is the present church" (homily 12).

(5) The falsehood appears from Luke 3:17: "He shall baptize you with the Holy Spirit and with fire, whose fan is in his hand, and he will cleanse his threshing-floor and gather the wheat into his garner; but the chaff he will burn with fire unquenchable." Here threshing-floor stands for the catholic church as the doctors expound, especially Augustine, who says of faith: "Hold most tenaciously and in no wise doubt that God's threshing-floor is the catholic church and that in it the chaff will remain mixed with the wheat till the end of the world" (*ad Petrum*). And this judgment of Augustine is confirmed by Christ's words: "The kingdom of heaven is like unto a man who sows good seed in his field," and Christ afterward says: "Let both grow until the harvest" (Matt. 13:30).

Now for the right understanding of these things and the things to be said, we must lay down out of the apostle's words that Christ is the head of the universal church, that she is his body and that everyone who is predestinate is one of her members and consequently a part of this church, which is Christ's mystical body, that is, hidden body, ruled by the power and influence of Christ, the Head, and compacted and welded together by the bond of predestination. This underlying proposition follows from that saying of the apostle: "He gave him to be head over all the church which is his body" (Eph. 1:22). It also follows from the words when, speaking as the representative of the predestinate, he says: "We being many are one body in Christ" (Rom. 12:5). It also follows from Eph. 4:11: "He gave some apostles, some prophets, some evangelists, and some pastors and teachers, for the perfecting of the saints for the work of the ministry unto the edifying of the body of Christ." And further on it is said: "Doing the truth in love, let us grow up in all things into him who is the head, even Christ, for whom all the body compacted together by that which every joint supplieth, according to the working in the measure of each several part, maketh increase of the body unto the edifying of itself in love" (Eph. 4:15).

Further it is to be noted that Christ is called the head of the church for the reason that he is the most exalted individual of the human family, imparting to all its members motion and feeling. For as in a man the most excellent part is the head, which gives to the body and to its parts motion and feeling, and without which neither the body nor any of its members could live the life of nature, so Christ is the individual, the true God and man, imparting spiritual life and motion to the church and every one of its members and without whose influence it could not live or feel. And as in a man's head are all the senses, so in Christ are hid all the treasures of the wisdom and knowledge of God (Col. 2:3). The above judgment is also involved in the apostle's words when he says: "All things were created by him and in him; and he is before all, and in him do all things consist and he is the head of the body, the church who is the beginning and the first born from the dead; that in all things he might have the pre-eminence, for in him it was pleasing that all fulness should dwell and through him to reconcile all things to himself" (Col. 1:20).

This unity of the body—that is, the church—the apostle proves by showing that the diversity of graces, ministries and operations proceeds from the one spiritual Lord who works in all (1 Cor. 12:3). For grace must precede: it is the beginning of ministration for clerics and of operation for laymen. The Spirit gives grace, the Lord receives ministration, and God demands ministration. "To one," the apostle says, "is given by the Spirit the word of wisdom, to another the word of knowledge by the same Spirit; to one faith in the same Spirit, to another the grace of healing, to another the working of miracles, to another prophecy, to another discerning of spirits, to another divers sorts of tongues, to another the interpretation of words" (1 Cor. 12:8-10). These nine the apostle seems to express one after the other, each in its own logical order in the men who receive the gifts. God, he says, has placed some in the church, first apostles, secondarily prophets, thirdly teachers, then miracles, then gifts of healings, interpretations of words, helps, governments, divers sorts of tongues, all nine of which seem to be correlated to the former nine. And in the same passage, comparing the body of Christ and its members to the body of the natural man, the apostle says: "As the body is one and hath many members, but all the members of the body, though they are many, are one body, so also is Christ" (1 Cor. 12:12).

There is to be noted a threefold correspondence and a threefold difference between the members of the mystical body and the human body. For as the members compose one body to which the soul is joined, and again as each member is necessary to every other, the one helping the other in the performance of its functions, so it is true of the members of the church by virtue of the power of communion and the bond of love. Again, as the members of the body keep themselves in their own function, so do also the members of the church. For, according to Chrysostom, a man is as a book in whom the whole Christian religion is written, therefore, just as there is an affinity from the head down to the feet, so reason and feeling are bound together (*de opere imperfecta*). Also, just as every member, comely or uncomely, serves the spirit without strife, so every member of the church serves Christ, without any strife concerning supremacy and obedience. And just as the superior members do not boast of their comeliness but perform their functions and follow the soul's rule unto the help of each single member, so ought it to be with members of the church. And just as the eyes and the countenance are in their activities without a covering lest, if veiled, they might defile and prepare for destruction, so Christ and the apostles, out of the fervor of their love and by reason of their exemption from the fervor of lust, were not involved in temporal interests in a secular way; and their vicars, yea, all clerics ought to be like eyes. But the members, less comely, as the secret parts, are more concealed and more tender and multiplex, and so it is with mean persons, by whom the dregs of the church are gotten rid of. But the difference between the members of these bodies is to be stated thus: (1) Since the parts of the church persist by grace, they are not concerned as to their place or corporal location, as are the members of the human body. (2) As the members are mystical, it is not inconsistent but fitting that single members should have functions of different kinds. For a man is, as it were, a totality so that it is fitting that he should act all at once, so far as he is able. (3) The members of the church should have vital forces flowing into them from Christ, just as the members of the body have vital forces flowing into them from the soul, from which these forces become part of the very essence of the members; nevertheless, the inflowing comes first, and the operation of the members is voluntary and gracious and meritorious.

Further, it is to be noted that, as there is in the human body an element which is not of the body itself, as spittle, phlegm, ordure, and fluid or urine, and this element is not of the body because it is not a part of the body—and it is another thing to be a part of the human body, as is every one of its members—so also there is something in the mystical body of Christ, which is the church, that is nevertheless not of the church, since it is not a part of it; and in this way every reprobate Christian is of the body just as ordure is of the body and to be finally separated from it. And so it is one thing to be of the church and another thing to be in the church. And it is clear that it does not follow of all pilgrims who are in the church that they are then of the church, but the opposite. For we know that the tares grow together with the wheat, the raven feeds on the same threshing-floor as the dove, and the chaff is gathered into the same garner with the grain. Nevertheless, there is an incommunicable distinction between them, just as has been illustrated by the human body. In this way, we ought to think of holy mother church, and to these things 1 John 2:18 has reference where it is said: "Now have there arisen many antichrists. They went out from us, but were not of us; for, if they had been of us, they would have continued with us." For just as superfluity proceeds from food and the solid members and yet is not of them, so the purgaments of the church, namely the reprobate, proceed from her and yet are not of her as parts, for none of her parts can fall away from her finally, because predestinating love, which binds her together, does not fail. This the apostle asserts (1 Cor. 13), and this he proves when he says: "We know that to them that love God all things work together for good, even to them that are called to be righteous according to his purpose" that is, the purpose of predestination. "For whom he foreknew, them he also predestinated to be conformed to the image of his Son, that he might be the first-born among many brethren. And whom he predestinated, them he also called; and whom he called, them he also justified" (Rom. 8:28-30). And he concludes by calling them predestinate after suffering a long trial when he said: "I am persuaded that neither death nor life, nor angels, nor principalities, nor powers, nor things present, nor things to come, nor might, nor depth, nor any creature shall be able to separate us from the love of God which is in Christ Jesus our Lord" (Rom. 8:38-39).

Besides, it is to be noted that, as many say, the relation of pilgrims to holy mother church is fourfold. Some are in the church in name and in fact, as are predestinate Catholics, obedient to Christ; some are neither in fact nor in name, as are the reprobate heathen; some in name only, as are reprobate hypocrites; and some are in the church in fact, although they may seem in name to be outside, as are predestinate Christians whom the satraps of antichrist seem to be damning before the very eyes of the church, for so pontiffs and Pharisees condemned by bitter death our Redeemer as a blasphemer, and consequently as an heretic, "who was predestinated to be the Son of God" (Romans 1:4).

Further, it is to be noted that no place, or human election, makes a person a member of the holy universal church, but divine predestination does in the case of everyone who persists in following Christ in love. And, according to Augustine predestination is the election of the divine will through grace; or, as it is commonly said, predestination is the preparation of grace—making ready—in the present time, and of glory in the future. But the position is taken that predestination is twofold: first, the one predestination by which a person is foreordained here to righteousness and the acceptance of the remission of sins, but not for the obtaining of the life of glory (*de Penitentia, Dist.* 4, *Hinc propheta*). To this predestination the second definition, as given above, does not apply. The other predestination is that whereby a person is predestinated to obtain eternal life in the future. The first kind of predestination follows this, and not vice versa. For if anyone is predestinated to eternal life, it necessarily follows that he is predestinated unto righteousness, and if he follows life eternal, he has also followed righteousness. But the converse is not true. For many are made partakers of present righteousness but from want of perseverance are not partakers of life eternal. Hence it is said: "Many seem to be predestinate by the merit of present righteousness and not by the predestination of eternal glory" (*de Penitentia,* 4, *Hoc ergo*). And Gratian grounds this position in the words of the apostle, "Blessed be the God and Father of our Lord Jesus Christ who has blessed us with every spiritual blessing in the heavenly places in Christ: even as He chose us in Him before the foundation of the world, that we should be holy and without blemish before Him in love, who predestinated us unto the adoption of sons through Jesus Christ, according to the good pleasure of His will to the praise of the glory of His grace, which is freely bestowed on us in His beloved Son, in whom we have our redemption through His blood unto the remission of sins" (Eph. 1:3-7).

Further, it is evident that men may be of holy mother church in two ways—either by predestination to life eternal, the way all who are finally holy are of holy mother church, or by predestination to present righteousness only, as are all such who at one time or another accept the grace of the remission of sins but do not persevere unto the end.

And, further, it is evident that grace is twofold—namely, the grace of predestination unto eternal life, from which a person foreordained cannot finally fall away. The other is the grace related to present righteousness, which now is present and now is absent, now comes and now goes. The first kind of grace makes sons for the holy universal church and makes a man infinitely more perfect than the second kind, because it bestows an infinite good to be enjoyed forever. But not so the second kind of grace. Again, the first makes sons of an eternal heritage, while the second makes officials acceptable to God only for time. Hence it seems probable that just as Paul was at the same time a blasphemer according to present unrighteousness and yet of holy mother church, and, consequently, one of the faithful and in grace in virtue of predestination unto eternal life—so Iscariot was at one and the same time in grace according to present righteousness and yet never of holy mother church by predestination unto life eternal, for that predestination was wanting in his case. And so Iscariot, howbeit he was an apostle and bishop elected by Christ—"bishop" being the name of an office—was nevertheless never a part of holy mother church. Even so Paul was never a member of the devil, howbeit he committed some acts which were like the acts of the church of the wicked. Similar was the case of Peter, who, by the Lord's permission, fell into grave perjury, but in order that he might rise the stronger, for as Augustine says, it is expedient that the predestinate fall into sins of that sort.

From what has been said, it is evident that there is a twofold separation from holy church. The first is permanent, and here belong the reprobate who are separated from the church. The second may be lost—and here belong heretics, who are separated by ruinous sin from holy church itself, but, nevertheless, are able by God's grace to come to the sheepfold of the Lord Jesus Christ. Of the latter Christ says: "Other sheep I have which are not of this fold, and them I must bring" (John 10:16). Other sheep he had by virtue of predestination, which are not of this fold and of his church according to present righteousness, which sheep of his grace he brought to life.

This distinction between predestination and present grace deserves to be strongly emphasized, for some are sheep by predestination and ravening wolves according to present righteousness, as Augustine deduces in his *Commentary on John*: "In like manner some are sons by predestination and not yet by present grace." And this same distinction in both its parts Augustine touches upon in his *Exposition of John 11:52*, where it is said: "That they might gather together into one the children of God who are scattered abroad." "Caiaphas," Augustine says, "was prophesying of the Jewish people only, to whom the sheep belonged whom the Lord had in mind when he said: 'I am not sent but unto the lost sheep of the house of Israel,' but the Evangelist knew that there were other sheep who were not of this fold which he had to bring. Therefore, he added: 'And not for that nation only, but that he might gather together into one the sons of God who are scattered abroad.' These things, moreover, were said according to the law of predestination. For up to that time they were neither his sheep nor the sons of God." So much Augustine. And in reference to these things it is said, "In this way they are not children except as they are partakers of eternal blessedness." And it is added: "They are called children in three ways: either by predestination alone, as those of whom John spoke that 'he might gather into one the children of God who are scattered abroad'; or by predestination and the hope of eternal blessedness, as were those to whom the Lord said: 'Little children, yet a little while I am with you'; or, thirdly, by the merit of faith and present righteousness, but not by predestination to eternal glory, as was the case with those of whom the Lord said: 'If his sons forsook my law and walked not in my statutes' (Psalm 89:31)" (*De Penitentia, Dist. 4, Hoc ergo*). [...]

Chapter X: The Power of Binding and Loosing

Now as to the power—authority—of Christ, given by himself to his vicars, which is touched upon in the words, "I will give unto thee the keys of the kingdom of heaven," that is, the power to bind and to loose sins—Augustine says, "The effects of this power are shown, when Christ adds, 'And whatsoever thou shalt bind on earth, shall be bound in heaven, and whatsoever thou shalt loose on earth shall be loosed in heaven.' This power is a spiritual power. Therefore, it is to be noted, that spiritual power is a power of the spirit, determining its acts of itself so that a rational creature, so far as gracious gifts go, may be guided and have his own distinctive place both as determined from the standpoint of the subject and the object" (*Com. on John 21*). Every man, however, is a spirit, since he has two natures, as the Savior in speaking to his disciples said: "Ye know not what spirit ye are of" (Luke 9:55), and "every spirit that confesseth not Jesus is not of God" (1 John 4:3). Here the spirit is subtle and heretical, denying Jesus to be very God and very man. And it is evident that whether power in respect to God and power in respect to rational creatures are analogous or the analogy is to be restricted to the powers of men and the powers of angels, it is true that all spiritual power is a power of the spirit. And, although a man does not give grace, he nevertheless administers the sacraments, so that the inferior is guided as to gifts of grace.

But although bodily power may be the result of gifts of grace, nevertheless it is immediate, so that the creature of God is ruled according to the law of natural things or of fortune. So every man is seen to have a double power, for every man ought to have the power over the movements of his members, and therefore has the power of walking in grace, so also the spiritual power has manifold subdivisions, for there is one power of orders and another common to all. The power of orders is called the spiritual power. This is that which the clergy has to administer the sacraments of the church that the clergy may profit itself and the laity, and such power is the power of consecrating the mass, absolving and performing the other sacramental acts. For the power of consecrating the mass exists of itself and immediately, that the priest may consecrate just as dispositions of moral virtue are ordained because of acts better than the dispositions. And as the priest, in order that he may consecrate worthily, is guided as to the gifts of grace, the above description holds.

But the spiritual power, which is common, is the power which every priest has in doing spiritual works whether in his own person or among others, and about these the verse reminds us: "Teach, counsel, punish, console, remit, bear, pray."

For as many as received Christ by faith to these hath he given the power to become the sons of God, so that they may guide themselves and their brethren in the way of their Father Christ, and by rebuking in love as Christ said: "If thy brother sin against thee, go show him his fault between thee and him alone" (Matt. 18:15).

Secular power is twofold, civil and common. Civil power, which is authoritative, belongs only to the civil lord. But civil power, which is vicarious, belongs to officials or servants. But secular power, which is common to all, is the power by which a man is able to rule himself and his own according to the gifts of nature and of fortune. And thus, just as a man cannot be a whole man without body and soul, nor is the adopted child of God complete without the gifts of nature and of grace, so the pilgrim cannot get along as a pilgrim unless he has both secular and spiritual power which are common to all, although this is bound in the case of infants and the dead. But spiritual power is everywhere the more perfect and the sacerdotal power exceeds the power of kings in dignity as appears from Heb. 7:7: "Greater is he that blesses and less is he who is blest."

Hence the spiritual power, which is sacerdotal, excels the royal in age, dignity, and usefulness. In age it excels, because the priesthood was instituted by God's command, as appears from Ex. 28. Later at God's command the kingly power was instituted by the priesthood, as appears from Deut. 17 and 1 Sam. 12. In dignity it excels, as already said, because the priest as the greater blesses, consecrates, and anoints the king. And the usefulness is evidently greater for the reason that the spiritual power is in and of itself sufficient for the ruling of the people, as appears from the history of Israel, which down to the time of Saul was salubriously administered independent of the kingly authority. Therefore, the spiritual power, inasmuch as it concerns the best things—things having their sufficiency in themselves—excels the earthly power, since the latter is of no avail independent of the spiritual power which is the chief regulative force. On the other hand, the spiritual power may act by itself without the aid of the earthly power. And, for this reason, the priests who abuse this power, which is so exalted, by pride or other open sin, fall all the lower with the devil into hell, and this is in accord with the rule of St. Gregory and other saints: "The higher the position the deeper the fall."

And it is to be noted, that power now means absolutely the ability to regulate and rule and now collectively such ability through authoritative notification and announcement. And when these senses are equally known, it is evident, there is nothing contradictory in the principles that there is no power but of God and yet to give power from God, that is, make an authoritative announcement before the church that a created being has from God power of this sort. Indeed, such a bestowal, so far as part of it is concerned, is given by man but not unless God primarily authorizes it. And from this we may further understand that power is not relaxed or stiffened, increased or diminished, so far as its essence goes, but only in respect to the exercise of the act which proceeds from the power itself. And this exercise ought only to be used when a reasonable ground exists for it from the side of God. This meaning is set forth in *Decretum 24:1, Miramur*, which says: "The official power is one thing, the exercise of it another. And official power is for the most part held in restraint in the case of monks and of others, such as those under suspension, who are inhibited from ministering, though the power itself is not taken away from them." In like manner it is conceded that the natural power, which is free will, may now be relaxed by grace and now tightened [increased and lessened]. And in this way the seeming discordances of the doctors which arise by ambiguity of language are solved, some of whom, as Anselm, say, "that free will cannot be lost or increased or diminished," while others, like Augustine say that free will may be lost through sin and increased through grace (*Enchiridion*). On this account, there is in the church great strife about the power of bestowment, withdrawal, or restriction. Nevertheless, it is known that when God and reason make it necessary for the profit of the church that a thing should be done by man, then and not otherwise does God give or withdraw or restrict power of this sort.

Hence, when Christ said to Peter: "I will give thee the keys of the kingdom of heaven," that is the power of binding and loosing sins, he said in the person of Peter to the whole church militant, that not does any person whatever of the church without distinction hold those keys, but that the whole church, as made up of its individual parts, as far as they are suitable for this, holds the keys. These keys, however, are not material things, but they are spiritual power and acquaintance with evangelical knowledge, and it was on account of this power and knowledge, as we believe, that Christ used the plural "keys." For this reason, the Master of Sentences [Peter Lombard] says: "He speaks in the plural 'keys,' for one is not sufficient. These keys are the wisdom of discernment and the power of judging, whereby the ecclesiastical judge is bound to receive the worthy and exclude the unworthy from the kingdom" (*12:18, cap. 2*). And it is to be noted that to the Trinity alone does it belong to have the chief power of this kind. And the humanity of Christ alone has chief subordinate power from within himself, for Christ is at the same time God and man. Nevertheless, prelates of the church have committed unto them instrumental or ministerial power, which is a judicial power, consisting chiefly of two things, namely, the power of knowing how to discriminate, and the power of judging judicially. The former of these is called in the court of penance the key of the conscience, reasonably disposing the mind to the exercise of the second function, that is, the judicial, for no one legally has the power of pronouncing a definite sentence unless he has the prior power of discerning in a case in which he is called upon to discriminate and pronounce sentence.

The first key, therefore, is neither an act nor a state of knowledge, but the power of antecedent discernment. Consequently, all the power of the sacerdotal order, namely, of being the instrument in opening to man the gate, which is Christ, or of shutting to an inferior the said kingdom, is the key of the church given to Peter and to others, as appears from the Savior's words: "Verily I say unto you whatsoever ye bind on earth, shall be bound in heaven, and whatsoever ye shall loose on earth shall be loosed in heaven" (Matt. 18:18). He also said: "Receive ye the Holy Spirit. Whosesoever sins ye forgive they are forgiven unto them; and whosesoever sins ye retain they are retained" (John 20:22). To Peter and the church in him were the words spoken: "Whatsoever thou shalt loose on earth," etc. (Matt. 16:19).

These words, because of a defect in their understanding, frighten many Christians so that they are filled with servile fear, while others are deceived by them and presume because of the fulness of power [they are supposed to convey]. Therefore, the following things are to be laid down: (1) that the Savior's dictum about the virtue of the words is necessary, because it is not possible for a priest to loose or bind anything, unless such loosing and binding take place in heaven, not only in the heavenly realm which also comprises the sublunary world [world below the moon] and all things which are therein, but also take place with the divine approval and the approval of angelic beings which are heavenly. Hence, it is to be noted that guilt inheres in the soul of him who sins mortally and grace is corrupted or ceases to be, for which reason he who sins mortally is under the debt of eternal damnation, provided he does not do penance, and, if he persists in this guilt, he is separated from the companionship of pilgrims in grace. But in penance there is a remedy, by which guilt is deleted, grace conferred, the chain of damnation broken, and man reunited with the church. This penance is performed by contrition, confession and satisfaction. Contrition, which is sorrow or full pain for sin committed, must include displeasure with the sin already committed, and the sin which may be committed and, in the case of necessity, such contrition is enough for salvation. Hence the Savior, knowing that the mind of the adulteress was full of sorrow, added the words: "Go and sin no more" (John 8:11). For this reason St. Augustine, St. Ambrose, and St. Gregory agree in saying that to be penitent is to lament evils done and not to wish to do evils that are to be lamented.

Secondly, it is to be noted that for the justification of the wicked man there is needed infinite power by which God cleanses from spot and stain and grants grace. Again, God's mercy is needed whereby he relaxes the offense done his Majesty, and the eternal punishment for the debt which would follow if he did not do penance. Therefore, the church often prays, "Almighty and most merciful God," urging the infinite power and mercy of God. But that infinite power is required for the justification of a wicked man is evident because, as Augustine says, "it is easier to create a world than to justify the wicked; the first demands infinite power and consequently also the second [act], and this is the reason why, in the justification of the wicked, the active bestowal of the Holy Spirit is required, which cannot be secured except from God," as Augustine proves in many places, as I have shown in my *Tract on Indulgences*. And the Master of Sentences concludes from these words of Augustine and says, "Therefore no men, however holy, can give the Holy Spirit" (1:14) and the same reasoning applies to the active remission of sins.

Hence in a unique sense the Baptist said of Christ: "Behold the Lamb of God that taketh away the sins of the world" (John 1:29). On these words Augustine says: "Let no one presume and say of himself that he takes away the sins of the world. Now, observe the proud against whom John lifted his finger were not yet heretics and yet they were already shown to be such against whom he cried from the river" (*Hom. on John, 4*). Wherefore the Jews often ascribed blasphemy to Christ because, esteeming him, though falsely, to be a mere man, they said he was not able of himself to forgive sins, because sin is not forgiven by a mere word except only as the offense against God is relaxed. But who forgives an injury except the person against whom it is done or against whose subject it is done? For God, in giving power of this kind, first forgives the injury against Himself before His vicar can forgive. Hence on this point Ambrose says: "He alone forgives sins who alone died for us. The Word of God forgives sins. The priest is the judge. The priest performs his function and does not exercise the way of any power" (*De Penitentia, 1*). To the same purport speaks Jerome, whom the Master of Sentences quotes and Gregory (*1:1, Paulus*). The same holds good for the retention and binding of sins. Hence the Master of Sentences, adducing these authorities and reasons, concludes that "God alone washes a man within clean from the stain of sin and from the debt of eternal punishment," and he closes thus: "By these and many other testimonies it is taught that God alone and of Himself forgives sins; and just as He forgives some so He retains the sins of others" (*4:18, 4*).

But someone will say, if God alone can forgive and retain sins, why did He say to the apostles and their vicars: "Whatsoever ye shall loose," etc., and "whosoever sins ye retain," etc.? What, therefore, is it for a priest to loose or bind sins, to remit or retain? To the first the Master of Sentences gives answer and says: "Priests also bind when they impose the satisfaction of penance upon those who confess. They loose when in view of the satisfaction they forgive anything or admit those purged by it to participation in the sacraments." To the second Richard answers well in his *Power of Loosing and Binding*, when he says: "What is it to remit sins except to relax the sentence of punishment which is due for sins, and by relaxing to absolve? And what is it to retain sins but not to absolve those not truly penitent? For many of those who confess seek absolution who nevertheless do not want to wholly abandon their sins. Many promise caution for the future but do not want to make satisfaction. All of this sort, insofar as they do not truly repent, beyond doubt ought not to be forgiven. For truly to repent is to be sorry for past wrongdoing, to confess with a strong purpose, to make satisfaction, and to take heed to oneself with all caution. Those who do penance in this way, they ought to be forgiven, and to be remitted in any other way without absolution, this is to retain sins. Now, from the things already said we may clearly understand that, in the forgiveness of sins, the Lord does by and of Himself what is done through his minister, that is, he does not by Himself and through the office of ministers, but He fully of Himself looses the bond of obduracy, and He looses by Himself and His minister the debt of eternal damnation; truly He looses by his ministers the debt of future purgation. The power of the first kind of forgiveness He reserves for Himself alone. The second kind of forgiveness He imparts by Himself and His minister. But the third kind, the Lord is accustomed to impart not as much by Himself as by his minister. Properly, indeed, is it said that the Lord absolves the truly penitent from the bond of damnation. Nonetheless it is true that the priest does this and the Lord, the Lord in view of the conversion of the heart, and the priest in view of the confession of the mouth. For the confession of the heart alone suffices in the case of the truly penitent unto salvation. And the case of necessity excludes both the confession of the mouth and absolution by the priest." Thus much Richard.

From these things the conclusion is drawn that God predestinates from eternity, and He executes in time the absolution of a person who is to be saved and the remission of his sin, before such a person is absolved on earth by the minister of the church. Again the minister of the church, the vicar of Christ, is not able to absolve or to bind, to forgive sins or to retain them, unless God has done this previously. This appears from John 15:5: "Apart from me ye can do nothing." That vessel of election knew this, and so he said: "Not that we are sufficient of ourselves to account anything as from ourselves, but our sufficiency is from God" (2 Cor. 3:5). Therefore, if we are not sufficient to think except as God imparts the thought, how are we sufficient to bind and loose except God have previously loosed and bound? And this the philosophers recognize when they say that a second cause can effect nothing without the coagency of a first cause.

Further, it is clear that no man may be loosed from sin or receive the remission of sins unless God have loosed him or given him remission. Hence the Baptist says: "A man can receive nothing except it first be given him from heaven" (John 3:27). Hence as an earthly lord first forgives in spirit the sin committed against himself, before this is announced by himself or by another, so it is necessary for God to do. Therefore, the presbyters are wildly beside themselves who think and say that they may of their own initiative loose and bind, without the absolution or binding of Jesus Christ preceding their act. For loosing and binding are in the first instance the simple [absolute] act of God. Therefore, the Gospel says, "Whatsoever is bound on earth shall be bound in heaven," but it does not say that it is bound in heaven at a later time and not previously.

Hence, the ignorant think that the priest binds and looses in time first and after him God. It is folly to have this opinion. But the logicians know well that priority is twofold: the one, priority of origin, taken from the material cause, and the other the priority of dignity, taken from the final cause. And these two priorities meet at one and the same time, and in this way the binding and loosing of the church militant is in a sense prior to the binding and loosing of the church triumphant and vice versa.

But God's act of binding or loosing is absolutely first. And it is evident it would be blasphemy to assert that a man may remit an offense done to so great a Lord, with the Lord himself approving the remission. For by the universal law and practice followed by the Lord, He himself must loose or bind first, if any vicar looses or binds. And for us no article of the faith ought to be more certain than the impossibility of any one of the church militant to absolve or bind except insofar as he is conformed to the head of the church, our Lord Jesus Christ.

Hence, the faithful should be on his guard against this form of statement: "If the pope or any other pretends that he binds or looses by a particular sign, then by that very fact the offender is loosed or bound." For by conceding this, they have to concede that the pope is impeccable as is God, for otherwise he is able to err and to misuse the key of Christ. And it is certain that as impossible as it is for the figure of a material key to open anything when the substance is wanting, so impossible is it for Christ's vicar to open or shut except as he conforms himself to the key of Christ which first opens and shuts. For just as Christ the firstborn of many brethren and the firstfruits of them that sleep was the first to enter the kingdom, so he alone and above all could have had committed to him the spiritual kingdom which was altogether closed from the time our first parents lied until he himself came. And the same is to be said in regard to any opening or closing whatever which pertains to the heavenly country. And it is plain that every vicar of Christ, so long as he continues to walk in this world, may err, even in those things which concern the faith and the keys of the church as those knew who wrote the Chronicles [*Histories of the Church of Ranulph Higden, Martinus Polanus*, etc]; for Peter himself, Christ's first vicar, sinned in these regards.

Likewise, God is the only being who cannot be ignorant as to whose sins may be remitted, and He the only being who cannot be moved by a wrong motive and judge unjust judgment. But any vicar may be ignorant as to whose sins ought to be remitted, and he may be moved by a wrong motive in binding or loosing. Therefore, if he refuse to impart absolution to one truly penitent and confessing, moved by anger or greed, he cannot by his act bind such a person in guilt. Similar would be the case with one who came with a lying confession, as happens very often, and the priest, not knowing his hypocrisy, should impart to him the words of absolution. Undoubtedly he does not thereby absolve, for the Scriptures say: "The Holy Spirit evades a feigned act of worship" (Wisdom 1:4). In the first case, just noted, the vicar alleges that he bound or forgave sins and did not; and in the second case he alleges that he loosed or remitted sins and did not. And it is evident how great the illusion may be of those who administer the keys and of those who do not truly repent. For it is necessary that a person, wishing to be absolved, be first so disposed in his will that he is sorry for his guilt, and then have the purpose to sin no more. Hence, all priests combined—who are at the same time vicars—are not able to absolve from sins him who wishes to go on sinning and who does not wish to lament his sins.

So all together are not able to bind a righteous man or retain his sins when he humbles himself with his whole heart and has a contrite heart, a thing which God does not despise. Wherefore St. Jerome, commenting on Matt. 16:19, "I will give unto thee the keys of the kingdom of heaven, and whatsoever thou shalt loose on earth shall be loosed in heaven," etc., says: "Some not understanding this passage appropriate something of the arrogance of the Pharisees so as to think that they can damn the guiltless and loose offenders, for with God not the judgment of priests is sought but the life of the guilty." To these words the Master of Sentences adds: "Here it is plainly shown that God does not follow the sentence of the church which judges in ignorance and deceitfully" (*4:18, cap. 6*). He also adds: "Sometimes he who is sent outdoors, that is, outside of holy church, by the priest, is, nevertheless, inside. And he who, by virtue of the truth, is outside, seems to be kept inside by the priest's false sentence" (*cap. 8*). And again he says that the priest who binds and looses others ought himself to be prudent and just, for otherwise he will put to death souls who do not die and revive souls which do not live, and in this way he turns his power of pronouncing judgment into an instrument of cursing—so that it is said in Mal. 2:2: "I will bless your cursings and curse your blessings" (*4:19, cap 4*). Therefore the vicars of Christ ought to take heed that they do not lightly presume to bind or loose whenever it pleases them. [...]

For every man who, being penitent, is according to the rite loosed on earth by Christ's vicar on the earth, he also is loosed in heaven—just as he who has believed and is baptized shall be saved, and he who has believed in love shall be saved finally. For "believe" here is to be accepted as in John 3:36, "He that believeth on the Son hath eternal life," and if it shall be argued that whosoever believeth on the Son hath eternal life: every Christian believes on the Son of God, therefore every Christian hath eternal life—or, again, if it be argued that whosoever believeth on the Son of God hath eternal life but that reprobate, who is in grace, believes on the Son of God, therefore that reprobate has eternal life—in these cases the conclusion is false. And both these conclusions are invalid, because "to believe" is one thing in the major premise and another thing in the minor. Hence, in order to correct the statement the argument must run in this way: whosoever believes with love in the Son of God and perseveres. In this case the consequence is good [he shall be finally saved]. But the minor statement the objector should prove [namely, that every Christian believes with love of God]. Similar is the case with the second conclusion and its minor premise: namely, "that reprobate who is in grace believes with love in the Son of God and perseveres." This reasoning is false.

From the things already said, it is clear what the power of the keys is and what is catholic belief on the subject, namely, that every priest of Christ ordained according to the rite has the sufficient power to confer the sacraments appertaining to him and consequently to absolve a person truly contrite from sin, howbeit power of this kind, so far as the exercise of it goes, is for good reasons bound in the case of many persons, as appears near the beginning of this chapter. But how this power belonged to the apostles equally is stated in the *Decretum, Dist. 21, in novo,* where it is said: "The other apostles with him, that is, Peter, by reason of equal fellowship received honor and power.... When these died, the bishops arose in their place." And here the Gloss, *Argumentum,* says that the bishops are all equal in apostolic power, so far as the order and ground of consecration go. St. Cyprian says: "He gave to all the apostles after his resurrection equal power" (24 *cap. Loquitur*).

Hence it would be foolish to believe that the apostles received from Christ no spiritual gifts except what were derived by them immediately and purely from Peter, for Christ said to all: "Whatsoever ye shall loose on earth" (Matt. 18:18); also, "Receive ye the Holy Spirit: whosesoever sins ye remit they are remitted unto them" (John 20:23); and again, "This do ye in remembrance of me" (Luke 22:19); and still again, "All power is given unto me in heaven and on earth. Go ye therefore and teach all nations, baptizing them in the name of the Father, and the Son, and the Holy Spirit, teaching them to observe all things whatsoever I have commanded you; and lo, I am with you all the days, even unto the consummation of the ages" (Matt. 28:19, 20).

INTRODUCTION TO DESIDERIUS ERASMUS'S *JULIUS EXCLUSUS*

ON THE EVE of the Reformation, the Papacy still faced significant rivals, not only in the vestiges of the conciliar movement, but in the ever-growing power and influence of the major monarchies of Europe. But rather than maintaining influence by exercising spiritual leadership, the popes of the later 15th and early 16th centuries were among the most wicked and corrupt ever to hold the office. Alexander VI (r. 1492–1503) made no secret of his numerous mistresses and illegitimate children, some of whom he elevated to high church offices and showered with ecclesiastical wealth. His successor, Julius II (r. 1503–1513), was less open about his own sexual scandals but more shameless in his Machiavellian connivings for political power.

In this period, then, the Papacy sustained its power by two related strategies. One was centralizing more and more of the Church's spiritual authority, so that the Pope alone had the authority to forgive certain sins or grant exceptions from various church laws. This helped not merely in keeping many ordinary Christians and churchmen dependent on the papacy, but also generated extraordinary wealth for the papal coffers. Of course, it was one of the most egregious instances of this profitable spiritual trade—the sale of indulgences by papal preacher Johann Tetzel in 1517—that prompted Luther's revolutionary protest against the Church. The Papacy's second strategy, though, was to become a political power player in its own right, both through the territory it controlled in central Italy (the Papal States) and through a cunning series of alliances between the rival powers that surrounded it. It was such brazen military campaigning and diplomatic scheming that Pope Julius II made the trademark of his papacy, from 1503-13. However, whatever gains in worldly power he may have achieved for the papacy came at the cost of widespread disgust throughout Christendom, which helped lay the groundwork for the Protestant Reformation that was to burst forth soon after.

No one so fully represented the reforming ferment of the early 16th century as Dutch humanist Desiderius Erasmus (1466–1536). Erasmus was the foremost scholar of the new classical learning that was sweeping Europe and also a peerless wordsmith able to make full use of the powerful new medium of the printing press. As a result, he was something of a rock star during the decade leading up to the Reformation. He traveled throughout western Europe researching, writing, and publishing, while being wined and dined by scholars and noblemen. A master satirist, he often upset the church authorities with his witty and irreverent critiques of the Pharisaism and immorality that dominated the late medieval church, most notably in his 1511 *The Praise of Folly*. However, Kelley Sowards writes that for Erasmus, "however comic, its [his satire's] purpose was deadly serious: no less than the moral-religious reform of society."[1]

Indeed, Erasmus was an ardent and earnest advocate not merely of reforming the most obvious corruptions of the Church, but of restoring her to true simple Christian faith and discipleship, which was found in the heart, not in outward pomp and power. He was also a strong advocate of returning to the original text of the Scriptures, a project to which he leant enormous momentum through his 1516 publication of a critical Greek text and revised Latin translation of the New Testament. This combination of biblical scholarship and commitment to a religion of simple, personal faith made Erasmus a seemingly natural ally for the Protestant Reformation. Indeed, it was commonly said that "Erasmus laid the

---

[1] J. Kelley Sowards, "Introduction" to *The Julius Exclusus of Erasmus*, trans. Paul Pascal (Bloomington, IN: Indiana University Press, 1968), 24.

egg that Luther hatched." Still, Erasmus shrunk back from fully endorsing Luther's reforming project, making him despised by Protestants and conservative Catholics alike. Erasmus was better at pointing out the faults in the existing Church than in proposing a comprehensive remedy for them.

Nowhere is he better at pointing out these faults with wit and rhetorical flair than in his 1517 satire *Julius Excluded from Heaven* (which Erasmus always studiously refused to admit writing), which narrates a conversation between the bombastic ghost of Pope Julius and the shocked St. Peter at the gates of heaven. In it, the full catalogue of Julius's vices is laid bare, with particular focus on the needless wars he started and his shameless maneuvering in ecclesiastical politics to prevent meaningful reform of the Church and protect his own wealth and position. Erasmus also shows his sympathy to the conciliar movement by chronicling at length Julius's successful efforts to thwart the work of the Council of Pisa. He also shows the absurdity of the pope's claims, against the conciliarists of the preceding century, to be wholly above any earthly judge and council, whatever wickedness he be guilty of. However, Erasmus also displays a deeper theological concern about the meaning of the church, one that was to resonate deeply with the Protestant Reformers, in the following lines (not appearing in this excerpt):

> *Julius*: What is more apostolic than to enlarge the Church of Christ?

> *Peter*: But if the Church is the Christian people, bound together by the spirit of Christ, I would say that you have subverted the Church...

> *Julius*: What *we* mean by the Church is sacred buildings, priests, and especially the Roman Curia.

This contest—between an essentially outward and institutional conception of the church, and the church as the whole body of believers united by the Spirit—was to erupt into a full-scale Reformation, beginning just a few months after the publication of the *Julius Exclusus*.

Further Reading

For further reading, see Erika Rummel, ed., *The Erasmus Reader* (Toronto: University of Toronto Press, 1990); John C. Olin, ed., *Christian Humanism and the Reformation: Selected Writings of Erasmus* (New York: Fordham University Press, 1987); Erika Rummel, *The Humanist-Scholastic Debate in the Renaissance and Reformation* (Cambridge, MA: Harvard University Press, 1998).

DESIDERIUS ERASMUS,
JULIUS EXCLUSUS (1517)[1]

JULIUS: What the devil is this? The doors don't open? Somebody must have changed the lock or broken it.

GENIUS: It seems more likely that you didn't bring the proper key; for this door doesn't open to the same key as a secret money-chest. Why didn't you bring both the keys you have? This is the key of power, not of wisdom.

JULIUS: I didn't have any other key but this; I don't see why we need a different one when we've got this.

GENIUS: I don't either; but the fact is, we're still on the outside.

JULIUS: Now I'm really getting mad; I'll knock the doors down. Ho! Ho! Somebody come and open this door right away! What's the hangup? nobody home? What's the matter with the doorman? He's asleep, I guess, or else drunk.

GENIUS: This fellow judges everyone else by himself.

PETER: A good thing our gates are of adamant, otherwise this one, whoever he is, would have kicked them in. He must be a giant of some sort, a general of the armies, a stormer of cities. But oh my God, what a sewer-stench is this! I certainly won't open the gates right away, but take a seat up here by a grated window where I can look out and keep an eye on the scene. Who are you and what do you want?

---

[1] Taken from Robert M. Adams, ed. and trans., *Desiderius Erasmus: The Praise of Folly and Other Writings* (New York: W.W. Norton, 1989), 143–55. Used by permission.

JULIUS: Open the door, will you? at least, if you can. And if you were really doing your job, it should have been open long ago, and decorated with all the heraldry of heaven.

PETER: Pretty lordly. But first tell me who you are.

JULIUS: As if you couldn't see for yourself.

PETER: See? What I see is new to me, like nothing I ever saw before, and I might say monstrous.

JULIUS: But if you're not stone-blind, you're bound to recognize this key, even if you aren't familiar with the golden oak tree. You can certainly see my triple crown, as well as my cloak all gleaming with gold and gems.

PETER: That silver key of yours I do recognize, though there's only one of them, and it's very different from those that were given to me long ago by the one true shepherd of the church, that is, Christ. But that glorious crown of yours, how could I possibly recognize it? No tyrant ruling over barbarian peoples ever ventured to wear one like it, much less anyone who came here asking for admission. Your cloak doesn't impress me either, for I always used to consider gold and jewels as trash to be despised. But what does this amount to really? In all this stuff—the key, the crown, the cloak—I recognize marks of that rascally cheat and impostor who shared a name with me but not a faith, that scoundrel Simon whom I once flung down with the aid of Christ.

JULIUS: Enough of these jokes, and watch yourself;, for I, if you don't know, am Julius of Liguria, and I don't doubt you recognize these two letters P. M., unless you've forgotten how to read.

PETER: I expect they stand for "Pestiferous Maximus."

GENIUS: Ha ha ha! This porter is as good as a wizard; he's got the needle's touch.

JULIUS: What it means is "Pontifex Maximus."

PETER: If you were triply great, greater even than Hermes Trismegistus, you still wouldn't get in here unless you were supremely good, that is, holy.

JULIUS: Well, if it comes down to comparative holiness, you've got some nerve to keep me waiting outside here when for all these centuries you've only been called "holy," whereas nobody ever called me anything but "most holy." I have six thousand bulls to prove it.

GENIUS: That's what he said, bulls!

JULIUS: —in which I am not only named "Lord most holy," but addressed as "your holiness," so that whatever I chose to do.

GENIUS: -Even when he was drunk—

JULIUS: —people used to say that the holiness of the most holy lord Julius had done it.

PETER: Then you'd better ask those flatterers of yours to let you into heaven, because they're the ones who made you so holy. They provided the holiness, now let them provide the bliss. By the way, though I know you don't think it matters, do you actually imagine you were a holy man?

JULIUS: You really vex me. If I were only allowed to go on living, I wouldn't envy you your holiness or your bliss, either one.

PETER: The proper expression of a pious mind! But apart from that, when I look you over from head to foot, I see many a sign of impiety and none of holiness. What's the meaning of these many comrades of yours? They're certainly not a papal retinue. You have almost twenty thousand men at your back, and in this entire crowd I can't find one single individual who has so much as the face of a Christian. I see a horrifying mob of ruffians, reeking of nothing but brothels, booze shops, and gunpowder. They look to me like plain highway robbers or spooks stolen out of hell and now intent on stirring up wars in heaven. As for yourself, the more I look at you, the fewer traces do I see of any apostolic character. What sort of unnatural arrangement is it, that while you wear the robes of a priest of God, under them you are dressed in the bloody armor of a warrior? Besides that, what a savage pair of eyes, what baleful features, what a menacing brow, what a disdainful and arrogant expression! I'm ashamed to say, and even to see, that there's no part

101

of your body not marked with traces of outrageous and abominable lust; in addition, you belch and stink like a man just come from a drunken debauch and fresh from a fit of vomiting. Judging from the appearance of your whole body, you seem to me, not worn out by age or disease, but broken down and shriveled up by drunken excesses.

GENIUS: How vividly he portrays the man in his own colors!

PETER: I see you threatening me with your lofty expression; but my feelings won't be suppressed. I suspect you may be that most pestilent pagan of all, Julius the Roman, returned from hell to make mock of our system. Certainly everything about you agrees well with him.

JULIUS: Ma di sì!

PETER: What did he say?

GENIUS: He's angry. At that expression, every one of the cardinals used to take flight, otherwise they'd feel the stick of his holiness on their backs, especially if he hadn't had his supper.

PETER: You seem to me to have some understanding of the man; tell me, who are you?

GENIUS: I am the particular Genius of Julius.

PETER: His bad Genius, no doubt.

GENIUS: Whatever I may be, I'm Julius's man.

JULIUS: Why don't you stop all this nonsense and open the doors? Perhaps you'd rather I broke them down. Why do we need all this palaver? You see the sort of troops I have at my command.

PETER: I do indeed see some highly practiced thieves. But you must be aware that these doors can only be opened in other ways.

JULIUS: Enough words, I say. If you don't hurry up and open the gates, I'll unleash my thunderbolt of excommunication with which I used to terrify great kings on earth and their kingdoms too. You see, I've already got a bull prepared for the occasion.

PETER: Just tell me, please, what you mean by all this bombast about bulls, bolts of thunder, and maledictions. I never heard from Christ a single one of these words.

JULIUS: You'll feel their full force, if you don't watch out.

PETER: Perhaps you used to terrify people with that bluster, but it counts for nothing here. Here we deal only in the truth. This is a fortress to be captured with good deeds, not ugly words. But let me ask you, since you threaten men with the thunder of excommunication; what's your legal authority for that?

JULIUS: Very well: I take it you are now out of office and have no more standing than any other unbeneficed priest; indeed, you're not even a complete priest, since you lack the power to consecrate.

PETER: Doubtless because I happen to be dead.

JULIUS: Obviously.

PETER: But for the same reason, you have no more standing with me than any other dead man.

JULIUS: But as long as the cardinals are arguing over the election of a new pope, it counts as my administration.

GENIUS: He's still dreaming dreams about being alive!

JULIUS: But now, open the door, I tell you.

PETER: And I won't do a thing, I tell you, unless you give me a full account of your merits.

JULIUS: What merits?

PETER: Let me explain the idea. Did you distinguish yourself in theology?

JULIUS: Not at all. I had no time for it, being continually engaged in warfare. Besides, there are plenty of priests to do that sort of work.

PETER: Then by the holiness of your life you gained many souls for Christ?

GENIUS: Many more for hell, I'd say.

PETER: You performed miracles?

JULIUS: You're talking old-fashioned nonsense.

PETER: You prayed earnestly and constantly?

JULIUS: This is pure foolishness.

PETER: You subdued the lusts of the flesh with fasts and long vigils?

GENIUS: Enough of this, please; with this line of questioning, you're just wasting your time.

PETER: I never heard of any other gifts that an outstanding pope was supposed to possess. If he has some more apostolic talents, let him tell me about them himself.

JULIUS: Though it's a disgraceful thing for Julius who never lowered his crest before anyone else to yield to Peter—who was, to say nothing worse, a lowly fisherman and almost a beggar. Still, just to let you know what sort of prince you're slighting in this way, now hear this. In the first place, I am from Liguria, not a Jew like you, but I'm afraid that like you I was once a boatman.

GENIUS: It's nothing to be ashamed of, for there's still this difference, that Peter fished for a living, while Julius plied the oar on a barge for minimum wages.

JULIUS: Then, as it happened that I was the nephew of Pope Sixtus the great.

GENIUS: Great in vices, he means.

JULIUS: —on his sister's side, his special favor combined with my industry first gave me access to ecclesiastical office, and so I gradually rose to the dignity of a cardinal's cap. Having undergone many reverses of fortune, and been tossed to and fro by various accidents—having suffered, among other diseases, from epilepsy and the pox they call French—I found myself quite overwhelmed; I was exiled, rejected, despised, despaired of, and almost given over as lost. Yet I never doubted that some day I would attain the papacy. That showed real strength of character, compared with you, who were terrified at the question of a serving girl, and gave up your faith on the spot. She weakened your courage, but I got new courage from a woman, a soothsayer and prophetess of sorts, who when she saw me overwhelmed with misfortunes secretly whispered in my ear, "Bear up, Julius! Don't be ashamed of anything you have to do or put up with; some day you will attain the triple crown. You will be king of kings and ruler of all rulers." And in fact neither her prophecy nor my own instincts deceived me. Beyond all expectations I achieved my goal, partly with the help of the French who sheltered me in my hour of need, partly by the marvelous power of money in large quantities, which I increased by taking usurious rates of interest. And finally my own ready wit helped me—

PETER: What's this ready wit you're talking about?

JULIUS: —to coin money from the bare promise of ecclesiastical offices, making skillful use of brokers in the process, since the sums I demanded couldn't have been paid in cash by a man as rich as Crassus. But it's useless to describe the schemes to you, since not even all my bankers understood them. Anyhow, that's how I made my way. Now as for how I bore myself in the pontificate, I'll venture to say that none of the early popes (who seem to me to have been popes in name only), nor even of the later ones, deserve so well of the church and of Christ himself as I do.

GENIUS: Only listen to the bragging of the beast!

PETER: I'm waiting to hear how you got away with it all.

JULIUS: I discovered a great many new offices (that's what they're called) which in themselves brought goodly sums into the papal treasury. Then I found a brand-new way by which bishoprics could be bought without any taint of simony. For my predecessors had made a law that any man appointed bishop should lay down his previous office. I interpreted it this way; "You are ordered to lay down your previous office; but if you don't have one you can't lay it down, therefore you must buy it." By this means each individual bishopric brought in its six or seven thousand ducats over and above those that are traditionally extorted for bulls. Also, the new money that I spread all over Italy brought in a very healthy sum.

And I never let up on accumulating money, understanding as I did that without it nothing is managed properly, whether sacred or profane. Now, to come to my major achievements, I conquered Bologna, which had long been ruled by the Bentivogli, and restored it to the control of Rome. The previously undefeated Venetians I crushed with my army. For a long time I harassed the duke of Ferrara, and nearly caught him in a trap. I cleverly escaped from a schismatic council set up against me by convoking a fraudulent counter-council, and so, as they say, drove out one nail with another. Finally, I expelled from Italy the French, who at that time were the terrors of the whole world, and I would have driven out the Spanish too (for I had that project under way), if the fates had not suddenly removed me from the earth. And I ask you to admire my undaunted spirit throughout these trials. When the French looked like winners, I was already looking around for a good hiding place; when my position seemed almost desperate, I grew a long white beard as a disguise. But then the golden messenger of victory alighted unexpectedly on me at Ravenna, where a good many thousand Frenchmen were killed; and that was the resurrection of Julius. In fact, for three days I was believed to be at death's door; I thought so myself; and yet here again, against everyone's hopes and even my own expectations, I lived anew. In fact, my power and my political shrewdness are so great to this day that there's none of the Christian kings whom I haven't brought to blows, breaking up the treaties by which they had painfully made peace with one another, ripping them to pieces, and trampling them underfoot. Indeed, I was so successful in abolishing the treaty of Cambrai, made between me, the king of France, the emperor Maximilian, and several other rulers, that nobody ever mentions it anymore. Over and above all this, I raised several different armies, celebrated many grandiose triumphs, put on splendid shows, built numerous impressive structures, and then at my death left at least five million ducats, which I would have increased even further if that Jewish physician who saved my life on one occasion had been able to stretch it out a little longer. And I really wish now that some magician could be found to restore my earthly existence, so that I could put the finishing touches on the really marvelous projects that I had under way. Still, on my deathbed I tried to ensure that none of the wars I had stirred up throughout the world should be settled; I ordered that money set aside for those wars should not be diverted elsewhere; and that was my last wish as I breathed out my dying breath. Now do you hesitate to open the gates for a pontiff who has deserved so well of Christ and the church? And I expect you to be all the more impressed because all this was achieved by my individual constancy of mind alone. I had none of those helpers and favoring circumstances that others have enjoyed; I had no ancestors, for I didn't even know my own father (which indeed I say proudly); I had no personal attractions, since most people shuddered at my face as at an ogre; I had no education, since with me it never took; I had no physical strength, for reasons mentioned above; I was not possessed of youthful energy, for I did all these things as an old man; popularity played no part, for there was nobody who didn't hate me; and I got no credit for clergency because I punished savagely those whom other rulers commonly let off scot-free.

PETER: What's this all about?

GENIUS: He talks very tough, but there's something soft in it.

JULIUS: Thus, with everything against me—fortune, age, strength, briefly, without help from gods or men, by the unaided power of my spirit and my money—I accomplished in a few years so much, that my successors will be busy for at least a decade deciding what to do next. I've said all this about myself with the utmost truth and also, for that matter, with the utmost honesty. If one of those preachers who orate before me in Rome had been here to cover my account with his decorations, you'd have thought a god was being described, not a man.

PETER: Unconquerable warrior, since all these things you talk about are new to me and unheard-of, I beg your pardon for my amazement or inexperience; I hope it won't be too tiresome for you to answer a few clumsy questions about the details. Who, for example, are these little curly-headed striplings?

JULIUS: I brought them up for my diversion.

PETER: Who are these smoke-blackened and mutilated fellows?

JULIUS: They are soldiers and warriors who in behalf of me and the church bravely encountered death in battle. Some died in the siege of Bologna, many in the war against the Venetians, others still at Ravenna. They are all to be admitted to heaven by the terms of our contract, in which I promised, by promulgating some mighty bulls, to send anyone straight to heaven who died fighting for Julius, whatever his previous life had been like.

PETER: As far as I can see, these people must have been the very lot who before your coming were most hateful to me because they were always trying to break in by force, using leaden bulls to force their way.

JULIUS: Then, as I understand it, you didn't let any of them in?

PETER: Not a single one of that crowd did I admit. That's what Christ told me; he didn't say to admit those who came here lugging heavy leaden bulls, but only those who had clothed the naked, fed the hungry, given drink to the thirsty, visited the prisoners, aided the pilgrims. If he wanted me to keep out those who prophesied in his name, cast out devils, and did wonderful works, do you suppose he would want people let in who just walk up with a bull in the name of Julius?

JULIUS: If I had only known!

PETER: I understand; if some demon out of hell had told you about it, you would have declared war on me.

JULIUS: I would have excommunicated you first.

PETER: But go on, why do you go about wearing armor?

JULIUS: As if you didn't know the holy pope wields two swords; you wouldn't want me to go into battle unarmed, would you?

PETER: When I held your position, I followed that rule in the word of God which says to use no sword save that of the spirit.

JULIUS: That would surprise Malchus, whose ear you cut off without a sword, no doubt.

PETER: I recall the event, and it's true; but at that time I was fighting for my master, Christ, not for myself; for the life of the Lord, not for loot or worldly booty; and I fought, not as pope, but as one to whom the keys had only been promised, not delivered, nor had I yet received the holy spirit. All the same, I was ordered to put up my sword as a clear warning that warfare of that sort was unbecoming to priests and even to Christians in general. But more of this elsewhere. Why are you so careful about calling yourself a Ligurian as if it mattered what part of the earth the vicar of Christ came from?

JULIUS: But I consider it an act of the highest piety to shed renown on my people; that's why I have this title inscribed on all my coins, statues, structures, and arches.

PETER: So a man can recognize his fatherland who doesn't know his father? At first, I thought you had in mind that heavenly Jerusalem, the home of all true believers and of its unique prince in whose name those believers are eager to be sanctified and exalted. But why do you describe yourself as "nephew to Sixtus on his sister's side"? I'm surprised that this man Sixtus never showed up here, though he was pope and related to such a leader as yourself. Do tell me, if you will, what kind of man he was: was he a priest?

JULIUS: A mighty soldier he was, and a man of exemplary religion too; he was a Franciscan.

PETER: Indeed, I once knew a man named Francis, a layman distinguished among his fellows for virtue as well as his scorn for wealth, pleasure, and ambition. Does that poor man now have command of military commanders like this?

JULIUS: As far as I can see, you don't want anyone to better himself; even Benedict was a poor man once, but now his followers are so rich that even I am envious of them.

PETER: Fine! but let's go back a ways: you are the nephew of Sixtus.

JULIUS: Glad to confirm it; I'd like to stop the mouths of those who say I'm his son. That's slanderous.

PETER: Slanderous indeed—unless perhaps it's true.

JULIUS: It's an insult to papal dignity, which must always be protected.

PETER: But I think popes should protect their own dignity by not doing anything offensive to the moral law. Speaking of papal dignity, let me ask you, is that the common and accepted way of achieving the papacy that you were describing just now?

JULIUS: For some centuries now, that's been the way of it, unless my successor is created by some other procedure. For as soon as I achieved the papacy myself, I issued a formidable bull that no one else should seek the office by the means I had used; and I renewed that bull shortly before my death. How it will be observed is up to other people.

PETER: I don't see how anyone could describe a bad state of affairs any better. But this puzzles me, how anybody can be found to undertake the job, since so much hard work attaches to the office and so many difficulties must be overcome to acquire it. When I was pope, hardly anyone could be persuaded to accept the office of a presbyter or a deacon.

JULIUS: No wonder; for in those days the reward of bishops was nothing but hard work, sleepless nights, constant study, and very often death: now, it's a kingdom, with the privileges of a tyrant. And who, if he has a chance of a kingdom, won't grab at it?

PETER: Well, tell me now about Bologna. Had it departed from the faith that it had to be brought back to Rome?

JULIUS: Absurd! That wasn't the question at all.

PETER: Perhaps the Bentivogli were poor administrators and destroying the prosperity of the city.

JULIUS: Not a bit of it; the town was flourishing as never before. They had enlarged it and adorned it with many new buildings. That only made me more eager for it.

PETER: I understand; they had taken possession of it illegally.

JULIUS: No, again; the city was theirs by treaty.

PETER: Perhaps the citizens hated their ruler?

JULIUS: On the contrary; they clung to him tooth and nail, whereas they almost all loathed me.

PETER: What was the reason for it then?

JULIUS: Because, as the ruler arranged things, out of the immense sums that he collected from the citizens, only a few paltry thousands ever reached my treasury. Besides, its capture helped on some other plans that I had in mind. And so, with the French doing the work (mostly out of fear of my thunderbolt), I drove out the Bentivogli and put bishops and cardinals in charge of the town, so that all the money collected there, down to the last penny, came into the hands of the church of Rome. Besides, in the old days, all the titles and dignities of imperial rule seemed to belong to him. Now you see everywhere statues of me; my titles are inscribed everywhere, my trophies are admired; nothing to be seen but stone and bronze images of Julius. Finally, if you had seen the royal procession in which I entered Bologna, you would surely despise all the triumphs celebrated by the Octavii and Scipios; you would understand that there were good reasons why I fought so hard for Bologna; and you would see that at the same time the church was fighting and triumphing alongside me.

PETER: So when you were the monarch, as I understand it, that condition had come about for which Christ ordered us to pray: "Thy kingdom come." Now tell me what the Venetians did wrong.

JULIUS: First of all, they ran after Greek fashions, and they treated me almost as a joke, putting all sorts of obstacles in my way.

PETER: Were they right or wrong?

JULIUS: What does that matter? It's sacrilege even to mumble about the pope of Rome, except in the way of praise. Then they bestowed their priesthoods as they saw fit; they wouldn't allow lawsuits to be transferred to Rome; and they wouldn't allow the selling of dispensations. Do I have to go on? They inflicted unbearable damage on the authority of Rome, and took command of a significant part of your patrimony.

PETER: My patrimony? What patrimony are you talking about to me, who left all my possessions behind to follow, unclad, a barefoot Christ?

JULIUS: I say that various cities are the property of the Roman church, and it has pleased the most holy fathers to call by that name these their own special possessions.

PETER: Thus you use my shame to cover your own greed. And so this is what you call unbearable damage?

JULIUS: Why not?

PETER: Were their manners corrupted? Was piety growing cold?

JULIUS: Forget it! You're talking about trifles. We were being deprived of thousands upon thousands of ducats, enough to furnish out a legion of soldiers.

PETER: A terrible loss for a usurer, I'm sure. And now about the duke of Ferrara, what was the matter with him?

JULIUS: What did he do, that most ungrateful of men? Alexander the vicar of Christ did this miserable rogue the honor of bestowing on him, as a wife, his second daughter, and with her he gave an enormous dowry, more than a man so base of birth could have expected. Yet, indifferent to such humane treatment, he made nothing but trouble for me, accusing me of simony, pederasty, and mental instability. And besides, he held back some taxes, not the major ones, I concede, but still important enough not to be overlooked by a diligent shepherd.

GENIUS: Or a skinflint.

JULIUS: Besides, which is more to the point, Ferrara helped along the main project I had in mind to join this territory to my own because of its strategic location. At first, I wanted to bestow the city on my kinsman, a man of energy who would have ventured anything in behalf of the dignity of the church. In fact, he recently killed the cardinal of Pavia with his own hands, in my behalf. As for my daughter's husband, he isn't the political sort.

PETER: What's this I hear? Do popes have wives and children nowadays?

JULIUS: Proper wives they don't have; but what's so strange about their having children, since they're men and not eunuchs?

PETER: But what sort of events led to the calling of that schismatic council?

JULIUS: It's a long story, but I'll cut it short. For a long time, some people have been discontented with the Roman church. They complained of the shameful money-grubbing, of monstrous and abominable lusts, of poisonings, sacrilege, murders, public sales of simoniacal positions, pollution of every description. They called me a simonist, a drunkard, a low villain swollen with earthly lusts, and on every count the man least worthy of occupying the position that in fact I occupied; they called me the greatest of all perils to the Christian community. And in this troubled state of affairs they thought help was to be sought from a general council of the church. They added that I had sworn when I was created pope to call a general council within two years, asserting that I was created pope only on that condition.

PETER: Were they right about that?

JULIUS: Absolutely. But when it suited my convenience to do so, I absolved myself of my own oath. When a king wants to break his solemn oath, who has any doubt that he can do it? Keep your piety for another occasion, as the first Julius, my other self, used to say. But only note the audacity of these men, the schemes they devised. Nine cardinals made a separation, notified me of a council to be called, and invited me to attend, even to preside. When I declined, they announced the council to the whole world in the name of the emperor Maximilian (under the pretext that years ago councils used to be called by Roman emperors) and likewise Louis of France, the twelfth of that name. What they proposed—I shudder to say it—

was to rip up the seamless garment of Christ, which even those who crucified the Savior left untorn.

PETER: But were you the sort of man they said?

JULIUS: What has that got to do with it? I was pope. Suppose I was a worse rascal than the Cercopes, stupider than a wooden statue or the log from which it was made, more foul than the swamp of Lerna; whoever holds this key of power must be revered as the vicar of Christ and reverenced as the holiest of men.

PETER: Even if he's openly evil?

JULIUS: As open as you like. It's just unthinkable that God's vicar on earth, who represents God himself before men, should be rebuked by any puny mortal or disturbed by any sort of popular outcry.

PETER: But common sense is outraged if we must feel warmly toward one whom we see to be evil, or speak well of one about whom we think ill.

JULIUS: Let every man think as he will, as long as he speaks well or at least holds his tongue. The pope of Rome cannot be censured by anyone, not by a general council.

PETER: This one thing I know, that Christ's vicar on earth should be as much like him as possible, and lead his life in such a way that nobody can blame any part of it, or justifiably speak evil of him. Things go badly with popes when, instead of earning men's commendations by good deeds, they extort praises with threats. Such popes cannot be praised without lying; indeed, they can't expect anything more than the sullen silence of those who hate them. Tell me now truly, is there no way at all to correct a criminal, infectious pope?

JULIUS: Absurd. Who is going to remove the highest authority of all?

PETER: That's exactly why he should be removed, because he's the highest figure; for the higher he is, the more pernicious his influence may be. If secular laws allow for a king who rules his land badly to be not only deposed but executed, why should the church be so helpless that it must put up with a pope who ruins everything, instead of expelling him as a public nuisance?

JULIUS: If the pope is to be corrected, it ought to be by a council; but against the will of the pope a council can't be called; otherwise it would be a mere convention, not a proper council. Even if it were called, it couldn't issue any decrees if the pope objected. And finally, my last defense is absolute power, of which the pope possesses more, all by himself, than an entire council. In short, the pope can't be removed from office for any crime whatever.

PETER: Not for homicide?

JULIUS: Not for parricide.

PETER: Not for fornication?

JULIUS: Ridiculous! not even for incest.

PETER: Not for the sin of simony?

JULIUS: Not for six hundred such sins.

PETER: Not for poisoning someone?

JULIUS: Not even for sacrilege.

PETER: Not for blasphemy?

JULIUS: No, I say.

PETER: Not for all these crimes poured together in a single sewer of a man?

JULIUS: Add if you like the names of six hundred other vices, each one worse than any of these, and still the pope cannot be removed from his throne for any such reasons.

PETER: This is a new doctrine about the dignity of the pope that I've picked up here; he alone, it seems, is entitled to be the worst of men. I've also learned about a new misery for the church, that she alone is unable to rid herself of such a monster, but is forced to adore a pope with a character that nobody would endure in a stable-boy.

JULIUS: Some say there is a single reason for which a pope can be removed.

PETER: What kind of good deed is that, please tell me—since he can't be removed for evil deeds, such as those I've mentioned.

JULIUS: For the crime of heresy; but only if he's been publicly convicted of it. In reality, this is just a flimsy thread of an exception, that doesn't limit papal authority by a single scintilla. The pope can always repeal the law, if it bothers him in the least. And then who would dare to accuse the pope himself, entrenched as he is behind so many lines of defense? Besides, if he were hard pressed by a council, it would be easy to save face with a recantation if a flat denial didn't dispose of the matter. Finally, there are a thousand different deceptions and evasions by which he could get away, unless he were a plain wooden stock instead of a man.

INTRODUCTION TO MARTIN LUTHER'S
NINETY-FIVE THESES

FEW DOCUMENTS in Christian history have become as iconic as Martin Luther's *Ninety-Five Theses*, the ringing denunciation of the corruptions of the late medieval church that was to spark the Protestant Reformation. Luther (1483–1546) may or may not have posted them on the church door in Wittenberg (he almost certainly did not nail them, in any case, as later legend would have it), but his dissemination of them on October 31, 1517 marked a turning point not only in Luther's life but in the life of the whole Christian church.

The document itself, however, is an unlikely candidate for the role of revolutionary text or Protestant manifesto: composed chiefly for an academic disputation on a practice now long-forgotten and scarce understood, the theses are a bit bewildering to the modern reader looking for familiar Reformation slogans. Indeed, neither of Luther's two great principles—justification by faith alone and the authority of Scripture alone—are to be found in these pages, even though the former had already begun to influence Luther's thinking and underlies several of his concerns in the *Theses*.

Judged by the standard of Luther's later work (even his writings from two or three years later), the *Theses* is a fairly conservative text, and Luther hardly expected them to unleash a full-scale reconception of Christian theology and division of the church. At this time, Luther was not so much interested in overthrowing the whole penitential system of the Catholic Church as in purifying it from obvious abuses, and he continued to accept many of the Pope's claims of authority. Indeed, in Theses 80-90 he says that one of his chief concerns is to defend the honor of the Pope against the easy attacks that to which the careless teaching of the indulgence preachers has exposed him.

On the other hand, it is easy to downplay too much the significance of the *Theses*. Luther was not, after all, just a random and inconsequential monk, as the Pope and his advisors were to try to dismiss him; he was at this time one of the highest-ranking leaders of the Augustinian Order in Germany and an increasingly-renowned professor at one of its leading universities. Moreover, Luther did not compose the *Theses* on a whim; he had been long wrestling over the indulgences issue and was well aware that by attacking the practice, he would likely be earning himself some very powerful enemies. Finally, although theses were normally composed for academic disputations only, Luther seems to have from the first intended these for a wider audience. As scholar Timothy J. Wengert notes, the *Theses* are full of rhetorical flourishes that suggest Luther wanted to reach and persuade many educated readers,[1] and, very unusually for such theses, Luther from the first invited scholars from around Germany to respond to the theses in writing. Indeed, there does not ever seem to have been an academic disputation in Wittenberg, as would normally have followed the proposal of such theses. Most striking of all, Luther took the extraordinary step of sending the *Theses* to Archbishop Albrecht of Mainz, the leading church authority in Germany, and exhorting him in no uncertain terms to restrain the indulgence preachers.

So who were these indulgence preachers and why was Luther so upset about them? The answer sheds light both on the astonishing depth of the late medieval church's corruption and on the often misunderstood heart of Luther's protest against it.

The theology and practice of indulgences had been around for centuries, although it had gotten increasingly out of hand in the

---

[1] Timothy J. Wengert, *Martin Luther's 95 Theses with Introduction, Commentary, and Study Guide* (Minneapolis: Fortress Press, 2015), 5.

decades leading up to 1517. At its root lay a long medieval distinction between guilt and punishment: although true repentance of sins and confession to a priest could give the believer absolution from *guilt* and therefore from hellfire, sin still demanded some kind of temporal punishment. Some of this punishment could be handled by taking penitential actions prescribed by the priest, but much of it would remain to be exacted after death. Accordingly, the medieval church came increasingly to teach the doctrine of purgatory, a place where the faithful must undergo a long term (perhaps even hundreds of thousands of years) of purifying torment before they could enter heaven. But there was some good news. By doing certain holy acts, like participating in or helping pay for a Crusade, Christians could receive an "indulgence" from the Pope, shortening their time in purgatory or perhaps even skipping it altogether. Eventually, recognizing in indulgences a potentially immense source of revenue, later popes began offering them for money more often than for good deeds, and, needing to continue to expand the market to keep the revenues flowing, they started allowing the faithful to buy indulgences for their dead relatives already in purgatory.

Johann Tetzel's (c. 1465–1519) indulgence campaign that prompted Luther's protest in 1517, though, was an extraordinary illustration of the corruption that came from mixing such absolute spiritual power with the wide-reaching worldly power of the late medieval church. Ostensibly ordered to help finance the construction of St. Peter's basilica in Rome, much of the money actually went into the coffers of Archbishop Albrecht of Mainz. Albrecht needed it to repay the Fugger banking family for immense debts he had contracted to buy from the Pope the most powerful church office in Germany at the age of 23. Since the most enthusiastic buyers of indulgences were the uneducated and gullible poor, Tetzel's indulgence campaign constituted an extraordinary redistribution of wealth upward from the poorest to the richest in Christendom.

Such exploitation of the poor infuriated Luther, and in thesis 45, he decries those who, instead of helping the needy, as Christ commanded for the truly penitent, spent all their spare money on indulgences. More fundamentally, though, Luther worried that indulgences were a form of cheap grace, a way for people to purchase false security for their souls without truly facing the depth of their sin and repenting from the heart. The earlier distinction between guilt and punishment had been thoroughly blurred so that indulgences had become, in the minds of the public, encouraged by salesmen like Tetzel, a substitute for true repentance, purchasing freedom from guilt as well as punishment. This point is key to grasp, given how readily Luther's gospel of salvation by faith alone is often distorted. Luther's concern with the late medieval church was less that it had made salvation too hard (by endless works rather than simple faith) and more that it had made salvation too easy (by thoughtless outward works or transactions rather than heartfelt repentance, being crucified with Christ). The real gospel of Christ, charged Luther, was both much more serious, more frightening, and more liberating than the spiritual economy the popes had created to fill their own coffers.

Further Reading

For further reading, see Scott H. Hendrix, *Martin Luther: Visionary Reformer* (New Haven: Yale University Press, 2015), ch. 5; Timothy J. Wengert, *Martin Luther's 95 Theses with Introduction, Commentary, and Study Guide* (Minneapolis: Fortress Press, 2015); David Bagchi, "Luther's *Ninety-five Theses* and the Contemporary Critique of Indulgences" in Robert N. Swanson, ed., *Promissory Notes on the Treaury of Merits: Indulgences in Late Medieval Europe* (Leiden: Brill, 2006): 331–56.

MARTIN LUTHER,
THE NINETY-FIVE THESES (1517)[1]

OUT OF LOVE for the truth and the desire to bring it to light, the following propositions will be discussed at Wittenberg, under the presidency of the Reverend Father Martin Luther, Master of Arts and of Sacred Theology, and Lecturer in Ordinary on the same at that place. Wherefore he requests that those who are unable to be present and debate orally with us, may do so by letter.

In the Name our Lord Jesus Christ. Amen.

1. Our Lord and Master Jesus Christ, when He said *Poenitentiam agite*[2], willed that the whole life of believers should be repentance.

2. This word cannot be understood to mean sacramental penance, i.e., confession and satisfaction, which is administered by the priests.

3. Yet it means not inward repentance only; nay, there is no inward repentance which does not outwardly work diverse mortifications of the flesh.

4. The penalty [of sin], therefore, continues so long as hatred of self continues; for this is the true inward repentance, and continues until our entrance into the kingdom of heaven.

5. The pope does not intend to remit, and cannot remit any penalties other than those which he has imposed either by his own authority or by that of the Canons.

---

[1] Translated by C.M. Jacobs in Henry Eyster Jacobs and Adolph Spaeth, eds., *Works of Martin Luther, with Introductions and Notes*, Vol. 1 (Philadelphia: A.J. Holman, 1915).

[2] Latin for "Do repentance."

6. The pope cannot remit any guilt, except by declaring that it has been remitted by God and by assenting to God's remission; though, to be sure, he may grant remission in cases reserved to his judgment. If his right to grant remission in such cases were despised, the guilt would remain entirely unforgiven.

7. God remits guilt to no one whom He does not, at the same time, humble in all things and bring into subjection to His vicar, the priest.

8. The penitential canons are imposed only on the living, and, according to them, nothing should be imposed on the dying.

9. Therefore the Holy Spirit in the pope is kind to us, because in his decrees he always makes exception of the article of death and of necessity.

10. Ignorant and wicked are the doings of those priests who, in the case of the dying, reserve canonical penances for purgatory.

11. This changing of the canonical penalty to the penalty of purgatory is quite evidently one of the tares that were sown while the bishops slept.

12. In former times the canonical penalties were imposed not after, but before absolution, as tests of true contrition.

13. The dying are freed by death from all penalties; they are already dead to canonical rules, and have a right to be released from them.

14. The imperfect health [of soul], that is to say, the imperfect love, of the dying brings with it, of necessity, great fear; and the smaller the love, the greater is the fear.

15. This fear and horror is sufficient of itself alone (to say nothing of other things) to constitute the penalty of purgatory, since it is very near to the horror of despair.

16. Hell, purgatory, and heaven seem to differ as do despair, almost-despair, and the assurance of safety.

17. With souls in purgatory it seems necessary that horror should grow less and love increase.

18. It seems unproved, either by reason or Scripture, that they are outside the state of merit, that is to say, of increasing love.

19. Again, it seems unproved that they, or at least that all of them, are certain or assured of their own blessedness, though we may be quite certain of it.

20. Therefore by "full remission of all penalties" the pope means not actually "of all," but only of those imposed by himself.

21. Therefore those preachers of indulgences are in error, who say that by the pope's indulgences a man is freed from every penalty, and saved;

22. Whereas he remits to souls in purgatory no penalty which, according to the canons, they would have had to pay in this life.

23. If it is at all possible to grant to any one the remission of all penalties whatsoever, it is certain that this remission can be granted only to the most perfect, that is, to the very fewest.

24. It must needs be, therefore, that the greater part of the people is deceived by that indiscriminate and high-sounding promise of release from penalty.

25. The power which the pope has, in a general way, over purgatory, is just like the power which any bishop or curate has, in a special way, within his own diocese or parish.

26. The pope does well when he grants remission to souls [in purgatory], not by the power of the keys (which he does not possess), but by way of intercession.

27. They preach man who say that so soon as the penny jingles into the money-box, the soul flies out [of purgatory].

28. It is certain that when the penny jingles into the money-box, gain and avarice can be increased, but the result of the intercession of the Church is in the power of God alone.

29. Who knows whether all the souls in purgatory wish to be bought out of it, as in the legend of Sts. Severinus and Paschal.

30. No one is sure that his own contrition is sincere; much less that he has attained full remission.

31. Rare as is the man that is truly penitent, so rare is also the man who truly buys indulgences, i.e., such men are most rare.

32. They will be condemned eternally, together with their teachers, who believe themselves sure of their salvation because they have letters of pardon.

33. Men must be on their guard against those who say that the pope's pardons are that inestimable gift of God by which man is reconciled to Him;

34. For these "graces of pardon" concern only the penalties of sacramental satisfaction, and these are appointed by man.

35. They preach no Christian doctrine who teach that contrition is not necessary in those who intend to buy souls out of purgatory or to buy confessionalia.

36. Every truly repentant Christian has a right to full remission of penalty and guilt, even without letters of pardon.

37. Every true Christian, whether living or dead, has part in all the blessings of Christ and the Church; and this is granted him by God, even without letters of pardon.

38. Nevertheless, the remission and participation [in the blessings of the Church] which are granted by the pope are in no way to be despised, for they are, as I have said, the declaration of divine remission.

39. It is most difficult, even for the very keenest theologians, at one and the same time to commend to the people the abundance of pardons and [the need of] true contrition.

40. True contrition seeks and loves penalties, but liberal pardons only relax penalties and cause them to be hated, or at least, furnish an occasion [for hating them].

41. Apostolic pardons are to be preached with caution, lest the people may falsely think them preferable to other good works of love.

42. Christians are to be taught that the pope does not intend the buying of pardons to be compared in any way to works of mercy.

43. Christians are to be taught that he who gives to the poor or lends to the needy does a better work than buying pardons;

44. Because love grows by works of love, and man becomes better; but by pardons man does not grow better, only more free from penalty.

45. Christians are to be taught that he who sees a man in need, and passes him by, and gives [his money] for pardons, purchases not the indulgences of the pope, but the indignation of God.

46. Christians are to be taught that unless they have more than they need, they are bound to keep back what is necessary for their own families, and by no means to squander it on pardons.

47. Christians are to be taught that the buying of pardons is a matter of free will, and not of commandment.

48. Christians are to be taught that the pope, in granting pardons, needs, and therefore desires, their devout prayer for him more than the money they bring.

49. Christians are to be taught that the pope's pardons are useful, if they do not put their trust in them; but altogether harmful, if through them they lose their fear of God.

50. Christians are to be taught that if the pope knew the exactions of the pardon-preachers, he would rather that St. Peter's church should go to ashes, than that it should be built up with the skin, flesh and bones of his sheep.

51. Christians are to be taught that it would be the pope's wish, as it is his duty, to give of his own money to very many of those from whom certain hawkers of pardons cajole money, even though the church of St. Peter might have to be sold.

52. The assurance of salvation by letters of pardon is vain, even though the commissary, nay, even though the pope himself, were to stake his soul upon it.

53. They are enemies of Christ and of the pope, who bid the Word of God be altogether silent in some Churches, in order that pardons may be preached in others.

54. Injury is done the Word of God when, in the same sermon, an equal or a longer time is spent on pardons than on this Word.

55. It must be the intention of the pope that if pardons, which are a very small thing, are celebrated with one bell, with single proces-

sions and ceremonies, then the Gospel, which is the very greatest thing, should be preached with a hundred bells, a hundred processions, a hundred ceremonies.

56. The "treasures of the Church," out of which the pope grants indulgences, are not sufficiently named or known among the people of Christ.

57. That they are not temporal treasures is certainly evident, for many of the vendors do not pour out such treasures so easily, but only gather them.

58. Nor are they the merits of Christ and the Saints, for even without the pope, these always work grace for the inner man, and the cross, death, and hell for the outward man.

59. St. Lawrence said that the treasures of the Church were the Church's poor, but he spoke according to the usage of the word in his own time.

60. Without rashness we say that the keys of the Church, given by Christ's merit, are that treasure;

61. For it is clear that for the remission of penalties and of reserved cases, the power of the pope is of itself sufficient.

62. The true treasure of the Church is the Most Holy Gospel of the glory and the grace of God.

63. But this treasure is naturally most odious, for it makes the first to be last.

64. On the other hand, the treasure of indulgences is naturally most acceptable, for it makes the last to be first.

65. Therefore the treasures of the Gospel are nets with which they formerly were wont to fish for men of riches.

66. The treasures of the indulgences are nets with which they now fish for the riches of men.

67. The indulgences which the preachers cry as the "greatest graces" are known to be truly such, insofar as they promote gain.

68. Yet they are in truth the very smallest graces compared with the grace of God and the piety of the Cross.

69. Bishops and curates are bound to admit the commissaries of apostolic pardons, with all reverence.

70. But still more are they bound to strain all their eyes and attend with all their ears, lest these men preach their own dreams instead of the commission of the pope.

71. He who speaks against the truth of apostolic pardons, let him be anathema and accursed!

72. But he who guards against the lust and license of the pardon-preachers, let him be blessed!

73. The pope justly thunders against those who, by any art, contrive the injury of the traffic in pardons.

74. But much more does he intend to thunder against those who use the pretext of pardons to contrive the injury of holy love and truth.

75. To think the papal pardons so great that they could absolve a man even if he had committed an impossible sin and violated the Mother of God—this is madness.

76. We say, on the contrary, that the papal pardons are not able to remove the very least of venial sins, so far as its guilt is concerned.

77. It is said that even St. Peter, if he were now pope, could not bestow greater graces; this is blasphemy against St. Peter and against the pope.

78. We say, on the contrary, that even the present pope, and any pope at all, has greater graces at his disposal; to wit, the Gospel, powers, gifts of healing, etc., as it is written in I Corinthians xii.

79. To say that the cross, emblazoned with the papal arms, which is set up [by the preachers of indulgences], is of equal worth with the Cross of Christ, is blasphemy.

80. The bishops, curates and theologians who allow such talk to be spread among the people will have an account to render.

81. This unbridled preaching of pardons makes it no easy matter, even for learned men, to rescue the reverence due to the pope from slander, or even from the shrewd questionings of the laity.

82. To wit: "Why does not the pope empty purgatory, for the sake of holy love and of the dire need of the souls that are there, if he redeems an infinite number of souls for the sake of miserable

money with which to build a Church? The former reasons would be most just; the latter is most trivial."

83. Again: "Why are mortuary and anniversary masses for the dead continued, and why does he not return or permit the withdrawal of the endowments founded on their behalf, since it is wrong to pray for the redeemed?"

84. Again: "What is this new piety of God and the pope, that for money they allow a man who is impious and their enemy to buy out of purgatory the pious soul of a friend of God, and do not rather, because of that pious and beloved soul's own need, free it for pure love's sake?"

85. Again: "Why are the penitential canons long since in actual fact and through disuse abrogated and dead, now satisfied by the granting of indulgences, as though they were still alive and in force?"

86. Again: "Why does not the pope, whose wealth is today greater than the riches of the richest, build just this one church of St. Peter with his own money, rather than with the money of poor believers?"

87. Again: "What is it that the pope remits, and what participation does he grant to those who, by perfect contrition, have a right to full remission and participation?"

88. Again: "What greater blessing could come to the Church than if the pope were to do a hundred times a day what he now does once, and bestow on every believer these remissions and participations?"

89. "Since the pope, by his pardons, seeks the salvation of souls rather than money, why does he suspend the indulgences and pardons granted heretofore, since these have equal efficacy?"

90. To repress these arguments and scruples of the laity by force alone, and not to resolve them by giving reasons, is to expose the Church and the pope to the ridicule of their enemies, and to make Christians unhappy.

91. If, therefore, pardons were preached according to the spirit and mind of the pope, all these doubts would be readily resolved; nay, they would not exist.

92. Away, then, with all those prophets who say to the people of Christ, "Peace, peace," and there is no peace!

93. Blessed be all those prophets who say to the people of Christ, "Cross, cross," and there is no cross!

94. Christians are to be exhorted that they be diligent in following Christ, their Head, through penalties, deaths, and hell;

95. And thus be confident of entering into heaven rather through many tribulations, than through the assurance of peace.

INTRODUCTION TO MARTIN LUTHER'S *LETTER TO THE CHRISTIAN NOBILITY OF THE GERMAN NATION*

THE REFORMATION was almost from its very beginning entangled with politics; indeed, it could hardly be otherwise, given that the late medieval papacy had been itself been profoundly entangled with politics, and many of its worst corruptions stemmed from its worldly ambitions. We have seen already in previous selections how there were no lack of voices to criticize the Church's over-reaching temporal claims and contend for the right of civil authorities to govern their territories without papal intervention.

Indeed, it was Elector Frederick the Wise's jealous sense of his own authority within Saxony that helped protect Luther from the early counterattacks of the Roman authorities, after his attack on indulgences began to provoke serious concerns. In summer 1518 Luther was initially summoned to a hearing in Rome, but protests by Frederick led to a hearing with leading theologian Cardinal Cajetan to be moved to Augsburg in southern Germany. Cajetan's insistence that Luther drop the theological debate and simply submit to papal authority hardened rather than weakened Luther's reforming resolve, and he began to reconsider many other elements of medieval theology that he had previously accepted. By his 1519 public debate with Johann Eck, the Leipzig Disputation, Luther had read and was willing to defend some of the writings of Jan Hus, the 15th-century Czech reformer burned for heresy. This scandalized Eck, who hastened to Rome to lobby for Luther's wholesale condemnation.

Meanwhile, a new Holy Roman Emperor had been crowned, Charles V (r. 1516–1556), at the age of 19. Uniting for the first time the crowns of the Empire and Spain—including Spain's rapidly growing possessions in the New World—Charles was on paper the most powerful man ever to be crowned in Europe. In reality, though, he was to be faced with a hopeless task, pinned between the papacy, to which he was spiritually loyal even if something of a political rival, the growing power of the Ottoman Turks to the east, and the restive German nobility to the north, some of whom were ardent supporters of Luther's ideas and reforms, and others of whom simply smelled an opportunity to increase their power and autonomy. It was to these nobles of the myriad German principalities, as well as to the young emperor himself, that Luther addressed his appeal in the remarkable text *The Letter to the Christian Nobility of the German Nation*.

In many respects, with its emphases on the authority of temporal rulers and the superiority of councils to Popes, it can be seen as an extension of many late medieval arguments, Erasmus's *Julius Exclusus* included. But Luther, expecting an excommunication from Rome any day and increasingly convinced that a wholesale reconfiguration of the Western Church was in order, went considerably further than all his predecessors.

His key innovation is found in his attack on what he calls the "first wall of the Romanists"—the distinction of clergy and laity. This distinction, and the treatment of clergy as an entirely separate, "spiritual" body of Christians subject to the Pope alone, had of course been a thorn in the side of lay rulers for centuries, unable as they were to tax the clergy or even prosecute them for crimes. Marsilius of Padua in particular had gone a long way to erasing clerical autonomy, but even he did not question the distinction itself— indeed, in some ways he intensified it with his sharp dichotomy between spiritual and temporal affairs. Luther, however, made a revolutionary claim, which became known as the "priesthood of all believers," arguing that "all Christians are truly of the spiritual estate, and there is no difference among them, save of office alone," so much so that in a pinch, laymen could choose a priest from among themselves and ordain him, without needing the consecration of a bishop.

Luther's doctrine of the universal priesthood was not meant as a call for an "every man for himself" religion—the church still needed teachers and authorities—but ordained teaching authority emerged out of the whole community of believers, much as Marsilius had argued that political authority must be delegated upwards from the whole community. Moreover, as leading members of the church, placed by God in positions of power to care for their people, Christian rulers had a duty to take action for the reform of the church if the ordained clergy were not doing their jobs. This insistence on the legitimate role of lay authority in the church was to be a consistent and transformative theme of the Reformation, though one that was to create many headaches for the Reformers as kings and princes tried to bend the church to worldly priorities and ambitions.

Having made his greatest argument in demolishing the "first wall of the Romanists," the latter two walls—that the Pope alone has authority both to declare the meaning of Scripture and to call councils—were easily dispensed of. Drawing on arguments of earlier conciliarists, direct appeals to Scripture, and his new conception of authority residing in the whole body of the Church, Luther argued that Scripture must take precedence over any papal claims, and if the pope was stubborn, councils or civil rulers should take steps to correct him.

In the remainder of the treatise, not included here, Luther goes on to offer a detailed indictment of the corruptions of wealth and power that had perverted the late medieval church, and detailed suggestions for how the papacy might be cut down to an appropriate size and properly spiritual function. He also offers extended advice for the reform of ecclesiastical and civil laws on such important matters as marriage, arguing above all that clergy should be allowed to marry. Many of his suggestions, and his expectation that godly rulers might actually implement them all, seem a bit idealistic; however, it should be recognized that the Reformation was no merely churchly affair and it was not long before Protestant princes and city councils undertook thoroughgoing moral, civil, and educational reforms that were to have nearly as far-reaching a legacy as Luther's doctrinal reforms.

Further Reading

For further reading, see Scott H. Hendrix, *Martin Luther: Visionary Reformer* (New Haven: Yale University Press, 2015), ch. 7; James A. Estes, ed., *To the Christian Nobility of the German Nation, 1520: The Annotated Luther, Study Edition* (Minneapolis: Fortress Press, 2016); James A. Estes, *Peace, Order, and the Glory of God: Secular Authority and the Church in the Thought of Luther and Melanchthon, 1518–1559* (Leiden: Brill, 2005).

MARTIN LUTHER,
LETTER TO THE CHRISTIAN NOBILITY OF THE GERMAN NATION (1520)[1]

Introduction

TO HIS MOST Serene and Mighty Imperial Majesty and to the Christian Nobility of the German Nation.

Dr. Martinus Luther.

The grace and might of God be with you, Most Serene Majesty, most gracious, well-beloved gentlemen!

It is not out of mere arrogance and perversity that I, an individual poor man, have taken upon me to address your lordships. The distress and misery that oppress all the Christian estates, more especially in Germany, have led not only myself, but everyone else, to cry aloud and to ask for help, and have now forced me too to cry out and to ask if God would give His Spirit to anyone to reach a hand to His wretched people. Councils have often put forward some remedy, but it has adroitly been frustrated, and the evils have become worse, through the cunning of certain men. Their malice and wickedness I will now, by the help of God, expose, so that, being known, they may henceforth cease to be so obstructive and injurious. God has given us a young and noble sovereign,[2] and by

---

[1] Translated by C. A. Buchheim in C.W. Eliot, ed., *The Prince, by Niccolo Machiavelli; Utopia, by Sir Thomas More; Ninety-five Theses, Address to the German Nobility, Concerning Christian Liberty, by Martin Luther; with introductions and notes*, Harvard Classics 36 (New York: P.F. Collier, 1910).

[2] Charles V was at that time not quite twenty years of age.

this has roused great hopes in many hearts; now it is right that we too should do what we can, and make good use of time and grace.

The first thing that we must do is to consider the matter with great earnestness, and, whatever we attempt, not to trust in our own strength and wisdom alone, even if the power of all the world were ours; for God will not endure that a good work should be begun trusting to our own strength and wisdom. He destroys it; it is all useless, as we read in Psalm xxxiii, "There is no king saved by the multitude of a host; a mighty man is not delivered by much strength." And I fear it is for that reason that those beloved princes the Emperors Frederick, the First and the Second, and many other German emperors were, in former times, so piteously spurned and oppressed by the popes, though they were feared by all the world. Perchance they trusted rather in their own strength than in God; therefore they could not but fall; and how would the sanguinary tyrant Julius II have risen so high in our own days but that, I fear, France, Germany, and Venice trusted to themselves? The children of Benjamin slew forty-two thousand Israelites, for this reason: that these trusted to their own strength (Judges xx, etc.).

That such a thing may not happen to us and to our noble Emperor Charles, we must remember that in this matter we wrestle not against flesh and blood, but against the rulers of the darkness of this world (Eph. vi. 12), who may fill the world with war and bloodshed, but cannot themselves be overcome thereby. We must renounce all confidence in our natural strength, and take the matter in hand with humble trust in God; we must seek God's help with earnest prayer, and have nothing before our eyes but the misery and wretchedness of Christendom, irrespective of what punishment the wicked may deserve. If we do not act thus, we may begin the game with great pomp; but when we are well in it, the spirits of evil will make such confusion that the whole world will be immersed in blood, and yet nothing be done. Therefore let us act in the fear of God and prudently. The greater the might of the foe, the greater is the misfortune, if we do not act in the fear of God and with humility. If popes and Romanists have hitherto, with the devil's help, thrown kings into confusion, they may still do so, if we attempt things with our own strength and skill, without God's help.

The Three Walls of The Romanists

The Romanists have, with great adroitness, drawn three walls round themselves, with which they have hitherto protected themselves, so that no one could reform them, whereby all Christendom has fallen terribly.

Firstly, if pressed by the temporal power, they have affirmed and maintained that the temporal power has no jurisdiction over them, but, on the contrary, that the spiritual power is above the temporal.

Secondly, if it were proposed to admonish them with the Scriptures, they objected that no one may interpret the Scriptures but the pope.

Thirdly, if they are threatened with a council, they pretend that no one may call a council but the pope.

Thus they have secretly stolen our three rods, so that they may be unpunished, and entrenched themselves behind these three walls, to act with all the wickedness and malice, which we now witness. And whenever they have been compelled to call a council, they have made it of no avail by binding the princes beforehand with an oath to leave them as they were, and to give moreover to the pope full power over the procedure of the council, so that it is all one whether we have many councils or no councils, in addition to which they deceive us with false pretenses and tricks. So grievously do they tremble for their skin before a true, free council; and thus they have overawed kings and princes, that these believe they would be offending God, if they were not to obey them in all such knavish, deceitful artifices.

Now may God help us, and give us one of those trumpets that overthrew the walls of Jericho, so that we may blow down these walls of straw and paper, and that we may set free our Christian rods for the chastisement of sin, and expose the craft and deceit of the devil, so that we may amend ourselves by punishment and again obtain God's favour.

(a) The First Wall: That the Temporal Power has no Jurisdiction over the Spirituality

Let us, in the first place, attack the first wall.

It has been devised that the pope, bishops, priests, and monks are called the spiritual estate, princes, lords, artificers, and peasants are the temporal estate. This is an artful lie and hypocritical device, but let no one be made afraid by it, and that for this reason: that all Christians are truly of the spiritual estate, and there is no difference among them, save of office alone. As St. Paul says (1 Cor. xii), we are all one body, though each member does its own work, to serve the others. This is because we have one baptism, one Gospel, one faith, and are all Christians alike; for baptism, Gospel, and faith, these alone make spiritual and Christian people.

As for the unction by a pope or a bishop, tonsure, ordination, consecration, and clothes differing from those of laymen—all this may make a hypocrite or an anointed puppet, but never a Christian or a spiritual man. Thus we are all consecrated as priests by baptism, as St. Peter says: "Ye are a royal priesthood, a holy nation" (1 Peter ii. 9); and in the book of Revelations: "and hast made us unto our God (by Thy blood) kings and priests" (Rev. v. 10). For, if we had not a higher consecration in us than pope or bishop can give, no priest could ever be made by the consecration of pope or bishop, nor could he say the mass, or preach, or absolve. Therefore the bishop's consecration is just as if in the name of the whole congregation he took one person out of the community, each member of which has equal power, and commanded him to exercise this power for the rest; in the same way as if ten brothers, co-heirs as king's sons, were to choose one from among them to rule over their inheritance, they would all of them still remain kings and have equal power, although one is ordered to govern.

And to put the matter even more plainly, if a little company of pious Christian laymen were taken prisoners and carried away to

137

a desert, and had not among them a priest consecrated by a bishop, and were there to agree to elect one of them, born in wedlock or not, and were to order him to baptize, to celebrate the mass, to absolve, and to preach, this man would as truly be a priest, as if all the bishops and all the popes had consecrated him. That is why in cases of necessity every man can baptize and absolve, which would not be possible if we were not all priests. This great grace and virtue of baptism and of the Christian estate they have quite destroyed and made us forget by their ecclesiastical law. In this way, the Christians used to choose their bishops and priests out of the community; these being afterwards confirmed by other bishops, without the pomp that now prevails. So was it that St. Augustine, Ambrose, and Cyprian were bishops.

Since, then, the temporal power is baptized as we are, and has the same faith and Gospel, we must allow it to be priest and bishop, and account its office an office that is proper and useful to the Christian community. For whatever issues from baptism may boast that it has been consecrated priest, bishop, and pope, although it does not beseem everyone to exercise these offices. For, since we are all priests alike, no man may put himself forward or take upon himself, without our consent and election, to do that which we have all alike power to do. For, if a thing is common to all, no man may take it to himself without the wish and command of the community. And if it should happen that a man were appointed to one of these offices and deposed for abuses, he would be just what he was before. Therefore a priest should be nothing in Christendom but a functionary; as long as he holds his office, he has precedence of others; if he is deprived of it, he is a peasant or a citizen like the rest. Therefore a priest is verily no longer a priest after deposition. But now they have invented *characteres indelebiles*,[3] and pretend that a priest after deprivation still differs from a simple layman. They even imagine that a priest can never be anything but

---

[3] In accordance with a doctrine of the Roman Catholic Church, the act of ordination impresses upon the priest an indelible character; so that he immutably retains the sacred dignity of priesthood.

a priest—that is, that he can never become a layman. All this is nothing but mere talk and ordinance of human invention.

It follows, then, that between laymen and priests, princes and bishops, or, as they call it, between spiritual and temporal persons, the only real difference is one of office and function, and not of estate; for they are all of the same spiritual estate, true priests, bishops, and popes, though their functions are not the same—just as among priests and monks every man has not the same functions. And this, as I said above, St. Paul says (Rom. xii; 1 Cor. xii), and St. Peter (1 Peter ii): "We, being many, are one body in Christ, and severally members one of another." Christ's body is not double or twofold, one temporal, the other spiritual. He is one Head, and He has one body.

We see, then, that just as those that we call spiritual, or priests, bishops, or popes, do not differ from other Christians in any other or higher degree but in that they are to be concerned with the word of God and the sacraments—that being their work and office—in the same way the temporal authorities hold the sword and the rod in their hands to punish the wicked and to protect the good. A cobbler, a smith, a peasant, every man, has the office and function of his calling, and yet all alike are consecrated priests and bishops, and every man should by his office or function be useful and beneficial to the rest, so that various kinds of work may all be united for the furtherance of body and soul, just as the members of the body all serve one another.

Now see what a Christian doctrine is this: that the temporal authority is not above the clergy, and may not punish it. This is as if one were to say the hand may not help, though the eye is in grievous suffering. Is it not unnatural, not to say unchristian, that one member may not help another, or guard it against harm? Nay, the nobler the member, the more the rest are bound to help it. Therefore I say, Forasmuch as the temporal power has been ordained by God for the punishment of the bad and the protection of the good, therefore we must let it do its duty throughout the whole Christian body, without respect of persons, whether it strikes popes, bishops, priests, monks, nuns, or whoever it may be. If it were sufficient reason for fettering the temporal power that it is inferior among the offices of Christianity to the offices of priest or confessor, or to the spiritual estate—if this were so, then we ought to restrain tailors, cobblers, masons, carpenters, cooks, cellarmen, peasants, and all secular workmen, from providing the pope or bishops, priests and monks, with shoes, clothes, houses or victuals, or from paying them tithes. But if these laymen are allowed to do their work without restraint, what do the Romanist scribes mean by their laws? They mean that they withdraw themselves from the operation of temporal Christian power, simply in order that they may be free to do evil, and thus fulfil what St. Peter said: "There shall be false teachers among you, [...] and in covetousness shall they with feigned words make merchandise of you" (2 Peter ii. 1, etc.).

Therefore the temporal Christian power must exercise its office without let or hindrance, without considering whom it may strike, whether pope, or bishop, or priest: whoever is guilty, let him suffer for it.

Whatever the ecclesiastical law has said in opposition to this is merely the invention of Romanist arrogance. For this is what St. Paul says to all Christians: "Let every soul" (I presume including the popes) "be subject unto the higher powers; for they bear not the sword in vain: they serve the Lord therewith, for vengeance on evildoers and for praise to them that do well" (Rom. xiii. 1–4). Also St. Peter: "Submit yourselves to every ordinance of man for the Lord's sake, [...] for so is the will of God" (1 Peter ii. 13, 15). He has also foretold that men would come who should despise government (2 Peter ii), as has come to pass through ecclesiastical law.

Now, I imagine, the first paper wall is overthrown, inasmuch as the temporal power has become a member of the Christian body; although its work relates to the body, yet does it belong to the spiritual estate. Therefore, it must do its duty without let or hindrance upon all members of the whole body, to punish or urge, as guilt may deserve, or need may require, without respect of pope, bishops, or priests, let them threaten or excommunicate as they will. That is why a guilty priest is deprived of his priesthood before being given over to the secular arm; whereas this would not be right, if the secular sword had not authority over him already by Divine ordinance.

It is, indeed, past bearing that the spiritual law should esteem so highly the liberty, life, and property of the clergy, as if laymen were not as good spiritual Christians, or not equally members of the Church. Why should your body, life, goods, and honour be free, and not mine, seeing that we are equal as Christians, and have received alike baptism, faith, spirit, and all things? If a priest is killed, the country is laid under an interdict[4]: why not also if a peasant is killed? Whence comes this great difference among equal Christians? Simply from human laws and inventions.

It can have been no good spirit, either, that devised these evasions and made sin to go unpunished. For if, as Christ and the Apostles bid us, it is our duty to oppose the evil one and all his works and words, and to drive him away as well as may be, how then should we remain quiet and be silent when the pope and his followers are guilty of devilish works and words? Are we for the sake of men to allow the commandments and the truth of God to be defeated, which at our baptism we vowed to support with body and soul? Truly we should have to answer for all souls that would thus be abandoned and led astray.

Therefore it must have been the arch-devil himself who said, as we read in the ecclesiastical law, "If the pope were so perniciously wicked, as to be dragging souls in crowds to the devil, yet he could not be deposed." This is the accursed and devilish foundation on which they build at Rome, and think that the whole world is to be allowed to go to the devil rather than they should be opposed in their knavery. If a man were to escape punishment simply

---

[4] By the Interdict, or general excommunication, whole countries, districts, or towns, or their respective rulers, were deprived of all the spiritual benefits of the Church, such as Divine service, the administering of the sacraments, etc.

because he is above the rest, then no Christian might punish another, since Christ has commanded each of us to esteem himself the lowest and the humblest (Matt. xviii. 4; Luke ix. 48).

Where there is sin, there remains no avoiding the punishment, as St. Gregory says, "We are all equal, but guilt makes one subject to another." Now let us see how they deal with Christendom. They arrogate to themselves immunities without any warrant from the Scriptures, out of their own wickedness, whereas God and the Apostles made them subject to the secular sword; so that we must fear that it is the work of antichrist, or a sign of his near approach.

(b) The Second Wall: That no one may interpret the Scriptures but the pope

The second wall is even more tottering and weak: that they alone pretend to be considered masters of the Scriptures; although they learn nothing of them all their life. They assume authority, and juggle before us with impudent words, saying that the pope cannot err in matters of faith, whether he be evil or good, albeit they cannot prove it by a single letter. That is why the canon law contains so many heretical and unchristian, nay unnatural, laws; but of these we need not speak now. For whereas they imagine the Holy Ghost never leaves them, however unlearned and wicked they may be, they grow bold enough to decree whatever they like. But were this true, where were the need and use of the Holy Scriptures? Let us burn them, and content ourselves with the unlearned gentlemen at Rome, in whom the Holy Ghost dwells, who, however, can dwell in pious souls only. If I had not read it, I could never have believed that the devil should have put forth such follies at Rome and find a following.

But not to fight them with our own words, we will quote the Scriptures. St. Paul says, "If anything be revealed to another that sitteth by, let the first hold his peace" (1 Cor. xiv. 30). What would be the use of this commandment, if we were to believe him alone that teaches or has the highest seat? Christ Himself says, "And they shall be all taught of God" (St. John vi. 45). Thus it may come to pass that the pope and his followers are wicked and not true Christians, and, not being taught by God, have no true understanding, whereas a common man may have true understanding. Why should we then not follow him? Has not the pope often erred? Who could help Christianity, in case the pope errs, if we do not rather believe another who has the Scriptures for him?

Therefore it is a wickedly devised fable—and they cannot quote a single letter to confirm it—that it is for the pope alone to interpret the Scriptures or to confirm the interpretation of them. They have assumed the authority of their own selves. And though they say that this authority was given to St. Peter when the keys were given to him, it is plain enough that the keys were not given to St. Peter alone, but to the whole community. Besides, the keys were not ordained for doctrine or authority, but for sin, to bind or loose, and what they claim besides this from the keys is mere invention. But what Christ said to St. Peter: "I have prayed for thee that thy faith fail not" (St. Luke xxii. 32), cannot relate to the pope, inasmuch as the greater part of the popes have been without faith, as they are themselves forced to acknowledge; nor did Christ pray for Peter alone, but for all the Apostles and all Christians, as He says, "Neither pray I for these alone, but for them also which shall believe on Me through their word" (St. John xvii). Is not this plain enough?

Only consider the matter. They must needs acknowledge that there are pious Christians among us that have the true faith, spirit, understanding, word, and mind of Christ: why then should we reject their word and understanding, and follow a pope who has neither understanding nor spirit? Surely this were to deny our whole faith and the Christian Church. Moreover, if the article of our faith is right, "I believe in the holy Christian Church," the pope cannot alone be right; else we must say, "I believe in the pope of Rome," and reduce the Christian Church to one man, which is a devilish and damnable heresy. Besides that, we are all priests, as I have said, and have all one faith, one Gospel, one Sacrament; how then should we not have the power of discerning and judging what is right or wrong in matters of faith? What becomes of St. Paul's words, "But he that is spiritual judgeth all things, yet he himself is judged of no man" (1 Cor. ii. 15), and also, "We having the same spirit of faith"? (2 Cor. iv. 13). Why then should we not perceive as well as an unbelieving pope what agrees or disagrees with our faith?

By these and many other texts we should gain courage and freedom, and should not let the spirit of liberty (as St. Paul has it) be frightened away by the inventions of the popes; we should boldly judge what they do and what they leave undone by our own believing understanding of the Scriptures, and force them to follow the better understanding, and not their own. Did not Abraham in old days have to obey his Sarah, who was in stricter bondage to him than we are to anyone on earth? Thus, too, Balaam's ass was wiser than the prophet. If God spoke by an ass against a prophet, why should He not speak by a pious man against the pope? Besides, St. Paul withstood St. Peter as being in error (Gal. ii). Therefore, it behooves every Christian to aid the faith by understanding and defending it and by condemning all errors.

(c) The Third Wall: That no one may call a council but the pope

The third wall falls of itself, as soon as the first two have fallen; for if the pope acts contrary to the Scriptures, we are bound to stand by the Scriptures, to punish and to constrain him, according to Christ's commandment, "Moreover, if thy brother shall trespass against thee, go and tell him his fault between thee and him alone; if he shall hear thee, thou hast gained thy brother. But if he will not hear thee, then take with thee one or two more, that in the mouth of two or three witnesses every word may be established. And if he shall neglect to hear them, tell it unto the Church; but if he neglect to hear the Church, let him be unto thee as a heathen man and a publican" (St. Matt. xviii. 15–17). Here each member is commanded to take care for the other; much more then should we do this, if it is a ruling member of the community that does evil, which by its

144

evil-doing causes great harm and offence to the others. If then I am to accuse him before the Church, I must collect the Church together. Moreover, they can show nothing in the Scriptures giving the pope sole power to call and confirm councils; they have nothing but their own laws; but these hold good only so long as they are not injurious to Christianity and the laws of God. Therefore, if the pope deserves punishment, these laws cease to bind us, since Christendom would suffer, if he were not punished by a council. Thus we read (Acts xv) that the council of the Apostles was not called by St. Peter, but by all the Apostles and the elders. But if the right to call it had lain with St. Peter alone, it would not have been a Christian council, but a heretical conciliabulum. Moreover, the most celebrated council of all—that of Nicaea—was neither called nor confirmed by the Bishop of Rome, but by the Emperor Constantine; and after him many other emperors have done the same, and yet the councils called by them were accounted most Christian. But if the pope alone had the power, they must all have been heretical. Moreover, if I consider the councils that the pope has called, I do not find that they produced any notable results.

Therefore, when need requires, and the pope is a cause of offence to Christendom, in these cases whoever can best do so, as a faithful member of the whole body, must do what he can to procure a true free council. This no one can do so well as the temporal authorities, especially since they are fellow-Christians, fellow-priests, sharing one spirit and one power in all things, and since they should exercise the office that they have received from God without hindrance, whenever it is necessary and useful that it should be exercised. Would it not be most unnatural, if a fire were to break out in a city, and every one were to keep still and let it burn on and on, whatever might be burnt, simply because they had not the mayor's authority, or because the fire perchance broke out at the mayor's house? Is not every citizen bound in this case to rouse and call in the rest? How much more should this be done in the spiritual city of Christ, if a fire of offence breaks out, either at the pope's government or wherever it may! The like happens if an enemy attacks a town. The first to rouse up the rest earns glory and thanks. Why then should not he earn glory that decries the coming of our enemies from hell and rouses and summons all Christians?

But as for their boasts of their authority, that no one must oppose it, this is idle talk. No one in Christendom has any authority to do harm, or to forbid others to prevent harm being done. There is no authority in the Church but for reformation. Therefore, if the pope wished to use his power to prevent the calling of a free council, so as to prevent the reformation of the Church, we must not respect him or his power; and if he should begin to excommunicate and fulminate, we must despise this as the doings of a madman, and, trusting in God, excommunicate and repel him as best we may. For this his usurped power is nothing; he does not possess it, and he is at once overthrown by a text from the Scriptures. For St. Paul says to the Corinthians "that God has given us authority for edification, and not for destruction" (2 Cor. x. 8). Who will set this text at naught? It is the power of the devil and of antichrist that prevents what would serve for the reformation of Christendom. Therefore we must not follow it, but oppose it with our body, our goods, and all that we have. And even if a miracle were to happen in favour of the pope against the temporal power, or if some were to be stricken by a plague, as they sometimes boast has happened, all this is to be held as having been done by the devil in order to injure our faith in God, as was foretold by Christ: "There shall arise false Christs and false prophets, and shall show great signs and wonders, insomuch that, if it were possible, they shall deceive the very elect" (Matt. xxiv. 23); and St. Paul tells the Thessalonians that the coming of antichrist shall be "after the working of Satan with all power and signs and lying wonders" (2 Thess. ii. 9).

Therefore let us hold fast to this: that Christian power can do nothing against Christ, as St. Paul says, "For we can do nothing against Christ, but for Christ" (2 Cor. xiii. 8). But, if it does anything against Christ, it is the power of antichrist and the devil, even if it rained and hailed wonders and plagues. Wonders and plagues prove nothing, especially in these latter evil days, of which false wonders are foretold in all the Scriptures. Therefore we must hold fast to the words of God with an assured faith; then the devil will soon cease his wonders.

And now I hope the false, lying spectre will be laid with which the Romanists have long terrified and stupefied our consciences. And it will be seen that, like all the rest of us, they are subject to the temporal sword; that they have no authority to interpret the Scriptures by force without skill; and that they have no power to prevent a council, or to pledge it in accordance with their pleasure, or to bind it beforehand, and deprive it of its freedom; and that if they do this, they are verily of the fellowship of antichrist and the devil, and having nothing of Christ but the name.

INTRODUCTION TO LUTHER'S *BABYLONIAN CAPTIVITY OF THE CHURCH* (1520)

HAVING THROWN down the gauntlet to Rome in the *Letter to the Christian Nobility*, Luther knew an excommunication was probably not long in coming. Accordingly, he did not hesitate to mount a still bolder assault on the very foundations of the late medieval church—its sacramental system.

It is difficult for us today to imagine just how much of late medieval society revolved around the Church's seven sacraments. These covered every period of life: Baptism for the beginning of life, Confirmation for puberty, Marriage or Ordination for adulthood, Extreme Unction for the deathbed, and the Eucharist and Penance continually throughout. The Eucharist especially had morphed into something almost unrecognizable by comparison with early church practice. Celebrated nearly always in private by individual priests, it was no longer a fellowship meal, or even a distribution of the body and blood of Christ to the faithful (laity had, since the 13th century, only been allowed to receive the bread, not the wine), but a sacrificial offering performed by the priest to merit forgiveness of sins. Like the indulgence system, what had begun as a salve for the souls of the living was soon expanded to include the dead, with the wealthy leaving money in their estates to hire priests to say masses for their souls. (Recall the famous prayer on the eve of Agincourt in the play *Henry V*, where Shakespeare has Henry, worried that God might be punishing him for his father's treatment of King Richard II, say, "I have built two chantries, where the sad and solemn priests sing still for Richard's soul.") To say this was a lucrative business is an understatement; a large share of clergy was kept employed full-time doing little else. Once consecrated, the Eucharistic elements could then be reserved for adoration or paraded through the streets on festival days as opportunities for the common people to show devotion and seek forgiveness, and for the Church to bring in some cash. The immense power claimed by the Church for the sacraments, and the exclusive power over them reserved to the clergy, helped entrench the sharp divide between clergy and laity that Luther had attacked in the *Letter to the Christian Nobility*.

Accordingly, Luther dedicates *The Babylonian Captivity of the Church* to the task of rethinking the sacraments from the ground up. Borrowing the common term for the Papacy's 14th-century "captivity" at Avignon for his title, he argued that the sacramental system, far from being an economy of grace, had become a tool for holding believers captive to the power of the clergy. He argues for only three sacraments, rather than seven—the Eucharist, Baptism, and Penance—and strips down Penance so that it is neither really a sacrament in the same sense as the others nor under the power of the priest. By far the largest section of the text (and the section we have chosen for this reader) is his discussion of the Eucharist, or "the Sacrament of the Altar."

The previous year, Luther had declared his sympathy for the Hussites, whose greatest offense had been their insistence that the laity receive communion in both kinds—that is, the bread and the wine. Here he openly defends their position, calling the restriction of wine to the priests "the first captivity of this sacrament." He spends several pages ridiculing the fanciful exegesis that the Roman Church had developed to justify this restriction, and argues from both Scripture and church history that both bread and wine belong to the laity. The next section goes further, forcefully rejecting the scholastic doctrine of transubstantiation as ridiculous philosophical juggling. Instead, he argues for a simple affirmation of what came to be called *consubstantiation*—that the real body and blood of Christ are present together with the real bread and wine. Although all the Protestant Reformers were to follow Luther in his rejection of transubstantiation, most would not endorse his somewhat over-reaching attacks on scholastic metaphysics; indeed, the Reformed came to believe the consubstantiation view led to no less nonsensical conclusions than transubstantiation.

In attacking "the third captivity of this sacrament," the sacrificial conception of the mass, which Luther calls "the most wicked of all," he gets to the real heart of the matter, and offers a comprehensive rethink of the meaning of the Eucharist and the sacraments in general. He is well aware of the consequences—that he will "alter almost the entire external form of the churches and introduce, or rather reintroduce, a totally different kind of ceremony" and will "overturn the practice and teaching of all the churches and monasteries, by virtue of which they have flourished all these centuries." At its root, he argues, the Eucharist is nothing else than Christ's promise of the forgiveness of sins (and thus, simply the Gospel itself in visible form) received by faith by believing communicants. In this last section, Luther's genius for distilling his doctrine to clear and beautifully simple explanations shines through, such as his example of the rich lord bequeathing his inheritance to a beggar. If the gospel heart of the sacrament is recognized and preserved, Luther has no objection to embellishing the ceremony with outward pomp. But we must not, he says (now adopting scholastic metaphysical terms for his own use) confuse the gospel substance with the outward accidents.

Although inspiring to his growing body of sympathizers, *The Babylonian Captivity* was shocking and scandalous to orthodox Catholic ears. Indeed, one of Luther's bitterest opponents, Thomas Murner, did Luther the favor of translating his Latin treatise into German, assuming that it would be self-refuting,[1] a scheme that backfired rather badly.

---

[1] Martin Luther, *Three Treatises*, 2nd ed. (Minneapolis: Fortress Press, 1990), 120.

Further Reading

For further reading, see Scott H. Hendrix, *Martin Luther: Visionary Reformer* (New Haven: Yale University Press, 2015), ch. 7; Paul W. Robinson, ed., *The Annotated Luther, Volume 3: Church and Sacraments* (Minneapolis: Fortress, 2016); Brian C. Brewer, *Martin Luther and the Seven Sacraments: A Contemporary Protestant Reappraisal* (Grand Rapids: Baker Academic, 2017).

MARTIN LUTHER,
THE BABYLONIAN CAPTIVITY OF THE CHURCH (1520)[1]

The Sacrament of the Altar

2.1 NOW, ABOUT the Sacrament of the Bread, the most important of all sacraments:

2.2 Let me tell you what progress I have made in my studies on the administration of this sacrament. For when I published my treatise on the Eucharist, I clung to the common usage, being in no way concerned with the question whether the papacy was right or wrong. But now, challenged and attacked, no, forcibly thrust into the arena, I shall freely speak my mind, let all the papists laugh or weep together.

2.3 In the first place, John 6 is to be entirely excluded from this discussion, since it does not refer in a single syllable to the sacrament. For not only was the sacrament not yet instituted, but the whole context plainly shows that Christ is speaking of faith in the Word made flesh, as I have said above. For He says, "My words are spirit, and they are life," which shows that He is speaking of a spiritual eating, whereby whoever eats has life, while the Jews understood Him to be speaking of bodily eating and therefore disputed with Him. But no eating can give life save the eating which is by

---

[1] Translated by Albert T.W. Steinhaeuser in Henry Eyster Jacobs and Adolph Spaeth, eds., *Works of Martin Luther, with Introductions and Notes*, Vol. 2 (Philadelphia: A.J. Holman, 1915). Modernized by Robert E. Smith for Project Wittenberg.

faith, for that is the truly spiritual and living eating. As Augustine also says: "Why make ready teeth and stomach? Believe, and you have eaten." For the sacramental eating does not give life, since many eat unworthily. Therefore, He cannot be understood as speaking of the sacrament in this passage.

2.4 These words have indeed been wrongly applied to the sacrament, as in the decretal *Dudum* and often elsewhere. But it is one thing to misapply the Scriptures, it is quite another to understand them in their proper meaning. But if Christ in this passage enjoined the sacramental eating, then by saying, "Except you eat my flesh and drink my blood, you have no life in you," He would condemn all infants, invalids and those absent or in any way hindered from the sacramental eating, however strong their faith might be. Thus Augustine, in the second book of his *Contra Julianum*, proves from Innocent that even infants eat the flesh and drink the blood of Christ, without the sacrament, that is, they partake of them through the faith of the Church. Let this then be accepted as proved—John 6 does not belong here. For this reason I have elsewhere written that the Bohemians have no right to rely on this passage in support of their use of the sacrament in both kinds.

2.5 Now there are two passages that do clearly bear upon this matter—the Gospel narratives of the institution of the Lord's Supper, and Paul in 1 Corinthians 11. Let us examine these. Matthew, Mark and Luke agree that Christ gave the whole sacrament to all the disciples, and it is certain that Paul delivered both kinds. No one has ever had the temerity to assert the contrary. Further, Matthew reports that Christ did not say of the bread, "All of you, eat of it," but of the cup, "Drink of it all of you." Mark likewise does not say, "They all ate from it," but, "They all drank from it."

Both Matthew and Mark attach the note of universality to the cup, not to the bread, as though the Spirit saw this schism coming, by which some would be forbidden to partake of the cup, which Christ desired should be common to all. How furiously, do you think, would they rave against us, if they had found the word "all" attached to the bread instead of the cup! They would not leave us a loophole to escape, they would cry out against us and set us down as heretics; they would damn us for schismatics. But now, since it stands on our side and against them, they will not be bound by any force of logic—these men of the most-free will, who change and change again even the things that are God's, and throw everything into confusion.

2.6 But imagine me standing over against them and interrogating my lords the papists. In the Lord's Supper, I say, the whole sacrament, or communion in both kinds, is given only to the priests or else it is given also to the laity. If it is given only to the priests, as they would have it, then it is not right to give it to the laity in either kind. It must not be rashly given to any to whom Christ did not give it when He instituted it. For if we permit one institution of Christ to be changed, we make all of His laws invalid, and every one will boldly claim that he is not bound by any law or institution of His. For a single exception, especially in the Scriptures, invalidates the whole. But if it is given also to the laity, then it inevitably follows that it ought not to be withheld from them in either form. And if any do withhold it from them when they desire it, they act impiously and contrary to the work, example and institution of Christ.

2.7 I confess that I am conquered by this, to me, unanswerable argument, and that I have neither read nor heard nor found anything to advance against it. For here the word and example of Christ stand firm, when He says, not by way of permission but of command, "All of you, drink from it." For if all are to drink, and the words cannot be understood as addressed to the priests alone, then it is certainly an impious act to withhold the cup from laymen who desire it, even though an angel from heaven were to do it. For when they say that the distribution of both kinds was left to the judgment of the Church, they make this assertion without giving any reason for it and put it forth without any authority. It is ignored just as readily as it is proved, and does not stand up against an opponent who confronts us with the word and work of Christ.

Such a one must be refuted with a word of Christ, but this we do not possess.

2.8 But if one kind may be withheld from the laity, then with equal right and reason a portion of baptism and penance might also be taken from them by this same authority of the Church. Therefore, just as baptism and absolution must be administered in their entirety, so the Sacrament of the Bread must be given in its entirety to all laymen, if they desire it. I am amazed to find them asserting that the priests may never receive only the one kind, in the Mass, on pain of committing a mortal sin—that for no other reason, as they unanimously say, than that both kinds constitute the one complete sacrament, which may not be divided. I beg them to tell me why it may be divided in the case of the laity, and why to them alone the whole sacrament may not be given. Do they not acknowledge, by their own testimony, either that both kinds are to be given to the laity, or that it is not a valid sacrament when only one kind is given to them?

How can the one kind be a complete sacrament for the laity and not a complete sacrament for the priests? Why do they flaunt the authority of the Church and the power of the pope in my face? These do not make void the Word of God and the testimony of the truth.

2.9 But further, if the Church can withhold the wine from the laity, it can also withhold the bread from them. It could, therefore, withhold the entire Sacrament of the Altar from the laity and completely annul Christ's institution so far as they are concerned. I ask, by what authority? But if the Church cannot withhold the bread, or both kinds, neither can it withhold the wine. This cannot possibly be contradicted. For the Church's power must be the same over either kind as over both kinds, and if she has no power over both kinds, she has none over either kind. I am curious to hear what the Roman flatterers will have to say to this.

2.10 What carries most weight with me, however, and quite decides the matter for me is this. Christ says: "This is my blood, which is shed for you and for many for the remission of sins."

Here we see very plainly that the blood is given to all those for whose sins it was shed. But who will dare to say it was not shed for the laity? Do you not see whom He addresses when He gives the cup? Doesn't He give it to all? Doesn't He say that it is shed for all? "For you," He says—well, we will let these be the priests— "and for many"—these cannot be priests. Yet He says, "All of you, drink of it." I too could easily trifle here and with my words make a mockery of Christ's words, as my dear trifler does. But they who rely on the Scriptures in opposing us, must be refuted by the Scriptures.

2.11 This is what has prevented me from condemning the Bohemians, who, whether they are wicked men or good, certainly have the word and act of Christ on their side, while we have neither, but only that hollow device of men—"the Church has appointed it." It was not the Church that appointed these things, but the tyrants of the churches, without the consent of the Church, which is the people of God.

2.12 But where in all the world is the necessity, where the religious duty, where the practical use, of denying both kinds, i.e., the visible sign, to the laity, when everyone concedes to them the grace of the sacrament without the sign? If they concede the grace, which is the greater, why not the sign, which is the lesser? For in every sacrament the sign as such is of far less importance than the thing signified. What then is to prevent them from conceding the lesser, when they concede the greater? I can see but one reason. It has come about by the permission of an angry God in order to give occasion for a schism in the Church. It is to bring home to us how, having long ago lost the grace of the sacrament, we contend for the sign, which is the lesser, against that which is the most important and the chief thing, just as some men for the sake of ceremonies contend against love. No, this monstrous perversion seems to date from the time when we began for the sake of the riches of this world to rage against Christian love. Thus God would show us, by this terrible sign, how we esteem signs more than the things they signify.

How preposterous would it be to admit that the faith of baptism is granted the candidate for baptism, and yet to deny him the sign of this faith, namely, the water!

2.13 Finally, Paul stands invincible and stops every mouth, when he says in 1 Corinthians 11, "I have received from the Lord what I also delivered to you." He does not say, "I permitted to you," as that friar lyingly asserts. Nor is it true that Paul delivered both kinds on account of the contention in the Corinthian congregation. For, first, the text shows that their contention was not about both kinds, but about the contempt and envy among rich and poor, as it is clearly stated: "One is hungry, and another is drunken, and you put to shame those that have nothing." Again, Paul is not speaking of the time when he first delivered the sacrament to them, for he does not say, "I receive from the Lord and give to you," but, "I received and delivered"—namely, when he first began to preach among them, a long while before this contention. This shows that he delivered both kinds to them. "Delivered" means the same as "commanded," for elsewhere he uses the word in this sense. Consequently, there is nothing in the friar's fuming about permission. It is an assortment of arguments without Scripture, reason or sense. His opponents do not ask what he has dreamed, but what the Scriptures decree in this matter. Out of the Scriptures he cannot adduce one dot of an I or cross of a T in support of his dreams, while they can bring forward mighty thunderbolts in support of their faith.

2.14 Come here then, popish flatterers, one and all! Fall in line and defend yourselves against the charge of godlessness, tyranny, treason against the Gospel, and the crime of slandering your brethren. You decry as heretics those who will not be wise after the vaporings of your own brains, in the face of such patent and potent words of Scripture. If any are to be called heretics and schismatics, it is not the Bohemians nor the Greeks, for they take their stand upon the Gospel. But you Romans are the heretics and godless schismatics, for you presume upon your own fictions and fly in the face of the clear Scriptures of God. Parry that stroke, if you can!

2.15 But what could be more ridiculous, and more worthy of this friar's brain, than his saying that the Apostle wrote these words and gave this permission, not to the Church universal, but to a particular church, that is, the Corinthian? Where does he get his proof? Out of his one storehouse, his own impious head. If the Church universal receives, reads and follows this epistle in all points as written for itself, why should it not do the same with this portion of it? If we admit that any epistle, or any part of any epistle, of Paul does not apply to the Church universal, then the whole authority of Paul falls to the ground. Then the Corinthians will say that what he teaches about faith in the epistle to the Romans does not apply to them. What greater blasphemy and madness can be imagined than this!

God forbid that there should be one dot of an I or cross of a T in all of Paul which the whole Church universal is not bound to follow and keep! Not so did the Fathers hold, down to these perilous times, in which Paul foretold there should be blasphemers and blind and foolish men, of whom this friar is one, no, the chief of them.

2.16 However, suppose we grant the truth of this intolerable madness. If Paul gave his permission to a particular church, then, even from your own point of view, the Greeks and Bohemians are in the right, for they are particular churches. Hence it is sufficient that they do not act contrary to Paul, who at least gave permission. Moreover, Paul could not permit anything contrary to Christ's institution. Therefore I throw in your face, O Rome, and in the face of all you flatterers, these sayings of Christ and Paul, on behalf of the Greeks and the Bohemians. You cannot prove that you have received any authority to change them, much less to accuse others of heresy for disregarding your arrogance. Rather you deserve to be charged with the crime of godlessness and despotism.

2.17 Furthermore, Cyprian, who alone is strong enough to hold all the Romanists at bay, bears witness, in the fifth book of his treatise *On the Lapsed*, that it was a wide-spread custom in his church to administer both kinds to the laity, and even to children, yes, to give the body of the Lord into their hands, of which he cites many instances. He condemns, for example, certain members of the congregation as follows: "The sacrilegious man is angered at the priests because he does not receive the body of the Lord right away with unclean hands, or drink the blood of the Lord with defiled lips." He is speaking, as you see, of laymen, and irreverent laymen, who desired to receive the body and the blood from the priests. Do you find anything to snarl at here, wretched flatterer? Say that even this holy martyr, a Church Father preeminent for his apostolic spirit, was a heretic and used that permission in a particular church.

2.18 In the same place, Cyprian narrates an incident that came under his own observation. He describes at length how a deacon was administering the cup to a little girl, who drew away from him, whereupon he poured the blood of the Lord into her mouth. We read the same of St. Donatus, whose broken chalice this wretched flatterer so lightly disposes of. "I read of a broken chalice," he says, "but I do not read that the blood was given." It is no wonder! He who finds what he pleases in the Scriptures will also read what he pleases in histories. But will the authority of the Church be established, or will heretics be refuted, in this way?

2.19 Enough of this! I did not undertake this work to reply to him who is not worth replying to, but to bring the truth of the matter to light.

2.20 I conclude, then, that it is wicked and despotic to deny both kinds to the laity, and that this is not in the power of any angel, much less of any pope or council.

Nor does the Council of Constance give me pause, for if its authority carries weight, why does not that of the Council of Basel also carry weight? For the latter council decided, on the contrary, after much disputing, that the Bohemians might use both kinds, as the extant records and documents of the council prove. And to that council this ignorant flatterer refers in support of his dream. In such wisdom does his whole treatise abound.

2.21 The first captivity of this sacrament, therefore, concerns its substance or completeness, of which we have been deprived by the despotism of Rome. Not that they sin against Christ, who use the one kind, for Christ did not command the use of either kind, but left it to everyone's free will, when He said: "As often as you do this, do it in remembrance of me." But they sin who forbid the giving of both kinds to such as desire to exercise this free will. The fault lies not with the laity, but with the priests. The sacrament does not belong to the priests, but to all, and the priests are not lords but ministers, in duty bound to administer both kinds to those who desire them, and as often as they desire them. If they wrest this right from the laity and forcibly withhold it, they are tyrants. But the laity are without fault, whether they lack one kind or both kinds. They must meanwhile be sustained by their faith and by their desire for the complete sacrament. The priests, being ministers, are bound to administer baptism and absolution to whoever seeks them, because he has a right to them. But if they do not administer them, he that seeks them has at least the full merit of his faith, while they will be accused before Christ as wicked servants. In like manner the holy Fathers of old who dwelt in the desert did not receive the sacrament in any form for many years together.

2.22 Therefore I do not urge that both kinds be seized by force, as though we were bound to this form by a rigorous command. But I instruct men's consciences that they may endure the Roman tyranny, knowing well they have been deprived of their rightful share in the sacrament because of their own sin. This only do I desire—that no one justify the tyranny of Rome, as though it did well to forbid one of the two kinds to the laity. We ought rather to abhor it, withhold our consent, and endure it just as we should do if we were held captive by the Turk and not permitted to use either kind. That is what I meant by saying it seemed well to me that this captivity should be ended by the decree of a general council, our Christian liberty restored to us out of the hands of the Roman tyrant, and every one left free to seek and receive this sacrament, just as he is free to receive baptism and penance. But now they compel us, by the same tyranny, to receive the one kind year after year. So utterly lost is the liberty which Christ has given us. This is but the due reward of our godless ingratitude.

2.23 The second captivity of this sacrament is less grievous so far as the conscience is concerned, yet the very gravest danger threatens the man who would attack it, to say nothing of condemning it. Here I shall be called a Wycliffite and a heretic a thousand times over. But what of that? Since the Roman bishop has ceased to be a bishop and become a tyrant, I fear none of his decrees, for I know that it is not in his power, nor even in that of a general council, to make new articles of faith. Years ago, when I was delving into scholastic theology, the Cardinal of Cambrai gave me food for thought, in his comments on the fourth Book of the *Sentences*, where he argues with great acumen that to hold that real bread and real wine, and not their accidents only, are present on the altar, is much more probable and requires fewer unnecessary miracles—if only the Church had not decreed otherwise. When I learned later what church it was that had decreed this—namely, the Church of Thomas, i.e., of Aristotle—I waxed bolder, and after floating in a sea of doubt, at last found rest for my conscience in the above view—namely, that it is real bread and real wine, in which Christ's real flesh and blood are present, not otherwise and not less really than they assume to be the case under their accidents. I reached this conclusion because I saw that the opinions of the Thomists, though approved by pope and council, remain but opinions and do not become articles of faith, even though an angel from heaven were to decree otherwise. For what is asserted without Scripture or an approved revelation, may be held as an opinion, but need not be believed. But this opinion of Thomas hangs so completely in the air, devoid of Scripture and reason, that he seems here to have forgotten both his philosophy and his logic. For Aristotle writes about subject and accidents so very differently from St. Thomas, that I think this great man is to be pitied, not only for drawing his opinions in matters of faith from Aristotle, but for attempting to base them on him without understanding his meaning—an unfortunate superstructure upon an unfortunate foundation.

2.24 I therefore permit every man to hold either of these views, as he chooses. My one concern at present is to remove all scruples of conscience, so that no one may fear to become guilty of heresy if he should believe in the presence of real bread and real wine on the altar, and that everyone may feel at liberty to ponder, hold and believe either one view or the other, without endangering his salvation. However, I shall now more fully set forth my own view. In the first place, I do not intend to listen or attach the least importance to those who will cry out that this teaching of mine is Wycliffite, Hussite, heretical, and contrary to the decision of the Church, for they are the very persons whom I have convicted of manifold heresies in the matter of indulgences, the freedom of the will and the grace of God, good works and sin, etc. If Wycliffe was once a heretic, they are heretics ten times over, and it is a pleasure to be suspected and accused by such heretics and perverse sophists, whom to please is the height of godlessness. Besides, the only way in which they can prove their opinions and disprove those of others, is by saying, "That is Wycliffite, Hussite, heretical!" They have this feeble retort always on their tongue, and they have nothing else. If you demand a Scripture passage, they say, "This is our opinion, and the decision of the Church—that is, of ourselves!" Thus these men, "reprobate concerning the faith" and untrustworthy, have the audacity to set their own fancies before us in the name of the Church as articles of faith.

2.25 But there are good grounds for my view, and this above all—no violence is to be done to the words of God, whether by man or angel. But they are to be retained in their simplest meaning wherever possible, and to be understood in their grammatical and literal sense unless the context plainly forbids, lest we give our adversaries occasion to make a mockery of all the Scriptures. Thus Origen was repudiated, in ancient times, because he despised the grammatical sense and turned the trees, and all things else written concerning Paradise, into allegories. For it might be concluded from this that God did not create trees. Even so here, when the Evangelists plainly write that Christ took bread and broke it, and the book of Acts and Paul, in their turn, call it bread, we have to think of real bread and real wine, just as we do of a real cup. For even they do not maintain that the cup is transubstantiated. But since it is not necessary to assume a transubstantiation wrought by Divine power, it is to be regarded as a figment of the human mind, for it rests neither on Scripture nor on reason, as we shall see.

2.26 Therefore it is an absurd and unheard-of juggling with words, to understand "bread" to mean "the form, or accidents of bread," and "wine" to mean "the form, or accidents of wine." Why do they not also understand all other things to mean their forms, or accidents? Even if this might be done with all other things, it would yet not be right thus to emasculate the words of God and arbitrarily to empty them of their meaning.

2.27 Moreover, the Church had the true faith for more than twelve hundred years, during which time the holy Fathers never once mentioned this transubstantiation—certainly, a monstrous word for a monstrous idea—until the pseudo-philosophy of Aristotle became rampant in the Church these last three hundred years. During these centuries many other things have been wrongly defined, for example, that the Divine essence neither is begotten nor begets, that the soul is the substantial form of the human body, and the like assertions, which are made without reason or sense, as the Cardinal of Cambray himself admits.

2.28 Perhaps they will say that the danger of idolatry demands that bread and wine be not really present. How ridiculous! The laymen have never become familiar with their subtle philosophy of substance and accidents, and could not grasp it if it were taught them.

Besides, there is the same danger in the case of the accidents which remain and which they see, as in the case of the substance which they do not see. For if they do not adore the accidents, but Christ hidden under them, why should they adore the bread, which they do not see?

2.29 But why could not Christ include His body in the substance of the bread just as well as in the accidents? The two substances of fire and iron are so mingled in the heated iron that every part is both iron and fire. Why could not much rather Christ's body be thus contained in every part of the substance of the bread?

2.30 What will they say? We believe that in His birth Christ came forth out of the unopened womb of His mother. Let them say here too that the flesh of the Virgin was meanwhile annihilated, or as they would more aptly say, transubstantiated, so that Christ, after being enfolded in its accidents, finally came forth through the accidents! The same thing will have to be said of the shut door and of the closed opening of the tomb, through which He went in and out without disturbing them. Hence has risen that Babylonian philosophy of constant quantity distinct from the substance, until it has come to such a pass that they themselves no longer know what are accidents and what is substance. For who has ever proved beyond the shadow of a doubt that heat, color, cold, light, weight or shape are mere accidents? Finally, they have been driven to the fancy that a new substance is created by God for their accidents on the altar—all on account of Aristotle, who says, "It is the essence of an accident to be in something," and endless other monstrosities, all of which they would be rid if they simply permitted real bread to be present. And I rejoice greatly that the simple faith of this sacrament is still to be found at least among the common people. They do not understand, so they do not dispute, whether accidents are present or substance, but believe with a simple faith that Christ's body and blood are truly contained in whatever is there, and leave to those who have nothing else to do the business of disputing about that which contains them.

2.31 But perhaps they will say: From Aristotle we learn that in an affirmative proposition's subject and predicate must be identical, or, to set down the beast's own words, in the sixth book of his Metaphysics: "An affirmative proposition demands the agreement of subject and predicate," which they interpret as above. Hence, when it is said, "This is my body," the subject cannot be identical with the bread, but must be identical with the body of Christ.

2.32 What shall we say when Aristotle and the doctrines of men are made to be the arbiters of these lofty and divine matters? Why do we not put aside such curiosity, and cling simply to the word of Christ, willing to remain in ignorance of what here takes place, and content with this, that the real body of Christ is present by virtue of the words? Or is it necessary to comprehend the manner of the divine working in every detail?

2.33 But what do they say to Aristotle's assigning a subject to whatever is predicated of the attributes, although he holds that the substance is the chief subject? Hence for him, "this white," "this large," etc., are subjects of which something is predicated. If that is correct, I ask: If a transubstantiation must be assumed in order that Christ's body is not predicated of the bread, why not also a trans-accidentation in order that it be not predicated of the accidents? For the same danger remains if one understands the subject to be "this white" or "this round" is my body, and for the same reason that a transubstantiation is assumed, a transaccidentation must also be assumed, because of this identity of subject and predicate.

2.34 If, however, going beyond our understanding, you get rid of *accidents*, and therefore refuse to understand that *accidents* are included in the subject when you say, "This is my body," then why do you not, with the same ease, ignore the *substance* of bread, so that you do not include the bread as the *subject*, and, therefore "this is my body" includes the *substance* no less than the *accident*? Especially, seeing that this is a divine work, accomplished with all powerful might, and can work in the same manner and to the same extent in the substance as much as in the accident.[2]

2.35 Let us not, however, dabble too much in philosophy. Does not Christ appear to have admirably anticipated such curiosity by saying of the wine, not, "Hoc est sanguis meus," but "Hic est

---

[2] This paragraph was not translated in the Steinhaeuser edition and so was translated for this volume by Jonathan Roberts.

sanguis meus"[3]? And yet more clearly, by bringing in the word
"cup," when He said, "This cup is the new testament in my blood."
Does it not seem as though He desired to keep us in a simple faith,
so that we might but believe His blood to be in the cup? For my
part, if I cannot fathom how the bread is the body of Christ, I will
take my reason captive to the obedience of Christ, and clinging
simply to His word, firmly believe not only that the body of Christ
is in the bread, but that the bread is the body of Christ. For this is
proved by the words, "He took bread, and giving thanks, He broke
it and said, Take, eat; this [i.e., this bread which He took and broke]
is my body." And Paul says: "The bread which we break, is it not
the communion of the body of Christ?" He says not, in the bread,
but the bread itself, is the communion of the body of Christ. What
does it matter if philosophy cannot fathom this? The Holy Spirit is
greater than Aristotle. Does philosophy fathom their transubstantiation, of which they themselves admit that here all philosophy
breaks down? But the agreement of the pronoun "this" with
"body," in Greek and Latin, is owing to the fact that in these languages the two words are of the same gender. But in the Hebrew
language, which has no neuter gender, "this" agrees with "bread,"
so that it would be proper to say, "Hic est corpus meum." This is
proved also by the use of language and by common sense. The
subject, certainly, points to the bread, not to the body, when He
says, "Hoc est corpus meum," "Das ist mein Leib,"—i.e., This
bread is my body.

2.36 Therefore it is with the sacrament even as it is with
Christ. In order that divinity may dwell in Him, it is not necessary
that the human nature be transubstantiated and divinity be con-

---

[3] Luther here relies on the gender of the Latin pronoun in the Vulgate:
sanguis or "blood" is neuter, requiring the pronoun *hoc*, whereas *calix*, the
Latin for "cup," is masculine, requiring the pronoun *hic*. Thus in the Latin
the sentence must mean "this cup is my blood." Wycliffe, intriguingly,
makes the same argument above in his *Trialogus*. Unfortunately, the argument does not work in the Greek text, where both *aima* ("blood") and
poterion ("cup") are neuter.—Davenant eds.

tained under its accidents. But both natures are there in their entirety, and it is truly said, "This man is God," and "This God is man." Even though philosophy cannot grasp this, faith grasps it, and the authority of God's Word is greater than the grasp of our intellect. Even so, in order that the real body and the real blood of Christ may be present in the sacrament, it is not necessary that the bread and wine be transubstantiated and Christ be contained under their accidents. But both remain there together, and it is truly said, "This bread is my body, this wine is my blood," and vice versa. Thus I will for now understand it, for the honor of the holy words of God, which I will not allow any petty human argument to override or give to them meanings foreign to them. At the same time, I permit other men to follow the other opinion, which is laid down in the decree *Firmiter*. Only let them not press us to accept their opinions as articles of faith, as I said above.

2.37 The third captivity of this sacrament is that most wicked abuse of all, in consequence of which there is today no more generally accepted and firmly believed opinion in the Church than this—that the mass is a good work and a sacrifice. This abuse has brought an endless host of others in its wake, so that the faith of this sacrament has become utterly extinct and the holy sacrament has truly been turned into a fair, tavern, and place of merchandise. Hence participations, brotherhoods, intercessions, merits, anniversaries, memorial days, and the like wares are bought and sold, traded and bartered in the Church, and from this priests and monks derive their whole living.

2.38 I am attacking a difficult matter, and one perhaps impossible to abate, since it has become so firmly entrenched through century-long custom and the common consent of men that it would be necessary to abolish most of the books now in vogue, to alter almost the whole external form of the churches, and to introduce, or rather re-introduce, a totally different kind of ceremony. But my Christ lives, and we must be careful to give more heed to the Word of God than to all the thoughts of men and of angels. I will perform the duties of my office, and uncover the facts in the case. I will give the truth as I have received it, freely and without malice. For the rest let every man look to his own salvation. I will faithfully do my part that none may cast on me the blame for his lack of faith and knowledge of the truth, when we appear before the judgment seat of Christ.

2.39 In the first place, in order to grasp safely and fortunately a true and unbiased knowledge of this sacrament, we must above all else be careful to put aside whatever has been added by the zeal and devotion of men to the original, simple institution of this sacrament—such things as vestments, ornaments, chants, prayers, organs, candles, and the whole pageantry of outward things. We must turn our eyes and hearts simply to the institution of Christ and to this alone, and put nothing before us but the very word of Christ by which He instituted this sacrament, made it perfect, and committed it to us. For in that word, and in that word alone, reside the power, the nature, and the whole substance of the mass. All else is the work of man, added to the word of Christ. And the Mass can be held and remain a mass just as well without it. Now the words of Christ, in which He instituted this sacrament, are these:

2.40 "And while they were at supper, Jesus took bread, and blessed, and broke it: and gave to His disciples, and said: 'Take it and eat. This is my body, which shall be given for you.' And taking the chalice, He gave thanks, and gave to them, saying: 'All of you, drink of this. This is the chalice, the new testament in my blood, which shall be shed for you and for many the remission of sins. This do to commemorate me.'"

2.41 These words the Apostle also delivers and more fully expounds in 1 Corinthians 11. On them we must lean and build as on a firm foundation, if we would not be carried about with every wind of doctrine, even as we have until now been carried about by the wicked doctrines of men, who turn aside the truth. For in these words nothing is omitted that concerns the completeness, the use and the blessing of this sacrament and nothing is included that is superfluous and not necessary for us to know. Whoever sets them aside and meditates or teaches concerning the mass, will teach monstrous and wicked doctrines, as they have done who made of the sacrament an *opus operatum* and a sacrifice.

2.42 Therefore let this stand at the outset as our infallibly certain proposition—the Mass, or Sacrament of the Altar, is Christ's testament which He left behind Him at His death, to be distributed among His believers. For that is the meaning of His word—"This is the chalice, the new testament in my blood." Let this truth stand, I say, as the immovable foundation on which we shall base all that we have to say, for we are going to overthrow, as you will see, all the godless opinions of men imported into this most precious sacrament. Christ, Who is the Truth, said truly that this is the new testament in His blood, which is shed for us. Not without reason do I dwell on this sentence. The matter is not at all trivial, and must be most deeply impressed upon us.

2.43 Let us inquire, therefore, what a testament is, and we shall learn at the same time what the Mass is, what its use is, what its blessing is, and what its abuse is.

2.44 A testament, as everyone knows, is a promise made by one about to die, in which he designates his bequest and appoints his heirs. Therefore a testament involves, first, the death of the testator, and secondly, the promise of the bequest and the naming of the heir. Thus St. Paul discusses at length the nature of a testament in Romans 4, Galatians 3 and 4, and Hebrews 9. The same thing is also clearly seen in these words of Christ. Christ testifies concerning His death when He says: "This is my body, which shall be given; this is my blood, which shall be shed." He designates the bequest when He says: "For remission of sins." And He appoints the heirs when He says: "For you, and for many"—i.e., for such as accept and believe the promise of the testator. For here it is faith that makes men heirs, as we shall see.

2.45 You see, therefore, that what we call the mass is the promise of remission of sins made to us by God—the kind of promise that has been confirmed by the death of the Son of God. For the one difference between a promise and a testament is that a testament is a promise which implies the death of him who makes it. A testator is a man who is about to die making a promise. While he that makes a promise is, if I may so put it, a testator who is not about to die. This testament of Christ was foreshadowed in all the promises of God from the beginning of the world. Yes, whatever value those ancient promises possessed was altogether derived from this new promise that was to come in Christ. This is why the words "covenant" and "testament of the Lord" occur so frequently in the Scriptures, which words signified that God would one day die. For where there is a testament, the death of the testator must follow (Hebrews 9). Now God made a testament. Therefore it was necessary that He should die. But God could not die unless He became man. Thus both the incarnation and the death of Christ are briefly understood in this one word "testament."

2.46 From the above it will at once be seen what is the right and what is the wrong use of the Mass, what is the worthy and what is the unworthy preparation for it. If the Mass is a promise, as has been said, it is to be approached, not with any work, strength or merit, but with faith alone. For where there is the word of God Who makes the promise, there must be the faith of man who takes it. It is plain, therefore, that the first step in our salvation is faith, which clings to the word of the promise made by God, Who without any effort on our part, in free and unmerited mercy makes a beginning and offers us the word of His promise. For He sent His Word, and by it healed them. He did not accept our work and thus heal us. God's Word is the beginning of all. Faith follows it, and love follows faith. Then love works every good work, for it does cause harm, no, it is the fulfilling of the law. In no other way can man come to God and deal with Him than through faith. That is, not man, by any work of his, but God, by His promise, is the author of salvation, so that all things depend on the word of His power, and are upheld and preserved by it, with which word He conceived us, that we should be a kind of firstfruits of His creatures.

2.47 Thus, in order to raise up Adam after the fall, God gave him this promise, addressing the serpent: "I will put hostility between you and the woman, and your seed and her seed. She shall crush your head, and you will lie in wait for her heel" [Gen. 3:16]. In this word of promise Adam, with his descendants, was carried as it were in God's arms, and by faith in it he was preserved, patiently waiting for the woman who should crush the serpent's head, as God had promised. And in that faith and expectation he died, not knowing when or in what form she would come, yet never doubting that she would come. For such a promise, being the truth of God, preserves, even in hell, those who believe it and wait for it. After this came another promise, made to Noah—to last until the time of Abraham—when a rainbow was set as a sign in the clouds, by faith in which Noah and his descendants found a gracious God. After that He promised Abraham that all nations should be blessed in his seed. This is Abraham's arms, in which his posterity was carried. Then to Moses and the children of Israel, and especially to David, He gave the plain promise of Christ, thereby at last making clear what was meant by the ancient promise to them.

2.48 So it came finally to the most complete promise of the new testament, in which with plain words life and salvation are freely promised, and granted to such as believe the promise. He distinguished this testament by a particular mark from the old, calling it the "new testament." For the old testament, which He gave by Moses, was a promise not of remission of sins or of eternal things, but of temporal things—namely, the land of Canaan—by which no man was renewed in his spirit, to lay hold of the heavenly inheritance. Therefore it was also necessary that irrational beasts should be slain, as types of Christ, that by their blood the testament might be confirmed. So the testament was like the blood, and the promise like the sacrifice. But here He says: "The new testament in my blood"—not in another's, but in His own. By this blood grace is promised, through the Spirit, for the remission of sins, that we may obtain the inheritance.

2.49 The Mass, according to its substance, is, therefore, nothing else than the words of Christ mentioned above—"Take and eat." It is as if He said: "Behold, condemned, sinful man, in the pure and unmerited love with which I love you, and by the will of the Father of all mercies, I promise you in these words, even though you do not desire or deserve them, the forgiveness of all your sins and life everlasting. And, so that you may be most certainly assured of this my irrevocable promise, I give my body and shed my blood, thus by my very death confirming this promise, and leaving my body and blood to you as a sign and memorial of this same promise. As often, therefore, as you partake of them, remember me, and praise, magnify, and give thanks for my love and bounty for you."

2.50 From this you will see that nothing else is needed to have a worthy Mass than a faith that confidently relies on this promise, believes these words of Christ are true, and does not doubt that these infinite blessings have been bestowed upon it. Following closely behind this faith there follows, by itself, a most sweet stirring of the heart, by which the spirit of man is enlarged and grows fat—that is love, given by the Holy Spirit through faith in Christ—so that he is drawn to Christ, that gracious and good Testator, and made quite another and a new man. Who would not shed tears of gladness, no, nearly faint for the joy he has for Christ, if he believed with unshaken faith that this inestimable promise of Christ belonged to him!

How could one help loving so great a Benefactor, who offers, promises and grants, all unasked, such great riches, and this eternal inheritance, to someone unworthy and deserving of something far different?

2.51 Therefore, it is our one misfortune that we have many Masses in the world, and yet none or but the fewest of us recognize, consider and receive these promises and riches that are offered, although truly we should do nothing else in the mass with greater zeal (yes, it demands all our zeal) than set before our eyes, meditate, and ponder these words, these promises of Christ, which truly are the Mass itself, in order to exercise, nourish, increase, and strengthen our faith by such daily remembrance. For this is what He commands, saying, "This do in remembrance of me." This should be done by the preachers of the Gospel, in order that this promise might be faithfully impressed upon the people and commended to them, to the awakening of faith in the same.

2.52 But how many are there now who know that the Mass is the promise of Christ? I will say nothing of those godless preachers of fables, who teach human traditions instead of this promise. And even if they teach these words of Christ, they do not teach them as a promise or testament, and, therefore, not to the awakening of faith.

2.53 O the pity of it! Under this captivity, they take every precaution that no layman should hear these words of Christ, as if they were too sacred to be delivered to the common people. So mad are we priests that we arrogantly claim that the so-called words of consecration may be said by ourselves alone, as secret words, yet so that they do not profit even us, for we too fail to regard them as promises or as a testament, for the strengthening of faith. Instead of believing them, we reverence them with I know not what superstitious and godless fancies. This misery of ours, what is it but a device of Satan to remove every trace of the mass out of the Church? although he is meanwhile at work filling every nook and corner on earth with masses, that is, abuses and mockeries of God's testament, and burdening the world more and more heavily with grievous sins of idolatry, to its deeper condemnation. For what worse idolatry can there be than to abuse God's promises with perverse opinions and to neglect or extinguish faith in them?

2.54 For God does not deal, nor has He ever dealt, with man otherwise than through a word of promise, as I have said. Again, we cannot deal with God otherwise than through faith in the word of His promise. He does not desire works, nor has He need of them. We deal with men and with ourselves on the basis of works. But He has need of this—that we deem Him true to His promises, wait patiently for Him, and thus worship Him with faith, hope and love. Thus He obtains His glory among us, since it is not of ourselves who run, but of God who shows mercy, promises and gives, that we have and hold every blessing. That is the true worship and service of God which we must perform in the mass. But if the words of promise are not proclaimed, what exercise of faith can there be? And without faith, who can have hope or love? Without faith, hope and love, what service can there be? There is no doubt, therefore, that in our day all priests and monks, together with all their bishops and superiors, are idolaters and in a most perilous state, by reason of this ignorance, abuse and mockery of the mass, or sacrament, or testament of God.

2.55 For any one can easily see that these two—the promise and faith—must go together. For without the promise there is nothing to believe, while without faith the promise remains without effect, for it is established and fulfilled through faith. From this everyone will readily gather that the mass, which is nothing else than the promise, is approached and observed only in this faith, without which whatever prayers, preparations, works, signs of the cross, or genuflections are brought to it, are incitements to impiety rather than exercises of piety. For they who come thus prepared are likely to imagine themselves on that account justly entitled to approach the altar, when in reality they are less prepared than at any other time and in any other work, by reason of the unbelief which they bring with them. How many priests will you find every day offering the sacrifice of the Mass, who accuse themselves of a horrible crime if they—wretched men!—commit a trifling blunder—such as putting on the wrong robe or forgetting to wash their hands or stumbling over their prayers—but that they neither regard nor believe the Mass itself, namely, the divine promise. This causes them not the slightest qualms of conscience. O worthless religion of this our age, the most godless and thankless of all ages! [...]

2.66 But you will say: "How is this? Will you not overturn the practice and teaching of all the churches and monasteries, by virtue of which they have flourished these many centuries? For the mass is the foundation of their anniversaries, intercessions, applications, communications, etc.—that is to say, of their fat income." I answer: This is the very thing that has constrained me to write of the captivity of the Church, for in this manner the adorable testament of God has been subjected to the bondage of a godless traffic, through the opinions and traditions of wicked men, who, passing over the Word of God, have put forth the thoughts of their own hearts and misled the whole world. What do I care for the number and influence of those who are in this error? The truth is mightier than they all. If you are able to refute Christ, according to Whom the Mass is a testament and sacrament, then I will admit that they are right. Or if you can bring yourself to say that you are doing a good work, when you receive the benefit of the testament, or when you use this sacrament of promise in order to receive it, then I will gladly condemn my teachings. But since you can do neither, why do you hesitate to turn your back on the multitude who go after evil, and to give God the glory and confess His truth? Which is, indeed, that all priests today are perversely mistaken, who regard the mass as a work whereby they may relieve their own necessities and those of others, dead or alive. I am uttering unheard-of and startling things. But if you will consider the meaning of the mass, you will realize that I have spoken the truth. The fault lies with our false sense of security, in which we have become blind to the wrath of God that is raging against us.

2.67 I am ready, however, to admit that the prayers which we pour out before God when we are gathered together to partake of the Mass, are good works or benefits, which we impart, apply and communicate to one another, and which we offer for one another. As James teaches us to pray for one another that we may be saved, and as Paul, in 1 Timothy 2, commands that supplications, prayers and intercessions be made for all men, for kings, and for all that are in high station. These are not the Mass, but works of the Mass—if the prayers of heart and lips may be called works—for they flow from the faith that is kindled or increased in the sacrament. For the Mass, being the promise of God, is not fulfilled by praying, but only by believing. But when we believe, we shall also pray and perform every good work. But what priest offers the sacrifice of the Mass in this sense and believes that he is offering up nothing but the prayers? They all imagine themselves to be offering up Christ

Himself, as all-sufficient sacrifice, to God the Father, and to be performing a good work for all whom they have the intention to benefit. For they put their trust in the work which the Mass accomplishes, and they do not ascribe this work to prayer. Thus, gradually, the error has grown, until they have come to ascribe to the sacrament what belongs to the prayers, and to offer to God what should be received as a benefit.

2.68 It is necessary, therefore, to make a sharp distinction between the testament or sacrament itself and the prayers which are there offered. And it is no less necessary to bear in mind that the prayers avail nothing, either for him who offers them or for those for whom they are offered, unless the sacrament be first received in faith, so that it is faith that offers the prayers, for it alone is heard, as James teaches in his first chapter. So great is the difference between prayer and the Mass. The prayer may be extended to as many persons as one desires. But the mass is received by none but the person who believes for himself, and only in proportion to his faith. It cannot be given either to God or to men, but God alone gives it, by the ministration of the priest, to such men as receive it by faith alone, without any works or merits. For no one would dare to make the mad assertion that a ragged beggar does a good work when he comes to receive a gift from a rich man. But the Mass is, as has been said, the gift and promise of God, offered to all men by the hand of the priest.

2.69 It is certain, therefore, that the Mass is not a work which may be communicated to others, but it is the object, as it is called, of faith, for the strengthening and nourishing of the personal faith of each individual. But there is yet another stumbling-block that must be removed, and this is much greater and the most dangerous of all. It is the common belief that the Mass is a sacrifice, which is offered to God. Even the words of the canon tend in this direction, when they speak of "these gifts," "these offerings," "this holy sacrifice," and farther on, of "this offering." Prayer also is made, in so many words, "That the sacrifice may be accepted even as the sacrifice of Abel," etc., and hence Christ is termed the "Sacrifice of the altar." In addition to this there are the sayings of the holy Fathers, the great number of examples, and the constant usage and custom of all the world.

2.70 We must resolutely oppose all of this, firmly entrenched as it is, with the words and example of Christ. For unless we hold fast to the truth, that the mass is the promise or testament of Christ, as the words clearly say, we shall lose the whole Gospel and all our comfort. Let us permit nothing to prevail against these words, even though an angel from heaven should teach otherwise. For there is nothing said in them of a work or a sacrifice. Moreover, we have also the example of Christ on our side. For at the Last Supper, when He instituted this sacrament and established this testament, Christ did not offer Himself to God the Father, nor did He perform a good work on behalf of others, but He set this testament before each of them that sat at table with Him and offered him the sign. Now, the more closely our mass resembles that first Mass of all, which Christ performed at the Last Supper, the more Christian will it be. But Christ's Mass was most simple, without the pageantry of vestments, genuflections, chants and other ceremonies. Indeed, if it were necessary to offer the mass as a sacrifice, then Christ's institution of it was not complete.

2.71 Not that anyone should condemn the Church universal for embellishing and amplifying the Mass with many additional rites and ceremonies. But this is what we contend for: no one should be deceived by the glamour of the ceremonies and entangled in the multitude of pompous forms, and thus lose the simplicity of the Mass itself, and indeed practice a sort of transubstantiation—losing sight of the simple substance of the Mass and clinging to the manifold accidents of outward pomp. For whatever has been added to the word and example of Christ is an accident of the Mass, and ought to be regarded just as we regard the so-called monstrances and corporal cloths in which the host itself is contained. Therefore, as distributing a testament, or accepting a promise, differs diametrically from offering a sacrifice, so it is a contradiction in terms to call the Mass a sacrifice. The former is something that we receive, while the latter is something that we offer. The same thing cannot be received and offered at the same time, nor can it be both given and taken by the same person. Just as little as our prayer can be the same as that which our prayer obtains, or the act of praying the same as the act of receiving the answer to our prayer.

2.72 What shall we say, then, about the canon of the Mass and the sayings of the Fathers? First of all, if there were nothing at all to be said against them, it would yet be the safer course to reject them all rather than admit that the Mass is a work or a sacrifice, lest we deny the word of Christ and overthrow faith together with the Mass. Nevertheless, not to reject altogether the canons and the Fathers, we shall say the following: The Apostle instructs us in 1 Corinthians 11 that it was customary for Christ's believers, when they came together to mass, to bring with them meat and drink, which they called "collections" and distributed among all who were in need, after the example of the apostles in Acts 4. From this store was taken the portion of bread and wine that was consecrated for use in the sacrament. And since all this store of meat and drink was sanctified by the word and by prayer, being "lifted up" according to the Hebrew rite of which we read in Moses, the words and the rite of this lifting up, or offering, have come down to us, although the custom of collecting that which was offered, or lifted up, has fallen long since into disuse. Thus, in Isaiah 37, Hezekiah commanded Isaiah to lift up his prayer in the sight of God for the remnant. The Psalmist sings: "Lift up your hands to the holy places" and "To you will I lift up my hands." And in 1 Timothy 2 we read: "Lifting up pure hands in every place." For this reason the words "sacrifice" and "offering" must be taken to refer, not to the sacrament and testament, but to these collections, from this also the word "collect" has come down to us, as meaning the prayers said in the Mass.

2.73 The same thing is indicated when the priest elevates the bread and the chalice immediately after the consecration, whereby he shows that he is not offering anything to God, for he does not

say a single word here about a victim or an offering. But this elevation is either a survival of that Hebrew rite of lifting up what was
received with thanksgiving and returned to God, or else it is an
admonition to us, to provoke us to faith in this testament which
the priest has set forth and exhibited in the words of Christ, so that
now he shows us also the sign of the testament. Thus the offering
of the bread properly accompanies the demonstrative this in the
words, "This is my body," by which sign the priest addresses us
gathered about him. In like manner the offering of the chalice accompanies the demonstrative this in the words, "This chalice is the
new testament, etc." For it is faith that the priest ought to awaken
in us by this act of elevation. I wish that, as he elevates the sign, or
sacrament, openly before our eyes, he might also sound in our ears
the words of the testament with a loud, clear voice, and in the language of the people, whatever it may be, in order that faith may be
the more effectively awakened. For why may mass be said in Greek
and Latin and Hebrew, and not also in German or in any other
language? [...]

2.78 Therefore, just as a wicked priest may baptize, that is,
apply the word of promise and the sign of the water to a candidate
for baptism, so he may also set forth the promise of this sacrament
and administer it to those who partake, and even himself partake,
like Judas the traitor, at the Lord's Supper. It still remains always
the same sacrament and testament, which works in the believer its
own work, in the unbeliever a "strange work." But when it comes
to offering a sacrifice the case is quite different. For not the Mass
but the prayers are offered to God, and therefore it is as plain as
day that the offerings of a wicked priest avail nothing, but, as
Gregory says again, when an unworthy intercessor is chosen, the
heart of the judge is moved to greater displeasure. We must, therefore, not confound these two—the Mass and the prayers, the sacrament and the work, the testament and the sacrifice. For the one
comes from God to us, through the ministration of the priest, and
demands our faith, the other proceeds from our faith to God,
through the priest, and demands His answer. The former descends,

the latter ascends. Therefore the former does not necessarily require a worthy and godly minister, but the latter does indeed require such a priest, because "God does not hear sinners." He knows how to send down blessings through evildoers, but He does not accept the work of any evildoer, as He showed in the case of Cain, and as it is said in Proverbs 15, "The victims of the wicked are abominable to the Lord" and in Romans 14, "All that is not of faith is sin."

2.79 But in order to make an end of this first part, we must take up one remaining point against which an opponent might arise. From all that has been said we conclude that the mass was provided only for such as have a sad, afflicted, disturbed, perplexed and erring conscience, and that they alone commune worthily. For, since the word of divine promise in this sacrament sets forth the remission of sins, that man may fearlessly draw near, whoever he be, whose sins distress him, either with remorse for past or with temptation to future wrongdoing. For this testament of Christ is the one remedy against sins, past, present and future, if you but cling to it with unwavering faith and believe that what the words of the testament declare is freely granted to you. But if you do not believe this, you will never, nowhere, and by no works or efforts of your own, find peace of conscience. For faith alone sets the conscience at peace, and unbelief alone keeps the conscience troubled.

INTRODUCTION TO LEO X'S *EXSURGE DOMINE*

AS LUTHER expected while he was writing his *Letter to the Christian Nobility*, his fate was already being sealed in Rome. A bull of excommunication, *Exsurge Domine*, was being prepared by Pope Leo X (1475–1521) and his advisors, including Luther's earlier interlocutors Cardinal Cajetan (1469–1534) and Johann Eck (1483–1543). There was indeed a sharp disagreement between Cajetan and Eck on the appropriate way to proceed, reflecting a deep-seated uncertainty within the Roman Church about how to handle calls for reform. It was clear to many, including Leo himself, that something had to change after the low point of worldliness reached by Popes Alexander VI and Julius II, and many of Leo's councilors were concerned to restore the Church to its spiritual mission of serving the faithful.

Cajetan was among these, and argued that Luther's errors must be considered carefully one-by-one rather than condemned wholesale. But he was overruled by the uncompromising Eck, for whom Luther's defiance of papal authority and sympathy with the heretical Hussites could not be tolerated for a moment. The result was a somewhat curious document indeed, which lists off no less than forty-one statements supposedly extracted from Luther's writings that were "either heretical, false, scandalous, or offensive to pious ears, as seductive of simple minds." Of course, it made quite a difference to the assessment of Luther's theology which of these were to be considered *heretical* and which were merely "seductive of simple minds," but there was no attempt to rank the errors in the bull. What we find then is a list of forty-one disjointed statements, some fairly trivial and others momentous, with no context or elaboration to explain what Luther might have meant by them or why they were rejected.

Of course, this manner of proceeding was probably by design rather than carelessness (even if all did not agree in the design): after all, what better way to insist on the unquestionable authority of the Pope than to simply declare by fiat, without explanation, what was and was not to be permitted? In this, the Pope and Eck misjudged the climate of the times and the power of the printing press: mere assertions of authority were no match for the eloquent but simple persuasive arguments that Luther was filling his pamphlets with.

To be sure, there was no lack of rhetorical crafting in *Exsurge Domine's* opening and closing sections. Framed as an invocation to Christ, St. Peter, St. Paul, and all the saints to rise up and defend the Church from the "wild boar" destroying the vineyard of the Church, the language of the opening paragraphs is a memorable cry of lamentation, positioning the papacy as the victim rather than the oppressor. After the harsh words of condemnation that follow, the document resumes a gentler tone, flattering the German princes by saying that they have always been the most pious defenders of orthodoxy, and painting the pope as a gracious father trying to recall his wandering prodigal, Martin, to the fold. The first bit of rhetorical posturing was to prove effective in gaining the support of Charles V to prosecute Luther's heresy; the latter, needless to say, was laughed at in Wittenberg, where Luther was undaunted by the bull when it arrived late that year.

Just as the *Ninety-Five Theses* hardly make a very fitting manifesto for the Reformation which was to follow, so *Exsurge Domine* strikes the modern reader as something of a puzzling refutation. Leo and his advisors, after all, had no access to most of Luther's more revolutionary and memorable theological writings, which were indeed just beginning to appear that year. They had to make do with scattered treatises from 1518 and 1519, in which Luther was still feeling his way toward his final position. Moreover, the scholar Hans Hillerbrand concluded after a close review that "no less than twelve of the forty-one propositions did not accurately quote Luther or cannot be taken to express his sentiment."[1] It is also noteworthy that the Pope and his theologians seem relatively uninterested in Luther's great doctrines of grace which were to be his greatest contribution, focusing instead on statements in which Luther emphasized the depth of sin and the hopelessness of human efforts to overcome it, especially the penitential system devised by the late medieval church for that purpose. Luther's insistence that Christ alone, by faith alone, could do far more than any rite of penance, went unmentioned in the bull, and was not tackled properly until the Council of Trent thirty years later.

Further Reading

For further reading, see Scott H. Hendrix, *Martin Luther: Visionary Reformer* (New Haven: Yale University Press, 2015), ch. 5; Timothy J. Wengert, *Martin Luther's 95 Theses with Introduction, Commentary, and Study Guide* (Minneapolis: Fortress Press, 2015); David Bagchi, "Luther's *Ninety-five Theses* and the Contemporary Critique of Indulgences" in Robert N. Swanson, ed. *Promissory Notes on the Treaury of Merits: Indulgences in Late Medieval Europe* (Leiden: Brill, 2006): 331–56.

---

[1] Hans Hillerbrand, "Luther and *Exsurge Domine*," *Theological Studies* 30, no. 1 (1969): 111.

LEO X,
EXSURGE DOMINE (1520)[1]

ARISE, O Lord, and judge your own cause. Remember your reproaches to those who are filled with foolishness all through the day. Listen to our prayers, for foxes have arisen seeking to destroy the vineyard whose winepress you alone have trod. When you were about to ascend to your Father, you committed the care, rule, and administration of the vineyard, an image of the triumphant church, to Peter, as the head and your vicar, and his successors. The wild boar from the forest seeks to destroy it and every wild beast feeds upon it.

Rise, Peter, and fulfill this pastoral office divinely entrusted to you as mentioned above. Give heed to the cause of the holy Roman Church, mother of all churches and teacher of the faith, whom you by the order of God, have consecrated by your blood. Against the Roman Church, you warned, lying teachers are rising, introducing ruinous sects, and drawing upon themselves speedy doom. Their tongues are fire, a restless evil, full of deadly poison. They have bitter zeal, contention in their hearts, and boast and lie against the truth.

We beseech you also, Paul, to arise. It was you that enlightened and illuminated the Church by your doctrine and by a martyrdom like Peter's. For now a new Porphyry rises who, as the old once wrongfully assailed the holy apostles, now assails the holy pontiffs, our predecessors.

---

[1] Taken from *Papal Encyclicals Online*, "Exsurge Domine: Condemning the Errors of Martin Luther, Pope Leo X – June 15, 1520."

Rebuking them, in violation of your teaching, instead of imploring them, he is not ashamed to assail them, to tear at them, and when he despairs of his cause, to stoop to insults. He is like the heretics "whose last defense," as Jerome says, "is to start spewing out a serpent's venom with their tongue when they see that their causes are about to be condemned, and spring to insults when they see they are vanquished." For although you have said that there must be heresies to test the faithful, still they must be destroyed at their very birth by your intercession and help, so they do not grow or wax strong like your wolves. Finally, let the whole church of the saints and the rest of the universal church arise. Some, putting aside her true interpretation of Sacred Scripture, are blinded in mind by the father of lies. Wise in their own eyes, according to the ancient practice of heretics, they interpret these same Scriptures otherwise than the Holy Spirit demands, inspired only by their own sense of ambition, and for the sake of popular acclaim, as the Apostle declares. In fact, they twist and adulterate the Scriptures. As a result, according to Jerome, "It is no longer the Gospel of Christ, but a man's, or what is worse, the devil's."

Let all this holy Church of God, I say, arise, and with the blessed apostles intercede with almighty God to purge the errors of His sheep, to banish all heresies from the lands of the faithful, and be pleased to maintain the peace and unity of His holy Church.

For we can scarcely express, from distress and grief of mind, what has reached our ears for some time by the report of reliable men and general rumor; alas, we have even seen with our eyes and read the many diverse errors. Some of these have already been condemned by councils and the constitutions of our predecessors, and expressly contain even the heresy of the Greeks and Bohemians. Other errors are either heretical, false, scandalous, or offensive to pious ears, as seductive of simple minds, originating with false exponents of the faith who in their proud curiosity yearn for the world's glory, and contrary to the Apostle's teaching, wish to be wiser than they should be. Their talkativeness, unsupported by the authority of the Scriptures, as Jerome says, would not win credence unless they appeared to support their perverse doctrine even with divine testimonies however badly interpreted. From their sight fear of God has now passed.

These errors have, at the suggestion of the human race, been revived and recently propagated among the more frivolous and the illustrious German nation. We grieve the more that this happened there because we and our predecessors have always held this nation in the bosom of our affection. For after the empire had been transferred by the Roman Church from the Greeks to these same Germans, our predecessors and we always took the Church's advocates and defenders from among them. Indeed it is certain that these Germans, truly germane to the Catholic faith, have always been the bitterest opponents of heresies, as witnessed by those commendable constitutions of the German emperors in behalf of the Church's independence, freedom, and the expulsion and extermination of all heretics from Germany. Those constitutions formerly issued, and then confirmed by our predecessors, were issued under the greatest penalties even of loss of lands and dominions against anyone sheltering or not expelling them. If they were observed today both we and they would obviously be free of this disturbance. Witness to this is the condemnation and punishment in the Council of Constance of the infidelity of the Hussites and Wyclifites as well as Jerome of Prague. Witness to this is the blood of Germans shed so often in wars against the Bohemians. A final witness is the refutation, rejection, and condemnation no less learned than true and holy of the above errors, or many of them, by the universities of Cologne and Louvain, most devoted and religious cultivators of the Lord's field. We could allege many other facts too, which we have decided to omit, lest we appear to be composing a history.

In virtue of our pastoral office committed to us by the divine favor we can under no circumstances tolerate or overlook any longer the pernicious poison of the above errors without disgrace to the Christian religion and injury to orthodox faith. Some of these errors we have decided to include in the present document; their substance is as follows:

1. It is a heretical opinion, but a common one, that the sacraments of the New Law give pardoning grace to those who do not set up an obstacle.

2. To deny that in a child after baptism sin remains is to treat with contempt both Paul and Christ.

3. The inflammable sources of sin, even if there be no actual sin, delay a soul departing from the body from entrance into heaven.

4. To one on the point of death imperfect charity necessarily brings with it great fear, which in itself alone is enough to produce the punishment of purgatory, and impedes entrance into the kingdom.

5. That there are three parts to penance: contrition, confession, and satisfaction, has no foundation in Sacred Scripture nor in the ancient sacred Christian doctors.

6. Contrition, which is acquired through discussion, collection, and detestation of sins, by which one reflects upon his years in the bitterness of his soul, by pondering over the gravity of sins, their number, their baseness, the loss of eternal beatitude, and the acquisition of eternal damnation, this contrition makes him a hypocrite, indeed more a sinner.

7. It is a most truthful proverb and the doctrine concerning the contritions given thus far is the more remarkable: "Not to do so in the future is the highest penance; the best penance, a new life."

8. By no means may you presume to confess venial sins, nor even all mortal sins, because it is impossible that you know all mortal sins. Hence in the primitive Church only manifest mortal sins were confessed.

9. As long as we wish to confess all sins without exception, we are doing nothing else than to wish to leave nothing to God's mercy for pardon.

10. Sins are not forgiven to anyone, unless when the priest forgives them he believes they are forgiven; on the contrary, the sin would remain unless he believed it was forgiven; for indeed the

remission of sin and the granting of grace does not suffice, but it is necessary also to believe that there has been forgiveness.

11. By no means can you have reassurance of being absolved because of your contrition, but because of the word of Christ: "Whatsoever you shall loose, etc." Hence, I say, trust confidently, if you have obtained the absolution of the priest, and firmly believe yourself to have been absolved, and you will truly be absolved, whatever there may be of contrition.

12. If through an impossibility he who confessed was not contrite, or the priest did not absolve seriously, but in a jocose manner, if nevertheless he believes that he has been absolved, he is most truly absolved.

13. In the sacrament of penance and the remission of sin the pope or the bishop does no more than the lowest priest; indeed, where there is no priest, any Christian, even if a woman or child, may equally do as much.

14. No one ought to answer a priest that he is contrite, nor should the priest inquire.

15. Great is the error of those who approach the sacrament of the Eucharist relying on this, that they have confessed, that they are not conscious of any mortal sin, that they have sent their prayers on ahead and made preparations; all these eat and drink judgment to themselves. But if they believe and trust that they will attain grace, then this faith alone makes them pure and worthy.

16. It seems to have been decided that the Church in common Council established that the laity should communicate under both species; the Bohemians who communicate under both species are not heretics, but schismatics.

17. The treasures of the Church, from which the pope grants indulgences, are not the merits of Christ and of the saints.

18. Indulgences are pious frauds of the faithful, and remissions of good works; and they are among the number of those things which are allowed, and not of the number of those which are advantageous.

19. Indulgences are of no avail to those who truly gain them, for the remission of the penalty due to actual sin in the sight of divine justice.

20. They are seduced who believe that indulgences are salutary and useful for the fruit of the spirit.

21. Indulgences are necessary only for public crimes, and are properly conceded only to the harsh and impatient.

22. For six kinds of men indulgences are neither necessary nor useful; namely, for the dead and those about to die, the infirm, those legitimately hindered, and those who have not committed crimes, and those who have committed crimes, but not public ones, and those who devote themselves to better things.

23. Excommunications are only external penalties and they do not deprive man of the common spiritual prayers of the Church.

24. Christians must be taught to cherish excommunications rather than to fear them.

25. The Roman Pontiff, the successor of Peter, is not the vicar of Christ over all the churches of the entire world, instituted by Christ Himself in blessed Peter.

26. The word of Christ to Peter: "Whatsoever you shall loose on earth," etc., is extended merely to those things bound by Peter himself.

27. It is certain that it is not in the power of the Church or the pope to decide upon the articles of faith, and much less concerning the laws for morals or for good works.

28. If the pope with a great part of the Church thought so and so, he would not err; still it is not a sin or heresy to think the contrary, especially in a matter not necessary for salvation, until one alternative is condemned and another approved by a general Council.

29. A way has been made for us for weakening the authority of councils, and for freely contradicting their actions, and judging their decrees, and boldly confessing whatever seems true, whether it has been approved or disapproved by any council whatsoever.

30. Some articles of John Hus, condemned in the Council of Constance, are most Christian, wholly true and evangelical; these the universal Church could not condemn.

31. In every good work the just man sins.

32. A good work done very well is a venial sin.

33. That heretics be burned is against the will of the Spirit.

34. To go to war against the Turks is to resist God who punishes our iniquities through them.

35. No one is certain that he is not always sinning mortally, because of the most hidden vice of pride.

36. Free will after sin is a matter of title only; and as long as one does what is in him, one sins mortally.

37. Purgatory cannot be proved from Sacred Scripture which is in the canon.

38. The souls in purgatory are not sure of their salvation, at least not all; nor is it proved by any arguments or by the Scriptures that they are beyond the state of meriting or of increasing in charity.

39. The souls in purgatory sin without intermission, as long as they seek rest and abhor punishment.

40. The souls freed from purgatory by the suffrages of the living are less happy than if they had made satisfactions by themselves.

41. Ecclesiastical prelates and secular princes would not act badly if they destroyed all of the money bags of beggary.

No one of sound mind is ignorant how destructive, pernicious, scandalous, and seductive to pious and simple minds these various errors are, how opposed they are to all charity and reverence for the holy Roman Church who is the mother of all the faithful and teacher of the faith; how destructive they are of the vigor of ecclesiastical discipline, namely obedience. This virtue is the font and origin of all virtues and without it anyone is readily convicted of being unfaithful.

Therefore we, in this above enumeration, important as it is, wish to proceed with great care as is proper, and to cut off the advance of this plague and cancerous disease so it will not spread any further in the Lord's field as harmful thornbushes. We have therefore held a careful inquiry, scrutiny, discussion, strict examination, and mature deliberation with each of the brothers, the eminent cardinals of the holy Roman Church, as well as the priors and ministers general of the religious orders, besides many other professors and masters skilled in sacred theology and in civil and canon law. We have found that these errors or theses are not Catholic, as mentioned above, and are not to be taught, as such; but rather are against the doctrine and tradition of the Catholic Church, and against the true interpretation of the sacred Scriptures received from the Church. Now Augustine maintained that her authority had to be accepted so completely that he stated he would not have believed the Gospel unless the authority of the Catholic Church had vouched for it. For, according to these errors, or any one or several of them, it clearly follows that the Church which is guided by the Holy Spirit is in error and has always erred. This is against what Christ at his ascension promised to his disciples (as is read in the holy Gospel of Matthew): "I will be with you to the consummation of the world"; it is against the determinations of the holy Fathers, or the express ordinances and canons of the councils and the supreme pontiffs. Failure to comply with these canons, according to the testimony of Cyprian, will be the fuel and cause of all heresy and schism.

With the advice and consent of these our venerable brothers, with mature deliberation on each and every one of the above theses, and by the authority of almighty God, the blessed Apostles Peter and Paul, and our own authority, we condemn, reprobate, and reject completely each of these theses or errors as either heretical, scandalous, false, offensive to pious ears or seductive of simple minds, and against Catholic truth. By listing them, we decree and declare that all the faithful of both sexes must regard them as condemned, reprobated, and rejected. [...] We restrain all in the virtue of holy obedience and under the penalty of an automatic major excommunication. [...]

Moreover, because the preceding errors and many others are contained in the books or writings of Martin Luther, we likewise condemn, reprobate, and reject completely the books and all the writings and sermons of the said Martin, whether in Latin or any other language, containing the said errors or any one of them; and we wish them to be regarded as utterly condemned, reprobated, and rejected. We forbid each and every one of the faithful of either sex, in virtue of holy obedience and under the above penalties to be incurred automatically, to read, assert, preach, praise, print, publish, or defend them. They will incur these penalties if they presume to uphold them in any way, personally or through another or others, directly or indirectly, tacitly or explicitly, publicly or occultly, either in their own homes or in other public or private places. Indeed immediately after the publication of this letter these works, wherever they may be, shall be sought out carefully by the ordinaries and others [ecclesiastics and regulars], and under each and every one of the above penalties shall be burned publicly and solemnly in the presence of the clerics and people.

As far as Martin himself is concerned, O good God, what have we overlooked or not done? What fatherly charity have we omitted that we might call him back from such errors? For after we had cited him, wishing to deal more kindly with him, we urged him through various conferences with our legate and through our personal letters to abandon these errors. We have even offered him safe conduct and the money necessary for the journey urging him to come without fear or any misgivings, which perfect charity should cast out, and to talk not secretly but openly and face to face after the example of our Savior and the Apostle Paul. If he had done this, we are certain he would have changed in heart, and he would have recognized his errors. He would not have found all these errors in the Roman Curia which he attacks so viciously, ascribing to it more than he should because of the empty rumors of wicked men. We would have shown him clearer than the light of day that the Roman pontiffs, our predecessors, whom he injuriously attacks beyond all decency, never erred in their canons or constitutions which he tries to assail. For, according to the prophet, neither is healing oil nor the doctor lacking in Galaad.

But he always refused to listen and, despising the previous citation and each and every one of the above overtures, disdained to come. To the present day he has been contumacious. With a hardened spirit he has continued under censure over a year. What is worse, adding evil to evil, and on learning of the citation, he broke forth in a rash appeal to a future council. This to be sure was contrary to the constitution of Pius II and Julius II our predecessors that all appealing in this way are to be punished with the penalties of heretics. In vain does he implore the help of a council, since he openly admits that he does not believe in a council.

Therefore we can, without any further citation or delay, proceed against him to his condemnation and damnation as one whose faith is notoriously suspect and in fact a true heretic with the full severity of each and all of the above penalties and censures. Yet, with the advice of our brothers, imitating the mercy of almighty God who does not wish the death of a sinner but rather that he be converted and live, and forgetting all the injuries inflicted on us and the Apostolic See, we have decided to use all the compassion we are capable of. It is our hope, so far as in us lies, that he will experience a change of heart by taking the road of mildness we have proposed, return, and turn away from his errors. We will receive him kindly as the prodigal son returning to the embrace of the Church.

Therefore let Martin himself and all those adhering to him, and those who shelter and support him, through the merciful heart of our God and the sprinkling of the blood of our Lord Jesus Christ by which and through whom the redemption of the human race and the upbuilding of holy Mother Church was accomplished, know that from our heart we exhort and beseech that he cease to disturb the peace, unity, and truth of the Church for which the Savior prayed so earnestly to the Father. Let him abstain from his pernicious errors that he may come back to us. If they really will obey, and certify to us by legal documents that they have obeyed, they will find in us the affection of a father's love, the opening of the font of the effects of paternal charity, and opening of the font of mercy and clemency.

We enjoin, however, on Martin that in the meantime he cease from all preaching or the office of preacher.

INTRODUCTION TO MARTIN LUTHER'S
THE FREEDOM OF A CHRISTIAN

WITH *THE Freedom of a Christian*, Luther's luminous and at times almost lyrical summary of the Christian life, we finally encounter the Protestant manifesto that was missing in his earlier works. Here is a statement no longer of what Luther was against, but of what he was *for*, the joyful rediscovery of the gospel that he wanted to share with Western Christendom. Having leveled a devastating critique in *The Babylonian Captivity* of Rome's sacramental system, Luther here proclaimed the freedom that believers have in Christ and which no church authority can take away from them. In fact, Luther's prose sets a very different tone than most of his earlier writings, especially his conciliatory letter to Pope Leo X, which served as the preface to the work (not included here). There he insisted he had never meant to attack Leo personally, considering him to be a well-intentioned pope surrounded by wicked advisors, and offering his own advice on what Leo should do about them. Needless to say, Leo would not be impressed by the letter, and his bull of excommunication was in any case already on its way, destroying the aspirations of would-be peacemaker Karl von Miltitz, who had convinced Luther to write the letter.

Luther's theology would certainly develop after 1520, but we find in *The Freedom of a Christian*, in succinct and admirably clear form, the central themes that were to dominate his mature theology and influence that of all the Protestant reformers who followed him. These include the famous dualities of *simul justus et peccator* (that a believer is at the same time righteous and a sinner), of Law and Gospel (that Scripture must be read as consisting of commandments and promises), of faith and works, of the imputation of sin and righteousness ("the believing soul can boast of and glory in whatever Christ has as though it were its own, and whatever the soul has Christ claims as his own"), and of the two kingdoms—the inward man, alive by faith, and the outward man, animated by love. Each set of dualities was to be nuanced in various ways by later reformers and sometimes by Luther himself, but Luther's formulations of them here may still be taken as broadly representative for the Protestant movement.

Luther's penchant for paradox is on full display in the book, above all in his summary statement: "A Christian is a perfectly free lord of all, subject to none. A Christian is a perfectly dutiful servant of all, subject to everyone." Luther goes on to explain that in his inward character, before God, the Christian is entirely free because justified by faith; outwardly, before men, he is enslaved by love to serve all. Only by virtue of such a radical distinction between the inward and the outward, Luther believes, can the freedom of a Christian conscience before God be guaranteed, for if the Christian is led to believe that his justification before God depends on any outward works, rather than the free gift of faith, he is in bondage. By this means Luther attacks the whole array of Catholic ceremonies, saying,

> It does not help the soul if the body is adorned with the sacred robes of priests or dwells in sacred places or is occupied with sacred duties or prays, fasts, abstains from certain kinds of food, or does any work that can be done by the body and in the body. The righteousness and the freedom of the soul require something far different.

That something, he says, is the "the most holy Word of God, the gospel of Christ."

It is crucial to understand that the purpose of this radical distinction is not to attack outward works *per se*, but merely to establish the priority of the inward, which is faith: the outward must never determine the inward, grace must never be conditioned upon works, but the inward life of grace will determine the outward, issuing forth in good works. The freedom of justification results in an overflow of love that willingly obeys the laws of Scripture and the needs of the neighbor without allowing such works to reign over his conscience: "A man does not live for himself alone in this mortal body to work for it alone, but he lives also for all men on earth; rather he lives only for others and not for himself."

The freedom of a Christian is thus not, as it was quickly twisted by some of Luther's more radical followers, a freedom *for* oneself but a freedom *from* oneself. It was a liberation from the preoccupation with one's own salvation and merit, from fear that one is not toeing the line and meeting the standards; instead, the believer can actually focus on serving his neighbor.

But although Luther offers a compelling account of the relation of faith and works in this treatise, it is certainly not without tensions or ambiguities. Luther clearly states toward the end of the treatise that just because the Christian is freed in conscience from considering Catholic ceremonies as necessary to salvation, he need not reject all such ceremonies out of hand. But the guidance he offers for how to handle such ceremonies was not easy to follow. He argued that toward "wolves" who urge ceremonies upon us as necessary, we "must resist, do the very opposite, and offend them boldly." He himself was later to provide a particularly shocking example of such bold offense by his 1525 marriage to Katerina von Bora, a former monk marrying a former nun. But in the same passage, Luther goes on to advise just the opposite course of action before the weak in faith who needed to be initiated slowly into Gospel liberty—continuing to practice fasts and ceremonies that they were accustomed to. The difficulty of discerning when one was dealing with wolves or sheep, Pharisees or weaker brethren, meant that it was hard to know just how to approach the practice of traditional Catholic ceremonies, and this ambiguity continues to create conflicts among Protestants today.

Further Reading

For further reading, see Scott H. Hendrix, *Martin Luther: Visionary Reformer* (New Haven: Yale University Press, 2015), ch. 7; Timothy J. Wengert, ed., *The Freedom of a Christian, 1520: The Annotated Luther, Study Edition* (Minneapolis: Fortress Press, 2016).

MARTIN LUTHER,
THE FREEDOM OF A CHRISTIAN (1520)[1]

Concerning Christian Liberty

CHRISTIAN FAITH has appeared to many an easy thing; nay, not a few even reckon it among the social virtues, as it were; and this they do, because they have not made proof of it experimentally, and have never tasted of what efficacy it is. For it is not possible for any man to write well about it, or to understand well what is rightly written, who has not at some time tasted of its spirit, under the pressure of tribulation. While he who has tasted of it, even to a very small extent, can never write, speak, think, or hear about it sufficiently. For it is a living fountain, springing up unto eternal life, as Christ calls it in the 4th chapter of St. John.

Now, though I cannot boast of my abundance, and though I know how poorly I am furnished, yet I hope that, after having been vexed by various temptations, I have attained some little drop of faith, and that I can speak of this matter, if not with more elegance, certainly with more solidity than those literal and too subtle disputants who have hitherto discoursed upon it, without understanding their own words. That I may open, then, an easier way for the ignorant—for these alone I am trying to serve—I first lay down these two propositions, concerning spiritual liberty and servitude.

---

[1] From C.A. Buchheim and Henry Wace, trans. and eds., *First Principles of the Reformation* (London: John Murray, 1883).

A Christian man is the most free lord of all, and subject to none; a Christian man is the most dutiful servant of all, and subject to everyone.

Although these statements appear contradictory, yet, when they are found to agree together, they will be highly serviceable to my purpose. They are both the statements of Paul himself, who says: "Though I be free from all men, yet have I made myself servant unto all" (1 Cor. ix. 19), and: "Owe no man anything, but to love one another" (Rom. xiii. 8). Now love is by its own nature dutiful and obedient to the beloved object. Thus even Christ, though Lord of all things, was yet made of a woman; made under the law; at once free and a servant; at once in the form of God and in the form of a servant.

Let us examine the subject on a deeper and less simple principle. Man is composed of a twofold nature, a spiritual and a bodily. As regards the spiritual nature, which they name the soul, he is called the spiritual, inward, new man; as regards the bodily nature, which they name the flesh, he is called the fleshly, outward, old man. The Apostle speaks of this: "Though our outward man perish, yet the inward man is relieved day by day" (2 Cor. iv. 16). The result of this diversity is that, in the Scriptures, opposing statements are made concerning the same man; the fact being that in the same man these two men are opposed to one another; the flesh lusting against the spirit, and the spirit against the flesh (Gal. v. 17).

We first approach the subject of the inward man, that we may see by what means a man becomes justified, free, and a true Christian; that is, a spiritual, new, and inward man. It is certain that absolutely none among outward things, under whatever name they may be reckoned, has any weight in producing a state of justification and Christian liberty, nor, on the other hand an unjustified state and one of slavery. This can be shown by an easy course of argument.

What can it profit the soul, that the body should be in good condition, free, and full of life; that it should eat, drink, and act according to its pleasure; when even the most impious slaves of every kind of vice are prosperous in these matters? Again, what harm can ill-health, bondage, hunger, thirst, or any other outward evil, do to the soul, when even the most pious of men, and the freest in the purity of their conscience, are harassed by these things? Neither of these states of things has to do with the liberty or the slavery of the soul.

And so it will profit nothing that the body should be adorned with sacred vestments, or dwell in holy places, or be occupied in sacred offices, or pray, fast, and abstain from certain meats, or do whatever works can be done through the body and in the body. Something widely different will be necessary for the justification and liberty of the soul, since the things I have spoken of can be done by any impious person, and only hypocrites are produced by devotion to these things. On the other hand, it will not at all injure the soul that the body should be clothed in profane raiment, should dwell in profane places, should eat and drink in the ordinary fashion, should not pray aloud, and should leave undone all the things abovementioned, which may be done by hypocrites.

And, to cast everything aside, even speculations, meditations and whatever things can be performed by the exertions of the soul itself, are of no profit. One thing, and one alone, is necessary for life, justification, and Christian liberty; and that is the most holy word of God, the Gospel of Christ, as He says: "I am the resurrection and the life; he that believeth in me shall not die eternally "(John xi. 25); and also (John viii. 36) "If the Son shall make you free, ye shall be free indeed;" and (Matt. iv. 4), "Man shall not live by bread alone, but by every word that proceedeth out of the mouth of God."

Let us therefore hold it for certain and firmly established, that the soul can do without everything, except the word of God, without which none at all of its wants are provided for. But, having the word, it is rich and want for nothing; since that is the word of life, of truth, of light, of peace, of justification, of salvation, of joy, of liberty, of wisdom, of virtue, of grace, of glory, and of every good thing. It is on this account that the prophet in a whole psalm

(Ps. cxix), and in many other places, sighs for and calls upon the word of God with so many groanings and words.

Again, there is no more cruel stroke of the wrath of God than when He sends a famine of hearing His words (Amos viii. 11); just as there is no greater favour from Him than the sending forth of His word, as it is said: "He sent his word and healed them, and delivered them from their destructions" (Ps. cvii. 20). Christ was sent for no other office than that of the word, and the order of apostles, that of bishops, and that of the whole body of the clergy, have been called and instituted for no object but the ministry of the word.

But you will ask:—"What is this word, and by what means is it to be used, since there are so many words of God?" I answer, the Apostle Paul (Rom. i) explains what it is, namely, the Gospel of God, concerning His Son, incarnate, suffering, risen, and glorified through the Spirit, the sanctifier. To preach Christ is to feed the soul, to justify it, to set it free, and to save it, if it believes the preaching. For faith alone, and the efficacious use of the word of God, bring salvation. "If thou shalt confess with thy mouth the Lord Jesus, and shalt believe in thine heart that God hath raised him from the dead, thou shalt be saved." (Rom. x. 9). And again: "Christ is the end of the law for righteousness to every one that believeth" (Rom. x. 4); and "The just shall live by faith." (Rom. i. 17). For the word of God cannot be received and honoured by any works, but by faith alone. Hence it is clear that, as the soul needs the word alone for life and justification, so it is justified by faith alone and not by any works. For if it could be justified by any other means, it would have no need of the word, nor consequently of faith.

But this faith cannot consist at all with works; that is, if you imagine that you can be justified by those works, whatever they are, along with it. For this would be to halt between two opinions, to worship Baal, and to kiss the hand to him, which is a very great iniquity, as Job says. Therefore, when you begin to believe, you learn at the same time that all that is in you is utterly guilty, sinful, and damnable; according to that saying: "All have sinned, and come short of the glory of God" (Rom. iii. 23). And also: "There is none righteous, no, not one; they are all gone out of the way; they are together become unprofitable; there is none that doeth good, no, not one" (Rom. iii. 10–12). When you have learnt this, you will know that Christ is necessary for you, since He has suffered and risen again for you, that, believing on Him, you might by this faith become another man, all your sins being remitted, and you being justified by the merits of another, namely, of Christ alone.

Since then this faith can reign only in the inward man, as it is said: "With the heart man believeth unto righteousness" (Rom. x. 10); and since it alone justifies, it is evident that by no outward work or labour can the inward man be at all justified, made free, and saved; and that no works whatever have any relation to him. And so, on the other hand, it is solely by impiety and incredulity of heart that he becomes guilty, and a slave of sin, deserving condemnation; not by any outward sin or work. Therefore the first care of every Christian ought to be, to lay aside all reliance on works, and strengthen his faith alone more and more, and by it grow in the knowledge, not of works, but of Christ Jesus, who has suffered and risen again for him, as Peter teaches, when he makes no other work to be a Christian one. Thus Christ, when the Jews asked Him what they should do that they might work the works of God, rejected the multitude of works, with which He saw that they were puffed up, and commanded them one thing only, saying: "This is the work of God, that ye believe on him whom He hath sent, for him hath God the Father sealed" (John vi. 27, 29).

Hence a right faith in Christ is an incomparable treasure, carrying with it universal salvation, and preserving from all evil, as it is said: "He that believeth and is baptized shall be saved; but he that believeth not shall be damned" (Mark xvi. 16). Isaiah, looking to this treasure, predicted: "The consumption decreed shall overflow with righteousness. For the Lord God of hosts shall make a consumption, even determined, in the midst of the land" (Is. x. 22, 23). As if he said: "Faith, which is the brief and complete fulfilling of the law, will fill those who believe with such righteousness, that they will need nothing else for justification." Thus too Paul says: "For with the heart man believeth unto righteousness" (Rom. x. 10).

But you ask how it can be the fact that faith alone justifies, and affords without works so great a treasure of good things, when so many works, ceremonies, and laws are prescribed to us in the Scriptures. I answer: before all things bear in mind what I have said, that faith alone without works justifies, sets free, and saves, as I shall show more clearly below.

Meanwhile it is to be noted, that the whole Scripture of God is divided into two parts, precepts and promises. The precepts certainly teach us what is good, but what they teach is not forthwith done. For they show us what we ought to do, but do not give us the power to do it. They were ordained, however, for the purpose of showing man to himself; that through them he may learn his own impotence for good, and may despair of his own strength. For this reason they are called the Old Testament, and are so.

For example: "Thou shalt not covet," is a precept by which we are all convicted of sin; since no man can help coveting, whatever efforts to the contrary he may make. In order therefore that he may fulfil the precept, and not covet, he is constrained to despair of himself and to seek elsewhere and through another the help which he cannot find in himself, as it is said: "O Israel, thou hast destroyed thyself; but in me is thine help" (Hosea xiii. 9). Now what is done by this one precept, is done by all; for all are equally impossible of fulfilment by us.

Now when a man has through the precepts been taught his own impotence, and become anxious by what means he may satisfy the law—for the law must be satisfied, so that no jot or tittle of it may pass away; otherwise he must be hopelessly condemned—then, being truly humbled and brought to nothing in his own eyes, he finds in himself no resource for justification and salvation.

Then comes in that other part of Scripture, the promises of God, which declare the glory of God, and say: "If you wish to fulfil the law, and, as the law requires, not to covet, lo! believe in Christ, in whom are promised to you grace, justification, peace, and liberty." All these things you shall have, if you believe, and shall be without them, if you do not believe. For what is impossible for you by all the works of the law, which are many and yet useless, you shall fulfil in an easy and summary way through faith, because God the Father has made everything to depend on faith, so that whosoever has it, has all things, and he who has it not, has nothing. "For God hath concluded them all in unbelief, that He might have mercy upon all." (Rom. xi. 32). Thus the promises of God give that which the precepts exact and fulfil what the law commands, so that all is of God alone, both the precepts and their fulfilment. He alone commands. He alone also fulfils. Hence the promises of God belong to the New Testament, nay, are the New Testament.

Now since these promises of God are words of holiness, truth, righteousness, liberty, and peace, and are full of universal goodness, the soul, which cleaves to them with a firm faith, is so united to them, nay, thoroughly absorbed by them, that it not only partakes in, but is penetrated and saturated by, all their virtue. For if the touch of Christ was healing, how much more does that most tender spiritual touch, nay, absorption of the word, communicate to the soul all that belongs to the word. In this way, therefore, the soul, through faith alone, without works, is from the word of God justified, sanctified, endued with truth, peace, and liberty, and filled full with every good thing, and is truly made the child of God; as it is said: "To them gave he power to become the sons of God, even to them that believe on his name" (John i. 12).

From all this it is easy to understand why faith has such great power, and why no good works, nor even all good works put together, can compare with it, since no work can cleave to the word of God, or be in the soul. Faith alone and the word reign in it; and such as is the word, such is the soul made by it, just as iron exposed to fire glows like fire, on account of its union with the fire. It is clear then that to a Christian man his faith suffices for everything, and that he has no need of works for justification. But if he has no need of works, neither has he need of the law; and, if he has no need of the law, he is certainly free from the law, and the saying is true: "The law is not made for a righteous man" (1 Tim. i. 9). This is that Christian liberty, our faith, the effect of which is, not that we should be careless or lead a bad life, but that no one should need the law or works for justification and salvation.

Let us consider this as the first virtue of faith, and let us look also to the second. This also is an office of faith, that it honours with the utmost veneration and the highest reputation him in whom it believes, inasmuch as it holds him to be truthful and worthy of belief. For there is no honour like that reputation of truth and righteousness, with which we honour him, in whom we believe. What higher credit can we attribute to any one than truth and righteousness, and absolute goodness? On the other hand, it is the greatest insult to brand any one with the reputation of falsehood and unrighteousness, or to suspect him of these, as we do when we disbelieve him.

Thus the soul, in firmly believing the promises of God, holds Him to be true and righteous, and it can attribute to God no higher glory than the credit of being so. The highest worship of God is to ascribe to Him truth, righteousness, and whatever qualities we must ascribe to one in whom we believe. In doing this the soul shows itself prepared to do His whole will; in doing this it hallows His, name, and gives itself up to be dealt with as it may please God. For it cleaves to His promises, and never doubts that He is true, just, and wise, and will do, dispose, and provide for all things in the best way. Is not such a soul, in this its faith, most obedient to God in all things? What commandment does there remain which has not been amply fulfilled by such an obedience? What fulfilment can be more full than universal obedience? Now this is not accomplished by works, but by faith alone.

On the other hand, what greater rebellion, impiety, or insult to God can there be, than not to believe His promises? What else is this, than either to make God a liar, or to doubt His truth—that is, to attribute truth to ourselves, but to God falsehood and levity? In doing this, is not a man denying God and setting himself up as an idol in his own heart? What then can works, done in such a state of impiety, profit us, were they even angelic or apostolic works? Rightly hath God shut up all—not in wrath nor in lust—but in unbelief, in order that those who pretend that they are fulfilling the law by works of purity and benevolence (which are social and human virtues), may not presume that they will therefore be saved, but, being included in the sin of unbelief, may either seek mercy, or be justly condemned.

But when God sees that truth is ascribed to Him, and that in the faith of our hearts He is honoured with all the honour of which He is worthy, then in return He honours us on account of that faith, attributing to us truth and righteousness. For faith produces truth and righteousness, in rendering to God what is His, and therefore in return God gives glory to our righteousness. It is a true and righteous thing that God is true and righteous, and to confess this and ascribe these attributes to Him is to be ourselves true and righteous. Thus He says: "Them that honour me I will honour, and they that despise me shall be lightly esteemed" (1 Sam. ii. 30). And so Paul, says that Abraham's faith was imputed to him for righteousness, because by it he gave glory to God; and that to us also, for the same reason, it shall be reputed for righteousness, if we believe (Rom. iv).

The third incomparable grace of faith is this, that it unites the soul to Christ, as the wife to the husband; by which mystery, as the Apostle teaches, Christ and the soul are made one flesh. Now if they are one flesh, and if a true marriage—nay, by far the most perfect of all marriages—is accomplished between them (for human marriages are but feeble types of this one great marriage), then it follows that all they have becomes theirs in common, as well good things as evil things, so that whatsoever Christ possesses, that the believing soul may take to itself and boast of as its own, and whatever belongs to the soul, that Christ claims as his.

If we compare these possessions, we shall see how inestimable is the gain. Christ is full of grace, life, and salvation; the soul is full of sin, death, and condemnation. Let faith step in, and then sin, death, and hell will belong to Christ, and grace, life, and salvation to the soul. For, if he is a husband, he must needs take to himself that which is his wife's, and, at the same time, impart to his wife that which is his. For, in giving her his own body and himself, how can he but give her all that is his? And, in taking to himself the body of his wife, how can he but take to himself all that is hers?

In this is displayed the delightful sight, not only of communion, but of a prosperous warfare, of victory, salvation, and redemption. For since Christ is God and man, and is such a person as neither has sinned, nor dies, nor is condemned—nay, cannot sin, die, or be condemned; and since his righteousness, life, and salvation are invincible, eternal, and almighty; when, I say, such a person, by the wedding-ring of faith, takes a share in the sins, death, and hell of his wife, nay, makes them his own, and deals with them no otherwise than as if they were his, and as if he himself had sinned; and when he suffers, dies, and descends to hell, that he may overcome all things, since sin, death, and hell cannot swallow him up, they must needs be swallowed up by him in stupendous conflict. For his righteousness rises above the sins of all men; his life is more powerful than all death; his salvation is more unconquerable than all hell.

Thus the believing soul, by the pledge of its faith in Christ, becomes free from all sin, fearless of death, safe from hell, and endowed with the eternal righteousness, life, and salvation of its husband Christ. Thus he presents to himself a glorious bride, without spot or wrinkle, cleansing her with the washing of water by the word; that is, by faith in the word of life, righteousness, and salvation. Thus he betrothes her unto himself "in faithfulness, in righteousness, and in judgment, and in lovingkindness, and in mercies" (Hosea ii. 19, 20).

Who then can value highly enough these royal nuptials? Who can comprehend the riches of the glory of this grace?

Christ, that rich and pious husband, takes as a wife a needy and impious harlot, redeeming her from all her evils, and supplying her with all his good things. It is impossible now that her sins should destroy her, since they have been laid upon Christ and swallowed up in Him, and since she has in her husband Christ a righteousness which she may claim as her own, and which she can set up with confidence against all her sins, against death and hell, saying: "If I have sinned, my Christ, in whom I believe, has not sinned; all mine is His, and all His is mine;" as it is written, "My beloved is mine, and I am his" (Song ii. 16). This is what Paul says: "Thanks be to God, which giveth us the victory through our Lord Jesus Christ;" victory over sin and death, as he says: "The sting of death is sin, and the strength of sin is the law" (I Cor. xv. 56, 57).

From all this you will again understand why so much importance is attributed to faith so that it alone can fulfil the law, and justify without any works. For you see that the first commandment, which says, "Thou shalt worship one God only," is fulfilled by faith alone. If you were nothing but good works from the soles of your feet to the crown of your head, you would not be worshipping God, nor fulfilling the first commandment, since it is impossible to worship God, without ascribing to Him the glory of truth and of universal goodness, as it ought in truth to be ascribed. Now this is not done by works, but only by faith of heart. It is not by working, but by believing, that we glorify God, and confess Him to be true. On this ground faith is the sole righteousness of a Christian man, and the fulfilling of all the commandments. For to him who fulfils the first, the task of fulfilling all the rest is easy.

Works, since they are irrational things, cannot glorify God; although they may be done to the glory of God, if faith be present. But at present we are enquiring, not into the quality of the works done, but into him who does them, who glorifies God, and brings forth good works. This is faith of heart, the head and the substance of all our righteousness. Hence that is a blind and perilous doctrine which teaches that the commandments are fulfilled by works. The commandments must have been fulfilled, previous to any good works, and good works follow their fulfilment, as we shall see.

But, that we may have a wider view of that grace which our inner man has in Christ, we must know that in the Old Testament God sanctified to Himself every first-born male. The birthright was of great value, giving a superiority over the rest by the double honour of priesthood and kingship. For the first-born brother was priest and lord of all the rest.

Under this figure was foreshown Christ, the true and only first-born of God the Father and of the Virgin Mary, and a true king and priest, not in a fleshly and earthly sense. For His kingdom is not of this world; it is in heavenly and spiritual things that He reigns and acts as priest; and these are righteousness, truth, wisdom, peace, salvation, etc. Not but that all things, even those of earth and hell, are subject to Him—for otherwise how could He defend and save us from them?—but it is not in these, nor by these, that His kingdom stands.

So too His priesthood does not consist in the outward display of vestments and gestures, as did the human priesthood of Aaron and our ecclesiastical priesthood at this day, but in spiritual things, wherein, in His invisible office, He intercedes for us with God in heaven, and there offers Himself, and performs all the duties of a priest, as Paul describes Him to the Hebrews under the figure of Melchizedek. Nor does He only pray and intercede for us; He also teaches us inwardly in the spirit with the living teachings of His Spirit. Now those are the two special offices of a priest, as is figured to us in the case of fleshly priests, by visible prayers and sermons.

As Christ by His birthright has obtained these two dignities, so He imparts and communicates them to every believer in Him, under that law of matrimony of which we have spoken above, by which all that is the husband's is also the wife's. Hence all we who believe on Christ are kings and priests in Christ, as it is said: "Ye are a chosen generation, a royal priesthood, an holy nation, a peculiar people; that ye should shew forth the praises of him who hath called you out of darkness into his marvelous light" (1 Pet. ii. 9).

These two things stand thus. First, as regards kingship, every Christian is by faith so exalted above all things, that, in spiritual power, he is completely lord of all things, so that nothing whatever can do him any hurt; yea, all things are subject to him, and are compelled to be subservient to his salvation. Thus Paul says: "All things work together for good to them who are the called" (Rom. viii. 28); and also; "Whether life, or death, or things present, or things to come: all are yours; and ye are Christ's" (I Cor. iii. 22, 23).

Not that in the sense of corporeal power any one among Christians has been appointed to possess and rule all things, according to the mad and senseless idea of certain ecclesiastics. That is the office of kings, princes, and men upon earth. In the experience of life we see that we subjected to all things, and suffer many things, even death. Yea, the more of a Christian any man is, to so many the more evils, sufferings, and deaths is he subject, as we see in the first place in Christ the first-born, and in all His holy brethren.

This is a spiritual power, which rules in the midst of enemies, and is powerful in the midst of distress. And this is nothing else than that strength is made perfect in my weakness, and that I can turn all things to the profit of my salvation, so that even the cross and death are compelled to serve me and to work together for my salvation. This is a lofty and eminent dignity, a true and almighty dominion, a spiritual empire, in which there is nothing so good, nothing so bad, as not to work together for my good, if only I believe. And yet there is nothing of which I have need—for faith alone suffices for my salvation—unless that, in it, faith may exercise the power and empire of its liberty. This is the inestimable power and liberty of Christians.

Nor are we only kings and the freest of all men, but also priests for ever, a dignity far higher than kinship, because by that priesthood we are worthy to appear before God, to pray for others, and to teach one another mutually the things which are of God. For these are the duties of priests, and they cannot possibly be permitted to any unbeliever. Christ has obtained for us this favour, if we believe in Him, that, just as we are His brethren, and co-heirs and fellow kings with Him, so we should be also fellow priests with Him, and venture with confidence, through the spirit of faith, to come into the presence of God, and cry "Abba, Father!" and to pray for one another, and to do all things which we see done and figured in the visible and corporeal office of priesthood. But to an unbelieving person nothing renders service or works for good. He himself is in servitude to all things, and all things turn out for evil to him, because he uses all things in an impious way for his own advantage and not for the glory of God. And thus he is not a priest, but a profane person, whose prayers are turned into sin; nor does he ever appear in the presence of God, because God does not hear sinners.

Who then can comprehend the loftiness of that Christian dignity which, by its royal power, rules over all things, even over death, life, and sin, and, by its priestly glory, is all powerful with God; since God does what He Himself seeks and wishes; as it is written: "He will fulfil the desire of them that fear Him: He also will hear their cry, and will save them"? (Ps. cxlv. 19). This glory certainly cannot be attained by any works, but by faith only.

From these considerations any one may clearly see how a Christian man is free from all things, so that he needs no works in order to be justified and saved, but receives these gifts in abundance from faith alone. Nay, were he so foolish as to pretend to be justified, set free, saved, and made a Christian, by means of any good work, he would immediately lose faith with all its benefits. Such folly is prettily represented in the fable, where a dog, running along in the water, and carrying in his mouth a real piece of meat, is deceived by the reflection of the meat in the water, and, in trying with open mouth to seize it, loses the meat and its image at the same time.

Here you will ask: "If all who are in the Church are priests by what character are those, whom we now call priests, to be distinguished from the laity?" I reply: By the use of these words, "priest," "clergy," "spiritual person," "ecclesiastic," an injustice has been done, since they have been transferred from the remaining body of Christians to those few, who are now, by a hurtful custom, called ecclesiastics. For Holy Scripture makes no distinction between them, except that those, who are now boastfully called popes, bishops, and lords, it calls ministers, servants, and stewards, who are to serve the rest in the ministry of the Word, for teaching the faith of Christ and the liberty of believers. For though it is true that we are all equally priests, yet we cannot, nor, if we could, ought we all to minister and teach publicly. Thus Paul says, "Let a man so account of us as of the ministers of Christ, and stewards of the mysteries of God" (1 Cor. iv. 1).

This bad system has now issued in such a pompous display of power, and such a terrible tyranny that no earthly government can be compared to it, as if the laity were something else than Christians. Through this perversion of things it has happened that the knowledge of Christian grace, of faith, of liberty, and altogether of Christ, has utterly perished, and has been succeeded by an intolerable bondage to human works and laws; and, according to the Lamentations of Jeremiah, we have become the slaves of the vilest men on earth, who abuse our misery to all the disgraceful and ignominious purposes of their own will.

Returning to the subject which we had begun, I think it is made clear by these considerations that it is not sufficient, nor a Christian course, to preach the works, life, and words of Christ in a historic manner, as facts which it suffices to know as an example how to frame our life; as do those who are now held the best preachers, and much less so, to keep silence altogether on these and to teach in their stead the laws of men and the decrees of the Fathers. There are now not a few persons who preach and read about Christ with the object of moving the human affections to sympathize with Christ, to indignation against the Jews, and other childish and womanish absurdities of that kind.

Now preaching ought to have the object of promoting faith in Him, so that He may not only be Christ, but a Christ for you and for me, and that what is said of Him, and what He is called, may work in us. And this faith is produced and is maintained by preaching why Christ came, what He has brought us and given to us, and to what profit and advantage He is to be received. This is done when the Christian liberty which we have from Christ Himself is rightly taught, and we are shown in what manner all we Christians are kings and priests, and how we are lords of all things, and may be confident that whatever we do in the presence of God is pleasing and acceptable to Him. Whose heart would not rejoice in its inmost core at hearing these things? Whose heart, on receiving so great a consolation, would not become sweet with the love of Christ, a love to which it can never attain by any laws or works? Who can injure such a heart, or make it afraid? If the consciousness of sin, or the horror of death, rush in upon it, it is prepared to hope in the Lord, and is fearless of such evils, and undisturbed, until it shall look down upon its enemies. For it believes that the righteousness of Christ is its own, and that its sin is no longer its own, but that of Christ, for, on account of its faith in Christ, all its sin must needs be swallowed up from before the face of the righteousness of Christ, as I have said above. It learns too, with the Apostle, to scoff at death and sin, and to say: "O death, where is thy sting? O grave, where is thy victory? The sting of death is sin, and the strength of sin is the law. But thanks be to God, which giveth us the victory through our Lord Jesus Christ" (1 Cor. xv. 55–57). For death is swallowed up in victory; not only the victory of Christ, but ours also, since by faith it becomes ours, and in it we too conquer.

Let it suffice to say this concerning the inner man and its liberty, and concerning that righteousness of faith, which needs neither laws nor good works; nay, they are even hurtful to it, if any one pretends to be justified by them.

And now let us turn to the other part, to the outward man. Here we shall give an answer to all those who, taking offence at the word of faith and at what I have asserted, say: "If faith does everything, and by itself suffices for justification, why then are good works commanded? Are we then to take our ease and do no works, content with faith?" Not so, impious man, I reply; not so. That would indeed really be the case, if we were thoroughly and completely inner and spiritual persons; but that will not happen until the last day, when the dead shall be raised. As long as we live in the flesh, we are but beginning and making advances in that which shall be completed in a future life. On this account the Apostle calls that which we have in this life, the first-fruits of the Spirit (Rom. viii. 23). In the future we shall have the tenths, and the fullness of the Spirit. To this part belongs the fact I have stated before, that the Christian is the servant of all and subject to all. For in that part in which he is free, he does no works, but in that in which he is a servant, he does all works. Let us see on what principle this is so.

Although, as I have said, inwardly, and according to the spirit, a man is amply enough justified by faith, having all that lie requires to have, except that this very faith and abundance ought to increase from day to day, even till the future life; still he remains in this mortal life upon earth, in which it is necessary that he should rule his own body, and have intercourse with men. Here then works begin; here he must not take his ease; here he must give heed to exercise his body by fastings, watchings, labour, and other moderate discipline, so that it may be subdued to the spirit, and obey and conform itself to the inner man and faith, and not rebel against them nor hinder them, as is its nature to do if it is not kept under. For the inner man, being conformed to God, and created after the image of God through faith, rejoices and delights itself in Christ, in whom such blessings have been conferred on it; and hence has only this task before it, to serve God with joy and for naught in free love.

In doing this he offends that contrary will in his own flesh, which is striving to serve the world, and to seek its own gratification. This the spirit of faith cannot and will not bear, but applies itself with cheerfulness and zeal to keep it down and restrain it, as Paul says: "I delight in the law of God after the inward man; but I see another law in my members, warring against the law of my mind, and bringing me into captivity to the law of sin" (Rom. vii.

22, 23). And again: "I keep under my body, and bring it into subjection, lest that by any means, when I have preached to others, I myself should be a castaway" (1 Cor. ix. 27). And: "They that are Christ's have crucified the flesh with the affections and lusts" (Gal. v. 24).

These works, however, must not be done with any notion that by them a man can be justified before God—for faith, which alone is righteousness before God, will not bear with this false notion—but solely with this purpose, that the body may be brought into subjection, and be purified from its evil lusts, so that our eyes may be turned only to purging away those lusts. For when the soul has been cleansed by faith and made to love God, it would have all things to be cleansed in like manner, and especially in its own body, so that all things might unite with it in the love and praise of God. Thus it comes that from the requirements of his own body a man cannot take his ease, but is compelled on its account to do many good works, that he may bring it into subjection. Yet these works are not the means of his justification before God; he does them out of disinterested love to the service of God, looking to no other end than to do what is well-pleasing to Him whom he desires to obey dutifully in all things.

On this principle every man may easily instruct himself in what measure, and with what distinctions, he ought to chasten his own body. He will fast, watch, and labour, just as much as he sees to suffice for keeping down the wantonness and concupiscence of the body. But those who pretend to be justified by works are looking, not to the mortification of their lusts, but only to the works themselves, thinking that, if they can accomplish as many works and as great ones as possible, all is well with them, and they are justified. Sometimes they even injure their brain, and extinguish nature, or at least make it useless. This is enormous folly, and ignorance of Christian life and faith, when a man seeks, without faith, to be justified and saved by works.

To make what we have said more easily understood, let us set it forth under a figure. The works of a Christian man, who is justified and saved by his faith out of the pure and unbought mercy of God, ought to be regarded in the same light as would have been those of Adam and Eve in Paradise, and of all their posterity, if they had not sinned. Of them it is said: "The Lord God took the man, and put him into the garden of Eden to dress it and to keep it" (Gen. ii. 15). Now Adam had been created by God just and righteous, so that he could not have needed to be justified and made righteous by keeping the garden and working in it, but, that he might not be unemployed, God gave him the business of keeping and cultivating Paradise. These would have indeed been works of perfect freedom, being done for no object but that of pleasing God, and not in order to obtain justification, which he already had to the full, and which would have been innate in us all.

So it is with the works of a believer. Being by his faith replaced afresh in Paradise and created anew, he does not need works for his justification, but that he may not be idle, but may keep his own body and work upon it. His works are to be done freely, with the sole object of pleasing God. Only we are not yet fully created anew in perfect faith and love; these require to be increased, not however through works, but through themselves.

A bishop, when he consecrates a church, confirms children, or performs any other duty of his office, is not consecrated as bishop by these works; nay, unless he had been previously consecrated as bishop, not one of those works would have any validity; they would be foolish, childish, and ridiculous. Thus a Christian, being consecrated by his faith, does good works, but he is not by these works made a more sacred person, or more a Christian. That is the effect of faith alone; nay, unless he were previously a believer and a Christian, none of his works would have any value at all; they would really be impious and damnable sins.

True then are these two sayings: Good works do not make a good man, but a good man does good works. Bad works do not make a bad man, but a bad man does bad works. Thus it is always necessary that the substance or person should be good before any good works can be done, and that good works should follow and proceed from a good person. As Christ says: "A good tree cannot bring forth evil fruit, neither can a corrupt tree bring forth good fruit" (Matt. vii. 18). Now it is clear that the fruit does not bear the tree, nor does the tree grow on the fruit; but, on the contrary, the trees bear the fruit and the fruit grows on the trees.

As then trees must exist before their fruit, and as the fruit does not make the tree either good or bad, but, on the contrary, a tree of either kind produces fruit of the same kind, so must first the person of the man be good or bad, before he can do either a good or a bad work; and his works do not make him tad or good, but he himself makes his works either bad or good.

We may see the same thing in all handicrafts. A bad or good house does not make a bad or good builder, but a good or bad builder makes a good or bad house. And in general, no work makes the workman such as it is itself; but the workman makes the work such as he is himself. Such is the case too with the works of men. Such as the man himself is, whether in faith or in unbelief, such is his work; good if it be done in faith, bad if in unbelief. But the converse is not true—that, such as the work is, such the man becomes in faith or in unbelief. For as works do not make a believing man, so neither do they make a justified man, but faith, as it makes a man a believer and justified, so also it makes his works good.

Since, then, works justify no man, but a man must be justified before he can do any good work, it is most evident that it is faith alone which, by the mere mercy of God through Christ, and by means of His word, can worthily and sufficiently justify and save the person, and that a Christian man needs no work, no law, for his salvation; for by faith he is free from all law, and in perfect freedom does gratuitously all that he does, seeking nothing either of profit or of salvation—since by the grace of God he is already saved and rich in all things through his faith—but solely that which is well-pleasing to God.

So, too, no good work can profit an unbeliever to justification and salvation, and on the other hand, no evil work makes him an evil and condemned person, but that unbelief, which makes the person and the tree bad, makes his works evil and condemned. Wherefore, when any man is made good or bad, this does not arise from his works, but from his faith or unbelief, as the wise man says: "The beginning of sin is to fall away from God;" that is, not to believe. Paul says: "He that cometh to God must believe" (Heb. xi. 6); and Christ says the same thing: "Either make the tree good, and his fruit good; or else make the tree corrupt, and his fruit corrupt" (Matt. xii. 33). As much as to say: He who wishes to have good fruit, will begin with the tree, and plant a good one; even so he who wishes to do good works must begin, not by working, but by believing, since it is this which makes the person good. For nothing makes the person good but faith, nor bad but unbelief.

It is certainly true that, in the sight of men, a man becomes good or evil by his works, but here 'becoming" means that it is thus shown and recognized who is good or evil, as Christ says: "By their fruits ye shall know them" (Matt. vii. 20). But all this stops at appearances and externals, and in this matter very many deceive themselves, when they presume to write and teach that we are to be justified by good works, and meanwhile make no mention even of faith, walking in their own ways, ever deceived and deceiving, going from bad to worse, blind leaders of the blind, wearying themselves with many works, and yet never attaining to true righteousness; of whom Paul says: "Having a form of godliness, but denying the power thereof; ever learning, and never able to come to the knowledge of the truth" (2 Tim. iii. 5, 7).

He then, who does not wish to go astray with these blind ones, must look further than to the works of the law or the doctrine of works; nay, must turn away his spirit from works, and look to the person, and to the manner in which he may be justified. Now he is justified and saved, not by works or laws, but by the word of God, that is, by the promise of His grace, so that the glory may be to the Divine majesty, which has saved us who believe, not by works of righteousness which we have done, but according to His mercy, by the word of His grace.

From all this it is easy to perceive on what principle good works are to be cast aside or embraced, and by what rule all teachings put forth concerning works are to be understood. For if works are brought forward as grounds of justification, and are done under the false persuasion that we can pretend to be justified by them, they lay on us the yoke of necessity, and extinguish liberty along with faith, and by this very addition to their use, they become no longer good, but really worthy of condemnation. For such works are not free, but blaspheme the grace of God, to which alone it belongs to justify and save through faith. Works cannot accomplish this, and yet, with impious presumption, through our folly, they take it on themselves to do so, and thus break in with violence upon the office and glory of grace.

We do not then reject good works; nay, we embrace them and teach them in the highest degree. It is not on their own account that we condemn them, but on account of this impious addition to them, and the perverse notion of seeking justification by them. These things cause them to be only good in outward show, but in reality not good, since by them men are deceived and deceive others, like ravening wolves in sheep's clothing.

Now this Leviathan, this perverted notion about works, is invincible, when sincere faith is wanting. For those sanctified doers of works cannot but hold it, till faith, which destroys it, comes and reigns in the heart. Nature cannot expel it by her own power, nay, cannot even see it for what it is, but considers it as a most holy will. And when custom steps in besides, and strengthens this depravity of nature, as has happened by means of impious teachers, then the evil is incurable, and leads astray multitudes to irreparable ruin. Therefore, though it is good to preach and write about penitence, confession, and satisfaction, yet if we stop there, and do not go on to teach faith, such teaching is without doubt deceitful and devilish. For Christ, speaking by His servant John, not only said: "Repent ye," but added: "For the kingdom of heaven is at hand" (Matt. iii. 2).

For not one word of God only, but both, should be preached; new and old things should be brought out of the treasury, as well the voice of the law, as the word of grace. The voice of the law should be brought forward, that men may be terrified and brought to a knowledge of their sins, and thence be converted to penitence and to a better manner of life. But we must not stop here; that would be to wound only and not to bind up, to strike and not to heal, to kill and not to make alive, to bring down to hell and not to bring back, to humble and not to exalt. Therefore the word of grace, and of the promised remission of sin, must also be preached, in order to teach and set up faith, since, without that word, contrition, penitence, and all other duties, are performed and taught in vain.

There still remain, it is true, preachers of repentance and grace, but they do not explain the law and the promises of God to such an end, and in such a spirit that men may learn whence repentance and grace are to come. For repentance comes from the law of God, but faith or grace from the promises of God, as it is said: "Faith cometh by hearing, and hearing by the word of God" (Rom. x. 17). Whence it comes that a man, when humbled and brought to the knowledge of himself by the threatenings and terrors of the law, is consoled and raised up by faith in the Divine promise. Thus "weeping may endure for a night, but joy cometh in the morning" (Ps. xxx. 5). Thus much we say concerning works in general, and also concerning those which the Christian practices with regard to his own body.

Lastly, we will speak also of those works which he performs towards his neighbor. For man does not live for himself alone in this mortal body, in order to work on its account, but also for all men on earth; nay, he lives only for others and not for himself. For it is to this end that he brings his own body into subjection, that lie may be able to serve others more sincerely and more freely; as Paul says: "None of us liveth to himself, and no man dieth to himself. For whether we live, we live unto the Lord; and whether we die, we die unto the Lord" (Rom. xiv. 7, 8). Thus it is impossible that he should take his ease in this life, and not work for the good of his neighbors; since he must needs speak, act, and converse among men, just is Christ was made in the likeness of men, and found in fashion as a man, and had His conversation among men.

Yet a Christian has need of none of these things for justification and salvation, but in all his works he ought to entertain this view, and look only to this object, that he may serve and be useful to others in all that he does, having nothing before his eyes but the necessities and the advantage of his neighbor. Thus the Apostle commands us to work with our own hands that we may have to give to those that need. He might have said, that we may support ourselves, but he tells us to give to those that need. It is the part of a Christian to take care of his own body for the very purpose that, by its soundness and wellbeing, be may be enabled to labour, and to acquire and preserve property, for the aid of those who are in want, that thus the stronger member may serve the weaker member, and we may be children of God, thoughtful and busy one for another, bearing one another's burdens, and so fulfilling the law of Christ.

Here is the truly Christian life; here is faith really working by love; when a man applies himself with joy and love to the works of that freest servitude, in which he serves others voluntarily and for naught; himself abundantly satisfied in the fulness and riches of his own faith.

Thus, when Paul had taught the Philippians how they had been made rich by that faith in Christ, in which they had obtained all things, he teaches them further in these words: "If there be therefore any consolation in Christ, if any comfort of love, if any fellowship of the Spirit, if any bowels and mercies, fulfil ye my joy, that ye be like-minded, having the same love, being of one accord, of one mind. Let nothing be done through strife or vainglory; but in lowliness of mind let each esteem other better than themselves. Look not every man on his own things, but every man also on the things of others" (Phil. ii. 1–4).

In this we see clearly that the Apostle lays down this rule for a Christian life, that all our works should be directed to the advantage of others, since every Christian has such abundance through his faith, that all his other works and his whole life remain over and above, wherewith to serve and benefit his neighbor of spontaneous good will.

To this end he brings forward Christ as an example, saying: "Let this mind be in you, which was also in Christ Jesus: who, being in the form of God, thought it not robbery to be equal with God: but made himself of no reputation, and took upon him the form of a servant, and was made in the likeness of men; and being found in fashion as a man, he humbled himself, and became obedient unto death" (Phil. ii. 5–8). This most wholesome saying of the Apostle has been darkened to us by men who, totally misunderstanding the expressions "form of God," "form of a servant," "fashion," "likeness of men," have transferred them to the natures of Godhead and manhood. Paul's meaning is this: Christ, when He was full of the form of God, and abounded in all good things, so that He had no need of works or sufferings to be justified and saved—for all those things He had from the very beginning—yet was not puffed up with these things, and did not raise Himself above us, and arrogate to Himself power over us, though He might lawfully have done so, but on the contrary so acted in labouring, working, suffering, and dying as to be like the rest of men, and no otherwise than a man in fashion and in conduct, as if he were in want of all things, and had nothing of the form of God; and yet all this He did for our sakes, that He might serve us, and that all the works He should do under that form of a servant, might become ours.

Thus a Christian, like Christ his head, being full and in abundance through his faith, ought to be content with this form of God, obtained by faith; except that, as I have said, he ought to increase this faith, till it be perfected. For this faith is his life, justification, and salvation, preserving his person itself and making it pleasing to God, and bestowing on him all that Christ has, as I have said above, and as Paul affirms: "The life which I now live in the flesh I live by the faith of the Son of God" (Gal. ii. 20). Though he is thus free from all works, yet he ought to empty himself of this liberty, take on him the form of a servant, be made in the likeness of men, be found in fashion as a man, serve, help, and in every way act towards his neighbor as he sees that God through Christ has acted and is acting towards him. All this he should do freely, and with regard to nothing but the good pleasure of God, and he should reason thus:

Lo! my God, without merit on my part, of His pure and free mercy, has given to me, an unworthy, condemned, and contemptible creature, all the riches of justification and salvation in Christ, so that I no longer am in want of anything, except of faith to believe that this is so. For such a Father then, who has overwhelmed me with these inestimable riches of His, why should I not freely, cheerfully, and with my whole heart and from voluntary zeal, do all that I know will be pleasing to Him, and acceptable in His sight? I will therefore give myself, as a sort of Christ, to my neighbor, as Christ has given Himself to me, and will do nothing in this life, except what I see will be needful, advantageous, and wholesome for my neighbor, since by faith I abound in all good things in Christ.

Thus from faith flow forth love and joy in the Lord, and from love a cheerful, willing, free spirit, disposed to serve our neighbor voluntarily, without taking any account of gratitude or ingratitude, praise or blame, gain or loss. Its object is not to lay men under obligations, nor does it distinguish between friends and enemies, or look to gratitude or ingratitude, but most freely and willingly spends itself and its goods, whether it loses them through ingratitude, or gains good will. For thus did its Father, distributing all things to all men abundantly and freely, make His sun to rise upon the just and the unjust. Thus too the child does and endures nothing, except from the free joy with which it delights through Christ in God, the giver of such great gifts.

You see then that, if we recognize those great and precious gifts, as Peter says, which have been given to us, love is quickly diffused in our hearts through the Spirit, and by love we are made free, joyful, all-powerful, active workers, victors over all our tribulations, servants to our neighbor, and nevertheless lords of all things. But for those who do not recognize the good things given to them through Christ, Christ has been born in vain; such persons walk by works, and will never attain the taste and feeling of these great things. Therefore, just as our neighbor is in want, and has need of our abundance, so we too in the sight of God were in want, and had need of His mercy. And as our heavenly Father has freely helped us in Christ, so ought we freely to help our neighbor by our body and works, and each should become to other a sort of Christ, so that we may be mutually Christ's, and that the same Christ may be in all of us; that is, that we may be truly Christians.

Who then can comprehend the riches and glory of the Christian life? It can do all things, has all things, and is in want of nothing; is lord over sin, death, and hell, and at all same time is the obedient and useful servant of all. But alas! it is at this day unknown throughout the world; it is neither preached nor sought after, so that we are quite ignorant about our own name, why we are and are called Christians. We are certainly called so from Christ, who is not absent, but dwells among us, provided, that is, that we believe in Him, and are reciprocally and mutually one the Christ of the other, doing to our neighbor as Christ does to us. But now, in the doctrine of men, we are taught only to seek after merits, rewards, and things which are already ours, and we have made of Christ a taskmaster far more severe than Moses.

The Blessed Virgin, beyond all others, affords us an example of the same faith, in that she was purified according to the law of Moses, and like all other women, though she was bound by no such law, and had no need of purification. Still she submitted to the law voluntarily and of free love, making herself like the rest of women, that she might not offend or throw contempt on them. She was not justified by doing this, but, being already justified, she did it freely and gratuitously. Thus ought our works too to be done, and not in order to be justified by them, for, being first justified by faith, we ought to do all our works freely and cheerfully for the sake of others.

St. Paul circumcised his disciple Timothy, not because he needed circumcision for his justification, but that he might not offend or contemn those Jews, weak in the faith, who had not yet been able to comprehend the liberty of faith. On the other hand, when they contemned liberty, and urged that circumcision was necessary for justification, he resisted them, and would not allow Titus to be circumcised. For as he would not offend or contemn any one's weakness in faith, but yielded for the time to their will, so again he would not have the liberty of faith offended or contemned by hardened self-justifiers, but walked in a middle path, sparing the weak for the time, and always resisting the hardened, that he might convert all to the liberty of faith. On the same principle we ought to act, receiving those that are weak in the faith, but boldly resisting these hardened teachers of works, of whom we shall hereafter speak at more length.

Christ also, when His disciples were asked for the tribute money, asked of Peter, whether the children of a king were not free from taxes. Peter agreed to this, yet Jesus commanded him to go to the sea, saying: "Lest we should offend them, go thou to the sea, and cast a hook, and take up the fish that first cometh up; and when thou hast opened his mouth, thou shalt find a piece of money; that take, and give unto them for me and thee" (Matt. xvii. 27).

This example is very much to our purpose; for here Christ calls Himself and His disciples free men, and children of a king, in want of nothing; and yet He voluntarily submits and pays the tax. Just as far then as this work was necessary or useful to Christ for justification or salvation, so far do all His other works or those of His disciples avail for justification. They are really free and subsequent to justification, and only done to serve others and set them an example.

Such are the works which Paul inculcated, that Christians should be subject to principalities and powers, and ready to every good work (Tit. iii. 1), not that they may be justified by these things, for they are already justified by faith, but that in liberty of spirit they may thus be the servants of others, and subject to powers, obeying their will out of gratuitous love.

Such too ought to have been the works of all colleges, monasteries, and priests, every one doing the works of his own profession and state of life, not in order to be justified by them, but in order to bring his own body into subjection, as an example to others, who themselves also need to keep under their bodies, and also in order to accommodate himself to the will of others, out of free love. But we must always guard most carefully against any vain confidence or presumption of being justified, gaining merit, or being saved by these works, this being the part of faith alone, as I have so often said.

Any man possessing this knowledge may easily keep clear of danger among those innumerable commands and precepts of the pope, of bishops, of monasteries, of churches, of princes, and of magistrates, which some foolish pastors urge on us as being necessary for justification and salvation, calling them precepts of the Church, when they are not so at all. For the Christian freeman will speak thus: I will fast, I will pray, I will do this or that, which is commanded me by men, not as having any need of these things for justification or salvation, but that I may thus comply with the will of the pope, of the bishop, of such a community or such a magistrate, or of my neighbor as an example to him, for this cause I will do and suffer all things, just as Christ did and suffered much more for me, though He needed not at all to do so on His own account, and made Himself for my sake under the law, when he was not under the law. And although tyrants may do me violence or wrong in requiring obedience to these things, yet it will not hurt me to do them, so long as they are not done against God.

From all this every man will be able to attain a sure judgment and faithful discrimination between all works and laws, and to know who are blind and foolish pastors, and who are true and good ones. For whatsoever work is not directed to the sole end, either of keeping under the body, or of doing service to our neighbor—provided he require nothing contrary to the will of God—is no good or Christian work. Hence I greatly fear that at this day few or no colleges, monasteries, altars, or ecclesiastical functions are Christian ones, and the same may be said of fasts and special prayers to certain Saints. I fear that in all these nothing is being sought but what is already ours; while we fancy that by these things our sins are purged away and salvation is attained, and thus utterly do away with Christian liberty. This comes from ignorance of Christian faith and liberty.

This ignorance, and this crushing of liberty, are diligently promoted by the teaching of very many blind pastors, who stir up and urge the people to a zeal for these things, praising such zeal and puffing up men with their indulgences, but never teaching faith. Now I would advise you, if you have any wish to pray, to fast, or to make foundations in churches, as they call it, to take care not to do so with the object of gaining any advantage, either temporal or eternal. You will thus wrong your faith which alone bestows all things on you, and the increase of which, either by working or by suffering, is alone to be cared for. What you give, give freely and without price, that others may prosper and have increase from you and from your goodness. Thus you will be a truly good man and a Christian. For what do you want with your goods and your works, which are done over and above for the subjection of the body, since you have abundance for yourself through your faith, in which God has given you all things?

We give this rule: the good things which we have from God ought to flow from one to another, and become common to all, so that every one of us may, as it were, put on his neighbor, and so behave towards him its if he were himself in his place. They flowed and do flow from Christ to us; he put us on, and acted for us as if he himself were what we are. From us they flow to those who have need of them, so that my faith and righteousness ought to be laid down before God as a covering and intercession for the sins of my neighbor, which I am to take on myself, and so labour and endure servitude in them, as if they were my own, for thus has Christ done for us. This is true love and the genuine truth of Christian life. But only there is it true and genuine, where there is true and genuine faith. Hence the Apostle attributes to Charity this quality, that she seeketh not her own.

We conclude therefore that a Christian man does not live in himself, but in Christ, and in his neighbor, or else is no Christian; in Christ by faith, in his neighbor by love. By faith he is carried upwards above himself to God, and by love he sinks back below himself to his neighbor, still always abiding in God and His love, as Christ says: "verily I say unto you, hereafter ye shall see heaven open, and the angels of God ascending and descending upon the Son of man" (John i. 51).

Thus much concerning liberty, which, as you see, is a true and spiritual liberty, making our hearts free from all sins, laws, and commandments, as Paul says: "The law is not made for a righteous man" (1 Tim. i. 9), and one which surpasses every other and outward liberty, as far as heaven is above earth. May Christ make us to understand and preserve this liberty. Amen.

Finally, for the sake of those to whom nothing can be stated so well but that they misunderstand and distort it, we must add a word, in case they can understand even that. There are very many persons, who, when they hear of this liberty of faith, straightway turn it into an occasion of license. They think that everything is now lawful for them, and do not choose to show themselves free men and Christians in any other way than by their contempt and reprehension of ceremonies, of traditions of human laws, as if they were Christians merely because they refuse to fast on stated days, or eat flesh when others fast, or omit the customary prayers, scoffing at the precepts of men, but utterly passing over all the rest that belongs to the Christian religion. On the other hand, they are most pertinaciously resisted by those who strive after salvation solely by their observance of and reverence for ceremonies, as if they would be saved merely because they fast on stated days, or abstain from flesh, or make formal prayers talking loudly of the precepts of the Church and of the Fathers, and not caring a straw about those things which belong to our genuine faith. Both these parties are plainly culpable, in that, while they neglect matters which are of weight and necessary for salvation, they contend noisily about such as are without weight and not necessary.

How much more rightly does the Apostle Paul teach us to walk in the middle path, condemning either extreme, and saying: "Let not him that eateth despise him that eateth not; and let not him which eateth not judge him that eateth" (Rom. xiv. 3). You see here how the Apostle blames those who, not from religious feeling, but in mere contempt, neglect and rail at ceremonial observances, and teaches them not to despise, since this "knowledge puffeth up." Again, he teaches the pertinacious upholders of these things not to judge their opponents. For neither party observes towards the other that charity which edifieth. In this matter we must listen to Scripture, which teaches us to turn aside neither to the right hand nor to the left, but to follow those right precepts of the Lord which rejoice the heart. For just as a man is not righteous merely because be serves and devotes himself to works and ceremonial rites, so neither will be accounted righteous, merely because lie neglects and despises them.

It is not from works that we are set free by the faith of Christ, but from the belief in works, that is, from foolishly presuming to seek justification through works. Faith redeems our consciences, makes them upright and preserves them, since by it we recognize the truth that justification does not depend on our works, although good works neither can nor ought to be wanting to it, just as we cannot exist without food and drink and all the functions of this mortal body. Still it is not on them that our justification is based, but on faith, and yet they ought not on that account to be despised or neglected. Thus in this world we are compelled by the needs of this bodily life, but we are not hereby justified. "My kingdom is not hence, nor of this world," says Christ; but He does not say: "My kingdom is not here, nor in this world." Paul too says, "Though we walk in the flesh, we do not war after the flesh" (2 Cor. x. 3), and: "The life which I now live in the flesh I live by the faith of the Son of God" (Gal. ii. 20). Thus our doings, life, and being, in works and ceremonies, are done from the necessities of this life, and with the motive of governing our bodies, but yet we are not justified by these things, but by the faith of the Son of God.

The Christian must therefore walk in the middle path, and met these two classes of men before his eyes. He may meet with hardened and obstinate ceremonialists, who, like deaf adders, refuse to listen to the truth of liberty, and cry up, enjoin, and urge on us their ceremonies, as if they could justify us without faith. Such were the Jews of old, who would not understand, that they might act well. These men we must resist, do just the contrary to what they do, and be bold to give them offence, lest by this impious notion of theirs they should deceive many along with themselves. In the sight of these men it is expedient to eat flesh, to break fasts, and to do in behalf of the liberty of faith things which they hold to be the greatest sins. We must say of them: "Let them alone; they be blind leaders of the blind" (Matt. xv. 14). In this way Paul also would not have Titus circumcised, though these men urged it; and Christ defended the Apostles, who had plucked ears of corn on the Sabbath day; and many like instances.

Or else we may meet with simple-minded and ignorant persons, weak in the faith, as the Apostle calls them, who are as yet unable to apprehend that liberty of faith, even if willing to do so. These we must spare, lest they should be offended. We must bear with their infirmity, till they shall be more fully instructed. For since these men do not act thus from hardened malice, but only from weakness of faith, therefore, in order to avoid giving them offence, we must keep fasts and do other things which they consider necessary. This is required of us by charity, which injures no one, but serves all men. It is not the fault of these persons that they are weak, but that of their pastors, who by the snares and weapons of their own traditions have brought them into bondage, and wounded their souls, when they ought to have been set free and healed by the teaching of faith and liberty. Thus the Apostle says:

"If meat make my brother to offend, I will eat no flesh while the world standeth" (I Cor. viii. 13). And again: "I know, and am persuaded by the Lord Jesus, that there is nothing unclean of itself; but to him that esteemeth anything to be unclean, to him it is unclean. It is evil for that man who eateth with offence" (Rom. xiv. 14, 20).

Thus, though we ought boldly to resist those teachers of tradition, and though those laws of the pontiffs, by which they make aggressions on the people of God, deserve sharp reproof, yet we must spare the timid crowd, who are held captive by the laws of those impious tyrants, till they are set free. Fight vigorously against the wolves, but on behalf of the sheep, not against the sheep. And this you may do by inveighing against the laws and lawgivers, and yet at the same time observing these laws with the weak, lest they be offended, until they shall themselves recognize the tyranny as such, and understand their own liberty. If you wish to use your liberty, do it secretly, as Paul says: "Hast thou faith? have it to thyself before God" (Rom. xiv. 22). But take care not to use it in the presence of the weak. On the other hand, in the presence of tyrants and obstinate opposers, use your liberty in their despite, and with the utmost pertinacity, that they too may understand that they themselves are tyrants, and their laws useless for justification, nay, that they had not right to establish such laws.

Since, then, we cannot live in this world without ceremonies and works; since the hot and inexperienced period of youth has need of being restrained and protected by such bonds; and since everyone is bound to keep under his own body by attention to these things; therefore the minister of Christ must be prudent and faithful in so ruling and teaching the people of Christ in all these matters that no root of bitterness may spring up among them, and so many be defiled, as Paul warned the Hebrews, that is, that they may not lose the faith, and begin to be defiled by a belief in works, as the means of justification. This is a thing which easily happens, and defiles very many, unless faith be constantly inculcated along with works. It is impossible to avoid this evil, when faith is passed over in silence, and only the ordinances of men are taught, as has been done hitherto by the pestilent, impious, and soul-destroying traditions of our pontiffs, and opinions of our theologians. An infinite number of souls have been drawn down to hell by these snares, so that you may recognize the work of Antichrist.

In brief, as poverty is imperiled amid riches, honesty amid business, humility amid honours, abstinence amid feasting, purity amid pleasures, so is justification by faith imperiled among ceremonies. Solomon says: "Can a man take fire in his bosom, and his clothes not be burned?" (Prov. vi. 27). And yet, as we must live among riches, business, honours, pleasures, feastings, so must we among ceremonies, that is, among perils. Just as infant boys have the greatest need of being cherished in the bosoms and by the care of girls, that they may not die and yet, when they are grown, there is peril to their salvation in living among girls, so inexperienced and fervid young men require to be kept in and restrained by the barriers of ceremonies, even were they of iron, lest their weak mind should rush headlong into vice. And yet it would be death to them to persevere in believing that they can be justified by these things. They must rather be taught that they have been thus imprisoned, not with the purpose of their being justified or gaining merit in this way, but in order that they might avoid wrong doing, and be more easily instructed in that righteousness which is by faith, a thing which the headlong character of youth would not bear, unless it were put under restraint.

Hence in the Christian life ceremonies are to be no otherwise looked upon than builders and workmen look upon those preparations for building or working which are not made with any view of being permanent or anything in themselves, but only because without them there could be no building and no work. When the structure is completed, they are laid aside. Here you see that we do not contemn these preparations, but set the highest value on them; a belief in them we do contemn, because no one thinks that they constitute a real and permanent structure. If anyone were so manifestly out of his senses as to have no other object in life but that of setting up these preparations with all possible expense, diligence, and perseverance, while he never thought of the structure itself, but pleased himself and made his boast of these useless preparations and props, should we not all pity his madness, and think that, at the cost thus thrown away, some great building might have been raised?

Thus too we do not contemn works and ceremonies; nay, we set the highest value on them, but we contemn the belief in works, which no one should consider to constitute true righteousness, as do those hypocrites who employ and throw away their whole life in the pursuit of works, and yet never attain to that for the sake of which the works are done. As the Apostle says, they are "ever learning, and never able to come to the knowledge of the truth" (2 Tim. iii. 7). They appear to wish to build, they make preparations, and yet they never do build, and thus they continue in a show of godliness, but never attain to its power.

Meanwhile they please themselves with this zealous pursuit, and even dare to judge all others, whom they do not see adorned with such a glittering display of works, while, if they had been imbued with faith, they might have done great things for their own and others' salvation, at the same cost which they now waste in abuse of the gifts of God. But since human nature and natural reason, as they call it, are naturally superstitious, and quick to believe that justification can be attained by any laws or works proposed to them, and since nature is also exercised and confirmed in the same view by the practice of all earthly lawgivers, she can never, of her own power, free herself from this bondage to works, and come to a recognition of the liberty of faith.

We have therefore need to pray that God will lead us, and make us taught of God, that is, ready to learn from God; and will Himself, as He has promised, write His law in our hearts, otherwise there is no hope for us. For unless He himself teach us inwardly this wisdom hidden in a mystery, nature cannot but condemn it and judge it to be heretical. She takes offence at it and it seems folly to her, just as we see that it happened of old in the case of the prophets and apostles, and just as blind and impious pontiffs, with their flatterers, do now in my case and that of those who are like me, upon whom, together with ourselves, may God at length have mercy, and lift up the light of His countenance upon them, that we may know His way upon earth and His saving health among all nations, Who is blessed for evermore. Amen. In the year of the Lord MDXX.

INTRODUCTION TO *THE SCHLEITHEIM ARTICLES*

DESPITE LUTHER'S attempts to guard against misunderstanding, his fulminations against the unbiblical corruptions of the Roman Church and proclamation of Christian freedom were readily misappropriated in the tumultuous context of the early Reformation. Whereas Luther had insisted that unbiblical ceremonies and practices did not necessarily have to be discarded, so long as they were recognized as merely human institutions and were not sources of superstition, some began to preach that all such ceremonies be purged right away. And although Luther had insisted that the freedom of a Christian was inward, compatible with outward bondage to lawful government as a form of loving one's neighbor, more radical followers taught that the true Christian had no need of civil government at all, and that civil government, accordingly, had nothing to do with the church. Such ideas, which became known as the "radical Reformation" in contrast to the "magisterial Reformation," initially appeared in Germany—first in the radical reforms of Luther's former associate, Andreas Karlstadt (1486–1541), in 1522-23, and then in the apocalyptic theology of Thomas Müntzer and the associated disastrous peasant uprising of 1525 (1489–1525).

The most enduring form of the Radical Reformation, however, was the movement known as Anabaptism, which, although a squabbling family of disparate groups and ideas rather than one united movement, is most associated with teachings that emerged in and around Zurich between 1523 and 1525. Since 1519, Zurich had been undergoing a sweeping reformation of its own under the influential leadership of Ulrich Zwingli (1484–1531), often considered the father of the Reformed branch of the Reformation. Zurich had embraced a particularly thoroughgoing partnership between the reforming ministers and the city magistrates, and although the Reformation there was real and resulted in the conversion of many, it proceeded at the pace of politics. Ministers such as Conrad Grebel (1498–1526) and Balthasar Hubmaier (1480–1528) were appalled by the slow pace of reform and the nominalism of so much of the populace. The church in Zurich was self-evidently not identical with the city's whole population, and Grebel and Hubmaier did not think that such an ambiguous state of affairs should be tolerated. Anabaptism is best known for its insistence on re-baptism and its critique of civil authority, but both of these positions must be understood against the larger background of the Anabaptist aim to establish a visible congregation of saints that truly was the church and nothing but the church. This soon led to the practice of limiting church membership to those who voluntarily committed themselves by baptism (hence the name Anabaptist, or "re-baptizer"), but also to an insistence on policing church membership by rigorous discipline ("the ban") to remove false Christians from the fellowship. Despite the complexity and variety of the Anabaptist movements, this emphasis on discipline was a consistent theme.

Perhaps the most famous Anabaptist teaching, however, that of pacifism or non-resistance (and the corresponding notion that Christians must have nothing to do with civil government) came slightly later. It does not seem to have really emerged until after Grebel and Hubmaier's movement failed to gain public support and instead became the object of bitter persecution.[1] In the chaotic situation that followed the outbreak of such persecution in 1526, an Anabaptist preacher named Michael Sattler (1490–1527) tried to

---

[1] James M. Stayer, "Swiss-South German Anabaptism," in John D. Roth and James M. Stayer, eds., *A Companion to Anabaptism and Spiritualism* (Leiden: Brill, 2007), 84.

bring unity to the movement by convening a gathering at the Swiss town of Schleitheim. There he gained general support for the document he penned, *the Brotherly Union of a number of children of God concerning Seven Articles*, which has since become known simply as the *Schleitheim Articles* or the *Schleitheim Confession*. In it we find the already-established emphasis on rebaptism and the ban (articles 1 and 2), and a treatment of the Lord's Supper that emphasizes the need to restrict it only to true believers (article 3). Articles 4 and 6, on the necessity for a strict separation between church and world, and the rejection of any use of "the sword," though reflecting existing Anabaptist themes, were the first explicit declaration of them. Article 7, forbidding oaths and thus further separating Anabaptist believers from participation in the legal affairs of the broader society, seems to have been a new contribution of Sattler.[2]

As an attempt to establish something like an Anabaptist confession of faith, the *Schleitheim Articles* were only partially successful. A dizzying variety of sometimes contradictory expressions of the movement long persisted, but the principles of Schleitheim quickly became broadly influential in Swiss and South German Anabaptist communities, and in most of their present-day descendants, such as the Mennonites.

Further Reading

For further reading, see C. Arnold Snyder, "Swiss Anabaptism: The Beginnings," in John D. Roth and James M. Stayer, *A Companion to Anabaptism and Spiritualism, 1521–1700* (Leiden: Brill, 2007), 45–82; James M. Stayer, "Swiss-South German Anabaptism, 1526–1540," in Roth and Stayer, *Companion to Anabaptism*, 83–118.

---

[2] Stayer, "Swiss-South German Anabaptism," 89–91.

MICHAEL SATTLER,
THE SCHLEITHEIM ARTICLES (1527)[1]

FIRST. Observe concerning baptism: Baptism shall be given to all those who have learned repentance and amendment of life, and who believe truly that their sins are taken away by Christ, and to all those who walk in the resurrection of Jesus Christ, and wish to be buried with Him in death, so that they may be resurrected with Him, and to all those who with this significance request it [baptism] of us and demand it for themselves. This excludes all infant baptism, the highest and chief abomination of the Pope. In this you have the foundation and testimony of the apostles (Mt. 28, Mk. 16, Acts 2, 8, 16, 19). This we wish to hold simply, yet firmly and with assurance.

Second. On the Ban[2]. We are agreed as follows: The ban shall be employed with all those who have given themselves to the Lord, to walk in His commandments, and with all those who are baptized into the one body of Christ and who are called brethren or sisters, and yet who slip sometimes and fall into error and sin, being inadvertently overtaken. The same shall be admonished twice in secret and the third time openly disciplined or banned according to the command of Christ (Mt. 18). But this shall be done according to the regulation of the Spirit (Mt. 5) before the breaking of bread, so that we may break and eat one bread, with one mind and in one love, and may drink of one cup.

---

[1] Taken from J.C. Wenger, trans., *The Schleitheim Confession of Faith,* in *The Mennonite Quarterly Review* 19, no. 4 (October 1945): 247–253.

[2] *ban:* excommunication.

Third. Eucharist or Communion: In the breaking of bread we are of one mind and are agreed [as follows]: All those who wish to break one bread in remembrance of the broken body of Christ, and all who wish to drink of one drink as a remembrance of the shed blood of Christ, shall be united beforehand by baptism in one body of Christ which is the church of God and whose Head is Christ. For as Paul points out we cannot at the same time be partakers of the Lord's table and the table of devils; we cannot at the same time drink the cup of the Lord and the cup of the devil. That is, all those who have fellowship with the dead works of darkness have no part in the light. Therefore all who follow the devil and the world have no part with those who are called unto God out of the world. All who lie in evil have no part in the good. Therefore it is and must be [thus]: Whoever has not been called by one God to one faith, to one baptism, to one Spirit, to one body, with all the children of God's church, cannot be made [into] one bread with them, as indeed must be done if one is truly to break bread according to the command of Christ.

Fourth. On separation of the saved: A separation shall be made from the evil and from the wickedness which the devil planted in the world; in this manner, simply that we shall not have fellowship with them [the wicked] and not run with them in the multitude of their abominations. This is the way it is: Since all who do not walk in the obedience of faith, and have not united themselves with God so that they wish to do His will, are a great abomination before God, it is not possible for anything to grow or issue from them except abominable things. For truly all creatures are in but two classes, good and bad, believing and unbelieving, darkness and light, the world and those who [have come] out of the world, God's temple and idols, Christ and Belial; and none can have part with the other.

To us then the command of the Lord is clear when He calls upon us to be separate from the evil and thus He will be our God and we shall be His sons and daughters. He further admonishes us to withdraw from Babylon and the earthly Egypt that we may not be partakers of the pain and suffering which the Lord will bring upon them. From this we should learn that everything which is not united with our God and Christ cannot be other than an abomination which we should shun and flee from. By this is meant all popish and anti-popish works and church services, meetings and church attendance, drinking houses, civic affairs, the commitments [made in] unbelief and other things of that kind, which are highly regarded by the world and yet are carried on in flat contradiction to the command of God, in accordance with all the unrighteousness which is in the world. From all these things we shall be separated and have no part with them for they are nothing but an abomination, and they are the cause of our being hated before our Christ Jesus, Who has set us free from the slavery of the flesh and fitted us for the service of God through the Spirit Whom He has given us.

Therefore there will also unquestionably fall from us the unchristian, devilish weapons of force—such as sword, armor and the like, and all their use [either] for friends or against one's enemies I would like the records —by virtue of the word of Christ, "Resist not [him that is] evil."

Fifth. On pastors in the church of God: The pastor in the church of God shall, as Paul has prescribed, be one who out-and-out has a good report of those who are outside the faith. This office shall be to read, to admonish and teach, to warn, to discipline, to ban in the church, to lead out in prayer for the advancement of all the brethren and sisters, to lift up the bread when it is to be broken, and in all things to see to the care of the body of Christ, in order that it may be built up and developed, and the mouth of the slanderer be stopped.

This one moreover shall be supported of the church which has chosen him, wherein he may be in need, so that he who serves the Gospel may live of the Gospel as the Lord has ordained. But if a pastor should do something requiring discipline, he shall not be dealt with except [on the testimony of] two or three witnesses. And when they sin they shall be disciplined before all in order that the others may fear.

But should it happen that through the cross this pastor should be banished or led to the Lord [through martyrdom] another shall be ordained in his place in the same hour so that God's little flock and people may not be destroyed.

Sixth. Concerning the sword: The sword is ordained of God outside the perfection of Christ. It punishes and puts to death the wicked, and guards and protects the good. In the Law, the sword was ordained for the punishment of the wicked and for their death, and the same [sword] is [now] ordained to be used by the worldly magistrates. In the perfection of Christ, however, only the ban is used for a warning and for the excommunication of the one who has sinned, without putting the flesh to death—simply the warning and the command to sin no more.

Now it will be asked by many who do not recognize [this as] the will of Christ for us, whether a Christian may or should employ the sword against the wicked for the defense and protection of the good, or for the sake of love.

Our reply is unanimously as follows: Christ teaches and commands us to learn of Him, for He is meek and lowly in heart and so shall we find rest to our souls. Also Christ says to the heathenish woman who was taken in adultery, not that one should stone her according to the law of His Father (and yet He says, "As the Father has commanded me, thus I do"), but in mercy and forgiveness and warning, to sin no more. Such [an attitude] we also ought to take completely according to the rule of the ban.

Secondly, it will be asked, whether a Christian shall pass sentence in worldly disputes and strife such as unbelievers have with one another. This is our united answer: Christ did not wish to decide or pass judgment between brother and brother in the case of the inheritance, but refused to do so. Therefore we should do likewise.

Thirdly, it will be asked concerning the sword, "Shall one be a magistrate if one should be chosen as such?" The answer is as follows: They wished to make Christ king, but He fled and did not view it as the arrangement of His Father. Thus shall we do as He did, and follow Him, and so shall we not walk in darkness. For He Himself says, "He who wishes to come after me, let him deny himself and take up his cross and follow me." Also, He Himself forbids the [employment of] the force of the sword saying, "The worldly princes lord it over them, etc., but not so shall it be with you." Further, Paul says, "Whom God did foreknow He also did predestinate to be conformed to the image of His Son, etc." Also Peter says, "Christ has suffered (not ruled) and left us an example, that ye should follow His steps."

Finally it will be observed that it is not appropriate for a Christian to serve as a magistrate because of these points: The government magistracy is according to the flesh, but the Christians' is according to the Spirit; their houses and dwelling remain in this world, but the Christians' are in heaven; their citizenship is in this world, but the Christians' citizenship is in heaven; the weapons of their conflict and war are carnal and against the flesh only, but the Christians' weapons are spiritual, against the fortification of the devil. The worldlings are armed with steel and iron, but the Christians are armed with the armor of God, with truth, righteousness, peace, faith, salvation and the Word of God. [...]

Seventh. Concerning the oath: The oath is a confirmation among those who are quarreling or making promises. In the Law it is commanded to be performed in God's Name, but only in truth, not falsely. Christ, who teaches the perfection of the Law, prohibits all swearing to His [followers], whether true or false—neither by heaven, nor by the earth, nor by Jerusalem, nor by our head—and that for the reason which He shortly thereafter gives, "For you are not able to make one hair white or black." So you see it is for this reason that all swearing is forbidden: we cannot fulfill that which we promise when we swear, for we cannot change [even] the very least thing on us.

Christ also taught us along the same line when He said, "Let your communication be Yea, yea; Nay, nay; for whatsoever is more than these cometh of evil" [Matt. 5:37]. He says, "Your speech or word shall be yea and nay." [However] when one does not wish to understand, he remains closed to the meaning. Christ is simply Yea and Nay, and all those who seek Him simply will understand His Word. Amen.

INTRODUCTION TO THOMAS MORE'S
DIALOGUE CONCERNING HERESIES

Sir Thomas More's is one of the few names from the Reformation era to remain something of a household name today. His legacy rests chiefly his authorship of the humanist classic *Utopia* in 1516 and his execution (martyrdom) by Henry VIII in 1535, memorably depicted in Robert Bolt's great 1960 play (and 1966 film), *A Man for All Seasons*. Few realize, however (and few are likely to imagine, based on Bolt's portrayal), that between these two events, he spent a significant phase of his life as Henry's most implacable prosecutor of Lutheran "heresy" in England.

More (1478–1535), was a true "Renaissance man," gifted and tireless in both contemplation and in action. A close friend of Erasmus, he was perhaps England's pre-eminent proponent of humanist study and reform, and an internationally-recognized writer and scholar; but as the loyal servant of King Henry VIII and the Catholic Church, he was also a renowned lawyer, cunning diplomat, and indefatigable administrator. His meteoric rise to succeed Cardinal Wolsey as Lord Chancellor of England in 1529, however, was also the beginning of his fall. Appointed to the post precisely because of Wolsey's failure to secure for Henry a divorce from Catherine of Aragon, More found himself in an increasingly difficult position as Henry began to question papal authority in his determination to secure the divorce. More's allegiance to the English Crown was topped only by his allegiance to the Roman Church, and, in the end, unwilling to renounce the latter in order to serve the former, he lost his head, but gained an immortal reputation as a champion of conscience. More's notion of conscience, however, was hardly ours. As John Guy notes, heretics like the Lutherans "were not allowed consciences," in More's thinking, "since they had deviated from the authority and tradition of the Catholic Church."[1] "Conscience" for More meant simply submission to the authoritative consensus of the church's teaching. It was precisely such an appeal to the church's teaching authority that More was to make the cornerstone of his argument in his most important anti-Lutheran work, the *Dialogue Against Heresies* (1529).

Although the *Dialogue* was the result of a formal commission by Bishop of London Cuthbert Tunstal for More to head up anti-heresy propaganda, and was penned particularly in response to the recent trial of English reformer Thomas Bilney, the Dialogue was rooted in several years of theological polemic by More. This began with Henry VIII's response to Luther's *Babylonian Captivity* of the Church with his own *Defence of the Seven Sacraments* in 1520, which More was asked to edit. When Luther responded in 1522, Henry commissioned More to respond, which he did in 1523 with the *Answer to Luther*. More wrote further against the Lutherans in the unpublished 1526 *Letter to Bugenhagen*, and when Lutheranism began to gain a foothold in England with William Tyndale's translation of the New Testament into English that year, More began to pull out all the stops. In the flurry of polemical writing that began in 1529, many scholars suggest that the normally cool and judicious More lost his sense of proportion, becoming, in the words of C.S. Lewis, "monotonously anxious to conquer and to conquer equally, at every moment: to show in every chapter that every heretical book is wrong about everything."[2] In the *Dialogue* itself, however, and especially its first half, More seeks to give at least something of a fair hearing to the opposition, at least by constructing the work as a dialogue in which both sides are presented. In Book I, "the Messenger" with whom More debates begins by mounting an attack on

---

[1] John Guy, *Thomas More* (London: Arnold, 2000), 201.

[2] C.S. Lewis, *English Literature in the Sixteenth Century, Excluding Drama*, The Oxford History of English Literature, Vol. 3 (Oxford: Clarendon Press, 1954), 174.

the liturgical corruptions of the late medieval church: praying to saints, worshipping images, going on pilgrimages, etc. More seeks to counter his long series of attacks first by insisting that the holy places and relics have been well-attested by miracles, before shifting the conversation to the more fundamental ground of authority, the issue on which More's critiques of Luther earlier in the 1520s had focused. Part of this key section, comprising chapters 18-31 of Book I, appears in the excerpt below. Since More appealed to the authority of "the Church," Book II moves on to the all-important Reformation ground of the definition of this church, with More rejecting Luther's insistence that the true church remains hidden in this world, before moving back to the debate over the worship of images. In Book III, More turns his attention to more immediate English affairs, seeking to justify the treatment of Thomas Bilney and other Lutheran heretics who had recently been prosecuted,[3] before turning in Book IV to a long harangue against "the most pestilent sect of these Lutherans," and especially Luther himself, and a justification of handing them over to be burned at the stake.

In the crucial section of Book I excerpted below, More articulates what has become a classic Roman Catholic argument against the Protestant doctrine of *sola Scriptura*. Beginning with Christ's promise to Peter that his faith will not fail, More argues that it must be understood as a promise that the faith of the church as a whole would not fail, throughout the centuries. By getting the Messenger to agree (with somewhat implausible ease) that this means that the church cannot then ever fail *either* to believe all the articles of the Christian faith that are necessary *or* to come to believe additional articles of faith beyond those that are necessary, More concludes that the church's traditional belief in the efficacy of relics, the worship of images, etc., cannot possibly be in error, since then faith would have failed in the church. To the Messenger's response that Christ, and the true faith, are always with the church in the form of

---

[3] Bilney initially recanted in 1529, but then regretted his cowardice and began preaching the Protestant gospel again, leading to his 1531 martyrdom.

Scripture, More argues that Scripture is worthless without a reliable right interpretation, and that, unless we concede that the faith of the church has ever failed, we must believe that God has maintained in the authoritative teaching of the church the true understanding of Scripture.

In chapters 22 and 23, More turns to argue against a misleading stereotype of the Protestant doctrine of Scripture that remains common today: namely, that Protestants seek to approach Scripture in blind faith alone, without the interpretive aids of reasoning and the Church Fathers. More scores many easy points against the Messenger here, but at the cost of some consistency in his own argument, since earlier he had chided the Messenger for his overly rationalist refusal to believe in the miracles of relics on the grounds of "reason and nature." Still, it is true that in the early stages of the Reformation in particular, the Reformers often spoke of faith and reason in ways that encouraged More's caricature of a simplistic biblicism, a stance that later 16th-century Protestants were to oppose with a judicious retrieval of the role of philosophy in theology.

Further Reading

For further reading, see John Guy, *Thomas More* (London: Arnold, 2000); Judith H. Paterson, *Thomas More* (Boston: Twayne, 1979); C.S. Lewis, *English Literature in the Sixteenth Century, Excluding Drama*, The Oxford History of English Literature, Vol. 3 (Oxford: Clarendon Press, 1954), Bk. II, ch. 1.

THOMAS MORE,
DIALOGUE CONCERNING HERESIES
(1529)[1]

The Nineteenth Chapter

THE AUTHOR proves that if the worship of images were idolatry, then the Church, believing it to be lawful and pleasant to God, were in a misbelief and in a deadly error. And then were the faith failed in the Church, whereof Christ has promised the contrary, as is proved in the chapter before.

"Surely, sir," said he, "that God made not his Church for a while, but to endure until the world's end, that is there no Christian man but he will well agree. And since His Church cannot stand without faith, which is the entry into Christendom, for as Saint Paul says, *accendentem ad deum oportet credere* ("whoso will come to God must needs believe"), no man will deny but that faith is and always shall be in His Church. And that His Church not in faith only, and the knowledge of the truths necessary to be known for our soul's health, but also to the doing of good works and avoiding of evil is, has been, and ever shall be specially guided and governed by God and the secret inspiration of his Holy Spirit."

---

[1] Modernized by Brian Marr from Thomas M.C. Lawler, Germain Marchadour, and Richard C. Marius, eds., *A Dialogue Concerning Heresies*, Vol. 6.1 of *The Yale Edition of the Complete Works of Sir Thomas More* (New Haven, CT: Yale University Press, 1981).

"Well," said I, "then if the Church have faith, it errs not in belief."

"That is true," says he.

"It should err," said I, "if it believed not all the truths that we are bound to believe."

"What else?" said he.

"What, and we believed," said I, "all that is true, and over that some other thing not only false, but also displeasing to God? Did we not then err in our necessary belief?"

"Whereby mean you that?" said he.

"As thus," said I, "if that one believed in all the three persons of the Trinity, the Father, the Son, and the Holy Ghost, and therewith were persuaded that there were a fourth Person besides, equal and one god with them."

"He must," said he, "needs err in his necessary belief, by which he is bound to believe in the Trinity. And that fellow believes in a Quaternity!"

"That is," said I, "the whole Trinity and one more."

"But we be not only not bound," said he, "to believe in any more, but also bound not to believe in any more."

"Very well," said I, "then errs he as much and as far lacks his right belief who believes too much, as he who believes too little, and he who believes something that he should not as he that believes not something that he should."

"What else?" said he. "And what then?"

"Marry, this," said I: "If we believe that it were lawful and well done to pray to saints, and to reverence their images, and do honor to their relics and visit pilgrimages. And then where we do these things, they were indeed not well done, but were displeasing to God, and by him reputed as a diminishment, and a withdrawing of the honor due to Himself, and therefore before His majesty reproved and odious and taken as idolatry. Were not this opinion a deadly, pestilent error in us and a plain lack of right faith?"

"Yes, before God," said he.

"But you grant," said I, "that the Church cannot err in the right faith necessary to be believed, which is given and always kept in the Church by God."

"True," said he.

"Then it follows," said I, "that the Church in that it believes saints to be prayed unto, relics and images to be worshipped, and pilgrimages to be visited and sought is not deceived, nor does not err, but that the belief of the Church is true therein. And thereupon it also follows that the wonderful works done above nature at such images and pilgrimages, at holy relics, by prayers made unto saints, be not done by the devil to delude the Church of Christ therewith, since the thing that the Church does is well done and not idolatry, but by the great honor done unto saints God Himself the more highly honored, in that His servants have so much honor for His sake. And thereof follows it that Himself makes the miracles, [as proof] thereof.

"Also, if it be true that you have granted, that God keeps, and ever shall keep in His Church the right faith and right belief by the help of His own hand that has planted it, then can it not be that He shall suffer the devil to work wonders like unto His own miracles to bring his whole Church into a wrong faith. And then if those things be not done by the devil, I dare say you will not then deny but they be done by God. And so is yet again our purpose double proved. First, in that you grant that God will not suffer His Church to err in His right faith. Secondly (which pursues thereupon) by that He has by many a visible miracle declared that this faith and manner of observance is very pleasant and acceptable unto Him, which miracles since they be proved to be done upon good ground and cause appear well to be done by God and not by our ghostly enemy."

The Twentieth Chapter

The messenger alleges that the perpetual being and assistance of Christ with His Church to keep it out of all damnable errors is nothing else but His being with His Church in Holy Scripture, whereof the author declares the contrary.

"How think you?" said I. "Is there anything in this matter amiss?"

"I cannot well tell," said he, "what I might answer thereto. But yet methinks that I come to this point by some oversight in granting."

"Well," said I, "men say sometimes when they would say or do a thing and cannot well come thereon but miss and oversee themselves in the assay, 'It makes no matter,' they say, 'you may begin again and amend it, for it is neither Mass nor Matins.'[2] And albeit in this matter you have nothing granted but that is in my mind as true as the Matins or the Mass either, yet if you reckon yourself overswift in granting, I give you leave to go back and call again what you will."

"In good faith," said he, "full hard were it in mine own mind otherwise to think but that God shall always keep the right belief in His Church. But yet since we come to this conclusion by the granting thereof, let us look once again thereupon. And what if men would say, as I heard once one say myself, that God does peradventure not keep always faith in His Church to give them warning with when they do well and when the contrary, but since He has given them and left with them the Scripture, in which they may sufficiently see both what they should believe and what they should do, He lets them alone therewith without any other special cure of His upon their faith and belief. For therein they may see all that them needs if they will look and labor therein. And if they will not, the fault is their own sloth and folly! And whoso be willing to amend and be better may always have light to see how by recourse to the reading of Holy Scripture, which shall stand him in like stead

---

[2] *neither Mass nor Matins:* Mass and Matins were solemn ceremonies of worship; if something is neither Mass nor Matins, it is unimportant.

as you said before, that God kept the faith for by His special means in His Church."

"If this," said I, "were thus, whereof should Christ's promise serve, *Ego vobiscum sum omnibus diebus usque ad finem saeculi* ('I am with you all the days till the end of the world')? Wherefore should He be here with His Church if His being here should not keep His right faith and belief in His Church?"

"Marry," said he, "these words well agree withal! For God is and shall be until the world's end with His Church in His Holy Scripture! As Abraham answered the rich man in hell, saying, 'They have Moses and the prophets,' not meaning that they had them all at that time present with them, but only that they had their books. And so Christ, forasmuch as the Scripture has His faith comprehended therein, according to His own words, *Scrutamini scripturas, quia scripturae sunt quae testimonium perhibent de me* ('Search you the Scriptures for they bear witness of me'), therefore he said, *Ego vobiscum sum usque ad finem saeculi* ('I am with you to the end of the world'), because His Holy Scripture shall never fail as long as the world endures. 'Heaven and earth,' he says, 'shall pass away, but my words shall never pass away.' And therefore in His holy writing is He with us still, and therein He keeps and teaches us His right faith if we list to look for it and else, as I said, our own fault and folly it is."

"If God," said I, "be none otherwise with us but in Holy Scripture, then be those words of Christ, 'I am with you to the world's end' somewhat strangely spoken, and unlike the words of Abraham whereunto you resemble them. For Christ left never a book behind Him of His own making as Moses did and the prophets. And in their books was He spoken of, as He was in the Gospel. Wherefore if He had spoken and meant of Scripture, He would have said that they should have with them still His evangelists and writers of His gospels, as Abraham said, 'They have Moses and the prophets', which were the writers of the books that the Jews had. Christ also said, 'I am with you till the end of the world,' not 'I shall be,' but 'I am,' which is the word appropriated to His Godhead. And therefore that word 'am' is the name by which our Lord would, as He told Moses, be named unto Pharaoh, as a name which from all creatures (since they be all subject to time) clearly discern His Godhead, which is ever being and present, without difference of time past or to come. In which wise He was not in His Holy Scripture, for that had beginning. And at those words spoken was not yet all written. For of the chief part, which is the New Testament, there was yet at that time never one word written. And also we be not sure by any promise made that the Scripture shall endure to the world's end, albeit I think verily the substance shall. But yet as I say, promise have we none thereof. For where our Lord says that His words shall not pass away, nor one iota thereof be lost, He spoke of His promises made indeed, as His faith and doctrine taught by mouth and inspiration. He meant not that of His Holy Scripture in writing there should never an iota be lost, of which some parts be already lost, more peradventure than we can tell of. And of that we have, the books in some part corrupted with miswriting. And yet the substance of those words that He meant be known, where some part of the writing is unknown. He says also that His Father and He should send the Holy Ghost, and also that He would come himself, whereto all this if He meant no more but to leave the books behind them and go their way? Christ is also present among us bodily in the Holy Sacrament. And is He there present with us for nothing? The Holy Ghost taught many things I think unwritten, and whereof some part was never comprised in the Scripture, yet unto this day, as the article which no good Christian man will doubt of, that our Blessed Lady was a perpetual virgin as well after the birth of Christ as before.

"Our Savior also said unto His apostles that when they should be accused and brought in judgment, they should not need to care for answer: it should even then be put in their minds. And that He meant not only the remembrance of Holy Scripture, which before the pagan judges were but a cold and bare alleging, but such words newly given them by God, inspired in their hearts so effectual and confirmed with miracles that their adversaries, though they were angry thereat, yet should not be able to resist it. And thus with secret help and inspiration is Christ with His Church, and will be to the world's end present and assistant, not only spoken of in writing."

The Twenty-first Chapter

The author shows that if it so were indeed as the messenger said, that is, to wit that Christ continued with His Church none otherwise but only by the leaving of His Holy Scripture to them, and that all the faith also were only therein, then should it yet follow that as far as the necessity of our salvation requires, God gives the Church the right understanding thereof. And thereupon [it] follows further that the Church cannot err in the right faith, whereupon is inferred soon afterwards all that the messenger would have fled from before. And thereon also specially [it] follows that all the texts of Holy Scripture which heretics allege against images or any point of the common belief of Christ's Catholic Church can nothing serve their purpose.

"But now would I wit, since you reckon him none otherwise present than in Holy Scripture, whether then does He give His Church the right understanding of Holy Scripture or not?"

"What if he do not?" said he.

"Marry," said I, "then yourself see well that they were as well without. And so should the Scripture stand them in as good stead as a pair of spectacles should stand a blind friar."

"That is very true," said he. "But therefore has His wisdom and goodness provided it so to be written that it may be well understood by the collation[3] and consideration of one text with another."

"May it not also be," said I, "that some of them which do read it diligently, and diligently compare and consider every text, how it may stand with other may yet for all that mistake and misunderstand it?"

---

[3] *collation:* collection or comparison.

"Yes," said he, "it may be so. For else had there not been so many heretics as there have been."

"Very true," said I. "But now if all the faith be in Holy Scripture and no part thereof anywhere else, but that it must be therein altogether learned, were it then sufficient to understand some part aright, and some other part wrong in the necessary points of our faith, or must we, as far forth as concerns the necessity thereof, misunderstand no part?"

"We must," said he, "mistake no part, as far as necessarily concerns our faith. But we must have so the right understanding of [it] all together, that we conceive no damnable error."

"Well said!" said I. "Then if we must, we may. For if we may not, we must not. For our Lord binds no man to an impossibility."

"We may," said he.

"If we may," said I, "then may we either by good hap fall into the right understanding, or else by natural reason come to it, or else by supernatural grace be led into it."

"That is truth," said he. "Needs must it be one of these ways."

"Well," said I, "we will not yet search which. But I would first wit whether Christ have a Church in the world continually and so shall have to the world's end, or else has one sometimes, and sometimes none at all. As we might think that He had one while He was here Himself, and peradventure a while after, and haply none at all ever since, nor shall not again we wot not when."

"Nay," said he, "that cannot be in no wise, but that He must needs have His Church continue still somewhere, for else how could He be with them continually to the world's end, in Scripture or otherwise, if they (with whom He promised to be and continue to the world's end) should not continually so long endure? Or how could those words of Christ be true, 'Lo, I am with you all the days to the world's end,' if before the world's end He were away some days, as He were indeed from the Church some days, if in some days He had no Church?"

"Well," said I, "yet would I wit one thing more. Can He have a Church without faith?"

"Nay," said he, "that were impossible."

"Forsooth," said I, "so were it. For His Church is a congregation of people gathered into His faith. And faith is the first substantial difference discerning Christian men from heathen, as reason is the difference dividing man from all the kinds of brute beasts. Now then, if His Church be and ever shall be continual without any times between (in which there shall be none), and without faith it may never be, and no part of the faith is as you say elsewhere had but in Holy Scripture, and all it must be had, and also as we were agreed a little while before, there must be none error adjoined thereto, and therefore as far as touches the necessity of faith, no part of Scripture may be mistaken, but all must be understood rightly and may be rightly understood either by hap, reason, or help of grace, it necessarily follows that by one or other of these ways the Church of Christ has always and never fails, the right understanding of Scripture, as far as belongs for our necessity."

"That follows indeed," said he.

"Well," said I, "let pass for the while what follows further. And since the Church so has let us first agree by which of these three ways the Church has it, whether by hap, reason, or grace."

"By hap,"[4] said he, "were a poor having. For so might it hap to have and hap to fail.

"Then," said I, "since it has it ever, it cannot be by hap. What think you, then, of reason?"

"As little," said he, "as any man thinks! For I take reason for plain enemy to faith!"

"You take peradventure wrong," said I. "But thereof shall we see further after. But now since you so think you leave but the third way, which is the help of grace."

"No, surely," said he.

---

[4] *hap:* chance or fortune.

"Verily," said I, "where reason may between divers texts stand in great doubt which way to lean, I think that God with His Holy Spirit leads His Church into the consent of the truth. As Himself said that the Holy Ghost (whom he would send) should lead them into all truth. He said not that the Holy Ghost should at His coming write them all truth, nor tell them all the whole truth by mouth, but that He should by secret inspiration lead them into all truth. And therefore surely for a true conclusion in such means by God Himself, by the help of His grace (as yourself grants), the right understanding of Scripture is ever preserved in His Church from all such mistaking whereof might follow any damnable error concerning the faith. And thereof does there first follow that besides the Scripture itself, there is another present assistance and special cure of God perpetual with His Church to keep it in the right faith, that it err not by misunderstanding of Holy Scripture, contrary to the opinion that you purposed when you said that Christ's being with his Church was only the leaving of His Holy Scripture to us. And over this, if God were no otherwise present than you speak of, yet since it is proved that His Church for all that ever has the right understanding of Scripture, we be come to the same point again that you would so fain flit from. For if the Scripture (and nothing but the Scripture) does contain all things that we be bound to believe and to do and to forbear, and that God also therefore provides for His Church the right understanding thereof, concerning everything necessary for us that is contained in Scripture, then must there needs follow thereupon the thing that you feared lest you had wrongly and unadvisedly granted, that is, to wit, that God always keeps the right faith in His Church. And thereupon [it] follows further [that] the remnant of all that is in question between us, that the faith of the Church in the worship that it believes to be well given unto saints, relics, and images is not erroneous but right. And thereupon [it] follows also that the miracles done at such places be none illusions of damned spirits, but the mighty hand of God, to show his pleasure in the corroboration thereof, and in the excitation of our devotion thereto."

"Indeed," said he, "we be come back here with going forward, as men walk in a maze."

"You have not, yet," said I, "lost all that labor. For though you have half a check in this point, yet have you (if you perceive it) mated me in another point by one thing that is agreed between us now."

"What is that?" said he.

"This," said I, "that I have agreed as well as you that God has given His Church the right understanding of Scripture in as far forth as belongs to the necessity of salvation."

"In what point," said he, "has that mated you?"

"Why," said I, "see you not that? Nay, then will I not tell you but if you hire me, or if I tell you, yet shall you not win the game thereby. For since you see it not yourself, it is but a blind-mate."

"Let me know it yet," said he, "and I am agreed to take none advantage thereof."

"On that bargain be it," said I.

"You wot⁵ well," said I, "that against the worshipping of images and praying to saints, you laid certain texts of Scripture to prove it forbidden and reputed of God for idolatry. For answer whereof when I laid that men must lean to the sentence that the Church and holy doctors of the Church give to those texts, you said they were but men's false glosses against God's true texts. And now, since you grant and I also that the Church cannot misunderstand the Scripture to the hindrance of the right faith in things of necessity, and that you also acknowledge this matter to be such that it must either be the right belief and acceptable service to God, or else a wrong and erroneous opinion and plain idolatry, it follows of necessity that the Church does not misunderstand those texts that you or any other can allege and bring forth for that purpose. But that all these texts be so to be taken and understood as they nothing make against the Church, but all against your own opinion in this matter.

---

⁵ *wot:* say.

"And thus have you suddenly answered yourself to all those texts out of hand, with a gloss of your own, as true as any text in the Bible, and which all the world will never avoid, except they would make the Scripture serve the Church of naught, or rather to their hindrance than furtherance in the faith. For so were it if it might be that God gives them not the good understanding thereof, but suffers them to be deceived and deluded in errors by the mistaking of the letter."

"Marry," said he, "this is a blind-mate indeed!"

"Surely," said I, "these two things seem to me two as true points and as plain to a Christian man as any petition of Euclid's geometry is to a reasonable man. For as true as it is that every whole thing is more than its own half, as true is it indeed, and to every Christian man, faith makes it as certain, first, that Christ's Church cannot err in any such article as God upon pain of loss of heaven will that we believe, and thereupon [it] necessarily follows that there is no text of Scripture well understood by which Christian people are commanded to do the thing which the Church believes that they may lawfully leave undone, nor any text whereby we be forbidden anything which the Church believes that they may lawfully do."

The Twenty-second Chapter

Because the messenger had in the beginning showed himself desirous and greedy upon the text of Scripture with little force of the old Fathers' glosses, and with dispraise of philosophy and almost all the seven liberal sciences, the author therefore incidentally shows what harm has happed sometimes to fall to divers of those young men whom he has known to give their study to the Scripture only, with contempt of logic and other secular sciences, and little regard of the old interpreters. Wherefore the author shows that in the study of Scripture, the sure way is with virtue and prayer first to use the judgment of natural reason, whereunto secular literature helps much. And secondly, the comments of holy doctors. And thirdly, above all things, the articles of the Catholic faith, received and believed through the Church of Christ.

"And for because we speak of Scripture now and that the Church in things needly requisite to salvation has the right understanding of Holy Scripture, wherein I perceive you [to] be studious of the text alone, without great force of the old Fathers' interpretations or any other science, of which you reckon all seven, save grammar, almost to serve for naught. I have of you so good opinion that I trust all your study shall turn you to good. But surely I have seen to some folk so much harm to grow thereof that I never would advise any man else in the study of Scripture to take that way."

"Why so?" said he.

"For I have known," said I, "right good wits that has set all other learning aside, partly for sloth, refusing the labor and pain to be sustained in that learning, partly for pride, by which they could not endure the redargution[6] that should sometimes fall to their part in dispicions.[7] Which affections their inward, secret favor toward themselves, covered and cloaked under the pretext of simplicity and good Christian devotion, borne to the love of Holy Scripture alone. But in little while after, the damnable spirit of pride that unawares to themselves lurked in their hearts has begun to put out his horns and show himself. For then have they longed under the praise of Holy Scripture to set out to show their own study, which because they would have seem the more to be set by, they have first fallen to the dispraise and derision of all other disciplines. And because in speaking or preaching of such common things as all Christian men know, they could not seem excellent, nor make it appear and seem that in their study they had done any great mastery, to show themselves therefore marvelous, they set out paradoxes and strange opinions against the common faith of Christ's whole Church. And because they have therein the old holy doctors against them, they fall to the contempt and dispraise of them, either preferring their own fond glosses against the old cunning and

---

[6] *redargution:* refutation.

[7] *dispicions:* disputations.

blessed fathers' interpretations, or else lean to some words of Holy Scripture that seem to say for them against many more texts that plainly make against them, without receiving or ever giving to any reason or authority of any man quick or dead, or of the whole Church of Christ to the contrary. And thus once proudly persuaded a wrong way, they take the bridle in the teeth and run forth like a headstrong horse, that all the world cannot pluck them back. But with sowing sedition, setting forth of errors and heresies, and spicing their preaching with rebuking of priesthood and prelacy for the people's pleasure, they turn many a man to ruin and themselves also. And then the devil deceives them in their blind affections.

"They take for good zeal to the people their malicious envy. And for a great virtue their ardent appetite to preach, wherein they have so great pride for the people's praise that preach I ween they would, though God would [with] His own mouth command them the contrary."

"Why should you ween[8] so?" said he. "Or whereby can you be sure that you do not now misconstrue their good mind? Hard is it oftentimes to judge another man's deed that has some appearance of evil, because the purpose and intent may make it good. And what peril is it then where the deed appears good, there to judge the mind and intent for naught which who can see but God? As the Scripture said, *Dominus autem intuetur cor* ('Only God beholds the heart'). And therefore said our Savior, 'Judge not before the time.'"

"I judge not," said I, "but upon open things and well apparent. For I speak but of those whose erroneous opinions in their preaching and their obstinate pride in the defense of their worldly worship well declares their minds. And some have I seen which when they have for their perilous preaching been by their prelates prohibited to preach have (that notwithstanding) proceeded on still. And for the maintenance of their disobedience have amended the matter with a heresy, boldly and stubbornly defending that

---

[8] *ween:* think or suppose.

since they had cunning to preach, they were by God bound to preach. And that no man, nor no law that was made or could be made had any authority to forbid them. And this they thought sufficiently proved by the words of the apostle, *Oportet magis oboedire Deo quam hominibus* ('We must obey God rather than man'), as though these men were apostles now specially sent by God to preach heresies and sow sedition among Christian men as the very apostles were indeed sent and commanded by God to preach his very faith to the Jews. One of this sort of this new kind of preachers being demanded why that he used to say in his sermons about that nowadays men preached not well the Gospel, answered that he thought so because he saw not the preachers persecuted, nor no strife nor business arise upon their preaching. Which things, he said and wrote was the fruit of the Gospel, because Christ said, *Non veni pacem mittere, sed gladium* ('I am not come to send peace into the world, but the sword'). Was not this a worshipful understanding, that because Christ would make a division among infidels, from the remnant of them to win some, therefore these apostles would sow some cockle[9] of dissension among the Christian people, whereby Christ might lose some of them? For the fruit of strife among the hearers and persecution of the preacher cannot lightly grow among Christian men but by the preaching of some strange novelties, and bringing up of some newfangled heresies, to the infection of our old faith.

"One wist[10] I that was for his pertinacity in that opinion that he would and might and was bound to preach (any prohibition notwithstanding) when he was, after divers bold and open defenses thereof, at last before folk honorable and few reasoned withal, and not only the law showed him to the contrary of his opinion, which law was made at a general council, but also by plain authority of Holy Scripture proved that his opinion was erroneous. He so perceived himself satisfied that he meekly acknowledged his error and

---

[9] *cockle:* weeds or tares.

[10] *wist:* knew.

offered to abjure it and to submit himself to penance. But on the morrow when he came forth in open presence of the people, and there saw many that had oft heard him preach, of his secret pride he fell in such an open passion of shame that those should hear him go back with his word, which had before had his sermons in great estimation, that at the first sight of the people he revoked his revocation and said out aloud that he might well be heard, that his opinion was true, and that he was the day before deceived in that he had confessed it for false. And thus he held his own stubbornly without reason till the books were showed him again and himself read them before all the people, so that he perceived the audience that stood about him to feel and understand his proud folly in the defense of his indefensible error. And thereupon at the last yielded himself again. Such secret pride had our ghostly enemy conveyed into the heart of him, which I assure you seemed in all his other outward manner as meek a simple soul as a man should have seen in a summer's day. And some of them let not with lies and perjury to defend themselves, and some to stand in defense of their errors, or false denying of their own deed, to their great peril of the fire if their judges were not more merciful than their malice deserves. And all this done because (as themselves do at last confess) they think if they abjure, they shall after be suffered to preach again. Such a scabbed itch of vainglory catch they in their preaching that, though all the world were the worse for it and their own life lie thereon, yet would they long to be pulpited. And this I say has come of some that have with contempt of all other learning given them to Scripture alone. Whose affections of pride and sloth have not in the beginning been perceived to themselves but have accounted their vices for devotion."

"Would ye, then," said he, "condemn that manner of study by which a man has so great affection to the Scripture alone that he for the delight thereof feels little savor in anything else, but that we should lose time in philosophy, the mother of heresies, and let Scripture alone?"

"Nay," said I, "that mind am I not of. There was never [a] thing written in this world that can in any wise be comparable with any part of Holy Scripture. And yet I think other liberal sciences a gift of God also, and not to be cast away but worthy to wait and as handmaids to give attendance, upon divinity. And in this point I think not thus alone. For you shall find Saint Jerome, Saint Augustine, Saint Basil, and many of the old holy doctors, openly and plainly of the same opinion. And of divinity reckon I the best part to be contained in Holy Scripture. And this I say for him that shall have time thereto, and from youth intends to the Church, and to make himself, with God's help, meet for the office of a preacher. Howbeit if any man either happen to begin so late that he shall peradventure have no time thereto, or else any man of youth to have that fervent appetite unto Scripture that he cannot find in his heart to read anything else (which affection whoso haps to have given him is very fortunate if he with grace and meekness guide it well), then would I counsel him specially to study for the virtuous framing of his own affections and using great moderation and temperance in the preaching to other men. And in all things to flee the desire of praise and show of cunning, ever mistrusting his own inclinations and living in dread and fear of the devil's subtle sleights and inventions, [that devil] who though he lie in continual wait upon every preacher to catch him into pride if he can, yet his highest enterprise and proudest triumph stands in the bringing of a man to the most abuse of that thing that is of his own nature the best. And therefore great labor makes he and great boast, if he bring it about, that a good wit may abuse his labor bestowed upon the study of Holy Scripture.

"For the sure avoiding whereof, my poor advice were in the study thereof, to have a special regard to the writings and comments of old holy fathers. And yet or he fall in hand with the one or the other next grace and help of God to be gotten with abstinence and prayer and cleanness of living, before all things were it necessary to come well and surely instructed in all such points and articles as the Church believes. Which things once firmly had and fastly for undoubted truths presupposed, then shall reason and they be two good rules to examine and expound all doubtful texts by, since the reader shall be sure that no text is so to be understood as it stands against them both or against any point of the catholic faith of Christ's Church. And therefore if it seem to stand against any of them, either shall the light of natural reason with the collation of other texts help to find out the truth, or else (which is the surest way) he shall perceive the truth in the comments of the good holy doctors of old, to whom God has given the grace of understanding. Or finally if all that he can either find in other men's works or invent by God's aid, of His own study cannot suffice to satisfy, but that any text yet seem unto him contrary to any point of the Church's faith and belief, let him then, as Saint Augustine said, make himself very sure that there is some fault either in the translator, or in the writer, or nowadays in the printer, or finally that for some one let or other he understands it not aright. And so let him reverently acknowledge his ignorance, lean and cleave to the faith of the Church as to an undoubted truth, leaving that text to be better perceived when it shall please our Lord with His light to reveal and disclose it. And in this wise shall he take a sure way by which he shall be sure of one of two things, that is to wit, either to perceive and understand the Scripture right, or else at the leastwise never in such wise to take it wrong, that ever may turn his soul to peril."

The Twenty-third Chapter

The messenger objects against the counsel of the author in that he would that the student of Scripture should lean to the commenters and unto natural reason, which he calls enemy to faith. And there upon the answer of the author to those objections, specially proving that reason is servant to faith and not enemy and must with faith and interpretation of Scripture needs be concurrent.

"Sir," said he, "I will not say nay but this way will do well. Howbeit I fear me that we were likely to build up many errors if we square our timber and stones by these three rules, men's glosses, reason and faith, not that we find in Scripture, but that we bring with us to Scripture. For first, as for the commenters that you speak of, either their comments tell us the same tale that the text does or else another. If they tell me the same, I believe them only because the text says the same. And if they tell me another, then believe I them not at all, nor naught I should, except I should believe men better than God. And as for reason, what greater enemy can you find to faith than reason is, which counterpleads faith in every point? And would you then send them twain forth to school together that can never agree together but be ready to fight together and either scratch out [the] other's eyes by the way? It seems also somewhat strange that when God has left us in His Holy Scripture well and sufficiently His doctrine whereby He would we should have warning of all such things as he would we should believe and do or leave undone, and has left us the Scripture for none other cause but for that it should stand unto us for the witness of his will, declared us by writing that we should not say nay but we were warned, and none other cause why the Scripture should be given us, but to tell us His pleasure and stir us to fulfill it we shall now not shape our faith after the Scripture, but first frame us a faith ourselves, and then shape the Scripture of God thereby, and make it agree thereto. This were indeed a good, easy way for a slothful mason that were an evil workman to make him a square and a ruler of lead, that when he list not to take the labor to hew the stone to the square, he may bend the square to the stone, and so shall he yet bring them together at the leastways."

"As for the old commenters," said I, "they tell you the same tale that the text does, but they tell it you more plain, as we shall more talk of hereafter. But surely you beguiled me now in that you set reason so short, for verily I would never have wot[11] that you would in Scripture like worse a wise man than an unreasonable reader. Nor I cannot see why you should reckon reason for an enemy to faith, except you reckon every man for your enemy that is

---

[11] *wot:* thought.

your better and hurts you not. Thus were one of your five wits enemy to another. And our feeling should abhor our sight because we may see further by four miles than we may feel. How can reason (but if reason be unreasonable) have more disdain to hear the truth of any point of faith than to see the proof of many things natural whereof reason can no more attain to the cause than it can in the articles of the faith. But still for any power that reason has to perceive the cause, she shall judge it impossible after she prove it true, but if she believe her eye better than her wit.

"When you see the adamant stone draw iron to it, it grieves not reason to look thereon but reason has a pleasure to behold the thing that passes her power to perceive. For it is as plainly against the rule of reason that a heavy body should move alone any other motion than downward or that any bodily thing should draw another without touching as is any article of the faith. Nor never was there yet cause by reason assigned that men may perceive for probable but only that it is a secret property of the stone, which is as much to say as 'I wot not what.' And yet as I say reason can believe that thing well enough and be not angry therewith, nor strive against it. And yet all the rules that ever she learned tell her still that it may not be."

"Yea," said he, "but a man's own eyes tell him that it may be. And that must needs content him."

"May a man then better trust his eyes," said I, "than his wit?"

"Yea, marry!" said he. "What may he better trust than his eyes?"

"His eyes may," said I, "be deceived and ween they see that they see not, if reason give over its hold except you think the juggler[12] blow his galls through the goblet's bottom[13] or cut your girdle[14] before your face in twenty pieces and make it whole again and

---

[12] *juggler:* magician.

[13] *blow his galls through the goblet's bottom:* the magician appears to put his balls through a goblet.

[14] *girdle:* belt.

put a knife into his eye and see never the worse. And turn a plum into a dog's turd in a boy's mouth."

Now happened it madly that even with this word came one of my folk and asked whether they should make ready for dinner!

"Abide," said I, "let us have better meat first!" And therewith your friend and I began to laugh.

"Well," said I, "make no haste yet for a little while." And so went he his way, half out of countenance, weening that he had done or said somewhat like a fool, as he was one that was not very wise indeed and wont so to do.

And then said I to your friend, "Now you see that reason is not so proud a dame as you take her for. She sees done indeed by nature that she cannot perceive how and is well contented therewith. She sees a fond fellow deceive her sight and her wit therewith, and takes it well and merrily, and is not angry that the juggler will not teach every man his craft. And ween you then that she will take it so highly that God Himself, her master and maker, should do what Him list, and then tell her what, and tell her not how? I pray you," said I, "that our Lord was born of a virgin, how know you?"

"Marry," said he, "by Scripture!"

"How know you," said I, "that you should believe the Scripture?"

"Marry," said he, "by faith!"

"Why," said I, "what does faith tell you therein?"

"Faith," said he, "tells me that Holy Scripture is things of truth written by the secret teaching of God."

"And whereby know you," said I, "that you should believe God?"

"Whereby?" said he. "This is a strange question. Every man," said he, "may well wot that!"

"That is true," said I. "But is there any horse, or any ass that wots that?"

"None," said he, "that I wot of but if Balaam's ass anything understood thereof. For he spoke like a good reasonable ass."

"If no brute beast can wit that," said I, "and every man may, what is the cause why that man may and other beasts may not?"

"Marry," said he, "for man has reason and they have none!"

"Ah well then," said I, "reason must he needs have then that shall perceive what he should believe. And so must reason not resist faith but walk with her and as her handmaid so wait upon her that as contrary as you take her, yet of a truth faith goes never without her. But likewise as if a maid be suffered to run on the bridle[15], or be cup-shotten[16], or wax too proud, she will then wax copious and chop logic with her mistress, and fare sometimes as she were frantic, so if reason be suffered to run out at riot and wax overly high-hearted and proud, she will not fail to fall in rebellion toward her mistress's faith. But on the other side, if she be well brought up and well guided and kept in good temper, she shall never disobey faith being in her right mind. And therefore let reason be well guided for surely faith goes never without her.

"Now, in the study of Scripture, in devising upon the sentence, in considering what you read, in pondering the purpose of divers comments, in comparing together divers texts that seem contrary and be not, albeit I deny not but that grace and God's especial help is the great thing therein, yet uses He for an instrument man's reason thereto. God helps us to eat also, but yet not without our mouth. Now as the hand is the more nimble by the use of some feats, and the legs and feet more swift and sure by custom of going and running, and the whole body the more wieldy and lusty by some kind of exercise, so is it no doubt but that reason is by study, labor, and exercise of logic, philosophy, and other liberal arts corroborated and quickened, and the judgment both in them and also in orators, laws, and stories much ripened. And albeit poets be with many men taken but for painted words, yet do they much help the judgment and make a man among other things well furnished of one special thing, without which all learning is half lame."

---

[15] *bridle:* run wild.

[16] *cup-shotten:* get drunk.

"What is that?" said he.

"Marry," said I, "a good mother wit! And therefore are, in mine opinion, these Lutherans in a mad mind that would now have all learning save Scripture only clean cast away, which things (if the time will serve) be as me thinks to be taken and had, and with reason brought as I said before, into the service of divinity. And as holy Saint Jerome said, the Hebrews well despoil the Egyptians when Christ's learned men take out of the pagan writers the riches and learning and wisdom that God gave unto them, and employ the same in the service of divinity about the profit of God's chosen children of Israel the Church of Christ, which he has of the hard, stony pagans made the children of Abraham."

INTRODUCTION TO PHILIPP MELANCHTHON'S *APOLOGY OF THE AUGSBURG CONFESSION*

DESPITE INTERNAL tensions and polemical opposition, the Lutheran reform movement in Germany gained far more traction than might have been expected, given the Catholic Church's history of brutal efficiency in suppressing many heresies of recent centuries. Politics had worked in the evangelicals' favor. True, the new Holy Roman Emperor, Charles V, was devoutly loyal to the Roman Church and was, on paper, the most powerful man that Europe had seen in centuries. In practice, though, he was distracted from dealing with Protestantism both by ongoing political rivalries with the French and the Papacy, and by the growing power of the Ottoman Turks. Under Suleiman the Magnificent, the Turks had won a crushing victory over King of Hungary, Charles's cousin, at the Battle of Mohács in 1526, and in 1529, with seemingly unstoppable momentum, they besieged Vienna itself.

Though the siege failed, the Turkish threat remained dire, and Charles recognized the urgent need to bring unity within Germany if he was to successfully oppose it. Accordingly, in 1530 he convened an Imperial Diet (an assembly of all the representatives in the realm) at Augsburg to try to re-establish religious peace and political unity. The Protestant princes of Germany, for their part, saw an unprecedented opportunity to win formal toleration for their cause, or even persuade the Emperor of its righteousness. Although both hopes proved over-optimistic, the Diet did represent a huge milestone for the new movement, as the Lutherans were invited to publicly present a confession of their faith before the Emperor, a confession that was to become the foundational document of the new movement: the Augsburg Confession.

Consisting of twenty-one articles of faith and seven articles rehearsing the abuses of Catholic practice that had been reformed, corrected, or abolished in the Protestant churches, the Confession was a remarkably irenic document. Its author was Philipp Melanchthon (1497–1560), Luther's close friend and colleague, who knew much better than Luther how to moderate his words when circumstances required, as they certainly did in this case. The twenty-one articles of faith focused on the positive content of Protestant faith (which on several points was identical with Catholic orthodoxy) rather than the errors of Catholic doctrine, and took care to condemn the excesses and errors of the Anabaptist radicals. But conciliatory as it may have been, the forthrightly Protestant character of the Confession was unmistakable: just four articles in, after declaring the doctrines of God, of sin, and of Christ, the Confession offered a succinct formulation of the Protestant doctrine of justification by faith:

> Also they [Protestants] teach that men cannot be justified before God by their own strength, merits, or works, but are freely justified for Christ's sake, through faith, when they believe that they are received into favor, and that their sins are forgiven for Christ's sake, who, by His death, has made satisfaction for our sins. This faith God imputes for righteousness in His sight.

A confutation of the confession was soon prepared by theologians loyal to Rome, with the implacable Johann Eck again in a leading role. In response, Melanchthon penned a lengthy *Apology* (or Defense) *of the Augsburg Confession*, offering what was at that point the fullest systematic articulation and defense of central Protestant doctrines. Particularly important was his thorough explanation of the article on justification, which appears in full here.

Although there is a fair bit of inside baseball here, with Melanchthon taking scholastic theologians to task on their use of distinctions such as "condign merit" and "congruent merit," to defend meritorious works while opposing Pelagianism, there is also a barrage of forthrightly biblical argumentation, particularly in the final section.

Melanchthon goes to some lengths to correct several key misunderstandings of the Protestant doctrine which are as common today as they were then. First, in the opening section he explains why it is that our righteousness cannot please God. It is not that we cannot do things that are outwardly just (what Melanchthon calls "civil righteousness," or "the righteousness of reason"), whether by reason alone or by unregenerate attention to the Law given in Scripture. Humans can, for instance, avoid theft, killing, and adultery, and many do. But, says Melanchthon,

> the Decalog[ue] requires not only outward civil works, which reason can in some way produce, but it also requires other things placed far above reason, namely, truly to fear God, truly to love God, truly to call upon God, truly to be convinced that God hears us, and to expect the aid of God in death and in all afflictions; finally, it requires obedience to God, in death and all afflictions.
> Confronted with the demands of such a heart-obedience, our sinful souls balk or despair, and can only enjoy fellowship with God by clinging to the promises given in Christ.

Melanchthon also corrects the misunderstanding that such saving faith is merely historical knowledge, accepting as true propositions about God and Christ's redeeming work in history. Rather, in perhaps the most beautiful passages of this whole section, Melanchthon declares, saving faith is the certainty or the certain trust in the heart, when, with my whole heart, I regard the promises of God as certain and true, through which there are offered me, without my merit, the forgiveness of sins, grace, and all salvation, through Christ the Mediator [...]. Faith is that my whole heart takes to itself this treasure. It is not my doing, not my presenting or giving, not my work or preparation, but that a heart comforts itself, and is perfectly confident with respect to this, namely, that God makes a present and gift to us, and not we to Him, that He sheds upon us every treasure of grace in Christ.

Thus Melanchthon also guards against the misconception that for Protestantism, faith itself becomes a meritorious work, as if justification by faith meant, "do this one meritorious thing, faith, and God will justify you." Rather, he clarifies, faith is no active work but a passive receiving of Christ's finished work: "For faith justifies and saves, not on the ground that it is a work in itself worthy, but only because it receives the promised mercy."

The Apology was certainly not to be the last word on the subject. But by crystallizing Protestant doctrine, especially on key points like justification, in lucid and systematic form, Melanchthon was to play almost as important a role in the new movement as Luther himself.

Further Reading

For further reading, see Charles P. Arand, Robert Kolb, and James A. Nestingen, *The Lutheran Confessions: History and Theology of the Book of Concord* (Minneapolis, MN: Fortress Press, 2012), chs. 4–5; Clyde L. Manschreck, *Melanchthon: The Quiet Reformer* (New York: Abingdon Press, 1958); Anthony N.S. Lane, *Justification by Faith in Protestant-Catholic Dialogue* (London: T&T Clark, 2006).

PHILIPP MELANCHTHON, *APOLOGY OF THE AUGSBURG CONFESSION* (1531)[1]

Article IV (II): Of Justification

1] IN THE Fourth, Fifth, Sixth, and, below, in the Twentieth Article, they condemn us, for teaching that men obtain remission of sins not because of their own merits, but freely for Christ's sake, through faith in Christ. They reject quite stubbornly both these statements. For they condemn us both for denying that men obtain remission of sins because of their own merits, and for affirming that, through faith, men obtain remission of sins, and through faith in Christ 2] are justified. But since in this controversy the chief topic of Christian doctrine is treated, which, understood aright, illumines and amplifies the honor of Christ, which is of especial service for the clear, correct understanding of the entire Holy Scriptures, and alone shows the way to the unspeakable treasure and right knowledge of Christ, and alone opens the door to the entire Bible, and brings necessary and most abundant consolation to devout consciences, we ask His Imperial Majesty to hear us with forbearance in regard to matters of such importance. 3] For since the adversaries understand neither what the remission of sins, nor what faith, nor what grace, nor what righteousness is, they sadly corrupt

---

[1] Taken from W.H.T. Dau and F. Bente, trans. and eds., *Triglot Concordia: The Symbolical Books of the Evangelical Lutheran Church: German-Latin-English* (St. Louis: Concordia Publishing House, 1921). Taken from "The Defense of the Augsburg Confession," at BookofConcord.org.

this topic, and obscure the glory and benefits of Christ, and rob devout consciences of the consolations offered in Christ. 4] But that we may strengthen the position of our Confession, and also remove the charges which the adversaries advance against us, certain things are to be premised in the beginning, in order that the sources of both kinds of doctrine, i.e., both that of our adversaries and our own, may be known.

5] All Scripture ought to be distributed into these two principal topics, the Law and the promises. For in some places it presents the Law, and in others the promise concerning Christ, namely, either when, in the Old Testament, it promises that Christ will come, and offers, for His sake, the remission of sins justification, and life eternal, or when, in the Gospel, in the New Testament, Christ Himself, since He has appeared, promises the remission of sins, justification, and life eternal. 6] Moreover, in this discussion, by Law we designate the Ten Commandments, wherever they are read in the Scriptures. Of the ceremonies and judicial laws of Moses we say nothing at present.

7] Of these two parts the adversaries select the Law, because human reason naturally understands, in some way, the Law (for it has the same judgment divinely written in the mind). The natural law agrees with the law of Moses, or the Ten Commandments] and by the Law they seek the remission of sins and justification. 8] Now, the Decalogue requires not only outward civil works, which reason can in some way produce, but it also requires other things placed far above reason, namely, truly to fear God, truly to love God, truly to call upon God, truly to be convinced that God hears us, and to expect the aid of God in death and in all afflictions; finally, it requires obedience to God, in death and all afflictions, so that we may not flee from these or refuse them when God imposes them.

9] Here the scholastics, having followed the philosophers, teach only a righteousness of reason, namely, civil works, and fabricate besides that without the Holy Ghost reason can love God above all things. For, as long as the human mind is at ease, and does not feel the wrath or judgment of God, it can imagine that it wishes to love God, that it wishes to do good for God's sake. But it is sheer hypocrisy. In this manner they teach that men merit the remission of sins by doing what is in them, i.e., if reason, grieving over sin, elicit an act of love to God, or 10] for God's sake be active in that which is good. And because this opinion naturally flatters men, it has brought forth and multiplied in the Church many services, monastic vows, abuses of the mass; and, with this opinion the one has, in the course of time, devised this act of worship and observances, the other that. 11] And in order that they might nourish and increase confidence in such works, they have affirmed that God necessarily gives grace to one thus working, by the necessity not of constraint but of immutability, not that He is constrained, but that this is the order which God will not transgress or alter.

12] In this opinion there are many great and pernicious errors, which it would be tedious to enumerate. Let the discreet reader think only of this: If this be Christian righteousness, what difference is there between philosophy and the doctrine of Christ? If we merit the remission of sins by these elicit acts that spring from our mind, of what benefit is Christ? If we can be justified by reason and the works of reason, wherefore is there need 13] of Christ or regeneration (as Peter declares, 1 Pet. 1:18ff)? And from these opinions the matter has now come to such a pass that many ridicule us because we teach that another than 14] the philosophic righteousness must be sought after. Alas! it has come to this, that even great theologians at Louvain, Paris, etc., have known nothing of any other godliness or righteousness (although every letter and syllable in Paul teaches otherwise) than the godliness which philosophers teach. And although we ought to regard this as a strange teaching, and ought to ridicule it, they rather ridicule us, yea, make a jest of Paul himself. We have heard that some after setting aside the Gospel, have, instead of a sermon, explained the ethics of Aristotle. (I myself have heard a great preacher who did not mention Christ and the Gospel, and preached the ethics of Aristotle. Is this not a childish, foolish way to preach to Christians?) Nor did such men err if those things are true which the adversaries defend (if the doctrine of the adversaries be true, the *Ethics* is a precious book of sermons, and a fine new Bible). For Aristotle wrote concerning civil morals so learnedly that nothing further concerning this need be demanded. 15] We see books extant in which certain sayings of Christ are compared with the sayings of Socrates, Zeno, and others, as though Christ had come for the purpose of delivering certain laws through which we might merit the remission of sins, as though we did not receive this 16] gratuitously because of His merits. Therefore, if we here receive the doctrine of the adversaries, that by the works of reason we merit the remission of sins and justification, there will be no difference between philosophic, or certainly pharisaic, and Christian righteousness.

17] Although the adversaries, not to pass by Christ altogether, require a knowledge of the history concerning Christ, and ascribe to Him that it is His merit that a habit is given us or, as they say, *prima gratia* ["first grace"], which they understand as a habit, inclining us the more readily to love God; yet, what they ascribe to this habit is of little importance (is a feeble, paltry, small, poor operation, that would be ascribed to Christ), because they imagine that the acts of the will are of the same kind before and after this habit. They imagine that the will can love God, but nevertheless this habit stimulates it to do the same the more cheerfully. And they bid us first merit this habit by preceding merits; then they bid us merit by the works of the Law an increase of this habit and 18] life eternal. Thus they bury Christ, so that men may not avail themselves of Him as a Mediator, and believe that for His sake they freely receive remission of sins and reconciliation, but may dream that by their own fulfilment of the Law they merit the remission of sins, and that by their own fulfilment of the Law they are accounted righteous before God, while, nevertheless, the Law is never satisfied, since reason does nothing except certain civil works, and, in the mean time, neither in the heart fears God, nor truly believes that God cares for it. And although they speak of this habit, yet, without the righteousness of faith, neither the love of God can exist in man, nor can it be understood what the love of God is.

19] Their feigning a distinction between *meritum congrui* and *meritum condigni* [due merit and true, complete merit] is only an artifice in order not to appear openly to Pelagianize. For, if God necessarily gives grace for the *meritum congrui* [due merit], it is no longer *meritum congrui*, but *meritum condigni* [a true duty and complete merit]. But they do not know what they are saying. After this habit of love [is there], they imagine that man can acquire merit *de condigno*. And yet they bid us doubt whether there be a habit present. How, therefore, do they know whether they acquire merit *de congruo* or 20] *de condigno* [in full, or half]? But this whole matter was fabricated by idle men (but, good God! these are mere inane ideas and dreams of idle, wretched, inexperienced men, who do not much reduce the Bible to practice), who did not know how the remission of sins occurs, and how, in the judgment of God and terrors of conscience, trust in works is driven out of us. Secure hypocrites always judge that they acquire merit *de condigno*, whether the habit be present or be not present, because men naturally trust in their own righteousness, but terrified consciences waver and hesitate, and then seek and accumulate other works in order to find rest. Such consciences never think that they acquire merit *de condigno*, and they rush into despair unless they hear, in addition to the doctrine of the Law, the Gospel concerning the gratuitous remission of sins and the righteousness of faith. Thus some stories are told that when the Barefooted monks had in vain praised their order and good works to some good consciences in the hour of death, they at last had to be silent concerning their order and St. Franciscus, and to say: "Dear man, Christ has died for you." This revived and refreshed in trouble, and alone gave peace and comfort.

21] Thus the adversaries teach nothing but the righteousness of reason, or certainly of the Law, upon which they look just as the Jews upon the veiled face of Moses; and, in secure hypocrites who think that they satisfy the Law, they excite presumption and empty confidence in works, they place men on a sand foundation, their own works, and contempt of the grace of Christ. On the contrary, they drive timid consciences to despair, which laboring with doubt, never can experience what faith is, and how efficacious it is; thus, at last they utterly despair.

22] Now, we think concerning the righteousness of reason thus, namely, that God requires it, and that, because of God's commandment, the honorable works which the Decalogue commands must necessarily be performed, according to the passage Gal. 3:24: The Law was our schoolmaster;" likewise 1 Tim. 1:9: "The Law is made for the ungodly." For God wishes those who are carnal, gross sinners, to be restrained by civil discipline, and to maintain this, He has given laws, letters, doctrine, magistrates, penalties. 23] And this righteousness reason, by its own strength, can, to a certain extent, work, although it is often overcome by natural weakness, and by the devil impelling it to 24] manifest crimes. Now, although we cheerfully assign this righteousness of reason the praises that are due it (for this corrupt nature has no greater good: in this life and in a worldly nature, nothing is ever better than uprightness and virtue, and Aristotle says aright: "Neither the evening star nor the morning star is more beautiful than righteousness," and God also honors it with bodily rewards), yet it ought not to be praised with reproach to Christ.

25] For it is false, I thus conclude, and am certain that it is a fiction, and not true, that we merit the remission of sins by our works.

26] False also is this, that men are accounted righteous before God because of the righteousness of reason, works and external piety.

27] False also is this that reason, by its own strength, is able to love God above all things, and to fulfil God's Law, namely, truly to fear God, to be truly confident that God hears prayer, to be willing to obey God in death and other dispensations of God, not to covet what belongs to others, etc.; although reason can work civil works.

28] False also and dishonoring Christ is this, that men do not sin who, without grace, do the commandments of God, who keep the commandments of God merely in an external manner, without the Spirit and grace in their hearts.

29] We have testimonies for this our belief, not only from the Scriptures, but also from the Fathers. For in opposition to the Pelagians, Augustine contends at great length that grace is not given because of our merits. And in *De Natura et Gratia* he says: "If natural ability, through the free will, suffice both for learning to know how one ought to live and for living aright, then Christ has died in vain, then the offense of the Cross is made void." 30] Why may I not also here cry out? Yea, I will cry out, and, with Christian grief, will chide them: "Christ has become of no effect unto you whosoever of you are justified by the Law; ye are fallen from grace" (Gal. 5:4; cf. 2:21). For they, being ignorant of God's righteousness, and going about to establish their own righteousness, have not submitted themselves unto the righteousness of God. "For Christ is the end of the Law for righteousness to every one that believeth" (Rom. 10:3, 4). 31] And John 8:36: "If the Son therefore shall make you free, ye shall be free indeed." Therefore by reason we cannot be freed from sins and merit the remission of sins. And in John 3:5 it is written: "Except a man be born of water and of the Spirit, he cannot enter into the kingdom of God." But if it is necessary to be born again of the Holy Ghost, the righteousness of reason does not justify us before God, and does not 32] fulfil the Law, Rom. 3:23: "All have come short of the glory of God," i.e., are destitute of the wisdom and righteousness of God, which acknowledges and glorifies God. Likewise Rom. 8:7–8: "The carnal mind is enmity against God; for it is not subject to the Law of God, neither indeed can be. So then they that are in the flesh cannot please God." 33] These testimonies are so manifest that, to use the words of Augustine which he employed in this case, they do not need an acute understanding, but only an attentive hearer. If the carnal mind is enmity against God, the flesh certainly does not love God; if it cannot be subject to the Law of God, it cannot love

God. If the carnal mind is enmity against God, the flesh sins, even when we do external civil works. If it cannot be subject to the Law of God, it certainly sins even when, 34] according to human judgment, it possesses deeds that are excellent and worthy of praise. The adversaries consider only the precepts of the Second Table which contain civil righteousness that reason understands. Content with this, they think that they satisfy the Law of God. In the mean time they do not see the First Table which commands that we love God, that we declare as certain that God is angry with sin, that we truly fear God, that we declare as certain that God hears prayer. But the human heart without the Holy Ghost either in security despises God's judgment, or in punishment flees from, and 35] hates, God when He judges. Therefore it does not obey the First Table. Since, therefore, contempt of God, and doubt concerning the Word of God, and concerning the threats and promises, inhere in human nature, men truly sin, even when, without the Holy Ghost, they do virtuous works, because they do them with a wicked heart, according to Rom. 14:23: "Whatsoever is not of faith is sin." For such persons perform their works with contempt of God, just as Epicurus does not believe that God cares for him, or that he is regarded or heard by God. This contempt vitiates works seemingly virtuous, because God judges the heart.

36] Lastly, it was very foolish for the adversaries to write that men who are under eternal wrath merit the remission of sins by an act of love, which springs from their mind since it is impossible to love God, unless the remission of sins be apprehended first by faith. For the heart, truly feeling that God is angry, cannot love God, unless He be shown to have been reconciled. As long as He terrifies us, and seems to cast us into eternal death, human nature is not able to take courage, so as to love 37] a wrathful, judging, and punishing God (poor, weak nature must lose heart and courage, and must tremble before such great wrath, which so fearfully terrifies and punishes, and can never feel a spark of love before God Himself comforts). It is easy for idle men to feign such dreams concerning love, as, that a person guilty of mortal sin can love God above all things, because they do not feel what the wrath or judgment of God is. But in agony of conscience and in conflicts with Satan conscience experiences the emptiness of these philosophical speculations. 38] Paul says, Rom. 4:15: "The Law worketh wrath." He does not say that by the Law men merit the remission of sins. For the Law always accuses and terrifies consciences. Therefore it does not justify, because conscience terrified by the Law flees from the judgment of God. Therefore they err who trust that by the Law, by their own works, they merit the remission of sins. 39] It is sufficient for us to have said these things concerning the righteousness of reason or of the Law, which the adversaries teach. For after a while, when we will declare our belief concerning the righteousness of faith, the subject itself will compel us to adduce more testimonies, which also will be of service in overthrowing the errors of the adversaries which we have thus far reviewed.

40] Because, therefore, men by their own strength cannot fulfil the Law of God, and all are under sin, and subject to eternal wrath and death, on this account we cannot be freed by the Law from sin and be justified, but the promise of the remission of sins and of justification has been given us for Christ's sake, who was given for us in order that He might make satisfaction for the sins of the world, and has been appointed as the only 41] Mediator and Propitiator. And this promise has not the condition of our merits (it does not read thus: Through Christ you have grace, salvation etc., if you merit it), but freely offers the remission of sins and justification as Paul says in Rom. 11:6: "If it be of works, then is it no more grace." And in another place, Rom. 3:21: "The righteousness of God without the Law is manifested," i.e., the remission of sins is freely offered. Nor does reconciliation depend 42] upon our merits. Because if the remission of sins were to depend upon our merits, and reconciliation were from the Law, it would be useless. For as we do not fulfil the Law, it would also follow that we would never obtain the promise of reconciliation. Thus Paul reasons, Rom. 4:14: "For if they which are of the Law be heirs, faith is made void, and the promise made of none effect." For if the promise would require the condition of our merits and the Law, which we never fulfil, it would follow that the promise would be useless.

43] But since justification is obtained through the free promise it follows that we cannot justify ourselves. Otherwise wherefore would there be need to promise? And why should Paul so highly extol and praise grace? For since the promise cannot be received except by faith, the Gospel which is properly the promise of the remission of sins and of justification for Christ's sake, proclaims the righteousness of faith in Christ, which the Law does not teach. Nor is this the righteousness of the Law. 44] For the Law requires of us our works and our perfection. But the Gospel freely offers, for Christ's sake, to us, who have been vanquished by sin and death, reconciliation which is received not by works, but by faith alone. This faith brings to God not confidence in one's own merits, but only confidence in the promise, or 45] the mercy promised in Christ. This special faith, therefore, by which an individual believes that for Christ's sake his sins are remitted him, and that for Christ's sake God is reconciled and propitious, obtains remission of sins and justifies us. And because in repentance, i.e. in terrors, it comforts and encourages hearts, it regenerates us and brings the Holy Ghost that then we may be able to fulfil God's Law, namely, to love God, truly to fear God, truly to be confident that God hears prayer, and to obey God in all afflictions; it mortifies concupiscence etc. 46] Thus, because faith, which freely receives the remission of sins, sets Christ, the Mediator and Propitiator, against God's wrath, it does not present our merits or our love (which would be tossed aside like a little feather by a hurricane). This faith is the true knowledge of Christ, and avails itself of the benefits of Christ, and regenerates hearts, and precedes the fulfilling of the Law. And 47] of this faith not a syllable exists in the doctrine of our adversaries. Hence we find fault with the adversaries, equally because they teach only the righteousness of the Law, and because they do not teach the righteousness of the Gospel, which proclaims the righteousness of faith in Christ.

What Is Justifying Faith?

48] The adversaries feign that faith is only a knowledge of the history, and therefore teach that it can coexist with mortal sin. Hence they say nothing concerning faith, by which Paul so frequently says that men are justified, because those who are accounted righteous before God do not live in mortal sin. But that faith which justifies is not merely a knowledge of history, (not merely this, that I know the stories of Christ's birth, suffering, etc.—that even the devils know) but it is to assent to the promise of God, in which, for Christ's sake, the remission of sins and justification are freely offered. It is the certainty or the certain trust in the heart, when, with my whole heart, I regard the promises of God as certain and true, through which there are offered me, without my merit, the forgiveness of sins, grace, and all salvation, through Christ the Mediator. And that no one may suppose that it is mere knowledge, we will add further: it is to wish and to receive the offered promise of the remission of sins and of justification. Faith is that my whole heart takes to itself this treasure. It is not my doing, not my presenting or giving, not my work or preparation, but that a heart comforts itself, and is perfectly confident with respect to this, namely, that God makes a present and gift to us, and not we to Him, that He sheds upon us every treasure of grace in Christ.

49] And the difference between this faith and the righteousness of the Law can be easily discerned. Faith is the *latreia* [divine service], which receives the benefits offered by God; the righteousness of the Law is the *latreia* [divine service] which offers to God our merits. By faith God wishes to be worshiped in this way, that we receive from Him those things which He promises and offers.

50] Now, that faith signifies, not only a knowledge of the history, but such faith as assents to the promise, Paul plainly testifies when he says, Rom. 4:16: "Therefore it is of faith, to the end the promise might be sure." For he judges that the promise cannot be received unless by faith. Wherefore he puts them together as things that belong to one another, and connects promise and faith.

There Paul fastens and binds together these two, thus: Wherever there is a promise faith is required, and conversely, wherever faith is required, there must be a promise. 51] Although it will be easy to decide what faith is if we consider the Creed, where this article certainly stands: The forgiveness of sins. Therefore it is not enough to believe that Christ was born, suffered, was raised again, unless we add also this article, which is the purpose of the history: The forgiveness of sins. To this article the rest must be referred, namely, that for Christ's sake, and not for the sake of our merits, 52] forgiveness of sins is given us. For what need was there that Christ was given for our sins if for our sins our merits can make satisfaction?

53] As often, therefore, as we speak of justifying faith, we must keep in mind that these three objects concur: the promise, and that, too, gratuitous, and the merits of Christ, as the price and propitiation. The promise is received by faith; the "gratuitous" excludes our merits and signifies that the benefit is offered only through mercy; the merits of Christ are the price, because there must be a certain propitiation for our sins. 54] Scripture frequently implores mercy, and the holy Fathers often say that we 55] are saved by mercy. As often, therefore, as mention is made of mercy, we must keep in mind that faith is there required, which receives the promise of mercy. And, again, as often as we speak of faith, we wish an object to be understood, namely, the promised mercy. 56] For faith justifies and saves, not on the ground that it is a work in itself worthy, but only because it receives the promised mercy.

57] And throughout the prophets and the psalms this worship, this *latreia*, is highly praised, although the Law does not teach the gratuitous remission of sins. But the Fathers knew the promise concerning Christ, that God for Christ's sake wished to remit sins. Therefore, since they understood that Christ would be the price for our sins, they knew that our works are not a price for so great a matter, could not pay so great a debt. Accordingly, they received gratuitous mercy and remission of sins by faith, just as the saints in the New Testament. 58] Here belong those frequent repetitions concerning mercy and faith, in the psalms and the prophets, as this, Ps. 130:3: "If Thou, Lord, shouldest mark iniquities, O Lord, who shall stand?" Here David confesses his sins, and does not recount his merits. He adds: "But there is forgiveness with Thee." Here he comforts himself by his trust in God's mercy, and he cites the promise: "My soul doth wait, and in His Word do I hope," i.e., because Thou hast promised the remission of sins, 59] I am sustained by this Thy promise. Therefore the Fathers also were justified, not by the Law, but by the promise and faith. And it is amazing that the adversaries extenuate faith to such a degree, although they see that it is everywhere praised as an eminent service, as in Ps. 50:15: "Call upon Me in the day of trouble: I will deliver thee." 60] Thus God wishes Himself to be known, thus He wishes Himself to be worshiped, that from Him we receive benefits, and receive them, too, because of His mercy, and not because of our merits. This is the richest consolation in all afflictions,physical or spiritual, in life or in death, as all godly persons know. And such consolations the adversaries abolish when they extenuate and disparage faith, and teach only that by means of works and merits men treat with God, that we treat with God, the great Majesty, by means of our miserable, beggarly works and merits.

That Faith in Christ Justifies

61] In the first place, lest any one may think that we speak concerning an idle knowledge of the history, we must declare how faith is obtained (how the heart begins to believe). Afterward we will show both that it justifies, and how this ought to be understood, and we will explain the objections of the adversaries. 62] Christ, in the last chapter of Luke (24:47), commands that repentance and remission of sins should be preached in His name. For the Gospel convicts all men that they are under sin, that they all are subject to eternal wrath and death, and offers, for Christ's sake, remission of sin and justification, which is received by faith. The preaching of repentance, which accuses us, terrifies consciences with true and grave terrors. For the preaching of repentance, or this declaration of the Gospel: Amend your lives! Repent! when it truly penetrates the heart, terrifies the conscience, and is no jest, but a great terror, in which the conscience feels its misery and sin, and the wrath of God. In these, hearts ought again to receive consolation. This happens if they believe the promise of Christ, that for His sake we have remission of sins. This faith, encouraging and consoling in these fears, receives remission of sins, justifies and quickens. For this consolation is a new and spiritual 63] life (a new birth and a new life). These things are plain and clear, and can be understood by the pious, and have testimonies of the Church (as is to be seen in the conversion of Paul and Augustine). The adversaries nowhere can say how the Holy Ghost is given. They imagine that the Sacraments confer the Holy Ghost *ex opere operato*, without a good emotion in the recipient, as though indeed, the gift of the Holy Ghost were an idle matter.

64] But since we speak of such faith as is not an idle thought, but of that which liberates from death and produces a new life in hearts, which is such a new light, life, and force in the heart as to renew our heart, mind, and spirit, makes new men of us and new creatures, and is the work of the Holy Ghost; this does not coexist with mortal sin (for how can light and darkness coexist?) but as long as it is present, produces good 65] fruits, as we will say after a while. For concerning the conversion of the wicked, or concerning the mode of regeneration, what can be said that is more simple and more clear? Let them, from so great an array of writers, adduce a single commentary upon the *Sententiae* that speaks 66] of the mode of regeneration. When they speak of the habit of love, they imagine that men merit it through works, and they do not teach that it is received through the Word, precisely as also the Anabaptists teach at this time. 67] But God cannot be treated with, God cannot be apprehended, except through the Word. Accordingly, justification occurs through the Word, just as Paul says, Rom. 1:16: "The Gospel is the power of God unto salvation to every one that believeth." Likewise Rom. 10:17: "Faith cometh by hearing." And proof can be derived even from this that faith justifies, because, if justification occurs only through the Word, and the Word is apprehended only by faith, it follows that faith justifies. 68] But there are other and more important reasons. We have said these things thus far in order that we might show the mode of regeneration, and that the nature of faith (what is, or is not, faith), concerning which we speak, might be understood.

69] Now we will show that faith, and nothing else, justifies. Here, in the first place, readers must be admonished of this, that just as it is necessary to maintain this sentence: Christ is Mediator, so is it necessary to defend that faith justifies without works. For how will Christ be Mediator if in justification we do not use Him as Mediator; if we do not hold that for His sake we are accounted righteous? But to believe is to trust in the merits of Christ, that for His sake God certainly wishes to be reconciled with us. 70] Likewise, just as we ought to maintain that, apart from the Law, the promise of Christ is necessary, so also is it needful to maintain that faith justifies. (For the Law does not preach the forgiveness of sin by grace.) For the Law cannot be performed unless the Holy Ghost be first received. It is, therefore, needful to maintain that the promise of Christ is necessary. But this cannot be received except by faith. Therefore, those who deny that faith justifies, teach nothing but the Law, both Christ and the Gospel being set aside.

71] But when it is said that faith justifies, some perhaps understand it of the beginning, namely, that faith is the beginning of justification or preparation for justification, so that not faith itself is that through which we are accepted by God, but the works which follow; and they dream, accordingly, that faith is highly praised, because it is the beginning. For great is the importance of the beginning, as they commonly say, "The beginning is half of everything," just as if one would say that grammar makes the teachers of all arts, because it prepares for other arts, although in fact it is his own art that renders every one an artist. We do not believe thus concerning faith, but we maintain this, that properly and truly, by faith itself, we are for Christ's sake accounted righteous, or are acceptable to God. 72] And because "to be justified" means that out of unjust men just men are made, or born again, it means also that they are pronounced or accounted just. For Scripture speaks in both ways. (The term "to be justified" is used in two ways: to denote, being converted or regenerated; again, being accounted righteous.) Accordingly we wish first to show this, that faith alone makes of an unjust, a just man, i.e., receives remission of sins.

73] The particle alone offends some, although even Paul says, Rom. 3:28: "We conclude that a man is justified by faith, without the deeds of the Law." Again, Eph. 2:8: "It is the gift of God; not of works, lest any man should boast." Again, Rom. 3:24: "Being justified freely." If the exclusive alone displeases, let them remove from Paul also the exclusives "freely," "not of works," "it is the gift," etc. For these also are very strong exclusives. It is, however, the opinion of merit that we exclude. We do not exclude the Word or Sacraments, as the adversaries falsely charge us. For we have said above that faith is conceived from the Word, and we honor the ministry of the Word in the highest degree. 74] Love also and works must follow faith. Wherefore, they are not excluded so as not to follow, but confidence in the merit of love or of works is excluded in justification. And this we will clearly show.

That We Obtain Remission of Sins by Faith Alone in Christ

75] We think that even the adversaries acknowledge that, in justification, the remission of sins is necessary first. For we all are under sin. Wherefore we reason thus:

76] To attain the remission of sins is to be justified, according to Ps. 32:1: "Blessed 77] is he whose transgression is forgiven." By faith alone in Christ, not through love, not because of love or works, do we acquire the remission of sins, although love follows faith. 78] Therefore by faith alone we are justified, understanding justification as the making of a righteous man out of an unrighteous, or that he be regenerated.

79] It will thus become easy to declare the minor premise (that we obtain forgiveness of sin by faith, not by love) if we know how the remission of sins occurs. The adversaries with great indifference dispute whether the remission of sins and the infusion of grace are the same change. Being idle men, they did not know what to answer. In the remission of sins, the terrors of sin and of eternal death, in the heart, must be overcome, as Paul testifies, 1 Cor. 15:56: "The sting of death is sin, and the strength of sin is the Law. But thanks be to God, which giveth us the victory through our Lord Jesus Christ." That is, sin terrifies consciences, this occurs through the Law, which shows the wrath of God against sin, but we gain the victory through Christ. How? By faith, when we comfort ourselves by confidence in the mercy promised for 80] Christ's sake. Thus, therefore, we prove the minor proposition. The wrath of God cannot be appeased if we set against it our own works, because Christ has been set forth as a Propitiator, so that for His sake, the Father may become reconciled to us. But Christ is not apprehended as a Mediator except by faith. Therefore, by faith alone we obtain remission of sins, when we comfort our hearts with confidence in the mercy promised for 81] Christ's sake. Likewise Paul, in Rom. 5:2, says: "By whom also we have access," and adds, "by faith." Thus, therefore, we are reconciled to the Father, and receive remission of sins when we are comforted with confidence in the mercy promised for Christ's sake. The adversaries regard Christ as Mediator and Propitiator for this reason, namely, that He has merited the habit of love; they do not urge us to use Him now as Mediator, but, as though Christ were altogether buried, they imagine that we have access through our own works, and, through these, merit this habit, and afterwards, by this love, come to God. Is not this to bury Christ altogether, and to take away the entire doctrine of faith? Paul on the contrary, teaches that we have access, i.e., reconciliation, through Christ. And to show how this occurs, he adds that we have access by faith. By faith, therefore, for Christ's sake, we receive remission of sins. We cannot set our own love and our own works over against God's wrath.

82] Secondly, it is certain that sins are forgiven for the sake of Christ, as Propitiator, Rom. 3:25: "Whom God hath set forth to be a propitiation." Moreover, Paul adds: "through faith." Therefore this Propitiator thus benefits us, when by faith we apprehend the mercy promised in Him, and set it against the wrath and judgment of God. And to the same effect it is written in Heb. 4:14, 16: "Seeing, then, that we have a great High Priest," etc., "let us therefore come with confidence." For the Apostle bids us come to God, not with confidence in our own merits, but with confidence in Christ as a High Priest; therefore he requires faith.

83] Thirdly. Peter, in Acts 10:43, says: "To Him give all the prophets witness that through His name, whosoever believeth on Him, shall receive remission of sins." How could this be said more clearly? We receive remission of sins, he says, through His name, i.e., for His sake; therefore, not for the sake of our merits, not for the sake of our contrition, attrition, love, worship, works. And he adds: When we believe in Him. Therefore he requires faith. For we cannot apprehend the name of Christ except by faith. Besides he cites the agreement of all the prophets. This is truly to cite the authority of the Church. For when all the holy prophets bear witness, that is certainly a glorious, great excellent, powerful decretal and testimony. But of this topic we will speak again after a while, when treating of repentance.

84] Fourthly, remission of sins is something promised for Christ's sake. Therefore it cannot be received except by faith alone. For a promise cannot be received except by faith alone. Rom. 4:16: "Therefore it is of faith that it might be by grace, to the end that the promise might be sure;" as though he were to say: "If the matter were to depend upon our merits, the promise would be uncertain and useless, because we never could determine when we would have sufficient merit." And this, experienced consciences can easily understand, and would not, for a thousand worlds have our salvation depend upon ourselves. Accordingly, Paul says, in Galatian 3:22: "But the Scripture hath concluded all under sin, that the promise by faith of Jesus Christ might be given to them that believe." He takes merit away from us, because he says that all are guilty and concluded under sin; then he adds that the promise, namely, of the remission of sins and of justification, is given, and adds how the promise can be received, namely, by faith. And this reasoning, derived from the nature of a promise, is the chief reasoning (a veritable rock) in Paul, and is often repeated. Nor can anything be devised or imagined whereby this argument of Paul can be overthrown. Wherefore 85] let not good minds suffer themselves to be forced from the conviction that we receive remission of sins for Christ's sake, only through faith. In this they have sure and firm consolation against the terrors of sin, and against eternal death, and against all the gates of hell. Everything else is a foundation of sand that sinks in trials.

86] But since we receive remission of sins and the Holy Ghost by faith alone, faith alone justifies, because those reconciled are accounted righteous and children of God, not on account of their own purity, but through mercy for Christ's sake, provided only they by faith apprehend this mercy. Accordingly, Scripture testifies that by faith we are accounted righteous (Rom. 3:26). We, therefore, will add testimonies which clearly declare that faith is that very righteousness by which we are accounted righteous before God, namely, not because it is a work that is in itself worthy, but because it receives the promise by which God has promised that for Christ's sake He wishes to be propitious to those believing in Him, or because He knows that Christ of God is made unto us wisdom, and righteousness, and sanctification, and redemption (1 Cor. 1:30).

87] In the Epistle to the Romans, Paul discusses this topic especially, and declares that, when we believe that God, for Christ's sake, is reconciled to us, we are justified freely by faith. And this proposition, which contains the statement of the entire discussion (the principal matter of all Epistles, yea, of the entire Scriptures), he maintains in the third chapter: We conclude that a man is justified by faith, without the deeds of the Law (Rom. 3:28). Here the adversaries interpret that this refers to Levitical ceremonies, not to other virtuous works. But Paul speaks not only of the ceremonies, but of the whole Law. For he quotes afterward (7:7) from the Decalogue: "Thou shalt not covet." And if moral works (that are not Jewish ceremonies) would merit the remission of sins and justification, there would also be no need of Christ and the promise, and all that Paul speaks of the promise would be overthrown. He would also have been wrong in writing to the Ephesians (2:8): "By grace are ye saved through faith, and that not of yourselves; it is the gift of God, not of works." Paul likewise refers to Abraham and David. "But they had the command of God concerning circumcision" (Rom. 4:1, 6). Therefore, if any works justified, these works must also have justified at the time that they had a command. But Augustine teaches correctly that Paul speaks of the entire Law, as he discusses at length in his book, *Of the Spirit and Letter*, where he says finally: "These matters, therefore having been considered and treated, according to the ability that the Lord has thought worthy to give us, we infer that man is not justified by the precepts of a good life, but by faith in Jesus Christ."

88] And lest we may think that the sentence that faith justifies, fell from Paul inconsiderately, he fortifies and confirms this by a long discussion in the fourth chapter to the Romans, and afterwards repeats it in all his epistles. 89] Thus he says: "To him that worketh is the reward not reckoned of grace, but of debt. But to him that worketh not, but believeth on Him that justifieth the ungodly, his faith is counted for righteousness" (Rom. 4:4, 5). Here he clearly says that faith itself is imputed for righteousness. Faith, therefore, is that thing which God declares to be righteousness, and he adds that it is imputed freely, and says that it could not be imputed freely, if it were due on account of works. Wherefore he excludes also the merit of moral works (not only Jewish ceremonies, but all other good works). For if justification before God were due to these, faith would not be imputed for righteousness 90] without works. And afterwards: For we say that faith was reckoned to Abraham for righteousness" (Rom. 4:9). 91] Romans 5:1 says: "Being justified by faith, we have peace with God," i.e., we have consciences that are tranquil and joyful 92] before God. Rom. 10:10: "With the heart man believeth unto righteousness." Here he declares that faith is 93] the righteousness of the heart. Gal. 2:16: "We have believed in Christ Jesus that we might be justified by the faith of Christ, and not by the works of the Law." Eph. 2:8: "For by grace are ye saved through faith, and that not of yourselves; it is the gift of God; not of works, lest any man should boast."

94] John 1:12: "To them gave He power to become the sons of God, even to them that believe on His name, which were born, not of blood, nor of the will of the flesh, nor of the will of man, but of God." 95] John 3:14-15: "As Moses lifted up the serpent in the wilderness, even so must the Son of man be lifted up, that whosoever believeth in Him should not perish." 96] Likewise, 3:17: "For God sent not His Son into the world to condemn the world, but that the world through Him might be saved. He that believeth on Him is not condemned."

97] Acts 13:38–39: "Be it known unto you therefore, men and brethren, that through this Man is preached unto you the forgiveness of sins; and by Him all that believe are justified from all things from which ye could not be justified by the Law of Moses." How could the office of Christ and justification be declared more clearly? The Law, he says, did not justify. Therefore Christ was given, that we may believe that for His sake we are justified. He plainly denies justification to the Law. Hence, for Christ's sake we are accounted righteous when we believe that God, for His sake, has been reconciled to us. 98] Acts 4:11–12: "This is the stone which was set at naught of you builders, which is become the head of the corner. Neither is there salvation in any other; for there is none other name under heaven given among men whereby we must be saved." But the name of Christ is apprehended only by faith. I cannot believe in the name of Christ in any other way than when I hear His merit preached, and lay hold of that. Therefore, by confidence in the name of Christ, and not by confidence in our works, we are saved. For "the name" here signifies the cause which is mentioned, because of which salvation is attained. And to call upon the name of Christ is to trust in the name of Christ, as the cause or price because of which we are saved. 99] Acts 15:9: "Purifying their hearts by faith." Wherefore that faith of which the Apostles speak is not idle knowledge, but a reality, receiving the Holy Ghost and justifying us (not a mere knowledge of history, but a strong powerful work of the Holy Ghost, which changes hearts).

100] Habakkuk 2:4: "The just shall live by his faith." Here he says, first, that men are just by faith, by which they believe that God is propitious, and he adds that the same faith quickens, because this faith produces in the heart peace and joy and eternal life, which begins in the present life.

101] Isaiah 53:11: "By His knowledge shall He justify many." But what is the knowledge of Christ unless to know the benefits of Christ, the promises which by the Gospel He has scattered broadcast in the world? And to know these benefits is properly and truly to believe in Christ, to believe that that which God has promised for Christ's sake He will certainly fulfill.

102] But Scripture is full of such testimonies since, in some places, it presents the Law and in others the promises concerning Christ, and the remission of sins, and the free acceptance of the sinner for Christ's sake.

103] Here and there among the Fathers similar testimonies are extant. For Ambrose says in his letter to a certain Irenaeus: "Moreover, the world was subject to Him by the Law for the reason that, according to the command of the Law, all are indicted, and yet, by the works of the Law, no one is justified, i.e., because, by the Law, sin is perceived, but guilt is not discharged. The Law, which made all sinners, seemed to have done injury, but when the Lord Jesus Christ came, He forgave to all sin which no one could avoid, and, by the shedding of His own blood, blotted out the handwriting which was against us. This is what he says in Romans 5:20: 'The Law entered that the offense might abound. But where sin abounded, grace did much more abound.' Because after the whole world became subject, He took away the sin of the whole world, as he [John] testified, saying John 1:29: 'Behold the Lamb of

God, which taketh away the sin of the world.' And on this account let no one boast of works, because no one is justified by his deeds. But he who is righteous has it given him because he was justified after the laver of Baptism. Faith, therefore, is that which frees through the blood of Christ, because he is blessed 'whose transgression is forgiven, whose sin is covered'" (Ps. 32:1). 104] These are the words of Ambrose, which clearly favor our doctrine; he denies justification to works, and ascribes to faith that it sets us free 105] through the blood of Christ. Let all the Sententiarists, who are adorned with magnificent titles, be collected into one heap. For some are called angelic; others, subtle, and others irrefragable (that is, doctors who cannot err). When all these have been read and reread, they will not be of as much aid for understanding Paul as is this one passage of Ambrose.

106] To the same effect, Augustine writes many things against the Pelagians. In *Of the Spirit and Letter* he says: "The righteousness of the Law, namely, that he who has fulfilled it shall live in it, is set forth for this reason, that when any one has recognized his infirmity he may attain and work the same and live in it, conciliating the Justifier not by his own strength nor by the letter of the Law itself (which cannot be done), but by faith. Except in a justified man, there is no right work wherein he who does it may live." But justification is obtained by faith. Here he clearly says that the Justifier is conciliated by faith, and that justification is obtained by faith. And a little after: "By the Law we fear God; by faith we hope in God. But to those fearing punishment grace is hidden; and the soul laboring, etc., under this fear betakes itself by faith to God's mercy, in order that He may give what He commands." Here he teaches that by the Law hearts are terrified, but by faith they receive consolation. He also teaches us to apprehend, by faith, mercy, before we attempt to fulfil the Law. We will shortly cite certain other passages.

107] Truly, it is amazing that the adversaries are in no way moved by so many passages of Scripture, which clearly ascribe justification to faith, and, indeed, 108] deny it to works. Do they think that the same is repeated so often for no purpose? Do they think that these words fell inconsiderately from the Holy Ghost? 109] But they have also devised sophistry whereby they elude them. They say that these passages of Scripture which speak of faith ought to be received as referring to a *fides formata,* i.e., they do not ascribe justification to faith except on account of love. Yea, they do not, in any way, ascribe justification to faith, but only to love, because they dream that faith can 110] coexist with mortal sin. Whither does this tend, unless that they again abolish the promise and return to the Law? If faith receive the remission of sins on account of love, the remission of sins will always be uncertain, because we never love as much as we ought, yea, we do not love unless our hearts are firmly convinced that the remission of sins has been granted us. Thus the adversaries, while they require in the remission of sins and justification confidence in one's own love, altogether abolish the Gospel concerning the free remission of sins, although, at the same time, they neither render this love nor understand it, unless they believe that the remission of sins is freely received.

111] We also say that love ought to follow faith, as Paul also says, Galatians 5:6: "For in Jesus Christ neither circumcision availeth anything, nor uncircumcision, but faith which worketh by love." 112] And yet we must not think on that account that by confidence in this love or on account of this love we receive the remission of sins and reconciliation, just as we do not receive the remission of sins because of other works that follow. But the remission of sins is received by faith alone, and, indeed, by faith properly so called, because the promise cannot be received except by faith. 113] But faith, properly so called, is that which assents to the promise, is when my heart, and the Holy Ghost in the heart, says: The promise of God is true and certain. 114] Of this faith Scripture speaks. And because it receives the remission of sins, and reconciles us to God, by this faith we are, like Abraham, accounted righteous for Christ's sake before we love and do the works of the Law, although love necessarily follows. 115] Nor, indeed, is this faith an idle knowledge, neither can it coexist with mortal sin, but it is a work of the Holy Ghost, whereby we are freed from death, and terrified minds are encouraged and quickened. 116] And because this faith alone receives the remission of sins, and renders us acceptable to God, and brings the Holy Ghost, it could be more correctly called *gratia gratum faciens*, grace rendering one pleasing to God, than an effect following, namely, love.

117] Thus far, in order that the subject might be made quite clear, we have shown with sufficient fulness, both from testimonies of Scripture, and arguments derived from Scripture, that by faith alone we obtain the remission of sins for Christ's sake, and that by faith alone we are justified, i.e., of unrighteous men made righteous, or regenerated. 118] But how necessary the knowledge of this faith is, can be easily judged, because in this alone the office of Christ is recognized, by this alone we receive the benefits of Christ; this alone brings sure and firm 119] consolation to pious minds. And in the Church (if there is to be a church, if there is to be a Christian Creed) it is necessary that there should be the [preaching and] doctrine, by which consciences are not made to rely on a dream or to build on a foundation of sand, from which the pious may receive the sure hope of salvation. For the adversaries give men bad advice (therefore the adversaries are truly unfaithful bishops, unfaithful preachers and doctors; they have hitherto given evil counsel to consciences, and still do so by introducing such doctrine) when they bid them doubt whether they obtain remission of sins. For how will such persons sustain themselves in death who have heard nothing of this faith, and think that they ought to doubt whether they obtain the remission of sins? 120] Besides, it is necessary that in the Church of Christ the Gospel be retained, i.e., the promise that for Christ's sake sins are freely remitted. Those who teach nothing of this faith, 121] concerning which we speak, altogether abolish the Gospel. But the scholastics mention not even a word concerning this faith. Our adversaries follow them, and reject this faith. Nor do they see that, by rejecting this faith they abolish the entire promise concerning the free remission of sins and the righteousness of Christ.

INTRODUCTION TO THOMAS CAJETAN'S *FOUR LUTHERAN ERRORS*

THOMAS DE Vio Cajetan (1469–1534), the foremost Roman Catholic theologian during the early decades of the Reformation, was to play a tragically ambivalent role in the sequence of events that led to the fragmentation of Western Christendom. Born in the Italian town of Gaieta, he showed early dedication to the Church and to scholarship, entering the Dominican order in 1484 and pursuing his studies at the prestigious universities of Naples, Bologna, and Padua.

He soon mastered the Thomist tradition of philosophy and theology, which although faithfully preserved within Aquinas's own Dominican order, had fallen into increasing neglect over the two centuries since Aquinas's death. Cajetan was, more than anyone, responsible for the Thomist revival of the 16th century, which was to bear rich fruit among both Catholic and Protestant theologians in the Reformation and well beyond. The decades leading up to the Reformation saw Cajetan write numerous authoritative expositions and defenses of the Thomistic and Aristotelian scholastic tradition, but neither did he neglect to begin cultivating the linguistic skills of the new humanist scholarship. In all this work, his strength was also his weakness, as was to appear in his meeting with Luther in 1518: a no-nonsense intellectual precision that prized clarity of thought over religious feeling.

By the outbreak of the Reformation, Cajetan had attained positions of considerable influence within the power centers of the Catholic Church, though by virtue of intellectual reputation, not ambition. He was the Master-General of the whole Dominican or-

302

der from 1508 to 1518, and became a trusted advisor and diplomat for Popes Julius II and Leo X, serving as the latter's legate to the Diet of the Holy Roman Empire in 1518. The tumult that Luther's critique of indulgences caused led Rome to divert Cajetan from his original diplomatic mission in order to confront Luther.

Cajetan's theological perspective made him both good and bad for the job. On the one hand, he too had recently been writing on the issue of indulgences, showing concern to restrain many of the same abuses that had upset Luther. On the other hand, he was also one of the foremost apologists for papal supremacy, and he had no sympathy for Luther's inclination to appeal behind the Pope's back to a council or even straight to Scripture. Cajetan's penchant for sharp scholastic distinctions enabled him to immediately narrow down the key matters of debate with Luther to just two, but it also led him to ignore the degree to which Luther's protest was rooted in deeply-felt religious experience. Cajetan's meetings with Luther in October 1518 ended up hardening the battle lines and setting in motion the series of events that culminated in Luther's 1520 excommunication.

Still, Cajetan was a moderate, and he had no interest in seeking to condemn outright the whole Protestant enterprise, as many of the loudest voices within the Catholic Church were doing. Indeed, during the 1520s, he dedicated himself chiefly to the study of Scripture, recognizing that the Reformers would have to be met on their own ground, rather than dismissed with appeals to tradition. Cajetan's biblical scholarship alarmed many Catholic theologians, as he turned his razor-sharp intellect upon many of the fanciful interpretations and corrupt textual readings that had undergirded key Catholic claims for centuries, and found them wanting. Condemnations of Cajetan's work flowed in from many quarters, but he retained the high confidence of Pope Clement VII.

During the last few years of his life, Cajetan re-engaged the Lutheran Reformers with a series of treatises which sought to carefully discriminate those points on which their concerns were well-grounded and those where, in his view, the traditional teachings of the Church must stand. In *Four Lutheran Errors* of 1531, we see both his moderate tone and how, despite his willingness to argue from Scripture, there remained a strong burden of proof on behalf of Church tradition and practice. Focusing on a range of issues that relate more to concrete religious practice rather than upstream theological principles, he seeks at each point to show that there is Scriptural ground for traditional practices rejected by the Reformers, or at least that the Scriptures provide insufficient basis for rejecting them.

All four issues are written as responses to statements from the Augsburg Confession of the previous year: the insistence on receiving both kinds (bread and wine) in the Eucharist, the rejection of the notion that one must enumerate all one's sins when confessing to receive forgiveness, the rejection of the idea of doing works of satisfaction after penance to pay the penalty for sin, and the rejection of prayers to the saints. Cajetan argues at greatest length on the first issue, and one can see in his method why, for all his effort at moderation, he was not a man well-suited to bridging the gap with the Protestants. He confines himself to arguing the very limited thesis that one cannot prove from Scripture that communion must always involve both kinds, but he neither makes a positive case for the restriction, nor takes into account concrete pastoral concerns. Likewise, on the matter of enumerating one's sins, he ends up on similar ground to the Confession, conceding that one cannot be responsible to list sins forgotten or unknown, but he does not seem to take seriously the pastoral danger of making believers feel pressured to enumerate every sin they can possibly remember. On the third issue, it is interesting to see the fruits of Cajetan's controversial study of the biblical text. He concedes, following Erasmus's important re-reading of Matthew 3:2, that the phrase translated "do penance" really just means, "repent." However, he still thinks he can make the argument for penitential works on the basis of Matthew 3:8.

In the end, Cajetan's scalpel-like precision reveals just how far apart the two sides in the Reformation remained on questions of basic method and purpose, even when the polemical smoke had cleared.

Further Reading

For further reading, see Jared Wicks, ed. and trans., *Cajetan Responds: A Reader in Reformation Controversy* (Washington, DC: The Catholic University of America Press, 1978); Michael O'Connor, *Cajetan's Biblical Commentaries: Motive and Method* (Leiden: Brill, 2017).

THOMAS CAJETAN, *FOUR LUTHERAN ERRORS (1531)*[1]

TO THE Supreme Pontiff, Clement VII:

I feel called to write by the stubbornness the Lutherans show, on alleged grounds of conscience, concerning reception by the people of both forms of the Eucharist, confession of less than all one's sins, the denial of satisfaction for sin, and rejection of the invocation of the saints. I do not plan to treat these points comprehensively, but only regarding their derivation from Holy Scripture, since the Lutherans accept only the authority of Holy Scripture and profess to stand on this. What I write will not profit the stubborn, but I hope it will be of some use in restraining others from imitating them. It should also be of consolation and of no little comfort to the hearts of the faithful to have shown from Scripture the erroneous views the heretics teach while boasting how they hold to the holy Gospel! Even though I have written this on behalf of the Catholic Church, I submit it to the judgment of your Holiness no less than all my other writings.

1: Communion Under Both Forms

It is not enough for the Lutherans to receive Communion under both forms; they cannot indeed be persuaded to admit that Communion under one form alone is allowable. They hold that both

---

[1] Taken from Jared Wicks, trans. and ed., *Cajetan Responds: A Reader in Reformation Controversy* (Washington, DC: The Catholic University of America Press, 1978).

Christ's practice and command require reception under both forms. We must therefore take up both points in the light of Holy Scripture and demonstrate that reception under one form alone by the people is prohibited neither by Christ's practice nor by his commands. When we have shown this, it will be evident that the people are not obligated by divine law to receive Communion under both forms.

Because at the Last Supper when Our Savior instituted the sacrament of the Eucharist he gave Communion to the Apostles under both forms, as the Evangelists bear witness, they conclude that a priest should give Communion only under both forms. Priests must distribute the Eucharist in the manner in which Christ distributed it, and we should all receive Communion in the manner the Apostles received.

We can easily show, however, that the practice of Christ and the Apostles does not have the force of a law obligating us to distribute the Eucharist to the people in a manner similar to theirs. For if Christ's practice had the force of law we would not be obligated to observe just certain parts of his way of distributing, while not observing other parts, but we would be obligated to follow every aspect of his practice. But we are obviously not obliged to follow every aspect of Christ's manner of distribution, and so we are not obliged in distributing the Eucharist to follow this one aspect of the two forms.

The fact that we are not obliged to observe every aspect is clear. Christ broke the bread and gave this broken form of bread, but it would be silly to say that a priest is bound to give a broken Host. As Christ distributed, he did not place the Eucharist in the mouths of the Apostles, but said, "Take and eat." But it would be inane to say a priest is prohibited from placing the Eucharist in the mouths of communicants but must place it in their hand so they can give it to themselves. Christ gave this sacrament to the Apostles after supper, but it would be quite ridiculous to say we are obliged to receive Communion after supper and it is forbidden to give the Eucharist to people who are fasting. Finally, Christ gave the Eucharist under the form of unleavened bread, but yet the whole Church admits there is no binding law requiring either unleavened or leavened bread. All these examples make it evident that Christ's practice in distributing the Eucharist does not have the force of law determining that we should distribute in a similar manner.

If one would argue that Christ's manner of distribution must be imitated in this one aspect of giving the Eucharist under both forms, then he should take note that Christ gave under both forms only to the Apostles, not to the seventy disciples nor to the multitudes who believed in him. All that one can therefore conclude from Christ's example is that the successors of the Apostles should be given the Eucharist under both forms. No more can be concluded from Christ's distribution, and so one cannot conclude that the Eucharist should be given all Christians under both forms. It is evident that one cannot conclude from the practice of Christ that communion for the people under only one form is prohibited. Much less can one conclude this from the practice of the church at Corinth, about which Paul speaks in 1 Corinthians. The practice of one local church does not establish a law for other churches. — So much on Christ's practice.

We must now turn to the commands Christ gave both before the institution of the Eucharist and in the institution itself. A first command was at one time seen by the Bohemians in the words of Our Lord in John 6[:53], "Unless you eat the flesh of the Son of Man and drink his blood, you will not have life in you." What, they ask, could be more evident? The necessity of receiving Communion under both forms is enunciated in the same manner as was the necessity of baptism. In the same manner as he spoke about baptism in John 3[:5], "Unless one is reborn of water and the Spirit, he cannot enter the kingdom of God," so he spoke of the Eucharist: "Unless you eat the flesh of the Son of Man and drink his blood you will not have life in you" [6:53].

We answer, however, that in their authentic sense these words of Christ should not be interpreted as referring to the practice of the Eucharist, nor can they be so understood in the context of what we believe as Christians concerning sacramental food and drink. This can be demonstrated quite easily, since if they were understood of the Eucharist this would undermine the sufficiency of Baptism for salvation. The necessity appears to be the same in both cases: concerning eating the flesh and drinking the blood of the Son of Man, and concerning the necessity of rebirth of water and the Spirit. Therefore it evidently follows that if the former words of Christ point to a necessity of receiving the Eucharist, then baptism is not sufficient for salvation. For one to have life, he would have both to be baptized and to receive the Eucharist.

Now we not only profess the contrary of this in the Creed, as we confess "one baptism for the forgiveness of sins," but Our Lord also said in the Gospel, "Whoever believes and is baptized will be saved" (Mark 16:16). Paul the Apostle wrote in Titus 3[:5], "He saved us ... by the washing of regeneration." Since, therefore, interpreting Christ's words in John 6[:53] as referring to food and drink in the sacrament of the Eucharist would entail denying the sufficiency of baptism for salvation, it becomes evident that those words cannot be interpreted as referring to food and drink in the Eucharist. The text, consequently, does not issue a command obligating to reception of the Eucharist under both forms. Arriving at the authentic sense of those words of Christ is not part of our present undertaking; for the present question, one only needs to know that there Our Lord was not speaking of sacramental food and drink.

We can now take up the command Christ issued as he instituted the sacrament of the Eucharist. Look through all the gospels, and the only command you will find about the Eucharist is in Luke [22:19], immediately after the Eucharist was given under the form of bread: "Do this in commemoration of me." In Paul the Apostle, in 1 Corinthians 11[:24f], there are two commands recorded as given by Christ in the institution of the Eucharist: one immediately after giving the Eucharist under the form of bread, "Do this in commemoration of me," and the other immediately after giving the

Eucharist under the form of wine, "Do this, as often as you drink it, in commemoration of me."

If each of these commands is examined carefully, it will become evident that none of them entails a command obligating to communion under both forms. The context itself shows that the command given immediately after the form of bread in both Luke and Paul obviously pertains to the Eucharist under the form of bread. The command recorded by Paul concerning the imitation of Christ in the Eucharist under the form of wine is, however, patently restricted to the times that we do drink in commemoration of Christ. It is not an absolute command, but one based on a supposition, namely, that if we drink in commemoration of Christ, we should do what Christ did. He did not command that we should drink in commemoration of him, but that whenever we do drink in his memory we should do what he did. As often as you use the chalice of the Eucharist, you should offer it in sacrifice. "To drink" manifestly refers to the use of the chalice, and consequently to doing a distinct action. "To drink" refers to consecrating it, and what is literally commanded is that we associate the use of the chalice with the sacrifice of the chalice.

By not commanding a similar association concerning use of the Eucharist under the form of bread, he suggests that use of the chalice outside of the sacrifice is forbidden, while use under the form of bread is allowed. The rite of the Church follows this rule, not reserving the Eucharist under the form of drink but only under the form of bread for the sick and for those who receive Communion outside solemn masses.

Someone could argue that because this command directly obligates priests, it binds the people as by a further consequence. Those who drink in commemoration of Christ are commanded, "Do this," from which evidently follows that priests celebrating masses (they clearly drink in commemoration of Christ) are commanded, "Do this," a command including as well the giving of the chalice to others. The command would embrace all that Christ did with the chalice, and so by this command a priest would be bound, whenever he drinks, to give the chalice to others and they are thereby bound to take and drink.

The person arguing this way should first take note of the words of the verse, since his interpretation does not fit with the verse's context. In the verse, "Do this" is distinguished from the drinking. Thus confecting the sacrament is distinguished from the use of the sacrament, and consequently "Do this" in this verse is not all-inclusive, but by the context is limited to indicating the sacrament itself, in distinction from the use of the sacrament, since it is distinguished from the use of the chalice. Whatever therefore refers to the use of the chalice is included here in the reference to drinking, while whatever refers to the sacrament itself is included under "Do this," in full accord with the meaning of the context. But it is evident that giving others the chalice refers to the use of the chalice and not to the sacrament itself. Consequently giving others the chalice is not included in this verse under "Do this." One should finally take note that the Lutherans' practice is not consistent with what they say, since the argument obviously leads to obligating the celebrating priest to give the chalice to all present. This follows if "Do this" enjoins giving the sacrament in the manner in which Christ gave it. Christ gave it to all present, but the Lutherans do not observe this. Therefore the Christian people are not obligated to drink of the sacrament of the Eucharist by reason of this command of Christ, if the interpretation is to rest on the plain sense of the text and fit smoothly with it.

Since no command concerning eucharistic Communion is had in Holy Scripture except in the verses cited, it is evident that Christians are not obliged to receive Communion under both forms by a written command of divine right. It is therefore arbitrary and not grounded in Scripture when they proclaim that communion under the form of bread alone is forbidden. This is sufficient answer to the Lutherans who recognize only the authority of the Holy Scripture.

This is what we have to say about communion under one form alone.

2: Integral Confession of Sin

The Lutherans not only deny that one must confess all the mortal sins he has committed, but they say that to do it would be contrary to Holy Scripture and is impossible, since it stands written [Psalm 18:13], "Who knows his offenses?"

We say in response that, first, confession of all one's mortal sins rests on the Gospel; and, second, that it is not against the view cited from the prophet. The first can be shown from the form of administering the sacrament of Penance that Christ handed on when he instituted the sacrament in John 20[:22f]. Christ said to the Apostles, "Whose sins you forgive, they are forgiven, and whose sins you retain, they are retained." With these words Christ empowered the minister of the sacrament for two actions, either forgiving or retaining the sins of all men. Since the minister is empowered to discern whether the sins of each penitent are to be forgiven or retained, it evidently follows that the minister must know—unless he wants to administer blindly—whether any sins of the penitent are to be retained. This is the same as knowing whether anything in the penitent hinders forgiveness, since any retained sin would hinder the forgiveness of every sin of the person confessing.

One sin cannot be forgiven while another is retained, since all the mortal sins of the same person are evidently connected, both in regard to forgiveness and to retention, in relation both to God and to the minister of Christ. This clearly holds in relation to God, since a person whose sins God forgives is made a friend of God, according to the text, "Blessed is he to whom God imputes no sin" [Psalm 31:2]. But the person whose sin is retained remains in that one sin and is the enemy of God, since he is guilty of all, according to James 2[:10], "One who offends in one matter becomes guilty of all." Since both God's forgiveness and retention embrace all one's mortal sins, both the forgiveness and retention by the minister of Christ must consequently embrace not just some of the mortal sins of the penitent but all of them. For the forgiveness and retention

312

by the minister should be such that his forgiveness is accompanied by divine forgiveness and his retention accompanied by divine retention. Otherwise Christ's words would not be verified, "Whose sins you forgive, they are forgiven, and whose sins you retain, they are retained." The forgiveness by the minister could not claim the accompaniment of divine forgiveness, if it were in discord with this divine forgiveness. But it would be in discord with the divine forgiveness if while God forgave all or retained all, the minister did not forgive all or retain all. So that the minister can either forgive all or retain all, he must have knowledge of all, unless he is to be a blind and rash minister of forgiveness and retention. Since the minister of Christ gains knowledge of the sins of the penitent through the latter's confession, the penitent must consequently confess all his mortal sins.

Let the knowledgeable reader examine, ponder, and weigh what I have said, and you will conclude that the confession of all one's sins derives from the very form of institution recorded in the Gospel.

It remains for us to refute the objections put forward by the Lutherans. We do this by distinguishing between confession taken absolutely and taken as a human act. To confess all one's sins absolutely is to leave no sin unconfessed. But to confess all, in so far as confession is a human act, is to confess all that by human power can be confessed.

Now since no one knows his offenses fully, it is impossible for one to confess all his sins absolutely, since unknown sins would remain unconfessed. Still, it does not thereby follow that one cannot humanly speaking confess all his sins, since an integral human confession does not include all sins absolutely speaking, but only those that are known and remembered. The confession of forgotten and unknown sins is beyond human ability. Since divine and human law obviously require of a person no action beyond his power, and since we have it from the Gospel that the confession of all sins is required for the sacrament of Penance, the confession of all sins absolutely cannot be meant, but rather the confession of all sins as that lies within human abilities. This is to say that the penitent is to confess all his sins, but not unknown or forgotten sins.

3: Satisfaction for Sin

The Lutherans reject satisfaction for sin, which is the third part of the sacrament of penance. They say satisfaction or punishment for sin can at times remain after sin is forgiven is witnessed by the twofold way God forgives sin. Sometimes God forgives both the guilt for sin and the punishment due, as in the case of the good thief, to whom Christ said, "Today you will be with me in Paradise" (Luke 23:43). This is also the manner in which baptism forgives sin, since the baptismal grace alone suffices for eternal salvation, if before he dies the newly baptized person poses no further obstacle through sin. The ultimate effect of baptism is eternal life, and with forgiveness granted in this manner, there is evidently no need of satisfaction.

We also read, however, that in other cases God forgives sin without removing all need of punishment, as in 2 Samuel 12[:13], where, after the prophet Nathan had accused David of adultery and murder, and after David had confessed, "I have sinned against the Lord," Nathan answered, "The Lord also has put away your sin and you will not die. Nevertheless, the child born to you shall die." God evidently forgave the sin as to the guilt and as to some of the punishment due, but he did not remit the punishment inflicted through the death of David's son, nor that suffered by his own son openly violating his wives (as recorded in Chapter 16), nor the punishment through that propensity to evil lodged in his own house. Because of his sin, David had to suffer much from his son Absalom. The prophet Nathan threatened David on behalf of God with all these punishments for that one sin. Since therefore God at times forgives sin while leaving an obligation of punishment after forgiveness, we must consequently say that God at times forgives sin without removing the full debt of punishment due for the sin. Thus the need arises to complete the remaining punishment not remitted when God forgave the sin.

This remaining punishment can be completed in two ways, either by suffering endured or by satisfaction rendered. David completed his satisfaction by suffering endured, since he did not inflict on himself the punishments due. Instead, God inflicted them on him. What remains is for us to show from Scripture that we can ourselves complete the remaining punishment by rendering satisfaction. If you read Chapter 3 of the Gospel of Matthew, you will see that John the Baptist preached two things: first, "Do penance" [3:2], and, second, "Bring forth fruit befitting penance" [3:8]. In the first, the Greek word indicated simply the act of repentance, obviously referring to the sin itself. But the second part of the words witness to our works following repentance, since the "fruits of penance" are works arising from penance as from a root or stock. He did not say, "Bring forth fruit befitting innocence," or, "… fruit befitting righteousness or goodness," but, "… fruit befitting righteousness or goodness," but, "… fruit befitting penance." Consequently, he clearly meant quite specifically the fruit of penance as such, that is, a fitting product derived from interior repentance as its root. Since repentance pertains to previous sins, evidently the fruit befitting penance consists of works restoring that of which one repents. This is to repair what we repent of having neglected or done. This we call rendering satisfaction for our sins, since this entails the removal of all the evil left in the penitent from his sin, part of which is the debt of remaining punishment for his sin. If repentance does not yield fruit leading to the full restoration of all that the sinner lost through his sin, then it does not attain to the fruits befitting itself. Repentance tends by its own nature toward the completion of what it has begun, and it is clearly not complete as long as any debt remains to be paid from the sin.

Consequently we have it on the authority of the Holy Scripture that at times one must make satisfaction after sin is forgiven, and this can be through works which are the fruits befitting repentance.

I think there is no need for further discussion of the objection that our works are neither meritorious nor satisfactory. Scripture abounds with statements on both sides, with some denying that our works are meritorious and others affirming this. But these two views are obviously not contrary to each other. The meaning is that insofar as our works proceed from ourselves they are not meritorious and consequently not of satisfactory value; but in so far as they proceed from the divine grace that precedes, accompanies, and completes them, our works are meritorious and consequently of satisfactory value. Both aspects are so obvious in myriad passages of Scripture as to be grasped with noonday clarity by those well grounded in the sacred text. We can therefore omit further treatment.

This answers the error on satisfaction for sin.

4: Invocation of the Saints

The Lutherans claim that invocation of the saints is not derived from Scripture. Although I suspect they are not referring to the invocation of the holy angels, but of sainted men and women, we will stay on safe ground by first treating in summary fashion the holy angels, and then sainted men and women, showing what Scripture says about their invocation.

The fact that angels intercede for us is evident in the prophet Zechariah, where an angel says to God, "Lord of hosts, how long will you have no mercy on Jerusalem and the cities of Judah, against which your anger has continued seventy years?" [1:12]. And in Matthew 18[:10], Our Lord says that the angels plead on behalf of little ones who are despised: "See that you do not despise one of these little ones; I tell you their angels in heaven continually behold the face of my Father," doubtless to gain protection for the little ones who are despised.

We are taught to invoke the holy angels in Genesis 32[:26], where Jacob asked the angel to bless him, saying, "I will not let you go, unless you bless me." Then in Daniel 7[:16] the prophet related of himself, "I approached one of those standing there and sought from him the truth." No doubt he was referring to one of the holy assisting angels. Hebrews 1[:14] also refers to the holy angels, saying, "They are all ministering spirits, sent to serve for the sake of those who will attain the inheritance of salvation." Since God has arranged to govern us through intermediary angels, not for his own sake, but for the sake of us, the heirs of eternal life, we understand that he has ordained that we should invoke the holy angels as intermediaries between ourselves and God. Or are we to be so stupid as to say that once a prince or a court assigns an advocate to aid a pilgrim or orphan, the pilgrim or orphan is not to invoke the protection of the advocate assigned?

Since Holy Scripture is clear on the subject of the invocation of the holy angels, we can leave this topic and move to the invocation of sainted men and women. There are two manners in which we ordinarily invoke the saints, either by asking them directly, as in, "Saint Peter, pray for us," or by asking God through the merits of the saints, as the Church is accustomed to pray in the Canon of the Mass, saying, "By their merits and prayers may you grant...." We hold that both manners are derived from Holy Scripture.

The fact that the souls of the saints intercede for us is attested in Revelation 6[:9f], "I saw under the altar the souls of those who had been killed for the word of God ... and they cried out with a loud voice, saying, 'How long, O Lord holy and true, before you will judge and avenge our blood upon those who dwell on the earth?'" Now if the souls of the saints pray to God against evil persons dwelling on earth, how much the more will they pray for the salvation of the elect. The will of the saints is turned much more toward our benefit than toward evil for us. Again, in Luke 16[:27f] Our Lord revealed that the rich man in hell interceded for his brothers still in this life. This revelation suggests how much more the saints will intercede for the salvation of their own. For when the rich man was in this life he showed no interest in the salvation of his brothers; but once he was in torment, he prayed urgently for their salvation. How much more will sainted men and women, whose efforts in this life were for the salvation of their brethren, once they have put off the flesh and come to blessedness, continue the work done out of charity and intercede for the salvation of their brethren.

Matthew 27[:52f] indicates that we are to invoke the saints. It is written there that many bodies of the saints who had died rose, came into the holy city, and appeared to many. This shows that after the resurrection of Christ God rules and instructs us not only through the holy angels but through sainted men and women. They did not without purpose appear to many, but instructed them about the true Messiah and about his resurrection. Since up to that time God ruled us through the holy angels and not through sainted men and women, the beginning then of rule through sainted men and women suggests he had new intermediaries for ruling the elect. God wanted to show forth the sainted men and women who were now, through the merits of Christ's passion and resurrection, associated with the order of divine rule over us. Otherwise he would have sent angels into Jerusalem to appear to many and instruct them. The fact God revealed the resurrection of Christ not only through the angels who appeared to the women at the tomb, but also through the sainted men and women appearing to many in Jerusalem, indicates that God has now joined to the angels' ministry for our eternal salvation the ministry of sainted men and women.

It thus follows from the very order of divine rule, in which He rules us also through sainted men and women, that we are to have recourse to the saints. Otherwise we would fall into the same absurdity noted above, that is, if we are not to invoke the holy angels, for the apparitions cited from Revelation 6 and Matthew 26 bear witness that the saints have been appointed for our benefit as intermediaries between God and ourselves. So it is obvious that we may have recourse to these divinely given intermediaries. It would be no less absurd than before if God arranged to rule us through the intercession of sainted men and women (as our Scripture texts show he has done), and then we were not permitted to have recourse to these our intercessors.

Finally, Exodus 32[:13] teaches that we are to pray to God through the merits of the saints. In Moses' prayer of petition to God, he said, "Remember Abraham, Isaac, and Israel, your servants." This is nothing other than asking through the merits of Abraham, Isaac, and Israel. If you join to this what was said above about the saints' intercession for us, you will evidently conclude that according to Scripture we are to supplicate God not only through the merits but through the prayers of the saints as well. You should add to this that praying to God through the merits and prayers of the saints comes down to the same thing as praying to the saints to offer their merits and prayers to God. The thing itself is the same, though the manner is different, but in both cases there is an invocation of the saints in one manner or another. Thus you may easily conclude that in every aspect the invocation of the saints is derived from Scripture.

Now that these answers have been given on the issues raised, let the reader recall that it is uneducated persons who demand the certitude of mathematical proof in matters of morality and the wider fields of our human actions.

Rome, August 25, 1531

INTRODUCTION TO JOHN CALVIN'S *INSTITUTES OF THE CHRISTIAN RELIGION*

WHILE THE struggles for Reformation intensified in Germany, other parts of Europe did not remain free from the contagion of unrest that Luther's writings spread. France, in particular, had long harbored reformist sympathies, both on account of the country's long history of conflict with the Papacy, and from the new flowering of the humanist movement. Emphasizing a return to the original sources of Scripture and the Church Fathers, the humanists found in these sources a stark contrast to the tangle of ceremonies, corruptions, and scholastic logic-chopping that dominated the late medieval church.

In the early 1520s, a circle gathered around the humanist leader Jacques Lefevre d'Etaples in the diocese of Meaux; he was involved in the translation of the Bible into French and the teaching of doctrines quite similar to those being developed at the same time by Luther. This naturally invited suspicion and hostility from conservative theologians, but because the movement enjoyed the enthusiastic patronage of King Francis's sister, Marguerite d'Angouleme, it escaped persecution until the early 1530s. By that time it had been joined by a brilliant young lawyer, John Calvin (1509–1564), who had studied theology and philosophy before switching to law at the insistence of his father. The date of Calvin's conversion to full-fledged Protestant faith is not entirely clear, but he does write of it as a "sudden conversion," and it was complete enough by 1533 that he was forced to flee Paris in the midst of a crackdown on Protestant sympathizers. Calvin took refuge with several friends for a time in the small kingdom of Navarre in the south of France, where Marguerite was now Queen, and began a period of focused study and writing there. In 1534 he resigned his salaried position in the Catholic Church, signaling his full commitment to the Protestant cause. By 1535 he was in Basel, Switzerland, hard at work on a book that was to become a landmark of Protestant theology and an enduring classic of Christian thought: *The Institutes of the Christian Religion*. Completed in August of that year, it was not published until early in 1536, when it immediately made a name for its young author (then just twenty-six years old). It was a relatively short volume (only a fraction of the length of the final 1559 edition, having been significantly expanded along the way in editions of 1539 and 1543), but it was composed with extraordinary clarity, stylistic beauty, and logical order, qualities it was to maintain through all subsequent expansions.

It should be noted that Calvin did not at this stage (nor indeed ever) view himself as the founder of a distinct "Reformed" tradition of Protestantism over against Lutheranism. The 1536 edition certainly contains differences of detail and emphasis from Luther's theology, but so did the work of Luther's friend and collaborator Melanchthon, and Calvin certainly identified more closely with Luther's flavor of Protestantism than Zwingli's. In fact, he did not hesitate to later subscribe to the Augsburg Confession, and it was only polemical developments within the 1550s that set Calvin at odds with more intransigent defenders of Luther's theology within Germany.

What is clear is that Calvin viewed himself as a Frenchman, with a passionate lifelong concern to see the Protestant cause flourish in his homeland, from which he was exiled for the last three decades of his life. The prefatory letter to King Francis, which he penned in 1535 but retained in all subsequent editions of the *Institutes* as a symbol of his hopes for France, even after the death of Francis, was no mere rhetorical flattery of a hoped-for powerful patron. It was an earnest plea for the King to hear out the true nature of the Protestant confession (of which the *Institutes* was meant to serve as an outline for the King) and to stop listening to its slanderers, who infected the ear of the king against it. In particular, events of 1534 and 1535 had not been favorable to the public perception of Protestantism. A radical Anabaptist sect under the leadership of the fanatic John of Leiden had seized the west German city of Munster and proclaimed it the New Jerusalem. Combining the disdain for established civil authorities that other Anabaptists shared with an embrace of violence that many did not, this radical group preached polygamy and other alarming practices before being destroyed by an imperial army in 1535. Catholic leaders were quick to try and paint such rebels and radicals as the natural fruit of Protestantism, and Francis was naturally alarmed. Still, political considerations had led him to seek an alliance with the German Protestant princes, and at the time of Calvin's writing of the *Institutes*, he had real reason to be optimistic that Francis might respond favorably to the book. In any event, it is unclear whether Francis ever read even the preface, and French royal policy was to remain mostly hostile to Protestantism until an official toleration was declared, after much bloodshed, in 1598.

Calvin's theology, as the excerpt here from the first six chapters of the 1559 *Institutes* shows, revolved not around the hidden and inscrutable decree of predestination, as often imagined, but around God's self-revelation. God is so near to us that we cannot scarcely begin to think without being drawn to consider God, and we can have no true knowledge of ourselves without considering ourselves in relation to Him. Calvin's theology is informed throughout by what he called the *duplex cognitio Dei*, the twofold knowledge of God—as Creator and as Redeemer. The first, Calvin argued, was made known even to the natural man by virtue of creation itself: "In the creation of the world, he displayed those glorious banners, on which, to whatever side we turn, we behold his perfections visibly portrayed." Calvin discusses at some length how even pagan philosophers attained to some understanding of God and his greatness. However, he emphasizes no less, especially in chapter four, how readily this knowledge is smothered by sin and turned to superstition and hypocrisy (no doubt having some of the Catholicism of his day in mind, although these opening chapters are free of any direct reference to 16th-century conflicts). Accordingly, we need Scripture to show us how to rightly understand God and His works, even of God as Creator. Of God as Redeemer in Christ, the natural man knows nothing, and Calvin does not turn to consider this subject until Book II of the *Institutes*. Book III of the *Institutes* then expounds the inward and hidden means by which we receive the redeeming work of Christ, and Book IV the external and visible aids—the ministry of the church and the support of the godly magistrate. Although Calvin was to massively expand the treatment of the visible church's ministry in later editions of the *Institutes*, laying more stress on it than Luther ever did, the persistence of the internal/external division of Books III and IV reveals the ongoing influence of Luther's two-kingdoms framework.

Further Reading

For further reading, see Susan E. Schreiner, *The Theater of His Glory: Nature and the Natural Order in the Thought of John Calvin* (Durham, NC: The Labyrinth Press, 1991); Herman J. Selderhuis, *John Calvin: A Pilgrim's Life* (Downer's Grove: Intervarsity Press, 2009).

JOHN CALVIN, *INSTITUTES OF THE CHRISTIAN RELIGION* (1536/1559)[1]

Prefatory Address to his most Christian Majesty, the Most Mighty and Illustrious Monarch, Francis, King of the French

SIRE, when I first engaged in this work, nothing was farther from my thoughts than to write what should afterwards be presented to your Majesty. My intention was only to furnish a kind of rudiments, by which those who feel some interest in religion might be trained to true godliness. And I toiled at the task chiefly for the sake of my countrymen the French, multitudes of whom I perceived to be hungering and thirsting after Christ, while very few seemed to have been duly imbued with even a slender knowledge of him. That this was the object which I had in view is apparent from the work itself, which is written in a simple and elementary form adapted for instruction.

But when I perceived that the fury of certain bad men had risen to such a height in your realm, that there was no place in it for sound doctrine, I thought it might be of service if I were in the same work both to give instruction to my countrymen, and also lay before your Majesty a Confession, from which you may learn what the doctrine is that so inflames the rage of those madmen who are this day, with fire and sword, troubling your kingdom. For I fear

---

[1] Taken from Henry Beveridge, trans., *Institutes of the Christian Religion: A New Translation* (Edinburgh: Calvin Translation Society, 1845).

not to declare that what I have here given may be regarded as a summary of the very doctrine which, they vociferate, ought to be punished with confiscation, exile, imprisonment, and flames, as well as exterminated by land and sea. [...]

Let not a contemptuous idea of our insignificance dissuade you from the investigation of this cause. We, indeed, are perfectly conscious how poor and abject we are: in the presence of God we are miserable sinners, and in the sight of men most despised—we are (if you will) the mere dregs and off-scourings of the world, or worse, if worse can be named, so that before God there remains nothing of which we can glory save only his mercy, by which, without any merit of our own, we are admitted to the hope of eternal salvation, and before men not even this much remains, since we can glory only in our infirmity, a thing which, in the estimation of men, it is the greatest ignominy even tacitly to confess. But our doctrine must stand sublime above all the glory of the world, and invincible by all its power, because it is not ours, but that of the living God and his Anointed, whom the Father has appointed King, that he may rule from sea to sea, and from the rivers even to the ends of the earth, and so rule as to smite the whole earth and its strength of iron and brass, its splendour of gold and silver, with the mere rod of his mouth, and break them in pieces like a potter's vessel, according to the magnificent predictions of the prophets respecting his kingdom (Daniel 2:34; Isaiah 11:4; Psalm 2:9).

Our adversaries, indeed, clamorously maintain that our appeal to the word of God is a mere pretext—that we are, in fact, its worst corrupters. How far this is not only malicious calumny, but also shameless effrontery, you will be able to decide, of your own knowledge, by reading our Confession. Here, however, it may be necessary to make some observations which may dispose, or at least assist, you to read and study it with attention.

When Paul declared that all prophecy ought to be according to the analogy of faith (Rom. 12:6), he laid down the surest rule for determining the meaning of Scripture. Let our doctrine be tested by this rule and our victory is secure. For what accords better and more aptly with faith than to acknowledge ourselves divested of all virtue that we may be clothed by God, devoid of all goodness that we may be filled by Him, the slaves of sin that he may give us freedom, blind that he may enlighten, lame that he may cure, and feeble that he may sustain us, to strip ourselves of all ground of glorying that he alone may shine forth glorious, and we be glorified in him? When these things, and others to the same effect, are said by us, they interpose, and querulously complain, that in this way we overturn some blind light of nature, fancied preparatives, free will, and works meritorious of eternal salvation, with their own supererogations also, because they cannot bear that the entire praise and glory of all goodness, virtue, justice, and wisdom, should remain with God. But we read not of any having been blamed for drinking too much of the fountain of living water; on the contrary, those are severely reprimanded who "have hewed them out cisterns, broken cisterns, that can hold no water" (Jer. 2:13). Again, what more agreeable to faith than to feel assured that God is a propitious Father when Christ is acknowledged as a brother and propitiator, than confidently to expect all prosperity and gladness from Him, whose ineffable love towards us was such that He "spared not his own Son, but delivered him up for us all" (Rom. 8:32), than to rest in the sure hope of salvation and eternal life whenever Christ, in whom such treasures are hid, is conceived to have been given by the Father? Here they attack us, and loudly maintain that this sure confidence is not free from arrogance and presumption. But as nothing is to be presumed of ourselves, so all things are to be presumed of God; nor are we stript of vainglory for any other reason than that we may learn to glory in the Lord. Why go farther? Take but a cursory view, most valiant King, of all the parts of our cause, and count us of all wicked men the most iniquitous, if you do not discover plainly, that "therefore we both labour and suffer reproach because we trust in the living God" (1 Tim. 4:10), because we believe it to be "life eternal" to know "the only true God, and Jesus Christ," whom he has sent (John 17:3). For this hope some of us are in bonds, some beaten with rods, some made a gazingstock, some proscribed, some most cruelly tortured, some obliged to flee; we are all pressed with straits, loaded with dire execrations, lacerated by slanders, and treated with the greatest indignity.

Look now to our adversaries (I mean the priesthood, at whose beck and pleasure others ply their enmity against us), and consider with me for a little by what zeal they are actuated. The true religion which is delivered in the Scriptures, and which all ought to hold, they readily permit both themselves and others to be ignorant of, to neglect and despise; and they deem it of little moment what each man believes concerning God and Christ, or disbelieves, provided he submits to the judgment of the Church with what they call implicit faith; nor are they greatly concerned though they should see the glow of God dishonoured by open blasphemies, provided not a finger is raised against the primacy of the Apostolic See and the authority of holy mother Church. Why, then, do they war for the mass, purgatory, pilgrimage, and similar follies, with such fierceness and acerbity, that though they cannot prove one of them from the word of God, they deny godliness can be safe without faith in these things—faith drawn out, if I may so express it, to its utmost stretch? Why? just because their belly is their God, and their kitchen their religion; and they believe, that if these were away they would not only not be Christians, but not even men. For although some wallow in luxury, and others feed on slender crusts, still they all live by the same pot, which without that fuel might not only cool, but altogether freeze. He, accordingly, who is most anxious about his stomach, proves the fiercest champion of his faith. In short, the object on which all to a man are bent is to keep their kingdom safe or their belly filled, not one gives even the smallest sign of sincere zeal.

Nevertheless, they cease not to assail our doctrine, and to accuse and defame it in what terms they may, in order to render it either hated or suspected. They call it new, and of recent birth; they carp at it as doubtful and uncertain; they bid us tell by what miracles it has been confirmed; they ask if it be fair to receive it against the consent of so many holy Fathers and the most ancient custom;

they urge us to confess either that it is schismatical in giving battle to the Church, or that the Church must have been without life during the many centuries in which nothing of the kind was heard. Lastly, they say there is little need of argument, for its quality may be known by its fruits, namely, the large number of sects, the many seditious disturbances, and the great licentiousness which it has produced. No doubt, it is a very easy matter for them, in presence of an ignorant and credulous multitude, to insult over an undefended cause; but were an opportunity of mutual discussion afforded, that acrimony which they now pour out upon us in frothy torrents, with as much license as impunity, would assuredly boil dry.

1. First, in calling it new, they are exceedingly injurious to God, whose sacred word deserved not to be charged with novelty. To them, indeed, I very little doubt it is new, as Christ is new, and the Gospel new; but those who are acquainted with the old saying of Paul, that Christ Jesus "died for our sins, and rose again for our justification" (Rom. 4:25), will not detect any novelty in us. That it long lay buried and unknown is the guilty consequence of man's impiety; but now when, by the kindness of God, it is restored to us, it ought to resume its antiquity just as the returning citizen resumes his rights.

2. It is owing to the same ignorance that they hold it to be doubtful and uncertain, for this is the very thing of which the Lord complains by his prophet, "The ox knoweth his owner, and the ass his master's crib; but Israel doth not know, my people doth not consider" (Isaiah 1:3). But however they may sport with its uncertainty, had they to seal their own doctrine with their blood, and at the expense of life, it would be seen what value they put upon it. Very different is our confidence—a confidence which is not appalled by the terrors of death, and therefore not even by the judgment—seat of God.

3. In demanding miracles from us, they act dishonestly, for we have not coined some new gospel, but retain the very one the truth of which is confirmed by all the miracles which Christ and the apostles ever wrought. But they have a peculiarity which we

have not—they can confirm their faith by constant miracles down to the present day! Nay rather, they allege miracles which might produce wavering in minds otherwise well disposed; they are so frivolous and ridiculous, so vain and false. But were they even exceedingly wonderful, they could have no effect against the truth of God, whose name ought to be hallowed always, and everywhere, whether by miracles, or by the natural course of events. The deception would perhaps be more specious if Scripture did not admonish us of the legitimate end and use of miracles. Mark tells us that the signs which followed the preaching of the apostles were wrought in confirmation of it (Mark 16:20); so Luke also relates that the Lord "gave testimony to the word of his grace, and granted signs and wonders to be done" by the hands of the apostles (Acts 14:3). Very much to the same effect are those words of the apostle, that salvation by a preached gospel was confirmed, "The Lord bearing witness with signs and wonders, and with divers miracles" (Heb. 2:4). Those things which we are told are seals of the gospel, shall we pervert to the subversion of the gospel? What was destined only to confirm the truth, shall we misapply to the confirmation of lies? The proper course, therefore, is, in the first instance, to ascertain and examine the doctrine which is said by the Evangelist to precede; then after it has been proved, but not till then, it may receive confirmation from miracles. But the mark of sound doctrine given by our Saviour himself is its tendency to promote the glory not of men, but of God (John 7:18; 8:50). Our Saviour having declared this to be test of doctrine, we are in error if we regard as miraculous, works which are used for any other purpose than to magnify the name of God. And it becomes us to remember that Satan has his miracles, which, although they are tricks rather than true wonders, are still such as to delude the ignorant and unwary. Magicians and enchanters have always been famous for miracles, and miracles of an astonishing description have given support to idolatry: these, however, do not make us converts to the superstitions either of magicians or idolaters. In old times, too, the Donatists used their power of working miracles as a battering-ram, with which they shook the simplicity of the common people. We now give to our opponents the answer which Augustine then gave to the Donatists (in Joan. Tract. 23), "The Lord put us on our guard against those wonder-workers, when he foretold that false prophets would arise, who, by lying signs and divers wonders, would, if it were possible, deceive the very elect" (Mt. 24:24). Paul, too, gave warning that the reign of antichrist would be "with all power, and signs, and lying wonders" (2 Thess. 2:9).

But our opponents tell us that their miracles are wrought not by idols, not by sorcerers, not by false prophets, but by saints: as if we did not know it to be one of Satan's wiles to transform himself "into an angel of light" (2 Cor. 11:14). The Egyptians, in whose neighbourhood Jeremiah was buried, anciently sacrificed and paid other divine honours to him (*Hieron. in Praef. Jerem*). Did they not abuse of the holy prophet of God? and yet, in recompense for so venerating his tomb, they thought that they were cured of the bite of serpents. What, then, shall we say but that it has been, and always will be, a most just punishment of God, to send on those who do not receive the truth in the love of it, "strong delusion, that they should believe a lie" (2 Thess. 2:11)? We, then, have no lack of miracles, sure miracles, that cannot be gainsaid, but those to which our opponents lay claim are mere delusions of Satan, inasmuch as they draw off the people from the true worship of God to vanity.

4. It is a calumny to represent us as opposed to the Fathers (I mean the ancient writers of a purer age), as if the Fathers were supporters of their impiety. Were the contest to be decided by such authority (to speak in the most moderate terms), the better part of the victory would be ours. While there is much that is admirable and wise in the writings of those Fathers, and while in some things it has fared with them as with ordinary men; these pious sons, forsooth, with the peculiar acuteness of intellect, and judgment, and soul, which belongs to them, adore only their slips and errors, while those things which are well said they either overlook, or disguise, or corrupt, so that it may be truly said their only care has been to gather dross among gold. Then, with dishonest clamour,

they assail us as enemies and despisers of the Fathers. So far are we from despising them, that if this were the proper place, it would give us no trouble to support the greater part of the doctrines which we now hold by their suffrages. Still, in studying their writings, we have endeavoured to remember that all things are ours, to serve, not lord it over us, but that we are Christ's only, and must obey him in all things without exception (1 Cor. 3:21–23; see also Augustine, Ep. 28). He who does not draw this distinction will not have any fixed principles in religion; for those holy men were ignorant of many things, are often opposed to each other, and are sometimes at variance with themselves. [...]

All the Fathers with one heart execrated, and with one mouth protested against, contaminating the word of God with the subtleties, sophists, and involving it in the brawls of dialecticians. Do they keep within these limits when the sole occupation of their lives is to entwine and entangle the simplicity of Scripture with endless disputes, and worse than sophistical jargon? So much so, that were the Fathers to rise from their graves, and listen to the brawling art which bears the name of speculative theology, there is nothing they would suppose it less to be than a discussion of a religious nature.

But my discourse would far exceed its just limits were I to show, in detail, how petulantly those men shake off the yoke of the Fathers, while they wish to be thought their most obedient sons. Months, nay, years would fail me; and yet so deplorable and desperate is their effrontery, that they presume to chastise us for overstepping the ancient landmarks! [...]

6. Their dilemma does not push us so violently as to oblige us to confess, either that the Church was a considerable time without life, or that we have now a quarrel with the Church. The Church of Christ assuredly has lived, and will live, as long as Christ shall reign at the right hand of the Father. By his hand it is sustained, by his protection defended, by his mighty power preserved in safety. For what he once undertook he will undoubtedly perform, he will be with his people always, "even to the end of the

world" (Mt. 28:20). With the Church we wage no war, since, with one consent, in common with the whole body of the faithful, we worship and adore one God, and Christ Jesus the Lord, as all the pious have always adored him. But they themselves err not a little from the truth in not recognizing any church but that which they behold with the bodily eye, and in endeavouring to circumscribe it by limits, within which it cannot be confined.

The hinges on which the controversy turns are these: first, in their contending that the form of the Church is always visible and apparent; and, secondly, in their placing this form in the see of the Church of Rome and its hierarchy. We, on the contrary, maintain, both that the Church may exist without any apparent form, and, moreover, that the form is not ascertained by that external splendour which they foolishly admire, but by a very different mark, namely, by the pure preaching of the word of God, and the due administration of the sacraments. They make an outcry whenever the Church cannot be pointed to with the finger. But how oft was it the fate of the Church among the Jews to be so defaced that no comeliness appeared? What do we suppose to have been the splendid form when Elijah complained that he was left alone (1 Kings 19:14)? How long after the advent of Christ did it lie hid without form? How often since has it been so oppressed by wars, seditions, and heresies, that it was nowhere seen in splendour? Had they lived at that time, would they have believed there was any Church? But Elijah learned that there remained seven thousand men who had not bowed the knee to Baal; nor ought we to doubt that Christ has always reigned on earth ever since he ascended to heaven. Had the faithful at that time required some discernible form, must they not have forthwith given way to despondency? And, indeed, Hilary accounted it a very great fault in his day that men were so possessed with a foolish admiration of Episcopal dignity as not to perceive the deadly hydra lurking under that mask. His words are, "One advice I give: Beware of Antichrist; for, unhappily, a love of walls has seized you; unhappily, the Church of God which you venerate exists in houses and buildings; unhappily, under these you find the name of peace. Is it doubtful that in these Antichrist will have his seat? Safer to me are mountains, and woods, and lakes, and dungeons, and whirlpools; since in these prophets, dwelling or immersed, did prophesy" (*Cont. Auxentium*).

And what is it at the present day that the world venerates in its horned bishops, unless that it imagines those who are seen presiding over celebrated cities to be holy prelates of religion? Away, then, with this absurd mode of judging! Let us rather reverently admit, that as God alone knows who are his, so he may sometimes withdraw the external manifestation of his Church from the view of men. This, I allow, is a fearful punishment which God sends on the earth, but if the wickedness of men so deserves, why do we strive to oppose the just vengeance of God? It was thus that God, in past ages, punished the ingratitude of men, for after they had refused to obey his truth, and had extinguished his light, he allowed them, when blinded by sense, both to be deluded by lying vanities and plunged in thick darkness, so that no face of a true Church appeared. Meanwhile, however, though his own people were dispersed and concealed amidst errors and darkness, he saved them from destruction. No wonder; for he knew how to preserve them even in the confusion of Babylon and the flame of the fiery furnace. [...]

7. Lastly, they are far from candid when they invidiously number up the disturbances, tumults, and disputes, which the preaching of our doctrine has brought in its train, and the fruits which, in many instances, it now produces, for the doctrine itself is undeservedly charged with evils which ought to be ascribed to the malice of Satan. It is one of the characteristics of the divine word, that whenever it appears, Satan ceases to slumber and sleep. This is the surest and most unerring test for distinguishing it from false doctrines which readily betray themselves, while they are received by all with willing ears, and welcomed by an applauding world. Accordingly, for several ages, during which all things were immersed in profound darkness, almost all mankind were mere jest and sport to the god of this world, who, like any Sardanapalus, idled and lux-

uriated undisturbed. For what else could he do but laugh and sport while in tranquil and undisputed possession of his kingdom? But when light beaming from above somewhat dissipated the darkness—when the strong man arose and aimed a blow at his kingdom—then, indeed, he began to shake off his wonted torpor, and rush to arms. And first he stirred up the hands of men, that by them he might violently suppress the dawning truth; but when this availed him not, he turned to snares, exciting dissensions and disputes about doctrine by means of his Catabaptists, and other portentous miscreants, that he might thus obscure, and, at length, extinguish the truth. And now he persists in assailing it with both engines, endeavouring to pluck up the true seed by the violent hand of man, and striving, as much as in him lies, to choke it with his tares, that it may not grow and bear knit. But it will be in vain, if we listen to the admonition of the Lord, who long ago disclosed his wiles, that we might not be taken unawares, and armed us with full protection against all his machinations. But how malignant to throw upon the word of God itself the blame either of the seditions which wicked men and rebels, or of the sects which impostors stir up against it! The example, however, is not new. Elijah was interrogated whether it were not he that troubled Israel. Christ was seditious, according to the Jews, and the apostles were charged with the crime of popular commotion. What else do those who, in the present day, impute to us all the disturbances, tumults, and contentions which break out against us? Elijah, however, has taught us our answer (1 Kgs. 18:17, 18). It is not we who disseminate errors or stir up tumults, but they who resist the mighty power of God.

But while this single answer is sufficient to rebut the rash charges of these men, it is necessary, on the other hand, to consult for the weakness of those who take the alarm at such scandals, and not unfrequently waver in perplexity. But that they may not fall away in this perplexity, and forfeit their good degree, let them know that the apostles in their day experienced the very things which now befall us. There were then unlearned and unstable men who, as Peter tells us, wrested the inspired writings of Paul to their own destruction (2 Pet. 3:16). There were despisers of God, who, when they heard that sin abounded in order that grace might more abound, immediately inferred, "We will continue in sin that grace may abound" (Rom. 6:1); when they heard that believers were not under the law, but under grace, forthwith sung out, "We will sin because we are not under the law, but under grace" (Rom. 6:15). There were some who charged the apostle with being the minister of sin. Many false prophets entered in privily to pull down the churches which he had reared. Some preached the gospel through envy and strife, not sincerely—maliciously even—thinking to add affliction to his bonds (Phil. 1:15). Elsewhere the gospel made little progress. All sought their own, not the things which were Jesus Christ's. Others went back like the dog to his vomit, or the sow that was washed to her wallowing in the mire. Great numbers perverted their spiritual freedom to carnal licentiousness. False brethren crept in to the imminent danger of the faithful. Among the brethren themselves various quarrels arose. What, then, were the apostles to do? Were they either to dissemble for the time, or rather lay aside and abandon that gospel which they saw to be the seed—bed of so many strifes, the source of so many perils, the occasion of so many scandals? In straits of this kind, they remembered that "Christ was a stone of stumbling, and a rock of offence," "set up for the fall and rising again of many," and "for a sign to be spoken against" ([Isaiah 8:14]; Luke 2:34); and, armed with this assurance, they proceeded boldly through all perils from tumults and scandals. It becomes us to be supported by the same consideration, since Paul declares that it is a never-failing characteristic of the gospel to be a "savour of death unto death in them that perish" (2 Cor. 2:16), although rather destined to us for the purpose of being a savour of life unto life, and the power of God for the salvation of believers. This we should certainly experience it to be, did we not by our ingratitude corrupt this unspeakable gift of God, and turn to our destruction what ought to be our only saving defense.

But to return, Sire. Be not moved by the absurd insinuations with which our adversaries are striving to frighten you into the belief that nothing else is wished and aimed at by this new gospel (for so they term it), than opportunity for sedition and impunity for all kinds of vice. Our God is not the author of division, but of peace; and the Son of God, who came to destroy the works of the devil, is not the minister of sin. We, too, are undeservedly charged with desires of a kind for which we have never given even the smallest suspicion. We, forsooth, meditate the subversion of kingdoms; we, whose voice was never heard in faction, and whose life, while passed under you, is known to have been always quiet and simple; even now, when exiled from our home, we nevertheless cease not to pray for all prosperity to your person and your kingdom. We, forsooth, are aiming after an unchecked indulgence in vice, in whose manners, though there is much to be blamed, there is nothing which deserves such an imputation; nor (thank God) have we profited so little in the gospel that our life may not be to these slanderers an example of chastity, kindness, pity, temperance, patience, moderation, or any other virtue. It is plain, indeed, that we fear God sincerely, and worship him in truth, since, whether by life or by death, we desire his name to be hallowed; and hatred herself has been forced to bear testimony to the innocence and civil integrity of some of our people on whom death was inflicted for the very thing which deserved the highest praise. But if any, under pretext of the gospel, excite tumults (none such have as yet been detected in your realm), if any use the liberty of the grace of God as a cloak for licentiousness (I know of numbers who do), there are laws and legal punishments by which they may be punished up to the measure of their deserts—only, in the mean time, let not the gospel of God be evil spoken of because of the iniquities of evil men.

Sire, that you may not lend too credulous an ear to the accusations of our enemies, their virulent injustice has been set before you at sufficient length; I fear even more than sufficient, since this preface has grown almost to the bulk of a full apology. My object, however, was not to frame a defense, but only with a view to the hearing of our cause, to mollify your mind, now indeed turned away and estranged from us—I add, even inflamed against us—but whose good will, we are confident, we should regain, would you but once, with calmness and composure, read this our Confession, which we desire your Majesty to accept instead of a defense. But if the whispers of the malevolent so possess your ear, that the accused are to have no opportunity of pleading their cause; if those vindictive furies, with your connivance, are always to rage with bonds, scourgings, tortures, maimings, and burnings, we, indeed, like sheep doomed to slaughter, shall be reduced to every extremity; yet so that, in our patience, we will possess our souls, and wait for the strong hand of the Lord, which, doubtless, will appear in its own time, and show itself armed, both to rescue the poor from affliction, and also take vengeance on the despisers, who are now exulting so securely.

Most illustrious King, may the Lord, the King of kings, establish your throne in righteousness, and your sceptre in equity. Basel, 1st August 1536.

Book I

Chapter 1. The Knowledge of God and of Ourselves Mutually Connected — Nature of the Connection

1. Our wisdom, in so far as it ought to be deemed true and solid Wisdom, consists almost entirely of two parts: the knowledge of God and of ourselves. But as these are connected together by many ties, it is not easy to determine which of the two precedes and gives birth to the other. For, in the first place, no man can survey himself without forthwith turning his thoughts towards the God in whom he lives and moves; because it is perfectly obvious that the endowments which we possess cannot possibly be from ourselves, nay, that our very being is nothing else than subsistence in God alone. In the second place, those blessings which unceasingly distil to us from heaven are like streams conducting us to the fountain.

Here, again, the infinitude of good which resides in God becomes more apparent from our poverty. In particular, the miserable ruin into which the revolt of the first man has plunged us compels us to turn our eyes upwards, not only that while hungry and famishing we may thence ask what we want, but being aroused by fear may learn humility. For as there exists in man something like a world of misery, and ever since we were stript of the divine attire our naked shame discloses an immense series of disgraceful properties every man, being stung by the consciousness of his own unhappiness, in this way necessarily obtains at least some knowledge of God. Thus, our feeling of ignorance, vanity, want, weakness, in short, depravity and corruption, reminds us that in the Lord, and none but He, dwell the true light of wisdom, solid virtue, exuberant goodness. We are accordingly urged by our own evil things to consider the good things of God; and, indeed, we cannot aspire to Him in earnest until we have begun to be displeased with ourselves. For what man is not disposed to rest in himself? Who, in fact, does not thus rest, so long as he is unknown to himself; that is, so long as he is contented with his own endowments, and unconscious or unmindful of his misery? Every person, therefore, on coming to the knowledge of himself, is not only urged to seek God, but is also led as by the hand to find him.

2. On the other hand, it is evident that man never attains to a true self-knowledge until he has previously contemplated the face of God, and come down after such contemplation to look into himself. For (such is our innate pride) we always seem to ourselves just, and upright, and wise, and holy, until we are convinced, by clear evidence, of our injustice, vileness, folly, and impurity. Convinced, however, we are not, if we look to ourselves only, and not to the Lord also—He being the only standard by the application of which this conviction can be produced. For, since we are all naturally prone to hypocrisy, any empty semblance of righteousness is quite enough to satisfy us instead of righteousness itself. And since nothing appears within us or around us that is not tainted with very great impurity, so long as we keep our mind within the confines of

human pollution, anything which is in some small degree less defiled delights us as if it were most pure just as an eye, to which nothing but black had been previously presented, deems an object of a whitish, or even of a brownish hue, to be perfectly white. Nay, the bodily sense may furnish a still stronger illustration of the extent to which we are deluded in estimating the powers of the mind. If, at mid-day, we either look down to the ground, or on the surrounding objects which lie open to our view, we think ourselves endued with a very strong and piercing eyesight, but when we look up to the sun, and gaze at it unveiled, the sight which did excellently well for the earth is instantly so dazzled and confounded by the refulgence, as to oblige us to confess that our acuteness in discerning terrestrial objects is mere dimness when applied to the sun. Thus too, it happens in estimating our spiritual qualities. So long as we do not look beyond the earth, we are quite pleased with our own righteousness, wisdom, and virtue; we address ourselves in the most flattering terms, and seem only less than demigods. But should we once begin to raise our thoughts to God, and reflect what kind of Being he is, and how absolute the perfection of that righteousness, and wisdom, and virtue, to which, as a standard, we are bound to be conformed, what formerly delighted us by its false show of righteousness will become polluted with the greatest iniquity; what strangely imposed upon us under the name of wisdom will disgust by its extreme folly, and what presented the appearance of virtuous energy will be condemned as the most miserable impotence. So far are those qualities in us, which seem most perfect, from corresponding to the divine purity.

3. Hence that dread and amazement with which as Scripture uniformly relates, holy men were struck and overwhelmed whenever they beheld the presence of God. When we see those who previously stood firm and secure so quaking with terror that the fear of death takes hold of them, nay, they are, in a manner, swallowed up and annihilated, the inference to be drawn is that men are never duly touched and impressed with a conviction of their insignificance, until they have contrasted themselves with the majesty of

God. Frequent examples of this consternation occur both in the Book of Judges and the Prophetical Writings; so much so, that it was a common expression among the people of God, "We shall die, for we have seen the Lord." Hence the Book of Job, also, in humbling men under a conviction of their folly, feebleness, and pollution, always derives its chief argument from descriptions of the Divine wisdom, virtue, and purity. Nor without cause: for we see Abraham the readier to acknowledge himself but dust and ashes the nearer he approaches to behold the glory of the Lord, and Elijah unable to wait with unveiled face for His approach, so dreadful is the sight. And what can man do, man who is but rottenness and a worm, when even the Cherubim themselves must veil their faces in very terror? To this, undoubtedly, the Prophet Isaiah refers, when he says, "The moon shall be confounded, and the sun ashamed, when the Lord of Hosts shall reign" (Isa. 24:23), i.e., when he shall exhibit his refulgence, and give a nearer view of it, the brightest objects will, in comparison, be covered with darkness.

But though the knowledge of God and the knowledge of ourselves are bound together by a mutual tie, due arrangement requires that we treat of the former in the first place, and then descend to the latter.

Chapter 2. What It Is to Know God—Tendency of This Knowledge

1. By the knowledge of God, I understand that by which we not only conceive that there is some God, but also apprehend what it is for our interest, and conducive to his glory, what, in short, it is befitting to know concerning him. For, properly speaking, we cannot say that God is known where there is no religion or piety. I am not now referring to that species of knowledge by which men, in themselves lost and under curse, apprehend God as a Redeemer in Christ the Mediator. I speak only of that simple and primitive knowledge, to which the mere course of nature would have con-

ducted us, had Adam stood upright. For although no man will now, in the present ruin of the human race, perceive God to be either a father, or the author of salvation, or propitious in any respect, until Christ interpose to make our peace, still it is one thing to perceive that God our Maker supports us by his power, rules us by his providence, fosters us by his goodness, and visits us with all kinds of blessings, and another thing to embrace the grace of reconciliation offered to us in Christ. Since, then, the Lord first appears, as well in the creation of the world as in the general doctrine of Scripture, simply as a Creator, and afterwards as a Redeemer in Christ—a twofold knowledge of him hence arises, of these the former is now to be considered, the latter will afterwards follow in its order. But although our mind cannot conceive of God, without rendering some worship to him, it will not, however, be sufficient simply to hold that he is the only being whom all ought to worship and adore, unless we are also persuaded that he is the fountain of all goodness, and that we must seek everything in him, and in none but him. My meaning is: we must be persuaded not only that as he once formed the world, so he sustains it by his boundless power, governs it by his wisdom, preserves it by his goodness, in particular, rules the human race with justice and Judgment, bears with them in mercy, shields them by his protection, but also that not a particle of light, or wisdom, or justice, or power, or rectitude, or genuine truth, will anywhere be found, which does not flow from him, and of which he is not the cause; in this way we must learn to expect and ask all things from him, and thankfully ascribe to him whatever we receive. For this sense of the divine perfections is the proper master to teach us piety, out of which religion springs. By piety I mean that union of reverence and love to God which the knowledge of his benefits inspires. For, until men feel that they owe everything to God, that they are cherished by his paternal care, and that he is the author of all their blessings, so that nought is to be looked for away from him, they will never submit to him in voluntary obedience, nay, unless they place their entire happiness in him, they will never yield up their whole selves to him in truth and sincerity.

2. Those, therefore, who, in considering this question, propose to inquire what the essence of God is, only delude us with frigid speculations—it being much more our interest to know what kind of being God is, and what things are agreeable to his nature. For, of what use is it to join Epicures in acknowledging some God who has cast off the care of the world, and only delights himself in ease? What avails it, in short, to know a God with whom we have nothing to do? The effect of our knowledge rather ought to be, first, to teach us reverence and fear; and, secondly, to induce us, under its guidance and teaching, to ask every good thing from him, and, when it is received, ascribe it to him. For how can the idea of God enter your mind without instantly giving rise to the thought that since you are his workmanship, you are bound, by the very law of creation, to submit to his authority?—that your life is due to him?—that whatever you do ought to have reference to him? If so, it undoubtedly follows that your life is sadly corrupted, if it is not framed in obedience to him, since his will ought to be the law of our lives. On the other hand, your idea of his nature is not clear unless you acknowledge him to be the origin and fountain of all goodness. Hence would arise both confidence in him, and a desire of cleaving to him, did not the depravity of the human mind lead it away from the proper course of investigation.

For, first of all, the pious mind does not devise for itself any kind of God, but looks alone to the one true God; nor does it feign for him any character it pleases, but is contented to have him in the character in which he manifests himself always guarding, with the utmost diligences against transgressing his will, and wandering, with daring presumptions from the right path. He by whom God is thus known perceiving how he governs all things, confides in him as his guardian and protector, and casts himself entirely upon his faithfulness—perceiving him to be the source of every blessing, if he is in any strait or feels any want, he instantly recurs to his protection and trusts to his aid—persuaded that he is good and merciful, he reclines upon him with sure confidence, and doubts not that, in the divine clemency, a remedy will be provided for his every time of need—acknowledging him as his Father and his Lord he considers himself bound to have respect to his authority in all things, to reverence his majesty, aim at the advancement of his glory, and obey his commands—regarding him as a just judge, armed with severity to punish crimes, he keeps the Judgment-seat always in his view. Standing in awe of it, he curbs himself, and fears to provoke his anger. Nevertheless, he is not so terrified by an apprehension of Judgment as to wish he could withdraw himself, even if the means of escape lay before him; nay, he embraces him not less as the avenger of wickedness than as the rewarder of the righteous, because he perceives that it equally appertains to his glory to store up punishment for the one, and eternal life for the other. Besides, it is not the mere fear of punishment that restrains him from sin. Loving and revering God as his father, honouring and obeying him as his master, although there were no hell, he would revolt at the very idea of offending him.

Such is pure and genuine religion, namely, confidence in God coupled with serious fear—fear, which both includes in it willing reverence, and brings along with it such legitimate worship as is prescribed by the law. And it ought to be more carefully considered that all men promiscuously do homage to God, but very few truly reverence him. On all hands there is abundance of ostentatious ceremonies, but sincerity of heart is rare.

Chapter 3. The Knowledge of God Naturally Implanted in the Human Mind

1. That there exists in the human minds and indeed by natural instinct, some sense of Deity, we hold to be beyond dispute, since God himself, to prevent any man from pretending ignorance, has endued all men with some idea of his Godhead, the memory of which he constantly renews and occasionally enlarges, that all to a man being aware that there is a God, and that he is their Maker,

may be condemned by their own conscience when they neither worship him nor consecrate their lives to his service. Certainly, if there is any quarter where it may be supposed that God is unknown, the most likely for such an instance to exist is among the dullest tribes farthest removed from civilization. But, as a heathen tells us, there is no nation so barbarous, no race so brutish, as not to be imbued with the conviction that there is a God. Even those who, in other respects, seem to differ least from the lower animals, constantly retain some sense of religion, so thoroughly has this common conviction possessed the mind, so firmly is it stamped on the breasts of all men. Since, then, there never has been, from the very first, any quarter of the globe, any city, any household even, without religion, this amounts to a tacit confession that a sense of Deity is inscribed on every heart. Nay, even idolatry is ample evidence of this fact. For we know how reluctant man is to lower himself, in order to set other creatures above him. Therefore, when he chooses to worship wood and stone rather than be thought to have no God, it is evident how very strong this impression of a Deity must be, since it is more difficult to obliterate it from the mind of man, than to break down the feelings of his nature—these certainly being broken down, when, in opposition to his natural haughtiness, he spontaneously humbles himself before the meanest object as an act of reverence to God.

2. It is most absurd, therefore, to maintain, as some do, that religion was devised by the cunning and craft of a few individuals, as a means of keeping the body of the people in due subjection, while there was nothing which those very individuals, while teaching others to worship God, less believed than the existence of a God. I readily acknowledge that designing men have introduced a vast number of fictions into religion, with the view of inspiring the populace with reverence or striking them with terror, and thereby rendering them more obsequious, but they never could have succeeded in this had the minds of men not been previously imbued with that uniform belief in God, from which, as from its seed, the religious propensity springs. And it is altogether incredible that

those who, in the matter of religion, cunningly imposed on their ruder neighbours, were altogether devoid of a knowledge of God. For though in old times there were some, and in the present day not a few are found who deny the being of a God, yet, whether they will or not, they occasionally feel the truth which they are desirous not to know. We do not read of any man who broke out into more unbridled and audacious contempt of the Deity than Caligula, and yet none showed greater dread when any indication of divine wrath was manifested. Thus, however unwilling, he shook with terror before the God whom he professedly studied to condemn. You may every day see the same thing happening to his modern imitators. The most audacious despiser of God is most easily disturbed, trembling at the sound of a falling leaf. How so, unless in vindication of the divine majesty, which smites their consciences the more strongly the more they endeavour to flee from it. They all, indeed, look out for hiding-places where they may conceal themselves from the presence of the Lord, and again efface it from their mind, but after all their efforts they remain caught within the net. Though the conviction may occasionally seem to vanish for a moment, it immediately returns, and rushes in with new impetuosity, so that any interval of relief from the gnawing of conscience is not unlike the slumber of the intoxicated or the insane, who have no quiet rest in sleep, but are continually haunted with dire horrific dreams. Even the wicked themselves, therefore, are an example of the fact that some idea of God always exists in every human mind.

3. All men of sound Judgment will therefore hold that a sense of Deity is indelibly engraven on the human heart. And that this belief is naturally engendered in all, and thoroughly fixed as it were in our very bones, is strikingly attested by the contumacy of the wicked, who, though they struggle furiously, are unable to extricate themselves from the fear of God. Though Diagoras, and others of like stamps make themselves merry with whatever has been believed in all ages concerning religion, and Dionysus scoffs at the Judgment of heaven, it is but a Sardonian grin; for the worm of conscience, keener than burning steel, is gnawing them within. I

do not say with Cicero, that errors wear out by age, and that religion increases and grows better day by day. For the world (as will be shortly seen) labours as much as it can to shake off all knowledge of God, and corrupts his worship in innumerable ways. I only say, that, when the stupid hardness of heart, which the wicked eagerly court as a means of despising God, becomes enfeebled, the sense of Deity, which of all things they wished most to be extinguished, is still in vigour, and now and then breaks forth. Whence we infer, that this is not a doctrine which is first learned at school, but one as to which every man is, from the womb, his own master; one which nature herself allows no individual to forget, though many, with all their might, strive to do so. Moreover, if all are born and live for the express purpose of learning to know God, and if the knowledge of God, in so far as it fails to produce this effect, is fleeting and vain, it is clear that all those who do not direct the whole thoughts and actions of their lives to this end fail to fulfil the law of their being. This did not escape the observation even of philosophers. For it is the very thing which Plato meant when he taught, as he often does, that the chief good of the soul consists in resemblance to God (in *Phæd. et Theact.*); i.e., when, by means of knowing him, she is wholly transformed into him. Thus Gryllus, also, in Plutarch, reasons most skillfully, when he affirms that, if once religion is banished from the lives of men, they not only in no respect excel, but are, in many respects, much more wretched than the brutes, since, being exposed to so many forms of evil, they continually drag on a troubled and restless existence: that the only thing, therefore, which makes them superior is the worship of God, through which alone they aspire to immortality (*lib. guod bruta anim. ratione utantur*).

Chapter 4. The Knowledge of God Stifled or Corrupted, Ignorantly or Maliciously

1. But though experience testifies that a seed of religion is divinely sown in all, scarcely one in a hundred is found who cherishes it in

his heart, and not one in whom it grows to maturity so far is it from yielding fruit in its season. Moreover, while some lose themselves in superstitious observances, and others, of set purpose, wickedly revolt from God, the result is that, in regard to the true knowledge of him, all are so degenerate that in no part of the world can genuine godliness be found. In saying that some fall away into superstition, I mean not to insinuate that their excessive absurdity frees them from guilt; for the blindness under which they labour is almost invariably accompanied with vain pride and stubbornness. Mingled vanity and pride appear in this, that when miserable men do seek after God, instead of ascending higher than themselves as they ought to do, they measure him by their own carnal stupidity, and, neglecting solid inquiry, fly off to indulge their curiosity in vain speculation. Hence, they do not conceive of him in the character in which he is manifested, but imagine him to be whatever their own rashness has devised. This abyss standing open, they cannot move one footstep without rushing headlong to destruction. With such an idea of God, nothing which they may attempt to offer in the way of worship or obedience can have any value in his sight, because it is not him they worship, but, instead of him, the dream and figment of their own heart. This corrupt procedure is admirably described by Paul, when he says, that "thinking to be wise, they became fools" (Rom. 1:22). He had previously said that "they became vain in their imaginations," but lest any should suppose them blameless, he afterwards adds that they were deservedly blinded, because, not contented with sober inquiry, because, arrogating to themselves more than they have any title to do, they of their own accord court darkness, nay, bewitch themselves with perverse, empty show. Hence it is that their folly, the result not only of vain curiosity, but of licentious desire and overweening confidence in the pursuit of forbidden knowledge, cannot be excused.

2. The expression of David, "The fool hath said in his heart, 'There is no God,'" is primarily applied to those who, as will shortly farther appear, stifle the light of nature, and intentionally stupefy themselves (Psalm 14:1, 53:1). We see many, after they have be-

come hardened in a daring course of sin, madly banishing all remembrance of God, though spontaneously suggested to them from
within, by natural sense. To show how detestable this madness is,
the Psalmist introduces them as distinctly denying that there is a
God, because although they do not disown his essence, they rob
him of his justice and providence, and represent him as sitting idly
in heaven. Nothing being less accordant with the nature of God
than to cast off the government of the world, leaving it to chance,
and so to wink at the crimes of men that they may wanton with
impunity in evil courses, it follows that every man who indulges in
security, after extinguishing all fear of divine Judgment, virtually
denies that there is a God. As a just punishment of the wicked,
after they have closed their own eyes, God makes their hearts dull
and heavy, and hence, seeing, they see not. David, indeed, is the
best interpreter of his own meaning, when he says elsewhere, the
wicked has "no fear of God before his eyes," (Psalm 36:1); and,
again, "He has said in his heart, God has forgotten; he hideth his
face; he will never see it" [Ps. 10:1]. Thus although they are forced
to acknowledge that there is some God, they, however, rob him of
his glory by denying his power. For, as Paul declares, "If we believe
not, he abideth faithful, he cannot deny himself," (2 Tim. 2:13); so
those who feign to themselves a dead and dumb idol, are truly said
to deny God. It is, moreover, to be observed that though they
struggle with their own convictions, and would fain not only banish
God from their minds, but from heaven also, their stupefaction is
never so complete as to secure them from being occasionally
dragged before the divine tribunal. Still, as no fear restrains them
from rushing violently in the face of God, so long as they are hur-
ried on by that blind impulse, it cannot be denied that their prevailing state of mind in regard to him is brutish oblivion.

3. In this way, the vain pretext which many employ to clothe
their superstition is overthrown. They deem it enough that they
have some kind of zeal for religion, how preposterous soever it
may be, not observing that true religion must be conformable to
the will of God as its unerring standard; that he can never deny

himself, and is no spectra or phantom, to be metamorphosed at each individual's caprice. It is easy to see how superstition, with its false glosses, mocks God, while it tries to please him. Usually fastening merely on things on which he has declared he sets no value, it either contemptuously overlooks, or even undisguisedly rejects, the things which he expressly enjoins, or in which we are assured that he takes pleasure. Those, therefore, who set up a fictitious worship, merely worship and adore their own delirious fancies; indeed, they would never dare so to trifle with God, had they not previously fashioned him after their own childish conceits. Hence that vague and wandering opinion of Deity is declared by an apostle to be ignorance of God: "Howbeit, then, when ye knew not God, ye did service unto them which by nature are no gods." And he elsewhere declares, that the Ephesians were "without God" at the time when they wandered without any correct knowledge of him (Eph. 2:12). It makes little difference, at least in this respect, whether you hold the existence of one God, or a plurality of gods, since, in both cases alike, by departing from the true God, you have nothing left but an execrable idol. It remains, therefore, to conclude with Lactantius, "No religion is genuine that is not in accordance with truth" (*Instit. Div. lib* 1:2, 6).

4. To this fault they add a second—viz. that when they do think of God it is against their will; never approaching him without being dragged into his presence, and when there, instead of the voluntary fear flowing from reverence of the divine majesty, feeling only that forced and servile fear which divine Judgment extorts Judgment which, from the impossibility of escape, they are compelled to dread, but which, while they dread, they at the same time also hate. To impiety, and to it alone, the saying of Statius properly applies: "Fear first brought gods into the world" (*Theb. lib.* 1). Those whose inclinations are at variance with the justice of God, knowing that his tribunal has been erected for the punishment of transgression, earnestly wish that that tribunal were overthrown. Under the influence of this feeling they are actually warring against God, justice being one of his essential attributes. Perceiving that

they are always within reach of his power, that resistance and eva-
sion are alike impossible, they fear and tremble. Accordingly, to
avoid the appearance of condemning a majesty by which all are
overawed, they have recourse to some species of religious observance, never ceasing meanwhile to defile themselves with every
kind of vice and add crime to crime, until they have broken the
holy law of the Lord in every one of its requirements and set his
whole righteousness at naught; at all events, they are not so restrained by their semblance of fear as not to luxuriate and take
pleasure in iniquity, choosing rather to indulge their carnal propen-
sities than to curb them with the bridle of the Holy Spirit. But since
this shadow of religion (it scarcely even deserves to be called a
shadow) is false and vain, it is easy to infer how much this confused knowledge of God differs from that piety which is instilled
into the breasts of believers, and from which alone true religion
springs. And yet hypocrites would fain, by means of tortuous wind-
ings, make a show of being near to God at the very time they are
fleeing from him. For while the whole life ought to be one perpetual course of obedience, they rebel without fear in almost all their
actions, and seek to appease him with a few paltry sacrifices; while
they ought to serve him with integrity of heart and holiness of life,
they endeavour to procure his favour by means of frivolous devices
and punctilios of no value. Nay, they take greater license in their
groveling indulgences, because they imagine that they can fulfil
their duty to him by preposterous expiations; in short, while their
confidence ought to have been fixed upon him, they put him aside,
and rest in themselves or the creatures. At length they bewilder
themselves in such a maze of error that the darkness of ignorance
obscures, and ultimately extinguishes, those sparks which were designed to show them the glory of God. Still, however, the conviction that there is some Deity continues to exist, like a plant which
can never be completely eradicated, though so corrupt, that it is
only capable of producing the worst of fruit. Nay, we have still
stronger evidence of the proposition for which I now contend—
viz. that a sense of Deity is naturally engraven on the human heart,

in the fact, that the very reprobate are forced to acknowledge it. When at their ease, they can jest about God, and talk pertly and loquaciously in disparagement of his power; but should despair, from any cause, overtake them, it will stimulate them to seek him, and dictate ejaculatory prayers, proving that they were not entirely ignorant of God, but had perversely suppressed feelings which ought to have been earlier manifested.

Chapter 5. The Knowledge of God Conspicuous in the Creation, and Continual Government of the World

1. Since the perfection of blessedness consists in the knowledge of God, he has been pleased, in order that none might be excluded from the means of obtaining felicity, not only to deposit in our minds that seed of religion of which we have already spoken, but so to manifest his perfections in the whole structure of the universe, and daily place himself in our view, that we cannot open our eyes without being compelled to behold him. His essence, indeed, is incomprehensible, utterly transcending all human thought; but on each of his works his glory is engraven in characters so bright, so distinct, and so illustrious that none, however dull and illiterate, can plead ignorance as their excuse. Hence, with perfect truth, the Psalmist exclaims, "He covereth himself with light as with a garment," (Psalm 104:2), as if he had said, that God for the first time was arrayed in visible attire when, in the creation of the world, he displayed those glorious banners, on which, to whatever side we turn, we behold his perfections visibly portrayed. In the same place, the Psalmist aptly compares the expanded heavens to his royal tent, and says, "He layeth the beams of his chambers in the waters, maketh the clouds his chariot, and walketh upon the wings of the wind," sending forth the winds and lightnings as his swift messengers. And because the glory of his power and wisdom is more refulgent in the firmament, it is frequently designated as his palace. And, first, wherever you turn your eyes, there is no portion of the world, however minute, that does not exhibit at least some sparks

of beauty, while it is impossible to contemplate the vast and beautiful fabric as it extends around, without being overwhelmed by the
immense weight of glory. Hence, the author of the Epistle to the
Hebrews elegantly describes the visible worlds as images of the
invisible, the elegant structure of the world serving us as a kind of
mirror, in which we may behold God, though otherwise invisible
(Heb. 11:3). For the same reason, the Psalmist attributes language
to celestial objects, a language which all nations understand, the
manifestation of the Godhead being too clear to escape the notice
of any people, however obtuse (Psalm 19:1). The apostle Paul, stat-
ing this still more clearly, says, "That which may be known of God
is manifest in them, for God has showed it unto them. For the invisible things of him from the creation of the world are clearly
seen, being understood by the things that are made, even his eternal power and Godhead" (Rom. 1:20).

2. In attestation of his wondrous wisdom, both the heavens
and the earth present us with innumerable proofs not only those
more recondite proofs which astronomy, medicine, and all the natural sciences, are designed to illustrate, but proofs which force
themselves on the notice of the most illiterate peasant, who cannot
open his eyes without beholding them. It is true, indeed, that those
who are more or less intimately acquainted with those liberal studies are thereby assisted and enabled to obtain a deeper insight into
the secret workings of divine wisdom. No man, however, though
he be ignorant of these, is incapacitated for discerning such proofs
of creative wisdom as may well cause him to break forth in admiration of the Creator. To investigate the motions of the heavenly
bodies, to determine their positions, measure their distances, and
ascertain their properties, demands skill, and a more careful examination; and where these are so employed, as the Providence of God
is thereby more fully unfolded, so it is reasonable to suppose that
the mind takes a loftier flight, and obtains brighter views of his
glory. Still, none who have the use of their eyes can be ignorant of
the divine skill manifested so conspicuously in the endless variety,
yet distinct and well-ordered array, of the heavenly host; and, there-

fore, it is plain that the Lord has furnished every man with abundant proofs of his wisdom. The same is true in regard to the structure of the human frame. To determine the connection of its parts, its symmetry and beauty, with the skill of a Galen, requires singular acuteness (*Lib. De Usu Partium*), and yet all men acknowledge that the human body bears on its face such proofs of ingenious contrivance as are sufficient to proclaim the admirable wisdom of its Maker.

3. Hence certain of the philosophers have not improperly called man a microcosm, as being a rare specimen of divine power, wisdom, and goodness, and containing within himself wonders sufficient to occupy our minds, if we are willing so to employ them. Paul, accordingly, after reminding the Athenians that they "might feel after God and find him," immediately adds, that "he is not far from every one of us" (Acts 17:27), every man having within himself undoubted evidence of the heavenly grace by which he lives, and moves, and has his being. But if, in order to apprehend God, it is unnecessary to go farther than ourselves, what excuse can there be for the sloth of any man who will not take the trouble of descending into himself that he may find Him? For the same reason, too, David, after briefly celebrating the wonderful name and glory of God, as everywhere displayed, immediately exclaims, "What is man, that thou art mindful of him?" and again, "Out of the mouths of babes and sucklings thou hast ordained strength" (Psalm 8:2, 4). Thus he declares not only that the human race are a bright mirror of the Creator's works, but that infants hanging on their mothers' breasts have tongues eloquent enough to proclaim his glory without the aid of other orators. Accordingly, he hesitates not to bring them forward as fully instructed to refute the madness of those who, from devilish pride, would fain extinguish the name of God. Hence, too, the passage which Paul quotes from Aratus, "We are his offspring," the excellent gifts with which he has endued us attesting that he is our Father (Acts 17:28). In the same way also, from natural instinct, and, as it were, at the dictation of experience, heathen poets call him the father of men. No one, indeed, will vol-

untarily and willingly devote himself to the service of God unless he has previously tasted his paternal love, and been thereby allured to love and reverence Him. […]

9. We see there is no need of a long and laborious train of argument in order to obtain proofs which illustrate and assert the Divine Majesty. The few which we have merely touched show them to be so immediately within our reach in every quarter that we can trace them with the eye, or point to them with the finger. And here we must observe again (see chap. 2 s. 2) that the knowledge of God which we are invited to cultivate is not that which, resting satisfied with empty speculation, only flutters in the brain, but a knowledge which will prove substantial and fruitful wherever it is duly perceived, and rooted in the heart. The Lord is manifested by his perfections. When we feel their power within us, and are conscious of their benefits, the knowledge must impress us much more vividly than if we merely imagined a God whose presence we never felt. Hence it is obvious that in seeking God, the most direct path and the fittest method is not to attempt with presumptuous curiosity to pry into his essence, which is rather to be adored than minutely discussed, but to contemplate him in his works, by which he draws near, becomes familiar, and in a manner communicates himself to us. To this the Apostle referred when he said that we need not go far in search of him, because, by the continual working of his power, he dwells in every one of us (Acts 17:27). Accordingly, David, after acknowledging that his greatness is unsearchable, proceeds to enumerate his works, declaring that his greatness will thereby be unfolded (Psalm 145). It therefore becomes us also diligently to prosecute that investigation of God which so enraptures the soul with admiration as, at the same time, to make an efficacious impression on it. And, as Augustine expresses it, since we are unable to comprehend Him, and are, as it were, overpowered by his greatness, our proper course is to contemplate his works, and so refresh ourselves with his goodness.

10. By the knowledge thus acquired, we ought not only to be stimulated to worship God, but also aroused and elevated to the

hope of future life. For, observing that the manifestations which the Lord gives both of his mercy and severity are only begun and incomplete, we ought to infer that these are doubtless only a prelude to higher manifestations, of which the full display is reserved for another state. Conversely, when we see the righteous brought into affliction by the ungodly, assailed with injuries, overwhelmed with calumnies, and lacerated by insult and contumely, while, on the contrary, the wicked flourish, prosper, acquire ease and honour, and all these with impunity, we ought forthwith to infer that there will be a future life in which iniquity shall receive its punishment and righteousness its reward. Moreover, when we observe that the Lord often lays his chastening rod on the righteous, we may the more surely conclude that far less will the unrighteous ultimately escape the scourges of his anger. There is a well-known passage in Augustine, "Were all sin now visited with open punishment, it might be thought that nothing was reserved for the final Judgment; and, on the other hand, were no sin now openly punished, it might be supposed there was no divine providence" (*De Civitat. Dei*, lib. 1 c. 8). It must be acknowledged, therefore, that in each of the works of God, and more especially in the whole of them taken together, the divine perfections are delineated as in a picture, and the whole human race thereby invited and allured to acquire the knowledge of God, and, in consequence of this knowledge, true and complete felicity. Moreover, while his perfections are thus most vividly displayed, the only means of ascertaining their practical operation and tendency is to descend into ourselves, and consider how it is that the Lord there manifests his wisdom, power, and energy—how he there displays his justice, goodness, and mercy. For although David justly complains of the extreme infatuation of the ungodly in not pondering the deep counsels of God, as exhibited in the government of the human race (Psalm 92:6), what he elsewhere says is most true, that the wonders of the divine wisdom in this respect are more in number than the hairs of our head (Psalm 40). But I leave this topic at present, as it will be more fully considered afterwards in its own place (Book I. c. 16, see. 6–9).

11. Bright, however, as is the manifestation which God gives both of himself and his immortal kingdom in the mirror of his works, so great is our stupidity, so dull are we in regard to these bright manifestations, that we derive no benefit from them. For in regard to the fabric and admirable arrangement of the universe, how few of us are there who, in lifting our eyes to the heavens, or looking abroad on the various regions of the earth, ever think of the Creator? Do we not rather overlook Him, and sluggishly content ourselves with a view of his works? And then in regard to supernatural events, though these are occurring every day, how few are there who ascribe them to the ruling providence of God—how many who imagine that they are casual results produced by the blind evolutions of the wheel of chance? Even when under the guidance and direction of these events, we are in a manner forced to the contemplation of God (a circumstance which all must occasionally experience), and are thus led to form some impressions of Deity, we immediately fly off to carnal dreams and depraved fictions, and so by our vanity corrupt heavenly truth. This far, indeed, we differ from each other, in that every one appropriates to himself some peculiar error, but we are all alike in this, that we substitute monstrous fictions for the one living and true God—a disease not confined to obtuse and vulgar minds, but affecting the noblest, and those who, in other respects, are singularly acute. How lavishly in this respect have the whole body of philosophers betrayed their stupidity and want of sense? To say nothing of the others whose absurdities are of a still grosser description, how completely does Plato, the soberest and most religious of them all, lose himself in his round globe? What must be the case with the rest, when the leaders, who ought to have set them an example, commit such blunders, and labour under such hallucinations? In like manner, while the government of the world places the doctrine of providence beyond dispute, the practical result is the same as if it were believed that all things were carried hither and thither at the caprice of chance, so prone are we to vanity and error. I am still referring to the most distinguished of the philosophers, and not to the

common herd, whose madness in profaning the truth of God exceeds all bounds.

12. Hence that immense flood of error with which the whole world is overflowed. Every individual mind being a kind of labyrinth, it is not wonderful, not only that each nation has adopted a variety of fictions, but that almost every man has had his own god. To the darkness of ignorance have been added presumption and wantonness, and hence there is scarcely an individual to be found without some idol or phantom as a substitute for Deity. Like water gushing forth from a large and copious spring, immense crowds of gods have issued from the human mind, every man giving himself full license, and devising some peculiar form of divinity, to meet his own views. It is unnecessary here to attempt a catalogue of the superstitions with which the world was overspread. The thing were endless, and the corruptions themselves, though not a word should be said, furnish abundant evidence of the blindness of the human mind. I say nothing of the rude and illiterate vulgar, but among the philosophers who attempted, by reason and learning, to pierce the heavens, what shameful disagreement! The higher any one was endued with genius, and the more he was polished by science and art, the more specious was the colouring which he gave to his opinions. All these, however, if examined more closely, will be found to be vain show. The Stoics plumed themselves on their acuteness, when they said that the various names of God might be extracted from all the parts of nature, and yet that his unity was not thereby divided: as if we were not already too prone to vanity, and had no need of being presented with an endless multiplicity of gods, to lead us further and more grossly into error. The mystic theology of the Egyptians shows how sedulously they laboured to be thought rational on this subject. And, perhaps, at the first glance, some show of probability might deceive the simple and unwary; but never did any mortal devise a scheme by which religion was not foully corrupted. This endless variety and confusion emboldened the Epicureans, and other gross despisers of piety, to cut off all sense of God. For when they saw that the wisest contradicted each other,

they hesitated not to infer from their dissensions, and from the frivolous and absurd doctrines of each, that men foolishly, and to no purpose, brought torment upon themselves by searching for a God, there being none: and they thought this inference safe, because it was better at once to deny God altogether, than to feign uncertain gods, and thereafter engage in quarrels without end. They, indeed, argue absurdly, or rather weave a cloak for their impiety out of human ignorance, though ignorance surely cannot derogate from the prerogatives of God. But since all confess that there is no topic on which such difference exists, both among learned and unlearned, the proper inference is that the human mind, which thus errs in inquiring after God, is dull and blind in heavenly mysteries. Some praise the answer of Simonides, who being asked by King Hero what God was, asked a day to consider. When the king next day repeated the question, he asked two days, and after repeatedly doubling the number of days, at length replied, "The longer I consider, the darker the subject appears." He, no doubt, wisely suspended his opinion, when he did not see clearly: still his answer shows that if men are only naturally taught, instead of having any distinct, solid, or certain knowledge, they fasten only on contradictory principles, and, in consequence, worship an unknown God.

13. Hence we must hold that whosoever adulterates pure religion (and this must be the case with all who cling to their own views), make a departure from the one God. No doubt, they will allege that they have a different intention, but it is of little consequence what they intend or persuade themselves to believe, since the Holy Spirit pronounces all to be apostates, who, in the blindness of their minds, substitute demons in the place of God. For this reason Paul declares that the Ephesians were "without God," until they had learned from the Gospel what it is to worship the true God (Eph. 2:12). Nor must this be restricted to one people only, since, in another place, he declares in general, that all men "became vain in their imaginations," after the majesty of the Creator was manifested to them in the structure of the world. Accordingly, in order to make way for the only true God, he condemns all

the gods celebrated among the Gentiles as lying and false, leaving no Deity anywhere but in Mount Zion where the special knowledge of God was professed (Hab. 2:18, 20). Among the Gentiles in the time of Christ, the Samaritans undoubtedly made the nearest approach to true piety; yet we hear from his own mouth that they worshipped they knew not what (John 4:22), whence it follows that they were deluded by vain errors. In short, though all did not give way to gross vice, or rush headlong into open idolatry, there was no pure and authentic religion founded merely on common belief. A few individuals may not have gone all insane lengths with the vulgar; still Paul's declaration remains true, that the wisdom of God was not apprehended by the princes of this world (1 Cor. 2:8). But if the most distinguished wandered in darkness, what shall we say of the refuse? No wonder, therefore, that all worship of man's device is repudiated by the Holy Spirit as degenerate. Any opinion which man can form in heavenly mysteries, though it may not beget a long train of errors, is still the parent of error. And though nothing worse should happen, even this is no light sin—to worship an unknown God at random. Of this sin, however, we hear from our Saviour's own mouth that all are guilty who have not been taught out of the law who the God is whom they ought to worship (John 4:22). Nay, even Socrates in Xenophon, lauds the response of Apollo enjoining every man to worship the gods according to the rites of his country, and the particular practice of his own city (lib. 1 *Memorabilia*). But what right have mortals thus to decide of their own authority in a matter which is far above the world; or who can so acquiesce in the will of his forefathers, or the decrees of the people, as unhesitatingly to receive a god at their hands? Every one will adhere to his own Judgment, sooner than submit to the dictation of others. Since, therefore, in regulating the worship of God, the custom of a city, or the consent of antiquity, is a too feeble and fragile bond of piety, it remains that God himself must bear witness to himself from heaven.

14. In vain for us, therefore, does Creation exhibit so many bright lamps lighted up to show forth the glory of its Author.

Though they beam upon us from every quarter, they are altogether insufficient of themselves to lead us into the right path. Some sparks, undoubtedly, they do throw out, but these are quenched before they can give forth a brighter effulgence. Wherefore, the apostle, in the very place where he says that the worlds are images of invisible things, adds that it is by faith we understand that they were framed by the word of God (Heb. 11:3), thereby intimating that the invisible Godhead is indeed represented by such displays, but that we have no eyes to perceive it until they are enlightened through faith by internal revelation from God. When Paul says that that which may be known of God is manifested by the creation of the world, he does not mean such a manifestation as may be comprehended by the wit of man (Rom. 1:19); on the contrary, he shows that it has no further effect than to render us inexcusable (Acts 17:27). And though he says, elsewhere, that we have not far to seek for God, inasmuch as he dwells within us, he shows, in another passage, to what extent this nearness to God is availing. God, says he, "in times past, suffered all nations to walk in their own ways. Nevertheless, he left not himself without witness, in that he did good, and gave us rain from heaven, and fruitful seasons, filling our hearts with food and gladness" (Acts 14:16, 17). But though God is not left without a witness, while, with numberless varied acts of kindness, he woos men to the knowledge of himself, yet they cease not to follow their own ways, in other words, deadly errors.

15. But though we are deficient in natural powers which might enable us to rise to a pure and clear knowledge of God, still, as the dullness which prevents us is within, there is no room for excuse. We cannot plead ignorance, without being at the same time convicted by our own consciences both of sloth and ingratitude. It were, indeed, a strange defense for man to pretend that he has no ears to hear the truth, while dumb creatures have voices loud enough to declare it; to allege that he is unable to see that which creatures without eyes demonstrate, to excuse himself on the ground of weakness of mind, while all creatures without reason are

able to teach. Wherefore, when we wander and go astray, we are justly shut out from every species of excuse, because all things point to the right path. But while man must bear the guilt of corrupting the seed of divine knowledge so wondrously deposited in his mind, and preventing it from bearing good and genuine fruit, it is still most true that we are not sufficiently instructed by that bare and simple, but magnificent testimony which the creatures bear to the glory of their Creator. For no sooner do we, from a survey of the world, obtain some slight knowledge of Deity, than we pass by the true God, and set up in his stead the dream and phantom of our own brain, drawing away the praise of justice, wisdom, and goodness, from the fountain-head, and transferring it to some other quarter. Moreover, by the erroneous estimate we form, we either so obscure or pervert his daily works as at once to rob them of their glory and the author of them of his just praise.

Chapter 6. The Need of Scripture, as a Guide and Teacher, in Coming to God as a Creator

1. Therefore, though the effulgence which is presented to every eye, both in the heavens and on the earth, leaves the ingratitude of man without excuse, since God, in order to bring the whole human race under the same condemnation, holds forth to all, without exception, a mirror of his Deity in his works, another and better help must be given to guide us properly to God as a Creator. Not in vain, therefore, has he added the light of his Word in order that he might make himself known unto salvation, and bestowed the privilege on those whom he was pleased to bring into nearer and more familiar relation to himself. For, seeing how the minds of men were carried to and fro, and found no certain resting-place, he chose the Jews for a peculiar people, and then hedged them in that they might not, like others, go astray. And not in vain does he, by the same means, retain us in his knowledge, since but for this, even those who, in comparison of others, seem to stand strong, would quickly fall away. For as the aged, or those whose sight is defective,

when any books however fair, is set before them, though they perceive that there is something written are scarcely able to make out two consecutive words, but, when aided by glasses, begin to read distinctly, so Scripture, gathering together the impressions of Deity, which, till then, lay confused in our minds, dissipates the darkness, and shows us the true God clearly. God therefore bestows a gift of singular value, when, for the instruction of the Church, he employs not dumb teachers merely, but opens his own sacred mouth; when he not only proclaims that some God must be worshipped, but at the same time declares that He is the God to whom worship is due; when he not only teaches his elect to have respect to God, but manifests himself as the God to whom this respect should be paid.

The course which God followed towards his Church from the very first, was to supplement these common proofs by the addition of his Word, as a surer and more direct means of discovering himself. And there can be no doubt that it was by this help, Adam, Noah, Abraham, and the other patriarchs, attained to that familiar knowledge which, in a manner, distinguished them from unbelievers. I am not now speaking of the peculiar doctrines of faith by which they were elevated to the hope of eternal blessedness. It was necessary, in passing from death unto life, that they should know God, not only as a Creator, but as a Redeemer also; and both kinds of knowledge they certainly did obtain from the Word. In point of order, however, the knowledge first given was that which made them acquainted with the God by whom the world was made and is governed. To this first knowledge was afterwards added the more intimate knowledge which alone quickens dead souls, and by which God is known not only as the Creator of the worlds and the sole author and disposer of all events, but also as a Redeemer, in the person of the Mediator. But as the fall and the corruption of nature have not yet been considered, I now postpone the consideration of the remedy (for which, see Book 2 c. 6 &c). Let the reader then remember, that I am not now treating of the covenant by which God adopted the children of Abraham, or of that branch of doctrine by which, as founded in Christ, believers have, properly speaking, been in all ages separated from the profane heathen. I am only showing that it is necessary to apply to Scripture, in order to learn the sure marks which distinguish God, as the Creator of the world, from the whole herd of fictitious gods. We shall afterward, in due course, consider the work of Redemption. In the meantime, though we shall adduce many passages from the New Testament, and some also from the Law and the Prophets, in which express mention is made of Christ, the only object will be to show that God, the Maker of the world, is manifested to us in Scripture, and his true character expounded, so as to save us from wandering up and down, as in a labyrinth, in search of some doubtful deity.

2. Whether God revealed himself to the fathers by oracles and visions, or, by the instrumentality and ministry of men, suggested what they were to hand down to posterity, there cannot be a doubt that the certainty of what he taught them was firmly engraven on their hearts, so that they felt assured and knew that the things which they learnt came forth from God, who invariably accompanied his word with a sure testimony, infinitely superior to mere opinion. At length, in order that, while doctrine was continually enlarged, its truth might subsist in the world during all ages, it was his pleasure that the same oracles which he had deposited with the fathers should be consigned, as it were, to public records. With this view the law was promulgated, and prophets were afterwards added to be its interpreters. For though the uses of the law were manifold (Book 2 c. 7 and 8), and the special office assigned to Moses and all the prophets was to teach the method of reconciliation between God and man (whence Paul calls Christ "the end of the law," Rom. 10:4), still I repeat that, in addition to the proper doctrine of faith and repentance in which Christ is set forth as a Mediator, the Scriptures employ certain marks and tokens to distinguish the only wise and true God, considered as the Creator and Governor of the world, and thereby guard against his being confounded with the herd of false deities. Therefore, while it becomes man seriously to employ his eyes in considering the works of God, since a place has been assigned him in this most glorious theatre

that he may be a spectator of them, his special duty is to give ear to the Word, that he may the better profit. Hence it is not strange that those who are born in darkness become more and more hardened in their stupidity, because the vast majority instead of confining themselves within due bounds by listening with docility to the Word, exult in their own vanity. If true religion is to beam upon us, our principle must be that it is necessary to begin with heavenly teaching, and that it is impossible for any man to obtain even the minutest portion of right and sound doctrine without being a disciple of Scripture. Hence, the first step in true knowledge is taken, when we reverently embrace the testimony which God has been pleased therein to give of himself. For not only does faith, full and perfect faith, but all correct knowledge of God, originate in obedience. And surely in this respect God has with singular Providence provided for mankind in all ages.

3. For if we reflect how prone the human mind is to lapse into forgetfulness of God, how readily inclined to every kind of error, how bent every now and then on devising new and fictitious religions, it will be easy to understand how necessary it was to make such a depository of doctrine as would secure it from either perishing by the neglect, vanishing away amid the errors, or being corrupted by the presumptuous audacity of men. It being thus manifest that God, foreseeing the inefficiency of his image imprinted on the fair form of the universe, has given the assistance of his Word to all whom he has ever been pleased to instruct effectually, we, too, must pursue this straight path, if we aspire in earnest to a genuine contemplation of God—we must go, I say, to the Word, where the character of God, drawn from his works is described accurately and to the life; these works being estimated, not by our depraved Judgment, but by the standard of eternal truth. If, as I lately said, we turn aside from it, how great soever the speed with which we move, we shall never reach the goal, because we are off the course. We should consider that the brightness of the Divine countenance, which even an apostle declares to be inaccessible, is a kind of labyrinth—a labyrinth to us inextricable, if the Word do

not serve us as a thread to guide our path, and that it is better to limp in the way, than run with the greatest swiftness out of it (1 Tim. 6:16). Hence the Psalmist, after repeatedly declaring (Psalm 93, 96, 97, 99, &c) that superstition should be banished from the world in order that pure religion may flourish, introduces God as reigning; meaning by the term, not the power which he possesses and which he exerts in the government of universal nature, but the doctrine by which he maintains his due supremacy, because error never can be eradicated from the heart of man until the true knowledge of God has been implanted in it.

4. Accordingly, the same prophet, after mentioning that the heavens declare the glory of God, that the firmament sheweth forth the works of his hands, that the regular succession of day and night proclaim his Majesty, proceeds to make mention of the Word: "The law of the Lord," says he, "is perfect, converting the soul; the testimony of the Lord is sure, making wise the simple. The statutes of the Lord are right, rejoicing the heart; the commandment of the Lord is pure, enlightening the eyes," (Psalm 19:1–9). For though the law has other uses besides (as to which, see Book 2 c. 7, sec. 6, 10, 12), the general meaning is, that it is the proper school for training the children of God, the invitation given to all nations, to behold him in the heavens and earth, proving of no avail. The same view is taken in the 29th Psalm, where the Psalmist, after discoursing on the dreadful voice of God, which, in thunder, wind, rain, whirlwind, and tempest, shakes the earth, makes the mountains tremble, and breaks the cedars, concludes by saying, "that in his temple does every one speak of his glory," unbelievers being deaf to all God's words when they echo in the air. In like manner another Psalm, after describing the raging billows of the sea, thus concludes, "Thy testimonies are very sure; holiness becometh thine house for ever" (Psalm 93:5). To the same effect are the words of our Saviour to the Samaritan woman, when he told her that her nation and all other nations worshipped they knew not what; and that the Jews alone gave worship to the true God (John 4:22). Since the human mind, through its weakness, was alto-

gether unable to come to God if not aided and upheld by his sacred word, it necessarily followed that all mankind, the Jews excepted, inasmuch as they sought God without the Word, were labouring under vanity and error.

INTRODUCTION TO THE COUNCIL OF TRENT'S *DECREE ON JUSTIFICATION*

BY JUST a couple of years into the Reformation, Luther had appealed his cause to a General Council of the Church. And although there were many in Rome who preferred to silence him by papal fiat or imperial force, his call for a Council found sympathetic ears throughout Christendom. Not only was the memory of the reforming councils of the previous century still relatively fresh, but it was clear to the majority of church leaders that Luther had gained such a large following because there was more than a kernel of truth in his denunciations of the Roman Church. Corruptions of both doctrine and practice were rife. Even many staunch traditionalists welcomed a council if it meant an opportunity to crystallize once and for all disputed and ambiguous Catholic teachings.

However, the interminable three-way political squabbles (and intermittent all-out wars) between the Pope, the French king Francis and Emperor Charles V delayed a council over and over. An abortive effort at Mantua in 1537 almost materialized, but soon dissolved. Meanwhile, remarkable reforming energies began to be felt within Italy itself, the heart of the Catholic Church. Moved partly by reading translations of Luther's writings and partly by their own religious experiences and reflections on the Augustinian legacy of the medieval Church, many prominent Italian churchmen came to views not too distant from Luther's doctrine of justification. When one of them, Gasparo Contarini (1483–1542), was chosen as papal representative to a conference with Protestant leaders, including Melanchthon and Bucer, at Regensburg in 1541, hopes were accordingly high for some sort of settlement. The Colloquy backfired, however, as Contarini's willingness to make concessions confirmed the suspicions of hardline traditionalists in Rome, leading to the arrest of Contarini and the launch of the Roman Inquisition in 1542.

It was thus in a climate exceedingly unfavorable to any concessions that a Council was at last convened at Trent after further negotiations, arguments, and delays in 1545. But though the Pope had obtained the grudging support of Charles for the Council, Francis still opposed it, and it was hardly the great General Council of Christendom that had been hoped for or that the moment required. Only a few dozen of the 600 bishops invited appeared, and almost all of them from Italy. Reform-minded bishops from Germany and France generally kept a wary distance, as did Protestant leaders.

This did not mean that no significant reforms were undertaken by the Council; on the contrary, it saw many important changes to the Church, including a purging of many of the worldly corruptions of the clergy that had made the church such a laughingstock to men like Erasmus and had earned Luther such a wide hearing. But the purpose of these reforms was to shore up the authority of the church, and when it came to doctrine, the result of the Council was to render the gap between Rome and Protestantism unbridgeable. To be sure, Trent condemned some of the more seriously aberrant formulations of church doctrine that had invited Protestant opposition, but they also set out to clarify many traditional teachings in such a way as to allow no more wiggle room, anathematizing errors on every side. Most significant in this regard were the fourth session of the Council, affirming the equal authority of church tradition alongside Scripture, and the sixth session of the Council, on justification.

The decree on justification proved the most trying and contentious of the Council, involving more than six months of debate and including a violent personal confrontation between one bishop who affirmed justification by faith alone and another who denounced him as "either a knave or a fool."[1] The final doctrinal statement epitomizes the legacy of Trent, on the one hand affirming much of what Protestants sought to affirm—the necessity of God's grace for every step of salvation—but at the same time conceiving justification as the infusion of a gracious power into the soul which then enabled the sinner to merit salvation by subsequent good works. Justification is by faith then only in the sense that faith is essential to begin the process. While Protestants of course would agree that the initial justifying faith is only a beginning, they stressed that the subsequent steps of the process must be understood as sanctification, the working out of a finished work of justification, and that these even these sanctified works did not merit God's favor but, being imperfect were only accepted for the sake of Christ. Trent was particularly adamant in rejecting this view, insisting that once justified, the believer could offer up to God a truly acceptable sacrifice of obedience.

The decree itself is structured as a series of sixteen short chapters, followed by thirty-three much shorter canons, each of which pronounces a summary anathema against any who teach contrary to the canon. Both the chapters and the canons intentionally agree with the Protestants in some matters—canons 1-3, 10, 22, 23a, 28, and 29a all seem to fall under this heading. Moreover, a large portion of the decree is directed against statements which, although apparently considered to be standard Protestant teachings, seem to have been largely misunderstood, so that most Protestant theologians would have said that the condemnations did not apply to them. Canons 4-6, 8, 14, 18-21, 26, and 31 seem to fall under this heading. There are also points where the Council attacks teachings that do seem to have been voiced by some Protestant writers and confessions, but which were disputed within the movement both in the 16th century and beyond. In particular, the Council was eager to refute the notion that the saved necessarily

---

[1] John W. O'Malley, *Trent: What Happened at the Council* (Cambridge, MA: The Belknap Press of Harvard University Press, 2013), 109.

experienced full assurance of salvation, such that failure to do so was a sign that one was not saved. While Protestants did insist, contra Catholic orthodoxy, that full assurance of salvation was possible, there were disputes as to whether it was necessary, or whether doubting was to be expected. The Council also clearly asserts the possibility of temporary justification—that is, that some might receive genuine grace through faith but not persevere. This was and remains a point of persistent disagreement among Protestants. Canons 13, 15, 16, 17, and 23b concerns such issues. This leaves Canons 7, 9, 11-12, 24, 25, 27, 29b, 30, and 32 as all reflecting a more or less accurate understanding of what the Protestants intended to teach, and forthrightly rejecting it. By declaring these statements anathema, or damnable errors, the Council closed the door to any likelihood of reunion with the Protestant reform movement.

Further Reading

For further reading, see John W. O'Malley, *Trent: What Happened at the Council* (Cambridge, MA: The Belknap Press of Harvard University Press, 2013); Anthony N.S. Lane, *Justification by Faith in Protestant-Catholic Dialogue* (London: T&T Clark, 2006).

THE COUNCIL OF TRENT, DECREE AND CANONS CONCERNING JUSTIFICATION (1545)[1]

WHEREAS there is, at this time, not without the shipwreck of many souls, and grievous detriment to the unity of the Church, a certain erroneous doctrine disseminated touching Justification; the sacred and holy, ecumenical and general Synod of Trent, lawfully assembled in the Holy Ghost—the most reverend lords, Giammaria del Monte, bishop of Palaestrina, and Marcellus of the title of the Holy Cross in Jerusalem, priest, cardinals of the holy Roman Church, and legates apostolic *a latere*, presiding therein, in the name of our most holy father and lord in Christ, Paul III., by the providence of God, Pope, purposes, unto the praise and glory of Almighty God, the tranquillising of the Church, and the salvation of souls, to expound to all the faithful of Christ the true and sound doctrine touching the said Justification; which (doctrine) the sun of justice, Christ Jesus, the author and finisher of our faith, taught, which the apostles transmitted, and which the Catholic Church, the Holy Ghost reminding her thereof, has always retained, most strictly forbidding that any henceforth presume to believe, preach, or teach, otherwise than as by this present decree is defined and declared.

---

[1] Taken from The Council of Trent.com,
http://www.thecounciloftrent.com/ch6.htm.

Chapter I. On the Inability of Nature and of the Law to justify man

The holy Synod declares first, that, for the correct and sound understanding of the doctrine of Justification, it is necessary that each one recognize and confess that, whereas all men had lost their innocence in the prevarication of Adam—having become unclean, and, as the apostle says, by nature children of wrath, as (this Synod) has set forth in the decree on original sin—they were so far the servants of sin, and under the power of the devil and of death that not the Gentiles only by the force of nature, but not even the Jews by the very letter itself of the law of Moses, were able to be liberated, or to arise, therefrom, although free will, attenuated as it was in its powers, and bent down, was by no means extinguished in them.

Chapter II. On the dispensation and mystery of Christ's advent

Whence it came to pass that the heavenly Father, the father of mercies and the God of all comfort, when that blessed fulness of the time was come, sent unto men, Jesus Christ, His own Son—who had been, both before the Law, and during the time of the Law, to many of the holy fathers announced and promised—that He might both redeem the Jews who were under the Law, and that the Gentiles, who followed not after justice, might attain to justice, and that all men might receive the adoption of sons. Him God hath proposed as a propitiator, through faith in his blood, for our sins, and not for our sins only, but also for those of the whole world.

Chapter III. Who are justified through Christ

But, though He died for all, yet do not all receive the benefit of His death, but those only unto whom the merit of His passion is communicated. For as in truth men, if they were not born propagated of the seed of Adam, would not be born unjust—seeing that, by that propagation, they contract through him, when they are conceived, injustice as their own—so, if they were not born again in

Christ, they never would be justified, seeing that, in that new birth, there is bestowed upon them, through the merit of His passion, the grace whereby they are made just. For this benefit the apostle exhorts us, evermore to give thanks to the Father, who hath made us worthy to be partakers of the lot of the saints in light, and hath delivered us from the power of darkness, and hath translated us into the Kingdom of the Son of his love, in whom we have redemption, and remission of sins.

Chapter IV. A description is introduced of the Justification of the impious, and of the Manner thereof under the law of grace

By which words, a description of the Justification of the impious is indicated, as being a translation, from that state wherein man is born a child of the first Adam, to the state of grace, and of the adoption of the sons of God, through the second Adam, Jesus Christ, our Saviour. And this translation, since the promulgation of the Gospel, cannot be effected, without the laver of regeneration, or the desire thereof, as it is written, unless a man be born again of water and the Holy Ghost, he cannot enter into the Kingdom of God [Jn. 3:5].

Chapter V. On the necessity, in adults, of preparation for Justification, and whence it proceeds

The Synod furthermore declares that in adults, the beginning of the said Justification is to be derived from the prevenient grace of God, through Jesus Christ, that is to say, from His vocation, whereby, without any merits existing on their parts, they are called; that so they, who by sins were alienated from God, may be disposed through His quickening and assisting grace, to convert themselves to their own justification, by freely assenting to and co-operating with that said grace in such sort that, while God touches the heart of man by the illumination of the Holy Ghost, neither is man himself utterly without doing anything while he receives that inspiration, forasmuch as he is also able to reject it; yet is he not able, by his own free will, without the grace of God, to move himself unto justice in His sight. Whence, when it is said in the sacred writings: Turn ye to me, and I will turn to you [Zech. 1:3], we are admonished of our liberty; and when we answer; Convert us, O Lord, to thee, and we shall be converted [Lam. 5:21], we confess that we are prevented by the grace of God.

Chapter VI. The manner of Preparation

Now they (adults) are disposed unto the said justice, when, excited and assisted by divine grace, conceiving faith by hearing, they are freely moved towards God, believing those things to be true which God has revealed and promised—and this especially, that God justifies the impious by His grace, through the redemption that is in Christ Jesus; and when, understanding themselves to be sinners, they, by turning themselves, from the fear of divine justice whereby they are profitably agitated, to consider the mercy of God, are raised unto hope, confiding that God will be propitious to them for Christ's sake; and they begin to love Him as the fountain of all justice; and are therefore moved against sins by a certain hatred and detestation, to wit, by that penitence which must be performed before baptism: lastly, when they purpose to receive baptism, to begin a new life, and to keep the commandments of God. Concerning this disposition it is written, He that cometh to God, must believe that he is, and is a rewarder to them that seek him [Heb. 11:6]; and, Be of good faith, son, thy sins are forgiven thee [Matt. 9:2]; and, The fear of the Lord driveth out sin [Ecclesiasticus 1:27]; and, Do penance, and be baptized every one of you in the name of Jesus Christ, for the remission of your sins, and you shall receive the gift of the Holy Ghost [Acts 2:38]; and, Going, therefore, teach ye all nations, baptizing them in the name of the Father, and of the Son, and of the Holy Ghost [Matt. 28:19]; finally, Prepare your hearts unto the Lord [1 Sam. 7:3].

Chapter VII. What the justification of the impious is, and what are the causes thereof

This disposition, or preparation, is followed by Justification itself, which is not remission of sins merely, but also the sanctification and renewal of the inward man, through the voluntary reception of the grace, and of the gifts, whereby man of unjust becomes just, and of an enemy a friend, that so he may be an heir according to hope of life everlasting.

Of this Justification the causes are these: the final cause indeed is the glory of God and of Jesus Christ, and life everlasting, while the efficient cause is a merciful God who washes and sanctifies gratuitously, signing, and anointing with the holy Spirit of promise, who is the pledge of our inheritance; but the meritorious cause is His most beloved only-begotten, our Lord Jesus Christ, who, when we were enemies, for the exceeding charity wherewith he loved us, merited Justification for us by His most holy Passion on the wood of the cross, and made satisfaction for us unto God the Father; the instrumental cause is the sacrament of baptism, which is the sacrament of faith, without which (faith) no man was ever justified; lastly, the alone formal cause is the justice of God, not that whereby He Himself is just, but that whereby He maketh us just, that, to wit, with which we being endowed by Him, are renewed in the spirit of our mind, and we are not only reputed, but are truly called, and are, just, receiving justice within us, each one according to his own measure, which the Holy Ghost distributes to every one as He wills, and according to each one's proper disposition and co-operation. For, although no one can be just, but he to whom the merits of the Passion of our Lord Jesus Christ are communicated, yet is this done in the said justification of the impious, when by the merit of that same most holy Passion, the charity of God is poured forth, by the Holy Spirit, in the hearts of those that are justified, and is inherent therein, whence, man, through Jesus Christ, in whom he is ingrafted, receives, in the said justification, together with the remission of sins, all these (gifts) infused at once, faith, hope, and charity. For faith, unless hope and charity be added thereto, neither unites man perfectly with Christ, nor makes him a living member of His body. For which reason it is most truly said, that Faith without works is dead and profitless [Jas. 2:17]; and, In Christ Jesus neither circumcision, availeth anything, nor uncircumcision, but faith which worketh by charity [Gal. 5:6]. This faith, Catechumen's beg of the Church—agreeably to a tradition of the apostles—previously to the sacrament of Baptism; when they beg for the faith which bestows life everlasting, which, without hope and charity, faith cannot bestow, whence also do they immediately hear that word of Christ, If thou wilt enter into life, keep the commandments [Matt. 19:17]. Wherefore, when receiving true and Christian justice, they are bidden, immediately on being born again, to preserve it pure and spotless, as the first robe given them through Jesus Christ in lieu of that which Adam, by his disobedience, lost for himself and for us, that so they may bear it before the judgment-seat of our Lord Jesus Christ, and may have life everlasting.

Chapter VIII. In what manner it is to be understood, that the impious is justified by faith, and gratuitously

And whereas the Apostle saith, that man is justified by faith and freely [Rom. 3:24], those words are to be understood in that sense which the perpetual consent of the Catholic Church hath held and expressed: to wit, that we are therefore said to be justified by faith, because faith is the beginning of human salvation, the foundation, and the root of all Justification, without which it is impossible to please God, and to come unto the fellowship of His sons: but we are therefore said to be justified freely, because that none of those things which precede justification—whether faith or works—merit the grace itself of justification. For, if it be a grace, it is not now by works, otherwise, as the same Apostle says, grace is no more grace [Rom. 11:6].

Chapter IX. Against the vain confidence of Heretics

But, although it is necessary to believe that sins neither are remitted, nor ever were remitted save gratuitously by the mercy of God for Christ's sake, yet is it not to be said that sins are forgiven, or have been forgiven, to anyone who boasts of his confidence and certainty of the remission of his sins, and rests on that alone, seeing that it may exist, yea does in our day exist, amongst heretics and schismatics; and with great vehemence is this vain confidence, and one alien from all godliness, preached up in opposition to the Catholic Church. But neither is this to be asserted that they who are truly justified must needs, without any doubting whatever, settle within themselves that they are justified, and that no one is absolved from sins and justified, but he that believes for certain that he is absolved and justified; and that absolution and justification are effected by this faith alone, as though whoso has not this belief, doubts of the promises of God, and of the efficacy of the death and resurrection of Christ. For even as no pious person ought to doubt of the mercy of God, of the merit of Christ, and of the virtue and efficacy of the sacraments, even so each one, when he regards himself, and his own weakness and indisposition, may have fear and apprehension touching his own grace, seeing that no one can know with a certainty of faith, which cannot be subject to error, that he has obtained the grace of God.

Chapter X. On the increase of Justification received

Having, therefore, been thus justified, and made the friends and domestics of God, advancing from virtue to virtue, they are renewed, as the Apostle says, day by day [2 Cor. 4:16]; that is, by mortifying the members of their own flesh, and by presenting them as instruments of justice unto sanctification [Rom. 6:13], they, through the observance of the commandments of God and of the Church, faith co-operating with good works, increase in that justice which they have received through the grace of Christ, and are still further justified, as it is written, He that is just, let him be justified still [Rev. 22:11]; and again, Be not afraid to be justified even to death [Rev. 2:10]; and also, Do you see that by works a man is justified, and not by faith only [Jas. 2:24]. And this increase of justification holy Church begs, when she prays, "Give unto us, O Lord, increase of faith, hope, and charity."

CHAPTER XI. On keeping the Commandments, and on the necessity and possibility thereof

But no one, how much soever justified, ought to think himself exempt from the observance of the commandments; no one ought to make use of that rash saying, one prohibited by the Fathers under an anathema, that the observance of the commandments of God is impossible for one that is justified. For God commands not impossibilities, but, by commanding, both admonishes thee to do what thou are able, and to pray for what thou art not able (to do), and aids thee that thou mayest be able; whose commandments are not heavy; whose yoke is sweet and whose burthen light. For whoso are the sons of God love Christ; but they who love him, keep his commandments, as Himself testifies, which, assuredly, with the divine help, they can do. For, although, during this mortal life, men, how holy and just soever, at times fall into at least light and daily sins, which are also called venial, not therefore do they cease to be just. For that cry of the just, Forgive us our trespasses [Matt. 6:12], is both humble and true. And for this cause, the just themselves ought to feel themselves the more obligated to walk in the way of justice, in that, being already freed from sins, but made servants of God, they are able, living soberly, justly, and godly, to proceed onwards through Jesus Christ, by whom they have had access unto this grace. For God forsakes not those who have been once justified by His grace, unless he be first forsaken by them. Wherefore, no one ought to flatter himself up with faith alone, fancying that by faith alone he is made an heir, and will obtain the inheritance, even though he suffer not with Christ, that so he may be also glorified with him. For even Christ Himself, as the Apostle saith, Whereas he was the son of God, learned obedience by the things which he suffered, and being consummated, he became, to all who obey him, the cause of eternal salvation [Heb. 5:8–9]. For which cause the same Apostle admonishes the justified, saying; Know you not that they that run in the race, all run indeed, but one receiveth the prize? So run that you may obtain. I therefore so run, not as at an uncertainty: I so fight, not as one beating the air, but I chastise my body, and bring it into subjection; lest perhaps, when I have preached to others, I myself should become a cast-away [1 Cor. 9:23–25]. So also the prince of the apostles, Peter; Labour the more that by good works you may make sure your calling and election [2 Pet. 1:10]. For doing those things, you shall not sin at any time. From which it is plain that those are opposed to the orthodox doctrine of religion, who assert that the just man sins, venially at least, in every good work; or, which is yet more insupportable, that he merits eternal punishments, as also those who state that the just sin in all their works, if, in those works, they, together with this aim principally that God may be gloried, have in view also the eternal reward, in order to excite their sloth, and to encourage themselves to run in the course, whereas it is written, I have inclined my heart to do all thy justifications for the reward [Ps. 119:12]; and, concerning Moses, the Apostle saith, that he looked unto the reward [Heb. 11:26].

Chapter XII. That a rash presumptuousness in the matter of Predestination is to be avoided

No one, moreover, so long as he is in this mortal life, ought so far to presume as regards the secret mystery of divine predestination, as to determine for certain that he is assuredly in the number of the predestinate, as if it were true, that he that is justified, either cannot sin any more, or, if he do sin, that he ought to promise himself an assured repentance; for except by special revelation, it cannot be known whom God hath chosen unto Himself.

Chapter XIII. On the gift of Perseverance

So also as regards the gift of perseverance, of which it is written, He that shall persevere to the end, he shall be saved [Matt. 24:13]—which gift cannot be derived from any other but Him who is able to establish him who standeth that he stand perseveringly, and to restore him who falleth: let no one herein promise himself any thing as certain with an absolute certainty, though all ought to place and repose a most firm hope in God's help. For God, unless men be themselves wanting to His grace, as he has begun the good work, so will he perfect it, working (in them) to will and to accomplish [Phil. 1:6]. Nevertheless, let those who think themselves to stand, take heed lest they fall, and, with fear and trembling work out their salvation, in labours, in watchings, in almsdeeds, in prayers and oblations, in fastings and chastity, for knowing that they are born again unto a hope of glory, but not as yet unto glory, they ought to fear for the combat which yet remains with the flesh, with the world, with the devil, wherein they cannot be victorious, unless they be with God's grace, obedient to the Apostle, who says, We are debtors, not to the flesh, to live according to the flesh; for if you live according to the flesh, you shall die; but if by the spirit you mortify the deeds of the flesh, you shall live [Rom. 8:12-13].

Chapter XIV. On the fallen, and their restoration

As regards those who, by sin, have fallen from the received grace of Justification, they may be again justified, when, God exciting them, through the sacrament of Penance they shall have attained to the recovery, by the merit of Christ, of the grace lost: for this manner of Justification is of the fallen the reparation, which the holy Fathers have aptly called a second plank after the shipwreck of grace lost. For, on behalf of those who fall into sins after baptism, Christ Jesus instituted the sacrament of Penance, when He said, Receive ye the Holy Ghost, whose sins you shall forgive, they are forgiven them, and whose sins you shall retain, they are retained [Jn. 20:23]. Whence it is to be taught that the penitence of a Christian, after his fall, is very different from that at (his) baptism; and that therein are included not only a cessation from sins, and a detestation thereof, or, a contrite and humble heart, but also the sacramental confession of the said sins—at least in desire, and to be made in its season—and sacerdotal absolution; and likewise satisfaction by fasts, alms, prayers, and the other pious exercises of a spiritual life, not indeed for the eternal punishment—which is, together with the guilt, remitted, either by the sacrament, or by the desire of the sacrament—but for the temporal punishment, which, as the sacred writings teach, is not always wholly remitted, as is done in baptism, to those who, ungrateful to the grace of God which they have received, have grieved the Holy Spirit, and have not feared to violate the temple of God. Concerning which penitence it is written, Be mindful whence thou art fallen; do penance, and do the first works [Rev. 2:5]. And again; The sorrow that is according to God worketh penance steadfast unto salvation [2 Cor. 7:10]. And again; Do penance, and bring forth fruits worthy of penance [Matt. 3:8].

Chapter XV. That, by every mortal sin, grace is lost, but not faith

In opposition also to the subtle wits of certain men, who, by pleasing speeches and good words, seduce the hearts of the innocent, it is to be maintained that the received grace of Justification is lost, not only by infidelity whereby even faith itself is lost, but also by any other mortal sin whatever, though faith be not lost; thus defending the doctrine of the divine law, which excludes from the kingdom of God not only the unbelieving, but the faithful also (who are) fornicators, adulterers, effeminate, liers with mankind, thieves, covetous, drunkards, railers, extortioners, and all others who commit deadly sins, from which, with the help of divine grace, they can refrain, and on account of which they are separated from the grace of Christ.

Chapter XVI. On the fruit of Justification, that is, on the merit of good works, and on the nature of that merit

Before men, therefore, who have been justified in this manner—whether they have preserved uninterruptedly the grace received, or whether they have recovered it when lost—are to be set the words of the Apostle: Abound in every good work, knowing that your labour is not in vain in the Lord, for God is not unjust, that he should forget your work, and the love which you have shown in his name; and, do not lose your confidence, which hath a great reward. And, for this cause, life eternal is to be proposed to those working well unto the end, and hoping in God, both as a grace mercifully promised to the sons of God through Jesus Christ, and as a reward which is according to the promise of God Himself, to be faithfully rendered to their good works and merits. For this is that crown of justice which the Apostle declared was, after his fight and course, laid up for him, to be rendered to him by the just judge, and not only to him, but also to all that love his coming. For, whereas Jesus Christ Himself continually infuses his virtue into the said justified—as the head into the members, and the vine into the branches, and this virtue always precedes and accompanies and follows their good works, which without it could not in any wise be pleasing and meritorious before God—we must believe that nothing further is wanting to the justified to prevent their being accounted to have, by those very works which have been done in God, fully satisfied the divine law according to the state of this life, and to have truly merited eternal life, to be obtained also in its (due) time, if so be, however, that they depart in grace, seeing that Christ, our Saviour, saith: If any one shall drink of the water that I will give him, he shall not thirst for ever; but it shall become in him a fountain of water springing up unto life everlasting [Jn. 4:14]. Thus, neither is our own justice established as our own as from ourselves, nor is the justice of God ignored or repudiated; for that justice which is called ours, because that we are justified from its being inherent in us, that same is (the justice) of God, because that it is infused into us of God, through the merit of Christ. Neither is this to be omitted that although, in the sacred writings so much is attributed to good works that Christ promises that even he that shall give a drink of cold water to one of his least ones, shall not lose his reward [Matt. 10:42], and the Apostle testifies that, That which is at present momentary and light of our tribulation, worketh for us above measure exceedingly an eternal weight of glory [2 Cor. 4:17]; nevertheless God forbid that a Christian should either trust or glory in himself, and not in the Lord, whose bounty towards all men is so great that He will have the things which are His own gifts be their merits. And forasmuch as in many things we all offend, each one ought to have before his eyes, as well the severity and judgment, as the mercy and goodness (of God); neither ought any one to judge himself, even though he be not conscious to himself of anything, because the whole life of man is to be examined and judged, not by the judgment of man, but of God, who will bring to light the hidden things of darkness, and will make manifest the counsels of the hearts, and then shall every man have praise from God, who, as it is written, will render to every man according to his works. After this Catholic doctrine on Justification, which whoso receiveth not faithfully and firmly cannot be justified, it hath seemed good to the holy Synod to subjoin these canons, that all may know not only what they ought to hold and follow, but also what to avoid and shun.

On Justification: Canons

Canon I. If any one saith, that man may be justified before God by his own works, whether done through the teaching of human nature, or that of the law, without the grace of God through Jesus Christ; let him be anathema.

Canon II. If any one saith that the grace of God, through Jesus Christ, is given only for this, that man may be able more easily to live justly, and to merit eternal life, as if, by free will without grace, he were able to do both, though hardly indeed and with difficulty; let him be anathema.

Canon III. If any one saith that without the prevenient inspiration of the Holy Ghost, and without his help, man can believe, hope, love, or be penitent as he ought, so as that the grace of Justification may be bestowed upon him; let him be anathema.

Canon IV. If any one saith that man's free will moved and excited by God, by assenting to God exciting and calling, nowise co-operates towards disposing and preparing itself for obtaining the grace of Justification; that it cannot refuse its consent, if it would, but that, as something inanimate, it does nothing whatever and is merely passive; let him be anathema.

Canon V. If any one saith that, since Adam's sin, the free will of man is lost and extinguished; or, that it is a thing with only a name, yea a name without a reality, a figment, in fine, introduced into the Church by Satan; let him be anathema.

Canon VI. If any one saith that it is not in man's power to make his ways evil, but that the works that are evil God worketh as well as those that are good, not permissively only, but properly, and of Himself, in such wise that the treason of Judas is no less His own proper work than the vocation of Paul; let him be anathema.

Canon VII. If any one saith that all works done before Justification, in whatsoever way they be done, are truly sins, or merit the hatred of God; or that the more earnestly one strives to dispose himself for grace, the more grievously he sins: let him be anathema.

Canon VIII. If any one saith that the fear of hell, whereby, by grieving for our sins, we flee unto the mercy of God, or refrain from sinning, is a sin, or makes sinners worse; let him be anathema.

Canon IX. If any one saith that by faith alone the impious is justified; in such wise as to mean, that nothing else is required to co-operate in order to the obtaining the grace of Justification, and that it is not in any way necessary, that he be prepared and disposed by the movement of his own will; let him be anathema.

Canon X. If any one saith that men are just without the justice of Christ, whereby He merited for us to be justified; or that it is by that justice itself that they are formally just; let him be anathema.

Canon XI. If any one saith that men are justified, either by the sole imputation of the justice of Christ, or by the sole remission of sins, to the exclusion of the grace and the charity which is poured forth in their hearts by the Holy Ghost, and is inherent in them; or even that the grace, whereby we are justified, is only the favour of God; let him be anathema.

Canon XII. If any one saith that justifying faith is nothing else but confidence in the divine mercy which remits sins for Christ's sake; or, that this confidence alone is that whereby we are justified; let him be anathema.

Canon XIII. If any one saith that it is necessary for every one, for the obtaining the remission of sins, that he believe for certain, and without any wavering arising from his own infirmity and disposition, that his sins are forgiven him; let him be anathema.

Canon XIV. If any one saith that man is truly absolved from his sins and justified, because that he assuredly believed himself absolved and justified; or, that no one is truly justified but he who believes himself justified; and that, by this faith alone, absolution and justification are effected; let him be anathema.

Canon XV. If any one saith that a man, who is born again and justified, is bound of faith to believe that he is assuredly in the number of the predestinate; let him be anathema.

Canon XVI. If any one saith that he will for certain, of an absolute and infallible certainty, have that great gift of perseverance unto the end, unless he have learned this by special revelation; let him be anathema.

Canon XVII. If any one saith that the grace of Justification is only attained to by those who are predestined unto life; but that all others who are called, are called indeed, but receive not grace, as being, by the divine power, predestined unto evil; let him be anathema.

Canon XVIII. If any one saith that the commandments of God are, even for one that is justified and constituted in grace, impossible to keep; let him be anathema.

Canon XIX. If any one saith that nothing besides faith is commanded in the Gospel; that other things are indifferent, neither commanded nor prohibited, but free; or, that the ten commandments nowise appertain to Christians; let him be anathema.

Canon XX. If any one saith that the man who is justified and how perfect soever is not bound to observe the commandments of God and of the Church, but only to believe; as if indeed the Gospel were a bare and absolute promise of eternal life, without the condition of observing the commandments; let him be anathema.

Canon XXI. If any one saith that Christ Jesus was given of God to men, as a redeemer in whom to trust, and not also as a legislator whom to obey; let him be anathema.

Canon XXII. If any one saith, that the justified, either is able to persevere, without the special help of God, in the justice received; or that, with that help, he is not able; let him be anathema.

Canon XXIII. If any one saith that a man once justified can sin no more, nor lose grace, and that therefore he that falls and sins was never truly justified; or, on the other hand, that he is able, during his whole life, to avoid all sins, even those that are venial, except by a special privilege from God, as the Church holds in regard of the Blessed Virgin; let him be anathema.

Canon XXIV. If any one saith that the justice received is not preserved and also increased before God through good works; but that the said works are merely the fruits and signs of Justification obtained, but not a cause of the increase thereof; let him be anathema.

Canon XXV. If any one saith that, in every good work, the just sins venially at least, or—which is more intolerable still—mortally, and consequently deserves eternal punishments; and that for this cause only he is not damned, that God does not impute those works unto damnation; let him be anathema.

Canon XXVI. If any one saith that the just ought not, for their good works done in God, to expect and hope for an eternal recompense from God, through His mercy and the merit of Jesus Christ, if so be that they persevere to the end in well doing and in keeping the divine commandments; let him be anathema.

Canon XXVII. If any one saith that there is no mortal sin but that of infidelity; or, that grace once received is not lost by any other sin, however grievous and enormous, save by that of infidelity; let him be anathema.

Canon XXVIII. If any one saith that, grace being lost through sin, faith also is always lost with it; or, that the faith which remains, though it be not a lively faith, is not a true faith; or, that he, who has faith without charity, is not a Christian; let him be anathema.

Canon XXIX. If any one saith that he, who has fallen after baptism, is not able by the grace of God to rise again; or, that he is able indeed to recover the justice which he has lost, but by faith alone without the sacrament of Penance, contrary to what the holy Roman and universal Church—instructed by Christ and his Apostles—has hitherto professed, observed, and taught; let him be anathema.

Canon XXX. If any one saith that, after the grace of Justification has been received, to every penitent sinner the guilt is remitted, and the debt of eternal punishment is blotted out in such wise, that there remains not any debt of temporal punishment to be discharged either in this world, or in the next in Purgatory, before the entrance to the kingdom of heaven can be opened (to him); let him be anathema.

Canon XXXI. If any one saith that the justified sins when he performs good works with a view to an eternal recompense; let him be anathema.

Canon XXXII. If any one saith that the good works of one that is justified are in such manner the gifts of God, as that they are not also the good merits of him that is justified; or, that the said justified, by the good works which he performs through the grace of God and the merit of Jesus Christ, whose living member he is, does not truly merit increase of grace, eternal life, and the attainment of that eternal life—if so be, however, that he depart in grace—and also an increase of glory; let him be anathema.

Canon XXXIII. If any one saith that, by the Catholic doctrine touching Justification, by this holy Synod inset forth in this present decree, the glory of God, or the merits of our Lord Jesus Christ are in any way derogated from, and not rather that the truth of our faith, and the glory in fine of God and of Jesus Christ are rendered (more) illustrious; let him be anathema.

INTRODUCTION TO THE COUNCIL OF TRENT'S *DECREE ON THE EUCHARIST*

BY EARLY 1547, the Council was at last beginning work on the important and controversial issues surrounding the sacraments, especially the Eucharist. Here, the issues under debate were myriad, and striking as they did at the heart of late medieval piety and church power, not to be dispensed with hastily. First were questions of eucharistic presence, on which nearly all Protestants, echoing the arguments of John Wycliffe from a century and a half before, dismissed as absurd the scholastic doctrine of transubstantiation. This had claimed that nothing that could really be called "bread" or "wine" remained after the consecration, but only the actual body and blood of Christ. Many Protestants (although not Luther himself) went further, denying that Christ's body and blood should be understood as really and truly present in the consecrated elements at all. Beyond such questions of presence was the debate over the notion of eucharistic sacrifice. Catholic doctrine and practice had evolved the view that when the priest consecrates the bread and wine into the body and blood of Christ, he also offers Christ up to be sacrificed anew for the remission of the sins of the living and dead. Indeed, this view was at the heart of the lucrative industry of "chantry chapels" in the late medieval period, in which priests would conduct masses for the sole purpose of propitiating the sins of a deceased wealthy donor.

In attacking Roman Catholic doctrine at both of these points, the Protestants were not concerned merely with bad doctrine, but with what they saw as a transformation of eucharistic practice away from a meal in which believers commune with Christ by faith and into a religious spectacle to be observed from a distance. Laity rarely (generally only once a year) communed, with the vast majority of masses involving priests alone, and when they did partake, it was only the bread, not the wine. Instead of partaking the elements, they adored them—praying before them and watching them paraded through the streets at the great annual Feast of Corpus Christi. Against all these abuses the Reformers vigorously protested, and in 1547, the bishops and theologians assembled at Trent were ready to consider their complaints.

Unfortunately, events were soon to conspire against their efforts. In March 1547, there were rumors of an epidemic of plague beginning at Trent, and the assembled delegates nervously began to consider moving the Council to another city, Bologna being the most feasible suggestion. However, lying as it did within the Papal States, rather than within the territory of Charles V's Holy Roman Empire, as Trent did, the choice of Bologna would be politically explosive, and torpedo any chances of Protestant participation. Still, fear won out (though no plague erupted in Trent after all), and the Council transferred to Bologna. Charles was furious as expected, and over two and a half years of fitful and wandering proceedings, there was never a quorum of delegates at Bologna sufficient to pass any new decrees.

Finally the Council was reconvened at Trent in 1551 and began to work through the sacraments. At Session XIII in the fall of that year, the Council re-affirmed the doctrines of the real presence and transubstantiation, and the practices of eucharistic veneration, the Feast of Corpus Christi, and the appropriateness of priests communing alone. There was, it seemed, little of the will to contemplate sweeping reforms that there had been in the debate over justification. Still, in several ways, concessions were at least contemplated. For one, the decree exhorts the faithful to "frequent" communion, although many Catholics continued to commune only once or twice a year. For another, the Council initially held off on re-affirming the appropriateness of restricting the laity from receiving the wine. Many theologians thought the Protestants had a very good point here, and hoped that they might soon persuade some Protestant delegates to attend the Council and discuss this point, so it was temporarily tabled.

As it turned out, the Council itself was also soon adjourned again, and for a variety of complex political and practical reasons, was not re-convened for a decade, until early 1562. At this point, the Council took up again the matter of communion in both kinds and re-affirmed the late medieval practice, before issuing, in Session XXII (not included here), a decree on the sacrifice of the mass, that is, the notion that the ritual constituted a propitiatory sacrifice of Christ's flesh that had value in remitting sins. The decree also reiterated the appropriateness of private masses as well as re-affirming the legitimacy of most of the disputed rites and ceremonies that surrounded the celebration of the mass. The Council was not, by this point, in a very conciliatory mood. For the Protestants, the open and stubborn defense of what seemed to them the most blasphemous features of late medieval piety offered definitive proof that the Roman church was not merely corrupt and in need of reform, but apostate and in need of separation.

Further Reading

For further reading, see John W. O'Malley, *Trent: What Happened at the Council* (Cambridge, MA: The Belknap Press of Harvard University Press, 2013); George Hunsinger, *The Eucharist and Ecumenism: Let us Keep the Feast* (New York: Cambridge University Press, 2008).

COUNCIL OF TRENT,
DECREE AND CANONS CONCERNING THE MOST HOLY SACRAMENT OF THE EUCHARIST (1551)[1]

BEING THE third under the Sovereign Pontiff, Julius III., celebrated on the eleventh day of October, MDLI.

The sacred and holy, ecumenical and general Synod of Trent, lawfully assembled in the Holy Ghost, the same Legate, and nuncios of the Apostolic See presiding therein, although the end for which It assembled, not without the special guidance and governance of the Holy Ghost, was, that It might set forth the true and ancient doctrine touching faith and the sacraments, and might apply a remedy to all the heresies, and the other most grievous troubles with which the Church of God is now miserably agitated, and rent into many and various parts, yet, even from the outset, this especially has been the object of Its desires, that It might pluck up by the roots those tares of execrable errors and schisms, with which the enemy hath, in these our calamitous times, overthrown the doctrine of the faith, in the use and worship of the sacred and holy Eucharist, which our Savior, notwithstanding, left in His Church as a symbol of that unity and charity, with which He would fain have all Christians be mentally joined and united together. Wherefore, this sacred and holy Synod delivering here, on this venerable and divine sacrament of the Eucharist, that sound and genu-

---

[1] Taken from The Council of Trent.com,
http://www.thecounciloftrent.com/ch13.htm.

ine doctrine, which the Catholic Church, instructed by our Lord Jesus Christ Himself, and by His apostles, and taught by the Holy Ghost, who day by day brings to her mind all truth, has always retained, and will preserve even to the end of the world, forbids all the faithful of Christ, to presume to believe, teach, or preach henceforth concerning the holy Eucharist, otherwise than as is explained and defined in this present decree.

Chapter I: On the real presence of our Lord Jesus Christ in the most holy sacrament of the Eucharist

In the first place, the holy Synod teaches, and openly and simply professes, that, in the august sacrament of the holy Eucharist, after the consecration of the bread and wine, our Lord Jesus Christ, true God and man, is truly, really, and substantially contained under the species of those sensible things. For neither are these things mutually repugnant, that our Savior Himself always sitteth at the right hand of the Father in heaven, according to the natural mode of existing, and that, nevertheless, He be, in many other places, sacramentally present to us in his own substance, by a manner of existing, which, though we can scarcely express it in words, yet can we, by the understanding illuminated by faith, conceive, and we ought most firmly to believe, to be possible unto God, for thus all our forefathers, as many as were in the true Church of Christ, who have treated of this most holy Sacrament, have most openly professed that our Redeemer instituted this so admirable a sacrament at the last supper, when, after the blessing of the bread and wine, He testified, in express and clear words, that He gave them His own very Body, and His own Blood, words which, recorded by the holy Evangelists, and afterwards repeated by Saint Paul, whereas they carry with them that proper and most manifest meaning in which they were understood by the Fathers, it is indeed a crime the most unworthy that they should be wrested by certain contentions and wicked men to fictitious and imaginary tropes, whereby the verity of the flesh and blood of Christ is denied, contrary to the universal sense of the Church, which, as the pillar and ground of truth, has detested as satanical these inventions devised by impious men; she recognizing, with a mind ever grateful and unforgetting, this most excellent benefit of Christ.

Chapter II: On the reason of the Institution of this most holy Sacrament

Wherefore, our Savior, when about to depart out of this world to the Father, instituted this Sacrament, in which He poured forth as it were the riches of His divine love towards man, making a remembrance of his wonderful works; and He commanded us, in the participation thereof, to venerate His memory and to show forth his death until He come to judge the world. And He would also that this sacrament should be received as the spiritual food of souls, whereby may be fed and strengthened those who live with His life who said, He that eateth me, the same also shall live by me, and as an antidote, whereby we may be freed from daily faults and be preserved from mortal sins. He would, furthermore, have it be a pledge of our glory to come, and everlasting happiness, and thus be a symbol of that one body whereof He is the head, and to which He would fain have us as members be united by the closest bond of faith, hope, and charity, that we might all speak the same things and there might be no schisms amongst us.

Chapter III: On the excellency of the most holy Eucharist over the rest of the Sacraments

The most holy Eucharist has indeed this in common with the rest of the sacraments: that it is a symbol of a sacred thing, and is a visible form of an invisible grace. But there is found in the Eucharist this excellent and peculiar thing: that the other sacraments have then first the power of sanctifying when one uses them, whereas in the Eucharist, before being used, there is the Author Himself of sanctity. For the apostles had not as yet received the Eucharist from the hand of the Lord, when nevertheless Himself affirmed with truth that to be His own body which He presented [to them]. And this faith has ever been in the Church of God, that, immediately after the consecration, the veritable Body of our Lord and His veritable Blood, together with His soul and divinity are under the species of bread and wine; but the Body indeed under the species of bread, and the Blood under the species of wine, by the force of the words; but the body itself under the species of wine, and the blood under the species of bread, and the soul under both, by the force of that natural connection and concomitancy whereby the parts of Christ our Lord, who hath now risen from the dead, to die no more, are united together; and the divinity, furthermore, on account of the admirable hypostatical union thereof with His body and soul. Wherefore it is most true that as much is contained under either species as under both, for Christ whole and entire is under the species of bread, and under any part whatsoever of that species; likewise the whole [Christ] is under the species of wine, and under the parts thereof.

Chapter IV: On Transubstantiation

And because that Christ, our Redeemer, declared that which He offered under the species of bread to be truly His own body, therefore has it ever been a firm belief in the Church of God, and this holy Synod doth now declare it anew, that, by the consecration of the bread and of the wine, a conversion is made of the whole substance of the bread into the substance of the body of Christ our Lord, and of the whole substance of the wine into the substance of His blood, which conversion is, by the holy Catholic Church, suitably and properly called Transubstantiation.

Chapter V: On the cult and veneration to be shown to this most holy Sacrament

Wherefore, there is no room left for doubt that all the faithful of Christ may, according to the custom ever received in the Catholic Church, render in veneration the worship of latria[2], which is due to the true God, to this most holy sacrament. For not therefore is it

---

[2] *latria:* supreme worship

the less to be adored on this account, that it was instituted by Christ, the Lord, in order to be received: for we believe that same God to be present therein, of whom the eternal Father, when introducing him into the world, says, "And let all the angels of God adore him" [Heb. 1:6]; whom the Magi falling down, adored; who, in fine, as the Scripture testifies, was adored by the apostles in Galilee.

The holy Synod declares, moreover, that very piously and religiously was this custom introduced into the Church, that this sublime and venerable sacrament be, with special veneration and solemnity, celebrated, every year, on a certain day, and that a festival; and that it be borne reverently and with honor in processions through the streets, and public places. For it is most just that there be certain appointed holy days, whereon all Christians may, with a special and unusual demonstration, testify that their minds are grateful and thankful to their common Lord and Redeemer for so ineffable and truly divine a benefit, whereby the victory and triumph of His death are represented. And so indeed did it behoove victorious truth to celebrate a triumph over falsehood and heresy, that thus her adversaries, at the sight of so much splendor and in the midst of so great joy of the universal Church, may either pine away weakened and broken, or, touched with shame and confounded, at length repent.

Chapter VI: On reserving the Sacrament of the sacred Eucharist, and bearing it to the Sick

The custom of reserving the holy Eucharist in the sacrarium is so ancient that even the age of the Council of Nicaea recognized that usage. Moreover, as to carrying the sacred Eucharist itself to the sick and carefully reserving it for this purpose in churches, besides that it is exceedingly conformable to equity and reason, it is also found enjoined in numerous councils and is a very ancient observance of the Catholic Church. Wherefore, this holy Synod ordains that this salutary and necessary custom is to be by all means retained.

Chapter VII: On the preparation to be given that one may worthily receive the sacred Eucharist

If it is unbeseeming for anyone to approach to any of the sacred functions unless he approach holily, assuredly, the more the holiness and divinity of this heavenly sacrament are understood by a Christian, the more diligently ought he to give heed that he approach not to receive it but with great reverence and holiness, especially as we read in the Apostle those words full of terror, "He that eateth and drinketh unworthily, eateth and drinketh judgment to himself." Wherefore, he who would communicate, ought to recall to mind the precept of the Apostle, "Let a man prove himself." Now ecclesiastical usage declares that necessary proof to be, that no one, conscious to himself of mortal sin, how contrite soever he may seem to himself, ought to approach to the sacred Eucharist without previous sacramental confession. This the holy Synod hath decreed is to be invariably observed by all Christians, even by those priests on whom it may be incumbent by their office to celebrate, provided the opportunity of a confessor do not fail them; but if, in an urgent necessity, a priest should celebrate without previous confession, let him confess as soon as possible.

Chapter VIII: On the use of this admirable Sacrament

Now as to the use of this holy sacrament, our Fathers have rightly and wisely distinguished three ways of receiving it. For they have taught that some receive it sacramentally only, to wit sinners; others spiritually only, those to wit who eating in desire that heavenly bread which is set before them, are, by a lively faith which worketh by charity, made sensible of the fruit and usefulness thereof; whereas the third [class] receive it both sacramentally and spiritually, and these are they who so prove and prepare themselves beforehand, as to approach to this divine table clothed with the wedding garment. Now as to the reception of the sacrament, it was always the custom in the Church of God that laymen should receive the communion from priests, but that priests when celebrating should communicate themselves, which custom, as coming down from an apostolical tradition, ought with justice and reason to be retained. And finally this holy Synod with true fatherly affection admonishes, exhorts, begs, and beseeches, through the bowels of the mercy of our God, that all and each of those who bear the Christian name would now at length agree and be of one mind in this sign of unity, in this bond of charity, in this symbol of concord; and that mindful of the so great majesty, and the so exceeding love of our Lord Jesus Christ, who gave His own beloved soul as the price of our salvation, and gave us His own flesh to eat, they would believe and venerate these sacred mysteries of His body and blood with such constancy and firmness of faith, with such devotion of soul, with such piety and worship as to be able frequently to receive that supersubstantial bread, and that it may be to them truly the life of the soul, and the perpetual health of their mind; that being invigorated by the strength thereof, they may, after the journeying of this miserable pilgrimage, be able to arrive at their heavenly country, there to eat, without any veil, that same bread of angels which they now eat under the sacred veils.

But forasmuch as it is not enough to declare the truth, if errors be not laid bare and repudiated, it hath seemed good to the holy Synod to subjoin these canons, that all, the Catholic doctrine being already recognized, may now also understand what are the heresies which they ought to guard against and avoid.

On The Most Holy Sacrament Of The Eucharist: Canons

CANON I. If anyone denieth that in the sacrament of the most holy Eucharist, are contained truly, really, and substantially, the body and blood together with the soul and divinity of our Lord Jesus Christ, and consequently the whole Christ, but saith that He is only therein as in a sign, or in figure, or virtue, let him be anathema.

CANON II. If anyone saith that in the sacred and holy sacrament of the Eucharist, the substance of the bread and wine remains conjointly with the body and blood of our Lord Jesus Christ, and denieth that wonderful and singular conversion of the whole substance of the bread into the Body, and of the whole substance of the wine into the Blood—the species Only of the bread and wine remaining—which conversion indeed the Catholic Church most aptly calls Transubstantiation, let him be anathema.

CANON III. If anyone denieth that in the venerable sacrament of the Eucharist the whole Christ is contained under each species, and under every part of each species, when separated, let him be anathema.

CANON IV. If anyone saith that after the consecration is completed, the body and blood of our Lord Jesus Christ are not in the admirable sacrament of the Eucharist, but [are there] only during the use, whilst it is being taken, and not either before or after, and that, in the hosts, or consecrated particles, which are reserved or which remain after communion, the true Body of the Lord remaineth not, let him be anathema.

CANON V. If anyone saith either that the principal fruit of the most holy Eucharist is the remission of sins, or that other effects do not result therefrom, let him be anathema.

CANON VI. If anyone saith that in the holy sacrament of the Eucharist, Christ, the only-begotten Son of God, is not to be adored with the worship, even external of latria, and is, consequently, neither to be venerated with a special festive solemnity, nor to be solemnly borne about in processions, according to the laudable and universal rite and custom of holy church, or, is not to be proposed publicly to the people to be adored, and that the adorers thereof are idolaters, let him be anathema.

CANON VII. If anyone saith that it is not lawful for the sacred Eucharist to be reserved in the sacrarium, but that, immediately after consecration, it must necessarily be distributed amongst those present, or that it is not lawful that it be carried with honor to the sick, let him be anathema.

CANON VIII. If anyone saith that Christ, given in the Eucharist, is eaten spiritually only, and not also sacramentally and really, let him be anathema.

CANON IX. If anyone denieth that all and each of Christ's faithful of both sexes are bound, when they have attained to years of discretion, to communicate every year, at least at Easter, in accordance with the precept of holy Mother Church, let him be anathema.

CANON X. If anyone saith that it is not lawful for the celebrating priest to communicate himself, let him be anathema.

CANON XI. If anyone saith that faith alone is a sufficient preparation for receiving the sacrament of the most holy Eucharist, let him be anathema. And for fear lest so great a sacrament may be received unworthily, and so unto death and condemnation, this holy Synod ordains and declares that sacramental confession, when a confessor may be had, is of necessity to be made beforehand by those whose conscience is burthened with mortal sin, how contrite even soever they may think themselves. But if anyone shall presume to teach, preach, or obstinately to assert, or even in public disputation to defend the contrary, he shall be thereupon excommunicated.

INTRODUCTION TO IGNATIUS OF LOYOLA'S *SPIRITUAL EXERCISES*

IT IS important to keep in mind what we mean by the Catholic Counter-Reformation which ramped up in the 1540s. It was not merely—indeed, not even primarily—a "Counter-Reformation" in the sense of "something that counteracted, or sought to resist, the Reformation." Rather, it was very much a "Counter-Reformation" in the same sense of a "counter-attack"—it was itself a reformation which sought to respond to that which the Protestants had undertaken, an internal reform and renewal movement that was, however, fiercely loyal to the Pope. Of course, what shape such internal reform and renewal should take was hotly contested, and all but the most traditionalist advocates of reform ran the risk of being accused of Protestant sympathizers.

So it was with probably the most famous and influential of all Counter-Reformation leaders, Ignatius of Loyola (1491–1556), founder of Society of Jesus, or Jesuit order. From its humble beginnings as a band of friends trying to travel to Jerusalem in the late 1530s, the order was nearly ubiquitous a century later, with well-established mission centers not only across Europe but in South America, North America, and East Asia.

No group did more to slow and in some places, such as Poland, to roll back the progress of the Reformation as the Jesuits. Key to their success was their imitation of key features of Protestantism. They stressed the importance of teaching and catechesis, realizing that ordinary Catholic laypeople could hardly be expected to just "shut up and obey the Pope" when presented with persuasive arguments from Protestant preachers. They also downplayed the barrier between clergy and laity that had been such a crucial part of Luther's early protest, acting neither as parish priests nor as monks living in their separated communities, but instead working closely with ordinary people. Indeed, their courageous and dedicated mission work in the Americas and Asia won countless converts from heathenism and set a model that later Protestant foreign missionaries were to seek to imitate. The Jesuits also laid great stress on individual religious experience and the discipleship of the soul, thus helping to rebut Protestant critiques of hypocritical outward ceremonialism.

This last emphasis grew directly out of Ignatius's own deep religious experience. Born in northern Spain under the name Íñigo de Loyola (his later name, Ignatius, was the result of a scribal error),[1] he aspired to rise to a position in the nobility and joined the army. Seriously wounded in the battle of Pamplona, he spent several months convalescing with little around to read but medieval devotional texts. The result was a powerful conversion experience that led Ignatius to commit himself to a missionary life. Although he was passionately devoted to the service of the Roman church, Ignatius's emphasis on personal religious experience savored a little too much of Protestantism and other heresies for the Spanish Inquisition, and he left Spain in 1528.

After a period of study in Paris, Ignatius and a group of companions vowed to make a pilgrimage to Jerusalem, but were thwarted in 1537 by a war with the Turks that shut down all shipping. Stranded in Italy, Ignatius and his companions went to Rome and determined to serve Jesus and His Church in whatever ways He called them to, and began calling themselves the Society of Jesus. In 1540, Ignatius succeeded in winning papal approval to formalize the Society as a religious order of the Catholic Church. Ignatius and his associates still faced suspicion and opposition from many members of the Roman hierarchy, however, and his devo-

---

[1] Diarmaid MacCulloch, *Reformation: Europe's House Divided, 1490–1700* (London: Penguin, 2003), 220.

tional guide, the *Spiritual Exercises*, was carefully screened by the Roman Inquisition before being approved for publication in 1548.

The *Exercises* is a curious book—not meant for reading so much as for use as a how-to manual by spiritual directors, which Ignatius trained his followers to be. Rather than playing the passive role of confessor that most parish priests did before the Reformation, Jesuit spiritual directors would lead believers in a prolonged process of self-examination, meditation, and contemplation of Christ to help them leave behind sin and strengthen their faith. Indeed, in their emphasis on the depth of our depravity that must be confessed, the Exercises are reminiscent of aspects of Luther's theology, particularly those that earned early condemnation in the bull *Exsurge Domine*. However, the difference between Reformation and Counter-Reformation spirituality is also clear in the excerpt below. For Luther, although awareness of one's deep sinfulness and helplessness was necessary to truly receive the grace of God, one was not supposed to wallow in self-examination, grief, or fear, but to turn immediately from it to the comfort of Christ's mercy. To be sure, the "First Week" excerpted here is followed by meditations on Christ's life, on his death, and on his resurrection; introspection and repentance is only the beginning. Still, it is a beginning that is never wholly left behind, since in Ignatian spirituality, as in all Roman Catholic spirituality, there is no room for the firm and confident assurance of salvation that Protestants proclaimed; indeed, as we saw in the last reading, such assurance was explicitly anathematized.

Further Reading

For further reading, see Diarmaid MacCulloch, *The Reformation: A History* (New York, Penguin, 2005), ch. 5; John Patrick Donnelly, S.J., *Ignatius of Loyola: Founder of the Jesuits* (New York: Longman, 2004); George E. Ganss, S.J., ed., *Ignatius of Loyola: Spiritual Exercises and Selected Works* (New York: Paulist Press, 1991).

IGNATIUS OF LOYOLA,
SPIRITUAL EXERCISES (1548)[1]

General Examen of Conscience to Purify Oneself and to Make One's Confession Better

I PRESUPPOSE that there are three kinds of thoughts in me: that is, one my own, which springs from my mere liberty and will; and two others, which come from without, one from the good spirit, and the other from the bad.

Thought

There are two ways of meriting in the bad thought which comes from without, namely:

First Way. A thought of committing a mortal sin, which thought I resist immediately and it remains conquered.

Second Way. The second way of meriting is: When that same bad thought comes to me and I resist it, and it returns to me again and again, and I always resist, until it is conquered.

This second way is more meritorious than the first.

A venial sin is committed when the same thought comes of sinning mortally and one gives ear to it, making some little delay, or receiving some sensual pleasure, or when there is some negligence in rejecting such thought.

There are two ways of sinning mortally:

---

[1] Elder Mullan, S.J., trans., *The Spiritual Exercises of St. Ignatius of Loyola* (New York: P.J. Kennedy & Sons, 1914). Excerpt from "First Week."

First Way. The first is, when one gives consent to the bad thought, to act afterwards as he has consented, or to put it in act if he could.

Second Way. The second way of sinning mortally is when that sin is put in act.

This is a greater sin for three reasons: first, because of the greater time; second, because of the greater intensity; third, because of the greater harm to the two persons.

Word

One must not swear, either by Creator or creature, if it be not with truth, necessity and reverence.

By necessity I mean, not when any truth whatever is affirmed with oath, but when it is of some importance for the good of the soul, or the body, or for temporal goods.

By reverence I mean when, in naming the Creator and Lord, one acts with consideration, so as to render Him the honor and reverence due.

It is to be noted that, though in an idle oath one sins more when he swears by the Creator than by the creature, it is more difficult to swear in the right way with truth, necessity and reverence by the creature than by the Creator, for the following reasons.

First Reason. The first: When we want to swear by some creature, wanting to name the creature does not make us so attentive or circumspect as to telling the truth, or as to affirming it with necessity, as would wanting to name the Lord and Creator of all things.

Second Reason. The second is that in swearing by the creature it is not so easy to show reverence and respect to the Creator, as in swearing and naming the same Creator and Lord, because wanting to name God our Lord brings with it more respect and reverence than wanting to name the created thing. Therefore swearing by the creature is more allowable to the perfect than to the imperfect, because the perfect, through continued contemplation and enlightenment of intellect, consider, meditate and contemplate more that God our Lord is in every creature, according to His own essence, presence and power, and so in swearing by the creature they are more apt and prepared than the imperfect to show respect and reverence to their Creator and Lord.

Third Reason. The third is that in continually swearing by the creature, idolatry is to be more feared in the imperfect than in the perfect.

One must not speak an idle word. By idle word I mean one which does not benefit either me or another, and is not directed to that intention. Hence words spoken for any useful purpose, or meant to profit one's own or another's soul, the body or temporal goods, are never idle, not even if one were to speak of something foreign to one's state of life, as, for instance, if a religious speaks of wars or articles of trade, but in all that is said there is merit in directing well, and sin in directing badly, or in speaking idly.

Nothing must be said to injure another's character or to find fault, because if I reveal a mortal sin that is not public, I sin mortally; if a venial sin, venially; and if a defect, I show a defect of my own.

But if the intention is right, in two ways one can speak of the sin or fault of another:

First Way. The first: When the sin is public, as in the case of a public prostitute, and of a sentence given in judgment, or of a public error which is infecting the souls with whom one comes in contact.

Second Way. Second: When the hidden sin is revealed to some person that he may help to raise him who is in sin—supposing, however, that he has some probable conjectures or grounds for thinking that he will be able to help him.

Act

Taking the Ten Commandments, the Precepts of the Church and the recommendations of Superiors, every act done against any of these three heads is, according to its greater or less nature, a greater or a lesser sin.

By recommendations of Superiors I mean such things as Bulls de Cruzadas and other Indulgences, as for instance for peace, granted under condition of going to Confession and receiving the Blessed Sacrament. For one commits no little sin in being the cause of others acting contrary to such pious exhortations and recommendations of our Superiors, or in doing so oneself.

Method For Making The General Examen

It contains in it five Points.

First Point. The first Point is to give thanks to God our Lord for the benefits received.

Second Point. The second, to ask grace to know our sins and cast them out.

Third Point. The third, to ask account of our soul from the hour that we rose up to the present Examen, hour by hour, or period by period: and first as to thoughts, and then as to words, and then as to acts, in the same order as was mentioned in the Particular Examen.

Fourth Point. The fourth, to ask pardon of God our Lord for the faults.

Fifth Point. The fifth, to purpose amendment with His grace.

OUR FATHER.

General Confession With Communion

Whoever, of his own accord, wants to make a General Confession, will, among many other advantages, find three in making it here.

First. The first: Though whoever goes to Confession every year is not obliged to make a General Confession, by making it there is greater profit and merit, because of the greater actual sorrow for all the sins and wickedness of his whole life.

Second. The second: In the Spiritual Exercises, sins and their malice are understood more intimately, than in the time when one was not so giving himself to interior things. Gaining now more knowledge of and sorrow for them, he will have greater profit and merit than he had before.

Third. The third is: In consequence, having made a better Confession and being better disposed, one finds himself in condition and prepared to receive the Blessed Sacrament: the reception of which is an aid not only not to fall into sin, but also to preserve the increase of grace.

This General Confession will be best made immediately after the Exercises of the First Week.

First Exercise: It Is a Meditation with the Three Powers on the First, the Second and the Third Sin

It contains in it, after one Preparatory Prayer and two Preludes, three chief Points and one *Colloquy.*

Prayer. The Preparatory Prayer is to ask grace of God our Lord that all my intentions, actions and operations may be directed purely to the service and praise of His Divine Majesty.

First Prelude. The First Prelude is a composition, seeing the place.

Here it is to be noted that, in a visible contemplation or meditation—as, for instance, when one contemplates Christ our Lord, Who is visible—the composition will be to see with the sight of the imagination the corporeal place where the thing is found which I want to contemplate. I say the corporeal place, as for instance, a Temple or Mountain where Jesus Christ or Our Lady is found, according to what I want to contemplate. In an invisible contemplation or meditation—as here on the Sins—the composition will be to see with the sight of the imagination and consider that my soul is imprisoned in this corruptible body, and all the compound in this valley, as exiled among brute beasts: I say all the compound of soul and body.

Second Prelude. The second is to ask God our Lord for what I want and desire.

The petition has to be according to the subject matter; that is, if the contemplation is on the Resurrection, one is to ask for joy with Christ in joy; if it is on the Passion, he is to ask for pain, tears and torment with Christ in torment.

Here it will be to ask shame and confusion at myself, seeing how many have been damned for only one mortal sin, and how many times I deserved to be condemned forever for my so many sins.

Note. Before all Contemplations or Meditations, there ought always to be made the Preparatory Prayer, which is not changed, and the two Preludes already mentioned, which are sometimes changed, according to the subject matter.

First Point. The first Point will be to bring the memory on the First Sin, which was that of the Angels, and then to bring the intellect on the same, discussing it; then the will, wanting to recall and understand all this in order to make me more ashamed and confound me more, bringing into comparison with the one sin of the Angels my so many sins, and reflecting, while they for one sin were cast into Hell, how often I have deserved it for so many.

I say to bring to memory the sin of the Angels, how they, being created in grace, not wanting to help themselves with their liberty to reverence and obey their Creator and Lord, coming to pride, were changed from grace to malice, and hurled from Heaven to Hell; and so then to discuss more in detail with the intellect: and then to move the feelings more with the will.

Second Point. The second is to do the same—that is, to bring the Three Powers—on the sin of Adam and Eve, bringing to memory how on account of that sin they did penance for so long a time, and how much corruption came on the human race, so many people going the way to Hell.

I say to bring to memory the Second Sin, that of our First Parents; how after Adam was created in the field of Damascus and placed in the Terrestrial Paradise, and Eve was created from his rib, being forbidden to eat of the Tree of Knowledge, they ate and so sinned, and afterwards clothed in tunics of skins and cast from

Paradise, they lived, all their life, without the original justice which they had lost, and in many labors and much penance. And then to discuss with the understanding more in detail; and to use the will as has been said.

Third Point. The third is likewise to do the same on the Third particular Sin of any one who for one mortal sin is gone to Hell—and many others without number, for fewer sins than I have committed.

I say to do the same on the Third particular Sin, bringing to memory the gravity and malice of the sin against one's Creator and Lord; to discuss with the understanding how in sinning and acting against the Infinite Goodness, he has been justly condemned forever; and to finish with the will as has been said.

Colloquy. Imagining Christ our Lord present and placed on the Cross, let me make a Colloquy, how from Creator He is come to making Himself man, and from life eternal is come to temporal death, and so to die for my sins.

Likewise, looking at myself, what I have done for Christ, what I am doing for Christ, what I ought to do for Christ.

And so, seeing Him such, and so nailed on the Cross, to go over that which will present itself.

The Colloquy is made, properly speaking, as one friend speaks to another, or as a servant to his master; now asking some grace, now blaming oneself for some misdeed, now communicating one's affairs, and asking advice in them.

And let me say an OUR FATHER.

Second Exercise: It Is a Meditation on the Sins and Contains in It after the Preparatory Prayer and Two Preludes, Five Points and One Colloquy

Prayer. Let the Preparatory Prayer be the same.

First Prelude. The First Prelude will be the same composition.

Second Prelude. The second is to ask for what I want. It will be here to beg a great and intense sorrow and tears for my sins.

First Point. The first Point is the statement of the sins; that is to say, to bring to memory all the sins of life, looking from year to year, or from period to period. For this three things are helpful: first, to look at the place and the house where I have lived; second, the relations I have had with others; third, the occupation in which I have lived.

Second Point. The second, to weigh the sins, looking at the foulness and the malice which any mortal sin committed has in it, even supposing it were not forbidden.

Third Point. The third, to look at who I am, lessening myself by examples:

First, how much I am in comparison to all men;

Second, what men are in comparison to all the Angels and Saints of Paradise;

Third, what all Creation is in comparison to God: (Then I alone, what can I be?)

Fourth, to see all my bodily corruption and foulness;

Fifth, to look at myself as a sore and ulcer, from which have sprung so many sins and so many iniquities and so very vile poison.

Fourth Point. The fourth, to consider what God is, against Whom I have sinned, according to His attributes; comparing them with their contraries in me—His Wisdom with my ignorance; His Omnipotence with my weakness; His Justice with my iniquity; His Goodness with my malice.

Fifth Point. The fifth, an exclamation of wonder with deep feeling, going through all creatures, how they have left me in life and preserved me in it; the Angels, how, though they are the sword of the Divine Justice, they have endured me, and guarded me, and prayed for me; the Saints, how they have been engaged in interceding and praying for me; and the heavens, sun, moon, stars, and elements, fruits, birds, fishes and animals—and the earth, how it has not opened to swallow me up, creating new Hells for me to suffer in them forever!

Colloquy. Let me finish with a Colloquy of mercy, pondering and giving thanks to God our Lord that He has given me life up to now, proposing amendment, with His grace, for the future.

OUR FATHER.

Third Exercise: It Is a Repetition of the First and Second Exercise, Making Three Colloquies

After the Preparatory Prayer and two Preludes, it will be to repeat the First and Second Exercise, marking and dwelling on the Points in which I have felt greater consolation or desolation, or greater spiritual feeling.

After this I will make three Colloquies in the following manner:

First Colloquy. The first Colloquy to Our Lady, that she may get me grace from Her Son and Lord for three things: first, that I may feel an interior knowledge of my sins, and hatred of them; second, that I may feel the disorder of my actions, so that, hating them, I may correct myself and put myself in order; third, to ask knowledge of the world, in order that, hating it, I may put away from me worldly and vain things.

And with that a HAIL MARY.

Second Colloquy. The second: The same to the Son, begging Him to get it for me from the Father.

And with that the SOUL OF CHRIST.

Third Colloquy. The third: The same to the Father, that the Eternal Lord Himself may grant it to me.

And with that an OUR FATHER.

Fourth Exercise: It Is a Summary of This Same Third

I said a summary, that the understanding, without wandering, may assiduously go through the memory of the things contemplated in the preceding Exercises.

I will make the same three Colloquies.

Fifth Exercise: It Is a Meditation on Hell

It contains in it, after the Preparatory Prayer and two Preludes, five Points and one Colloquy:

Prayer. Let the Preparatory Prayer be the usual one.

First Prelude. The first Prelude is the composition, which is here to see with the sight of the imagination the length, breadth and depth of Hell.

Second Prelude. The second, to ask for what I want: it will be here to ask for interior sense of the pain which the damned suffer, in order that, if, through my faults, I should forget the love of the Eternal Lord, at least the fear of the pains may help me not to come into sin.

First Point. The first Point will be to see with the sight of the imagination the great fires, and the souls as in bodies of fire.

Second Point. The second, to hear with the ears wailings, howlings, cries, blasphemies against Christ our Lord and against all His Saints.

Third Point. The third, to smell with the smell smoke, sulphur, dregs and putrid things.

Fourth Point. The fourth, to taste with the taste bitter things, like tears, sadness and the worm of conscience.

Fifth Point. The fifth, to touch with the touch; that is to say, how the fires touch and burn the souls.

Colloquy. Making a Colloquy to Christ our Lord, I will bring to memory the souls that are in Hell, some because they did not believe the Coming, others because, believing, they did not act according to His Commandments; making three divisions:

First, Second, and Third Divisions. The first, before the Coming; the second, during His life; the third, after His life in this world; and with this I will give Him thanks that He has not let me fall into any of these divisions, ending my life.

Likewise, I will consider how up to now He has always had so great pity and mercy on me.

I will end with an OUR FATHER.

Note: The first Exercise will be made at midnight; the second immediately on rising in the morning; the third, before or after Mass; in any case, before dinner; the fourth at the hour of Vespers; the fifth, an hour before supper.

This arrangement of hours, more or less, I always mean in all the four Weeks, according as his age, disposition and physical condition help the person who is exercising himself to make five Exercises or fewer.

Additions: To Make the Exercises Better and to Find Better What One Desires

First Addition. The first Addition is, after going to bed, just when I want to go asleep, to think, for the space of a HAIL MARY, of the hour that I have to rise and for what, making a resume of the Exercise which I have to make.

Second Addition. The second: When I wake up, not giving place to any other thought, to turn my attention immediately to what I am going to contemplate in the first Exercise, at midnight, bringing myself to confusion for my so many sins, setting examples, as, for instance, if a knight found himself before his king and all his court, ashamed and confused at having much offended him, from whom he had first received many gifts and many favors: in the same way, in the second Exercise, making myself a great sinner and in chains; that is to say going to appear bound as in chains before the Supreme Eternal Judge; taking for an example how prisoners in chains and already deserving death, appear before their temporal judge. And I will dress with these thoughts or with others, according to the subject matter.

Third Addition. The third: A step or two before the place where I have to contemplate or meditate, I will put myself standing for the space of an OUR FATHER, my intellect raised on high, considering how God our Lord is looking at me, etc.; and will make an act of reverence or humility.

Fourth Addition. The fourth: To enter on the contemplation now on my knees, now prostrate on the earth, now lying face upwards, now seated, now standing, always intent on seeking what I want.

We will attend to two things. The first is that if I find what I want kneeling, I will not pass on; and if prostrate, likewise, etc. The second; in the Point in which I find what I want, there I will rest, without being anxious to pass on, until I content myself.

Fifth Addition. The fifth: After finishing the Exercise, I will, during the space of a quarter of an hour, seated or walking leisurely, look how it went with me in the Contemplation or Meditation; and if badly, I will look for the cause from which it proceeds, and having so seen it, will be sorry, in order to correct myself in future; and if well, I will give thanks to God our Lord, and will do in like manner another time.

Sixth Addition. The sixth: Not to want to think on things of pleasure or joy, such as heavenly glory, the Resurrection, etc. Because whatever consideration of joy and gladness hinders our feeling pain and grief and shedding tears for our sins, but to keep before me that I want to grieve and feel pain, bringing to memory rather Death and Judgment.

Seventh Addition. The seventh: For the same end, to deprive myself of all light, closing the blinds and doors while I am in the room, if it be not to recite prayers, to read and eat.

Eighth Addition. The eighth: Not to laugh nor say a thing provocative of laughter.

Ninth Addition. The ninth: To restrain my sight, except in receiving or dismissing the person with whom I have spoken.

Tenth Addition. The tenth Addition is penance.

This is divided into interior and exterior. The interior is to grieve for one's sins, with a firm purpose of not committing them nor any others. The exterior, or fruit of the first, is chastisement for the sins committed, and is chiefly taken in three ways.

First Way. The first is as to eating. That is to say, when we leave off the superfluous, it is not penance, but temperance. It is penance when we leave off from the suitable; and the more and more, the greater and better—provided that the person does not injure himself, and that no notable illness follows.

Second Way. The second, as to the manner of sleeping. Here too it is not penance to leave off the superfluous of delicate or soft things, but it is penance when one leaves off from the suitable in the manner: and the more and more, the better—provided that the person does not injure himself and no notable illness follows. Besides, let not anything of the suitable sleep be left off, unless in order to come to the mean, if one has a bad habit of sleeping too much.

Third Way. The third, to chastise the flesh, that is, giving it sensible pain, which is given by wearing haircloth or cords or iron chains next to the flesh, by scourging or wounding oneself, and by other kinds of austerity.

Note. What appears most suitable and most secure with regard to penance is that the pain should be sensible in the flesh and not enter within the bones, so that it give pain and not illness. For this it appears to be more suitable to scourge oneself with thin cords, which give pain exteriorly, rather than in another way which would cause notable illness within.

First Note. The first Note is that the exterior penances are done chiefly for three ends: First, as satisfaction for the sins committed;

Second, to conquer oneself—that is, to make sensuality obey reason and all inferior parts be more subject to the superior;

Third, to seek and find some grace or gift which the person wants and desires; as, for instance, if he desires to have interior contrition for his sins, or to weep much over them, or over the pains and sufferings which Christ our Lord suffered in His Passion, or to settle some doubt in which the person finds himself.

Second Note. The second: It is to be noted that the first and second Addition have to be made for the Exercises of midnight and at daybreak, but not for those which will be made at other times; and the fourth Addition will never be made in church in the presence of others, but in private, as at home, etc.

Third Note. The third: When the person who is exercising himself does not yet find what he desires—as tears, consolations, etc.—it often helps for him to make a change in food, in sleep and in other ways of doing penance, so that he change himself, doing penance two or three days, and two or three others not. For it suits some to do more penance and others less, and we often omit doing penance from sensual love and from an erroneous judgment that the human system will not be able to bear it without notable illness; and sometimes, on the contrary, we do too much, thinking that the body can bear it; and as God our Lord knows our nature infinitely better, often in such changes He gives each one to perceive what is suitable for him.

Fourth Note. The fourth: Let the Particular Examen be made to rid oneself of defects and negligences on the Exercises and Additions. And so in the SECOND, THIRD AND FOURTH WEEKS.

INTRODUCTION TO HEINRICH BULLINGER'S *DECADES II.7: OF THE MAGISTRATE*

ONE OF the aspects of Reformation theology that is most liable to puzzle a modern reader is its pervasive influence on the God-given calling of the civil magistrate to oversee and where necessary reform the church. Although we are apt to try and excuse it as simply a pragmatic effort to seek the protection of powerful princes against oppressing prelates, it does not take much reading to realize that, on the contrary, this principle was deeply anchored in their theology. We have seen already how Luther's *Letter to the Christian Nobility* articulated the doctrine of the "priesthood of all believers," empowering lay authorities to take a role in reforming the church. Although Luther, recognizing that "a wise prince is a mighty rare bird, and an upright prince even rarer,"[1] was always cautious about entrusting too much ecclesiastical power to grasping rulers, both he and Melanchthon eventually filled out an account of church and society in which Christian rulers played an indispensable role in maintaining the good order and administration of reformed churches, and helping protect them against heresy and schism.

The fullest theology of the role of the Christian magistrate, however, was outlined by the Zurich reformers, Ulrich Zwingli

---

[1] Martin Luther, *On Temporal Authority: To What Extent it Should be Obeyed*, in Jaroslav Pelikan and Helmut T. Lehmann, eds., *Luther's Works: American Edition* (St. Louis: Concordia Publishing House, and Philadelphia: Muhlenberg Press, 1955–1970), 45: 113.

(1484–1531) and especially his successor Heinrich Bullinger (1504–1575). Although the broad outlines of their ecclesiology were the same as Luther's (resting on the same basic distinction of two realms or kingdoms), several factors impelled them in the direction of a more robust and optimistic account of the "godly magistrate." First was the need to respond to the threat of Anabaptism with its frontal attack on the idea of Christians playing a role in civil government; the Anabaptists, as discussed previously, had a strong early presence in Zurich. Second was the close-knit city-state polity of Switzerland; with republican governments overseeing relatively small areas, a close partnership of ministers and magistrates was feasible. Third, and most theologically important, was the Zurich reformers' emphasis on the continuity of Old and New Testaments, which was to become a distinctive of the Reformed tradition over against the Lutheran. It is, after all, readily evident to any reader of the Old Testament that civil and religious responsibilities were closely intertwined, with the kings of Israel and Judah being judged primarily on the extent to which they did or did not enforce true religion and root out idolatry. Since the Zurich reformers did not hesitate to treat Israel and the church as one people under two phases of the administration of the one covenant of grace, neither did they hesitate to argue strenuously for Christian rulers to take up the duties of their Old Testament counterparts, looking to godly kings like Hezekiah and Josiah as their examples.

Heinrich Bullinger was one of the most extraordinary men of the Reformation, though one largely forgotten and rarely quoted today. His long life witnessed nearly all the decisive phases of the Reformation, and although he almost never left the small city of Zurich, his influence, wielded largely through an extraordinary letter-writing network, spanned the length and breadth of the Continent. At age 27, Bullinger stepped into Zwingli's larger-than-life shoes as leading minister of Zurich following Zwingli's death at the Battle of Kappel. He adeptly shepherded the church there through the tense political situation that followed, navigating the ecclesiastical isolation that had been created by Luther's hostility, and eventually forging strong ties with Bucer in Strasbourg, Calvin in Geneva, and many other centers of what was to eventually become the Reformed tradition.

Perhaps most significant and lasting, however, was his forty-year-long role as a prophetic mentor to the English Reformation. Recognizing early on the enormous strategic importance for the Protestant cause of Henry VIII's defection from Rome, Bullinger dedicated his treatise on Scripture to Henry in 1538, and was to similarly dedicate treatises to Edward VI and Queen Elizabeth. By the 1560s, he was the leading theological authority for the Church of England, consulted by bishops and theologians on myriad questions. His strong view of the role of the godly magistrate in ordering and governing the church was to help shape and sustain the English understanding of the monarch's position as head of the church.

Perhaps nowhere does Bullinger so clearly and forcibly articulate his understanding of this doctrine than in the seventh sermon of Vol. II of his *Decades*. This mighty five-volume tome, consisting of fifty lengthy "sermons," was written by Bullinger in 1549 and dedicated to the young Edward VI of England (r. 1547–1553) to help guide him in his reforming task. Volume II is dedicated primarily to an exposition of the Ten Commandments, and Sermons 6-8 relate to the sixth commandment, which Bullinger sees as the most suitable heading under which to treat the civil magistrate's duties. Bullinger considers the magistrate's religious responsibilities as important enough to spend one-half of Sermon 7 expounding.

In this sermon, you will see his heavy methodological reliance on the Old Testament, reasoning that if Christ and the Apostles had intended for the New Testament church to chart a completely different course when it came to the role of magistrates, they would have said so. Moreover, he points out, from the earliest Christian Roman emperors on, Christian magistrates have understood their task vis-à-vis the church in terms not unlike those of Old Testament kings. Of course, we should be clear on what this task is. Bullinger is emphatic that there is still a clear distinction of offices, denying "that we would have the king to preach, to baptize, and to minister the Lord's supper." Rather, it is an ordering role, taking thought for the external structure of the church and its temporal affairs, to ensure it is effectively governed, peaceable, and well provided for. Moreover, Bullinger defends the ministers' God-given responsibility to proclaim the Word of God to the king so that he knows how he ought to govern the church, although he does allow that if the ministers are slack, corrupt, or inattentive to the Word of God, the godly prince will go directly to the Scriptures for guidance and correct ungodly ministers accordingly.

The doctrine of the godly prince was certainly to create headaches for Protestant churches who found themselves stuck with ungodly princes, but it was not until centuries later that most Protestants took the step of removing ecclesiastical affairs from civil oversight.

Further Reading

For further reading, see W.J. Torrance Kirby, *The Zurich Connection and Tudor Political Theology* (Leiden: Brill, 2007); Bruce Gordon and Emidio Campi, eds., *Architect of the Reformation: An Introduction to Heinrich Bullinger, 1504-1575* (Grand Rapids: Baker Academic, 2004); Paul D.L Avis, *The Church in the Theology of the Reformers* (Atlanta: John Knox Press, 1981), chs. 9–10.

HEINRICH BULLINGER,
DECADES II.7: OF THE MAGISTRATE[1]

Whether the care of religion appertain to him or no, and whether he may make laws and ordinances in cases of religion

THE FIRST and greatest thing that chiefly ought to be in a magistrate is easily perceived by the declaration of his office and duty. In my yesterday's sermon I shewed you what the magistrate is, how many kinds of magistrates there are, of whom the magistrate had his beginning, for what causes he was ordained, the manner and order how to choose peers, and what kind of men should be called to be magistrates. To this let us now add what the office and duty of a magistrate properly is.

The whole office of a magistrate seemeth to consist in these three points: to order, to judge, and to punish, of every one whereof I mean to speak severally in order as they lie. The ordinance of the magistrate is a decree made by him for maintaining of religion, honesty, justice, and public peace: and it consisteth on two points: in ordering rightly matters of religion, and making good laws for the preservation of honesty, justice, and common peace. But before I come to the determining and ordering of religion, I will briefly, and in few words, handle their question which demand whether the care of religion do appertain to the magistrate as part

---

[1] Taken from Thomas Harding, ed., *The Decades of Henry Bullinger, Minister of the Church of Zurich: The First and Second Decades*, trans. H.I. (Cambridge: Cambridge University Press, 1849).

of his office or no? For I see many that are of opinion that the care and ordering of religion doth belong to bishops alone, and that kings, princes, and senators ought not to meddle therewith.

But the catholic verity teacheth that the care of religion doth especially belong to the magistrate, and that it is not in his power only, but his office and duty also to dispose and advance religion. For among them of old their kings were priests, I mean, masters and overseers of religion. Melchizedek, that holy and wise prince of the Canaanite people, who bare the type or figure of Christ our Lord, is wonderfully commended in the holy scriptures; now he was both king and priest together. Moreover, in the book of Numbers, to Joshua, newly ordained and lately consecrated, are the laws belonging to religion given up and delivered. The kings of Judah also, and the elect people of God, have for the well ordering of religion (as I will by examples anon[2] declare unto you) obtained very great praise, and again, as many as were slack in looking to religion are noted with the mark of perpetual reproach. Who is ignorant that the magistrate's especial care ought to be to keep the commonweal in safeguard and prosperity? Which undoubtedly he cannot do unless he provide to have the word of God preached to his people and cause them to be taught the true worship of God, by that means making himself, as it were, the minister of true religion. In Leviticus and Deuteronomy the Lord doth largely set down the good prepared for men that are religious and zealous indeed, and reckoneth up on the other side the evil appointed for the condemners of true religion (Lev. 26, Deut. 28). But the good magistrate is commanded to retain and keep prosperity among his people, and to repel all kind of adversity. Let us hear also what the wise man, Solomon, saith in his Proverbs: "Godliness and truth preserve the king, and in godliness his seat is holden up." "When the just are multiplied, the people rejoice, and when the wicked ruleth, the people lamenteth. The king by judgment stablisheth his dominion, but a tyrant overthroweth it. When the wicked increase,

---

[2] *anon:* presently.

iniquity is multiplied, and the just shall see their decay. Where the word of God is not preached, the people decay, but happy is he that keepeth the law" (Prov. 20:28, 29:2, 4, 16, 18). Whereby we gather, that they which would not have the care of religion to appertain to princes do seek and bring in the confusion of all things, the dissolution of princes and their people, and lastly, the neglecting and oppression of the poor.

Furthermore, the Lord commandeth the magistrate to make trial of doctrines, and to kill those that do stubbornly teach against the scriptures, and draw the people from the true God. The place is to be seen in the thirteenth of Deuteronomy God also forbade the magistrate to plant groves or erect images, as is to be seen in the seventeenth of Deuteronomy. And by those particularities he did insinuate things general, forbidding to ordain, to nourish, and set forth superstition or idolatry, wherefore he commanded to advance true religion, and so consequently it followeth that the care of religion belongeth to the magistrate. What may be thought of that moreover that the most excellent princes and friends of God among God's people did challenge to themselves the care of religion as belonging to themselves, insomuch that they exercised and took the charge thereof, even as if they had been ministers of the holy things? Joshua in the mount Ebal caused an altar to be builded, and fulfilled all the worship of God, as it was commanded of God by the mouth of Moses (Josh. 8:30). David, in bringing in and bestowing the ark of God in his place, and in ordering the worship of God, was so diligent that it is wonder to tell. So likewise was Solomon, David's son. Neither do I think that any man knoweth not how much Asa, Jehoshaphat, Hezekiah, and Josiah labored in the reformation of religion, which in their times was corrupted and utterly defaced. The very heathen kings and princes are praised, because, when they knew the truth, they gave out edicts for the confirmation of true religion against blasphemous mouths. Nebuchadnezzar, the Chaldean, the most mighty monarch of all the world, than who I doubt whether any more great and mighty did reign in the world, publisheth a decree that he should be torn in pieces and his house made a jakes,[3] whosoever spake reproachfully against the true God which made both heaven and earth. The place is extant in the third chapter of Daniel's prophecy. Darius the Mede, the son of Ahasuerus, king Cyrus his uncle, saith: "I have decreed that all men in the whole dominion of my kingdom do fear the God of Daniel," as is to be seen in the sixth of Daniel. Cyrus, king of Persia, looseth the Jews from bondage and giveth them in charge to repair the temple and restore their holy rites again (Ezra 1). Darius of Persia, the son of Hystaspes, saith: "I have decreed for every man which changeth anything of my determination touching the reparation of the temple, and the restoring of the worship of God, that a beam be taken out of his house, and set up, and he hanged thereon, and his house to be made a jakes" (Ezra 6:11). The very same Darius again, who was also called Artaxerxes, saith: "Whosoever will not do the law of thy God, and the law of the king, let judgment straightway pass upon him, either to death, or to utter rooting out, or to confiscation of his goods, or imprisonment" (Ezra 8:26). All this we find in the book of Ezra.

The men, which are persuaded that the care and ordering of religion doth belong to bishops alone, do make an objection and say that these examples, which I have alleged, do nothing appertain to us which are Christians, because they are examples of the Jewish people. To whom mine answer is: the men of this opinion ought to prove that the Lord Jesus and his apostles did translate the care of religion from the magistrate unto bishops alone, which they shall never be able to do. But we, on the other side, will briefly shew that those ancient princes of God's people, Joshua, David, and the rest were Christians verily and indeed, and that therefore the examples which are derived from them and applied to Christian princes, both are and ought to be of force and effect among us at this day. I will in the end add also the prophecy of the prophet Isaiah, whereby it may appear that even now also kings have in the church at this day the same office that those ancient kings had in that congregation

---

[3] *jakes:* dunghill.

which they call the Jewish church. There is no doubt but that they ought to be accounted true Christians, which, being anointed with the Spirit of Christ do believe in Christ and are in the sacraments made partakers of Christ. For Christ (if ye interpret the very word) is as much to say as "anointed." Christians therefore, according to the etymology of their name, are anointed. That anointing, according to the apostle's interpretation (1 Jn. 2:20, 27), is the Spirit of God, or the gift of the Holy Ghost. But St Peter testifieth that the Spirit of Christ was in the kings and prophets (1 Pet. 1:11). And Paul affirmeth flatly that we have the very same Spirit of faith (1 Cor. 10:2-4) that they of old had, and doth moreover communicate our sacraments with them, where he saith that they were baptized under the cloud and that they all drank of the spiritual rock that followed them, which rock was Christ (2 Cor. 14:13).

Since then the case is so, the examples, truly, which are derived from the words and works of those ancient kings, for the confirmation of faith and charity, both are and ought to be of force with us. And yet I know that everything doth not consequently follow upon the gathering of examples. But here we have, for the making good of our argument, an evident prophecy of Isaiah, who foretelleth that kings and princes, after the times of Christ and the revealing of the gospel, should have a diligent care of the church and should by that means become the feeders and nurses of the faithful. Now it is evident what it is to feed and to nourish, for it is all one as if he should have said that they should be the fathers and mothers of the church. But he could not have said that rightly, if the care of religion did not belong to princes, but to bishops alone. The words of Isaiah are these: "Behold, I will stretch out my hand unto the Gentiles, and set up my token to the people, and they shall bring thee thy sons in their laps, and thy daughters on their shoulders. And kings shall be thy nursing fathers, and queens thy nursing mothers, they shall fall before thee with their faces flat upon the earth, and lick up the dust of thy feet," &c. Shall not we say, that all this is fully performed in some Christian princes? Among whom the first was the holy emperor Constantine, who, by calling a general council, did determine to establish true and sincere doctrine in the church of Christ, with a settled purpose utterly to root out all false and heretical phantasies and opinions. And when the bishops did not go rightly to work by the true rule and touchstone of the gospel and of charity, he blamed them, upbraiding them with tyrannical cruelty and declaring therewithal what peace the Lord had granted by his means to the churches, adding moreover that it were a detestable thing if the bishops, forgetting to thank God for his gifts of peace, should go on among themselves to bait one another with mutual reproaches and taunting libels, thereby giving occasion of delight and laughter to wicked idolaters, when as of duty they ought rather to handle and treat of matters of religion. For [saith he] the books of the evangelists, apostles, and oracles of the ancient prophets are they which must instruct us in the understanding of God's holy law. Let us expel, therefore, this quarrelling strife, and think upon the questions proposed, to resolve them by the words of scripture inspired from above. After him again, the holy emperors, Gratian, Valentinian, and Theodosius, make a decree and give out the edict in these very words: "We will and command all people that are subject to our gracious empire to be of that religion, which the very religion, taught and conveyed from Peter till now, doth declare that the holy apostle Peter did teach to the Romans." And so forward.

By this, dearly beloved, ye perceive how kings and princes among the people of the new Testament have been the foster-fathers and nourishers of the church, being persuaded that the care of religion did first of all and especially belong to themselves.

The second objection that they make is the leprosy of Uzziah king of Judah, which he gat by challenging to himself the office of the priest, while he presumed to burn incense on the incense-altar (2 Chron. 26:18, 19). They object the Lord's commandment, who bad Joshua stand before Eleazar the priest and gave the king in charge to receive the book of the law at the Levites' hands (Num. 27:22; Deut. 17:18). But our disputation tendeth not to the confounding of the offices and duties of the magistrate and ministers of the church, as that we would have the king to preach, to baptize, and to minister the Lord's supper, or the priest, on the other side, to sit in the judgment-seat and give judgment against a murderer, or by pronouncing sentence to take up matters in strife. The church of Christ hath and retaineth several and distinguished offices, and God is the God of order, and not of confusion. Hereunto tendeth our discourse, by demonstration to prove to all men that the magistrate of duty ought to have a care of religion, either in ruin to restore it, or in soundness to preserve it, and still to see that it proceed according to the rule of the word of God. For to that end was the law of God given into the king's hands by the priests that he should not be ignorant of God's will touching matters ecclesiastical and political, by which law he had to govern the whole estate of all his realm. Joshua, the captain of God's people, is set before Eleazar indeed, but yet he hath authority to command the priests, and, being a politic governor, is joined as it were in one body with the ecclesiastical ministers. The politic magistrate is commanded to give ear to the ecclesiastical ruler, and the ecclesiastical minister must obey the politic governor in all things which the law commandeth. So then the magistrate is not made subject by God to the priests as to lords, but as to the ministers of the Lord: the subjection and duty which they owe is to the Lord himself and to his law, to which the priests themselves also ought to be obedient, as well as the princes. If the lips of the priest err from the truth, and speak not the word of God, there is no cause why any of the common sort, much less the prince, should either hearken unto, or in one tittle reverence the priest. "The lips of the priest," saith Malachi, "keep knowledge, and they seek the law at his mouth, because he is the messenger of the Lord of hosts" (Mal. 2:7). To refuse to hear such priests is to repel God himself. Such priests as these the godly princes of Israel did always aid and assist, false priests they did disgrade, those which neglected their offices they rebuked sharply, and made decrees for the executing and right administering of every office.

Of Salomon we read, that he put Abiathar beside the priesthood of the Lord (that he might fulfil the word of the Lord, which he spake to Eli in Shiloh), and made Zadok priest in Abiathar's stead (1 Kings 2:27). In the second book of Chronicles it is said: "And Salomon set the sorts of priests to their offices, as David his father had ordered them, and the Levites in their watches, for to praise and minister before the priests day by day, as their course did require" (2 Chron. 8:14). In the same book again, Jehoiada the priest doth indeed anoint Joash king, but, nevertheless, the king doth call the priest, and give him a commandment to gather money to repair the temple (2 Chron. 24). Moreover, that religious and excellent prince, Hezekiah, called the priests and Levites, and said unto them: "Be ye sanctified, and sanctify ye the house of the Lord our God, and suffer no uncleanness to remain in the sanctuary. My sons, be not slack now, because the Lord hath chosen you to minister unto himself" (2 Chron. 29:5, 11). He did also appoint singers in the house of the Lord, and those that should play on musical instruments in the Lord's temple. Furthermore, king Hezekiah ordained sundry companies of priests and Levites, according to their sundry offices, everyone according to his own ministry. What may be said of that too, that even he did divide to the priests their portions and stipends throughout the priesthood? The same king gave charge to all the people to keep holy the feast of Passover, writing to them all such letters as priests are wont to write, to put them in mind of religion and hearty repentance. And after all this there is added: "And the king wrought that which was good, right, and just before the Lord his God" (2 Chron. 31:20). When princes therefore do order religion according to the word of God, they do the thing that pleaseth the Lord. This and the like is spoken again by the godly prince Josiah. Who therefore will hereafter say that the care of religion belongeth unto bishops alone?

The Christian emperors, following the example of the ancient kings as of their fathers, did with great care provide for the state of true religion in the church of Christ. Arcadius and Honorius did determine that, so often as matters of religion were called in question, the bishops should be summoned to assemble a council. And before them again, the emperors Gratian, Valentinian, and Theodosius, established a law, wherein they declared to the world what faith and religion they would have all men to receive and retain, to wit, the faith and doctrine of St Peter, in which edict, also, they proclaimed all them to be heretics which thought or taught the contrary, allowing them alone to be called Catholics, which did persevere in St Peter's faith. By this we gather that the proper office of the priests is to determine of religion by proofs out of the word of God, and that the prince's duty is to aid the priests in advancement and defense of true religion. But if it happen at any time that the priests be slack in doing their duty, then is it the prince's office by compulsion to enforce the priests to live orderly according to their profession, and to determine in religion according to the word of God. The emperor Justinian, in *Novellis Constitut. 3*, writing to Epiphanius, archbishop of Constantinople, saith: "We have, most reverend patriarch, assigned to your holiness the disposition of all things that are honest, seemly, and agreeable to the rule of holy scriptures, touching the appointing and ordering of sacred bishops and reverend clerks." And in the seventeenth constitution he saith: "We give charge and commandment that no bishop have license to sell or make away any immovables, whether it be in houses or lands belonging to the churches." Again, in the fifty-seventh constitution, he forbiddeth to celebrate the holy mysteries in private houses. He addeth the penalty, and saith: "For the houses, wherein it is done, shall be confiscate and sold for money, which shall be brought into the emperor's exchequer." In the sixty-seventh constitution, he chargeth all bishops not to be absent from their churches, but if they be absent, he willeth that they should receive no commodity or stipend of the provincial stewards, but that their revenue should be employed on the church's necessities. In the hundred and twenty-third constitution, the lieutenants of every province are commanded to assemble a council for the use and defense of ecclesiastical laws, if the bishops be slack to look thereunto. And immediately after he saith: "We do utterly forbid all bishops, prelates, and clerks, of what degree soever, to play at tables, to keep company with dice-players, to be lookers on upon gamesters, or to run to gaze upon may-games or pageants." I do not allege all this as canonical scriptures, but as proofs to declare that princes in the primitive church had power, official authority, and a usual custom, granted by God (as Isaiah did prophesy), and derived from the examples of ancient kings, to command bishops and to determine of religion in the church of Christ.

As for them which object the church's privilege, let them know that it is not permitted to any prince, nor any mortal man, to grant privileges contrary to the express commandments and very truth of God's word. St Paul affirmed that he had power given him to edify, but not to destroy (2 Cor. 13:10). I am the briefer, because I will not stand to prove that they are unworthy of indifferent privileges, which are not such as priests and Christ his ministers should be, but are soldiers rather and wicked knaves, full of all kind of mischief. Among other things in the canon law, *Distinct.* 40, we find this written: "See to yourselves, brethren, how ye sit upon the seat: for the seat maketh not the priest, but the priest the seat: the place sanctifieth not the man, but the man the place. Every priest is not a holy man, but every holy man is a priest. He that sitteth well upon the seat receiveth the honor of the seat: but he that sitteth ill upon the seat, doth injury unto the seat. Therefore an evil priest getteth blame by his priesthood, and not any dignity." And thus much thus far touching this matter.

Since now that I have declared unto you, dearly beloved, that the care of religion doth belong to the magistrate too, and not to the bishops alone, and that the magistrate may make laws also in cases of religion, it is requisite that I inquire what kind of laws those are that the magistrates what may make in matters of religion. There is no cause why the king or magistrate should suppose that power is given to him to make new laws touching God, the worship of God, or his holy mysteries, or to appoint a new kind of true justice and goodness. For as every magistrate is ordained of God and is God's minister, so must he be ruled by God and be obedient to God's holy word and commandment, having evermore an eye unto that, and depending still upon that alone. The scripture, which is the word of God, doth abundantly enough set down all that which is proper to true religion: yea, the Lord doth flatly forbid to add to or take anything from his holy word. The magistrate therefore maketh no new laws touching God, and the honor to be given to God, but doth religiously receive and keep, doth put in ure[4] and publish those ancient laws in that kingdom which God hath allotted him unto. For hereunto appertaineth the giving of the book of God's law unto the kings of Israel (Deut. 17:18, 19; 2 Kings 11:12) that they might learn thereby the way to do the things which they of duty ought to see done. To Joshua the Lord doth say: "See that thou dost observe and do according to all the law that Moses my servant commanded thee: thou shalt not turn from it either to the right hand or to the left. Neither shall the book of this law depart out of thy mouth, but occupy thy mind therein day and night, that thou mayest observe and do according to all that is written therein. For then thou shalt make thy way prosperous, and then thou shalt do wisely" (Josh. 1:7, 8). Devout and holy princes therefore did do their faithful and diligent endeavor to cause the word of God to be preached to the people, to retain and preserve among the people the laws, ceremonies, and statutes of God, yea, they did their best to spread it to all men as far as they could, and, as time and place required, to apply it holily to the states and persons; on the other side, they were not slack to banish and drive away false doctrine, profane worshippings of God, and blasphemies of his name, but settled themselves utterly to overthrow and root it out for ever. In this sort (I say) godly magistrates did make and ordain devout laws for the maintenance of religion. In this sort they bore a godly and devout care for matters of religion. The cities which the Levites had to possess were of old their schools of Israel. Now Joshua did appoint those cities for studies' sake, and the cause of godliness (Josh. 21). King Hezekiah was no less careful for the sure payment

---

[4] *ure:* use.

and revenue of the ministers' stipends than he was for the restoring and renewing of every office (2 Chron. 31). For honor and advancement maketh learning to flourish, when need and necessity is driven to seek out sundry shifts: beggary setteth religion to sale, much more the invented lies of men's own mouths. Josaphat sendeth senators and other officers with the priests and teachers through all his kingdom (2 Chron. 17:7-9): for his desire was by all means possible to have God's word preached with authority and certain majesty, and, being preached, to have it defended and put in ure to the bringing forth of good works. King Josiah doth, together with idolatry and profane worshippings of God, destroy the false priests that were to be found, setting up in their steads the true teachers of God's word, and restoring again sincere religion (2 Kings 23), even as also king Joash, having rebuked the Levites, did repair the decayed buildings of the holy temple (2 Kings 12). I am not able to run through all the scriptures and rehearse all the examples in them expressed: let the godly prince or magistrate learn by these few what and how he ought to determine touching laws for religion.

On the other side, Ahijah, the Shilonite, saith to Jeroboam: "Thus saith the Lord: Thou shalt reign according to all that thy soul desireth, and shalt be king over Israel. And if thou hearken unto all that I command thee, and wilt walk in my ways, and do that is right in my sight, that thou keep my statutes and my commandments as David my servant did, then will I be with thee, and build thee a sure house" (1 Kings 11:38). But the wretch despised those large promises, and rejecting God's word, his temple at Jerusalem, and his lawful worship, refusing also the Levites, he made him priests of the dregs and rascal sort of people, he built himself new temples, which he decked, nay, rather disgraced, with images and idols, ordaining and offering sacrifices not taught in God's word, by that means inventing a certain new kind of worshipping God and a new manner of religion. And although his desire was to seem to be willing to worship God, yet is he by God condemned for a wicked man. Hearken, I pray, the sentence of the Lord, which he denounceth against him: "Thou hast done evil," saith Ahijah, as the Lord had taught him, "above all that were before thee. For thou hast gone and made thee other gods and molten images, to provoke me, and hast cast me behind thy back. Therefore I will bring evil upon the house of Jeroboam, and will root out from Jeroboam even him that pisseth against the wall, and him that is in prison and forsaken in Israel, and will take away the remnant of the house of Jeroboam, as one carrieth away dung till all be gone" (1 Kings 14:9-10). And all these things were fulfilled according to the saying of the Lord, as the scripture witnesseth in these words: "When Baasha was king, he smote all the house of Jeroboam, and left nothing that breathed of that that was Jeroboam's" (1 Kings 15:29). But the very same king, being nothing the better or wiser by another's mishap and miserable example of his predecessor, sticketh not to continue to teach the people, to publish and defend the strange and foreign religion, contrary to the word of God, which Jeroboam had begun. But what followed thereupon? Forsooth, the Lord by the preaching of Hanani the prophet doth say unto him: "Forasmuch as I exalted thee out of the dust, and made thee prince over my people Israel, and thou hast walked in the way of Jeroboam, and hast made my people Israel to sin, to anger me with their sins, behold, I will root out the posterity of Baasha, and the posterity of his house, and will make thy house like the house of Jeroboam" (1 Kings 16:2-3). Which was performed (as the scripture saith) by Zimri, captain of the host of Israel: for he destroyed king Elah, the son of Baasha, when he was drunken, and all his posterity (1 Kings 16:9-13). Omri succeeded in the kingdom, who was the father of Ahab, that mischievous cut-throat, whom the Syrians slew in fighting a battle (1 Kings 22:34). After him reigned his sons Amaziah and Joram. But when they left the religion taught in the word of God to follow the new tradition of king Jeroboam, and had thereunto added the worshipping of the shameful idol Baal, they were utterly (at last) destroyed by the means of Jehu, a very just, although a rigorous prince (2 Kings 9, 10). The offspring of Omri reigned about the space of forty years, not without the shedding of much innocent blood, but it was at last destroyed, when the measure of iniquity was fulfilled, and was utterly plucked up at the roots by the just judgment of Almighty God.

Let all princes and magistrates therefore learn by these wonderful and terrible examples to take heed to themselves how they devise any new religion, or alter the lawful and ancient manner of worshipping, which God himself hath ordained already. Our faithful Lord is our good God, who hath fully, simply, and absolutely set down in his word his true religion and lawful kind of worship, which he hath taught all men to keep alone and for evermore; let all men therefore cleave fast unto it, and let them die in defense thereof that mean to live eternally. They are punished from above, whosoever do add to or take away anything from the religion and kind of worship first ordained and appointed of God. Mark this, ye great men and princes of authority. For the keeping or not keeping of true religion is the root from whence abundant fruit of felicity, or else utter unhappiness, doth spring and bud out. He therefore that hath ears to hear, let him hear. Let no man suffer himself to be seduced and carried away with any colored intent, how goodly to the eye soever it be, which is indeed a mere vanity and detestable iniquity. To God obedience is much more acceptable than sacrifices are. Neither do the decrees of the Highest need any whit at all our fond additions.

Here followeth now the second part of the magistrates' ordinance, which consisteth in making good laws for the preservation of honesty, justice, and public peace, which is likewise accomplished in good and upright laws. But some there are who think it mere tyranny to lay laws on free men's backs, as it were a yoke upon necks not used to labor, supposing that everyone ought rather to be left to his own will and discretion. The apostle indeed did say, "The law is not given for the just, but for the unjust" (1 Tim. 1:9), but the cause why the law is not given to the just, is because he is just, for the just worketh justice, and doth of his own accord the thing which the law exacteth of every mortal man. Wherefore the law is not troublesome to the just man, because it is agreeable to the mind and thoughts of upright livers, who do embrace it with all their hearts. But the unjust desireth nothing more than to live as he lusteth; he is not conformable in any point to the law, and therefore must he by the law be kept under, and bridled from marring himself and hurting other[s]. So then, since to good men the laws are no troublesome burden but an acceptable pleasure, which are also necessary for the unjust, as ordained for the bridling of lawless and unruly people, it followeth consequently that they are good and profitable for all men, and not to be rejected of any man. What may be said of that, moreover, that God himself, who did foresee the disposition of us men, what we would be, and hath still favored the true liberty which he desired always to have preserved among his people, as one that ever meant them good, and never did ordain the thing that should turn to their hindrance or discommodity, that God himself (I say) was their lawgiver, and hath not suffered any age at any time to live as people without a law? Yea too, those commonweals have been happy always, that have admitted laws and submitted themselves to be governed by laws, when as, contrarily, those kingdoms have of all other been most miserable and torn in pieces by civil dissensions and foreign enemies, which, having banished upright laws, did strive to maintain their own kind of freedom, their uncontrolled dealing and licentious liberty, that is, their beastly lust and uncivil rudeness. Good laws therefore are for the health and preservation of the people, and necessary for the peace and safeguard of commonweals and kingdoms.

Wherefore it is a wonder to see the folly of some Christians, since the very heathens have given so honest report of laws and lawgivers. They took their lawgivers for gods, confessing thereby that good laws are the gift of God. But the gift of God cannot be superfluous and unprofitable. Plutarch called laws the life of cities. Demosthenes did expressly confess that laws are the gifts of God. Cicero named laws the bonds of the city (because without laws it is loosed and dispersed), the foundation of liberty, and the wellspring of justice and perfect honesty. For laws undoubtedly are the strongest sinews of the commonweal, and life of the magistrates, so that neither the magistrates can without the laws conveniently live and rule the weal public, nor the laws without the magistrates shew forth their strength and lively force. The magistrate therefore is the living law, and the law is the dumb magistrate. By executing and applying the law, law is made to live and speak, which those princes do not consider that are wont to say, *Wir sind das recht,* "We are the right, we are the law." For they suppose that they at their pleasure may command what they list, and that all men by and by must take it for law. But that kind of ruling, without all doubt, is extreme tyranny. The saying of the poet is very well known, which representeth the very words of a tyrant:

> I say, and it shall be so,
> My lust shall be the law.

The prince, indeed, is the living law, if his mind obey the written laws, and square not from the law of nature. Power and authority, therefore, is subject unto laws, for unless the prince in his heart agree with the law, in his breast do write the law, and in his words and deeds express the law, he is not worthy to be called a good man, much less a prince. Again, a good prince and magistrate hath power over the law, and is master of the laws, not that they may turn, put out, undo, make and unmake them as they list at their pleasure, but because he may put them in practice among the people, apply them to the necessity of the state, and attemper their interpretation to the meaning of the maker.

They therefore are deceived as far as heaven is wide, which think for a few privileges, of emperors and kings granted to the magistrate to add, diminish, or change some point of the law, that therefore they may utterly abolish good laws, and live against all law and seemliness. For, as no emperors or kings are permitted to grant any privileges contrary to justice, goodness, and honesty, so, if they do grant any such privilege, it ought not to be received or taken of good subjects for a good turn or benefit, but to be counted rather (as it is indeed) their utter destruction and clean overthrow. Among all men, at all times and of all ages, the meaning and substance of the laws touching honesty, justice, and public peace, is kept inviolable: if change be made, it is in circumstances, and the law is interpreted as the case requireth, according to justice and a good end. The law saith, "Let no man kill another: let him that killeth another be killed himself." That law remaineth for ever unchangeable, neither is it lawful for any man at any time to put it out or wipe it away. And yet the rigor of the law may be diminished, and the law itself favorably interpreted, as, for example, if a man kill one whom he loveth entirely well, and kill him by chance, and not of set purpose or pretended malice, so that, when he hath done, he is sorry for it at the very heart, and would (if it were possible) buy his life again with whatsoever he hath to give for it, in such a case the killer ought not to be killed, and therein the magistrate may dispense with the rigor of the law. Another beareth a deadly and continual grudge to one, whom he killeth, and goeth about to color the matter under the pretense of hap and misfortune; for he sought occasion, that he might for himself have a shew of chance-medley [killing in self-defense]. In such a case as this the magistrate cannot change any jot of the law, but must needs kill him whom the meaning of the law commandeth to kill. I could allege more examples like unto these, but my care is, of purpose, so much as I may, not to be too tedious unto you with too long a discourse. By this that I have spoken it is apparently evident that laws are good and not to be broken, and how far forth they do admit the prince's *epieikeian,* that is, the prince's moderation, interpretation, limitation, or dispensation, lest peradventure that old and accustomed proverb be rightly applied unto them, "Law with extremity is extreme injury."

Hitherto I have declared that laws are good, profitable, necessary, and not to be broken; it remaineth now to tell what and what kind of laws the magistrate ought most chiefly to use for the ordering and maintaining of honesty, justice, and public peace, according to his office. Some there are whose opinion is that the magistrate ought not to use any written laws, but that he should rather give sentence as he thought best according to natural equity, as the circumstances of place, time, persons, and cases do seem to require. Other some there are that do their endeavor to thrust into all kingdoms and commonweals the judicial laws of Moses. And some there are which, having once rejected the law of Moses, will have no judgment given in law, but what is derived out of the laws of heathen princes. But since they that have the preeminence and magistrate's authority are men either good or bad, and since that, even in the best men, covetousness, anger, hatred, favor, grief, fear, and other affections are rife to be found, to whom, I pray you, have they committed the commonweal, which, rejecting all written law statutes and certain laws, would have every man that is a magistrate to give judgment as he himself thinketh best? Have they not committed their commonweal to the rule of a beast? But what shall I say then of evil men that are in authority, since in the best men things are so amiss? As good were a kingdom subject to the furies of hell, as bound to the judgments of naughty men. But we will (say they) have them give judgment according to the equity of nature's law, and not after the lust of their corrupt affection. Mine answer is to that, that they will give judgment as affection leadeth them without controlment, and say that they judged by natural equity. They cannot, they will say, judge otherwise, nor otherwise understand the pith of the matter. They think that best which they have determined, and nothing is done contrary to conscience, and thou for thy labor shalt be called *coram nobis* [before us] for daring find fault with their sentence in judgment. And so shall the just man perish, barbarous affections shall have the upper hand, and naughty men rule all the roost. Yea, and admit we grant all men are good that are called to be magistrates, yet diversity of opinions, that will rise in giving of judgment, will stir up among them endless brawls and continual troubles. If all things therefore be well considered, the best way by a great deal is to put written laws in ure.

Let us learn this by the example of our eternal, wise, excellent, and mighty God, who gave to the Jews, his peculiar people, such laws as at his commandment were set down in writing. The magistrate hath otherwise business enough to judge, that is, to apply and confer the causes with the laws, to see how far and wherein they agree or disagree, and to judge who hath offended against the law, and who have not transgressed the law. Now it is to be marked that in Moses' judicial law to be enforced there are many things proper and peculiar to the Jewish nation, and so ordained, according to the state of the place, time, and persons, that if we should go about to thrust on and apply them all to other nations, we should seem to shew ourselves more than half mad. And to what end should we bring back and set up again among the people of God the offscourings of the heathen that were cast out a great while ago? The apostles of our Lord Jesus Christ did bind or burden no man with the laws of Moses, they never condemned good laws of the heathens, nor commended to any man naughty laws of the Gentiles, but left the laws, with the use and free choice of them, for the saints to use as they thought good. But therewithal they ceased not most diligently to beat into all men's heads the fear of God, faith, charity, justice, and temperance, because they knew that they, in whose hearts those virtues were settled, can either easily make good laws themselves, or pick and choose out the best of those which other men make. For it maketh no matter whether the magistrate pick out of Moses' Jewish laws, or out of the allowable laws of the heathen, sufficient laws for him and his countrymen, or else do keep still the old and accustomed laws which have before been used in his country, so that he have an eye to cut off such wicked, unjust, and lawless laws, as are found to be thrust in among the better sort. For I suppose that upright magistrates ought to take off curiosity and new invented novelties. "Seldom," saith the proverb, "is the crow's eye picked out without troublesome stirs," and curious men's new laws are for the most part worse than the old, that are broken by them and utterly abolished.

Furthermore, all laws are given for ordering of religion or outward worship of God, or else for the outward conversation of life and civil behavior. Touching the laws of religion, I have spoken of them before. For civil and politic laws, I add thus much, and say that those seem to be the best laws, which, according to the circumstance of every place, person, state, and time, do come nearest unto the precepts of the ten commandments and the rule of charity, not having in them any spot of iniquity, licentious liberty, or shameless dishonesty. Let them, moreover, be brief and short, not stretched out beyond measure, and wrapped in with many expositions; let them have a full respect to the matter whereto they are directed, and not be frivolous and of no effect.

Now mark that politic laws do for the most part consist in three especial and principal points: honesty, justice, and peace. Let laws therefore tend to this end, that discipline and honesty may be planted and maintained in the commonweal, and that no unseemly, licentious, and filthy act be therein committed. Let law forbid all uncleanness, wantonness, lightness, sensuality, and riotousness, in apparel, in building, in bibbing [drinking] and banqueting. Let wedlock be commanded by law to be kept holy. Let stews and brothelhouses be banished the realm. Let adulteries, whoredoms, rapes, and incests be put to exile. Let moderate feastings be allowed and admitted. Let thriftiness be used, which is the greatest revenue that a man can enjoy. Briefly, whatsoever is contrary to honesty and seemliness, let it by law be driven out and rejected.

Let justice by laws be strongly fortified. Let it by laws be provided that neither citizen nor foreigner be hurt or hindered in fame, in goods, in body, or life. Let upright laws be made for the obtaining of legacies and inheritances, for the performing of contracts and bargains, for covenants and agreements, for suretyships, for buying and selling, for weights and measures, for leases and things let to hire, for lending and borrowing, for pawns in mortgage, for use, commodity, and usury of money. Let order be taken for maintenance of peace between the father and his children, betwixt man and wife, betwixt the master and the servant, and, to be short, that every man may have his own. For my meaning is not here to reckon up particularly every several point and tittle of the law. Lastly, means must be made by giving of laws, that peace may be established, whereby every man may enjoy his own. All violent robberies and injuries must be expelled, privy grudges and close conspiracies must not be thought of. And war must be quieted by wisdom, or else undertaken and finished with manly fortitude.

But, that we may have such a magistrate and such a life, the apostle commanded us earnestly to pray, where he saith: "I exhort you that, first of all, prayers, supplications, intercessions, and giving of thanks, be made for all men, for kings and for all that are in authority, that we may live a quiet and peaceable life in all godliness and honesty" (1 Tim. 2:1, 2).

I am now again compelled to end my Sermon before the matter be finished. That which remaineth I will add tomorrow. Make ye your earnest prayers, with your minds lift up into heaven, &c.

INTRODUCTION TO PETER MARTYR VERMIGLI'S *OXFORD TREATISE ON THE EUCHARIST*

BY THE time Peter Martyr Vermigli (1499–1562) arrived in England in December 1547 at the invitation of Archbishop Thomas Cranmer (1489–1556) to take up the Regius Chair of Divinity at Oxford, he was no stranger to controversy. Born in Florence, Italy in 1499 and educated at the prestigious University of Padua beginning in 1518, Vermigli, like Luther, had entered the Augustinian Order of monks and risen rapidly through its ranks to become the head of the Order in Italy. Although we now in hindsight think of the Reformation as largely a northern European phenomenon, and the Mediterranean countries as staunchly Catholic, this was hardly a foregone conclusion at the time. On the contrary, during the 1530s, Vermigli was at the heart of a robust home-grown Italian Reform movement, nourished by the careful reading of Scripture, the Church Fathers, and often Protestant writings from Germany or Switzerland clandestinely smuggled in. First at Naples in southern Italy and then at Lucca in the north, Vermigli established a reputation as a gifted preacher and expositor of Scripture, and a band of disciples, increasingly Protestant in fact if not in name, gathered around him. Many were subsequently to play key roles in the wider Reformation, especially his star student, Girolamo Zanchi (1516–1590).

Vermigli himself, however, found his position in Italy untenable in 1542 after a rapid change in the ecclesiastical climate had hardened the Church's opposition to reform and led to the establishment of a Roman Inquisition dedicated to rooting out heresy in Italy. Vermigli packed his bags (and his books) and fled north to Zurich, where he presented himself to Heinrich Bullinger and openly declared his Protestant convictions. He soon won Bullinger's trust and esteem and was recommended to a teaching post in Strasbourg, working alongside the great reformer, Martin Bucer (1491–1551). Conflict with a hardline Lutheran party there, followed by a decisive Catholic victory over German Protestants at the Battle of Mühlberg in 1547, however, soon rendered their position in Strasbourg difficult. England, however, had suddenly become newly hospitable to the evangelical cause by the death of Henry VIII and accession of the boy-king, Edward VI. Archbishop Cranmer, now with something of a free hand to direct religious policy, invited first Vermigli and then Bucer to England. Vermigli was by this point establishing a reputation as a Reformed theological luminary, unrivalled in his mastery not only of the Biblical languages, but also in his knowledge of the Fathers and of the scholastic philosophical and theological tradition. He was eminently suited for the unpleasant task of confronting the staunchly conservative Oxford theologians on their home turf, as Cranmer asked him to do. Cranmer, after all, may have helped hold the reins of government, but he recognized that a successful reformation required not merely laws but persuasion. The persuasion of the common people depended mostly on liturgy; hence Cranmer's hard labors on the Book of Common Prayer.[1] But the persuasion of intellectuals depended largely on academic theological disputation.

Vermigli's first major opportunity for such disputation came about a year into his teaching stint at Oxford. Having spent his first year lecturing on the book of 1 Corinthians, Vermigli seems to have provoked controversy by his remarks on chapters 10 and 11, where Paul addresses the Lord's Supper. Many of the theologians at Oxford, led by Richard Smith (whose professorship Vermigli

---

[1] For more on this, and more context on the Edwardian phase of the Reformation in England, see the introduction to chapter 24 below.

had been given) were still deeply committed to the traditional Catholic doctrine of transubstantiation, which, as we have seen, had been a flashpoint of controversy from John Wyclif's abortive reform onward.

In being called to address the doctrine of the Eucharist, however, Vermigli was being drawn into an even wider battle, one that had threatened to tear apart the Protestant ranks since the first decade of the Reformation. While nearly all the Reformers united in opposing transubstantiation, Luther had nonetheless insisted that the true flesh and blood of Christ are locally present in the consecrated elements in some mysterious fashion. Zwingli, on the other hand, had stressed the integrity of Christ's flesh as a human body, one that must be locally confined to heaven, such that believers received its benefits by faith and the agency of the Spirit. Many theologians, Vermigli among them, were coming toward something of a middle position by the 1540s, emphasizing that Christ truly makes himself present to the souls of believers in the partaking of the sacrament, but this presence is not to be sought outwardly in the elements. Still, the subject was a fraught one, and especially in England, where there were representatives of every position vying for influence.

Vermigli's 1549 Treatise on the Eucharist and the accompanying Oxford Disputation, however, constituted something of a turning point, as Cranmer himself and other key church leaders publicly embraced Vermigli's Reformed position. Unfortunately, the 1549 texts do not themselves provide a great summary of Vermigli's own positive theology of the Eucharist, constrained as he was by the polemical context to focus nearly all his efforts on refuting the doctrine of transubstantiation. Still, his prefatory dedication to Cranmer provides a neat and eloquent summary of the pastoral rationale for his simple evangelical doctrine, shorn of superstition or needless paradoxes. Vermigli is emphatic that to say something is spiritually or metaphorically true does not mean it is untrue, and that it is no more strange to say that Christ can present himself without being physically present, than to say that an object may make itself present by light or sound without being physically present. But since the organ by which we receive Christ is faith, it follows that the consecrated elements are nothing in themselves, but only in the course of faithful reception.

His key arguments against transubstantiation, excerpted below, give a good sense of his theological method: a deft combination of Scriptural exegesis, judicious appeal to the Church Fathers, and rational argumentation (without needless philosophical subtleties). A few arguments are particularly effective in turning the tables on his adversaries. In one, he notes that if the Reformed are accused of not taking the "is" in "This is my body" literally, neither do the Romanists, since they actually must interpret it as "This [bread] is at this moment being transformed into my body." In another, he notes that it is strange that they will so willingly admit the "new birth" of baptism to be metaphorical while stubbornly refusing to treat the Eucharist similarly. But perhaps most striking is his claim that if the doctrine of transubstantiation be allowed, and the testimony of our senses about what is bread and what is wine be contradicted, we will have no ground to take seriously the testimony of our senses elsewhere. And if this be so, the ground on which Scripture itself attests the reality of the incarnation and resurrection will be undermined—what is to prevent skepticism regarding the real earthly body of Christ if common sense observation be thrown out the window? This argument crisply demonstrates Vermilgi's Reformed concern to maintain the harmony of reason and faith, rather than setting them needlessly at odds.

Although the rapidly changing religious politics in England were to see Vermigli's time there cut short, his theological legacy there and elsewhere put down deep roots that have remained to the present day, even as his name has been largely forgotten.

Further Reading

For further reading, see Joseph C. McLelland, "Introduction" to *The Oxford Treatise and Disputation On the Eucharist, 1549*, The Peter

Martyr Library, Vol. 7 (Kirksville, MO: Truman State University, 2000); W. J. Torrance Kirby, Emidio Campi, and Frank A. James III, eds., *A Companion to Peter Martyr Vermigli* (Leiden: Brill, 2009); John Williamson Nevin, *The Mystical Presence and the Doctrine of the Reformed Church on the Lord's Supper*, edited by Linden J. DeBie (Eugene, OR: Wipf and Stock, 2012).

PETER MARTYR VERMIGLI,
OXFORD TREATISE ON THE EUCHARIST
(1549)[1]

I HAVE decided to explain certain matters in a few words, lest by keeping silent I might be held unwise, an innovator, a bold, rash and ungodly man, as though I robbed the sacrament of the Eucharist of its honor and dignity, or thrust the holy Supper on the church without Christ, or encouraged such other things as tend to impiety and the neglect of religion. I should rather die, or be nothing at all, or suffer the greatest grief, than disseminate such doctrine. For my part, I attribute so much to this sacrament as to say that through its use the faithful obtain the greatest benefits to be hoped for from God in this life, if they themselves are not hindered through vice or faithlessness.

I hold that all people earnestly desire three sorts of good. First, to continue their life received at birth as long as possible. Second, they wish God to be reconciled to them, and gracious. For the wise live most miserably, knowing that they are never faultless, and that by divine justice a certain punishment is due for every fault, unless they have a sure expiation to hand. Last, the prudent wish to live with one another in justice and goodwill, in happiness and peace; for without these we live most miserably and unhappily. Such are in substance the things universally desired by all who act

---

[1] Taken from Joseph C. McLelland, trans., *The Peter Martyr Library, Volume Seven: The Oxford Treatise and Disputation On the Eucharist, 1549*, Vol. 56 of *Sixteenth Century Essays & Studies* (Kirksville, MO: Truman State University, 2000). Used by permission.

wisely. And the chief and principal point of these three is that life may be sustained a long span of time, which we obtain by a beneficial and wholesome kind of diet. We have this most clearly in the holy Supper. Just as the bread and wine (which feed the body) are given outwardly to the communicants, so is it truly granted to their minds that by faith they eat the body and blood of Christ, given for our redemption, so that the whole person, both inward and outward, is restored to the greatest happiness. This is the only way that Scripture allows and knows of eating the body and drinking the blood of the Lord, namely when we apprehend by a constant and firm faith that Jesus the Son of God our Savior and Lord gave his own body on the cross and shed his blood for us, and that he has so embraced us who are given to him by the Father, and so joined and incorporated us to himself that he is our head and we flesh of his flesh and bone of his bones, while he dwells in us and we in him. In this stands the whole power and reason of this meat and drink, to which our faith is stirred up and kindled by the threefold Word: sometimes inwardly, while the Holy Spirit, by his secret yet mighty power, clearly incites our souls to renew these things in ourselves, that they may be embraced with lively and willing faith; to the same end we are often moved by the help of God's words, piercing us by outward sound or by writing; and finally, to provide every help for our infirmity, Christ added bread and wine in the Supper as signs. By his words and institution they become sacraments, that is instruments by which the Holy Spirit excites faith in our minds so that we may be spiritually yet truly fed and sustained by his body and blood.

What more could there be to lead the faithful to life than this kind of food? Do we not by such eating dwell in Christ and Christ in us? Can we ask for so great a good to be more clearly promised us than when he himself said, "Who eats me shall live by me?" (Jn. 6:51).

Moreover, in John 6 the Lord taught this simple, unadorned, yet true and genuine, eating of his body and drinking of his blood. Afterward the Lord desired that this should be helped by means of the outward word and the sensation of bread and wine, when we come to the holy table. Therefore whoever does not reject a holy life (I mean life eternal and most happy), must he not cherish the Eucharist above all things? Will he not embrace it as a sweet pledge of his salvation? Will he not use it in the congregation of the saints as often as it is given? Indeed he will, if he ponders these matters earnestly within himself.

Next to life, which all wish to lead happily, for the most part men desire to have God well pleased with them. If we are unsure of this, our mind is anxious, our thoughts troublesome, our conscience tormenting, creatures terrify us as avengers and harsh servants of God, nothing is quiet inside us or out, we fear both heaven and hell alike, showing the same hatred to God as to the devil, for the one we fear as an executioner and the other as a judge. In this condition the holy Scriptures help us, teaching that the heavenly Father is at peace with humankind by no other means than by the sacrifice of his only begotten Son. Through this sacrifice God has made an everlasting covenant with his people, has forgiven our sins, has adopted those who believe as his children, has committed them to his first begotten Son for salvation, and has incorporated them and made them heirs of his heavenly kingdom.

Now in receiving the sacrament of the Eucharist, the memory of the Lord's death and of the whole mystery of our redemption through the incarnate Word of God is reopened, the acknowledgment of God's testament is renewed, and the blessed communion of Christ and remission of sins through his sacrifice given on the altar of the cross is offered. So in this sacrament, if received rightly and with faith, not by any power of the work but by the free benefit of Christ which we apprehend in believing, we acknowledge that our sins are forgiven, the covenant between God and ourselves confirmed, and God's very Son, who possesses life in himself through the Father, is received in such a way that whoever partakes of his flesh and blood in true faith lives through him, so that the heavenly inheritance is possessed by the faithful, as far as the state of this life permits.

Therefore we claim not only life, but a life safe and calm in face of divine wrath. What joy and delights and honest pleasures are lacking to us who have God merciful and favorable towards us, and the Son of God dwelling in us? None of them whatever, if we seek those things that are true and solid, not fantasies and shadows. In the institution of this sacrament, when he gave his body and blood to be eaten and drunk by faith, Christ referred to the sustenance and nourishment of life through faith. For in the Gospel of Luke he said, "Do this in remembrance of me." Paul expressed this more plainly, saying: "For as often as you eat this bread and drink this cup, you declare the Lord's death till he come." Finally, it is said by both Luke and Paul, "This cup is the new testament through my blood which shall be shed for you" (Lk. 22:19-20; 1 Cor. 11:25-26). Therefore, in regard to reconciliation with God, the forgiveness of sins, and the confirmation of the testament, I have imagined nothing, devised nothing, invented nothing which is not from holy Scripture.

Lastly, because man is not made for solitude, but desires social and civil life, therefore when once convinced that he has the gracious divine will through Christ, and that through him his sins are forgiven, nothing else is required for his perfect and absolute life while he abides here, except to live with others (called in Scripture neighbors) not only in harmony but with the greatest justice and charity. Now this sacrament teaches us this most effectively and earnestly. For in the mysteries we become sharers in one table: What else should we have in mind than that we are one body, members one of another under Christ our head? And one bread, united among ourselves just as almost innumerable grains of wheat coalesce in that bread which we take? Those who are not persuaded by such reasons to maintain mutual concord and charity among brethren have without doubt hardened their hearts like stone and iron, and will be considered more savage and brutish than tigers and the crudest beasts. For, knowing that the Son of God gave his life for his enemies, they themselves are not moved to do good, so far as they are able, to their brothers and neighbors for whom Christ died.

If a secular table reconciles men to one another when they meet together, why should not the table of Christ effect this the more? Since the wildest beasts are tamed by food, why are men not made gentle by this heavenly food? If treaties and covenants are usually sealed by food and drink, why do not the children of God establish peace and friendship among themselves by communicating together?

We are directed to such things by this divine rite, and by the word of holy Scripture recited in it. In view of our obstinacy, opposed as we are to just, honest, and holy things, even if the admonition seem feeble or ineffectual, yet on condition that faith is not absent, the power of the Holy Spirit seizes our hearts by the sacraments and words of God. This always stimulates harmony, peace, and mutual love, so that while we communicate together not only do we use an outward occasion, but our minds also experience the inward moving of divine inspiration. So you see, most great leader, what notable and excellent goods which I show are given us through the Eucharist. Let those who would scourge Martyr complain as much as they please that I violate the sacrament of the Lord's Supper. Let them step forward and demonstrate what they have accomplished more than I by their transubstantiations, their marvels and wonders, what more solid fruit and genuine profit they have brought by this sacrament either to communicants or to churches. Will they speak of the benefit of our dwelling in Christ and Christ in us? So will I. Will they speak of obtaining a holy life and heavenly blessedness? I propose that too. Will they speak of receiving the body and blood of Christ? No less do I, yet such as is had by faith and the soul. Will they object to the remission of sins, the confirmation of the covenant, the remembrance of the cross and Christ's death that is effected? I think not, for I have often taught all of this to large gatherings. Will they oppose the incorporation, so to speak, which in communicating we obtain by faith, both with Christ and among ourselves his members? They cannot,

452

for this also have I constantly emphasized. What then do they say, since besides these nothing else is taught about the Eucharist in Scripture? I know what they will say now: you take away transubstantiation—corporeal, carnal, real, and substantial presence—this we deplore; this we affirm more fully than you; in this we dissent from you. I hear them quite well, but have decided to make no reply just now, because transubstantiation is an empty thing, and because I have dealt with it enough in both the *Disputation* and the *Treatise* prefixed to it.

Now concerning Christ's body, which I deny to be present—as you complain so much—I wish to say something openly to explain myself. If I should ask you why one should assert such a presence as you imagine for yourself, I think you will answer: in order that the body and blood of Christ may be joined to us. But since the whole work of this union is heavenly and spiritual, this presence of yours so zealously argued, relating to locality, is not required at all. What need is there either of physical contact or of nearness of places? Tell me this: since holy Scripture declares not only that we are united with Christ but also that we are members together with our brethren, being made one body, will you not agree that the faithful in Spain, Italy, Germany, and France are so joined with us as to be (as Paul says) members together with us (1 Cor. 10:17)? I know you will not deny that. Therefore if separation of places and physical contact, which are impossibilities, do not hinder this unity by which we are joined together in one through Christ, why do you deny that we are truly joined to him without any real and corporeal presence? And if you do not deny it, why do you insist on promoting such a presence?

To use a plainer and more expressive simile: as you know, in holy Scripture, man and wife both are and are called one flesh. For Adam, or God through Adam, said: "This is now bone of my bones, and flesh of my flesh; for this cause a man shall leave father and mother, and cleave to his wife, and they shall become one flesh" (Gen. 2:23-24). So appropriate is this likeness to the matter at hand that in Ephesians Paul takes the Church as the body of

Christ in the same manner as the wife is the bone and flesh of her husband (Eph. 5:21ff). If it sometimes happens that a man stays in London while his wife remains at Cambridge or Oxford, this union of flesh between husband and wife is not prevented. Their separation and lack of physical contact which cannot then exist shows only that wife and husband themselves remain one and the same flesh.

Thus in order to enter into union with Christ, there is no need for you to attempt to tie his body and blood, or as you say to hide them, under the appearance of bread and wine. We are truly joined to Christ without these wonders. Apart from such fancied devices, the Eucharist is a whole and perfect sacrament; nor are Christ's words diminished without these delusions when he said, "This is my body," delivering bread to his apostles, as the following treatise will declare more fully. Thus in order to establish and confirm all these things, the church needs no corporeal or substantial presence of the body of Christ.

Yet I would not have it thought on account of these similes I bring that I regard lightly or depreciate the union we have and daily enter into with Christ. For I well know that in order to demonstrate its closeness, Scripture is accustomed to declare that we are not only endowed with the Spirit, merit, and intercession of Jesus, and act and live by his inspiration and Spirit, but also that he himself is with us and dwells in our hearts by faith: he is our head, he dwells in us and we in him, we are born again in him, his flesh is both given and received to be eaten and drunk. But I understand statements of this kind to be metaphorical, since proper speech cannot easily be found for these things—words signify this or that as they are appointed to serve human ends. Therefore when it comes to heavenly and divine things, the natural man who does not understand such great secrets cannot as much as name them.

In this way the Holy Spirit attends to our weakness: having granted us light and understanding beyond our nature, he also humbled himself to these metaphors, namely abiding, dwelling, eating, and drinking, so that in a certain sense he may make known to us this divine and heavenly union which we have with Christ. Since these forms of speech consist of two things, the highest efficacy and a significance not proper but transferred, they must not be interpreted rashly but with prudent and spiritual caution. This is observed if we do not extend their sense more than is fitting nor attribute too much to them, especially when applied to sacraments. The hyperboles of the Fathers and contempt of Anabaptists greatly confused the sacraments (particularly this one with which we are dealing). The latter judge it only a token of mutual love, a cold and bare sign of Christ's death; the former attribute everything divine to it, by which they step arrogantly into dreadful idolatry.

The median position we hold can be retained in no other way than by interpreting the phrases we have mentioned according to the analogy or convenience of holy Scripture. This requires us not to tear asunder the hypostatic union of Christ (as they call it), on account of which the properties of the two natures, divine and human, communicate with each other; yet also to distinguish with sound understanding exactly what we have communicated by alternation of the properties, so that the divinity is not made subject to human infirmities, nor the humanity so deified that it leave the bounds of its own nature and be destroyed. Therefore by a spiritual wisdom, such as only holy Scripture provides, we must discern what is agreeable to Christ in respect of one nature and the other. In this regard, the presence of the body of Christ which I remove from the Eucharist is that by which it is everywhere diffused, or else in many places at once, so that it frees itself from the quantity and limitation necessary to a human body.

Thus if by *presence* someone understands the perception of faith by which we ourselves ascend to heaven, by mind and spirit embracing Christ in his majesty and glory, I willingly consent to him. But I totally reject their opinion who contend that the body is enclosed and covered in the bread and wine, and affirm that it is under their forms, so that they should worship and adore him there; in brief, they have set up an idol. This is the head, origin, and source of all contention; here in general the state of all the present controversy rests. Therefore if we do not resolve this point sincerely, well, and clearly, our adversaries will continue to have some means of making a fair show of maintaining and defending their superstitions and idolatries (which they force on the church) through sophistical arguments decked out with painted face.

To cover the whole matter in few words, I heartily affirm these two things. One, that this sacrament of the holy Supper is nothing without use. How true this is other sacraments testify. The other point is that when we make use of it we grasp Christ's body and blood by faith alone. Those who teach otherwise speak what they do not understand themselves, nor are they understood by others; they fling themselves by choice into obscurities and labyrinths where the Scriptures do not lead. And this is the basis, the strength and foundation of the opinion I have declared, namely that it belongs properly only to the divine nature to be by substance everywhere and to fill all things; while conversely the state and condition of human nature is to be contained in a definite place, measurable and spatial, unable to spread itself over many places or everywhere at the same time. Our senses witness to this fact, confirmed by human reason, nor does any divine Scripture prove it to be otherwise; the Fathers asserted it in many places. If this is reversed and the opposite taught, as many do, we derive no profit, since we already have as much when we hold our opinion, just expressed.

Let those who cry against me that I teach a reception of the Lord's Supper without Christ, that is without his body and blood, take this for an answer: if they desire the presence of the body of Christ as an apprehension through faith, offered to us by signification of words and signs and exhibited by the Lord's kindness, I gladly and willingly admit it, as I have said. For just as light, color, sound, and so on can exist in a remote place yet are said to be present to our senses while we perceive them, so the body of Christ may be termed present, in this meaning of presence, because we grasp it by faith. And if this is understood with right and sound judgment in the way we have explained, one may say that the body of Christ is much more present to those who believe than are those qualities which are distant in place yet received by the senses. For apprehension by faith is more certain; more firmly do we adhere to what we believe than do the senses or reason to what they comprehend by its natural power. [...]

Arguments Against Transubstantiation

6. Now we must look at the contrary arguments by which this opinion is overthrown.

First, holy Scripture lays down that this is bread; therefore it is not true that its substance is changed. The evangelists say that Christ took bread, broke it, and gave it to his disciples. Paul mentions bread five times: "Is not the bread which we break a participation in the body of Christ?" "We who are many are one bread, and one body, who participate in one bread." "As often as you eat this bread you announce the Lord's death till he come." "Whoever eats this bread and drinks this cup of the Lord unworthily will be guilty of the body and blood of the Lord." Finally, "Let a man prove himself, and so eat that bread and drink that cup" (1 Cor. 10:16-17, 11:26-28). Since these things are clear and open, if an angel from heaven should preach otherwise let him be accursed. I could also propose what is often said about the breaking of bread, but I see that it might be understood otherwise, as if it is spoken of common food, as in Isaiah 58[:7], "Break your bread to the hungry," and by Jeremiah in Lamentations 4[:4], "The little ones beg for their bread, but no one breaks it for them." Therefore I will restrain myself, and advance only what is firm. Since the passages cited are quite clear, they ought to be taken as they stand.

Some cavil that it is called bread because of the natures which are exchanged; to speak in their style, they say that the name is a *terminus a quo* [boundary from which], and offer examples. When a serpent was made from Aaron's rod it devoured the serpents of the magicians (Ex. 7:12), which they had also made from their rods; it is said the rod of Aaron devoured the serpents of the magicians. Again, in the sacred writings man is often called earth, since his body was made from it. Woman also was called by Adam bone of his bones and flesh of his flesh, because she was formed from them by God (Gen. 2:23). But these are empty objections, because Scripture clearly takes note of these changes, so that the necessity of history and of the words forces us to these tropes, and we admit them. First let them show us in Scripture that this change was made (namely of bread and wine into the body and blood of Christ) and we will also grant them the tropes, that is, the bread is called not what it is now but what it was before. By the same token they might say: if someone gives me wine which at once turns sour, and I put the vinegar in a pot, I might well say, this is your wine. Not that it was then wine, but because it was wine before. But here one's sense judges the change of wine into vinegar, which does not occur in the Eucharist. For in that case, neither sense nor reason nor holy Scripture drives us to admit such a change.

7. They object a passage in John, chapter 2, "when the governor of the feast had tasted the water made into wine," by which they wish to show that the wine just produced by the miracle of Christ still retains the name of water (Jn. 2:9). But the Evangelist did not simply say water, but "made into wine." Nor will they find in holy Scripture this declaration that bread is said to be turned into the body of Christ. They jump to John, chapter 6, and say that here the apostle calls bread not ordinary wheat bread but the Lord's body; as in the sixth of John it is called bread when Christ said, "I am the bread of life" (Jn. 6:35). And what Paul said counts against them: "The bread which we break, is it not the communion of the body of Christ?" (1 Cor. 10:16) since it cannot suit the body of Christ to be broken—as it is written, "Not a bone of him will be broken" (Ps. 34:20; Jn. 19:36).

Where will these sharp wits who find in John 6 that Christ called himself bread, find that he called himself wine? For in this Supper the other symbol is called wine, in fact in those words of the Evangelist, "I shall not drink hereafter of this fruit of the vine" (Matt. 26:29). But without doubt vines do not produce accidents, but wine. Nor is it of consequence that the Fathers say with such agreement that the mystical body is signified by the symbols of this sacrament, bread being made of many grains and wine pressed out of many grapes; such things do not possess reality through accidents. We really marvel at these men who, when they hear us bringing similes (the rock was Christ; the lamb or victim is the passover; circumcision is the covenant), claim that these allegories do not apply, while they themselves pile up tropes and allegories everywhere. They also say that bread is taken for everything that can be eaten, as in the Hebrew tongue *Lehem* is taken for all kinds of food. But the evangelists are against them, for they restrict this kind of food to bread. Others imagine that bread signifies the accidents and form of bread; they beg the question, and take as already proved what is in dispute, namely that accidents are present without a subject, which they should have proved first. Nor should miracles be multiplied without some necessity.

8. Another argument is that the ancients had the same sacraments as we, yet had no need of transubstantiation. Neither the rock, nor the water flowing out of the rock, nor manna was transubstantiated, for this was impossible; therefore, it is not required for our sacraments. We read the first proposition in Paul: "The fathers and we had the same food" (1 Cor. 10:3). Our opponents deny this and would have our sacraments completely distinguished from the mysteries of the ancients in many ways. We grant this too, as to different symbols and also different times as well as other properties. But concerning the reality of the sacraments, which was received by the holy patriarchs, we hold that it was the very same meat and drink that form the substance of our sacraments. Augustine writes to Marcellinus about the difference between these sacraments: "For an astute man it is enough that Christ's future coming was foretold by some sacraments, and that after his coming others should proclaim this." Here Augustine seems to regard only the difference in time. And in his little work *On the usefulness of true penance* he states quite clearly that when the ancients had manna they ate the very same thing we eat: "For they ate the same spiritual

food." What is "the same" but what we also have here? And because to some it might seem unworthy that we have no more than the Jews, he stresses Paul's testimony. Paul, he says, thought it not enough to say that the ancients had spiritual food, and added "the very same," that by this "same" we might understand that in their manna they ate what we do. Nor is it a serious objection of some that he spoke of spiritual eating, that is, the patriarchs believed in the Christ that was to come. First, they cannot confirm their own carnal eating of Christ; second, the fathers not only believed with the mind but also received a symbol of the object of faith, that is, manna or water. So the reality did not exist only in faith, and Augustine's saying stands that the food of the fathers was not only spiritual but "the very same."

9. It matters little if one brings from the same Augustine the prologue to Psalm 73, where he considers three differences between the new and old sacraments. First, the Savior is promised there but given here. Second, our sacraments are easier, fewer, nobler, and felicitous. Lastly, theirs were like toys in the hands of children, whereas in ours there is something more profitable and solid. The first of these should be understood concerning the promise of Christ's coming, even though he had not yet taken actual flesh; still, in the food he was given spiritually to the fathers who believed in the promise. But ours are said to give Christ, since they testify that he has come and is no longer expected.

Next, it is certain that our sacraments are fewer and easier, for they signify in a more powerful way, since their words are clearer than in the Old Testament. Moreover, the joy is greater, for we are free from the yoke of ceremonies and live in the last hour and have advanced all the nearer to Christ's kingdom. More plentiful also is the Spirit, and the church more extensive than at that time, when many kings and prophets desired to see the things you see (Lk. 10:24). Again, the sacraments of the Law were like toys in the hands of children, because it suited the age of the fathers to be like children busy with many ceremonies, various first principles and numerous instructions. But all these do not prove that the sacraments of the ancients lacked what makes for reality in a mystery, the same as ours.

Cyprian states in the second book, epistle 3: "Our Lord Jesus Christ offered the very same thing as Melchizedek," that is, "bread and wine, namely his body and blood." Augustine wrote against Faustus, book 19, chapter 16: "What error do they embrace who think that when the signs and sacraments are changed, the things themselves are different." In the same work, book 20, chapter 21: "Before Christ's advent the flesh and blood of this sacrifice was promised through the likeness of sacrificial victims; in Christ's passion, it was represented through the truth itself; after Christ's ascension it is celebrated through the sacrament of remembrance." On John, *tract 26*: "Those sacraments differed in the signs, but were equal in the thing signified." Later he adds: "Therefore it was the same food and drink, to those who understood and believed; but to those who understood not the one was only manna, the other water, and to believers the same as now." For then Christ was to come, now Christ has come; *venturus* [to come] and *venit* [come] are different words, but it is the same Christ.

More recently, Bertram writes: "Now St. Paul affirms that our fathers ate the same spiritual food and drank the same spiritual drink. Perhaps you ask what 'same'? Just this: the same which the faithful in the Church eat and drink today. For it is not proper to suppose a difference, since it is one and the same Christ who not only fed the people with his flesh and gave them drink with his blood when they were in the desert, in the cloud and baptized in the sea, but also in the church now feeds believers with the bread of his body and gives them drink with the water of his blood." He adds: "Here is surely a wonder, incomprehensible and matchless: he had not yet assumed manhood, nor yet tasted death for the salvation of the world, nor yet redeemed us with his blood, but our fathers in the desert already ate his body and drank his blood by a spiritual food and invisible drink; as the apostle testifies saying 'The same spiritual meat.'" Again: "For this very one who in the church converts bread and wine into the flesh of his body and the water of his blood spiritually by his omnipotence, in those days by an invisible operation gave manna from heaven as his body and water coming down from heaven as his blood."

10. Moreover, we see that in the sacrament of baptism the Holy Spirit and the remission of sins are conferred, yet we do not say that they lie concealed in the water. In fact we put on Christ, yet no one holds that the water is transubstantiated. [They say that] Christ is in the Eucharist in one way and in baptism in another; I do not deny it, so long as they agree to his presence in baptism. As to the mode, I confess that in baptism Christ is given to us as mediator, reconciler, to speak more properly, as regenerator. Here he is given to us truly as food and nourishment.

Further, with their transubstantiation they come close to the Marcionite trope, for they say: it seems to be bread, but is not. This is the very thing Marcion said about Christ's flesh and body, that it was not true flesh, but only an appearance.

Christ is no conjurer, nor does he delude our senses; indeed he proved his resurrection by the senses: "Touch and see, because a spirit has not flesh and bones" (Lk. 24:40). The apostles might have said, "We touch and see, it appears to be flesh and body, but is not." Thus it would be an empty proof by which Christ established that he was no fantasy but had a true body. He showed that he had received his own and not another by the nail wounds and by the opening in his side. His argument would be of no strength if room is given for these tricks.

The Fathers also argue from the properties and qualities of human nature: Christ was truly man because he hungered, slept, was surprised and saddened, wept and suffered. Such arguments are lost if substance is not demonstrated by these qualities, so that one could no longer say: it is the form, the same taste, the same color as bread; therefore it is really bread. For heretics will confess that Christ hungered, slept, showed surprise, wept and suffered, but when you infer from this that he was therefore truly man, they deny the conclusion. They hold that these properties can be present in Christ without their reality, namely human nature. As to

Marcion's argument, they say that perhaps he took his error from the Gospel, where it is written that Christ walked on the water with dry feet, that he ascended to heaven, and escaped from the hands of the Jews so that they did not see him, but that such things from the Gospel should not be used because of this Marcionite peril. To this we reply that in the Gospels Christ is described as once or twice doing these miracles, while you treat them as constant.

And since we have not invented what is in Scripture, we ought not to be accused of providing excuses. Where we invent, expound, and theologize without the express Word of God, we must beware lest we open a window to heretics.

11. Further, this corrupts the nature of the sacrament. Augustine states (on John): "The word comes to the element and is made a sacrament." Its nature is to be composed of these two things, but they would remove the elements, bread and wine. Then Augustine should not have said the word comes to the element, but rather it destroys or removes the element.

When they remove the natures of the elements, the analogy of signification is lost. Bread signifies the body of Christ because it feeds, strengthens, and sustains, and this we cannot attribute to accidents. It is also a signification of many grains gathered into one, representing the mystical body, and that cannot be attributed to accidents. Paul has said, "We many are one bread and one body, who participate in one bread" (1 Cor. 10:17). In baptism, water is said to be the fountain of regeneration, and since its substance is preserved that is quite fitting, for the accidents of water are not suitable.

In removing the substance of bread and wine in the proposition *Hoc est corpus meum* they abuse the verb substantive *est*, for it is transubstantiated, converted, or transmuted. For when [*cum*] they utter those words of the Lord the bread is not yet the body of Christ; if they accept "is" in its true meaning they state a falsehood. This is why some of the Scholastics hold that the verb "is" ought to be taken for: to be made, to be changed or transformed.

They attribute this power of efficacy to those few words of the Lord, which make this change whenever used, yet in the Scripture they have not a word about such a thing. If some relate those words of Paul, Matthew, Mark, or Luke, they do not think of consecration, for the whole power is ascribed to their own canon. We know that the sacrament is present when we do what Christ did and commanded to be done. Not only did he say those words; he gave thanks, broke bread, ate, and gave others to eat. Since many things are here, all concur with the truth of the sacrament, nor should any be neglected. I overlook their ignorance of whether consecration is in Christ's words or in the prayers.

They expose themselves to great danger, for an evil priest and impostor could refrain from those words, could change or invert them.

Since an intention (as they say) is required of him that is to consecrate, it could happen that when doing these things he has no thought of consecration, or even rejects it.

12. They fall into many absurdities and perplexities, for they hold that a body may be in infinite places at one and the same time. They claim that this is no problem, since if the body of Christ is there it is not in a quantitative manner. Here is a wonder, how they can have a body, a quantum, truly present and yet not by way of quantity! Since they affirm his presence truly, corporeally, and carnally, as they say, yet not locally, who cannot see that these arguments are invented to deceive? They object that this was permitted to the body of St. Ambrose, who while in Milan was present at the funeral of St. Martin in Tours and was seen there. They ask why what was granted to Ambrose should not be allowed the body of Christ even more? But they assume what we do not, for it could have been revealed to Ambrose and have seemed to him that he was present at those rites, and perhaps he was represented to the people's vision by the work of angels; but that his body was in both places we do not allow. Besides, we can leave the truth of the reported miracle to the mind of its author.

Another objection concerns souls. Although they are creatures, yet each is in the head and all the members of our body. But this is rash, to compare spirit with body, and allow to bodies what we grant spirits. Christ said plainly: "A spirit has not flesh and bones," thus putting a great distance between them. Even if we allow to the body what is proper to our soul, it does not follow that the body of Christ can be in many places, just because our spirits and angels can be in various places at one and the same time. For they are creatures, and therefore of limited and finite power.

13. Many other disasters follow, for if mice nibble the sacred bread they say they have eaten accidents; if they are filled and satisfied, this is the work of accidents. If a priest happens to utter those words over a cask of wine and a chest of bread, both full to the top, and you ask what fills the cask and the chest—as well as the bellies of those who eat and drink—they will reply: accidents. And since those who eat are nourished, some of them dare to claim that God creates in the bellies of those who eat and drink either phlegm or some other humor, which can be changed into blood, whence they are nourished.

But if that sacrament is burned, as happened in the time of Hesychius, as he testified on Leviticus, and Origen also on the same book, ashes will surely remain, and so a substance will be created out of accidents. Worms may breed in the consecrated bread, and here too they say that substance is produced from accidents. The more daring of them pretend that the former substance is restored by a miracle so that such things may occur. But if one can add and invent miracles like this, any theologian can easily escape. For no matter how difficult the problem he will apply a miracle and thus solve all arguments that may be brought against him.

They affirm these things not only by miracles but by sophistries, just as Scotus was urged to tell us what is demonstrated in the subject of the proposition, when uttering those words *Hoc est corpus meum* [this is my body]. At length he replied: what is demonstrated is something singular or individual of a more general substance, which with the predicate refers to the same thing, or as they say is made the subject of the same thing; no difference exists between those things signified by the subject and the predicate, except by different ways of conceiving.

See where they rush, yet still do not escape. For they have not yet replied as to what is described when one says, "This is my body." Rochester says that in these propositions when one thing is changed into another it is not absurd that one describe what went before. Thus he admits that in "This is my body" the former bread is demonstrated, and is changed into the body of Christ while those words are spoken. In that case I maintain that the proposition is not properly formed, for it should have been: this becomes my body or this is changed into my body, otherwise to say "This is my body" is improper speech.

14. Those who hold that the body of Christ is really joined to the symbols while the natures of bread and wine are preserved, argue against transubstantiation as follows. What dignity or privilege do accidents have that they can be joined with Christ's body, while this is denied to the substance and nature of bread? And if accidents can remain, why not also the substance of bread? Indeed many Fathers supposed that this was done and used a likeness, showing that in Christ the human and divine natures truly remain, in such a way that one does not pass into the other; these opinions we shall introduce in their place.

They fall into another absurdity: when they break the sacrament, what is broken, we ask? On this they hedge; some have said, according to the Master of the Sentences in book 4, that the essence or substance of the body of Christ is broken. But he refutes this opinion, since the body of Christ is immortal and therefore not affected by such things or new events. Others have said that it is not a true fraction, but only looks like it, for so our senses take it. This is also rejected, lest we establish a permanent illusion. At last they say that accidents are broken, positing a sort of mathematical quantity, separated from matter, so that if it is divided it is so only by the power of mind and the capacity of intellect. They divide reality, so that the separated parts are readily visible.

We read in Jeremiah, "Let us send wood into his bread"—a place cited by Tertullian and Lactantius. They interpret it to mean putting the wood of the cross on the body of Christ, and assume that bread is mentioned because through bread Christ was to give himself to us. They take the prophet's words as a figure of the sacramental bread. But since these others remove it, leaving us only a figure, they therefore assert a figure of a figure, so that nothing solid remains. This can be inferred from the Fathers' familiar statement about Melchizedek, who brought bread and wine: the analogy [*typos*] is not observed by these men when they remove bread and wine. The same result occurs in relation to the showbread.

15. Let us submit an argument from baptism. Just above we held that the truth of that sacrament does not require that water is transubstantiated. Now let us reason from those who are themselves baptized, of whom Scripture clearly says that they put away the old man and are born again (Eph. 4:22). No transubstantiation is imagined in them, even though generation is defined as a motion by which new sub-stance is acquired. Little wonder that Nicodemus balked at the words of the Lord, announcing that he must be born anew. He hesitated, considering the new beginning proclaimed to someone already existing and advanced in years (Jn. 3:4). But if we interpret that beginning to be new and the nativity spiritual, why refuse the same thing in the Eucharist? And why not refer everything to spiritual eating? I gladly link these two sacraments, baptism and Eucharist, because Paul does so in this letter, chapter 12: "We were all by one Spirit baptized into one body, and all made to drink of one Spirit" (1 Cor. 12:13). Nor is it valid to say that we are baptized into one body in terms of a mystical body, since Christ is not absent from the mystical body, being its head. Elsewhere Paul says clearly, "In baptism we put on Christ" (Gal. 3:27).

We see also that Christian authors draw much from John chapter 6 concerning the sacrament of the Eucharist; no Father interprets that chapter without writing copiously about the Eucha-

rist. Therefore we conclude: what is said there either applies to this
sacrament or not; if not, why is it cited, or the Eucharist discussed
in that context? If it does apply, it means a spiritual eating only,
that is, through faith, by which the true body and blood of Christ
are received. Why is it necessary to introduce another new reception there, and to imagine a carnal eating by which the same thing
is received again? For they must admit that if someone who is pious and faithful comes, he eats Christ's body twice, first by a spiritual eating through faith, afterward in their carnal eating, which
they have never proved. So you see that they block their own way,
since they cannot truly cite those testimonies concerning the Eucharist from John 6.[23] When they affirm transubstantiation, they
are branded with the same error as the Capernaites (Jn. 6:24, 65).
These also had in mind who knows not what corporeal eating of
the flesh of Christ. Christ called them back from this idea immediately, by saying that his words were spirit and life, the flesh profiting nothing. And he introduces the thought of his ascension into
heaven: "What if you see the Son of Man ascending into heaven
where he was before?" But these men say they are not of the same
opinion as the Capernaites. They hold that the latter thought
Christ's flesh should be cut in pieces and torn with the teeth, which
they abhor. Whatever the special fantasy of the Capernaites was
one cannot say, but probably it was a carnal sense, so that they
were disturbed by the mention of ascension into heaven. Why do
these men who dare to say that Christ is eaten both carnally and
corporeally not learn from this example? What is the difference
whether you receive him in parts or swallow him whole?

16. What Christ said to his apostles at the end of his life is
relevant here, that he would leave the world and depart from them.
This would not be true if he were with us through transubstantiation, as they wish. They usually reply that Christ left the world as to
the conditions of mortality, of intimacy and human conversation.
This may be subtle but it misses the point. For when Christ spoke
the words in question, Philip replied, "Behold now you speak plainly and without parables" (Jn. 16:29). But if it had been taken in

their sense, it would have been an obscure and parabolic utterance. Moreover, if Christ remains with us corporeally in the Eucharist, by the same token he might remain in our hearts and lives. Thus after his ascension he could still rule the church in person and be present in the apostles. But he said that he would give a substitute [*vicarius*] in his place, namely the Holy Spirit, who would not be necessary if the whole Christ in divinity and humanity were present, as they have it. For since according to their doctrine his flesh and body is in each of us through communicating, and his divinity is present, he could act in person without the Holy Spirit as counselor.

When Mary the Lord's mother, the most blessed Virgin, heard from the angel that the Word of God would take flesh and that she was chosen to conceive and bear the Son of God, she considered them new and wonderful things, asked how they were possible, and so on (Luke 1:26ff). But since this transmuting of bread into Christ's body is not less than the mystery of incarnation and nativity from a virgin, it is astonishing that one finds in Scripture neither wonder nor questioning about it. Nor is such faith in transubstantiation, although of such great moment, commended to us in the writings of the evangelists or apostles. We do not bother about those who say that in John's sixth chapter a question had been asked, for they wish to transfer the answer given there concerning spiritual eating to this sacramental eating, holding it to be distinct. That question and answer therefore serves our purpose, but is little help to those who imagine this eating now being discussed, another beside the spiritual.

17. Such fabrications lead to other improprieties and absurdities. Christ said "I will that where I am, there my servant shall be also," and made the same statement to the apostles (Jn. 12:26, 14:3). In Revelation we read of certain martyrs, "They follow him wherever he shall go" (Rev. 14:4). From this we should conclude that in the Eucharist transubstantiation is not only into the body of Christ but into all the saints! If they do not like it, let them leave Christ in heaven with his saints, or else they will follow him as at-

tendants. They say, we also grant that he is in heaven, visible and in his majesty and glory, but we claim that in the sacrament he is invisible. The objection about the company of saints and martyrs is true when applied to Christ, since he is visible in his glory and majesty in heaven. Their answer rests on ground already destroyed, for it allows the body of Christ to be present in many places at once, which the Fathers deny. It grants that Christ is with us as body and flesh, whereas he said that he would send another in his place, the Holy Spirit.

They cannot avoid giving Christ two bodies: when he took bread in his hands at the Supper, if it had been transubstantiated into his body then [*tum*] he would have carried his body with his body. Then one must say the body that carried and the body that was carried are one, whereas you cannot have active and passive in regard to the same thing at the same time. You can see into what absurdities they throw themselves.

They like to bring in Augustine on the Psalms, who states that Christ carried himself in his own hands. But if the passage on Psalm 73 is considered, that in one sense he carried himself in his own hands we will grant it, because he carried in his hands the sacrament of his body, but not really and properly his body. You could add that it follows from Christ's eating with his apostles that he ate himself! Invariably they reply that these matters are exercises of our faith. But we have many statements of Scripture in which our faith may occupy itself other than in human inventions. We believe that the Son of God was incarnate, born of a virgin, suffered and died for us, was raised from the dead and ascended to heaven, and many similar things in which our faith is sufficiently exercised.

Because sense does not apprehend this transubstantiation, nor can reason understand it or experience teach it, how can it be known? I'm sure you will say: through faith. But if it is a question of acting in faith, this cannot happen without the Word of God, and of that you are quite destitute.

INTRODUCTION TO MARTIN CHEMNITZ'S *EXAMINATION OF THE COUNCIL OF TRENT*

AS THE Council of Trent finally came to its conclusion in 1563 after eighteen fitful years, many Protestants, despairing of reconciliation with a reforming Rome, had begun to turn their attention to internal disputes. In particular, divisions were deepening within Germany between strict or "Gnesio"-Lutherans, "Philippists," who followed Philipp Melanchthon, and those more aligned with Calvin and the Swiss theologians. Meanwhile, the Roman Catholic Church had at last overcome the internal divisions on matters of doctrine and practice that had paralyzed it since 1517, settling in binding fashion just what would and would not be reformed, and what errors would be rejected. Newly confident Catholic polemicists began to step up their attacks on Protestant doctrine, and a new generation of theologians, raised and trained in the Protestant faith, undertook to restate their central protests and defend them with massive erudition.

A leading figure in both of these emerging battlefields—the intra-Protestant confessional quarrels and the polemics with Rome—was Martin Chemnitz (1522–1586), often called "the Second Martin" because of his central and crucial role in clarifying and systematizing Lutheran doctrine in a form that would serve the Lutheran churches for centuries to come. Born in 1522 to a family of modest means in a small town near Brandenburg, Martin showed early intellectual promise and was sent to Wittenberg to study in 1536. Financial challenges forced interruptions and relocations of his schooling several times, but in 1545, he returned to Wittenberg and made the acquaintance of Melanchthon, who was extremely impressed and encouraged Chemnitz in his study of mathematics and astrology. While serving as ducal librarian in Konigsberg, Prussia, Chemnitz began to develop an interest in theology, and had progressed so far by 1553 that, on his third stint in Wittenberg, Melanchthon appointed him to lecture on theology in the University there for a year.

Although encouraged to stay on there the following year, Chemnitz went instead to the influential north German city of Braunschweig to serve as assistant to his friend Joachim Mörlin, who had just been appointed superintendent there, a position in which he succeeded Mörlin in 1568. The position of superintendent, essentially the Lutheran version of the office of bishop, was as much a pastoral and administrative one as a theological one, and Chemnitz, renowned for his piety and peaceable nature no less than his intellectual acumen, excelled in the post and left a lasting legacy in Lower Saxony.

He is most known today, however, for his crucial role in the battles over Lutheran theological orthodoxy that roiled Germany in the 1550s through 1580s, particularly on the doctrine of the Eucharist (and the understanding of Christology that undergirded it). Breaking with his mentor Melanchthon, Chemnitz defended a certain understanding of the ubiquity of Christ's body that became the standard of Lutheran orthodoxy in the 1577 Formula of Concord that Chemnitz helped author. Although Chemnitz was a moderate compared to many of the contentious theologians around him, the Formula served to drive a final wedge between Lutherans and Reformed and was not well-received even in much of Lutheran Germany and Scandinavia.

Chemnitz's greatest legacy, though, was surely his massive four-volume *Examen Decretorum Concilii Tridentini*, the *Examination of the Council of Trent*, published between 1566 and 1573. J.A.O. Preus calls it "one of the greatest theological masterpieces ever produced in Lutheranism"[1] and the *Schaff-Herzog Encyclopedia of Religious Knowledge* says of it that "no book of the period was more damaging to Roman claims."[2] It emerged out of a short polemic that Chemnitz had written in 1560 against the Jesuit order, which called forth a withering reply from Portuguese Jesus Jacob Andrada. Andrada, who had been a delegate at Trent, made use of its newly completed compendium of anti-Protestant decisions to take the offensive. Chemnitz, in response, resolved to take the opportunity to subject the whole range of Trent's doctrinal determinations to a thorough theological and historical examination. The result was the masterful *Examen.*

The *Examen* works systematically through the key decrees of Trent in the order that they were promulgated, beginning in volume 1 with the key issues of Scripture and tradition, depravity and free will, and justification and good works (issues addressed in Sessions IV, V, and VI of the Council). Volume 2 tackles the sacraments (Sessions VII, XIII, and XIV), and volumes 3 and 4 wade through more practical and liturgical questions of church reform, such as clerical celibacy, invocation of saints, indulgences, and relics (Sessions XXIIII and XXV of the Council). Selections from any of these volumes would make for an edifying read, but we have chosen here to excerpt from Chemnitz's examination of priesthood and ordination in volume 2.

Crucial among Luther's early teachings, of course, had been his concept of "the priesthood of all believers," a radical redefinition of the concept of the church that emphasized the whole body of Christians, not just the clerical hierarchy. But where did this leave the office of ordained priest, or minister? Were congregants simply to take preaching and the sacraments into their own hands?

[1] J.A.O. Preus, *The Second Martin: The Life and Theology of Martin Chemnitz* (St. Louis: Concordia Publishing House, 1994), 126.

[2] Samuel Macauley Jackson, ed., *The New Schaff-Herzog Encyclopedia of Religious Knowledge* (Grand Rapids: Baker, 1908–14), III:25. Available at the *Christian Classics Ethereal Library:* http://www.ccel.org/ccel/schaff/encyc03/Page_25.html (accessed October 7, 2017).

Some of the radical groups took this step, but the magisterial Reformers always defended the importance of the ordained ministry as an office established by God for the upbuilding and good order of the church. Despite its roots in the apostolic ministry, however, the priesthood is not dependent on a strict succession of ordination by bishops, as the Catholic Church maintained, but emerges out of a divine calling, recognized and formalized by the community of believers. Nor, crucially, is the function of the priesthood to mediate God's grace to believers, and make propitiation on behalf of sinners before God, as in the Mass-centered understanding of the ministry that Rome had embraced. No, the office for which ordination set a man apart was fundamentally a preaching office, the ministry of the Word.

The following excerpts of Chemnitz's *Examen* offer a clear, learned, and forceful statement of these central Protestant convictions, as well as arguing vigorously that the distinction between bishop and presbyter (or priest) is a pragmatic distinction, rather than a theologically significant one.

Further Reading

For further reading, see J.A.O Preus, *The Second Martin: The Life and Theology of Martin Chemnitz* (St. Louis: Concordia Publishing House, 1994); Charles P. Arand, Robert Kolb, and James A. Nestingen, *The Lutheran Confessions: History and Theology of the Book of Concord* (Minneapolis, MN: Fortress Press, 2012), chs. 12–15; Paul D.L Avis, *The Church in the Theology of the Reformers* (Atlanta: John Knox Press, 1981).

MARTIN CHEMNITZ,
EXAMINATION OF THE COUNCIL OF TRENT (1565–73)[1]

Ninth Topic Concerning Holy Orders, from the 23rd Session of the Council of Trent

Section I: Concerning the Sacrament of Order, etc.

Chapter I

SACRIFICE and priesthood are by the ordinance of God linked together in such a way that both have existed under every law. Since therefore the Catholic Church has in the New Testament received from the institution of the Lord the holy, visible sacrifice of the Eucharist, one must also confess that there is in her a new visible and external priesthood, into which the old has been changed. And the sacred writings show and the tradition of the Catholic Church has always taught that this was instituted by the same Lord, our Savior, and given to the apostles and their successors in the priesthood for consecrating, offering, and administering the body and blood and also for remitting and retaining sins.

---

[1] Taken from Fred Kramer, trans., *Chemnitz's Works, Vol. 2: Examination of the Council of Trent* (1978; Saint Louis: Concordia Publishing House, 2007). Excerpted under Fair Use.

Canon I

If anyone says that there is not in the New Testament a visible and external priesthood, or that there is no power of consecrating and offering the body and blood of the Lord and of remitting and retaining sins, but only an office and bare ministry of preaching the Gospel, or that those who do not preach are not priests at all, let him be anathema.

Examination

1. The explanation is short and easy once it is shown what the controversy is about. They shout loudly that those who do not approve the priesthood of the papalists take away all order out of the church, that with infinite confusion they prostitute the ministry to any one of the common people and (something which Tertullian ascribes to the heretics) make laymen out of priests and enjoin priestly functions to laymen, with the result that there is neither any authority nor dignity of the ministry, etc. Therefore this slander must first of all be removed.

Now the Anabaptists and Enthusiasts are rightly disapproved, who either take the use of the external ministry of Word and sacrament entirely out of the church, or imagine that it is useless and unnecessary. For they teach that new and special revelations should rather be sought and expected from God without the use of the external ministry of Word and sacrament, and that this kind of calling, illumination, and conversion is much more excellent and worthy of honor than if we use the voice of the ministry. And indeed, it is God by whose power, working, efficacy, impulse, and inspiration whatever pertains to calling, illumination, conversion, repentance, faith, renewal, and in short, to the business of our salvation is begun, effected, increased, and preserved in men. But God arranged by a certain counsel of His that He wills to dispense these things, not by infusing new and special revelations, illuminations, and movements into the minds of men without any means, but through the outward ministry of the Word. This ministry He did not commit to angels, so that their appearances are to be sought and expected, but He put the Word of reconciliation into men, and He wills that the proclamation of the Gospel, divinely revealed, should sound forth through them.

2. All Christians are indeed priests (1 Pet. 2:9; Rev. 1:6), because they offer spiritual sacrifices to God. Everyone also can and should teach the Word of God in his own house (Deut. 6:7; 1 Cor. 14:35). Nevertheless, not everyone ought to take and arrogate to himself the public ministry of Word and sacrament. For not all are apostles; not all are teachers (1 Cor. 12:29), but those who have been set apart for this ministry by God through a particular and legitimate call (Acts 13:2; Jer. 23:21; Rom. 10:15). This is done either immediately or mediately. Paul prescribes a legitimate manner of calling which is made through the voice of the church (1 Tim. 3:2–7; Titus 1:5–9). Christ Himself indeed called certain men to this ministry immediately, in order to show that He approves the ministry of those who are chosen and called by the voice of the church according to the rule prescribed by the apostles, as will be explained more fully later. There is added also the promise that God will truly work effectively through the ministry of those who teach the Gospel, which the Son of God wills to preserve in the church through perpetual calling, as Paul says in Eph. 4:8ff: He ascended; He gave gifts to men; and He gave some to be apostles, some prophets, others evangelists, others however pastors and teachers for perfecting of the saints in the work of ministry, in edification of the body of Christ. To this use of the ministry, which God both instituted and preserves in the church, men must therefore be guided and taught that through this ministry there are offered to us eternal blessings, and indeed that God in this way receives us, rescues us from sin and the power of the devil and from eternal death, and restores to us righteousness and eternal life.

3. This ministry does indeed have power, divinely bestowed (2 Cor. 10:4–6; 13:2–4), but circumscribed with certain duties and limitations, namely, to preach the Word of God, teach the erring, reprove those who sin, admonish the dilatory, comfort the trou-

bled, strengthen the weak, resist those who speak against the truth, reproach and condemn false teaching, censure evil customs, dispense the divinely instituted sacraments, remit and retain sins, be an example to the flock, pray for the church privately and lead the church in public prayers, be in charge of care for the poor, publicly excommunicate the stubborn and again receive those who repent and reconcile them with the church, appoint pastors to the church according to the instruction of Paul, with consent of the church institute rites that serve the ministry and do not militate against the Word of God nor burden consciences but serve good order, dignity, decorum, tranquility, edification, etc. For these are the things which belong to these two chief points, namely, to the power of order and the power of jurisdiction.

4. We are not fighting about words. Paul, with a general term, calls teachers and pastors "ministers." In the Scripture of the New Testament the terms "priests" and "priesthood" are nowhere applied to the ministry of the New Testament. But in the use of the ecclesiastical writers a strong trend developed to call the ministry "priesthood" and the ministers "priests." Thus Chrysostom calls whatever pertains to the ministry of the New Testament "priesthood." Augustine, *De civitate Dei*, Bk. 20, says: "Bishops and presbyters are now properly called priests in the church." Now, if the papalists wanted only this, that there is in the New Testament an external priesthood, that is, an external ministry of the Word and the sacraments, as we have already explained, there would be no controversy, neither would disturbances arise on account of the term "priesthood" so long as matters which are true and necessary were inviolate.

5. But there is no obscurity about what they want and seek. For in this first canon they say expressly that by the priesthood for which they are contending they do not understand the office and ministry of preaching the Gospel, but declare in the first chapter that they are fighting in behalf of the sacrifice of the Mass, about their external and visible priesthood, which they define as being chiefly the power of sacrificing Christ in the Mass. And they think

that such a priesthood is necessary in order that the church may have mediators who can plead their cause before Christ, the supreme Judge, and by this act of sacrifice placate the wrath of the Father and obtain for the church propitiation and other gifts, both such as are spiritual and necessary for salvation and also bodily gifts that pertain to this life, yes, the liberation of souls from purgatory.

6. But we have shown above, under the topic of the Mass, that this sacrifice is not only fabricated but injurious to and blasphemous against Christ. There is therefore no need to undertake a special refutation at this point. For such as the sacrifice is, such also is the priesthood. I shall only add this reminder that the first canon devotes their priesthood to sacrifice in such a way that it frees it from the ministry of the Word. This they profess much more openly elsewhere, namely, that the ministry of teaching, the dispensation of Baptism, and the distribution of the Eucharist, which can be done through deacons, is not part of the substance of the papalist priesthood.

Therefore let a comparison be made! Christ says: "Go, teach, preach, baptize" (Matt. 28:19–20; Mark 16:15). Paul says: "A bishop must hold firm to the sure Word as taught, so that he may be able to give instruction in sound doctrine and also to confute those who contradict it" (Titus 1:9). He must be an apt teacher (1 Tim. 3:2), must attend to reading and teaching (1 Tim. 4:13), must rebuke those who sin, in the presence of all (1 Tim 5:20), etc. Therefore the apostles unburdened themselves of other duties, in order that they might be able to devote themselves to teaching and prayer (Acts 6:4). Paul says: "Christ did not send me to baptize but to preach the Gospel" (1 Cor. 1:17). These things, which Christ and the apostles declare to belong to the ministry of the Word, that is, the priesthood, the papalists remove from the substance of their priesthood. Also they do not want the dispensation of Baptism and the distribution of the Eucharist to belong properly to their priesthood. Therefore the papalists remove and separate from their priesthood all the things of which, according to the teaching of Scripture, the ministry of the New Testament consists. They establish as the essence of their priesthood the sacrifice of the body and blood of Christ in the Mass, which was brought into the church without, yes, contrary to Scripture, as was shown under the topic concerning the Mass.

They add also the remission and retention of sins. But this they are unwilling to have happen through the voice and proclamation of the Gospel, as Christ instituted it, but by that judicial act of which we spoke under a previous topic. Therefore the papalist priesthood is not the ministry of the New Testament but truly an abomination of Antichrist, standing in the holy place.

The ancients do, indeed, at times say that it is the duty of priests to offer the body and blood of Christ, but we have shown above, under the topic of the Mass, that they understand this of the administration of the Lord's Supper according to Christ's institution. For Paul also calls the preaching of the Gospel a sacrifice. Many among the papalists who heretofore displayed a certain degree of moderation indicated that they desired a reformation of the priesthood in which the ministry of teaching, which according to the heritage of Scripture belongs to the ministry of the New Testament, might again be enjoined to the care of the priests. But the Council of Trent simply defines the priesthood as the action of sacrificing, and Canon 1 pronounces the anathema on anyone who says that those who do not exercise the ministry of the Word and the sacraments are not priests.

7. They have only one argument, namely, that in the Old Testament there was a priesthood for offering sacrifices and that there is in the New Testament a fulfillment of the shadows of the Old. But you cannot construct the priesthood of the papalists from this. For the Epistle to the Hebrews teaches at great length that the sacrifices of the Old Testament have been fulfilled and completed in the New by the one sacrifice of Christ, our true High Priest. But they say: yet Paul argues (2 Cor. 3:7–11) that if the ministry of the Old Testament had its own splendor, the splendor of the ministry of the New Testament will be much greater. I answer: what this ministry of the New Testament is and what duties belong to it must

not be established by a bad imitation of the ceremonies of the Old Testament but must be learned from the description of Christ and the apostles in the New Testament. [...]

Section IV: Concerning the Ecclesiastical Hierarchy and Ordination

Chapter IV

Since, in the sacrament of order, just as in baptism and confirmation, a character is imprinted which can be neither obliterated nor taken away, the holy synod deservedly condemns the opinion of those who assert that priests of the New Testament have only a temporary power and that those who have once been rightly ordained can again become laymen if they do not exercise the ministry of the Word of God. But if anyone asserts that all Christians without distinction are priests of the New Testament or that all are mutually endowed with equal spiritual power, it is clear that he does nothing but throw into disorder the ecclesiastical hierarchy (which is set in order as a battle line before a camp), as though contrary to the teaching of blessed Paul all were apostles, all prophets, all evangelists, all pastors, all teachers. Accordingly the most holy synod declares that, beside the other ecclesiastical ranks, the bishops, who succeeded to the place of the apostles, belong chiefly to this hierarchical order and that they are placed there, as the same apostle says, by the Holy Spirit to rule the Church of God, that they are superior to priests, and confer the sacrament of confirmation, ordain ministers of the church, and that they are able to perform very many other functions which the rest, who are of an inferior order, have no power to perform. The most holy synod further teaches that in the ordination of bishops, priests, and the other orders the consent, call, or authority either of the people or of any secular power and magistrate is not required in such a way that without it the ordination is invalid; rather, it decrees that those who, called and appointed only by the people or by a secular power and magistrate, ascend to the exercise of these ministries and those who have taken them to themselves by their own rashness are all to be considered not ministers of the church but thieves and robbers who have not entered by the door. These, in general, are the things which it seemed good to the sacred synod to teach the faithful of Christ about the sacrament of order.

Canon VI

If anyone says that there is not in the Catholic Church a hierarchy, instituted by divine ordination, which consists of bishops, presbyters,[2] and ministers [or deacons], let him be anathema.

Canon VII

If anyone says that bishops are not superior to presbyters, or that they do not have the power of confirming and ordaining, or that the power they have is common to them together with the presbyters, or that orders conferred by them without the consent or call of the people or of the secular power are invalid, or that those who have neither been validly ordained nor sent by ecclesiastical and canonical power, but have come from elsewhere, are lawful ministers of the Word and the sacraments, let him be anathema.

Canon VIII

If anyone says that bishops who are obtained by authority of the Roman pontiff are not legitimate and true bishops but a human creation, let him be anathema.

Examination

1. I shall record nothing here about the things treated in the first part of this chapter—about the character which is said to be imprinted in the sacrament of order and about the priesthood which all Christians have in common. For of the character imprinted in

---

[2] The Greek word *presbyteros* (presbyter in Latin) first meant "elder" and later "priest." We have translated it "presbyter."

the sacraments we have spoken in connection with the ninth canon under "Concerning the Sacraments in General." That not any and every Christian should rashly, without a lawful call, take the ministry of the Word and the sacraments to himself, even though all are spiritual priests, we have explained in connection with the 10th canon under "Concerning the Sacraments in General" [pp. 98–100] and in the first section of this topic [pp. 677–678]. There remain, therefore, two questions: about bishops, and about what is a legitimate call. About these questions certain things must be said.

2. Now in order that what is judged here about bishops may be more rightly understood, certain things from Scripture and from testimonies of the true antiquity must first be repeated. The terms *episkopos* [bishop] and *episkopee* [office of bishop] are found used of the ecclesiastical ministry in the apostolic writings (Acts 1:20; 20:28; Phil. 1:1; Titus 1:7; 1 Tim. 3:1–2; 1 Peter 5:2). These terms were, however, taken from the use of everyday language and were adapted to the ministry of the church because it has the duty of administration and inspection. Suidas[3] says that in the Athenian republic those were called *episkopoi*, and "guards," who were sent to territories which were subject to them, not in order that they might preside with naked power, as Lindanus interprets, but to look into the affairs of each, that is, as Budaeus translates it from Livy, to look into the affairs of their allies. Plutarch says, on Pericles: "Phidias was *episkopos*, that is, inspector of all works." In Homer's *Iliad*, 9 and 24, Hector is called *episkopos* of the city. With Demosthenes, in verses of Solon, Pallas is called *episkopos* of Athens. In Plutarch, on Numa, he is called *episkopos* of the vestal virgins. In the same place Venus is *episkopos* over the dead. Cicero, *Ad Atticum*, Bk. 7: "Pompey wants me to be the one whom the whole Campagna and the people of the maritime districts have as *episkopos*, to whom all the recruiting and the revenue is committed." In *Pandectis*,[4] *episkopoi* are people placed over things offered for sale.

---

[3] Byzantine lexicographer c. A.D. 1000.

[4] An early kind of encyclopedia.

3. The apostles accommodated these words more willingly to the ecclesiastical ministry because they were at that time generally known from the Greek version of the Old Testament. For the words *paqad*, *pequdah*, and *pequdim*, which mean visitation, inspection, office, care, administration committed to someone, a duty demanded—these the Greeks translated *episkopein*, *episkopee*, and *episkopos*. In Num. 31:14 the officers of the army are called *episkopoi*; in Judges 9:28[5] Abimelech had Zebul as his *episkopos*. 2 Kings 11:15 speaks of the captains who are *episkopoi* over all the army. There also guards were placed over the house of the Lord [2 Kings 11:7]. This is explained thus by the Greeks: He placed *episkopos* over the house of the Lord. In 2 Chron. 39:12 the inspectors of works are called *episkopoi*. Num. 4:16: the office or duty of Eleazar in the tabernacle of God is called *episkopee*. Thus in Ps. 109:8 the office of Judas is called *episkopee*. I have noted down these examples which I had observed, in order that consideration might be given to the source from which the apostles took this term, the peculiar emphasis of which can also be gathered and understood from these passages. Jerome translated it *superattendens* (superintendent), Ambrose *superinspector* (overseer).

4. The question, however, is what rank in the ecclesiastical ministry the office of bishop is and what the duties of a bishop are. We can complete the explanation of this question more briefly because it has been treated *ex professo* by Jerome. He shows and proves that at the time of the apostles, bishops and presbyters were one and the same, or that one and the same person was both presbyter and bishop, one of these being a term for his office and dignity, the other for his age. For Paul says (Phil. 1:1) that in that one church there were bishops and deacons. In Acts 20:17 Luke says that the presbyters of the church at Ephesus were called out. When Paul has assembled them, he calls them bishops ["overseers," KJV and RSV; Acts 20:28]. In Titus 1:5ff. Paul speaks of appointing presbyters in every town. And as he explains what kind of presby-

---

[5] The text erroneously has Judith 9.

ter ought to be ordained, he says: "For a bishop must be blameless." In 1 Peter 5:1–2 Peter, addressing the presbyters calls himself a fellow presbyter and ascribes to the office of presbyters to *episkopein* ["oversight," KJV]. That the same ordination was common to [bishops and] presbyters Jerome shows from 1 Tim. 4:14, which speaks of the laying on of hands of the presbyters.

This opinion did not fall from the lips of Jerome accidentally while he was concerned about something else, but he argues it *ex professo* and repeats it in a number of places, e.g., on the Epistle to Titus, in his Letter to Evagrius, likewise to Oceanus. Ambrose follows this opinion, likewise Bede in the chapter on Philippians, likewise Isidore, dist. 21, ch. *Cleros*. The same Jerome also explains what was the cause and origin of the difference which was later made between a bishop and the presbyters, why and for what use this difference was accepted by the church. Thus he says, on Titus 1: "Before, by an impulse of the devil, a zeal in religion developed and it was said among the people, 'I belong to Paul; I to Apollos; I to Cephas,' the churches were governed by the common counsel of the presbyters. But after everyone thought that those whom he had baptized were his, not Christ's, it was decreed that in the whole city one who was elected from among the presbyters should be placed over the rest, to whom the care of the whole church should belong, and the seeds of schisms would be removed." Likewise: "With the ancients, presbyters and bishops were one and the same. But little by little, in order that the seedbeds of dissensions might be rooted out, the whole responsibility was conferred on one." The same says in the *Letter to Evagrius* (and this is quoted in dist. 93, ch. *Legimus*): "However, that later on one was elected who was placed over the rest, this was done as a remedy against schisms, lest everyone draw the church of Christ to himself and split it. For also at Alexandria, from the time of Mark the Evangelist until Dionysius, the presbyters always chose one from among themselves and placed him in a higher rank. Him they called *episcopus*, just as if the army would make a commander-in-chief for itself," etc.

Moreover, a little before the time of Jerome, Aerius began to urge this equality of presbyters and bishops, which existed at the time of the apostles, in such a way that he simply condemned the custom of the church which made the bishop superior to and placed him over the presbyters and gave him the supervision of the whole church as a remedy against dissensions and for the sake of order and harmony. However, when this opinion of Aerius was seen to give occasion for confusion and dissensions, it was rejected and disapproved. Then the bishops grew arrogant, despised the presbyters, and thought this prerogative was due them by divine right.

Because these controversies were still raging in his time, Jerome, as he himself declares, interposes his opinion from Scripture and shows that at the time of the apostles and with the ancients there was no distinction, but that presbyters and bishops were one and the same and that the churches were governed by their common counsel. Then he explains for what reason, for what purpose and use one bishop was placed over the others as head, namely, to remove the seedbeds of dissensions and schisms. To this extent Jerome approves this arrangement. But the pride of the bishops he curbs with these words: "Therefore as the presbyters know that, from the custom of the church, they are subject to the one who has been placed over them, so the bishops should know that they are greater than the presbyters more by custom than by the truth of an arrangement of the Lord, and that they ought to govern the church in common." Of the office of bishops Jerome says to Evagrius that the bishop does the same thing a presbyter does. Therefore the ministry of the Word and the sacraments and the care of ecclesiastical discipline were at that time the joint duty of the bishop and the presbyters. So far were bishops removed from shrinking back from the ministry of the presbyters that Jerome complains, *Ad Rusticum Narbonensem*, dist. 93, ch. *Diaconi*: "The bishop alone uses the ministry; he alone claims everything for himself; he alone invades areas belonging to others." At that time ordination was specifically the duty of the bishops, as Jerome says: "What does a bishop do

486

that a presbyter does not do, ordination excepted?" And Chrysostom says, on 1 Timothy, that a bishop is greater than a presbyter only in that he performs ordinations. Afterward more special duties began to be assigned to the bishops, as Leo lists them in dist. 98: the ordination of clerics, the arrangement, blessing and anointing of an altar, the consecration of a church, the reconciliation of heretics and penitents through the laying on of hands, preparing the chrism, marking the forehead with chrism, sending out prepared epistles, etc. As they gradually relaxed the ministry of the Word and the sacraments, the bishops began to devote themselves entirely to these actions. Finally, after they had cast off the ministry of the Word and the sacraments, also these small duties were relegated to the subsidiary bishops, and the episcopal offices were turned into overlordships. Such are now the bishops who are created by the Roman pontiff, of whom it is rightly said that they are not true and lawful bishops but a human invention, because they have entirely cast off from themselves the episcopal office as it was at the time of the apostles, at the time of Jerome, and even at the time of Leo, and have become chiefs of peoples, who rule because, while Christ said to the apostles, "It shall not be so among you" [Matt. 20:26], perhaps He said to the successors of the apostles, "It shall be so among you." And although these things ought to have been reformed at the council, the Tridentine canon only declares: "If anyone says that bishops who are obtained by authority of the Roman pontiff are not legitimate and true bishops but a human creation, let him be anathema." And so the order of bishops has been duly reformed!

5. Now that these things have been explained, it will be clear what the Council of Trent establishes about bishops. For when they reckon the bishops over and above the other ecclesiastical ranks, they appear to want to terminate the controversy which is going on between the scholastics and the canonists about the ecclesiastical orders or ranks, where the latter forge a special order for the bishops while the former count the bishops as belonging to the order of presbyters. If, when they say that the bishops are superior

to the presbyters, they were speaking of true bishops and would understand this as Jerome explains it, it could be tolerated. But the sixth canon asserts that the hierarchy, which consists of bishops, presbyters, and ministers [or deacons], was instituted by a divine decree. And they pronounce the anathema on anyone who holds otherwise. But we have already reported what Jerome, whom the other ancients follow, states about this question from Scripture. Therefore the Council of Trent pronounces the anathema on them.

6. This is truly a strange artifice, that when they need to speak about the power of the bishops, they make no mention whatever of the ministry of the Word and the sacraments, but, after mentioning the anointing with chrism, and ordination, they add by means of a general conclusion that the bishops are able also to do many other things, namely maintain horses and dogs, if not also harlots, exercise royal dominion, and similar episcopal duties. They pronounce the anathema if anyone holds that the power to ordain is held by the bishops in common with the presbyters, although Jerome, *Ad Evagrium*, proves this from Paul, who says in 1 Tim. 4:14 that Timothy was ordained through the laying on of the hands of the presbytery. So great is the Tridentine outpouring of anathemas!

7. The final question of this chapter is: what is a legitimate call of ministers of the Word and the sacraments? With this supplement they try openly, not so much to beat our churches but to cut their throat once and for all and to overthrow them utterly. With this supplement they wanted to strengthen the cries of those who contend that there is no true and lawful ministry of the Word and the sacraments in our churches, that God does not work through our ministry, that there is no true absolution or forgiveness of sins in our ministry, that our churches are not able to have a true sacrament of the body and blood of Christ, but that all who discharge the ministry of the Word and the sacraments in our churches are thieves and robbers who have not come in through the true door. Surely, a fearful threat! But they add no other reason

for this than that the ministers of our churches have not been called, sent, ordained, shaven, and anointed by papalist bishops.

8. Now, because the ministry of the Word and the sacraments is the ordinary means or instrument which God employs in matters pertaining to the dispensation of salvation, it is absolutely necessary to show to the church sure and firm arguments from Scripture in this question, namely, what is a true, lawful, orderly, and therefore divine call of ministers of the Word and the sacraments. Therefore we shall briefly draw them together as called for by our purpose.

9. To begin with, it is certain that no one is a legitimate minister of the Word and the sacraments—nor is able rightly and profitably to exercise the ministry for the glory of God and the edification of the church—unless he has been sent, that is, unless he has a legitimate call (Jer. 23:21; Rom. 10:15). The nature of this call is not, however, the same as when political or domestic offices are established either by the head of a family or by those who have the highest power in the state, that those who take onto themselves the rule in the church also do it in the same way and are able to order the ministries of the church according to their own will and by their own authority. But God, the author, preserver, governor, and (if I may use this term) husbandman of the ecclesiastical ministry, has reserved for Himself the right and authority of calling and sending those whom He wants to receive as co-workers in this ministry, and wants it to belong to Himself as Lord of the harvest. Therefore Christ says in Matt. 9:38: "Pray the Lord of the harvest to send out laborers into His harvest." Jer. 23:21: "I did not send the prophets, yet they ran." Eph. 4:11: Christ gives apostles, evangelists, pastors, teachers. Acts 20:28: "The Holy Ghost has made you overseers to feed the church of God." Acts 13:4: "They were sent out by the Holy Spirit." Therefore it is necessary for a legitimate call to the ministry of the church that the person who is to be a legitimate minister of the Word and the sacraments be called and sent by God, so that both the minister and the church can truthfully declare, as it is written in Is. 59:21: "I have put My words in your

mouth." 2 Cor. 5:19–20: "He has entrusted to us the message of reconciliation. So we are ambassadors for Christ, God making His appeal through us." Luke 10:16: "He who hears you hears Me." John 20:21: "As the Father has sent Me, even so I send you."

10. These things must be considered in a call of the church, in order that both the minister and also the church can state with certainty that God is present with this ministry and works through it, as He says in Matt. 28:20: "I am with you." John 20:22: "Receive the Holy Spirit." 2 Cor. 3:6: "He has qualified us to be ministers ... not of the letter but of the Spirit." 1 Cor. 3:5–9: "You are God's field, God's building." "We are God's assistants." "Paul plants; Apollos waters; God gives the growth." John 20:23: "If you forgive the sins of any, they are forgiven; if you retain the sins of any, they are retained." Matt. 16:19: "I will give you the keys of the kingdom of heaven, and whatever you loose on earth shall be loosed in heaven, and whatever you bind on earth shall be bound in heaven." Therefore Paul says in Rom. 10:14ff. that those who are not sent by God cannot preach in such a way that faith is received from that preaching—faith which calls upon the name of God, so that we are justified and saved. These things are certain from Scripture.

11. Now when God Himself speaks immediately to men and with His own voice makes known His will, as He often did in the Old Testament, and as later, in the time of the New Testament, He spoke through a Son (Heb. 1:2), then there is no doubt about the efficacy of the Word. However, God did not always want to set His Word before the church without means, with His own voice, but determined by sure counsel to use the voice of the ministry as His ordinary means or instrument. Nevertheless there remains also in this medium what is appropriate to the prophets: "Thus says the Lord: ... because I have put My words in your mouth ..." [Is. 59:21]. "... God making His appeal through us" [2 Cor. 5:20]. "Do you seek proof that Christ is speaking in me?" (2 Cor. 13:3). That these things are right and proper in those who are called immediately by the divine voice, not through men but by God Himself, as were the prophets in the Old Testament and the Baptist and the

apostles—this no sane person is able to doubt. But God called few men in this immediate manner. For those who at the time of the apostles were prophets, evangelists, pastors, teachers, bishops, presbyters, and deacons were called to the ministry not immediately but by the voice of the church. Now are the things which Scripture teaches about the presence and efficacy of God through the ministry doubtful, uncertain, or false in the case of a mediate call? Surely, this is a very great and comforting promise, that Scripture declares that also that call which is issued by the voice of the church is divine, or from God. Eph. 4:11: the Son of God gives pastors and teachers, who certainly were not, like the apostles, called immediately. And in Acts 20:28 Paul addresses the presbyters, who had been appointed either by Paul or by Timothy, thus: "The Holy Spirit has made you overseers." Therefore Paul, in the signature of 1 Corinthians, links Sosthenes to himself; in 2 Corinthians, Timothy; in 1 Thessalonians, Sylvanus. Therefore Paul applies the sayings: "We are God's fellow workers" [1 Cor. 3:9]; "He has entrusted to us the message of reconciliation ... God making His appeal through us" [2 Cor. 5:19–20], also to those who had been called mediately. Likewise, he declares that God works efficaciously also through the ministry of those who were called through the voice of the church: "Apollos waters; God gives the growth" [1 Cor. 3:6]. And in 1 Tim. 4:16 he says to Timothy: "You will save both yourself and your hearers." Eph. 4:11ff.: he gives teachers for building up the body of Christ, that we may attain to unity of faith, and doing the truth may grow in Christ. The promises are most delightful, and very necessary, namely, that the call also of those who have been called by the voice of the church is divine, that God is present with and works effectively through their ministry. Therefore Paul says that there is in Timothy a grace and a gift through the laying on of hands. He does not say only, "of my hands" [2 Tim. 1:6], but adds, "when the ... elders laid their hands upon you" (1 Tim. 4:14), lest it be thought that it makes a difference whether a person is ordained by apostles or by presbyters.

12. However, in order that this mediated call may enjoy these privileges, it is necessary that it be legitimate, i.e., that it be made in the manner and by the persons prescribed by Scripture. With respect to the kind of persons who should be called to the ministry a certain rule has been prescribed (Acts 6:3; Titus 1:6–9; 1 Tim. 3:2–13). But the question here is by whose voice and vote this election and call ought to be made in order that it may be possible to declare that it is divine, that is, that it is God Himself who through these means chooses, calls, and sends laborers into His harvest. Of this there are sure and clear examples in Scripture. In Acts 1:15–26, when another person had to be substituted in place of Judas, Peter laid the matter not before the apostles alone, but also before the rest of the disciples, for that is how the believers were at that time called, their number, gathered together, being about 120. There Peter set forth from Scripture what sort of person it should be and how they ought to choose him, to which they added their prayers. Lots were cast because the call was not to be simply mediated, but apostolic. For this reason lots were not used in calls thereafter. In Acts 6:2–6, when deacons are to be chosen and called, the apostles are not willing to arrogate the right of calling to themselves alone, but they call the church together. They do not, however, wholly renounce oversight over the calling and commit it to the pleasure of the common people or of the blind and confused crowd, but they are as it were steersmen and directors of the election and calling, for they set forth the principle and rule as to the sort of persons they should be and how they should be chosen. The men are placed before the apostles in order that the election might be examined, to see whether in their judgment it has been rightly made. They prayed, and approved the election by the laying on of hands. In Acts 14:23 Paul and Barnabas appoint elders in all churches to which they had preached the Gospel. However, they did not take the right and authority of choosing and calling to themselves alone. Luke uses the word *cheirotoneesantes*, which in 2 Cor. 8:19 is used of an election which is made by the voice or votes of the church, for it is taken from the Greek custom of voting with uplifted hands, and

signifies to create or designate someone by vote or to show agreement. Therefore Paul and Barnabas did not force presbyters on unwilling people, without the consent of the church. And in Acts 15:22, when men had to be elected who were to be sent to the church at Antioch with commands, Luke says: "It seemed good to the apostles and the elders, with the whole church, to choose … Barnabas and Silas." It is useful to observe in the apostolic history that sometimes both the ministers and the rest of the congregation jointly proposed and chose those whom they considered suitable (e.g., Acts 1:23). At other times the church proposed and chose; however, the election was submitted to the judgment of the apostles for their approval (Acts 6:3–6). Thus Paul sends to the churches Timothy, Titus, Sylvanus, etc. In Acts 14:23 presbyters were proposed, whom the church accepted by raising of hands. Meanwhile some also offered their services to the church, 1 Tim. 3:1: "If any one aspires to the office of bishop, he desires a noble task." Always, however, in a legitimate call at the time of the apostles the consent of the church and the judgment and approval of the presbytery was present and required.

Thus Titus was put in charge of guiding and moderating the election of presbyters on Crete, in order that it might be done rightly and that he might by means of ordination approve it and confirm the rightly performed election. For in Titus 1:5, in speaking of appointing elders, Paul uses the same word which is found in Acts 14:23, where likewise both *cheirotonia* and the appointing of elders are mentioned. And he instructs Titus that he should rebuke sharply those who are not sound in doctrine nor teach what they should, that is, as he says more clearly in 1 Tim. 5:12: "Do not be hasty in the laying on of hands, nor partake in another man's sins," namely, by approving an election or call which was not rightly done.

13. These examples from the apostolic history show clearly that election or calling certainly belongs in some way to the whole church, so that in their choosing and calling both presbyters and people are partners. This apostolic manner of choosing and calling

was retained and practiced in the church also later on. Dist. 24, Canon 3, of a Council of Carthage says: "No cleric shall be ordained unless he has been tested either by examination of the bishops or by testimony of the people." Leo says, Dist. 62: "No reason allows that any should be accounted as bishops who have neither been elected by the clergy nor desired by the people nor consecrated by the provincial bishop in accord with the judgment of the metropolitan." Dist. 67: "The other priests shall be ordained by their own bishop in such a way that the citizens and the other priests may give their assent." Dist. 24, from the Fourth Council of Carthage: "The bishop shall not ordain clerics without the counsel of his clerics, in order that he may seek the agreement and testimony of the citizens." Dist. 23, from the same council, ch. *Qui episcopus*: "When the person examined shall have been found fully instructed in all these things, then he shall with the total consent of clergy and laity, and with the agreement of the bishops of the whole province, and most of all either by order or in the presence of the metropolitan, be ordained a bishop."

VIII.[6] Quest. 1 is quoted as from Jerome, but it is from Origen, ch. *Licet*: "Therefore in the ordination of a priest the presence of the people is also required, in order that all may know and be certain that he who is the most outstanding among all the people is chosen for the priesthood, and that in the presence of the people, lest there remain later on a reconsideration or some doubt in anyone's mind." Dist. 65, ch. *Plebs*: "It is necessary that you bishops should frequently call together the presbyters, deacons, and the whole multitude in order that they may, not according to everyone's whim but with one mind, with your admonition, seek out such a person whom no opposition can keep back from the written decisions." Likewise: "You are not to consecrate bishops through Emilion except after election or consent of clergy and people." Ch. *Metropolitano*: "After the will of all the clerics and citizens has been discussed, let the best one be ordained." Ch. *Si in plebibus*: "The

---

[6] We are uncertain as to what this refers to.

archdeacon together with the clerics and people of his community shall do the choosing." Ch. *Sacrorum canonum*: "The emperors Charles and Louis decree that bishops are to be chosen through an election by the clergy and the people, according to the statutes of the canons." Jerome, *Ad Rusticum monachum*: "So live in the monastery that you may deserve to be a priest. When you shall have arrived at a mature age, and either the people or the bishop elect you to the priesthood, then perform the duties of a priest." Ambrose, Bk. 10, Letter No. 82: "He has deservedly become a great man whom the whole church has chosen, and it is rightly believed that he whom all the people requested has been elected according to the judgment of God."

14. Later on, when emperors and kings had embraced the Christian religion, their will, judgment, and authority also began to be brought to bear and to be requested in the matter of electing and calling, because they ought to be nurses of the church and according to the examples of Jehoshaphat, Hezekiah, and Josiah the oversight was committed to them in order that the ministries of the church might be rightly set up and administered. There are many canons about this matter, dist. 63. According to Sozomen, Bk. 7, ch. 7, the emperor gives the first place at the synod to Gregory of Nazianzus, and all the bishops support him. A very beautiful example of modesty is described in ch. *Valentinianus*, where the synod asks that the emperor, as a wise and pious man, should choose or propose someone. The emperor, however, answers: "The election is up to you. For you, possessing divine grace, and shining with such splendor, are better able to choose." Afterward he gave his assent to the election.

15. The fact that certain examples of the ancient church seem to deviate somewhat from this format is due to the following cause. This glorious harmony of bishops, clergy, the Christian magistrate, and the people in choosing and calling ministers of the church was very often disturbed. Clerics who were either heretics or schismatics, or were corrupted by other ignoble passions, often abused the right of election or arrogated it to themselves alone. In

that case both the magistrates and the Christian people were compelled to interpose themselves. Thus, when after the death of Aelurus the clergy on their own authority had elected Peter Mongo as bishop, Emperor Zeno was so angry that he even caused some to be punished, *Evagrius*, Bk. 3, ch. 11. When at Antioch, in the absence of the people, Porphyry had been ordained as bishop by a few bishops, a frightful tumult followed, *Nicephorus*, Bk. 13, ch. 30. Courtiers also repeatedly abused this, as though in their own right. In that case the clergy opposed them. A number of statutes of this kind are found in dist. 63. The most discreet regulation of all is that of Charles and Louis, which reads thus: "Mindful of the sacred canons, in order that the holy church may more freely possess her honor in the name of God, we proffer our assent to the ecclesiastical arrangement that bishops shall, according to the rules of the canons, be chosen by election of clergy and people."

16. Also the people very often abused their right in a way that led to tumults, dissensions, and all kinds of disorder. There bishops and Christian governments stepped in, as in the election of Ambrose. As a result a Laodicean canon says: "It must not be permitted to bring about by tumult[7] the election of those who are to be advanced to the priesthood." According to Sozomen, Bk. 7, ch. 8, when the votes of the bishops and those of the people were against each other, the emperor chose Nectarius, and this election was afterward held valid by a synod. But the people or the Christian magistrates were not for this reason simply excluded from choosing and calling, but this moderation was added, dist. 62: "The people must be taught, not followed. We also ought to inform them, if they do not know what is lawful or what is not lawful, not give them our consent." A decree of Leo says: "Let the desires of the citizens, the testimonies of the people, the will of those who are respected, and the choice of the clerics be determined in the ordination of priests." Likewise: "Let those who are to become priests

---

[7] The Latin word is *turbis*, which may also be translated "crowds" or "mobs." Nigrinus so understands it, and translates: *Es ist dem gemeinen Volk nicht zuzulassen*, etc.

be asked for peaceably and quietly; the election must have the subscription of the clerics, the testimony of those who are respected,
the consent of the order and of the people." Likewise: "Let the
consent and desire of the clergy and of the people be sought." And
in ch. *Nosse*: "When clergy and people have been summoned, let
such a one be chosen whom the sacred canons do not make ineligible. For it is in fact an election of priests, and the consent of the
faithful people must be added, because the people must be taught,
not followed." In the *Historia tripartita* the common people were
able to choose and to offer someone with their petition. Being a
bishop, Cyprian, Bk. 3, *Letters*, and Bk. 4, proposes Saturus, Opta-
tus, and Celerinus to the church. Valerius, desiring Augustine as his
assistant and successor, proposes this to the people. And Augustine
himself, *Letter No. 110*, in a lovely plea informs the people that he
desires Eradius as his successor, "Because I know," says he, "that
the churches are usually troubled after the death of bishops by ambitious and contentious men, and I ought, as far as I am able, to
take forethought for this city, that this may not happen." This
choice of Augustine is confirmed by the people, and this is made
known to the Emperors Theodosius and Valentinian. Augustine
also relates the example of Severus of Mileve, who had thought it
sufficient to point out his successor to the clergy and had therefore
not spoken before the people. As a result a disturbance arose afterward. Augustine says about this: "However, somewhat too little
had been done." Cyprian describes the manner of election in use at
his time thus, Bk. 1, Letter No. 4: "Therefore the people, in obedience to the Lord's commands and in the fear of God, ought to
separate themselves from a sinner who is placed over them, nor to
attend the sacrifices of a sacrilegious priest, since they especially
have the power either to choose worthy priests or to refuse unworthy ones. For we see that also this comes down to us by divine authority, that a priest should be selected in the presence of the people, before the eyes of all, and be approved as worthy and fit by
public judgment and testimony." And a little later: "God commands that a priest should be appointed before the whole assem-

bly, i.e., He teaches and shows that it should not be done except with the knowledge of the people who assist, so that either the misdeeds of the wicked may be revealed or the merits of the good made known in the presence of the people, and let that be a just and lawful ordination which has been examined by the vote and judgment of all, and let this be observed in action afterward according to the divine instructions." In the same place: "We sometimes see unworthy persons ordained, not according to the will of God but by human presumption. That whatever does not proceed from a legitimate and just ordination is displeasing to God, God Himself shows through the prophet Hosea, when he says: 'They made kings, but not through Me' (Hos. 8:4). Therefore the divine teaching and the apostolic custom must be diligently preserved and adhered to, which is held also among us and throughout nearly all the provinces, that for rightly conducted ordinations the five closest bishops of that province come together to the people for whom an overseer is to be ordained, and a bishop be chosen in the presence of the people who know the life of the individual candidates well and have insight into the actions and way of life of each," etc. The same says, Bk. 1, Letter No. 3, that the vote of the people and the consensus of fellow bishops is a divine judgment.

17. However, because it was not convenient for the whole multitude of the people always to be called together, and to ascertain the vote of every individual, the custom was observed among Christians, as Lampridius reports in a biography of Alexander, that the names of those who had been proposed for choosing and calling were openly published before the ordination, and the people were admonished that if anyone had anything against a man who was to be ordained, he should bring it up and set it forth. And in short, according to the statement of Gregory, it was always judged a grave abuse if anyone was given to such as were unwilling and did not ask for him.

18. This is the opinion of the primitive apostolic and ancient church about the lawful election of ministers of the Word and the sacraments, which opinion is followed in the churches which have

now been ordered according to the Word of God, where there is a presbytery which embraces the faithful Word as taught, a godly government, and people who know the doctrine and love godliness. But where there were at the time of the apostles idle priests, wicked rulers, people who walked in darkness, there at first the ministry could not be established through such an election, but there the apostles either went themselves or sent others who had been rightly elected elsewhere, that they should first lay the foundations. Thus Paul and Barnabas are sent to the Gentiles (Acts 13:2–3). And thus the Gospel was spread all the way to Phoenicia and Cyprus, and indeed thus it was first proclaimed to the Gentiles at Antioch (Acts 11:19). Thus Paul had many around him whom he sent here and there to the churches. But where the churches had been in a measure grounded, the ministries in the churches were soon ordered in the manner we have described (Acts 14:23). And although there the magistrates and priests continued in idolatry, the calling which was done by pure teachers together with faithful people was nevertheless lawful. Thus when the chief priests and priests had in part given up, in part devoted themselves to groves and high places, etc., and the people walked in darkness, Jehoshaphat himself set up ministries (2 Chron. 17 and 19).

19. I undertook this report in order to show that our churches have restored the true and lawful manner of choosing and calling, which was in use in the apostolic, primitive, and ancient church, and that from the contrast it might be seen more clearly what kind the ordination that of the papalist church is. From the things we have said until now, the examination of the Tridentine decree concerning the lawful calling and sending of ministers of the Word and the sacraments will be easy. For the fourth chapter and the seventh canon declare that those are lawful ministers of the Word and the sacraments who have been called, ordained, and sent by the papalist bishops and their subordinates alone, and that neither the consent nor the call and authority of the faithful people or of a pious government are required. Yes, they pronounce the anathema on anyone who says that for a legitimate call the consent

of the faithful people or of a pious government is required. But we have already clearly shown that the manner of a lawful election or call which the men of Trent condemn with the anathema is the manner of the apostolic, primitive, and ancient church. But we must remember that the concern which was laid on the Tridentine fathers by the Roman pontiff was not that they should restore the custom of the apostolic and ancient church but that they should preserve and strengthen the present state of the papalist kingdom in any way they could. What therefore they have until now practiced they want to have permitted to them with impunity hereafter, namely, that they be able to place over the churches any and all men who have been rendered suitable by partiality, request, or bribery, without a petition, consent, or vocation either of the faithful people or of a pious government, and to foist unknown men on the people. The assistants to the bishops do not even see fit to ask questions about the call so long as a person provides them an allowance and offers them money for the ordination. And the good fathers are not ashamed to establish with no more than a word things which clearly and diametrically are opposed to Scripture and to the true antiquity, and at once to append the anathema.

20. In our churches, however, the ministers of the Word and the sacraments are not only called and placed into office by the people and the secular government, as the Tridentine chapter imagines, but there comes to these the very weighty judgment, examination, and approval of the true presbytery. That this is a legitimate call we have already abundantly shown.

21. But why, they ask, do you not seek ordination from our bishops? I answer: if they were true bishops, and professed sound doctrine, they would rightly claim this for themselves. But now they are enemies and persecutors of the true doctrine. Does a shepherd ask that the care of a flock should be entrusted to him by a wolf? And they are not willing to ordain anyone who adheres to sound doctrine unless he first rejects and abjures it. Neither do they admit to ordination those who have been legitimately called according to the apostolic manner, lest damage arise from this for their

kingdom. Nor do they ordain their priests to the ministry of the Word and the sacraments, but to the impious sacrifice of the Mass. They also ensnare those whom they ordain in ungodly obligations, and apply their blasphemous chrism. Therefore we have the most weighty and just causes why we do not ask ordination from the enemies of the sound doctrine.

22. But they say: "Those who have not been called, ordained, and sent by the usual ecclesiastical authority are thieves and robbers." That will make thieves and robbers of the apostles, evangelists, pastors, teachers, presbyters, and deacons of the apostolic church, who were not ordained by the chief priests, who at that time had the regular ecclesiastical power. That is the same question with which the chief priests once attacked the ministry of the Baptist (John 1:19–25) and of Christ Himself, (Matt. 21:23): "Who gave You this authority?"

INTRODUCTION TO ZACHARIAS URSINUS'S *COMMENTARY ON THE HEIDELBERG CATECHISM*

WE NOTED in the introduction to the selection from Ignatius of Loyola, the one note that most differentiated Reformation from Counter-Reformation spirituality was that of comfort or assurance. Although Catholic apologists frequently chided the Reformers, as Enlightenment intellectuals were later to do also, for an overemphasis on the depth of human sin and depravity, the focal point of all good Protestant theology was always calm comfort in the mercy of Christ. This sentiment was given its most memorable expression in the great words of Question 1 of the Heidelberg Catechism:

Q. What is your only comfort in life and in death?

> That I am not my own, but belong, body and soul, in life and in death, to my faithful Savior Jesus Christ, who has fully paid for all my sins and delivered me from the dominion of the devil. He also watches over me in such a way that not a hair can fall from my head without the will of my father in heaven; in fact, all things must work together for my salvation. Because I belong to him, Christ, by his Holy Spirit, assures me of eternal life, and makes me wholeheartedly willing and ready from now on to live for him.

This document, however, was to emerge out of a decidedly uncomfortable moment in the history of Protestantism: the moment when the Lutheran and Reformed branches of the Reformation began to draw clear battle lines as opposing parties. There had, to be sure, been different teachings and emphases among the leading Reformers from the beginning, and on the matter of the Lord's Supper in particular, the early disagreement between Luther and Zwingli in the 1520s, although largely ironed out, or papered over (depending on your perspective) in the 1530s and 1540s, remained a source of tension between churches more influenced by Wittenberg and those more influenced by Zurich.

However, conflict did not seriously erupt until the 1550s, precipitated chiefly by intra-Lutheran squabbles as to who represented the truer heirs of Luther's theology. Melanchthon had always reserved the right to disagree with Luther when necessary, and as his own thinking on the matter of the Lord's Supper in particular evolved, he taught a doctrine that had clear affinities with that of Calvin, prompting loud denunciations from a party that came to be called Gnesio (that is, "authentic")-Lutherans. Still, until Melanchthon's death in 1560, there was a fair bit of wiggle room between the emerging confessional boundaries.

It was into this fast-disappearing wiggle room that Elector Frederick III of the Palatinate (1515–1576), an important principality in western Germany, tried to squeeze in the late 1550s and early 1560s. Frederick was determined to make the Palatinate, and especially the university in his capital city, Heidelberg, a beacon of the Reformation. To that end, he surrounded himself with leading disciples of Melanchthon and also some theologians trained in Zurich and Geneva, inviting increasing condemnations from Gnesio-Lutheran leaders around Germany. Seeking a full confessional statement that would highlight the common ground among Protestants, and that would serve as an effective teaching tool for his people, Frederick commissioned the Heidelberg Catechism, which appeared in 1563.

Its lead author, Zacharias Ursinus (1534–1583), epitomized the middle way Frederick was seeking to forge. Born in 1534, he had trained in theology at Wittenberg under the tutelage of Melanchthon, quickly becoming one of his star students and developing a close friendship with the great teacher. As intra-Lutheran conflict became more fierce, however, he went to Zurich in 1560 to study with one of the giants of the emerging Reformed tradition, Peter Martyr Vermigli. A year later he was called to Heidelberg to teach in the University, and the next year, appointed to the drafting committee of the Catechism, in which he seems to have taken the leading role. Despite his success in producing a document which breathes the spirit of Melanchthon and Calvin equally, not to mention showing the influence of other leading theologians, the Heidelberg Catechism was to provoke even sharper opposition than Frederick had faced before, and the Palatinate found itself increasingly isolated from other territories in Lutheran Germany.

Indeed, when Frederick died in 1576, his son Louis sought to align the Palatinate fully with the Gnesio-Lutherans, and drove out Ursinus and the other theologians at Heidelberg, an effort that was cut short by his own death in 1583. Ursinus, sadly, died that same year when only 48 years old, too soon to return to Heidelberg. Fortunately, however, he had succeeded before his death in producing, alongside many other brilliant works of theology, a series of lectures comprising a complete commentary on the Catechism, thoroughly elaborating the doctrines so succinctly stated in it. This text was edited into publishable form by his student David Pareus (1548–1622), who was subsequently to become one of the brightest luminaries of German Reformed theology. The Catechism itself, meanwhile, was to find before long a much wider sphere of influence than the Palatinate, being officially adopted by the Dutch Reformed Church in 1618 as one of their Three Forms of Unity, and has continued to serve as the official catechism of the Dutch and German Reformed down to the present.

The following excerpt provides the text of questions 86–91 of the Catechism, together with Ursinus's commentary. In this section, Ursinus turns to consider the role of good works in the life of a Christian as the fruits of gratitude which the justified believer should display to God and neighbor. This reflects a growing emphasis within the second generation of the Reformation, as well as within the Reformed tradition generally, which sought to counteract concerns that the proclamation of justification by faith alone might lead to an aimless antinomianism, rather than a disciplined and holy life.

However, Ursinus does not in any way back down from the affirmation that works in no way contribute to justification. In a theological *tour de force* that is particularly on display in his lengthy treatment of Q. 91, he answers such vexing questions and objections as these:

- In what sense are good works necessary to salvation?
- Are all our works before justification displeasing to God?
- If so, how can we still distinguish between moral and immoral works of the unregenerate?
- Are all our works after justification still tainted with sin?
- If so, how can they be pleasing to God?

Ursinus's careful answers to these questions represent a powerful clarification and defense of the Protestant position against Roman Catholic critiques that had been voiced from *Exsurge Domine* down to the Council of Trent and beyond.

Further Reading

For further reading, see Lyle D. Bierma, et. al., eds., *An Introduction to the Heidelberg Catechism: Sources, History, Theology* (Grand Rapids: Baker Academic, 2005); Lyle D. Bierma, *The Theology of the Heidelberg Catechism: A Reformation Synthesis* (Louisville, KY: Westminster John Knox Press, 2013).

ZACHARIAS URSINUS, *COMMENTARY ON THE HEIDELBERG CATECHISM* (1585)[1]

Heidelberg Catechism Question 86

> **Question 86.** Since then we are delivered from our misery, merely of grace through Christ, without any merit of ours, why must we still do good works?
>
> **Answer.** Because that Christ, having redeemed and delivered us by his blood, also renews us by his Holy Spirit, after his own image; that so we may testify, by the whole of our conduct, our gratitude to God for his blessings, and that he may be praised by us; also, that every one may be assured in himself of his faith, by the fruits thereof; and that by our godly conversation others may be gained to Christ.

Exposition

This Question, with respect to the moving causes of good works, is placed first, even before the Question relating to man's conversion, not because good works precede conversion, but because the things which follow are in this way more strikingly connected with

---

[1] Taken from George W. Williard, trans., *The Commentary of Dr. Zacharias Ursinus on the Heidelberg Catechism* (Cincinnati, OH: Elm Street Printing, 1888).

what precedes. Human reason argues in this way from the doctrine of free satisfaction: He is not bound to make satisfaction, for whom another has already satisfied. Christ has satisfied for us. Therefore, there is no need that we should perform good works. We reply that there is more in the conclusion than in the premises. All that legitimately follows is: Therefore, we ourselves are not bound to make satisfaction, which we grant, 1. In respect to the justice of God, which does not demand a double payment. 2. In respect to our salvation, which, in other respects, would be no salvation. Yet we are, nevertheless, bound to render obedience, and perform good works, for the reasons which are referred to, and explained in the above Question of the Catechism:

1. Because good works are the fruits of our regeneration by the Holy Spirit, which are always connected with our free justification. "Whom he called, them he also justified, and whom he justified, them he also glorified"; "Such were some of you; but ye are washed; but ye are sanctified; but ye are justified," &c. (Rom. 8:30; 1 Cor. 6:11). Those, therefore, who do not perform good works show that they are neither regenerated by the Spirit of God, nor redeemed by the blood of Christ.

2. That we may express our gratitude to God for the benefit of redemption. "Yield your members as instruments of righteousness unto God"; "That ye present your bodies, a living sacrifice, holy, acceptable unto God, which is your reasonable service," &c. (Rom. 6:13; 12:1).

3. That God may be glorified by us. "Let your light so shine before men, that they may see your good works, and glorify your Father which is in heaven"; "That they may, by your good works, which they shall behold, glorify God in the day of visitation." (Matt. 5:16; 1 Pet. 2:12).

4. Because they are the fruits of faith—that by which our own faith, as well as the faith of others is judged of. "Give diligence, to make your calling and election sure;" after which certain copies add the words, by good works. "Every good tree bringeth forth good fruit; but a corrupt tree bringeth forth evil fruit"; "Faith

worketh by love"; "But the fruit of the Spirit is love, joy, peace, long-suffering, gentleness, goodness, faith, meekness, temperance" (2 Pet. 1:10; Matt. 7:17; Gal. 5:6, 22).

5. That we may bring others to Christ. "When thou art converted, strengthen thy brethren"; "Ye wives, be in subjection to your own husbands, that, if any obey not the word, they also may, without the word, be won by the conversation of their wives"; "Let us follow after the things which make for peace, and things wherewith one may edify another" (Luke 22:32; 1 Pet. 3:1; Rom. 14:19). These causes, now, must be explained and urged with great diligence, in our sermons and exhortations to the people; and here we may cite, as being in point, the whole of the sixth chapter, and the first part of the eighth chapter of Paul's epistle to the Romans, down to the sixteenth verse.

For a further explanation of the first cause, we may remark that the benefit of justification is not given without regeneration: 1. Because Christ has merited both; viz., the remission of sins, and the habitation of God within us by the Holy Spirit. The Holy Spirit, now, is never inactive, but is always efficacious, and so brings it to pass that those in whom he dwells are made conformable to God. 2. Because the heart is purified by faith: for in all those to whom the merits of Christ are applied by faith, there is kindled the love of God, and a desire to do those things which are pleasing in his sight. 3. Because God bestows the benefit of justification upon none, but such as render true gratitude. But no one ever renders true gratitude except those who receive the benefit of regeneration. Therefore, neither of these can be separated from the other.

We must also observe the difference which exists between the first and second causes. The first shows what Christ effects in us by virtue of his death; whilst the second teaches to what we are bound in view of the benefits received.

Heidelberg Catechism Question 87

> **Question 87.** Cannot they then be saved, who, continuing in their wicked and ungrateful lives, are not converted to God?
>
> **Answer.** By no means; for the holy Scripture declares that no unchaste person, idolater, adulterer, thief, covetous man, drunkard, slanderer, robber, or any such like shall inherit the kingdom of God.

Exposition

This Question naturally grows out of the preceding one; for since good works are the fruits of our regeneration—since they are the expression of our thankfulness to God, and the evidences of true faith; and since none are saved but those in whom these things are found, it follows, on the other hand, that evil works are the fruits of the flesh—that they are manifestations of ingratitude, and evidences of unbelief, so that no one that continues to produce them can be saved. Hence, all those who are not converted to God from their evil works, but continue in their sins, are condemned for ever, according to the following declarations of the word of God: "Know ye not that the unrighteous shall not inherit the kingdom of God? be not deceived; neither fornicators, nor idolaters, nor adulterers, nor effeminate, &c., shall inherit the kingdom of God"; "Of the which I have told you in times past that they which do such things, shall not inherit the kingdom of God"; "For this ye know; that no whoremonger, nor unclean person, nor covetous man, who is an idolater, hath any inheritance in the kingdom of Christ and of God; for because of these things cometh the wrath of God upon the children of disobedience"; "He that loveth not his brother abideth in death" (1 Cor. 6:9; Gal. 5:21; Eph. 5:5, 6; 1 John 3:14).

We may also observe that another reason for good works may be deduced from the consequence which results from evil works; viz., that all those who perform evil works, and continue in their wicked and ungrateful lives, cannot be saved, inasmuch as they are destitute of true faith, and conversion.

Heidelberg Catechism Questions 88-90

Question 88. In how many parts doth the true conversion of man consist?
Answer. In two parts; in the mortification of the old, and in the quickening of the new man.

Question 89. What is the mortification of the old man?
Answer. It is a sincere sorrow of heart, that we have provoked God by our sins; and more and more to hate and flee from them.

Question 90. What is the quickening of the new man?
Answer. It is a sincere joy of heart in God, through Christ, and with love and delight to live according to the will of God in all good works.

Exposition

The doctrine touching man's conversion to God now claims our attention, concerning which we must inquire:

Is conversion necessary?
What is it?
Of how many parts does it consist?
What are the causes of it?
What are the effects of it?
Is it perfect in this life?
In what does the conversion of the godly differ from the repentance of the wicked?

I. Is The Conversion Of Man To God Necessary?

Man's conversion in this life is so necessary that without it no one can obtain everlasting life in the world to come, according to what the Scriptures teach: "Except a man be born of water and of the Spirit, he cannot enter into the kingdom of God"; "Except ye repent, ye shall all likewise perish"; "They which do such things shall not inherit the kingdom of God"; "If so be that being clothed we shall not be found naked" (John 3:5; Luke 13:3; 1 Cor. 6:9; 2 Cor. 5:3). The example of the foolish virgins (Matt. 25:1-10) who were excluded from the marriage, because they had not their lamps burning and filled with oil, is here in point. We may also here cite the following declarations of Christ: "Let your loins be girded about, and your lights burning"; "Be ye ready also; for the Son of man cometh at an hour when ye think not"; "The Lord of that servant will come in a day when he looketh not for him, and at an hour when he is not aware, and will cut him in sunder, and will appoint him his portion with the unbelievers" (Luke 12:35, 40, 46). We may here also quote the notable saying of Cyprian against Demetrius: "When we have once departed this life, there is no more room for repentance, or work of satisfaction. Here life is either lost or gained: here we secure our eternal salvation by the worship of God and the fruit of faith. Nor let any one be hindered, either by sin or external opposition, from coming to obtain salvation. No repentance is too late for any one still remaining in the world," &c. From this it appears how necessary conversion is for those who are to be saved. Hence all our exhortations to repentance must be based upon the absolute necessity of conversion to God, in all those who are to be justified.

II. What Is Man's Conversion To God?

The Hebrew expresses the idea of conversion by the word *Teschubah*; the Greek by μετανοια and μεταμελεια. There are some who affirm that these Greek words differ from each other in this: that the former is used only in reference to the repentance of the godly, whilst the latter is used also in reference to the repentance of the ungodly. Of Judas it is said, that he repented himself (Matt. 27:3), where the word μεταμεληθας, is used. Of Esau it is said, he found no place of repentance (μετανοιας). (Heb. 12:17.) Of God it is said (Rom. 11:29), the gifts of God are without repentance, where the word αμεταμελητα is used, that is, they are of such a kind that he himself cannot repent of them. The Septuagint, in speaking of God, uses both words without making any distinction. It repents me (μεταμελομα) that I have set up Saul to be king (1 Sam. 15:11). The Strength of Israel will not lie nor repent (ου μετανοησει). The difference, therefore, is either very small, or none at all, unless that the former Greek word above mentioned properly signifies a change of the mind, whilst the latter expresses a change of the will or purpose. In conversion, however, there is a change both of the understanding and the will.

The Latins have a number of words by which they express the same thing. They call it *regeneratio, renovatio, resipiscentia, conversio, pœnitentia. Resipiscentia* seems properly to correspond with the Greek μετανοια; for as *resipiscentia* is derived from *resipisco*, which means to become wise after having done a thing, so μετανοια is from μετανοεω, which means to become wise after having committed something wrong, to change the mind, and to alter the purpose. *Pœnitenia* is said to be derived either from *pœnitet* or from *pœna*, because the sorrow which is in repentance is, as it were, a punishment. Or else, as Erasmus supposes, it is from *pone tenendo*, as if to repent were to lay hold of a later purpose, or to understand a thing after it is done. But whatever may be the derivation of the word *pœnitentia* or repentance, it is more obscure than the term conversion. For repentance does not comprehend the whole extent of the subject—it does not express from what, and to what we are changed, but merely signifies the sorrow which is felt after the commission of some sin. Conversion, on the other hand, embraces the whole, as it adds that which is the beginning of a new life by faith.

The term repentance is, moreover, of a broader signification than conversion: for conversion is spoken of only in reference to the godly, who alone are converted to God. The same thing may be said of μετανοια and *resipiscentia*—that they refer merely to the godly, for by these three terms the new life of the godly is signified. But *pœnitentia* is spoken of the ungodly also, as of Judas, who did indeed repent of his wicked deed, but was not converted, because the ungodly, when they sorrow, are not converted or reformed. Thus far we have spoken of the terms which have reference to this subject; we must now proceed to inquire into the thing itself.

A definition, with respect to the parts of conversion, may be obtained from the 88th Question of the Catechism, where it is defined to be the mortification of the old, and the quickening of the new man. It is more fully expressed in the following definition: Man's conversion to God consists in a change of the corrupt mind and will into that which is good, produced by the Holy Ghost through the preaching of the law and the gospel, which is followed by a sincere desire to produce the fruits of repentance, and a conformity of the life to all the commands of God. This definition is confirmed by the following passages of Scripture: "If thou wilt return, return unto me"; "Wash you, make you clean"; "But ye are washed; but ye are sanctified in the name of the Lord Jesus, and by the Spirit of our God"; "Depart from evil, and do good" (Jer. 4:1; Is. 1:16; 1 Cor. 6:11; Ps. 34:14.) The whole definition is expressed in Acts 26:18, 20: "I send thee to open their eyes, and to turn them from darkness to light, and from the power of Satan unto God, that they may receive forgiveness of sins, and inheritance among them which are sanctified by faith that is in me. ... But shewed that they should repent, and turn to God, and do works meet for repentance."

III. Of How Many Parts Does Conversion Consist?

Conversion consists of two parts: the mortification of the old man, and the quickening of the new man. We speak more properly in this way, using the language of Paul, than if we were, as some do, to make conversion consist in contrition and faith. By contrition they understand mortification; and by faith the joy which follows the desire of righteousness and new obedience, which are indeed effects of faith, but not faith itself. Contrition also precedes conversion, but is not conversion itself, nor any part of it, being only a preparation, or that which leads to conversion; and that only in the elect. The old man which is mortified is the sinner only, or the corrupt nature of man. The new man which is quickened is he who begins to depart from sin, or it is the nature of man as regenerated. The mortification of the old man, or of the flesh, consists in the laying off and subduing of the corruption of our nature, and includes, 1. A knowledge of sin, and of the wrath of God. 2. Sorrow for sin, and on account of having offended God. 3. Hatred of sin, and an earnest desire to avoid it. The Scriptures speak of this mortification of sin in the following places: "If ye through the Spirit do mortify the deeds of the body, ye shall live"; "Rend your hearts, and not your garments"; "Come and let us return unto the Lord; for he hath torn, and he will heal us; he hath smitten, and he will bind us up" (Rom. 8:13; Joel 2:13; Hosea 6:1). From this it appears that mortification, or conversion, is very improperly attributed to the wicked, in whom there is no hatred or shunning of sin, nor sorrow for sin, all of which is embraced in the mortification of the old man. A knowledge of sin precedes sorrow, because the affections of the heart follow knowledge. Sorrow may follow a knowledge of sin on the part of the ungodly, from a sense of present, and from a fear of future evil, viz: of temporal and eternal punishment; yet this sorrow is not properly a part of conversion, nor a preparation to it, but rather a flight and turning away from God, and a rushing into desperation, as in the case of Cain, Saul, Judas, &c. It is called a sorrow, not unto salvation—the sorrow of the world, working death—a sorrow not after a godly sort, &c. In the godly, however, this sorrow arises from a sense of the displeasure of God, which they sincerely acknowledge and lament, and is connected with a hatred and abhorrence of all past sins, and with a shunning or turning away from all present and future sin. This sorrow is a part of conversion, or at least a preparation to it, and is called a sorrow unto salvation—a sorrow which is after a godly sort, working repentance unto salvation. The knowledge of sin, sorrow for sin, and a flying from it, differ in their subject, or as it respects that part of our being in which they have their proper seat. The knowledge of sin is in the mind, sorrow for sin in the heart, and fleeing from it in the will. The turning, which is included in conversion, is in the heart and will, and is a turning from one thing to another—from evil to good, according to what the Psalmist says: "Depart from evil and do good" (Ps. 34:14).

It is called in Scripture mortification, 1. Because, as one that is dead cannot perform the actions of a living man, so our nature, when its corruption is once removed, no more performs the actions peculiar to it in its corrupt state; that is, it does not produce actual sin when original sin is once circumscribed and kept under proper restraint. "For he that is dead as freed from sin" (Rom. 6:7). 2. Because this mortification is not without wrestling and pain: "for the flesh lusteth against the Spirit" (Gal. 5:17). It is for this reason that this mortification is called a crucifixion of the flesh. "They that are Christ's have crucified the flesh with the affections and lusts" (Gal. 5:24). 3. Because it is a ceasing from sin. It is, moreover, not simply called mortification, but the mortification of the old man, because, by it not the substance of man, but sin in man, is destroyed. The expression, old man, is also added for the purpose of distinguishing between the repentance of the godly and ungodly; for in the godly, not the man, but the old man is destroyed, whilst in the ungodly it is not the old man, but the man.

The quickening of the new man is a true joy and delight in God, through Christ, and an earnest and sincere desire to regulate the life according to the will of God, and to perform all good works. It embraces three things which are different from what is included in mortification: 1. A knowledge of the mercy of God, and an application of it in Christ. 2. Joy and delight arising from the fact that God is reconciled to us through Christ, and that obedience is begun in us and shall be perfected. 3. An ardent desire to perform new obedience, or to sin no more, but to render gratitude to God during our whole life, and to retain his love, which desire is itself new obedience according to the following declarations of Scripture: "Being justified by faith we have peace with God through our Lord Jesus Christ"; "The kingdom of God is righteousness, and peace, and joy in the Holy Ghost"; "I dwell in the high and holy place; with him also that is of a contrite and humble spirit to revive the spirit of the humble, and to revive the heart of the contrite ones"; "Likewise, reckon ye also yourselves to be dead indeed unto sin, but alive unto God through Jesus Christ our Lord"; "Nevertheless I live; yet not I, but Christ liveth in me; and the life which I now live in the flesh, I live by the faith of the Son of God, who loved me and gave himself for me" (Rom. 5:1; 14:17; Is. 57:15; Rom. 6:11; Gal. 2:20).

This part of conversion is called quickening, 1. Because, as a living man performs the actions of one that is alive, so this quickening includes the kindling of new light in the understanding, and the producing of new qualities and activities in the will and heart, from which a new life and new works proceed. 2. Because it includes on the part of those who are converted, joy and delight in God, which affords great comfort and consolation. It is added through Christ, because we cannot rejoice in God, unless he be reconciled unto us. It is now only through Christ that God is reconciled unto us. Hence, we only rejoice in God through Christ.

These two parts of conversion spring from faith. The reason is, because no one can hate sin and draw nigh to God, unless he loves God. But no one loves God who is not possessed of faith. Hence, although there is no express mention made of faith in either part of conversion, this is done, not because faith is excluded from conversion, but because the whole doctrine of conversion and thankfulness presupposes it, as a cause is presupposed from the presence of its own peculiar effect.

Obj. But faith produces joy. Therefore, it does not produce grief and mortification.

Ans. It is not absurd to affirm that the same cause produces different effects by a different kind of operation and in different respects. So faith produces grief, not of itself, but by an accident, which is sin, by which we offend God our kind and gracious father. Of itself it produces joy, because it assures us of God's fatherly will towards us, by and for the sake of Christ.

Reply. The preaching of the law precedes faith, since the preaching of repentance commences with the law. But the preaching of the law works sorrow and wrath. Therefore, there is a certain sorrow before faith.

Ans. We grant that there is a certain sorrow before faith, but not such as constitutes a part of conversion, for the sorrow of the ungodly which is before and without faith is rather a turning away from God, than a return to him, which being contrary, cannot agree neither wholly nor in part. But the contrition and sorrow which the elect experience is a certain preparation, leading to conversion, as we have already shown.

IV. What Are The Causes Of Conversion?

The Holy Spirit, or God himself, is the chief efficient cause of our conversion. Hence, it is that the saints pray that God would convert them, and that repentance is frequently called in the Scriptures the gift of God. "Turn thou me and I shall be turned, for thou art the Lord my God"; "Turn thou us unto thee, O Lord, and we shall be turned"; "Him hath God exalted with his right hand to be a Prince and a Saviour to give repentance to Israel, and forgiveness of sins," from which we may draw a most forcible argument in proof of the Divinity of Christ, inasmuch as it is peculiar to God alone to grant repentance and forgiveness of sins; "Then hath God also to the Gentiles granted repentance unto life"; "If God, peradventure, will give them repentance to the acknowledging of the truth, and that they may recover themselves out of the snare of the devil," &c. (Jer. 31:18; Lamen. 5:21; Acts 5:31; 11:18; 2 Tim. 2:25).

The means or instrumental causes of conversion are the law—the gospel, and again, the doctrine of the law after that of the gospel. For the preaching of the law goes before, preparing and leading us to a knowledge of the gospel: "for by the law is the knowledge of sin" (Rom. 3:20). Hence, there can be no sorrow for sin without the law. After the sinner has once been led to a knowledge of sin, then the preaching of the gospel follows, encouraging contrite hearts by the assurance of the mercy of God through Christ. Without this preaching there is no faith, and without faith there is no love to God, and hence no conversion to him. After the preaching of the gospel, the preaching of the law again follows, that it may be the rule of our thankfulness and of our life. The law, therefore, precedes, and follows conversion. It precedes that it may lead to a knowledge and sorrow for sin; it follows that it may serve as a rule of life to the converted. It is for this reason that the prophets first charge sin upon the ungodly, threaten punishment, and exhort to repentance; then comfort and promise pardon and forgiveness; and lastly, again exhort and prescribe the duties of piety and godliness. Such was, also, the character of the preaching of John the Baptist. It is in this way, that the preaching of repentance comprehends the law and the gospel, although in effecting conversion each has a part to perform peculiar to itself.

The next instrumental and internal cause of conversion is faith. Without faith there is no love to God, and unless we know what the will of God towards us is, viz., that he will remit unto us our sins by and for the sake of Christ, conversion will never be begun in us, neither as its respects the mortification of the old man, nor as it respects the quickening of the new: for by faith the heart is purified (Acts 15:9). Without faith we can have no true joy or delight in God; without faith we cannot love God; and whatsoever is not of faith is sin (Rom. 14:23). All good works proceed from faith, as their fountain. "Being justified by faith, we have peace with God through our Lord Jesus Christ" (Rom. 5:1).

The causes which contribute to our conversion are the cross, with the chastisements inflicted upon ourselves and others; also the benefits, punishments and example of others, &c. "Thou hast chastised me, and I was chastised, as a bullock unaccustomed to the yoke"; "It is good for me that I have been afflicted, that I might learn thy statutes"; "Let your light so shine before men, that they may see your good works and glorify your Father which is in heaven" (Jer. 31:18; Ps. 119:71; Matt. 5:16). The subject, or matter in which conversion is grounded, is the understanding, the will, the heart, and all the affections of man in which a change is produced.

The form of conversion is the turning itself with all the circumstances that are connected with it, which includes, 1. As it respects the mind and understanding, a correct judgment of God, together with his will and works; 2. As it respects the will, a sincere and earnest desire to avoid those falls and things which offend God, with a steady purpose to obey him, according to all his commandments; 3. As it respects the heart, new and holy desires and affections in accordance with the divine law; 4. As it respects the external actions and life, rectitude and obedience begun, according to the law of God. The object of conversion is, 1. Sin, or disobedience, which is the thing from which we are converted; 2. Righteousness, or new obedience, which is the thing to which we are converted. The chief end of conversion is the glory of God; the next end, which is subordinate to the glory of God, is our good, which consists in our blessedness and enjoyment of eternal life. The conversion of others is another end, still less principal, than those just mentioned. "And when thou art converted, strengthen thy brethren"; "Let your light so shine before men, that they may see your good works and glorify your Father which is in heaven" (Luke 22:32; Matt. 5:16).

The questions respecting Pelagianism are here properly in place: Whether a man can convert himself without the grace of the Holy Spirit, and, Whether a man can, by the exercise of his free power of choice, prepare himself for the reception of divine grace. Pelagius maintained the first, in opposition to what the Scriptures most plainly affirm. "Turn thou me, and I shall be turned;" "It is God which worketh in you, both to will and to do, of his good pleasure"; "A corrupt tree cannot bring forth good fruit" (Jer. 31:18; Phil. 2:13; Matt. 7:18). The Schoolmen and Papists at this day defend the last proposition respecting Pelagianism, in opposition to the explicit declarations of the word of God just cited, and also in contradiction to what Christ himself affirms, when he says, "No man can come to me, except the Father which hath sent me draw him" (John 6:44). Thomas Aquinas attributes a certain preparation to the free-will of man, but not conversion. He speaks however of this preparation, as though it contributed to the grace of conversion, which it does by the gracious aid of God, moving us inwardly. (*Vide sum. theol. partis primæ, parte secunda, quæst. 109, ad 6.*)

V. What Are The Effects Of Conversion?

The effects of conversion are, 1. A true and ardent love to God, and our neighbor; 2. An earnest desire to obey God, without any exception, according to all his commandments; 3. All good works, or new obedience itself; 4. A desire to convert others, and bring them in the way of salvation. In a word, the fruits of true repentance are the duties of piety towards God, and of charity towards our neighbor.

VI. Is Conversion Perfect In This Life?

Our conversion to God is not perfect in this life, but is here continually advancing, until it reaches the perfection which is proposed in the life to come. "We know in part" (1 Cor. 13:9). All the complaints and prayers of the saints are confirmations of this truth. "Cleanse thou me from secret faults"; "O wretched man that I am, who shall deliver me from the body of this death" (Ps. 19:13; Rom. 7:24). The conflict which is continually going on in those who are converted bears testimony to the same truth. "The flesh lusteth against the Spirit, and the Spirit against the flesh," &c. (Gal. 5:17). The same thing may be said of the exhortations of the prophets and apostles, in which they exhort those who are converted to turn more fully unto God. "He that is righteous, let him be righteous still, and he that is holy, let him be holy still" (Rev. 22:11). We may also establish the same thing in the following manner: Neither the mortification of the flesh, nor the quickening of the Spirit, is absolute or perfect in the saints in this life. Therefore, neither is conversion, which consists of these two parts, perfect. As it respects the mortification of the old man, the case is clear, and does not admit of doubt that it is not perfect in this life, because the saints do not only continually strive against the lust of the flesh, but they also often for a time yield, and give over in this conflict—often do they sin, fall and offend God, although they do not defend their sins, but detest, deplore, and endeavor to avoid them. As it regards the imperfection of the quickening of the new man, the same conflict is a sufficient testimony; and surely as our knowledge is now only in part, the renovation of the will and heart must also be imperfect: for the will follows the knowledge which we have.

There are two plain reasons why the will, in the case of those who are converted, tends imperfectly to the good in this life: 1. Because the renovation of our nature is never made perfect in this life, neither as it respects our knowledge of God, nor the inclination which we have to obey him. The single complaint and acknowledgment which the apostle Paul made is a sufficient proof of what we have just said. "I know that in me, that is, in my flesh dwelleth no good thing," &c. (Rom. 7:18, 19). 2. Because those who are converted are not always governed by the Holy Spirit, but are sometimes for a season deserted by God, either for the purpose of trying, or chastising, or humbling them; yet they are nevertheless brought to repentance, so as not to perish. "Lord, I believe, help thou mine unbelief" (Mark 9:24).

But why does God not perfect conversion in the case of his people in this life, seeing that he is able to effect it? The reasons are, 1. That the saints may be humbled and exercised in faith, patience, prayer and wrestling against the flesh, and that they may not boast of their perfection, thinking of themselves more highly than they ought, but daily pray; "Enter not into judgment with thy servant;" "Forgive us our sins" (Ps. 143:2; Matt. 6:12). 2. That they may press forward more and more unto perfection, and desire it more earnestly. That, trampling the world under their feet, they may run with greater alacrity in the Christian course, and aspire after those joys that are laid up in heaven, knowing that it will not be until then that they shall fully enjoy their promised inheritance. "Set your affection on things above, not on things on the earth, for ye are dead, and your life is hid with Christ in God"; "Mortify, therefore, your members which are upon the earth"; "It doth not yet appear what we shall be; but we know that when he shall appear, we shall be like him." (Col. 3:2, 3, 5; John 3:2).

Concerning this imperfection Calvin writes in the following expressive language: "This restoration is not accomplished in a single moment, or day, or year, but by continual, and sometimes even slow advances, the Lord destroys the carnal corruptions of his chosen, purifies them from all pollution, and consecrates them as temples to himself, renewing all their senses to real purity, that they may employ their whole life in the exercise of repentance, and know that this war are will be terminated only in death" (*Inst.* lib. 3. cap. 3. sec. 9). The sections following the one from which we have quoted, down to the fifteenth, may also be read to advantage, in which there is a disputation learnedly set forth against the Cathari and Anabaptists, in reference to the remains of sin which cleave to the godly as long as they remain in the flesh.

VII. In What Does The Conversion Of The Godly Differ From The Repentance Of The Ungodly?

The term repentance is used in reference to the ungodly as well as to the godly, because there are certain things in which they agree, as in a knowledge of sin, and sorrow on account of it. As it respects other things, however, there is a wide difference. They differ, 1. In the moving cause of repentance, or in the sorrow which is felt. The wicked are sorrowful, not on account of having offended God, but merely because of the punishment which they have brought upon themselves, and which necessarily attaches itself to the violation of God's law. If it were not for this, they would never manifest any sorrow for sin. So Cain was sorrowful merely on account of the punishment which God inflicted upon him for his sin. "My iniquity" (that is the punishment of my iniquity) "is greater than I can bear. Behold thou hast driven me out this day from the face of the earth," &c. The godly, however, do, indeed, dread the punishment of sin, but they are pained and grieved more particularly on account of sin itself, and the offence which they have committed against God. So it was in the case of David: "Against thee, thee only have I sinned: my sin is ever before me" (Ps. 51:3, 4). So it was also in the case of Peter, who wept bitterly on account of having offended Christ. The sorrow of Judas, however, did not arise on account of the evil of sin, but merely on account of the punishment which followed his crime. Horace expresses this distinction in the following language (lib. 1. epist. 16):

Oderunt peccare boni, virtutis amore,
Tu nihil admittes in te, formidine pœnæ.

2. The repentance of the godly differs from that of the ungodly as it respects the efficient cause of it. The repentance of the ungodly proceeds from distrust and despair, so that their despair, disquietude and hatred to God increases. The repentance of the godly, however, proceeds from faith, or the confidence which they have in the mercy of God, and in a gracious reconciliation with him by and for the sake of Christ.

3. They differ in form. The repentance of the godly is a turning to God from the devil, sin and their old nature; because they do not only sorrow, but also encourage themselves by exercising confidence in the mediator—they confide in Christ, rejoice in God, and trust in him saying with David, "Purge me with hyssop, and I shall be clean" (Ps. 51:7). The repentance of the ungodly is a turning away from God to the devil, to hatred and repining against God, and to despair.

4. They differ in their effects. The repentance of the godly is followed by new obedience; and in proportion to the depth of their repentance is the old man mortified in them, and the desire of righteousness increased. But the repentance of the ungodly is not followed by new obedience, but they continue in sin and return to their vomit, although for a time they feigned to repent of their sins, as Ahab did. They are, indeed, mortified, and destroyed, but the

corruption of their nature is not subdued: yea, by how much the more they repent, by so much the more is hatred, distrust, and aversion to God increased in them, so that they are continually being brought more and more under the power and dominion of Satan.

Heidelberg Catechism Question 91

> **Question 91.** But what are good works?
> **Answer.** Only those which proceed from a true faith, are performed according to the law of God, and to his glory, and not such as are founded on our imaginations, or the institutions of men.

Exposition

The doctrine concerning good works belongs properly to this Question of the Catechism, concerning which we must enquire particularly:

What are good works?

How may they be performed?

Are the works of the saints pure and perfectly good?

How can our works please God since they are only imperfectly good?

Why must we perform good works?

Do your good works merit any thing in the sight of God?

I. What Are Good Works?

Good works are such as are performed according to the law of God, such as proceed from a true faith, and are directed to the glory of God. Three things, therefore, claim our attention in the exposition of this question: 1. The conditions necessary to constitute a work good in the sight of God; 2. The difference between the works of the regenerate and the unregenerate; 3. In what respect, or how far the moral works of the ungodly are sins.

First, that a work may be good and pleasing in the sight of God these three conditions are necessary:

1. It must be commanded by God. No creature has the right, or power to institute the worship of God. But good works (we speak of moral good) and the worship of God are the same. Moral good differs widely from natural good, inasmuch as all actions, in as far as they are actions, including even those of the wicked, are naturally good; but all actions are not morally good, or in accordance with the justice of God. This condition excludes all will-worship, as well as the figment of good intentions, as when men do evil that good may come, or when they perform works founded upon their own imaginations, which they endeavor to thrust upon God in the place of worship, which, indeed, are not evil in themselves, but yet are not commanded by God. It is not sufficient for the worship of God that a work be not evil, or not prohibited: it must also be commanded by God, according to what the Scriptures declare, "To obey is better than sacrifice, and to hearken than the fat of rams"; "Walk in my statutes"; "In vain do they worship me, teaching for doctrines the commandments of men" (1 Sam. 15:22; Ez. 20:19; Matt. 15:9).

But some one may object and say, that works of indifference, such as may be done, or left undone, are not commanded by God, and yet many of them are pleasing to him, to which we reply that they are not pleasing to God in themselves, but by an accident, in as far as they partake of the general nature of love, and in as far as they are performed for the purpose of avoiding offence, and for the sake of contributing to the salvation of our fellow men. In this respect they are commanded by God in general, although not specially.

2. That a work may be good it must proceed from a true faith, which rests upon the merit and intercession of Christ, and from which we may know that we, together with our works, are acceptable to God for the sake of the mediator. To do any thing from a true faith is, 1. To believe that we are acceptable to God for the sake of the satisfaction of Christ; 2. That our obedience itself is

pleasing to God, both because it is commanded by him, and because the imperfection which attaches itself to it is made acceptable to God for the sake of the same satisfaction of Christ on account of which God is well pleased with us. Without faith it is impossible for any one to please God. Nor is the faith, by which any one may assure himself, that God wills and commands any particular work sufficient; for if this were all that is necessary, then the wicked, who know and do what God wills, would also act from faith. To act from a true faith, however, includes much more than this, because it includes in itself historical faith, and what is the most important of all, it applies unto itself the promise of the gospel. The Scriptures speak of this true faith in the following references: "Whatsoever is not of faith is sin"; "Without faith it is impossible to please God" (Rom. 14:23; Heb. 11:6). Nor is it difficult to perceive the reason and force of what is here affirmed, because without faith there is no love to God, and consequently no love to our neighbor. Every work now that does not proceed from love to God is hypocrisy, yea a reproach and contempt of God; for he who has the presumption to do any thing, whether it be pleasing to God or not, despises God, and casts a reproach upon him. Nor is it possible for us to have a good conscience without faith; and what is not done with a good conscience cannot please God.

3. That a work may be good, it must be referred principally to the honor and glory of God. Honor embraces love, reverence, obedience and gratitude. Hence, to do any thing to the honor of God, is to do it, that we may testify our love, reverence and obedience to God, and that for the sake of showing our thankfulness for the benefits which we have received. There is a necessity that our works, in order that they may be good and acceptable to God, should be referred to the divine glory, and not to our own praise or advantage; otherwise they will not proceed from the love of God, but from a desire to advance our own selfish interests, and will thus be mere hypocrisy. God must, therefore, be respected first whenever we do any thing: nor must we care what men may say, whether they praise or reproach us, if we have the assurance that we please

God in what we do, according to what the Apostle says, "Do all to the glory of God" (1 Cor. 10:31). Yet we may at the same time lawfully and profitably desire and seek true glory, according as it is written, "Let your light so shine before men that they may see your good works, and glorify your Father which is in heaven" (Matt. 5:16).

Briefly, faith is required in good works, because if we are not firmly persuaded that our works are pleasing to God, they proceed from contempt of God. The divine command is necessary, because faith has respect to the word of God. Inasmuch, therefore, as there cannot be any faith apart from the word, there can likewise be no good works independent of it. Finally, it is necessary that whatever we do, be referred to the glory of God, because, if we seek our own praise, or advantage in what we do, our works cannot please God.

By these conditions we exclude from the category of good works all those works, 1. Which are sins in themselves, being contrary to the divine law, and the will of God as revealed in his word; 2. Also those which are not opposed to the divine law, which in themselves are neither good nor evil, being actions of indifference, but which may, nevertheless, become evil by an accident. For works which are not opposed to the divine law, and which are not commanded by God, but by men, become evil and sinful when they are done with the conceit and expectation of worshipping God, or with offence and injury to our neighbor. Works of this character are deficient as it respects the first two conditions which we have specified as being indispensably necessary to constitute an action good in the sight of God; 3. Those works which are good in themselves, and which are commanded by God, but which, nevertheless, become sins by accident, in that they are not performed lawfully, not being done in the manner, nor with the design which God requires, that is, they do not proceed from a true faith, and are not done with the end that God may be glorified thereby. Works of this character are deficient in the last two conditions specified as necessary in order that our action may be pleasing to God.

Secondly, the works of the regenerate and the unregenerate differ, in this, that the good works of the regenerate are done according to the conditions which we have here specified, whilst those of the unregenerate, although God may have commanded them, do, nevertheless, not proceed from faith, and are not joined with internal obedience, but are done without sincerity, and are, therefore, works of hypocrisy, and, as they do not spring from a right cause, which is faith, so they are nor directed to the glory of God which is the chief end to which all our actions ought to be referred. The actions of the unregenerate do not, therefore, deserve to be called good works.

Thirdly, the difference which exists between the works of the righteous and the wicked, goes to prove that the moral works of the wicked are sins, but yet not such sins as those which are in their own nature opposed to the law of God: for these are sins in themselves, and according to their very nature, whilst the moral works of the wicked are sins merely by an accident, viz., on account of some defect, either because they do not proceed from a true faith, or are not done to the glory of God. This consequence, therefore, is of no force: The good works of the heathen and such as are unregenerate. are sins. Therefore they are all to be avoided and condemned: this consequence, we say, is not legitimate, because it is only the defects which attach themselves to these works, that are to be avoided and guarded against, as we have shown, in the former part of this work, when treating the subject of sin.

II. How May Good Works Be Performed?

The explanation of this question is necessary on account of the Pelagians, who affirm that the unregenerate may also, as well as the regenerate, perform good works; and also on account of the Papists and semi-Pelagians who imagine certain preparatory works of free-will. Good works are possible only by the grace and assistance of the Holy Spirit, and that by the regenerate alone, whose hearts have been truly regenerated by the Spirit of God, through the preaching of the gospel, and that not only in their first conversion and regeneration, but also by the perpetual and constant influence and direction of the same Spirit, who works in them a knowledge of sin, faith and a desire of new obedience, and also daily increases and confirms more and more the same gifts in them. St. Jerome endorses this doctrine when he says, "Let him be accursed, who says that it is possible to render obedience to the law, without the grace of the Holy Spirit." Without the grace and continual direction of the Holy Spirit, even the most holy persons on earth can do nothing but sin, as is evident from the examples of David, Peter, and others. Yea, without regeneration, no part of any work that is good in the sight of God, can ever be begun, inasmuch as we are all by nature evil and dead in sin (Matt. 7:11; Eph. 2:1). "All our righteousnesses," says the prophet Isaiah, in which declaration he comprehends both himself and the most holy amongst men, "are as filthy rags" (Is. 64:6). Now if nothing but sin is found before God in the saints, what will that be which is found in those who are unregenerated? What good these are able to perform, the apostle Paul describes in a most graphic manner, in the first and second chapters of his Epistle to the Romans. That the unregenerate are unable to perform such works as are acceptable to God, is also taught in the following passages of Scripture: "A corrupt tree cannot bring forth good fruit"; "Can the Ethiopian change his skin, or the leopard his spots? then may ye also do good, that are accustomed to do evil"; "Without me ye can do nothing"; "It is God, which worketh in you, both to will and to do of his good pleasure" (Matt. 7:18; Jer. 13:23; John, 15:5; Phil. 2:13). Without the righteousness of Christ imputed unto us, we are altogether unclean and abominable in the sight of God, and all our works are as dung. But the righteousness of Christ is not imputed unto us before our conversion. It is impossible, therefore, either that we, or our works should be pleasing to God before our conversion. Faith is the cause of good works. Faith comes from God: Therefore good works which are the fruits of faith, are from God; neither can they be before faith and conversion, or else the effect would be before its cause.

It is asked by some, in connection with this subject, are there not works that are preparatory to conversion? To which we reply that if by preparatory works are meant such as are the occasion of repentance, or which God uses for the purpose of effecting repentance in us, which may be said to be true of the outward deportment and discipline of the life, in as far as it is in accordance with the divine law; hearing, reading and meditating upon the word of God; also the cross, and adverse circumstances—if such works as these are meant, we may admit that there are such works as are preparatory. But if by preparatory works are meant works which are performed according to the law before conversion, by which, as by men's good efforts, God is enticed and moved to grant true conversion, as well as his other gifts, to those who do these things, we deny that there are any such works, because, according to the declaration of the Apostle Paul, "Whatsoever is not of faith is sin" (Rom. 14:23). The Papists call such works merits of congruity, as if they would say that they are indeed such as are imperfect in themselves and deserve nothing, but on account of which it may seem proper for the mercy of God to grant unto men conversion and eternal life. But God hath mercy on whom he will have mercy, and not upon those who deserve mercy (Rom. 9:18). No one deserves anything of God, but punishment, and banishment from his presence. "When ye shall have done all those things which are commanded you, say, We are unprofitable servants; for we have done that which was our duty to do" (Luke 17:10).

III. Are The Works Of The Regenerate Perfectly Good?

The works of the saints are not perfectly good or pure in this life: 1. Because even those who are regenerated do many things which are evil, which are sins in themselves, on account of which they are guilty in the sight of God, and deserve to be cast into everlasting punishment. Thus, Peter denied Christ thrice; David committed adultery, slew Uriah, attempted to conceal his wickedness, numbered the children of Israel, &c. The law now declares, "Cursed be he that confirmeth not all the words of this law to do them" (Deut.

27:26). 2. Because they omit doing many good things which they ought to do according to the law. 3. Because the good works which they perform are not so perfectly good and pure as the law requires, for they are always marred with defects, and polluted with sins. The perfect righteousness which the law requires is wanting, even in the best works of the saints. The reason of this is easily understood, inasmuch as faith, regeneration, and the love of God and our neighbor, from which good works proceed, continue imperfect in us in this life. As the cause is, therefore, imperfect, it is impossible that the effects which flow from this cause should be perfect. "I see another law in my members, warring against the law of my mind" (Rom. 7:23). This is the reason why the works of the godly cannot stand in the judgment of God. "Enter not into judgment with thy servant; for in thy sight shall no man living be justified"; "Cursed be he that confirmeth not all the words of this law to do them" (Ps. 143:2; Deut. 27:26). Inasmuch, therefore, as all our works are imperfect, it becomes us to acknowledge and lament our sinfulness and infirmity, and press forward so much the more towards perfection.

From what has now been said, it is evident that the figment, or conceit of the Monks in reference to works of supererogation—by which they understand such works as are done over and above what God and the law require from them, is full of impiety, for it makes God a debtor to man. Yea, it is a blasphemous doctrine, for Christ himself has said: "When ye shall have done all those things which are commanded you, say, We are unprofitable servants; for we have done that which was our duty to do" (Luke 17:10).

Obj. 1. But it is said, Luke 10:35: "Whatsoever thou spendest more, when I came again I will repay thee." Therefore there are at least some works of supererogation.

Ans. It is a sufficient reply to this objection to remark that in the interpretation of parables we must be careful not to press every minute circumstance too closely: for that which is similar is not altogether the same. The Samaritan says, Whatsoever thou spendest more, not in reference to God, but to the man that was bruised and wounded.

Obj. 2. Paul says, 1 Cor. 7:25: "Concerning virgins I have no commandment of the Lord, yet I give my judgment." Therefore judgment or advice may be given concerning things not commanded or required.

Ans. But Paul's meaning is, I give my advice that it is suitable and profitable for this life, but not that it merits eternal life.

Obj. 3. But Christ said, Matt. 19:21: "If thou wilt be perfect, go and sell what thou hast," &c. Therefore there are certain directions, which, being followed, make those who comply therewith perfect.

Ans. This is a special command, by which Christ designed to call this proud young man to humility, to the love of his neighbor, and to the office of an apostle in Judea. We may also remark that Christ did not require from him supererogation, but perfection, which requirement he made in order that he might bring him to see his great deficiency.

IV. How Can Our Good Works Please God, Since They Are Only Imperfectly Good?

If our works were not pleasing to God, they would be performed to no purpose. We must, therefore, know in what way it is that they please God. As they are imperfect in themselves, and defiled in many respects, they cannot of themselves please God, on account of his extreme justice and rectitude. Yet they are, nevertheless, acceptable to God in Christ the Mediator, through faith, or on account of the merit and satisfaction of Christ imputed unto us by faith, and on account of his intercession with the Father in our behalf. For just as we ourselves do not please God in ourselves, but in his Son, so our works being imperfect and unholy in themselves, are acceptable to God on account of the righteousness of Christ, which covers all their imperfection or impurity, so that it does not appear before God. It is necessary that the person who performs good works should be acceptable to God; then the works of the person are also accepted; otherwise, when the person is without faith, the best works are but an abomination before God, inasmuch as they are altogether hypocritical. As now the person is acceptable to God, so are the works. But the person is acceptable to God on account of the Mediator; that is, by the imputation of the merit and righteousness of Christ, with which the person is covered as with a garment in the presence of God. Hence the works of the person are also pleasing to God, for the sake of the Mediator. God does not look upon and examine our righteousness and imperfect works as they are in themselves, according to the rigor of his law in respect to which he would rather condemn them, but he beholds and considers them in his Son. It is for this reason that God is said to have had respect to Abel and his offering, viz., in his Son, in whom Abel believed, for it was by faith that he presented his sacrifice (Gen. 4:4. Heb. 11:4). So Christ is also called our High Priest, by whom our works are offered unto God. He is also called the altar, on which our prayers and works being placed, they are acceptable unto God, which otherwise would be detestable in his sight. It follows, therefore, that every defect and every imperfection respecting ourselves and our works is covered, and, as it were, repaired in the judgment of God, by the perfect satisfaction of Christ. It is in view of this that Paul says, "That I may be found in him, not having mine own righteousness, which is of the law, but that which is through the faith of Christ, the righteousness which is of God by faith" (Phil. 3:9).

V. Why Good Works Are To Be Done, Or Why Are They Necessary?

We have already, under the 86th Question, enumerated certain moving causes of good works which properly belong here, such as the connection which holds necessarily between regeneration and justification, the glory of God, the proof of our faith and election, and a good example by which others are won to Christ. These causes may be very appropriately dwelt upon to a much greater extent, if, having reduced them to three principal heads, we say that good works are to be performed by us for the sake of God, ourselves and our neighbor.

I. Good works are to be done in respect to God,

1. That the glory of God our heavenly Father, may be manifested. The manifestation of the glory of God is the chief end why God commands and wills that good works should be performed by us, that we may honor him by our good works, and that others seeing them may glorify our Father which is in heaven, as it is said, "Let your light so shine before men that they may see your good works, and glorify your Father which is in heaven" (Matt. 5:16).

2. That we may render unto God the obedience which he requires, or on account of the command of God. God requires the commencement of obedience in this life, and the perfection of it in the life to come. "This is my commandment, That ye love one another"; "This is the will of God even your sanctification"; "Being then made free from sin, ye became the servants of righteousness"; "Yield your members as instruments of righteousness unto God" (John 15:12; 1 Thes. 4:3; Rom. 6:18, 13).

3. That we may thus render unto God the gratitude which we owe unto him. It is just and proper that we should love, worship and reverence him by whom we have been redeemed, and from whom we have received the greatest benefits, and that we should declare our love and gratitude by our obedience and good works. God deserves our obedience and worship on account of the benefits which he confers upon us. We do not merit his benefits by anything that we do. Hence our gratitude, which shows itself by our obedience and good works, is due unto God for his great benefits. "I beseech you, brethren, by the mercies of God, that ye present your bodies a living sacrifice, holy, acceptable unto God, which is your reasonable service"; "Ye are an holy priesthood to offer up spiritual sacrifices acceptable to God by Jesus Christ" (Rom. 12:1; Pet. 2:5, 9, 20).

II. Good works are to be done on our own account,

1. That we may thereby testify our faith, and be assured of its existence in us by the fruits which we produce in our lives. "Every

good tree bringeth forth good fruit"; "Being filled with the fruits of righteousness which are by Jesus Christ, unto the praise and glory of God"; "Faith without works is dead" (Matt. 7:17; Phil. 1:11; James 2:17). It is by our good works, therefore, that we know that we possess true faith, because the effect is not without its own proper cause, which is always known by its effect; so that if we are destitute of good works and new obedience, we are hypocrites, and have an evil conscience instead of true faith; for true faith (which is never wanting in all the fruits which are peculiar to it) as a fruitful tree produces good works, obedience and repentance; which fruits distinguish true faith from that faith which is merely historical and temporary, as well as from hypocrisy itself.

2. That we may be assured of the fact that we have obtained the forgiveness of sins through Christ, and that we are justified for his sake. Justification and regeneration are benefits which are connected and knit together in such a way as never to be separated from each other. Christ obtained both for us at the same time, viz: the forgiveness of sins and the Holy Spirit, who through faith excites in us the desire of good works and new obedience.

3. That we may be assured of our election and salvation. "Give diligence to make your calling and election sure" (2 Pet. 1:10). This cause naturally grows out of the preceding one; for God out of his mercy chose from everlasting only those who are justified on account of the merit of his Son. "Whom he did predestinate, them he also called; and whom he called, them he also justified" (Rom. 8:30). We are, therefore, assured of our election by our justification; and that we are justified in Christ (which benefit is never granted unto the elect without sanctification) we know from faith, of which we are, again, assured by the fruits of faith, which are good works, new obedience and true repentance.

4. That our faith may be exercised, nourished, strengthened and increased by good works. Those who indulge in unclean lusts and desires against their consciences cannot have faith, and so are destitute of a good conscience and of confidence in God as reconciled and gracious; for it is only by faith that we obtain a sense of

the divine favor towards us and a good conscience. "If ye live after the flesh, ye shall die"; "I put thee in remembrance, that thou stir up the gift of God, which is in thee" (Rom. 8:13; 2 Tim. 1:6).

5. That we may adorn and commend our profession, life and calling by our good works. "I beseech you, that ye walk worthy of the vocation wherewith ye are called" (Eph. 4:1).

6. That we may escape temporal and eternal punishment. "Every tree that bringeth not forth good fruit is hewn down and cast into the fire"; "If ye live after the flesh ye shall die"; "Thou with rebukes dost correct man for iniquity" (Matt. 7:19; Rom. 8:13; Ps. 39:11).

7. That we may obtain from God those temporal and spiritual rewards, which, according to the divine promise, accompany good works both in this and in a future life. "Godliness is profitable unto all things, having promise of the life that now is, and of that which is to come" (1 Tim. 4:8). And if God did not desire that the hope of reward, and the fear of punishment should be moving causes of good works, he would not use them as arguments in the promises and threatenings which he addresses unto us in his word.

III. Good works are to be done for the sake of our neighbor,

1. That we may be profitable unto our neighbor, and edify him by our example and godly conversation. "All things are for your sakes, that the abundant grace might, through the thanksgiving of many, redound to the glory of God," &c.; "Nevertheless to abide in the flesh is more needful for you." (2 Cor. 4:15; Phil. 1:24).

2. That we may not be the occasion of offences and scandal to the cause of Christ. "Woe to that man by whom the offence cometh"; "The name of God is blasphemed among the Gentiles through you" (Matt. 18:7; Rom. 2:24).

3. That we may win the unbelieving to Christ. "And when thou art converted, strengthen thy brethren" (Luke 22:32).

The question, whether good works are necessary to salvation, belongs properly to this place. There have been some who have maintained simply and positively that good works are necessary to salvation, whilst others, again, have held that they are pernicious and injurious to salvation. Both forms of speech are ambiguous and inappropriate, especially the latter, because it seems not only to condemn confidence, but also the desire of performing good works. It is, therefore, to be rejected. The former expression must be explained in this way: that good works are necessary to salvation, not as a cause to an effect, or as if they merited a reward, but as a part of salvation itself, or as an antecedent to a consequent, or as a means without which we cannot obtain the end. In the same way we may also say that good works are necessary to righteousness or justification, or in them that are to be justified, viz., as a consequence of justification, with which regeneration is inseparably connected. But yet we would prefer not to use these forms of speech, 1. Because they are ambiguous; 2. Because they breed contentions, and give our enemies room for caviling; 3. Because these expressions are not used in the Scriptures with which our forms of speech should conform as nearly as possible. We may more safely and correctly say that good works are necessary in them that are justified, and that are to be saved. To say that good works are necessary in them that are to be justified, is to speak ambiguously, because it may be so understood as if they were required before justification, and so become a cause of our justification. Augustine has correctly said: "Good works do not precede them that are to be justified, but follow them that are justified." We may, therefore, easily return an answer to the following objection: That is necessary to salvation without which no one can be saved. But no one who is destitute of good works can be saved, as it is said in the 87th Question. Therefore, good works are necessary to salvation. We reply to the major proposition, by making the following distinction: That without which no one can be saved is necessary to salvation, viz., as a part of salvation, or as a certain antecedent necessary to salvation, in which sense we admit the conclusion, but not as a cause, or as a merit of salvation. We, therefore, grant the conclusion of the major proposition if understood in the sense in which we have just explained it. For good works are necessary to salvation, or, to speak more properly, in them that are to be saved (for it is better thus to speak for the sake of avoiding ambiguity) as a part of salvation itself, or, as an antecedent of salvation, but not as a cause or merit of salvation.

VI. Do Our Good Works Merit Any Thing In The Sight Of God?

This question naturally grows out of the preceding one, as the fourth grew out of the third. For when we say that we obtain rewards from God by our own good works, men immediately conclude that our good works must merit something at the hands of God. We must know, therefore, that our good works are necessary, and that they are also to be done for the rewards which are consequent thereon, but that they are, nevertheless, not meritorious, by which we mean that they deserve nothing from God, not even the smallest particle of spiritual or temporal blessings. The reasons of this are most true and evident.

1. Our works are imperfect, both in respect to their parts and degrees. As it respects the parts of our works, they are imperfect, for the reason that we omit many good things which the law prescribes, and do many evil things which the law prohibits; and always mingle much that is evil with the good we do, as both Scripture and experience testify. "The flesh lusteth against the Spirit and the Spirit against the flesh; and these are contrary, the one to the other, so that ye cannot do the things that ye would" (Gal. 5:17). Works, now, that are imperfect not only merit nothing, but are even condemned in the judgment of God. "Cursed be he that confirmeth not all the words of this law to do them" (Deut. 27:26). Our works are also imperfect in degree, because the best works of the saints are unclean and defiled in the sight of God, not being performed by those who are perfectly regenerated, nor with that love to God and our neighbor which the law requires. The prophet Isaiah declares even in reference to good works, "We are all as an unclean thing, and all our righteousnesses are as filthy rags" (Is. 64:6). So the apostle Paul passes the same judgment in regard to his own works, saying, "I count all things but loss, for the excellency

of the knowledge of Christ Jesus my Lord; for whom I have suffered the loss of all things; and do count them but dung that I may win Christ" (Phil. 3:8). It is in this way, now, that all the saints speak and judge concerning their own righteousness and merits.

2. No creature, performing even the best works, can merit any thing at the hand of God, or bind him to give any thing as though it were due from him, and according to the order of divine justice. The Apostle assigns the reason of this when he says, "Who hath first given to him, and it shall be recompensed unto him again"; "Is it not lawful for me to do what I will with mine own" (Rom. 11:35; Matt. 20:15). We deserve our preservation no more than we did our creation. God was not bound to create us; nor is he bound to preserve those whom he has created. But he did, and does, both of his own free-will and good pleasure. God receives no benefit from us, nor can we confer any thing upon our Creator. Now, where there is no benefit, there is no merit, for merit presupposes some benefit received.

3. Our works are all due unto God, for all creatures are bound to render worship and gratitude to the Creator, so that if we were even never to sin, yet we could not render unto God the worship and gratitude which is due from us. "When ye have done all those things which are commanded you, say, We are unprofitable servants; we have done that which was our duty to do" (Luke 17:10).

4. If we do any works which are good, these works are not ours, but God's, who produces them in us by his Holy Spirit. "It is God which worketh in you, both to will and to do, of his good pleasure"; "What hast thou, that thou didst not receive?" (Phil. 2:13; 1 Cor. 4:7). We are by nature the children of wrath—dead in trespasses and sins—evil trees, which cannot produce good fruit (Eph. 2:1, 3; Matt. 7:18). If we are by nature evil trees, God must by his grace make us good trees, and produce good fruit in us, as it is said; "We are his workmanship, created in Christ Jesus unto good works, which God hath before ordained, that we should walk in them" (Eph. 2:10). Hence, if we perform any thing that is good,

it is the gift of God, and not any merit on our part. It would, indeed, be foolish on the part of any one, if, when he were to receive a hundred florins as a present from a rich man, he should think he deserved a thousand for receiving the hundred, seeing that he is under obligations to the rich man for the gift which he has received, and not the rich man to him.

5. There is no proportion between our works, which are altogether imperfect, and those exceedingly great benefits which the Father freely grants unto us in his Son.

6. "He that glorieth, let him glory in the Lord" (1 Cor. 1:31). But if we deserve the remission of our sins by our good works, we should then have something whereof to glory; nor should we attribute the glory of our salvation to God, as it is said, "If Abraham were justified by works, he hath whereof to glory, but not before God" (Rom. 4:2).

7. We are justified before we perform good works. "For the children being not yet born, neither having done any good or evil, that the purpose of God according to election might stand, not of works, but of him that calleth; it was said unto her, the elder shall serve the younger: As it is written, Jacob have I loved, but Esau have I hated" (Rom. 9:11–14). We are, therefore, not justified before God at the time when we do good works, but we perform good works when we are justified.

8. The conceit of merit and justification by our good works is calculated to shake true Christian consolation, to disturb the conscience and lead men to doubt and despair in reference to their salvation. For when they hear the denunciation of the law, cursed be he that confirmeth not all the words of this law to do them, and consider their own imperfection, their conscience tells them that they can never perform all these things, so that they are continually led to cherish doubts, and to live in dread of the curse of the law. Faith, however, imparts sure and solid comfort to the conscience, because it grounds itself in the promise of God, which cannot disappoint the soul. "The inheritance is of faith, that it might be by

grace, to the end the promise might be sure to all the seed" (Rom. 4:16).

9. If we were to obtain righteousness by our own works, the promise would then be made of none effect, and Christ would have died in vain.

10. If the conceit concerning the merit of good works be admitted, then there would not be one and the same method of salvation. Abraham and the Thief on the cross would have been justified differently, which might also be said of us. But there is only one way of salvation: "I am the Way, and the Truth, and the Life; no man cometh unto the Father, but by me"; "There is one Mediator between God and men"; "There is one Lord, one faith, one baptism"; "Jesus Christ the same yesterday, to-day, and forever"; "There is none other name under heaven given among men, whereby we must be saved" (John 14:6; 1 Tim. 2:5; Eph. 4:5; Heb. 13:8; Acts 4:12).

11. Christ would not accomplish the whole of our salvation, and thus would not be a perfect Saviour if any thing were to be added by us to our righteousness by way of merit, for there would be as much detracted from his merit as would be added thereto from our merit. But Christ is our perfect Saviour, as the Scriptures sufficiently testify. "In whom we have redemption through his blood, the forgiveness of sins, according to the riches of his grace"; "By grace are ye saved, through faith, and that not of yourselves; it is the gift of God; not of works, lest any man should boast"; "The blood of Jesus Christ his Son cleanseth us from all sin"; "Neither is there salvation in any other" (Eph. 1:7; 2:8, 9; 1 John 1:7; Acts 4:12).

Obj. Reward presupposes merit. God also calls those good things which he promises, and grants unto them that perform good works, rewards. Therefore good works presuppose merit, and are meritorious in the sight of God.

Ans. The major proposition, sometimes, holds true among men, but never with God, because no creature can merit any thing at the hands of God, seeing that he is indebted to no one. Yet they are, nevertheless, called the rewards of our good works in respect to God, because he, out of his mere grace, recompenses them. This recompense, however, is not due; for we can add nothing to God, neither does he stand in need of our works. Yea, something is rather added unto us by our good works, because they are a conformity of ourselves with God, and his benefits, by which we are bound to render gratitude to God, and not God to us. It is, therefore, not less absurd to say that we merit salvation at the hands of God, than if a certain one should say, Thou hast given me one hundred florins. Therefore thou oughtest to give me a thousand florins. Yet God commands us to perform good works, and promises a gracious reward to those who do them, as a father promises rewards to his children.

INTRODUCTION TO THE 1559 *BOOK OF COMMON PRAYER*

THE REFORMATION was not a straightforward affair anywhere in Europe where it took root, but it encountered a particularly rocky and tortuous road in England. Nurtured in its earliest stages by a king (Henry VIII) who was temperamental, paranoid, autocratic, and deeply attached to the old Roman Catholic religion himself, the English Reformation seemed unlikely to amount to much for its first twenty years. Its leading architects, foremost among them the unlikely Archbishop of Canterbury, Thomas Cranmer (who was appointed to this lofty position in the Roman Catholic Church while himself a closet Protestant, with a closet wife to boot!) had to learn nothing so much as the art of diplomacy, and several met untimely deaths by misjudging the king's religious mood. Still, the authority of the Pope in England had been decisively rejected in 1533 and 1534, and Cranmer carefully laid the groundwork laid for deeper and more fully Protestant reform in the years that followed.

Reform accelerated rapidly when Henry died in 1547 and left the throne to his nine-year-old son, Edward VI, who was hailed as a "new Josiah." Edward himself was devoutly Protestant, as were several of his most influential councilors. In 1548 communion was offered for the first time in both kinds (that is, both bread and wine), and in 1549, a full Book of Common Prayer in English was published and prescribed for use throughout the country. Cranmer himself was the primary composer of the new text, though he made substantial use of existing liturgies; the peculiar beauty of expression that the new English texts displayed was to make an enduring impact on the development of the English language and centuries of Anglican worshippers. Although the orders of service in this book were relatively conservative, maintaining significant continuity with centuries of Catholic practice and even many points of theology, the mere fact of a liturgy celebrated entirely in English was a dramatic change. Worship was no longer to be a mere ceremonial display by the priests, with ordinary parishioners gawking on while the clergy mumbled in Latin. Now it was to be an opportunity for the whole congregation to gather together and worship the Lord, and to be instructed in the truth of Scripture through the readings and prayers.

However, the 1549 Prayer Book was only a beginning. With the Protestant cause on the Continent in a tenuous position after important military victories by Charles V, Cranmer was able to invite leading reformers such as Martin Bucer and Peter Martyr Vermigli to England to help advance the cause of the Reformation there. Bolstered by their support, he was able to begin work on a much more dramatic revision of the liturgy in a simpler, more biblical direction. Moreover, as all of these reformers had a more Reformed than Lutheran bent, Cranmer's own thought seems to have progressively evolved in that direction, particularly on the matter of the Eucharist. Given that transubstantiation was the greatest bulwark of the old Catholic religion, Cranmer encountered fiercer resistance here than anywhere, but in perhaps the boldest change of all in the new 1552 Book of Common Prayer, he changed the Words of Administration in Holy Communion as follows:

1549 version:

"The body of our Lord Jesus Christ which was given for thee, preserve thy body and soul unto everlasting life."
"The blood of our Lord Jesus Christ which was shed for thee, preserve thy body and soul unto everlasting life."

1552 version:

"Take and eat this, in remembrance that Christ died for thee, and feed on him in thy heart by faith, with thanksgiving."
"Drink this in remembrance that Christ's blood was shed for thee, and be thankful."

Still, the 1552 Prayer Book did not satisfy everyone. Some of the more zealous reformers, especially the fiery Scotsman, John Knox (c. 1513–1572), newly-arrived at court, felt that it was still much too popish, and they particularly decried the continuation of the practice of kneeling at communion. Whatever the words said, they complained, this physical practice would continue to encourage the common people in the superstition of transubstantiation. Accordingly, a last-minute change was made to include a rubric (the so-called "black rubric," because it was not printed in red like all the others) offering an explanation to worshippers that the kneeling signaled the penitent heart of the worshipper, not any adoration of Christ's flesh physically present in the consecrated elements. It was a compromise that was to please no one, and with the accession of Queen Elizabeth in 1559, it was tossed out to avoid antagonizing the conservatives. Indeed, the revision of 1559 attempted another compromise, fusing the Words of Administration from the 1549 and 1552 editions, so that different theologies of the Eucharist could all find a place in this most intimate moment of worship. Aside from these small but significant changes, and a few other minor alterations, the 1559 Prayer Book was substantially identical to that of 1552, and was to remain in use in the English Reformed church (the term "Anglican" was not to come till much later) for over a century, although maligned by Puritans as still too full of popish abuses.

The excerpts below comprise the original Preface and "On Ceremonies" that first appeared in the 1552 Prayer Book, as well as the Order for Holy Communion as it was crystallized in 1559. A couple points are worth highlighting from each.

The Preface emphasizes in good Protestant fashion the importance of people hearing the Word of God in their own tongue and lays considerable stress on the reform of the lectionary so as to ensure that as much of Scripture as possible be publicly read and understood. However, it also emphasizes, in very English fashion, the importance of uniformity in worship, a uniformity that was to prove so contentious in later decades. Anticipating already some of these contentions, the brief essay "On Ceremonies" seeks to offer a rationale for which old Catholic ceremonies were to be abolished, which reformed, and which retained. The focus was on edification, and readers were warned "to be more studious of unity and concord than of innovations and newfangleness," recognizing that antiquity deserved respect.

The Order for Holy Communion, it should be noted, was not simply an order of worship for the communion part of the service, but for a full worship service, one that was envisioned as only taking place a few times a year (no less than three, the Prayer Book prescribed). Although the Reformers by and large wanted to see much more frequent communion, the late medieval practice had been increasingly to commune only once per year, and it proved unrealistic to revise this practice too dramatically. Once we realize this, we may be a bit more forgiving of what may seem the excessively wordy and laborious explanations and warnings that the priest is to offer to the congregants before communing. Moreover, Cranmer intended the Prayer Book to be not merely a form of worship, but an opportunity to instruct the common people in the basics of Protestant theology, especially as there were few parish priests capable of preaching competently on their own. Centuries later, the extraordinary theological richness that he managed to pack into many of the prayers remains a source of instruction and inspiration to worshippers today.

Further Reading

For further reading, see Diarmaid MacCulloch, *Thomas Cranmer: A Life*, rev. ed. (New Haven: Yale University Press, 2016), chs. 10–11; Charles Hefling and Cynthia Shattuck, eds., *The Oxford Guide to the Boo of Common Prayer* (Oxford: Oxford University Press, 1998), Pts. I-II; Diarmaid MacCulloch, *Tudor Church Militant: Edward VI and the Protestant Reformation* (London: Allen Lane, 199).

THE CHURCH OF ENGLAND, *BOOK OF COMMON PRAYER* (1559)[1]

Preface

THERE WAS never anything by the wit of man so well devised or so sure established which in continuance of time hath not been corrupted, as among other things it may plainly appear by the common prayers in the church, commonly called divine service, the first original and ground whereof, if a man would search out by ancient fathers, he shall find that the same was not ordained but of a good purpose and for a great advancement of godliness. For they so ordered the matter that all the whole Bible (or the greatest part thereof) should be read over once in the year, intending thereby that the clergy and especially such as were Ministers of the congregation, should by often reading and [by the] meditation of God's word be stirred up to godliness themselves, and be more able also to exhort other[s] by wholesome doctrine, and to confute them that were adversaries to the truth. And further, that the people by daily hearing of holy scripture read in the Church should continually profit more and more in the knowledge of God and be the more inflamed with the love of His true religion. But, these many years [having] passed, those godly and decent order[s] of the ancient fathers hath been so altered, broken, and neglected by planting in uncertain stories, legends, responses, verses, vain repetitions, commemorations, and synodals that commonly when any book of the Bible was begun before three or four Chapters were read out,

---

[1] Spelling modernized by Brian Marr.

all the rest were unread. And in this sort the book of Isaiah was begun in Advent, and the book of Genesis in Septuagesima, but they were only begun, and never read through. After like sort were other books of holy scripture used. And moreover, whereas St. Paul would have such language spoken to the people in the Church as they might understand and have profit by hearing the same, the service in this church of England these many years hath been read in Latin to the people, which they understood not, so that they have heard with their ears only, and their hearts, spirit, and mind have not been edified thereby. And furthermore, notwithstanding that the ancient fathers have divided the Psalms into seven portions, whereof every one was called a nocturn, now of late time, a few of them have been daily said (and oft repeated) and the rest utterly omitted. Moreover, the number and hardness of the rules, called the Pie, and the manifold changings of the service was the cause that to turn the book only was so hard and intricate a matter that many times there was more business to find out what should be read than to read it when it was found out.

These inconveniences therefore considered, here is set forth such an order whereby the same shall be redressed. And for a readiness in this matter, here is drawn out a calendar for that purpose, which is plain and easy to be understood, wherein (so much as may be) the reading of holy scriptures is so set forth that all things shall be done in order, without breaking one piece thereof from another. For this cause be cut off anthems, responds, invitatories, and such like things as did break the continual course of the reading of the scripture. Yet because there is no remedy but that of necessity there must be some rules, therefore certain rules are here set forth, which as they be few in number, so they be plain and easy to be understand. So that here you have an order for prayer (as touching the reading of holy scripture) much agreeable to the mind and purpose of the old fathers, and a great deal more profitable and commodious than that which of late was used. It is more profitable, because here are left out many things, whereof some be untrue, some uncertain, some vain and superstitious, and is ordained nothing to be read but the very pure word of God, the holy scriptures, or that which is evidently grounded upon the same, and that in such a language and order as is most easy and plain for the understanding both of the readers and hearers. It is also more commodious, both for the shortness thereof and for the plainness of the order, and for that the rules be few and easy. Furthermore, by this order the Curates shall need none other books for their public service, but this book and the Bible, by the means whereof the people shall not be at so great charge for books, as in time past they have been.

And where heretofore there hath been great diversity in saying and singing in churches within this realm—some following Salisbury use, some Hereford use, some the use of Bangor, some of York, and some of Lincoln—now from henceforth all the whole realm shall have but one use. And if any would judge this way more painful because that all things must be read upon the book, whereas before by the reason of so often repetition they could say many things by heart, if those men will weigh their labor, with the profit and knowledge which daily they shall obtain by reading upon the book, they will not refuse the pain in consideration of the great profit that shall ensue thereof.

And forasmuch as nothing can almost be so plainly set forth, but doubts may rise in the use and practicing of the same, to appease all such diversity (if any arise) and for the resolution of all doubts concerning the manner how to understand, do, and execute the things contained in this book, the parties that so doubt or diversely take anything shall always resort to the Bishop of the diocese, who by his discretion shall take order for the quieting and appeasing of the same, so that the same order be not contrary to anything contained in this book. And if the Bishop of the diocese be in any doubt, then may he send for the resolution thereof unto the Archbishop.

Though it be appointed in the afore written Preface that all things shall be read and sung in the Church, in the English tongue to the end that the congregation may be thereby edified, yet it is not meant, but when men say morning and evening prayer privately, they may say the same in any language that they themselves do understand.

And all priests and deacons shall be bound to say daily, the morning and evening prayer, either privately or openly, except they be letted[2] by preaching, studying of divinity, or by some other urgent cause.

And the curate that ministereth in every parish church or chapel, being at home and not being otherwise reasonably letted shall say the same in the parish church or chapel where he ministereth and shall toll a bell thereto a convenient time before he begin that such as be disposed may come to hear God's word and to pray with him.

Of Ceremonies

Of such ceremonies as be used in the church and have had their beginning by the institution of man, some at the first were of godly intent and purpose devised, and yet at length turned to vanity and superstition; some entered into the Church by undiscrete devotion and such a zeal as was without knowledge, and for because they were winked at in the beginning, they grew daily to more and more abuses, which not only for their unprofitableness, but also because they have much blinded the people and obscured the glory of God are worthy to be cut away and clean rejected; other there be which, although they have been devised by man, yet it is thought good to reserve them still, as well for a decent order in the church (for the which they were first devised) as because they pertain to edification, whereunto all things done in the Church (as the Apostle teacheth) ought to be referred. And although the keeping or omitting of a ceremony (in itself considered) is but a small thing, yet the willful and contemptuous transgression and breaking of a common order and discipline is no small offence before God.

---

2 *letted:* prevented or hindered.

Let all things be done among you (saith St. Paul) in a seemly and due order. The appointment of the which order pertaineth not to private men, therefore no man ought to take in hand, nor presume to appoint or alter any public or common order in Christ's Church, except he be lawfully called and authorized thereunto.

And whereas as in this our time, the minds of men are so diverse that some think it a great matter of conscience to depart from a piece of the least of their ceremonies (they be so addicted to their old customs), and again on the other side some be so newfangled that they would innovate all thing[s] and so do despise the old that nothing can like them but that is new, it was thought expedient not so much to have respect how to please and satisfy either of these parties as how to please God and profit them both. And yet, lest any man should be offended (whom good reason might satisfy), here be certain causes rendered why some of the accustomed ceremonies be put away, and some retained and kept still.

Some are put away because the great excess and multitude of them hath so increased in these latter days that the burden of them was intolerable, whereof St. Augustine in his time complained that they were grown to such a number that the state of Christian people was in worse case (concerning that matter) then were the Jews. And he counselled that such [a] yoke and burden should be taken away, as time would serve quietly to do it.

But what would St. Augustine have said if he had seen the ceremonies of late days used among us, whereunto the multitude used in his time was not to be compared? This our excessive multitude of ceremonies was so great and many of them so dark that they did more confound and darken than declare and set forth Christ's benefits unto us.

And besides this, Christ's Gospel is not a ceremonial law (as much of Moses' law was) but it is a religion to serve God, not in bondage of the figure or shadow, but in the freedom of spirit, being content only with those ceremonies which do serve to a decent order and godly discipline, and such as be apt to stir up the dull mind of man to the remembrance of his duty to God by some notable and special signification whereby he might be edified.

Furthermore, the most weighty cause of the abolishment of certain ceremonies was that they were so far abused, partly by the superstitious blindness of the rude and unlearned, and partly by the insatiable avarice of such as sought more their own lucre than the glory of God that the abuses could not well be taken away, the thing remaining still. But now as concerning those persons, which peradventure will be offended, for that some of the old ceremonies are retained still, if they consider that without some ceremonies it is not possible to keep any order or quiet discipline in the Church, they shall easily perceive just cause to reform their judgements. And if they think much that any of the old do remain and would rather have all devised new, then such men granting some ceremonies convenient to be had, surely where the old may be well used, there they cannot reasonably reprove the old only for their age without betraying of their own folly. For in such a case, they ought rather to have reverence unto them for their antiquity, if they will declare themselves to be more studious of unity and concord than of innovations and newfangledness, which, as much as may be with the true setting forth of Christ's religion, is always to be eschewed. Furthermore, such shall have no just cause with the ceremonies reserved to be offended, for as those be taken away which were most abused and did burden men's consciences without any cause, so the other that remain are retained for a discipline and order which (upon just causes) may be altered and changed, and therefore are not to be esteemed equal with God's law. And moreover they be neither dark nor dumb ceremonies, but are so set forth that every man may understand what they do mean and to what use they do serve so that it is not like that they in time to come should be abused, as the other have been. And in these our doings, we condemn no other nations, nor prescribe anything but to our own people only. For we think it convenient that every country should use such ceremonies as they shall think best to the setting forth of God's honor or glory, and to the reducing of the people to a most perfect and godly living, without error or superstition. And that they should put away other things, which from time to time, they perceive to be most abused, as in men's ordinances, it often chanceth diversely in divers countries.

The Order for the Administration of the Lord's Supper or Holy Communion

So many as intend to be partakers of the Holy Communion shall signify their names to the curate over night, or else in the morning afore the beginning of morning prayer or immediately after.

And if any of those be an open and notorious evil liver, so that the congregation by him is offended, or have done any wrong to his neighbors by word or deed, the curate having knowledge thereof, shall call him and advertise him in any wise not to presume to the Lord's table until he have openly declared himself to have truly repented and amended his former naughty life, that the congregation may thereby be satisfied which afore were offended, and that he have recompensed the parties who he hath done wrong unto, or at the least declare himself to be in full purpose so to do, as soon as he conveniently may.

The same order shall the Curate use with those betwixt whom he perceiveth malice and hatred to reign, not suffering them to be partakers of the Lord's table until he know them to be reconciled. And if one of the parties so at variance, he content to forgive from the bottom of his heart all that the other hath trespassed against him and to make amends for that he himself hath offended, and the other party will not be persuaded to a godly unity, but remain still in his frowardness and malice, the Minister in that case ought to admit the penitent person to the Holy Communion, and not him that is obstinate.

The table, having at the Communion time a fair white linen cloth upon it, shall stand in the body of the church or in the chancel where morning prayer and evening prayer be appointed to be said. And the priest, standing at the north side of the table, shall say the Lord's prayer with this collect following:

Almighty God, unto whom all hearts be open, all desires known, and from whom no secrets are hid, cleanse the thoughts of our hearts by the inspiration of thy Holy Spirit, that we may perfectly love Thee and worthily magnify Thy holy name, through Christ our Lord. Amen.

Then shall the Priest rehearse distinctly at the ten commandments, and the people kneeling shall after every commandment ask God's mercy for their transgression of the same, after this sort:

Minister: God spake these words and said, "I am the Lord thy God, thou shalt have none other gods but me."

People: Lord have mercy upon us, and incline our hearts to keep this law.

Minister: "Thou shalt not make to thyself any graven image, nor the likeness of anything that is in heaven above, or in the earth beneath, or in the water under the earth. Thou shalt not bow down to them, nor worship them, for I the Lord thy God am a jealous God and visit the sin of the fathers upon the children unto the third and fourth generation of them that hate me, and shew mercy unto thousands, in them that love me and keep my commandments."

People: Lord have mercy upon us, and incline our hearts to keep this law.

Minister: "Thou shalt not take the name of the Lord thy God in vain, for the Lord will not hold him guiltless that taketh His name in vain."

People: Lord have mercy upon us, and incline our hearts to keep this law.

Minister: "Remember that thou keep holy the Sabbath day: six days shalt thou labor and do all that thou hast to do, but the seventh day is the Sabbath of the Lord thy God. In it thou shalt do no manner of work, thou and thy son and thy daughter, thy manservant, and thy maidservant, thy cattle, and the stranger that is within thy gates, for in six days the Lord made heaven and earth, the sea and all that in them is, and rested the seventh day. Wherefore the Lord blessed the seventh day and hallowed it."

People: Lord have mercy upon us, and incline our hearts to keep this law.

Minister: "Honor thy father and thy mother, that thy days may be long in the land which the Lord thy God giveth thee."

People: Lord have mercy upon us, and incline our hearts to keep this law.

Minister: "Thou shalt not do murder."

People: Lord have mercy upon us, and incline our hearts to keep this law.

Minister: "Thou shalt not commit adultery."

People: Lord have mercy upon us, and incline our hearts to keep this law.

Minister: "Thou shalt not steal."

People: Lord have mercy upon us, and incline our hearts to keep this law.

Minister: "Thou shalt not bear false witness against thy neighbor."

People: Lord have mercy upon us, and incline our hearts to keep this law.

Minister: "Thou shalt not covet thy neighbor's house. Thou shalt not covet thy neighbor's wife, nor his servant, nor his maid, nor his ox, nor his ass, nor any thing that is his."

People: Lord have mercy upon us, and write all these thy laws in our hearts we beseech thee.

Then shall follow the Collect of the day with one of these two Collects following for the Queen, the Priest standing up and saying,

Let us pray. Almighty God, whose kingdom is everlasting and power infinite, have mercy upon the whole congregation, and so rule the heart of thy chosen servant Elizabeth our Queen and governor that she (knowing whose minister she is) may above all things seek Thy honor and glory, and that we her subjects (duly considering whose authority she hath) may faithfully serve, honor, and humbly obey her in Thee and for Thee, according to Thy blessed word and ordinance, through Jesus Christ our Lord, who with Thee and the Holy Ghost liveth and reigneth ever one God, world without end. Amen.

Almighty and everlasting God, we be taught by Thy holy word that the hearts of Princes are in Thy rule and governance and that thou dost dispose and turn them as it seemeth best to Thy Godly wisdom: we humbly beseech Thee so to dispose and govern the heart of Elizabeth, Thy servant, our Queen and governor, that in all her thoughts, words, and works she may ever seek Thy honor and glory, and study to preserve Thy people committed to her charge, in wealth, peace, and godliness. Grant this, O merciful Father, for Thy dear Son's sake Jesus Christ our Lord. Amen.

Immediately after the Collects, the Priest shall read the Epistle beginning thus:

The Epistle written in the __th chapter of _____.

And the Epistle ended, he shall say the Gospel, beginning thus:

The Gospel written in the __th chapter of _____.

And the Epistle and Gospel being ended, shall be said the Creed:

I believe in one God, the Father Almighty, maker of heaven and earth, and of all things visible and invisible, and in one Lord Jesus Christ, the only-begotten Son of God, begotten of His Father before all worlds, God of God, light of light, very God of very God, gotten, not made, being of one substance with the Father, by whom all things were made, who for us men, and for our salvation came down from heaven, and was incarnate by the Holy Ghost, of the Virgin Mary, and was made man, and was crucified also for us, under Pontius Pilate. He suffered and was buried, and the third day he rose again, according to the Scriptures, and ascended into heaven, and sitteth at the right hand of the Father, and He shall come again with glory, to judge both the quick and the dead, whose kingdom shall have none end; and I believe in the Holy Ghost, the Lord and giver of life, who proceedeth from the Father and the Son, who with the Father and the Son together is worshipped and glorified, who spake by the Prophets; and I believe one catholic and Apostolic Church. I acknowledge one Baptism, for the remission of sins. And I look for the resurrection of the dead, and the life of the world to come. Amen.

After the Creed, if there be no sermon, shall follow one of the homilies already set forth, or hereafter to be set forth by common authority.

After such sermon, homily, or exhortation, the curate shall declare unto the people whether there be any holy days or fasting days the week following, and earnestly exhort them to remember the poor, saying one, or more of these sentences following, as he thinketh most convenient by his discretion:

"Let your light so shine before men that they may see your good works and glorify your Father which is in heaven" (Matt. 5:16).

"Lay not up yourselves treasure upon the earth, where the rust and moth doth corrupt, and where thieves break through and steal, but lay up for yourselves treasures in heaven, where neither rust, nor moth doth corrupt, and where thieves do not break through and steal" (Matt. 6:19–20).

"Whatsoever you would that men should do unto you, even so do unto them, for this is the law and the Prophets" (Matt. 7:12).

"Not everyone that sayeth unto me, 'Lord, Lord,' shall enter into the Kingdom of heaven; but he that doeth the will of my Father which is in heaven" (Matt. 7:21).

"Zacchaeus stood forth and said unto the Lord, 'behold Lord, the half of my goods I give to the poor, and if I have done any wrong to any man, I restore fourfold'" (Luke 19:8).

"Who goeth a warfare at any time of his own cost? Who planteth a vineyard and eateth not of the fruit thereof? Or who feedeth a flock, and eateth not of the milk of the flock?" (1 Cor. 9:7).

"If we have sown unto you spiritual things, is it a great matter if we shall reap your worldly things?" (1 Cor. 9:11).

"Do ye not know that they which minister about holy things, live off the sacrifice? Which wait off the altar are partakers with the altar. Even so hath the Lord also ordained that they which preach the Gospel should live off the gospel" (1 Cor. 9:13).

"He which soweth little shall reap little, and he that soweth plenteously shall reap plenteously. Let every man do according as he is disposed in his heart, not grudgingly or of necessity, for God loveth a cheerful giver" (2 Cor. 9:6–7).

"Let him that is taught in the word minister unto him that teacheth in all good things. Be not deceived: God is not mocked, for whatsoever a man soweth, that shall he reap" (Gal. 6:6).

"While we have time, let us do good unto all men, and specially unto them which are of the household of faith" (Gal. 6:10).

"Godliness is great riches if a man be content with that he hath, for we brought nothing into the world, neither may we carry anything out" (1 Tim. 6:6).

"Charge them which are rich in this world that they be ready to give and glad to distribute, laying up in store for themselves a good foundation against the time to come, that they may attain eternal life" (1 Tim. 6:17).

"God is not unrighteous that He will forget your works and labor that proceedeth of love, which love ye have shewed for His name's sake which have ministered unto saints, and yet do minister" (Heb. 6:10).

"To do good and to distribute, forget not, for with such sacrifices God is pleased" (Heb. 13:16).

"Whoso hath this world's good and seeth his brother have need and shutteth up his compassion from him, how dwelleth the love of God in him?" (1 Jn. 3:17).

"Give alms of thy goodness, and turn never thy face from any poor man, and then the face of the Lord shall not be turned away from thee" (Tob. 4:5).

"Be merciful after thy power. If thou hast much, give plenteously; if thou hast little, do thy diligence gladly to give of that little, for so gatherest thou thyself a good reward in the day of necessity" (Tob. 4:8).

"He that hath pity upon the poor lendeth unto the Lord, and look what he layeth out: it shall be paid him again" (Prov. 19:17).

Blessed be the man that provideth for the sick and needy, the Lord shall deliver him, in the time of trouble (Ps. 41:1).

Then shall the Church wardens, or some other by them appointed, gather the devotion of the people and put the same into the poor men's box, and upon the offering days appointed, every man and woman shall pay to the Curate the due and accustomed offerings, after which done, the Priest shall say:

Let us pray for the whole estate of Christ's Church militant here in earth.

Almighty and everliving God, which by Thy holy Apostle hast taught us to make prayers and supplications and to give thanks for all men, we humbly beseech thee most mercifully (to accept our alms) and to receive these our prayers which we offer unto thy divine majesty, beseeching Thee to inspire continually the universal Church with the spirit of truth, unity, and concord, and grant that all they that do confess Thy holy name may agree in the truth of Thy holy word and live in unity and godly love. We beseech Thee also to save and defend all Christian kings, princes, and governors, and specially thy servant, Elizabeth our Queen that under her we may be godly and quietly governed, and grant unto her whole Counsel and to all that be put in authority under her that they may truly and indifferently[3] minister justice to the punishment of wickedness and vice, and to the maintenance of God's true religion and virtue. Give grace, O heavenly Father, to all Bishops, Pastors and Curates that they may both by their life and doctrine set forth Thy true and lively word and rightly and duly administer Thy holy Sacraments, and to all Thy people give thy heavenly grace, and espe-

---

[3] *indifferently*: impartially.

cially to this congregation here present, that with meek heart and due reverence they may hear and receive thy holy word, truly serving Thee in holiness and righteousness all the days of their life. And we most humbly beseech Thee of Thy goodness, O Lord, to comfort and succor all them which in this transitory life be in trouble, sorrow, need, sickness, or any other adversity. Grant this, O father, for Jesus Christ's sake our only Mediator and advocate. Amen.

Then shall follow this exhortation at certain times when the Curate shall see the people negligent to come to the holy Communion:

We be come together at this time, dearly beloved brethren, to feed at the Lord's supper, unto the which in God's behalf I bid you all that be hear present, and beseech you for the Lord Jesus Christ's sake that ye will not refuse to come thereto, being so lovingly called and bidden of God Himself. Ye know how grievous and unkind a thing it is when a man hath prepared a rich feast, decked his table with all kind of provision so that there lacketh nothing but the guests to sit down, and yet they which be called without any cause most unthankfully refuse to come. Which of you in such a case would not be moved? Who would not think a great injury and wrong done unto him? Wherefore, most dearly beloved in Christ, take ye good heed lest ye, withdrawing yourselves from this holy supper, provoke God's indignation against you; it is an easy matter for a man to say, 'I will not communicate, because I am otherwise letted with worldly business', but such excuses be not so easily accepted and allowed before God. If any man say, 'I am a grievous sinner, and therefore am afraid to come', wherefore then do ye not repent and amend? When God calleth you, be you not ashamed to say ye will not come? When you should return to God, will you excuse yourself and say that you be not ready? Consider earnestly with yourselves how little such feigned excuses shall avail before God. They that refused the feast in the Gospel, because they had bought a farm, or would try their yokes of oxen, or because they were married, were not so excused, but counted unworthy of the heavenly feast. I for my part am here present and according to mine office I bid you in the name of God; I call you in

Christ's behalf; I exhort you, as you love your own Salvation that ye will be partakers of this holy Communion. And as the Son of God did vouchsafe to yield up His soul by death upon the cross for your health, even so it is your duty to receive the Communion together in the remembrance of His death as He Himself commanded. Now, if ye will in no wise thus do, consider with yourselves how great injury ye do unto God, and how sore punishment hangeth over your heads for the same. And whereas ye offend God so sore in refusing this holy banquet, I admonish, exhort, and beseech you that unto this unkindness ye will not add anymore, which thing ye shall do if ye stand by as gazers and lookers of them that do Communicate, and be no partakers of the same yourselves. For what thing can this be accounted else than a further contempt and unkindness unto God? Truly it is a great unthankfulness to say nay when ye be called, but the fault is much greater when men stand by, and yet will neither eat, nor drink this holy Communion with other[s]. I pray you what can this be else but even to have the mysteries of Christ in derision. It is said unto all: Take ye and eat, take and drink ye all of this, do this in remembrance of me. With what face then, or with what countenance shall ye hear these words? What will this be else, but a neglecting, a despising, and mocking of the Testament of Christ? Wherefore rather than you should so do, depart you hence, and give place to them that be godly disposed. But when you depart, I beseech you ponder with yourselves from whome ye departe: ye departe from the Lord's Table: ye depart from your brethren, and from the banquet of most heavenly food. These things, if ye earnestly consider, ye shall by God's grace return to a better mind, for the obtaining whereof we shall make our humble petitions while we shall receive the holy Communion.

And some time shall be said this also, at the discretion of the Curate:

Dearly beloved, forasmuch as our duty is to render to almighty God our heavenly Father most hearty thanks for that He hath given His Son our Savior Jesus Christ, not only to die for us, but also to be our Spiritual food and sustenance, as it is declared unto us, as well by God's word as by the holy sacraments of His blessed body and blood, the which being so comfortable a thing to them which receive it worthily and so dangerous to them that will presume to receive it unworthily, my duty is to exhort you to consider the dignity of the holy mystery, and the great peril of the unworthy receiving thereof, and so to search and examine your own consciences, as you should come holy and clean to a most godly and heavenly feast. So that in no wise you come but in the marriage garment, required of God in holy scripture, and so come and be received as worthy partakers of such a heavenly Table, the way and means thereto is:

First to examine your lives and conversation by the rule of God's commandments and whereinsoever ye shall perceive yourselves to have offended either by will, word, or deed, there bewail your own sinful lives, confess yourselves to almighty God, with full purpose of amendment of life. And if ye shall perceive your offenses to be such as be not only against God, but also against your neighbors, then ye shall reconcile yourselves unto them, ready to make restitution and satisfaction according to the uttermost of your powers for all injuries and wrongs done by you to any other, and likewise being ready to forgive other[s] that have offended you as you would have forgiveness of your offenses at God's hand. For otherwise the receiving of the holy Communion doth nothing else, but increase your damnation.

And because it is requisite that no man should come to the holy Communion but with a full trust in God's mercy and with a quiet conscience, therefore if there be any of you which by the means aforesaid cannot quiet his own conscience, but requireth further comfort or counsel, then let him come to me, or some other discrete and learned minister of God's word, and open his grief, that he may receive such Ghostly counsel, advice, and comfort as his conscience may be relieved, and that by the ministry of God's word, he may receive comfort, and the benefit of absolution, to the quieting of his conscience and avoiding of all scruple and doubtfulness.

Then shall the Priest say this exhortation:

Dearly beloved in the Lord, ye that mind to come to the holy Communion of the body and blood of our savior Christ must consider what St. Paul writeth unto the Corinthians, how he exhorteth all persons diligently to try and examine themselves before they presume to eat of that bread and drink of that cup. For as the benefit is great, if with a truly penitent heart and lively faith we receive that holy sacrament (for then we spiritually eat the flesh of Christ, and drink His blood, then we dwell in Christ and Christ in us, we be one with Christ, and Christ with us), so is the danger great if we receive the same unworthily. For then we be guilty of the body and blood of Christ our savior. We eat and drink our own damnation, not considering the Lord's body. We kindle God's wrath against us. We provoke him to plague us with diverse diseases and sundry kinds of death. Therefore if any of you be a blasphemer of God, a hinderer or slanderer of His word, an adulterer, or be in malice or envy, or in any other grievous crime, bewail your sins and come not to this holy table, lest after the taking of that holy sacrament, the devil enter into you, as he entered into Judas, and fill you full of all iniquities and bring you to destruction both of body and soul. Judge therefore yourselves, brethren, that ye be not judged of the Lord. Repent you truly for your sins past, have a lively and steadfast faith in Christ our savior. Amend your lives, and be in perfect charity with all men, so shall ye be mete partakers of those holy mysteries. And above all things ye must give most humble and hearty thanks to God the Father, the Son, and the Holy Ghost, for the redemption of the world by the death and passion of our savior Christ, both God and man, who did humble himself, even to the death upon the cross for us miserable sinners which lay in darkness and shadow of death that He might make us the children of God and exalt us to everlasting life. And to the end that we should always remember the exceeding great love of our master and only savior Jesus Christ, thus dying for us, and the innumerable benefits which by His precious bloodsheding He hath obtained to us, He hath instituted and ordained holy mysteries as pledges of His love, and continual remembrance of His death, to our great and endless comfort. To Him therefore with the Father and the Holy Ghost, let us give (as we are most bounden) continual thanks, submitting ourselves wholly to His holy will and pleasure, and studying to serve Him in true holiness and righteousness, all the days of our life. Amen.

Then shall the Priest say to them that come to receive the holy Communion:

You that do truly and earnestly repent you of your sins and be in love and charity with your neighbors and intend to lead a new life, following the commandments of God, and walking from hence further in His holy ways, draw near and take this holy Sacrament, to your comfort make your humble confession to almighty God, before this congregation here gathered together in His holy name, meekly kneeling upon your knees.

Then shall this general confession be made in the name of all those that are minded to receive this holy Communion, either by one of them, or else by one of the ministers, or by the priest himself, all kneeling humbly upon their knees.

Almighty God, Father of our Lord Jesus Christ, maker of all things, Judge of all men, we acknowledge and bewail our manifold sins and wickedness, which we from time to time most grievously have committed, by thought, word, and deed, against Thy divine Majesty, provoking most justly Thy wrath and indignation against us. We do earnestly repent and be heartily sorry for these our misdoings. The remembrance of them is grievous unto us; the burden of them is intolerable. Have mercy upon us, have mercy upon us, most merciful Father. For Thy Son our Lord Jesus Christ's sake, forgive us all that is past and grant that we may ever hereafter serve and please Thee in newness of life, to the honor and glory of Thy name, through Jesus Christ our Lord. Amen.

Then shall the priest or the Bishop, being present, stand up and, turning himself to the people, shall say thus:

Almighty God, our Heavenly Father, who of His great mercy hath promised forgiveness of sins to all them which with hearty repentance and true faith turn to him, have mercy upon you, pardon and deliver you from all your sins, confirm and strengthen you in all goodness, and bring you to everlasting life, through Jesus Christ our Lord. Amen.

Then shall the Priest also say:

Hear what comfortable words our savior Christ saith to all them that truly turn to him:

"Come unto me all that travail and be heavy laden, and I shall refresh you. So God loved the world that he gave His only begotten Son, to the end that all that believe in Him should not perish but have life everlasting" (Matt. 11:28; Jn. 3:16).

Hear also what St. Paul saith:

"This is a true saying, and worthy of all men to be received: that Jesus Christ came into the world to save sinners" (1 Tim. 1:15).

Hear also what St. John sayeth:

"If any man sin, we have an advocate with the Father, Jesus Christ the righteous, and He is the propitiation for our sins" (1 Jn. 2:1).

After the which the priest shall proceed saying:

Priest: Lift up your hearts.

Answer: We lift them up unto the Lord.

Priest: Let us give thanks unto our Lord God.

Answer: It is meet and right so to do.

Priest: It is very meet, right, and our bounden duty that we should at all times and in all places give thanks to Thee, O Lord holy Father, almighty, everlasting God.

Here shall follow the proper prefaces, according to the time, if there be any specially appointed, or else immediately shall follow:

Therefore with Angels and Archangels, and with all the company of heaven, we laud and magnify Thy glorious name, evermore praising Thee, and saying: Holy, holy, holy, Lord God of hosts, heaven and earth are full of Thy glory, glory be to Thee, O Lord most high.

Proper Prefaces

Upon Christmas day and seven days after:

Because thou didst give Jesus Christ, Thine only Son, to be born as this day for us, who by the operation of the Holy Ghost was made very man of the substance of the virgin Mary His mother, and that without spot of sin, to make us clean from all sin. Therefore with Angels and Archangels, and with all the company of heaven, we laud and magnify Thy glorious name, evermore praising Thee, and saying: Holy, holy, holy, Lord God of hosts, heaven and earth are full of Thy glory, glory be to Thee, O Lord most high.

Upon Easter day, and seven days after:

But chiefly are we bound to praise Thee for the glorious resurrection of Thy Son Jesus Christ our Lord, for He is the very paschal lamb which was offered for us and hath taken away the sin of the world, who by His death hath destroyed death, and by His rising to life again hath restored to us everlasting life. Therefore with Angels and Archangels, and with all the company of heaven, we laud and magnify Thy glorious name, evermore praising Thee, and saying: Holy, holy, holy, Lord God of hosts, heaven and earth are full of Thy glory, glory be to Thee, O Lord most high.

Upon the Ascension day, and seven days after:

Through Thy most dear beloved Son, Jesus Christ our Lord, who after His most glorious resurrection, manifestly appeared to all His Apostles, and in their sight ascended up into heaven to prepare a place for us, that, where He is, thither might we also ascend and reign with Him in glory. Therefore with Angels and Archangels, and with all the company of heaven, we laud and magnify Thy glorious name, evermore praising Thee, and saying: Holy, holy, holy, Lord God of hosts, heaven and earth are full of Thy glory, glory be to Thee, O Lord most high.

Upon Whitsunday, and six days after:

Through Jesus Christ our Lord, according to whose most true promise, the Holy Ghost came down this day from heaven, with a sudden great sound, as it had been a mighty wind in the likeness of fiery tongues lighting upon the Apostles, to teach them, and to lead them to all truth, giving them both the gift of divers languages, and also boldness with fervent zeal, constantly to preach the gospel unto all nations, whereby we are brought out of darkness and error into the clear light and true knowledge of Thee, and of thy Son Jesus Christ. Therefore with Angels and Archangels, and with all the company of heaven, we laud and magnify Thy glorious name, evermore praising Thee, and saying: Holy, holy, holy, Lord God of hosts, heaven and earth are full of Thy glory, glory be to Thee, O Lord most high.

Upon the feast of Trinity only:

It is very meet, right, and our bounden duty that we should at all times and in all places give thanks to Thee, O Lord, almighty and everlasting God, which art one God, one Lord, not one only person, but three persons in one substance, for that which we believe of the glory of the Father, the same we believe of the Son, and of the Holy Ghost, without any difference or inequality.

After which preface, shall follow immediately.

Therefore with Angels and Archangels, and with all the company of heaven, we laud and magnify Thy glorious name, evermore praising Thee, and saying: Holy, holy, holy, Lord God of hosts, heaven and earth are full of Thy glory, glory be to Thee, O Lord most high.

Then shall the priest, kneeling down at God's board, say in the name of all them that shall receive the communion, this prayer following:

We do not presume to come to this Thy table, O merciful Lord, trusting in our own righteousness, but in Thy manifold and great mercies, we be not worthy so much as to gather up the crumbs under Thy Table, but Thou art the same Lord, whose property is always to have mercy. Grant us therefore, gracious

Lord, so to eat the flesh of Thy dear Son Jesus Christ, and to drink His blood that our sinful bodies may be made clean by His body, and our souls washed through his most precious blood, and that we may evermore dwell in Him, and He in us.

Then the priest standing up, shall say as followeth:

Almighty God, our heavenly Father which of thy tender mercy didst give thine only Son Jesus Christ to suffer death upon the Cross for our redemption, who made there (by His one oblation of Himself once offered) a full, perfect, and sufficient sacrifice, oblation, and satisfaction for the sins of the whole world, and did institute and, in His holy gospel, command us to continue a perpetual memory of that His precious death, until his coming again, hear us O merciful father, we beseech Thee, and grant that we receiving these Thy creatures of bread and wine, according to Thy Son our savior Jesus Christ's holy institution, in remembrance of His death and passion, may be partakers of His most blessed body and blood, who in the same night that He was betrayed, took bread, and when He had given thanks, He brake it, and gave it to His disciples, saying: "Take, eat, this is my body, which is given for you. Do this in remembrance of me." Likewise after supper he toke the cup, and when He had given thanks, He gave it to them, saying: "Drink ye all of this, for this is my blood of the new Testament, which is shed for you and for many, for remission of sins. Do this as oft as ye shall drink it in remembrance of me."

Then shall the minister first receive the Communion in both kinds himself, and next deliver it to other Ministers (if any be there present that they may help the chief minister) and after to the people in their hands kneeling. And when he delivereth the bread, he shall say:

The body of our Lord Jesus Christ, which was given for thee, preserve thy body and soul into everlasting life, and take and eat this in remembrance that Christ died for thee: feed on Him in thine heart by faith, with thanksgiving.

And the minister that delivereth the cup shall say:

The blood of our Lord Jesus Christ, which was shed for thee, preserve thy body and soul into everlasting life, and drink this in remembrance that Christ's blood was shed for thee, and be thankful.

Then shall the priest say the Lord's prayer, the people repeating after him every petition.

After shall be said as followeth:

O Lord and heavenly Father, we thy humble servants, entirely desire Thy fatherly goodness mercifully to accept this our Sacrifice of praise and thanksgiving most humbly beseeching thee to grant that by the merits and death of thy Son Jesus Christ, and through faith in His blood, we (and all thy whole church) may obtain remission of our sins, and all other benefits of His passion. And here we offer and present unto Thee, O Lord, ourselves, our souls and bodies, to be a reasonable, holy, and lively sacrifice unto Thee, humbly beseeching Thee that all we which be partakers of this holy communion may be filled with Thy grace and heavenly benediction. And although we be unworthy through our manifold sins to offer unto Thee any sacrifice, yet we beseech Thee to accept this our bounden duty and service, not weighing our merits, but pardoning our offenses through Jesus Christ our Lord, by whom and with whom, in the unity of the Holy Ghost, all honor and glory be unto Thee, O Father Almighty, world without end. Amen.

Or this:

Almighty and everlasting God, we most heartily thank Thee, for that Thou dost vouchsafe to feed us which have duly received these holy mysteries with the spiritual food of the most precious body and blood of Thy Son, our savior Jesus Christ, and dost assure us thereby of Thy favor and goodness toward us, and that we be very members incorporate in Thy mystical body, which is the blessed company of all faithful people, and be also heirs through hope of Thy everlasting kingdom, by the merits of the most precious death and passion of Thy dear Son. We now most humbly beseech Thee, O heavenly Father, so to assist us with Thy grace that we may continue in that holy fellowship and do all such good works as Thou hast prepared for us to walk in, through Jesus Christ our Lord, to whom with Thee and the Holy Ghost be all honor and glory, world without end. Amen.

Then shall be said or sung:

Glory be to God on high, and in earth peace, goodwill towards men. We praise Thee, we bless Thee, we worship Thee, we glorify Thee, we give thanks to Thee, for Thy great glory. O Lord God, heavenly King, God the Father Almighty. O Lord the only-begotten Son Jesus Christ. O Lord God, Lamb of God, Son of the Father, that takest away the sins of the world, have mercy upon us: Thou that takest away the sins of the world, have mercy upon us. Thou that takest away the sins of the world, receive our prayer. Thou that sittest at the right hand of God the Father, have mercy upon us. For thou only art holy: Thou only art the Lord, thou only O Christ with the Holy Ghost art most high in the Glory of God the Father. Amen.

Then the Priest or the Bishop, if he be present, shall let them depart with this blessing:

The peace of God, which passeth all understanding, keep your hearts and minds in the knowledge and love of God, and of His Son Jesus Christ, our Lord. And the blessing of God almighty, the Father, the Son, and the Holy Ghost, be among you, and remain with you always. Amen.

Collects to be said after the offertory when there is no Communion; every such day one. And the same may be said also as often as occasion shall serve after the Collects, either of Morning and Evening Prayer, Communion, or Litany, by the discretion of the minister.

Assist us mercifully, O Lord, in these our Supplications and Prayers, and dispose the way of Thy servants toward the attainment of everlasting salvation, that among all the changes and chances of this mortal life they may ever be defended by Thy most gracious and ready help, through Christ our Lord. Amen.

O Almighty Lord and everliving God, vouchsafe we beseech Thee, to direct, sanctify, and govern both our hearts and bodies in the ways of Thy laws, and in the works of Thy commandments, that through Thy most mighty protection, both here and ever, we may be preserved in body and soul, through our Lord and Savior Jesus Christ. Amen.

Grant, we beseech Thee, almighty God, that the words which we have heard this day with our outward ears, may through Thy grace be so grafted inwardly in our hearts that they may bring forth in us the fruit of good living, to the honor and praise of Thy name, through Jesus Christ our Lord. Amen.

Prevent[4] us, O Lord, in all our doings, with Thy most gracious favor, and further us with Thy continual help that in all our works begun, continued, and ended in Thee, we may glorify Thy holy name, and finally by Thy mercy, obtain everlasting life, through Jesus Christ our Lord. Amen.

Almighty God, the fountain of all wisdom, which knowest our necessities before we ask and our ignorance in asking, we beseech Thee to have compassion upon our infirmities and those things which for our unworthiness we dare not, and for our blindness we cannot ask, vouchsafe to give us for the worthiness of Thy Son Jesus Christ our Lord. Amen.

Almighty God, which hast promised to hear the petitions of them that ask in Thy Son's name, we beseech Thee mercifully to incline Thine ears to us that have made known now our prayers and supplications unto Thee, and grant that those things which we have faithfully asked, according to Thy will, may effectually be obtained to the relief of our necessity, and to the setting forth of Thy glory through Jesus Christ our Lord. Amen.

Upon the holy days (if there be no Communion) shall be said that that is appointed at the Communion, until the end of the homily, concluding with the

---

[4] *prevent:* go before.

general prayer for the whole estate of Christ's Church militant here in earth, and one, or more of these Collects before rehearsed, as occasion shall serve.

And there shall be no celebration of the Lord's supper except there be a good number to Communicate with the Priest, according to his discretion.

And if there be not above twenty persons in the parish of discretion to receive the Communion, yet there shall be no communion except four or three at the least communicate with the priest And in cathedral and collegiate churches, where be many Priests and Deacons, they shall all receive the communion with the minister every Sunday at the least, except they have a reasonable cause to the contrary.

And to take away the superstition which any person hath or might have in the bread and wine, it shall suffice that the bread be such as is usual to be eaten at the table with other meats, but the best and purest wheat bread that conveniently may be gotten. And if any of the bread or wine remain, the Curate shall have it to his own use.

The bread and wine for the Communion shall be provided by the Curate, and the church wardens, at the charges of the Parish, and the parish shall be discharged of such sums of money or other duties which hitherto they have paid for the same by order of their houses every Sunday.

And note that every Parishioner shall communicate at the least three times in the year, of which Easter to be one, and shall also receive the sacraments and other rites according to the order in this book appointed. And yearly at Easter, every Parishioner shall reckon with his Parson, Vicar or Curate, or his or their deputy or deputies, and pay to them or him all ecclesiastical duties, accustomably due then and at that time to be paid.

INTRODUCTION TO JOHN FOXE'S *ACTS AND MONUMENTS*

THE ENGLISH Reformation nearly came to a sudden and violent end with the death of untimely death of Edward VI in the summer of 1553. Next in line for the succession was Mary (r. 1553–1558), the daughter of Catherine of Aragon, Henry VIII's first wife, from whom he had sought the divorce that had begun the English Reformation twenty years before. Mary had every reason to want to roll back the progress of Protestantism in England: not only was she anxious to revenge the insult upon her mother, but she had been raised a devout Catholic, and felt it her religious duty to return England to the obedience of the Pope as quickly as possible. Protestant leaders recognized the danger, and hastily scrambled to rewrite the laws of succession so as to bring Edward's young Protestant cousin, Lady Jane Grey, to the throne. Unfortunately, popular support for Mary as the rightful heir proved irresistible, and the leaders such as Cranmer only succeeded in adding the stigma of treason to that of heresy.

Many made their way in haste to safety on the Continent, including many who were to be later bishops in Queen Elizabeth's church, but Cranmer himself did not. Devoutly loyal to the English crown and deeply conflicted about the treason he had been involved in, he determined to remain, hoping for the best and preparing for the worst. The worst was indeed to soon fall on many of his co-religionists. By late 1554, Mary had bent Parliament largely to her will and began trying many Protestants for heresy. Beginning early in 1555, hundreds were burned at the stake. Cranmer, however, was left to wait in increasing psychological agony under arrest in Oxford.

The delay in executing Cranmer was due to a number of factors. Some were simply legal and procedural; he was after all the Archbishop of Canterbury, and he had to be duly deprived by both authorities in church and state before judicial proceedings could commence. There was also some hope by the Catholic authorities that he might be brought to publicly recant his Protestant opinions and profess again his obedience to the Pope. Even those determined to see him executed hoped to achieve this result first, thus winning a public relations victory for the Roman cause unlike any that they had yet managed anywhere in Europe. This was indeed the plan that was soon put into action, and with cunning persistence and precision.

Cranmer was confined in increasing isolation for a year, brought out only to witness the excruciating execution of his friends, Bishops Ridley and Latimer, and to undergo various interrogations and mock trials, all the while his resolve being slowly worn down. At the end of 1555, a Spanish friar, Juan de Villagarcia, began meeting with him to persuade him of his errors and convince him to repent. Skillfully playing on Cranmer's gnawing guilt and loneliness, Villagarcia and his allies eventually succeeded in eliciting a series of increasingly abject recantations from Cranmer's pen, so that by March 1556 he seemed ready to fully return to the bosom of the Roman Catholic Church and the obedience of the pope.

His execution, however, was not to be stayed even by such repentance. But before he was brought to the stake, the authorities were determined to make a public show of his recantation, thus crushing, they hoped, all psychological resistance by remaining Protestants in England. Instead, the elaborate event on March 21st must go down as one of the greatest public-relations catastrophes of history. Cranmer, marshaling all his courage, recanted his recantation in the most dramatic manner, and went to the stake with dignity, dying in the Protestant faith in which he had so long lived.

The result was a strengthening of growing popular resistance to Mary, which helped Elizabeth rapidly re-establish Protestant religion at Mary's death in 1558.

The account below of Cranmer's final weeks and death is taken from the book traditionally known as Foxe's Book of Martyrs, which became a classic of English religious literature. John Foxe (c. 1516–1587) was an English Protestant scholar who had, with many others, taken flight to the Continent at Mary's accession, to return when Elizabeth took the throne. Seeking to memorialize the lives and deaths of the Marian martyrs, and set them alongside classic stories of martyrs from earlier ages of the church, Foxe composed the massive tome Acts and Monuments in 1563. It was to prove matchless as a piece of propaganda for the Protestant cause in an England that, although now formally Protestant, still harbored many lukewarm or Catholic holdouts. Subsequently expanded, reprinted, and abridged many times, Acts and Monuments was instrumental in helping the Protestant English church come to see itself as a continuation of the faithful testimony of the early Christians against tyrannical persecutors.

Although blatantly one-sided, it has been generally recognized as a relatively reliable source at least for its core subject matter, the English Reformation. For Cranmer's martyrdom in particular, so public were the events surrounding it that there was little room for either Catholic or Protestant propagandists to distort it, and the following account may be taken as substantially accurate.

Further Reading

For further reading, see Diarmaid MacCulloch, *Thomas Cranmer: A Life*, rev. ed. (New Haven: Yale University Press, 2016), chs. 10–11; Susan Doran and Thomas S. Freeman, eds., *Mary Tudor: Old and New Perspectives* (New York: Palgrave MacMillan, 2011); John N. King, *Foxe's 'Book of Martyrs' and Early Modern Print Culture* (Cambridge: Cambridge University Press, 2006).

JOHN FOXE, *ACTS AND MONUMENTS* (1563)[1]

The Martyrdom of Thomas Cranmer

DR. THOMAS Cranmer was descended from an ancient family, and was born at the village of Arselacton, in the county of Northampton. After the usual school education, he was sent to Cambridge, and was chosen fellow of Jesus College. Here he married a gentleman's daughter, by which he forfeited his fellowship, and became a reader in Buckingham college, placing his wife at the Dolphin inn, the landlady of which was a relation of hers, whence arose the idle report that he was an ostler. His lady shortly after dying in childbed, to his credit he was re-chosen a fellow of the college before mentioned. In a few years after, he was promoted to be Divinity Lecturer, and appointed one of the examiners over those who were ripe to become Bachelors or Doctors in Divinity. It was his principle to judge of their qualifications by the knowledge they possessed of the Scriptures, rather than of the ancient fathers, and hence many popish priests were rejected, and others rendered much improved.

He was strongly solicited by Dr. Capon to be one of the fellows on the foundation of Cardinal Wolsey's college, Oxford, of which he hazarded the refusal. While he continued in Cambridge, the question of Henry VIII's divorce with Catharine was agitated.

---

[1] John Foxe, *Fox's Book of Martyrs, or a History of the Lives, Sufferings, and Triumphant Deaths of the Primitive Protestant Martyrs* (Philadelphia: John C. Winston, 1926).

At that time, on account of the plague, Dr. Cranmer removed to the house of a Mr. Cressy, at Waltham Abbey, whose two sons were then educating under him. The affair of divorce, contrary to the king's approbation, had remained undecided above two or three years, from the intrigues of the canonists and civilians, and though the cardinals Campeius and Wolsey were commissioned from Rome to decide the question, they purposely protracted the sentence. It happened that Dr. Gardiner (secretary) and Dr. Fox, defenders of the king in the above suit, came to the house of Mr. Cressy to lodge, while the king removed to Greenwich. At supper, a conversation ensued with Dr. Cranmer, who suggested that the question, whether a man may marry his brother's wife or not, could be easily and speedily decided by the word of God, and this as well in the English courts as in those of any foreign nation. The king, uneasy at the delay, sent for Dr. Gardiner and Dr. Foxe, to consult them, regretting that a new commission must be sent to Rome, and the suit be endlessly protracted. Upon relating to the king the conversation which had passed on the previous evening with Dr. Cranmer, his majesty sent for him, and opened the tenderness of conscience upon the near affinity of the queen. Dr. Cranmer advised that the matter should be referred to the most learned divines of Cambridge and Oxford, as he was unwilling to meddle in an affair of such weight; but the king enjoined him to deliver his sentiments in writing, and to repair for that purpose to the Earl of Wiltshire's, who would accommodate him with books, and every thing requisite for the occasion. This Dr. Cranmer immediately did, and in his declaration, not only quoted the authority of the Scriptures, of general councils and the ancient writers, but maintained that the bishop of Rome had no authority whatever to dispense with the word of God. The king asked him if he would stand by this bold declaration, to which replying in the affirmative, he was deputed ambassador to Rome, in conjunction with the Earl of Wiltshire, Dr. Stokesley, Dr. Carne, Dr. Bennet, and others, previous to which, the marriage was discussed in most of the universities of Christendom and at Rome; when the pope presented his toe to be kissed, as customary, the Earl of Wiltshire and his party refused. Indeed, it is affirmed that a spaniel of the Earl's, attracted by the glitter of the pope's toe, made a snap at it, whence his holiness drew in his sacred foot, and kicked at the offender with the other. Upon the pope demanding the cause of their embassy, the Earl presented Dr. Cranmer's book, declaring that his learned friends had come to defend it. The pope treated the embassy honourably, and appointed a day for the discussion, which he delayed, as if afraid of the issue of the investigation. The Earl returned, and Dr. Cranmer, by the king's desire, visited the emperor, and was successful in bringing him over to his opinion. Upon the Doctor's return to England, Dr. Warham, archbishop of Canterbury, having quitted this transitory life, Dr. Cranmer was deservedly, and by Dr. Warham's desire, elevated to that eminent station.

In this function, it may be said that he followed closely the charge of St. Paul. Diligent in duty, he rose at five in the morning, and continued in study and prayer till nine: between then and dinner, he devoted to temporal affairs. After dinner, if any suitors wanted hearing, he would determine their business with such an affability, that even the defaulters were scarcely displeased. Then he would play at chess for an hour, or see others play, and at five o'clock he heard the Common Prayer read, and from this till supper he took the recreation of walking. At supper his conversation was lively and entertaining; again he walked or amused himself till nine o'clock, and then entered his study.

He ranked high in favour with king Henry and ever had the purity and the interest of the English church deeply at heart. His mild and forgiving disposition is recorded in the following instance: An ignorant priest, in the country, had called Cranmer an ostler, and spoken very derogatory of his learning. Lord Cromwell receiving information of it, the man was sent to the fleet, and his case was told to the archbishop by a Mr. Chertsey, a grocer, and a relation of the priest's. His grace, having sent for the offender, reasoned with him, and solicited the priest to question him on any learned subject. This the man, overcome by the bishop's good nature, and knowing his own glaring incapacity, declined, and entreated his forgiveness, which was immediately granted, with a charge to employ his time better when he returned to his parish. Cromwell was much vexed at the lenity displayed, but the bishop was ever more ready to receive injury than to retaliate in any other manner than by good advice and good offices.

At the time that Cranmer was raised to be archbishop, he was king's chaplain, and archdeacon of Taunton; he was also constituted by the pope penitentiary general of England. It was considered by the king that Cranmer would be obsequious; hence the latter married the king to Anne Boleyn, performed her coronation, stood godfather to Elizabeth, the first child, and divorced the king from Catharine. Though Cranmer received a confirmation of his dignity from the pope, he always protested against acknowledging any other authority than the king's, and he persisted in the same independent sentiments when before Mary's commissioners in 1555. One of the first steps after the divorce was to prevent preaching throughout his diocese, but this narrow measure had rather a political view than a religious one, as there were many who inveighed against the king's conduct. In his new dignity Cranmer agitated the question of supremacy, and by his powerful and just arguments induced the parliament to "render to Cæsar the things which are Cæsar's." During Cranmer's residence in Germany, 1531, he became acquainted with Ossiander, at Nurenburgh, and married his niece, but left her with him while on his return to England; after a season he sent for her privately, and she remained with him till the year 1539, when the Six Articles compelled him to return her to her friends for a time.

It should be remembered that Ossiander, having obtained the approbation of his friend Cranmer, published the laborious work of the Harmony of the Gospels in 1537. In 1534 the archbishop completed the dearest wish of his heart, the removal of every obstacle to the perfection of the Reformation, by the subscription of the nobles and bishops to the king's sole supremacy. Only bishop Fisher and Sir Thomas More made objection; and their agreement not to oppose the succession, Cranmer was willing to consider as sufficient, but the monarch would have no other than an entire concession. Not long after, Gardiner, in a private interview with the king, spoke inimically of Cranmer, (whom he maliciously hated) for assuming the title of Primate of all England, as derogatory to the supremacy of the king; this created much jealousy against Cranmer, and his translation of the Bible was strongly opposed by Stokesley, bishop of London. It is said, upon the demise of queen Catharine, that her successor Anne Boleyn rejoiced—a lesson this to show how shallow is the human judgment! since her own execution took place in the spring of the following year, and the king, on the day following the beheading of this sacrificed lady, married the beautiful Jane Seymour, a maid of honour to the late queen. Cranmer was ever the friend of Anne Boleyn, but it was dangerous to oppose the will of the carnal tyrannical monarch.

In 1538, the holy Scriptures were openly exposed to sale; and the places of worship overflowed every where to hear its holy doctrines expounded. Upon the king's passing into a law the famous Six Articles, which went nearly again to establish the essential tenets of the Romish creed, Cranmer shone forth with all the lustre of a Christian patriot, in resisting the doctrines they contained, and in which he was supported by the bishops of Sarum, Worcester, Ely, and Rochester, the two former of whom resigned their bishoprics. The king, though now in opposition to Cranmer, still revered the sincerity that marked his conduct. The death of Lord Cromwell in the Tower, in 1540, the good friend of Cranmer, was a severe blow to the wavering protestant cause, but even now Cranmer, when he saw the tide directly adverse to the truth, boldly waited on the king in person, and by his manly and heartfelt pleading, caused the book of Articles to be passed on his side, to the great confusion of his enemies, who had contemplated his fall as inevitable.

Cranmer now lived in as secluded a manner as possible, till the rancour of Winchester preferred some articles against him, relative to the dangerous opinion he taught in his family, joined to other treasonable charges. These the king delivered himself to Cranmer, and believing firmly the fidelity and assertions of innocence of the accused prelate, he caused the matter to be deeply investigated, and Winchester and Dr. Lenden, with Thornton and Barber, of the bishop's household, were found by the papers to be the real conspirators. The mild forgiving Cranmer would have interceded for all remission of punishment, had not Henry, pleased with the subsidy voted by parliament, let them be discharged; these nefarious men, however, again renewing their plots against Cranmer, fell victims to Henry's resentment, and Gardiner forever lost his confidence. Sir G. Gostwick soon after laid charges against the archbishop, which Henry quashed, and the primate was willing to forgive.

In 1544, the archbishop's palace at Canterbury was burnt, and his brother-in-law with others perished in it. These various afflictions may serve to reconcile us to an humble state; for of what happiness could this great and good man boast? since his life was constantly harassed either by political, religious, or natural crosses. Again the inveterate Gardiner laid high charges against the meek archbishop and would have sent him to the tower; but the king was his friend, gave him his signet that he would defend him, and in the council not only declared the bishop one of the best affected men in his realm, but sharply rebuked his accusers for their calumny.

A peace having been made, Henry, and the French king Henry the Great, were unanimous to have the mass abolished in their kingdom, and Cranmer set about this great work; but the death of the English monarch, in 1546, suspended the procedure, and king Edward his successor continued Cranmer in the same functions, upon whose coronation he delivered a charge that will ever honour his memory, for its purity, freedom, and truth. During this reign he prosecuted the glorious reformation with unabated zeal, even in the year 1552, when he was seized with a severe ague, from which it pleased God to restore him that he might testify by his death the truth of that seed he had diligently sown.

The death of Edward, in 1553, exposed Cranmer to all the rage of his enemies. Though the archbishop was among those who supported Mary's accession, he was attainted at the meeting of parliament, and in November adjudged guilty of high treason at Guildhall, and degraded from his dignities. He sent an humble letter to Mary, explaining the cause of his signing the will in favor of Edward, and in 1554 he wrote to the council, whom he pressed to obtain a pardon from the queen, by a letter delivered to Dr. Weston, but which the latter opened, and on seeing its contents, basely returned. Treason was a charge quite inapplicable to Cranmer, who supported the queen's right; while others, who had favoured Lady Jane, upon paying a small fine were dismissed. A calumny was now spread against Cranmer that he complied with some of the popish ceremonies to ingratiate himself with the queen, which he dared publicly to disavow, and justified his articles of faith. The active part which the prelate had taken in the divorce of Mary's mother had ever rankled deeply in the heart of the queen, and revenge formed a prominent feature in the death of Cranmer. We have in this work, noticed the public disputations at Oxford, in which the talents of Cranmer, Ridley, and Latimer shone so conspicuously, and tended to their condemnation. The first sentence was illegal, inasmuch as the usurped power of the pope had not yet been re-established by law. Being kept in prison till this was effected, a commission was despatched from Rome, appointing Dr. Brooks to sit as the representative of his Holiness, and Drs. Story and Martin as those of the queen. Cranmer was willing to bow to the authority of Drs. Story and Martin, but against that of Dr. Brooks he protested. Such were the remarks and replies of Cranmer, after a long examination, that Dr. Brooks observed, "We come to examine you, and methinks you examine us." Being sent back to confinement, he received a citation to appear at Rome within eighteen days, but this was impracticable, as he was imprisoned in England; and as he stated, even had he been at liberty, he was too poor to employ an advocate. Absurd as it must appear, Cranmer was condemned at Rome, and February 14, 1556, a new commission was appointed by which, Thirdly, bishop of Ely, and Bonner, of London, were deputed to sit in judgment at Christ-church, Oxford. By virtue of this instrument, Cranmer was gradually degraded, by putting mere rags on him to represent the dress of an archbishop; then stripping him of his attire, they took off his own gown, and put an old worn one upon him instead. This he bore unmoved, and his enemies, finding that severity only rendered him more determined, tried the opposite course, and placed him in the house of the dean of Christchurch, where he was treated with every indulgence. This presented such a contrast to the three years hard imprisonment he had received, that it threw him off his guard. His open, generous nature was more easily to be seduced by a liberal conduct than by threats and fetters. When Satan finds the Christian proof against one mode of attack, he tries another; and what form is so seductive as smiles, rewards, and power, after a long, painful imprisonment? Thus it was with Cranmer: his enemies promised him his former greatness if he would but recant, as well as the queen's favour, and this at the very time they knew that his death was determined in council. To soften the path to apostasy, the first paper brought for his signature was conceived in general terms; this one signed, five others were obtained as explanatory of the first, till finally he put his hand to the following detestable instrument:

"I, Thomas Cranmer, late archbishop of Canterbury, do renounce, abhor, and detest all manner of heresies and errors of Luther and Zuinglius, and all other teachings which are contrary to sound and true doctrine. And I believe most constantly in my heart, and with my mouth I confess one holy and catholic church visible, without which there is no salvation; and therefore I acknowledge the bishop of Rome to be supreme head on earth, whom I acknowledge to be the highest bishop and pope, and Christ's vicar, unto whom all Christian people ought to be subject.

"And as concerning the sacraments, I believe and worship in the sacrament of the altar the body and blood of Christ, being contained most truly under the forms of bread and wine; the bread, through the mighty power of God being turned into the body of our Saviour Jesus Christ, and the wine into his blood.

"And in the other six sacraments, also, (alike as in this) I believe and hold as the universal church holdeth, and the church of Rome judgeth and determineth.

"Furthermore, I believe that there is a place of purgatory, where souls departed be punished for a time, for whom the church doth godlily and wholesomely pray, like as it doth honour saints and make prayers to them.

"Finally, in all things I profess, that I do not otherwise believe than the catholic church and the church of Rome holdeth and teacheth. I am sorry that I ever held or thought otherwise. And I beseech Almighty God, that of his mercy he will vouchsafe to forgive me whatsoever I have offended against God or his church, and also I desire and beseech all Christian people to pray for me.

"And all such as have been deceived either by mine example of doctrine, I require them by the blood of Jesus Christ that they will return to the unity of the church, that we may be all of one mind, without schism or division.

"And to conclude, as I submit myself to the catholic church of Christ, and to the supreme head thereof, so I submit myself unto the most excellent majesties of Philip and Mary, king and queen of this realm of England, &c. and to all other their laws and ordinances, being ready always as a faithful subject ever to obey them. And God is my witness, that I have not done this for favour or fear of any person, but willingly and of mine own conscience, as to the instruction of others."

"Let him that standeth take heed lest he fall!" said the apostle, and here was a falling off indeed! The papists now triumphed in their turn: they had acquired all they wanted short of his life. His recantation was immediately printed and dispersed, that it might have its due effect upon the astonished protestants; but God counter-worked all the designs of the Catholics by the extent to which they carried the implacable persecution of their prey. Doubtless, the love of life induced Cranmer to sign the above declaration; yet death may be said to have been preferable to life to him who lay under the stings of a goaded conscience and the contempt of every gospel Christian; this principle he strongly felt in all its force and anguish.

The queen's revenge was only to be satiated in Cranmer's blood, and therefore she wrote an order to Dr. Cole, to prepare a sermon to be preached March 21, directly before his martyrdom, at St. Mary's, Oxford; Dr. Cole visited him the day previous, and was induced to believe that he would publicly deliver his sentiments in confirmation of the articles to which he had subscribed. About nine in the morning of the day of sacrifice, the queen's commissioners, attended by the magistrates, conducted the amiable unfortunate to St. Mary's church. His torn, dirty garb, the same in which they habited him upon his degradation, excited the commiseration of the people. In the church he found a low, mean stage, erected opposite to the pulpit, on which being placed, he turned his face, and fervently prayed to God. The church was crowded with persons of both persuasions, expecting to hear the justification of the late apostacy: the Catholics rejoicing, and the Protestants deeply wounded in spirit at the deceit of the human heart. Dr. Cole, in his sermon, represented Cranmer as having been guilty of the most atrocious crimes, encouraged the deluded sufferer not to fear death, not to doubt the support of God in his torments, nor that masses would be said in all the churches of Oxford for the repose of his soul. The Doctor then noticed his conversion, and which he ascribed to the evident working of Almighty Power, and in order that the people might be convinced of its reality, asked the prisoner to give them a sign. This Cranmer did, and begged the congregation to pray for him, for he had committed many and grievous sins, but, of all, there was one which awfully lay upon his mind, of which he would speak shortly.

During the sermon Cranmer wept bitter tears: lifting up his hands and eyes to heaven, and letting them fall, as if unworthy to live; his grief now found vent in words; before his confession he fell upon his knees, and, in the following words unveiled the deep contrition and agitation which harrowed up his soul.

"O Father of heaven! O Son of God, Redeemer of the world! O Holy Ghost, three persons and one God! have mercy on me, most wretched caitiff and miserable sinner. I have offended both against heaven and earth, more than my tongue can express. Whither then may I go, or whither may I flee? To heaven I may be ashamed to lift up mine eyes, and in earth I find no place of refuge or succour. To thee, therefore, O Lord, do I run; to thee do I humble myself, saying, O Lord, my God, my sins be great, but yet have mercy upon me for thy great mercy. The great mystery that God became man, was not wrought for little or few offences. Thou didst not give thy Son, O Heavenly Father, unto death for small sins only, but for all the greatest sins of the world, so that the sinner return to thee with his whole heart, as I do at present. Wherefore, have mercy on me, O God, whose property is always to have mercy, have mercy upon me, O Lord, for thy great mercy. I crave nothing for my own merits, but for thy name's sake, that it may be hallowed thereby, and for thy dear Son Jesus Christ's sake. And now therefore, O Father of Heaven, hallowed be thy name," &c.

Then rising, he said he was desirous before his death to give them some pious exhortations by which God might be glorified and themselves edified. He then descanted upon the danger of a love for the world, the duty of obedience to their majesties of love to one another and the necessity of the rich administering to the wants of the poor. He quoted the three verses of the fifth chapter of James, and then proceeded, "Let them that be rich ponder well these three sentences: for if they ever had occasion to show their charity, they have it now at this present, the poor people being so many, and victual so dear.

"And now forasmuch as I am come to the last end of my life, whereupon hangeth all my life past, and all my life to come, either to live with my master Christ for ever in joy, or else to be in pain for ever with the wicked in hell, and I see before mine eyes presently, either heaven ready to receive me, or else hell ready to swallow me up, I shall therefore declare unto you my very faith how I believe, without any colour of dissimulation: for now is no time to dissemble, whatsoever I have said or written in times past.

"First, I believe in God the Father Almighty, maker of heaven and earth, &c. And I believe every article of the Catholic faith, every word and sentence taught by our Saviour Jesus Christ, his apostles and prophets, in the New and Old Testament.

"And now I come to the great thing which so much troubleth my conscience, more than any thing that ever I did or said in my whole life, and that is the setting abroad of a writing contrary to the truth, which now here I renounce and refuse, as things written with my hand contrary to the truth which I thought in my heart, and written for fear of death, and to save my life, if it might be; and that is, all such bills or papers which I have written or signed with my hand since my degradation, wherein I have written many things untrue. And forasmuch as my hand hath offended, writing contrary to my heart, therefore my hand shall first be punished; for when I come to the fire, it shall first be burned.

"And as for the Pope, I refuse him as Christ's enemy, and antichrist, with all his false doctrine.

"And as for the sacrament, I believe as I have taught in my book against the bishop of Winchester, which my book teacheth so true a doctrine of the sacrament, that it shall stand in the last day before the judgment of God, where the papistical doctrines contrary thereto shall be ashamed to show their face."

Upon the conclusion of this unexpected declaration, amazement and indignation were conspicuous in every part of the church. The Catholics were completely foiled, their object being frustrated; Cranmer, like Sampson, having completed a greater ruin upon his enemies in the hour of death, than he did in his life.

Cranmer would have proceeded in the exposure of the popish doctrines, but the murmurs of the idolaters drowned his voice, and the preacher gave an order to lead the heretic away! The savage command was directly obeyed, and the lamb about to suffer was torn from his stand to the place of slaughter, insulted all the way by the revilings and taunts of the pestilent monks and friars. With thoughts intent upon a far higher object than the empty threats of man, he reached the spot dyed with the blood of Ridley and Latimer. There he knelt for a short time in earnest devotion, and then arose, that he might undress and prepare for the fire. Two friars who had been parties in prevailing upon him to abjure, now endeavoured to draw him off again from the truth, but he was steadfast and immoveable in what he had just professed, and before publicly taught. A chain was provided to bind him to the stake, and after it had tightly encircled him, fire was put to the fuel, and the flames began soon to ascend. Then were the glorious sentiments of the martyr made manifest—then it was, that stretching out his right hand, he held it unshrinkingly in the fire till it was burnt to a cinder, even before his body was injured, frequently exclaiming, "This unworthy right hand!" Apparently insensible of pain, with a countenance of venerable resignation, and eyes directed to Him for whose cause he suffered, he continued, like St. Stephen, to say, "Lord Jesus receive my spirit!" till the fury of the flames terminated his powers of utterance and existence. He closed a life of high sublunary elevation, of constant uneasiness, and of glorious martyrdom, on March 21, 1556.

Thus perished the illustrious Cranmer, the man whom king Henry's capricious soul esteemed for his virtues above all other men. Cranmer's example is an endless testimony that fraud and cruelty are the leading characteristics of the catholic hierarchy. They first seduced him to live by recantation, and then doomed him to perish, using perhaps the sophistical arguments, that, being brought again within the catholic pale, he was then most fit to die. His gradual change from darkness to the light of the truth proved that he had a mind open to conviction. Though mild and forgiving in temper, he was severe in church discipline, and it is only on this ground that one act of cruelty of his can in any way be excused. A poor woman was in Edward's reign condemned to be burnt for her religious opinions; the pious young monarch reasoned with the archbishop upon the impropriety of Protestants resorting to the same cruel means they censured in papists, adding humanely,

"What! would you have me send her quick to the devil in her error?" The prelate however was not to be softened, and the king signed the death warrant with eyes steeped in tears. There is however a shade in the greatest characters, and few characters, whether political or religious, were greater than Cranmer's.

INTRODUCTION TO *AN ADMONITION TO THE PARLIAMENT*

ELIZABETH'S RESTORATION of Protestant worship and doctrine in 1558-9 was initially hailed by Protestant leaders and ministers throughout England and abroad as a God-sent deliverance from the tyranny and superstition of Mary's reign. But it was not long before dissatisfaction began to fester in the young Church of England. The sources of the trouble are not hard to find; as we saw in the introduction to the Book of Common Prayer selection, there were some tensions even in Edward's reign between those who felt that many traditional liturgical elements could be harmlessly retained and those who favored a simplified and, as they saw it, more biblical liturgy. When many Protestant leaders fled abroad during Mary's reign, they had the freedom to improvise their own forms of worship, and many came to prefer the pared-down and more word-centered liturgies of Reformed churches on the Continent. In a series of contentious episodes in Frankfurt, different parties within the English exile community there quarreled over whether or not to retain the liturgies of the 1552 Book of Common Prayer, and the city magistrates had to intervene.

Although both parties to this dispute happily re-united in England after Elizabeth took the throne, the liturgy she established was in certain respects even more conservative than the 1552 Prayer Book, concerned as she was to avoid antagonizing too much Catholic nobles at home and Catholic monarchs abroad. Indeed, many churchmen, including high-ranking bishops such as John Jewel of Salisbury (1522–1571) and Edmund Grindal (c. 1519–1583) of London, who had been in exile and seen Continental

models of worship first-hand, expected that there would be considerable leeway in the actual practice of the liturgy, and that more
progressive-minded ministers would be free to leave out portions
that they considered too tainted with the popish past.

But while most bishops might have been fine with a more
flexible policy, Queen Elizabeth (r. 1558–1603) certainly was not.
Although her own commitment to Protestant faith cannot be
doubted, her personal sense of piety was still relatively traditional,
and she was a shrewd enough politician to recognize her position
would become tenuous indeed if she appeared too openly anti-
Catholic. Accordingly, as the 1560s went on, she made clear to her
Archbishop of Canterbury, Matthew Parker (1504–1575), that she
expected him to enforce full conformity to the Book of Common
Prayer, including in the matter of clerical vestments (the various
ceremonial garments that priests and bishops were expected to
wear). These were a particular sticking point among more reform-
minded Protestants, who saw them as the uniform of Antichrist,
and a series of conflicts known as the Vestiarian Controversy broke
out from 1564 to 1567. However, the anti-Vestiarian party lost a lot
of steam when they appealed for advice to the Reformed leader
Heinrich Bullinger in Zurich and were exhorted to conform to the
law, such vestments being "things indifferent"—neither commanded nor forbidden in Scripture.

Between 1567 and 1572, however, the Elizabethan Church
entered upon a decisive new stage, engendering a movement which
was to leave a wide and lasting legacy on the Reformed world over
succeeding centuries, particularly in Britain and America, a movement traditionally known as "puritanism." A great deal seems to
have changed between the conclusion of this controversy in 1567
and the outbreak of the Admonition Controversy in 1572, when
young radicals John Field (c. 1545–1588) and Thomas Wilcox (c.
1549–1608), frustrated by the lack of official response to reforming
overtures and complaints, published and disseminated a scandal-
ously rancorous *Admonition to Parliament*.

The document, although framed as a petition to the Parliament that was then assembling (Parliament meeting, back then, only every few years) was clearly intended as a piece of public propaganda;[1] indeed, Elizabeth had already made clear, and would make increasingly clear over the next couple decades, that she did not see it as Parliament's task to deliberate on matters of church government. Unsurprisingly, the document ignited a firestorm of controversy: Field and Wilcox were imprisoned, an official *Answere by John Whitgift* was commissioned, and battle lines were drawn as pamphlets and counter-pamphlets, treatises and counter-treatises, began to multiply. The immediate literary controversy, in which Whitgift emerged as the spokesman for the establishment, and Thomas Cartwright as the spokesman for the puritans, lasted until 1577. However, the movement that the *Admonition* called into being lasted in organized form until the early 1590s, when it had grown so militant that the bishops and Privy Council took dramatic steps to quash it. The cast of this new act in the drama, however, were quite different from those who had fought it out with the bishops over vestments in 1565–67, most of whom had grudgingly submitted when it was clear the policy was inflexible. Of the twenty scrupulous Protestants who presented a supplication to the bishops over vestments in 1565, only three, says Puritan scholar Patrick Collinson, "remained staunch to the radical cause until their deaths," and most "at once dissociated themselves from the new extremism." So much so, in fact, that from 1572 on, "we are evidently witnessing the beginnings of a new movement rather than the conversion of the old."[2]

And indeed, the issues at stake in the Admonition Controversy are far different, and broader, than those in the Vestiarian. No longer is the question one of when scrupulous consciences can legitimately resist imposition of certain ceremonies, a dispute on

---

[1] Patrick Collinson, *The Elizabethan Puritan Movement* (Berkeley: University of California Press, 1967), 118–120.

[2] Collinson, *Elizabethan Puritan Movement*, 75, 120.

the margins of the Elizabethan settlement. Instead, the new dispute concerned the basic validity of that settlement in its essential features. "We in England are so far off from having a church rightly reformed, according to the prescript of God's word, that as yet we are not come to the outward face of the same," the *Admonition* fulminates, throwing down a gauntlet to the bishops and the government.[3] At stake now is not whether the bishops should enforce strict conformity, but whether the bishops have power to govern the church at all; not whether civil law should presume to bind ministers to wear the cap and surplice, but whether civil authority has any role in determining ceremonies. A fundamental platform of the *Admonition* is the presbyterian doctrine of church government, which, aside from a general sense that lower clergy ought to have more authority in determining church affairs, had been nowhere on the radar in the earlier controversy. This system of polity is not presented as a suggestion, as that best suited to the edification and good government of the churches, but as a biblical requirement. This emphasis reflects a shift in attitudes toward "things indifferent" across the board, with the new Admonitionists suggesting not so much that indifferent ceremonies were being used unedifyingly, but that they were not indifferent in the first place. Indeed, it was no longer enough for ceremonies not to be forbidden by Scriptural teaching, as Catholic rites had been considered by earlier Protestants, but they must be positively affirmed and required by Scripture. Such was the principle that Thomas Cartwright was to hammer out in conflict with Whitgift, a principle that has since become known as the "regulative principle of worship" and has

---

[3] John Field and Thomas Wilcox, *An Admonition to Parliament*, in W.H. Frere and C.E. Douglas, eds., *Puritan Manifestoes: A Study of the Origin of the Puritan Revolt* (London: SPCK, 1907), 9. This sentence was quickly amended in the second edition of the *Admonition* to the somewhat more moderate, "as yet we are *scarce* come to the outward face of the same"; but the damage was done—conformists would hereafter charge the Presbyterians with denying that the church of England was a true church.

exercised great influence on the Presbyterian and Reformed traditions through the centuries.

Further Reading

For further reading, see Patrick Collinson, *The Elizabethan Puritan Movement* (Berkeley: University of California Press, 1967); Stephen Brachlow, *The Communion of Saints: Radical Puritan and Separatist Ecclesiology, 1570–1625* (Oxford: Oxford University Press, 1988); Francis J. Bremer, *Puritanism: A Very Short Introduction* (Oxford: Oxford University Press, 2009).

JOHN FIELD AND THOMAS WILCOX,
AN ADMONITION TO THE PARLIAMENT (1572)[1]

SEEING THAT nothing in this mortal life is more diligently to be sought for and carefully to be looked unto than the restitution of true religion and reformation of God's church, it shall be your parts, dearly beloved, in this present Parliament assembled, as much as in you lieth to promote the same, and to employ your whole labor and study, not only in abandoning all popish remnants, both in ceremonies and regiment, but also in bringing in and placing in God's church those things only which the Lord himself in His word commandeth, because it is not enough to take pains in taking away evil, but also to be occupied in placing good in the stead thereof. Now because many men see not all things, and the world in this respect is marvelously blinded, it hath been thought good to proffer to your godly considerations a true platform of a church reformed, to the end that, it being laid before your eyes to behold the great unlikeness betwixt it and this our English Church, you may learn either with perfect hatred to detest the same, and with singular love to embrace and carefully endeavor to plant the other, or else to be without excuse before the majesty of our God, who, for the discharge of our conscience and manifestation of his truth, hath by us revealed unto you, at this present, the sincerity and simplicity of his Gospel. Not that you should either willfully

---

[1] Spelling modernized by Brian Marr. Taken from *Early English Books Text Creation Partnership*.

withstand or ungraciously tread the same under your feet, for God doth not disclose His will to any such end, but that you should yet now a length with all your main and might endeavor that Christ, whose easy yoke and light burthen we have of long time cast off from us, might rule and reign in his church by the scepter of His word only.

May it therefore please your wisdoms to understand that we in England are so far off from having a church rightly reformed according to the prescript of God's word that, as yet, we are scarce come to the outward face of the same. For to speak of that wherein the best consent, and whereupon all good writers accord the outward marks whereby a true Christian church is known are preaching of the word purely, ministering of the sacraments sincerely, and ecclesiastical discipline, which consisteth in admonition and correction of faults severely. Touching the first, namely the ministry of the word, although it must be confessed that the substance of doctrine by many delivered is sound and good, yet herein it faileth: that neither the ministers thereof are according to God's word proved, elected, called, or ordained, nor the function in such sort so narrowly looked unto as of right it ought and is of necessity required. For whereas in the old church a trial was had, both of their ability to instruct and of their godly conversation also, now by the letters commendatory of some one man, noble or other, tag and rag, learned and unlearned, of the basest sort of the people (to the slander of the gospel in the mouths of the adversaries) are freely received. In those days no idolatrous sacrificers or heathenish priests were appointed to be preachers of the Gospel, but we allow and like well of popish mass-mongers, men for all seasons, King Henry's priests, Queen Mary's priests, who of a truth (if God's word were precisely followed) should from the same be utterly removed. Then they taught others; now they must be instructed themselves, and therefore like young children they must learn catechisms, and so first they consecrate them and make them ministers, and then they set them to school. Then election was made by the elders with the common consent of the whole church; now everyone picketh out for himself some notable good benefice, he obtaineth the next advowson, by money or by favor and so thinketh himself to be sufficiently chosen. Then the congregation had authority to call ministers; in stead thereof now they run, they ride, and by unlawful suite and buying, prevent other suiters also. Then no minister placed in any congregation but by the consent of the people; now, that authority is given into the hands of the bishop alone, who by his sole authority thrusteth upon them such as they many times as well for unhonest life, as also for lack of learning may and do [instantly] dislike. Then, none admitted to the ministry but a place was void beforehand to which he should be called, but now bishops (to whom the right of ordering ministers doth at no hand appertain) do make sixty, eighty, or a hundred at a clap, and send them abroad into the country like masterless men. Then, after just trial and vocation they were admitted to their function by laying on of the hands of the company of the eldership only; now there is (neither of these being looked unto) required a surplice, a vestment, a pastoral staff, beside that ridiculous and (as they use it to their new creatures) blasphemous saying: "receive the Holy Ghost." Then every pastor had his flock, and every flock his shepherd, or else shepherds; now they do not only run fisking from place to place (a miserable disorder in God's church), but covetously join living to living, making shipwreck of their own consciences, and being but one shepherd (nay, would to God they were shepherds and not wolves) have many flocks. Then the ministers were preachers; now bare readers. And if any be so well disposed to preach in their own charges, they may not without my lord's license. In those days known by voice, learning, and doctrine; now they must be discerned from other by popish and Antichristian apparel, as cap, gown, tipper and etc. Then, as God gave utterance they preached the word only; now they read homilies, articles, injunctions, etc. Then it was painful; now gainful. Then poor and ignominious in the eyes of the world; now rich and glorious. And therefore titles, livings, and offices by Antichrist devised are given to them, as metropolitan, archbishop, lord's grace, lord bishop, suffragan, dean, archdeacon, prelate of the garter, earl, county palatine, honor, high commissioners, justices of peace and quorum, etc.—all which, together with their offices, as they are strange and unheard of in Christ's church, nay plainly in God's word forbidden, so are they utterly with speed out of the same to be renounced. Then ministers were not so tied to any one form of prayers but as the spirit moved them and as necessity of time required, so they might pour forth hearty supplications to the Lord. Now they are bound of necessity to a prescript order of service and book of common prayer in which a great number of things contrary to God's word are contained, as baptism by women private, communions, Jewish purifyings, observing of holy days, etc. patched (if not all together, yet the greatest piece) out of the Popes' portius. Then, feeding the flock diligently; now, teaching quarterly. Then, preaching in season and out of season; now once in a month is thought of some sufficient, if twice, it is judged a work of supererogation. Then, nothing taught but Gods word; now princes' pleasures, men's devices, popish ceremonies, and Antichristian rites in public pulpits descended. Then they sought them; now they seek theirs.

These, and a great many other abuses are in the ministry remaining, which unless they be removed and the truth brought in, not only God's justice shall be poured forth, but also God's church in this realm shall never be built. For if they which seem to be workmen are no workmen in deed, but in name, or else work not so diligently and in such order as the workmaster commandeth, it is not only unlikely that the building shall go forward, but altogether impossible that ever it shall be preferred. The way therefore to avoid these inconveniences and to reform these deformities is this: your wisdoms have to remove advowsons, patronages, impropriations, and bishops' authority, claiming to themselves thereby right to ordain ministers and to bring in the old and true election which was accustomed to be made by the congregation. You must displace those ignorant and unable ministers already placed, and in their rooms appoint such as both can and will by God's assistance feed the flock. You must pluck down and utterly overthrow without hope of restitution the court of faculties, from whence not only licenses to enjoy many benefices are obtained, as pluralities, trialities, totquots, etc., but all things for the most part, as in the court of Rome are set on sale: licenses to marry, to eat flesh in times prohibited, to live from benefices and charges, and a great number beside of such like abominations. Appoint to every congregation a learned and diligent preacher. Remove homilies, articles, injunctions, and that prescript order of service made out of the massbook. Take away the lordship, the loitering, the pomp, the idleness, and livings of bishops, but yet employ them to such ends as they were in the old church appointed for. Let a lawful and a godly seignory look that they preach, not quarterly or monthly, but continually, not for filthy lucre's sake, but of a ready mind. So God shall be glorified, your consciences discharged, and the flock of Christ, purchased with his own blood, edified.

Now to the second point, which concerneth ministration of sacraments: in the old time, the word was preached before they were ministered; now it is supposed to be sufficient if it be read. Then they were ministered in public assemblies; now in private houses. Then by ministers only; now by midwives, and deacons equally. But because in treating of both the sacraments together, we should deal confusedly, we will therefore speak of them severally. And first for the Lord's supper, or holy communion.

They had no introite, for Celestinus a pope brought it in, about the year 430; but we have borrowed a piece of one out of the mass-book. They read no fragments of the Epistle and Gospel; we use both. The Nicene Creed was not read in their communion; we have it in ours. There was then accustomed to be an examination of the communicants, which now is neglected. Then they ministered the sacrament with common and usual bread; now with wafer cakes, brought in by Pope Alexander, being in form, fashion, and substance, like their god of the altar. They received it sitting; we, kneeling, according to Honorius' Decree. Then it was delivered generally and indefinitely, "Take ye and eat ye"; we particularly, and singularly, "Take thou, and eat thou." They used no other words but such as Christ left; we borrow from papists, "The body of our Lord Jesus Christ which was given for thee." They had no Gloria in excelsis in the ministry of the Sacrament then, for it was put to afterward; we have now. They took it with conscience; we without. They shut men by reason of their sins from the Lord's Supper; we thrust them in their sin to the Lord's Supper. They ministered the sacrament plainly; we, pompously with singing, piping, surplice and cope wearing. They simply, as they received it from the Lord; we sinfully, mixed with man's inventions and devices. And as for baptism, it was enough with them if they had water and the party to be baptized, faith, and the minister to preach the word and minister the sacraments.

Now, we must have surplices devised by Pope Aidan, interrogatories ministered to the infant, holy sorts invented by Pope Pius, crossing and such like pieces of Popery which the church of God in the Apostles' times never knew (and therefore not to be used), nay, which we are sure of, were and are man's devices, brought in long after the purity of the primitive church. To redress these, your wisdoms have to remove (as before) ignorant ministers, to take away private communions and baptisms, to enjoin deacons and midwives not to meddle in ministers' matters, [and] if they do, to see them sharply punished; to join assistance of elders and other officers that, seeing men will not examine themselves, they may be examined and brought to render a reason of their hope; that the statute against wafer-cakes may more prevail then an Injunction; that people be appointed to receive the Sacrament, rather sitting for avoiding of superstition than kneeling, having in it the outward show of evil, from which we must abstain; that excommunication be restored to his old former force; that papists, nor other, neither constrainedly nor customably communicate in the mysteries of salvation; that both the sacrament of the Lord's supper and Baptism also may be ministered according to the ancient purity and simplicity; that the parties to be baptized, if they be of the years of discretion, by themselves and in their own persons, or if they be infants, by their parents (in whose room if upon necessary occasions and businesses they be absent, some of the congregation knowing the good behavior and sound faith of the parents) may both make rehearsal of their faith, and also if their faith be sound and agreeable to holy scriptures, desire to be in the same baptized; and finally that nothing be done in this or any other thing but that which you have the express warrant of God's word for.

Let us come now to the third part, which concerneth ecclesiastical discipline: the officers that have to deal in this charge are chiefly three: ministers, preachers, or pastors of whom before; seniors or elders; and deacons. Concerning seniors, not only their office but their name also is out of this English church utterly removed. Their office was to govern the church with the rest of the ministers, to consult, to admonish, to correct, and to order all things appertaining to the state of the congregation. Instead of these seigniors in every church, the pope hath brought in and we yet maintain the Lordship of one men over many churches, yea over sundry Shires. These seigniors then did execute their offices in their own persons without substitutes. Our lord bishops have their under-officers, as suffragans, chancellors, archdeacons, officials, commissaries, and such like. Touching deacons, though their names be remaining, yet is the office foully perverted and turned upside down, for their duty in the primitive church was to gather the alms diligently and to distribute it faithfully, also for the sick and impotent persons to provide painfully, having ever a diligent care that the charity of godly men were not wasted upon loiterers and idle vagabonds. Now it is the first step to the ministry, nay, rather a mere order of priesthood. For they may baptize in the presence of a bishop or priest, or in their absence (if necessity so require) minister the other Sacrament, likewise read the holy Scriptures and homilies in the congregation, instruct the youth in the catechism, and also preach, if he be commanded by the bishop. Again, in the old church, every congregation had their deacons; now they are tied to cathedral churches only, and what do they there? Gather the alms and distribute to the poor? Nay, that is the least piece or rather no part of their function. What then? To sing a gospel when the bishop ministereth the communion. If this be not a perverting of this office and charge, let everyone judge. And yet, lest the reformers of our time should seem utterly to take out of God's church this necessary function, they appoint somewhat to it concerning the poor, and that is, to search for the sick, needy, and impotent people of the parish, and to intimate their estates, names, and places where they dwell to the curate, that by his exhortation they may be relieved by the parish or other convenient alms. And this as you see is the nighest part of his office, and yet you must understand it to be in such places where there is a curate and a deacon, every parish cannot be at that cost to have both, nay, no parish so far as can be gathered as this present hath. Now then, if you will restore the church to his ancient officers, this you must do: instead of an archbishop or lord bishop, you must make equality of ministers. Instead of chancellors, archdeacons, officials, commissaries, proctors, summoners, church wardens, and such like, you have to put in every congregation a lawful and godly seigniory. The deaconship must not be confounded with the ministry, nor the collectors for the poor may not usurp the deacon's office, but he that hath an office must look to his office, and every man must keep himself within the bounds and limits of his own vocation. And to these three jointly, that is, the ministers, seniors, and deacons, is the whole regiment of the church to be committed. This regiment consisteth especially in ecclesiastical discipline, which is an order left by God unto his church, whereby men learn to frame their wills and doings according to the law of God, instructing and admonishing one another, yea and by correcting and punishing all willful persons, and condemners of the same. Of this discipline there is kinds, one private, wherewith we will not, because it is impertinent to our purpose, another public, which although it hath been long banished, yet if it might now at the length be restored, would be very necessary and profitable for the building up of God's house. The final end of this discipline is the reframing of the disordered, and to bring them to repentance, and to bridle such as would offend. The chiefest part and last punishment of this discipline is excommunication, by the consent of the church determined if the offender be obstinate, which how miserably it hath been by the pope's proctors, and is by our new canonists abused, who seeth not? In the primitive church it was in many men's hands; now one alone excommunicateth. In those days it was the last censure of the church, and never went forth but for notorious crimes; now it is pronounced for every light trifle. Then excommunication was greatly regarded and feared; now because it is a money matter, no whit at all esteemed. Then for great sins, severe punishment, and for small offenses, censures according. Now great sins either not at all punished, as blasphemy, usury, drunkenness, etc., or else slightly passed over with pricking in a blanket, or pinning in a sheet, as adultery, whoredom, etc. Again, such as are no sins (as if a man conform not himself to popish orders and ceremonies, if he come not at the whistle of him who hath by God's word no authority to call, we mean, chancellors, officials, and all that rule) are grievously punished, not only by excommunication, suspension, deprivation and other (as they term it) spiritual coercion, but also by banishing, imprisoning, revilings, taunting, and what not? Then the sentence was tempered according to the notoriousness of the fact; now on the one side either hatred against some persons carrieth men headlong into rash and cruel judgement, or else favor, affection, or money mitigateth the rigor of the same, and all this cometh to pass because the regiment left of Christ to his church is committed into one man's hands, whom alone it shall be more easy for the wicked by bribing to pervert than to overthrow the faith and piety of zealous and godly company, for such manner of men in deed should the seigniors be. Then it was said, 'tell the church'; now it is spoken, 'complain to my lord's grace, primate, and metropolitan of all England, or to his inferior, my lord bishop of the diocese, [and] if not to him, show the chancellor or official, or commissary'. Again, whereas the excommunicate were never received till they had publicly confessed their offense, now for paying the fees of the court, they shall by master official or chancellor easily be absolved in some private place. Then the congregation, by the wickedness of the offender grieved, was by his public penance satisfied. Now absolution shall be pronounced, though that be not accomplished. Then the party offending should in his own person hear the sentence of absolution pronounced; now, bishops, archdeacons, chancellors, officials, commissaries and such like absolve one man for another. And this is that order of ecclesiastical discipline which all godly wish to be restored, to the end that everyone by the same may be kept within the limits of his vocation, and a great number be brought to line in godly conversation. Not that we mean to take away the authority of the civil magistrate and chief governor, to whom we wish all blessedness, and for the increase of whose godliness we daily pray, but that, Christ being restored into his kingdom, to rule in the same by the scepter of his word and severe discipline, the prince may be better obeyed, the realm more flourish in godliness, and the Lord himself more sincerely and purely according to His revealed will served than heretofore He hath been, or yet at this present is. Amend therefore these horrible abuses, and reform God's church, and the Lord is on your right hand, you shall not be removed forever. For He will deliver and defend you from all your enemies, either at home or abroad, as He did faithful Jacob and good Jehoshaphat. Let these things alone, and God is a righteous judge; He will one day call you to your reckoning. Is a reformation good for France, and can it be evil for England? Is discipline meet for Scotland and is it unprofitable for this realm? Surely God hath set these examples before your eyes to encourage you to go forward to a thorough and a speedy reformation. You may not do as heretofore you have done, patch and piece, nay rather go backward, and never labor or contend to perfection. But altogether remove whole Antichrist, both head and tail, and perfectly plant that purity of the word, that simplicity of the sacraments, and severity of discipline which Christ hath commanded and commended to His church. And here to end, we desire all to suppose that we have not attempted this enterprise for vainglory, gain, preferment, or any other worldly respect, neither yet judging ourselves so exactly to have set out the state of a church reformed as that nothing more could be added, or a more perfect form and order drawn, for that were great presumption to arrogate so much unto ourselves, seeing that, as we are but weak and simple souls, so God hath raised up men of profound judgment and notable learning. But thereby to declare our good wills towards the setting forth of God's glory, and the building up of his church, accounting this, as it were, but an entrance into further matter, hoping that our God, who hath in us begun this good work, will not only in time hereafter make us strong and able to go forward therein, but also move other[s], upon whom he hath bestowed greater measure of his gifts and graces, to labor more thoroughly and fully in the same.

The God of all glory so open your eyes to see His truth that you may not only be inflamed with a love thereof, but with a continual care seek to promote, plant, and place the same amongst us, that we the English people and our posterity, enjoying the sincerity of God's gospel forever, may say always: "The Lord be praised!" To whom, with Christ Jesus His Son, our only Savior, and the Holy Ghost, our alone comforter, be honor, praise, and glory, forever and ever. Amen.

INTRODUCTION TO RICHARD HOOKER'S *LAWS OF ECCLESIASTICAL POLITY*

THE CONFLICT provoked by the *Admonition to Parliament* was not only heated but prolonged, lasting until at least 1593, though there were more dormant phases within the ongoing rounds of controversy. The first round lasted until 1577, as Puritan champion Thomas Cartwright (1535–1603) duked it out in print with John Whitgift (c. 1530–1604), an unbending defender of the establishment. After a few years of relative quiet, in which some bishops were tolerant toward Puritan dissenters in their dioceses, Whitgift was appointed the new Archbishop of Canterbury in 1583 and wasted little time in doing the bidding of his royal mistress by trying to enforce complete uniformity on the Church of England. His somewhat harsh measures, however, backfired by helping the Puritans win support from sympathetic noblemen. They also provoked the more militant to map out a blueprint for a complete overhaul of the Church of England along Presbyterian lines, and even to begin putting certain elements in practice despite the bishops' opposition.

It is difficult to understand why this might have been such a radical notion from our 21st-century standpoint, but it bears remembering that at the time, it had scarcely occurred to anyone that a society could accommodate multiple churches (what we would now call "denominations") within a single political unit. If you lived in Geneva, you were expected to be a member of the Church of Geneva, with a single city-wide church government. If you lived in

England, you were expected to be a member of the Church of England, with a single nation-wide church government. To either replace that single government against the will of the Queen, or to carve out a separate church within the one nation, was seen by some defenders of the Church as scarcely less treasonous than the plots of English Catholics to bring back in papal authority.

As a result, a new burst of publishing war ramped up from 1585 onward, but the turning point was 1588, when a group of radical Puritans ghostwriting under the name Martin Marprelate published a series of satirical pamphlets impugning the character of the bishops that were seen even by many Puritan leaders as a shocking violation of propriety. Public opinion started to swing against the presbyterians, particularly when a somewhat deranged fanatic named William Hacket in 1591 declared himself a prophet anointed by God for the task of overthrowing the Queen and establishing presbyterianism. By 1593, the authorities had largely quashed the presbyterian movement. However, the deep-seated dissatisfaction with the Church's structure and liturgy that had prompted the movement remained unresolved.

Enter Richard Hooker (c. 1553–1600). Born near the city of Exeter, he was a student in Oxford during the years of the Admonition Controversy and a teacher during the uneasy peace that followed it. With friends among both Puritan sympathizers and more moderate bishops (and with Walter Travers as his brother-in-law), Hooker sought to chart a middle course until the late 1580s, when the increasing stridency of the presbyterian rhetoric seems to have prompted him to decisively reject the movement. He recognized, however, that the Church would scarcely succeed in its mission of bringing the grace and peace of Christ to the people of England unless it addressed the root cause of the complaints, and persuaded Puritan dissenters that the Prayer Book worship, and government by bishops, were biblically acceptable and spiritually upbuilding.

Hooker realized that this task would require a much more systematic analysis of the dispute than anyone had yet offered, an analysis he undertook in his *magnum opus*, *The Laws of Ecclesiastical*

Polity, the first part of which appeared in 1593. In the lengthy Preface, he sought to understand the psychology behind the Puritan complaint: legitimate dissatisfaction with imperfections in the Church led to the search for a scapegoat—the bishops—and a comprehensive solution—Scriptural rules. But this was not, he contended, how Scripture functioned; just because it tells us all we need to be saved does not mean it contains the answer for every question we might want answered. After all, God gave us rational minds for the purpose of making wise judgments in the absence of direct revelations of his will (Books I and II). Hooker argued in Book III that many matters of church government fell within this absence, since they were certainly not matters necessary to salvation. Moreover, many Puritan complaints were motivated by irrational fear of anything tainted with "popery," as if, just because some practice had been followed in the medieval Catholic church, that alone meant it could not be followed in a Protestant church (Book IV). Hooker went on in Books V through VIII to offer a detailed defense of the rationale behind various Prayer Book ceremonies and the governmental structure of the English church, arguing that even if not always perfect, they were more than adequate to foster a godly and faithful church.

Hooker's work retains a startling relevance right down to the 21st century, as both of the tendencies that he particularly singles out—an insistence on finding detailed rules in Scripture even for relatively minor questions, and a fear of doing anything that Catholics do—remain alive and well in Protestant churches today. Unfortunately, his original prose, though masterful ("for its purpose, perhaps the most perfect in English" according to C. S. Lewis)[1] was challenging to read even in its time and is nearly impossible today, given how much the language has evolved. The following text therefore represents part of a project to "translate" Hooker's *Laws* into modern English by the Davenant Institute.

---

[1] C. S. Lewis, *English Literature in the Sixteenth Century, Excluding Drama*, The Oxford History of English Literature, Vol. 3 (Oxford: Clarendon Press, 1954), 462.

Further Reading

For further reading, see W. Bradford Littlejohn, *Richard Hooker: A Companion to His Life and Work* (Eugene, OR: Cascade, 2015); Daniel Eppley, *Reading the Bible with Richard Hooker* (Minneapolis, MN: Fortress Press, 2016); Charles Miller, *Richard Hooker and the Vision of God: Exploring the Origins of 'Anglicanism'* (Cambridge: James Clarke & Co., 2013).

RICHARD HOOKER,
OF THE LAWS OF THE ECCLESIASTICAL POLITY (1593)[1]

Preface

1. The Cause and Occasion for Writing this Work and what Is Hoped for from those for whom Such Pains Are Taken

(1.) THOUGH for no other cause, yet for this—that posterity may know we have not loosely through silence permitted things to pass away as in a dream—for this I write, offering to posterity an account of the present state and legal establishment of the Church of England, and a vindication of those who have fought so hard to preserve and uphold it. I know I have little reason, beloved, to expect from you anything but your usual harshness and bitterness toward all who disagree with you, but this bitterness will never drown the love which we have for all who claim the name of Christ. Man is naturally impatient when it comes to insults and slanders, but we hope that the God of peace will give us the grace to be patient, for the sake of the work which we desire to complete.

(2.) I first decided to undertake this project when I saw how fervently you presbyterians protested against the established government and liturgy of our church; was it true, as all your books

---

[1] Modernized text by W. Bradford Littlejohn and the Davenant Institute; published in *Radicalism: When Reform Becomes Revolution* (Moscow, ID: The Davenant Press, 2016) and in forthcoming translations of books III and IV.

insisted, that all good Christians were obliged to join with you in promoting this new church government, which you call "the Lord's Discipline"? I will confess that, initially, I was disposed to think there must be some very strong reasons why so many well-intentioned and pious men were so worked up about this issue. Unfortunately, however, when I looked into the matter (at least, as far as my own poor abilities would permit) in obedience to St. Paul's admonition to "prove all things" and to "hold fast that which is good," (1 Thess. 5:21), I had no choice but to conclude otherwise. Specifically, I arrived at two conclusions. First, no law of God nor reason of man has yet been offered that would prove we do ill to stubbornly resist the alteration of the present form of church-government which the laws of this land have established. Second, the new presbyterian scheme which you propose in its place has no compelling claim to be called "the ordinance of Jesus Christ," since you have at least thus far offered no clear proof to this effect.

(3.) In this book, I have undertaken to offer for you a proof of these two theses. I heartily beseech you, for the love you have for Jesus Christ, that if you really care for the peace and quietness of this church, if you have in you that gracious humility which is the crown of Christian virtues, if you care, as I am sure you do, for the integrity of your souls, hearts, and consciences (which cannot with integrity refuse to acknowledge truth merely on account of personal animus), you will "hold not the faith of our Lord Jesus Christ, the Lord of glory, with respect of persons" (Jas. 2:1) and you will regard the truth of what I am writing, not the fact that it is I who am writing it. Please do not think that you are reading the words of someone who is out to oppose the truths that you have embraced, but rather the words of someone who is eager to embrace the same truths, insofar as they are indeed truths. God knows this is the only reason that I have undertaken such a laborious and painstaking project as this. […]

4. What Has Made the More Learned Approve This Discipline

(1.) AS FOR those of you who are a lantern to the rest and mold the hearts of others (not seeking to manipulate, I trust, but because you have already been swayed by greater men), it is your burden to defend this cause by argument. For this you bring forth many verses from Scripture, but such that those things which you say logically and necessarily follow from Scripture turn out to be cobbled together only by poor and slight conjecture. I need not bring up any particular example of you doing this, since it would in fact be hard to find any examples of you doing otherwise. It is rather peculiar that your presbyterian government should be so clearly taught by Christ and His Apostles in Scripture, but never discovered by any church until now, while the sort of church government which you so resolutely oppose has been observed by Christians everywhere, and none of them noticed that it was forbidden by Scripture. I challenge you to find one church upon the face of the earth that has had such a church government, or that has not been episcopally-governed since the time of the Apostles!

(2.) You offer many examples from history trying to show that the early church followed this discipline in this way and that it remains a pattern for us, a mirror of what Scripture supposedly teaches. But you do not really mean it, and only say this because everyone else does; whenever someone brings up the example of antiquity, you complain that anyone should look for examples of church government from prior times. You plainly think that, from the time of the Apostles to the present age, when you have at last discovered the truth, no age is a safe example to follow.[2] You then cite from Eusebius the report of Hegesippus that "until then the Church had remained a virgin, pure and uncorrupted.... But when the sacred band of the apostles and the generation of those who heard the divine wisdom with their own ears passed on, then god-

---

[2] Thomas Cartwright, *A Replye to an Answere made of M. doctor Whitgifte* [Hemel Hepstead: J. Shroud, 1573], 97; John Whitgift, *The Works of John Whitgift*, ed. John Ayre (Cambridge: The University Press, 1851-53), 2:181-84.

less error began."[3] Clement also confirms that there was corruption immediately after the Apostles' time, quoting the old proverb that "few sons are like their fathers,"[4] and Socrates Scholasticus says that around 430 AD the Roman and Alexandrian bishops stopped being sacred rulers, and fell to the level of merely secular rulers.[5] From this you conclude that no form of church government is safe to follow except for that from the Apostolic age.

(3.) By the way, note that when you propose the pattern of the Apostolic church as a pattern for all times, although you all agree about church government, you do not all have the same intentions. Laymen who are anxious for reform want the clergy to follow the pattern of Apostolic poverty and be poor just as they were. This sort would be happy if the church was led by none but a company of begging friars! If it did add to the glory of God and the good of His church for His clergy to be as poor as the Apostles when they had neither staff nor purse, then I hope that God also would give them the accompanying spirit, which Paul describes when he says he knew "both to abound and to be in want" (Phil. 4:12). This would be a fit mark of true episcopacy. The Church of Christ is a mystical body, and a body cannot stand unless all the parts are properly fitted and proportioned to one another. Please apply the same standard to both sides: if the clergy are to be poor like the Apostles, let the laity also be like the laity of the Apostles' days! Such an arrangement might not be very wise, but it would at least be fair.

(4.) But you who are clergy (if you still do not mind me calling you clergy!) sometimes seem to want more than even this. You think that perfect reform of the church means making the church just as it was in the time of the Apostles, which is neither possible, nor certain, nor fitting. Not *possible*, because Scripture does not fully describe what form of church government existed in the time of

[3] Eusebius, *The Church History*, translated by Paul L. Maier (Grand Rapids: Kregel Publications, 2007), 106-107.

[4] Clement of Alexandria, *Stromateis: Books 1-3*, trans. Paul Ferguson, vol. 85 of *The Fathers of the Church* (Washington, DC: Catholic University of America Press, 1991), 30.

[5] Socrates, *Ecclesiastical History* 7.11.

the Apostles, so you are setting up a standard that cannot be known, and thus certainly cannot be practiced. Not *certain*, because even within the apostolic period, later times saw policies that had not been anticipated in earlier times, so that a general appeal to "apostolic practice" is much too vague, especially given that you yourselves vary in defining when the authoritative apostolic period ends. You say that, although the finishing touches of Antichrist's building were not yet completed, the foundations for it were secretly laid even in the Apostles' times! So you reject all times except the Apostolic period, yet you only half-heartedly approve of even that period, leaving it rather doubtful by what principles we should follow their example. Finally, your appeal to the apostolic standard is not *fitting* for our present time. While the masses often go astray by favoring ancient custom, insisting that we return to it if things are going badly, and do not attempt to examine why things have changed, we can hardly tolerate such naïveté in learned men like you, who should understand well enough how the church must sometimes adapt itself to changing circumstances.

To be sure, it is a good general rule, as Arnobius says, that the older a ceremony, the better; not as an absolute rule, however, but only so far as the good intention behind such rites, orders, and ceremonies continues to apply in different times and circumstances.[6] For instance, there are certain Apostolic customs, which if we tried to revive would be scandalous, such as the holy kiss (Rom. 16:16), and others, such as the love feasts (Jude 12), which no one now thinks needful. Conversely, there are many things not found in apostolic times, such as providing for the clergy by tithes, building almshouses for the poor, sorting people into parishes, and so forth, not practical in the Apostles' times, which are much more convenient and fitting for the church to retain than to remove merely for the sake of better conforming to the most ancient practice.

(5.) The Apostolic order of the church should not be put forward as a sufficient or necessary rule for all churches. Even if it were, you would still have to prove that your discipline was the

---

[6] Minucius Felix, *Octavius*, Loeb Classical Library 250 (Cambridge: CUP, 1931), 328-329. Minucius Felix's dialogue was preserved in Arnobius' *Adversus Nationes*.

Apostolic form of church government. You have even failed to prove those things that you say are all-important, concerning the authority of lay elders and the distinction between doctors and pastors. In short, we can conclude that with the exception of our own time, one in which insolence, pride, and contempt of all authority are at their worst, there has been no time when the complete form or even the basic substance of your model of church government was practiced.

(6.) When this argument from antiquity fails you, you appeal to learned men that seem to claim all Christians should abandon our form of church government and adopt yours. While you mention many men worthy of respect, there are others whom you cite, it would seem, only to impress the more gullible who judge by quantity, not quality. Yet surely those who know the quality and value of these men will think you are scraping the bottom of the barrel! But even if every one of them were as good as the best of them, their opinions and conjectures should not overrule the laws of the Church of England. This is doubly true since they do not in fact all agree, and those few who do agree do so because they followed one man as their guide, one who is not unlikely to have strayed. But if any writer happens to say that in the Apostles' time there were probably lay-elders, or does not dislike having them in the church today, or says that "bishop" was at first merely a synonym for "presbyter," or in any way praises churches without an episcopal government, or attacks those bishops that abuse their office—all these men you claim as full adherents of your side, just as convinced as you that the law of God obligates every Christian church to remove bishops and replace them with elders. Anyone who thinks that all the names you invoke are on your side is greatly deceived indeed.

(7.) On some of the main points about your church government, I concede that there is a general agreement among many of the Reformed churches abroad. Certainly, the learned in other churches were inclined to do as did the church of Geneva, since the tedious workings of public authority made reform come a little too slowly for a people eager to change everything right away. They had no time to think up a form of church government other than that form which had already been devised and was ready to hand, had already been tried in similar situations, could be established without delay, and easily pleased the people because of the power it gave them. Therefore since the example of this one church was followed by the rest, due to the necessity of circumstances, it should not surprise us to find among them all a remarkable consensus about the key points of church-order. We should not marvel greatly when people who do the same thing agree about why they are doing it.

(8.) Consider also what Galen once said about philosophy, in which people decide their beliefs in the same way they evaluate rumors. "People will often be persuaded by a credible man, but when two, three, or four good men agree about something, the issue is thought to be beyond debate, and thus often they are all led astray, either by all erring in judgment at the same point, or by too credulously deferring to the testimony of one."[7] Even if ten people offer the same testimony, if it turns out that their knowledge comes from only one of them, then we should treat their testimony as if there had only been one of them. It is the same in the issue at hand, when daughter churches speak their mother church's dialect, when many sing one song because their choirmaster sings it (a man whose authority amongst the greatest divines we have already described).

You might very well ask why so many learned men follow one man's judgment, without being compelled by an argument.[8] To ask the question is to answer it. You are reluctant to imagine that those who have, in matters of doctrine, achieved a knowledge unsurpassed since the time of the Apostles, should err when it comes to church government. Such is our human tendency, that whenever we admire somebody for their achievements in great things, it is hard to persuade us that they err in anything. The reason for this is that "Dead flies cause the oil of the perfumer to send forth an evil odor; so doth a little folly outweigh wisdom and honor" (Eccles.

---

[7] Cf. Galen, *Concerning the Diagnosis and Cure of the Errors of Every Soul* in *Opera*, ed. C.G. Kühn (Leipzig: in officina Libraria C. Cnoblochii, 1821-33), 5:96-97.

[8] *A Petition Directed to Her most excellent Majesty* [Middleburg: R. Schilders], 14.

10:1). In virtually every profession, this has given the opinions of a few undue influence, so that Luther can do no wrong in the eyes of the Germans, and Calvin none in the eyes of many of the Reformed churches. We see, however, that God presents many models of virtue in Scripture, yet none of them is totally without sin, in order that to Him alone we might say, "Thou only art holy, thou only art just." Thus we are not able to say whether God in His wisdom might permit some worthy vessels of His glory to be blemished with the stain of human frailty so that we would not esteem anyone more than he deserves. [...]

Book III

2. Must Scripture Contain a Complete System of Church Government?

(1) JUST because someone might point out that speech is necessary for all men throughout the world, this does not mean that all men must speak the same language. In the same way, while all churches need a polity and order of some sort, not all need to have exactly the same sort. Of course, no form of polity can be good unless God be its author. As Tertullian says, "Those things that are not of God can have no other than God's adversary for their author."[9] Whatever be in the Church of God, if it is not of God, we hate it. Therefore it must come from God, and can come in one of two ways: either as supernaturally revealed by God, like those things delivered by Moses for the government of the commonwealth of Israel, or something which men can discover with the light of reason given to them by God for that purpose. No one can deny that the law of nature itself is instituted by God, which it cannot be unless God be considered to speak in the latter way as well as in the former. Therefore, since our opponents say that no form of church polity is lawful, or of God, unless God has set it down in Scripture, I cannot help but ask whether they mean set down in Scripture *in whole* or *in part*. If they say *in whole*, I challenge them to

---

[9] Tertullian, *On the Apparel of Women* 8, trans. S. Thewall, in *The Ante-Nicene Fathers*, 4:17: "For there is no other whose they can be, if they are not God's."

show any form of polity that ever was set down this way. They will not dare to claim that their own is indeed comprehensively laid out in Scripture, nor will they deny that even ours, which they so detest, is at least in part taken from Scripture. I must also ask whether, when they speak of a polity "taken from Scripture," whether they mean explicitly and specifically set down there, or simply that the general principles and rules can be found in Scripture? They cannot pretend the former, since not every part of their own discipline is spelled out in Scripture; and as for the latter, if this is all they mean, they can hardly object against other forms of polity! After all, such general principles do not prescribe any one particular form of polity, but allow for many different sorts which may all embody these principles in different ways.

(2.) However, let us cut them some slack and try to give their objections as fair a hearing as possible, when they earnestly oppose other Christians who deny that we need to find a complete form of church polity in Scripture. We have already established that matters of faith and salvation are in a completely different category than matters having to do with ceremonies, order, and kinds of church government.[10] The former are necessarily contained in the word of God, either explicitly or by clear deduction; the latter are not. We may not accept anything in the former category unless it is *found* in Scripture, but we *may* accept anything in the latter unless it is *denied* in Scripture. Although I do not see any just or reasonable cause for questioning this distinction, it is hard to satisfy minds that are so brainsick in their errors that they always find something to take issue with. We are here rebuked for two things: first for failing to rightly distinguish (since they say that matters of discipline and church government are "matters necessary to salvation and of faith," while we distinguish them) and second for demeaning Scripture as if it contained only

> the principal points of religion, some crude and
> unfashioned manner of building the Church, but
> had left out that which belongs to the form and

---

[10] [We have here omitted a footnote of Hooker's which is substantially identical to what he goes on to say in the main body text, and which includes a lengthy quotation from Cartwright, *A Replye*, 26.]

fashion of it; as if there were in the Scriptures only enough to cover the Church's nakedness, and not to adorn her with necklaces, bracelets, rings, and jewels; enough to quench her thirst, to kill her hunger, but not to provide a more liberal, and (as it were) a more delicious and dainty diet.11

If this is all they have to say, our response will be an easy one.

3. Church Government Is Not a Matter of Salvation

TO LUMP together in speech things which are different in reality is the mother of all error. To remove all confusions which give birth to errors, it is necessary to distinguish, and to rightly distinguish, the mind must sever things of different natures and discern how they are different. If we imagine a difference where there is none, we obviously misdistinguish. The only way to know whether we are committing this error is to compare our conceptions with the nature of things as they actually are.

(2.)Things having to do with the Church of Christ are not all of the same sort. Some things are matters of faith, which we must merely know and believe; others are matters of action, which must be both known and done. The doctrine of the Trinity is simply a matter of faith to be believed. Precepts concerning works of charity are matters of action, and we must not only know them, but practice them. Since this is obvious to all men, I marvel that our opponents find it ridiculous for us to distinguish church government, which is clearly a matter of action, from matters of faith, since they themselves distinguish between "doctrine" and "discipline."[12] For if they rightly distinguish matters of discipline from matters of doctrine, why may we not reasonably distinguish matters of government from matters of faith? Do not they include under doctrine what we call matters of faith? Do they not include

---

[11] Cartwright, *A Replye*, 26.

[12] Hooker's footnote: "Cartwright says, 'We offer to show the discipline to be a part of the Gospel.' And again, he says, 'I speak of the discipline as part of the Gospel" (*Second Replie*, 1, 5). If the discipline is one part of the Gospel, what can the other part be but doctrine?"

church government under discipline? When they blame us for doing what they themselves do, it is hard to avoid the conclusion that something besides reason motivates their protests.

(3.) We learn what God's Church is obligated to know or do partly from nature. But nature teaches this only incompletely— neither as fully nor as clearly as we need in order to have knowledge sufficient for salvation. Therefore, God has revealed in Scripture that which we need for salvation and could never know without supernatural revelation, and has also restated more clearly the most important truths that nature teaches. So then, we affirm that Scripture contains all that is *needful* for the Church, and even the chief of those things that are not needful, yet we are still charged with error. We all teach that whatever is said to be necessary for salvation—whatever all men must know or do to be saved, so that failure to believe and do it is eternal death and damnation, such as the articles of the Christian faith and the sacraments of the Church—these things must be contained in Scripture for God's church to be able to measure the length and breadth of the way in which she must walk. But unlike them, we also teach that those things which are mere aids to sanctification may be changed, just as a gravel path, if it is then paved with stone, still remains the same path. Since discretion may teach the Church what is beneficial in these matters, Scripture here only binds the Church in this sense: that whatever it forbids, the Church must not permit, lest the path which should always be clear become overgrown with brambles and thorns.

(4.) If this is not a sound argument, where does it go astray? It cannot be that we make some things necessary and others mere aids, for our Lord and Savior Himself makes such a distinction by calling justice and mercy and faith "the weightier matters of the law" (Matt. 23:23). Is our mistake then counting ceremonies as mere aids, not as things necessary to salvation?[13] (Note that by "ceremonies," we do not mean sacraments or other means of

---

13 [Hooker's footnote:] "Dudley Fenner (assuming Fenner was indeed the author) himself grants the government of the Church of Christ to be, although a matter of great importance, still not of the substance of religion." (See *A Defence of the godlie ministers against the slaunders of D. Bridges* [Middelberg: R. Schilders, 1587], 121.)

grace, but only the external rites which accompany them.) Let those who blame us for this consider their words carefully. Do not they themselves plainly compare things necessary for salvation to garments which cover the body of the Church, and those that are merely accessory to rings, bracelets, and jewels that adorn it? Do they not compare the one to the food by which the Church lives, and the other to that which makes her diet liberal, dainty, and delicious? Is dainty fare necessary for sustenance? Is rich attire necessary to clothe the body? If not, how can they urge as necessary the very things which their own metaphors imply are not necessary? What logician is there who can show us how these similes can be true while our distinction is untrue, a distinction between external aids and things necessary to salvation?

4. We Do Not Dishonor Scripture

(1.) IT IS no insult to nature to say, as Plato and Aristotle have, that she provides all living creatures with sufficient nourishment and that she brings forth no kind of creature who needs that which she cannot provide, even if we do not so magnify her bounty as to say she brings sons of men into the world adorned with dazzling attire or that she makes costly buildings to spring up out of the earth for them.[14] In the same way, we in no way diminish the perfection of Scripture and the honor due to it by saying that Scripture leaves some things to the Church's discretion. All we are saying is that Scripture must teach the Church whatever is necessary for salvation, and it is no disgrace for Scripture to leave some things at the Church's liberty, just as nature has left it to men to design their own attire, instead of providing coverings for them as it does for the beasts of the field. Therefore let them show where it is that we say, as they accuse us, that Scripture contains no more than the bare essentials. We acknowledge that Scripture contains infinite treasures of wisdom, which are applicable to the myriad circumstances of life, and indeed that there is scarcely any noble branch of knowledge worthy of study to which it does not give direction and light. Not only that, but even in the disputed

---

[14] Aristotle, *Politics* I.8 [1258a]; Plato, *Menexenus* [237E].

matter of church government, although Scripture does not prescribe a particular form of church polity, it gives many general precepts for how to govern rightly, and many examples of good governance even in particulars; indeed, that it even contains those things which are of principal weight in determining the particular form of church polity (though, it should be added, these things point more to our episcopal form than to the form that they imagine). If we so willingly grant all this, why do they accuse us of "so narrowing the scope of Scripture that it can only direct us in the principal points of our religion, as if Scripture gave us only a rough and unfinished framework of the Church and left out everything pertaining to its form and fashion"[15]? Let such accusers judge in their consciences whether we deserve this accusation. [...]

Book IV

1. How Useful Ceremonies Are in the Church

IN ANCIENT TIMES, such simplicity and gentleness of spirit once prevailed in the world that highly esteemed leaders were always reluctant to pass judgment against anything that was publicly received by the Church of God, unless it was obviously evil. They were less inclined to a severity that delights to find fault with every small error, and more inclined to that charity which wants to give everything the benefit of the doubt. In this present age, zeal has conquered charity, and rhetoric has drowned meekness. Anyone can criticize anything, and no one is surprised by it. The rites and ceremonies of the Church—the very same ones that holy and virtuous men defended in face of profane and scornful foes—are now mocked by Christians themselves! Whether these criticisms are deserved or not will become apparent once we have heard everything they have to say about the established rituals of our church. Since our opponents themselves compare these matters to "mint and cumin,"[16] thereby admitting that they are not weighty matters of polity, we hope that their wrangling over small things will be neither too earnest nor long.

---

15 Cartwright, *A Replye*, 26.

16 Thomas Cartwright, *The Rest of the Second Replie*, p. 171

(2.) Here we will not consider their particular objections against the orders of the church, but merely their general objections. Let us plainly discern the nature and use of these ceremonies, so that we may better know their different qualities. First we must take note that every public duty which God requires the Church to perform has not only essential, defining elements, but also a particular outward manner in which they are properly administered. The substance of all religious actions is declared to us by God Himself in few words; for example, in the case of the sacraments. Of these, St. Augustine says, "The word is added to the elemental substance, and it becomes a sacrament."[17] Baptism is given by the element of water and with the prescribed words which the Church of Christ uses. The sacrament of the body and blood of Christ is administered in the elements of bread and wine, if the mystical words are added to them. However, a great deal more is necessary to properly administer these holy sacraments.

(3.) In determining the outward form of any religious action, our chief goal should be the edification of the church. Men are edified either when their minds are led by these actions to the consideration of some truth that demands our attention, or when their hearts are moved with any suitable affection—when they are in any way stirred up to the appropriate reverence, devotion, attention, and due regard. Therefore, not only speech, but also many different sensible means have always been thought necessary for this purpose. Of these, the eye is the most active and receptive of all our senses, the organ by which to best make a deep and lasting impression, and therefore we have not only prayers, readings, questions, and exhortations, but also visible signs, which are very effective at helping men to carefully know and remember the purpose for which they carry out such ceremonies. Nature itself must teach this, for do not men always mark any public actions of great weight (whether civil or sacred) with pomp and ceremony? Such visible solemnity, setting them apart from common actions, compels the eyes of the people to give them close attention. Words, both be-

---

[17] Saint Augustine, *Tractates on the Gospel of John 55–111*, trans. John W. Rettig, Vol. 90 of *The Fathers of the Church* (Washington DC: Catholic University of America Press, 1994), 117 [Tractate 80, section 3].

cause they are commonly used and do not so strongly move our imagination, often fail to engage our attention, and so God has wisely provided that the public deeds of men should be marked not only with words, but also with certain visible actions, which make an easier and more memorable impression than mere speech does. Let us not presume to condemn as follies the things which the long experience of all ages has proven profitable, just because we do not always know the reason for them. A mind disposed to mock whatever it does not understand might ask why Abraham told his servant to put his hand under his thigh and swear (Gen. 24:9), instead of simply showing the strength of his oath by naming the Lord God of heaven and earth without that strange ceremony. In contracts and bargains, a man's word is sufficient to express his will. However, "Now this was the custom in former time in Israel concerning redeeming and concerning exchanging, to confirm all things: a man drew off his shoe, and gave it to his neighbor; and this was the manner of attestation in Israel" (Ruth 4:7). The Romans had a similarly strange ceremony when freeing a slave: the master presented his slave in a court, took him by the hand, and not only said before the public magistrate, "I will that this man become free," but also struck him on the check, turned him around, and shaved off his hair, before the magistrate touched him three times with a rod, and he was given a cap and white garment. What was the point of all these things? How strange and seemingly unreasonable it was among the Hebrews that when someone wanted to make himself a perpetual servant, he was not only to testify in the presence of a judge, but, as a visible token of it he was to have his ear bored through with an awl! There are innumerable examples of such things in both civil and religious actions, for they have use and force in both. "Sacred symbols are actually the perceptible tokens of the conceptual things. They show the way to them and lead to them."[18]

---

[18] *Pseudo-Dionysius: The Complete Works*, trans. Colm Luibheid (New York: Paulist Press, 1987), 205 [2.2]. Hooker translated it as "the sensible things which religion hath hallowed, are resemblances framed according to things spiritually understood, whereunto they serve as a hand to lead, and a way to direct."

(4.) Someone might object that if we add significant rites and ceremonies to religious duties, we are instituting new sacraments. However, I am sure they will not say that Numa Pompilius ordained a sacrament when he commanded the priests to "make sacrifices with their hands wrapped as far as the fingers, thus signifying that faith must be kept and that when men clasp hands, there too is the sacred temple of faith."[19] Again, we must remind our opponents that they themselves do not think that all significant ceremonies are sacraments, since they deny that laying on of hands is a sacrament, yet they still deem it a forceful sign and reminder, as they say: "The party ordained by this ceremony was reminded that he had been separated to the work of the Lord, and so that he might remember that he had been taken as it were by the hand of God from among others and learn not to account himself his own, nor to act according to his own will, but to consider that God has set him to a duty. If he discharges and accomplish this duty, he can rest assured of a reward at the hands of God, but if not, he can expect vengeance."[20] Among great ceremonies, some of them *are* sacraments, some are merely *like* sacraments. Sacraments are the signs and tokens of some general promised grace, which always truly descends from God to the soul that duly receives them. Other significant tokens are only like sacraments, yet not sacraments: which is not our distinction, but theirs. For concerning the Apostles' laying on of hands, they themselves say: "they used this sign, or as it were sacrament."[21]

2. First, They Accuse Our Ceremonies of Not Having Apostolic Simplicity, and Instead Having Greater Pomp and Show

(1.) RITES and ceremonies may be objected against for being of the wrong sort or being too numerous. The first charge leveled at

---

[19] Livy, *The History of Rome, Books 1–5*, trans. Valerie M. Warrior (Indianapolis: Hackett Publishing, 2006), 33 [1.21].

[20] Travers, *Ecclesiastical Discipline*, fol. 51.

[21] Travers, fol. 52.

our ceremonies is that they are of the wrong sort: that we have departed from the ancient simplicity of Christ and His apostles, replacing it with outward show, so that we now have rituals which those who best pleased God best and most devoutly served Him never had.[22] For our opponents take it for granted that the first condition of the church was the best, that the faith of the Christian religion was soundest in its beginning, that God's Scriptures were then best understood by all men, and that all manner of godliness then abounded. Thus they conclude that the customs, laws, and ordinances devised since then must not be as good for the Church of Christ, and that we ought to sweep away all later innovations to return the Church to its former condition. We consider this principle to be either uncertain, or at the very least insufficient, if not both.

(2.) For if this principle were certain, then they should have no difficulty showing us where it is so clear that we can say without dispute 'these alone were all the ceremonies and customs of the Apostle's times, neither more nor less than these.' It is true that many things of this sort are alluded to in Scripture—indeed, many things are either explicitly declared in or necessarily deduced from the Apostles' writings—but must all the apostolic customs of the Church be found in the Scriptures? Surely not, for if one closely observes the scope of their writings, it is clear that they mentioned no more details than particular occasions required. So will our opponents admit any other record besides the apostolic writings? Obviously not. Whereas St. Augustine says that those things done by the whole Church may be thought apostolic, even though they are not written, they utterly condemn his judgment.[23] I will not defend here St. Augustine's opinion, which is actually that such universal practices were either of apostolic origin or else rooted in the decrees of a general council (he could imagine no other source of positive laws and orders received by the Christian world besides

---

[22] Travers, fols. 1–2, 11, 12, 98, and Thomas Cartwright, *The Rest of the Second Replie*, p. 181.

[23] Augustine, *On Baptism, Against the Donatists* 5.23. Cartwright condemns it in *The First Replie*, p. 31.

these two).[24] But, setting aside St. Augustine, those who condemn his opinion here must confess that it is very uncertain what the customs of the Church were in the times of the Apostles, since the Scriptures do not mention them and our opponents utterly reject all other sources. Therefore, by restricting the Church to the orders of the Apostolic times, they tie it to a remarkably vague standard, unless they require that no orders be observed except for those found in the writings of the Apostles themselves, in which case their standard hardly suffices as a benchmark against which to measure the church's ceremonies forever after.

(3.) Our end must always be the same; our ways and means to reaching that end, need not be. The Apostles were pursuing the glory of God, and the good of His Church, and therefore these are the marks at which we too must aim. However, since rites and orders may be better suited to one time than to another, why should we insist on one age as the ideal for the rest to follow? I am quite sure that they do not mean that we must worship God in secret meetings; or that we should use common rivers and brooks for baptism; or that the Eucharist should be administered after mealtime; or that we must reinstitute love feasts; or that ministers should no longer have regular salaries and must become dependent on voluntary donations. In such cases, they easily enough perceive how what was fitting enough for the first age of the church is unfit for the present. We rightly honor the faith, zeal, and godliness of former times, but does this prove that our Church orders must be identical to theirs or that we may not lawfully add or subtract anything from their practices? Those who call for the Church to return to its former state cannot help but qualify their claims. If any practice has appeared which violates the spirit of what was first established in the Church, then we must return to the former things. However, where the new practice is consistent with the old principles, our respect for the ancient practice need not cause us to reject the new.

(4.) If we compare the Israelites' worship of God when they were slaves in a strange land with their worship in the land of Canaan and Jerusalem, then who will not admit what a great differ-

---

[24] Augustine, 118.

ence there was between the two conditions? In Egypt, they were perhaps glad to take some corner of a poor hovel and serve God upon their knees, perhaps covered in dust and straw. Yet their worship was just as accepted by God, whose deliverance of them from bondage showed that they had not served Him in vain. Nonetheless, no sooner do they have any possessions to call their own in the desert, than the Lord requires a tabernacle of them. Having planted them in the land, God gave them David as their king and gave him rest from all his enemies. Then David grieved at the contrast between his own flourishing palace and the lowly state of the house of worship: "See now, I dwell in a house of cedar, but the ark of God dwelleth within curtains" (2 Sam. 7:2). But it was God's pleasure for Solomon his son to carry out this purpose, and to do so in a manner consistent not with their former poverty, but with their present prosperity. For this reason Solomon writes to the king of Tyre, "And the house which I build is great; for great is our God above all gods" (2 Chr. 2:5). From this it is clear that the orders of the Church may be equally acceptable to God, whether they are framed for the splendor of later times, or for the reverent simplicity of former times. Therefore, the mere fact that our orders differ from those of the Apostles does not prove that they are wrong.

3. Second, they criticize many of our ceremonies for being the same as those of the church of Rome

AND YET, our opponents say, we have accommodated ourselves to the customs of the church of Rome, and our orders and ceremonies are popish! They note that the founders of our church were not as careful in this matter as they should have been, being content with practices taken from the church of Rome, and we should correct their oversight by abolishing all popish ceremonies. They say we must have no communion or fellowship with papists, neither in doctrine, nor ceremonies, nor government. It is not enough for us to be divided from the church of Rome by a wall of doctrine alone while retaining part of their ceremonies and almost all of their form of government—away with all such government and ceremonies! They demand nothing less than the utter rejection all things popish.

We must answer them according to the plain meaning of their words, not allowing for any ambiguity which may cause endless disputes. If their main position is simply that 'nothing should be established in the Church except what God has commanded in His Word,' then everything Rome does beyond this they must call popish. And therefore, anything of this sort that our church retains, they call popish, even if it is lawful and consistent with the Word of God. For they plainly affirm that, "Even if the forms and ceremonies which the church of Rome used were not unlawful and contained nothing contrary to the Word of God, nonetheless neither the Word of God, nor reason, nor the examples of the oldest Jewish and Christian churches permit us to use the same forms and ceremonies, since they are not commanded by God, and there are always better ones that could be put in their place." Therefore, the question is whether we may follow the church of Rome in its orders, rites, and ceremonies as long as they are not defective, or whether we must always devise others and have no conformity with Rome even in minor things. If this, then, is what they mean by saying that we should abolish whatever is popish, we wholeheartedly reject their argument.

(2.) To try and prove that all popish orders and ceremonies should be utterly abolished, they argue as follows: "First, we do respect St. Augustine's judgment that where nothing is commanded or forbidden in Scripture, we must observe the custom of the people of God and the decree of our forefathers.[25] But why should we retain the customs and constitutions of the papists in such things, since they were neither the people of God nor our forefathers?" Second, "even if the forms and ceremonies which the church of Rome used were not unlawful and contained nothing contrary to the word of God, nonetheless neither the Word of God, nor reason, nor the examples of the oldest Jewish and Christian churches permit us to use the same forms and ceremonies"—especially since the papists are heretics and so close at hand—"since they are neither commanded by God, and there are always better ones that

---

[25] Cartwright, *The First Replie*, p. 30.

could be put in their place."[26] Thus it is against the Word of God to be in agreement with the church of Rome in such things.[27] . . .

4. When They Explain Which Popish Ceremonies They Are Referring to, They Contradict their Own Arguments against Popish Ceremonies

Before we answer our opponents' further arguments, we must cut off that escape route which they so often use when the strength of their argument fails. For since we only retain those ceremonies that seem to us good and profitable (indeed, so good and profitable that it would have been worse to replace them with others), then the plainest and most direct way for them to counter this would be to prove that the ceremonies in question are in fact harmful to the church (or at least worse than some alternative). However, when they saw how difficult it would be to prove this, they took the easy way out, deriding the ceremonies of our church as "popish." They preferred this way because the term "popery" is to the common people more odious than paganism itself, so that whenever they hear something called "popish," they come to loathe it, imagining that anything that merits that label must be detestable. They have therefore filled the ears of the people with a great clamor: 'The church of England is fraught with popish ceremonies! Those who favor the cause of reformation do nothing more than maintain the sincerity of the Gospel of Jesus Christ, and all who resist them fight for the laws of Jesus' sworn enemy, upholding the filthy relics of Antichrist by defending that which is popish!' These are the notes which draw so many sighs from the hearts of the multitude; these are the tunes that so exasperate their minds against the lawful guides and governors of their souls; these are the voices that fill them with a general discontent, as if the bosom of the famous church in which they lived reeked more than any dungeon. However, when the authors of such seductive speeches are examined and asked to answer directly whether it is lawful for us to retain any

---

[26] Cartwright, *The First Replie*, p. 131.

[27] Cartwright, *The First Replie*, p. 131.

ceremonies not commanded in the Word of God and used by the church of Rome, they equivocate. Since they cannot deny that some ceremonies like this must be lawful, they try to convince us that they agree with us and they only think such ceremonies must be avoided when they are unprofitable or "when ones that are just as good or better may be established."[28] This answer adds nothing to what we already believe, and seems to contradict their own arguments.

(2.) It adds nothing to our convictions, because they know that any ceremonies we have kept in common with the church of Rome, we retain because we judge them to be profitable and better than alternatives. So when they say that we should abolish any Romish ceremonies that are unprofitable or could be improved upon, they are tilting at windmills, unless they mean that we should abolish all Romish ceremonies which in their judgment are unprofitable. But then they must show who authorized them to be the judges in such matters and why we are required to agree with them. Otherwise, they will not get much of a hearing when they oppose their "It seems to me..." to the orders of the church of England, as in the question of surplices[29] one of them does: "It seems to me black is a more decent color, and a garment down to the foot is a great deal more comely."[30] If they think that the burden of proof is on us to show that these ceremonies are best, they are sadly deceived. For it is only right and fair that anything long received and formally approved of in the Church should be presumed good until proven otherwise. If we as defendants answer that the ceremonies in question are godly, comely, decent, and profitable for the Church, their reply is childish and disorderly when they say that we are begging the question and we thereby reveal the weakness of our cause. On the contrary, orderly proceeding demands that we answer this way; the burden of proof rests on them. It is hardly fair for them to first say that we must not use any ceremonies of the church of Rome that are bad, and then to presume until proven otherwise that all those which they happen to dislike qualify as bad.

---

[28] Cartwright, *The Rest of the Second Replie*, p. 171.

[29] A white vestment worn over the cassock.

[30] Travers, *Ecclesiastical Discipline*, fol. 100.

(3.) Moreover, it contradicts their own arguments. To prove that a ceremony cannot be good or profitable for us, they often appeal to the mere fact that the church of Rome uses it. This manner of arguing shows that they not only exclude those Romish ceremonies that are unprofitable, but that they judge all to be unprofitable which are Romish—that is, any either devised by the church of Rome, or used by them without scriptural command. Indeed, this is the only way they can render this exclusion consistent with their other positions. For they do think it is lawful to retain certain good doctrines and customs of discipline which they have in common with the church of Rome as long as those good things are "perpetual commandments in whose place no other can come," while ceremonies, they say, are changeable. So in reality, their judgment is that whatever the church of Rome practices, except for what is immutably commanded by God, reformed churches have reason enough to change and to dismiss as neither good nor profitable. Lest we seem to be attributing to them something that they do not believe, let them read their own words in which they complain that "our church is forced to be like the papists in any of their ceremonies" and urge that this alone should make them do away with them "inasmuch as these are their ceremonies," and that the writings of Bishop John Jewel justify their complaint. Their appeal to Bishop Jewel is false, but their words here at least show that we do them no wrong in identifying that the point of contention between us is whether we should abolish all orders, rites, and ceremonies in the church of England that are used in the Church of Rome and not prescribed in the Word of God.

INTRODUCTION TO ROBERT BELLARMINE'S *CONTROVERSIES OF THE CHRISTIAN FAITH*

WHILE Protestants in England and on the Continent increasingly fell to wrangling among themselves over matters of both doctrine and church government, the Roman Catholic Church seemed to be getting a fresh burst of energy. The increasing territorial definition of those areas that had become Protestant versus those that remained Catholic meant that the Roman Church could concentrate and coordinate its resources better than in the tumultuous early decades of the Reformation. More importantly, the increasing theological definition provided by Trent enabled Rome's apologists to know exactly what doctrines they were called on to defend and which they were called on to refute. Of the cohort of Catholic apologists who arose in the later 16th century, none was more respected for his erudition and clarity of thought than Robert Bellarmine (1542–1621).

Born with powerful connections in Montepulciano, Italy, Bellarmine seemed destined for a life in the service of the church; his uncle, Marcello Spannochi, was to become Pope Marcellus II in 1555. Seven years after entering the Jesuit novitiate in 1560, Bellarmine went off to study at the University of Padua and continued his studies at the University of Leuven in Flanders. With his studies concluded, he taught at the University of Leuven for seven years, during which he earned a reputation as a teacher and preacher. Such was his reputation by 1576 that Pope Gregory XIII commissioned him to teach polemical theology in Rome.

Over the following decades he continued to gain influence and titles; his name was even floated for pope on a few occasions, though he was too conscientious and opposed to corruption to ever have much chance (or any desire) of obtaining this highest office. He epitomized the Counter-Reformation in both senses of the term, being zealous for the internal reform of corruptions within the Church, and equally zealous to repress the heresies of the Protestant Reformation. His learning and zeal were such that in 1599 Pope Clement VIII made him Cardinal Inquisitor. It was while he held that post that Bellarmine condemned Giordano Bruno (1548–1600), the noted philosopher and cosmologist, to death by burning for holding to a number of heretical positions. Consistent with his actions, Bellarmine, unsurprisingly, defended the Church's authority to coerce in matters of faith and the subjugation of the state to the Church.[1] For instance, Bellarmine wrote:

> Also, they [Christians] can, as a punishment for different sins, not only be obliged by their confessors in the internal forum to atone for their sins by giving alms, but also be fined by the bishops in the external forum with pecuniary sanctions and also be put in prison.[2]

Such views, even though controversial amongst Roman Catholics today, ruled the day both in theory and practice during Bellarmine's day. Late in his life, Bellarmine was also to play a key role in the controversial trial of Galileo over heliocentrism.

Bellarmine did not simply hold important posts of authority throughout his adult life, but was highly respected for his intellect

---

[1] Thomas Pink, "Suarez and Bellarmine on the Church as Coercive Lawgiver," in Riccardo Saccenti and Cinzia Sulas, eds., *Legge e Natura I dibattiti teologici e giuridici fra XV e XVII secolo* (Arricia: Aracne editrice, 2016), 287–332.

[2] Robert Bellarmine, *Tractatus de Potestate Summi Pontificis in Rebus Temporalibus, adversus Gulielmum Barclay,* c. 3, in *On Temporal and Spiritual Authority: Robert Bellarmine,* ed. by S. Turtino (Liberty Fund, Indianapolis 2012), 169; quoted in Pink, "Suarez and Bellarmine," 208.

and loyalty to the Roman Catholic Church. His reputation was such that in the 1930s he was made both a Saint and a Doctor of the Roman Catholic Church. This makes his makes his writings of particular historical interest and means that Bellarmine's writings can be trusted to accurately represent the views of 16th Century Roman Catholicism.

Given this, his *Disputationes De Controversiis Christianae Fidei (Controversies of the Christian Faith)* is significant because it is amongst the first Roman Catholic attempts to systematize the debate between Protestants and Roman Catholics. Arising out of the lectures he began giving at Rome in 1576, the *Disputationes* were published in several volumes from 1581 to 1593. It was at last translated into English by Kenneth Baker in 2016, offering a rich resource for modern readers to gain insight into how post-Tridentine Catholicism understood the nature of scripture, the church, the sacraments, and much more.

Volume 1 of the *Controversies* focuses on the doctrine of the Word of God, expounding the Catholic understanding of Scripture, church tradition, and the interpretive authority of the pope. Like many Catholic apologists from the 1520s down the present day, Bellarmine makes a great deal of the interpretive pluralism that seemed to result from the Protestant reliance on Scripture alone as the rule of faith. In this excerpt, Bellarmine argues forcefully that the Scriptures are not sufficiently clear to end theological controversies: if the Scriptures are so clear, why are there so many disagreements about what the Scriptures mean? The teaching of the church, not the Scriptures alone, must provide the rule of faith. Bellarmine's argument here may thus be taken as a significant expansion and refinement of that which we saw Thomas More presenting in the excerpt from the *Dialogue Concerning Heresies* above. The idea of a single, finally authoritative earthly interpreter had been an alluring prospect before the Reformation, and for many, the chaos unleashed by Luther's protest against such authority further confirmed the church's need for it.

The *Controversies* were to provoke fierce responses from Protestant apologists around Europe, particularly in England. Volume 1 in particular provided the occasion for one of the finest Protestant clarifications and defenses of *sola Scriptura*, William Whitaker's *Disputation on Holy Scripture*, which appears in the next chapter, forming the other half of the conversation begun here in Bellarmine's *Controversies*.

Further Reading

For further reading, see Stefania Tutino, *Empire of Souls: Robert Bellarmine and the Christian Commonwealth* (Oxford: Oxford University Press, 2010); James Brodrick, *Robert Bellarmine: Saint and Scholar* (London: Burns and Oates, 1966).

ROBERT BELLARMINE,
THE FIRST GENERAL CONTROVERSY: ON THE WORD OF GOD (1581)[1]

Book 3: On the Interpretation and True Meaning of Scripture

Chapter I: Scripture is not so clear by itself that, without some explanation, it suffices to end controversies about the faith

FOR THE Scriptures in this third book on the interpretation of the divine letters I decided to begin with this question: Are the divine Scriptures by themselves easily and clearly understood, or do they need some interpretation? Indeed, Martin Luther says in the preface to the letter condemned by Pope Leo: "It is necessary, according to the judgment of Scripture, to draw this conclusion— that it cannot happen, unless we give to Scripture the first place in all things which often is given to the Fathers, that is, that Scripture by itself is most certain, easy, open for the interpretation of itself, proving, judging and illuminating all things, etc." In the same place he contends that Scripture is clearer than the Commentaries of all the Fathers. He teaches similar things in his book on free will and elsewhere.

---

[1] Taken from Kenneth Baker, trans., *Controversies of the Christian Faith by St. Robert Cardinal Bellarmine, S.J.* (Saddle River, NJ: Keep the Faith, 2016). Used by permission.

But since Luther saw that one could immediately raise the objection: Why are there so many controversies, if Scripture is so clear? He invented two escapes from this. One, that Scripture, although it is obscure in some places, still those points are clarified elsewhere. The second, that Scripture, although by itself is very clear, still for proud persons and infidels it is obscure because of their blindness and hardness of heart.

Brentius in his Prologue against Peter a Soto adds a third escape, namely, that sometimes it is obscure because to phrases in a foreign language, that is, Hebrew and Greek, but its meaning is clear. This opinion is manifestly false, for Scripture itself bears witness to its own obscurity and difficulty in Ps. 119: "Give me understanding, that I may keep thy law" (v. 34). In the same place: "Open my eyes, that I may behold the wondrous things out of thy law" (v. 18). And in the same place: "Make thy face shine upon thy servant, and teach me thy statutes" (v. 135). And certainly David knew all the Scripture, which existed at the time, and he knew the expressions of the Hebrew language, nor was he proud of unbelieving. Therefore rightly St. Jerome in his letter to Paulinus, while treating these words, says this: "If such a great prophet professes the darkness of ignorance, do you not realize that we little ones, who have just been weaned, are surrounded by a night of ignorance?"

Moreover, in Luke 24 the Lord interpreted the Scriptures for his disciples, who certainly knew the Hebrew expressions, since they were Hebrews, and they were not proud or unbelieving. In Acts 8:28 the Eunuch of the Queen of the Ethiopians was reading the Scriptures, and he was reading them diligently; he was also holy, pious and humble, as Jerome says in his letter to Paulinus on the Study of Scripture, and still when he was asked by Philip: "Do you understand what you are reading?" He answered: "How can I, unless someone guides me?"

Finally, in 2 Pet. 3:15-16 Peter says that in the letters of Paul there are some things hard to understand, "which the ignorant and unstable twist to their own destruction." There it should be noted

that the Apostle Peter did not say that there are some things difficult for the unlearned and the unstable, as the heretics explain it,
but difficult absolutely. For. St. Augustine, who certainly was not
unlearned or unstable, in his book of Faith and Works, chapters 15
and 16, admits that it was very difficult for him to understand the
text in 1 Cor. 3:12, "Now if anyone builds on the foundation, etc.,"
and he says that this is one of the places concerning which St. Peter
warned that it is difficult to understand.

Then besides the testimony of Scripture, the same point can
be shown from the common consent of the ancient Fathers [....]

In order to prove this point, besides the authorities, there is
also the confirmation of reason. For in the Scriptures two things
can be considered—the things that are said, and the way in which
they are said. It you consider the things, it is necessary to admit that
the Scriptures are very obscure, since they speak about the greatest
mysteries—the divine Trinity, the Incarnation of the Word, the
heavenly Sacraments, the nature of the angels, the operation of
God on the minds of men, eternal predestination and reprobation,
and all kinds of arcane and supernatural things, which are investigated not without a lot of study and hard work, and not without
the danger of falling into grave errors. Certainly, if the science of
Metaphysics is more difficult and obscure than all other natural
disciplines, because it considers the first causes, why will not sacred
Scripture be obscure, which is treating things much more lofty?
This is evident, because a great part of Scripture contains prophecies about future things, and prophecies written as songs, than
which certainly nothing is more difficult, nothing more obscure.

Then if we consider the way of speaking, we will find innumerable causes of difficulty. First, in Scripture there are many
things which at first sight seem to be contradictory, as the following in Ex. 20:5, "I the Lord your God am a jealous God, visiting
the iniquity of the fathers upon the children to the third and fourth
generation." And then in Ez. 18:20, "The son shall not suffer for
the iniquity of the father, hut the soul that sins shall die." Second,
there are ambiguous words and prayers, as in John 8:25 to the Jews

who asked, "Who are you?" And Christ answered them: "the beginning (*principium*), who is also speaking to you." In an amazing way all the commentators anguish over this text, and even now it is not known what this means: "the beginning, who," and in the Greek it is even more obscure where the word "Beginning" is in the accusative case, τήν αρτχήν. Third, there are incomplete sentences, as in Rom. 5:12, "Therefore as sin came into the world through one man and death through sin, and so death spread to all men because all men sinned," and what follows; here in the whole periodic sentence there is no principal verb. Fourth, there are distorted sentences, like Gen. 10:32: "These are the families of the sons of Shem, by their families, their languages, their lands, and their nations," for immediately following is the beginning of chapter 11: "Now the whole earth had one language and few words." Fifth, there are expressions proper to the Hebrews, as in Ps. 89:29: "his throne as the days of heaven." Likewise in Ps. 119:109: "My soul is in my hands continually," and there are many more like these. Sixth, there are many figurative statements, tropes, metaphors, allegories, hyperboles, ironies, and others of the same kind without number.

Finally there is the testimony of the adversaries, which willy-nilly forces them to admit this truth. For if Scripture were so clear, as they say, why did Luther and the Lutherans write so many commentaries? Why have they published such different versions of Scripture? Why do they explain Scripture in such different ways? Certainly Osiander in his refutation of a writing, which Philippus had published against him, says that there are twenty different opinions about justification according to the Scriptures just among Confessionists. And Luther himself in book 1 against Zwingli and Oecolampadius wrote this: "If the world were to last longer, it would again be necessary, because of the different interpretations of Scripture which exist now, in order to preserve the unity of faith, for us to accept the decrees of the Councils, and to have recourse to them." And I ask, where do so many interpretations of

Scripture come from, if Scripture is so easy and clear? Why do they fight with each other so intensely over this matter?

Luther in one of his articles said that Scripture of itself is intelligible and clear; and in his book on free choice he said that there are no difficulties in the sacred Writings, and that no text could be proposed to him that he could not easily interpret. We find the same idea in his preface to the Psalms, where he said: "I do not wish that it should be presumed about me by anyone, which no one hitherto has been able to do concerning the holy and learned Psalms, that I cannot understand and teach their true meaning. It is sufficient to have understood some of them and those partially. The Spirit has reserved many things to himself so that he might always keep us as disciples; many things he only shows in order to attract, many things he hands on in order to move us." And after that: "I know that it is a mark of impudent temerity for anyone to dare to say that he has understood one book of Scripture in all of its parts." And in his book on the Council (page 12) he said: "Twenty years ago I was forced to think little of the commentaries of the Fathers, since Scripture had to be read in the Schools, and we had to search with great effort for their true and genuine meaning."

Brentius in the prolegomena against Peter a Soto said: "They talk nonsense when they say that Scripture is obscure, and therefore needs an interpretation." And further on he says: "It is only for the impious and the unbelieving that the Scripture is obscure, but it is not for pious believers." But he himself in the Confession of Wittenberg, in the chapter on sacred Scripture, says this: "It is not obscure that the gift of interpreting Scripture is not a matter of human prudence, but a gift of the Holy Spirit. The Holy Spirit is totally free, and he is not obligated to a certain kind of men, but he distributes his gifts to men according to his own good pleasure."

But why, Brentius, I ask, is the gift of interpretation necessary if, as you yourself just said, Scripture does not need any interpretation?

Now Martin Kemnitius in his Examination of session 4 of the Council of Trent said: "God wanted the gift of interpretation to be in the Church, which like the gift of healings, miracles and languages is not common to all." And after that he said: "Gratefully and reverently we use the works of the Fathers, who have usefully illuminated many passages of Scripture with their commentaries." Your parent Luther was indeed very grateful to the works of the Fathers, since in his book on the Council (page 52) he wrote that the commentaries of the Fathers are pieces of coal instead of gold. The Centuriatorians are no less opposed to Luther, even though they are rigid Lutherans (see Centuries 1, book 2, chapter 4, col. 52), since they write the following: "The Apostles knew that the Scriptures cannot be understood without the Holy Spirit and an interpreter. Now we will consider the arguments of Luther and Brentius."

Chapter 2: The Objections of the Adversaries are Answered

They take their first objection from these words of Deut. 30:11: "This commandment which I command you this day is not too hard for you, neither is it far off. It is not in heaven ... neither is it beyond the sea," etc. In these words the great facility of Scripture is shown: "So that it is not necessary," Brentius said, "to conquer mountains and to go to Rome for the interpretation of the Scriptures."

I respond that this text is usually understood in two ways. Several Fathers understand this text to be not about the facility of understanding the Scriptures, but about the facility of fulfilling the precepts of the Decalogue, because there is the assistance of grace. This is contrary to all Lutherans, who teach that the precepts of God are impossible to observe. In this way Tertullian explains it in book 4 against Marcion; Origen, Ambrose, Chrysostom, and others in their comments on Rom. 10:8-9; and Augustine in his book on perfect justice (see the next to last response).

Others, however, among whom is Abulensis in comments on this text, understand these words to be about the facility of knowing, not indeed the Holy Scriptures, which perhaps at that time did not yet exist, but only the precepts of the Decalogue, which, since they are natural can be easily understood, and those Jews especially could understand them easily, who heard Moses explaining them, and confessed that they understood everything, and promised that they would observe them. Therefore he adds: "The word is very near you: it is in your mouth and in your heart," that is, in your heart, since you have already understood what must be done; and it is in your mouth, because you have confessed that you understand it. And there is no contradiction to this explanation in what David said in the quote given above, namely, that it was difficult for him to understand the Law of the Lord. For David, under the name of the Law, does not understand only the ten precepts, but all the divine Scriptures. The Lord also uses the same idea in the Gospel, when he says: "It is to fulfill the word that is written in their law, 'they hated me without cause'" (John 15:25).

The second argument is based on Ps. 19:9, "The ordinances of the Lord are true, enlightening the eyes," and Ps. 118:105, "Thy word is a lamp to my feet." And "The unfolding of thy words," etc. (v. 130). And Proverbs 6:23, "The commandment is a lamp and the teaching a light."

I respond first: the author in this place is not dealing with all Scripture, but only with the precepts of the Lord, which are said to be enlightening, a lamp and a light. Not that they are easily understood, although this also is true; For what is easier than, "You shall love your neighbor?" But since they are understood and known they direct man in his actions. Secondly, it can be said that he is indeed talking about all the Scriptures, but that the Scriptures are said to be enlightening, a light and a lamp, not because they are easily understood, but because when they have been understood they enlighten the mind. For the Prophet in Ps. 19 had spoken about the knowledge of the Philosophers, which they acquired from creatures, when he says: "The heavens are telling the glory of

God," etc. Further on. in order to show that they did not arrive at that light which was obtained by those whom God deigns to instruct, and to whom he gave the written law, he adds: "the law of the Lord is perfect, reviving the soul," etc. (v. 7). Similarly, in Ps. 119 he wants to demonstrate that the knowledge which is had from the revealed word of God is greater than that derived from creatures; and because of this he compared the word of God to a lamp, which in order to dissipate the darkness of the night is much more useful for us than the light of all the stars.

The third argument is Matt. 5:14: "You are the light of the world." But if the Apostles are the light of the world, why is it that the preaching and Scriptures of the Apostles are not clear?

I respond: the Lord is speaking about the light of good example, probity and morals. For he wanted the Apostles to be examples of holiness proposed to the whole world for imitation. Therefore, he adds immediately: "Let your light so shine before men, that they may see your good works." For this, if the Lord were speaking about the light of doctrine, it would not make sense that the Scriptures of the Apostles are very easy to understand, but it does that having been understood they enlighten the mind, they instruct about lofty things and escape the darkness of all errors.

The fourth argument is from 2 Pet. 1:19: "We have the prophetic word made more sure. You will do well to pay attention to this as to a lamp shining in a dark place."

I respond: in this place also the words of the Prophets are called a lamp, not because they are easily understood, but because, having been understood, they enlighten, and show the way to Christ, who is the true Sun of justice.

The fifth argument is from 2 Cor. 4:3: "And even if our gospel is veiled, it is veiled only to those who are perishing. In their case the god of this world has blinded the eyes of the unbelieving, to keep them from seeing the light of gospel of the glory of Christ, who is the image of God." Therefore Scripture is open and easy for all the faithful.

I respond: The Apostle is not speaking about the understanding of the Scriptures, but the knowledge and faith in Christ, which the Apostles were preaching. For he had said in the previous chapter that there is a difference between the Old Testament and the New, namely, that in the Old men did not see the mysteries of Christ, the Incarnation, the passion, etc., except through the veil of figures and shadows. That is what the veil signified, with which Moses covered his face, when he spoke to the people, but in the New Testament, now that the figures have all been fulfilled, with an uncovered face we behold the glory of Christ, and there is no old woman, nor Christian boy, who does not know the God incarnate, who suffered, etc.

Therefore, someone can ask, if that is the case, why is it that after the preaching of the gospel still so many do not believe, and, especially the Jews, see nothing but shadows and figures? For this reason the Apostle says that the gospel is veiled to certain persons because their internal eyes have been blinded by perverse affections, about which the Lord said in John 5.44, "How can you believe, who receive glory from one another?" Moreover, the God of this world is understood as a God who is the creator of material things distinct from the true God, as the Marcionists and Manicheans interpret it, as Chrysostom says here, but he also says that the phrase "of this world" should be joined, not with "God but with "unbelievers," as Ambrose, Chrysostom, and others say regarding this passage, and Augustine also in book 21, chapter 2 of his treatise against Faustus. Certainly the Devil is called the God of this world, not because he is God in the absolute sense, but because he is the God of the infidels, as it is said in Ps. 96: "The Gods of the nations are demons." Augustine says this in book 21, chapter 9 against Faustus and Cyril against Oecumenius.

The sixth argument. St. Augustine says in book 2. chapter 6 of his books on Christian Doctrine: "Thus the Holy Spirit has magnificently and wholesomely modulated the Holy Scriptures so that the more open places present themselves to hunger and the more obscure places may deter a disdainful attitude. Hardly anything may be found in these obscure places which is not found plainly said elsewhere."

I respond that St. Augustine did not add that "hardly" in vain. For some very obscure things are found, which are never explained in the total Scripture, like a great part of the book of Revelation, the beginning and the end of Ezekiel, etc. Then this is very difficult, namely, to find something that is said very obscurely in one place, to be said clearly elsewhere. Otherwise, how could the same Augustine say in letter 119, chapter 21, that there is more that he does not know in the sacred Scriptures than what he knows? What about the situation concerning some texts, which seem very clear to us, and perhaps seem obscure to someone else? Therefore, Scripture alone does not suffice to eliminate controversies.

Certainly the words in Matt. 26:26, This is my body, seem to us to be so clear that the Evangelist could not have spoken more clearly. But to the Zwinglians they seem obscure and figurative. And the words in the same place, "Drink of it, all of you," seem clear to us, and to Lutherans they are explained in very different ways. For when we read Mark 14:23, "And they all drank of it," which is understood to be about the twelve disciples, interpreting Scripture through Scripture we say that the Lord said to his twelve disciples: "All of you drink of this." But Brentius in his prolegomena says clearly that here the command is not just for the Apostles, but also for all others that they should drink from the cup. And when we ask whether also the Turks, and the Jews, and infants should drink it? Then they add a gloss to the text: "All," that is, "all believing adults."

The seventh argument. The summary of all Scripture, which consists in the precepts of the Decalogue, the Creed, the Lord's Prayer, and the Sacraments, has very clear testimonies in the Scriptures; therefore all Scripture is very clear.

I respond: "The consequence and the antecedent are denied." I deny the consequence because, although everything in some way can be reduced to them, nevertheless in themselves they are obscure, as is clear from the prophecies of the prophets, from the Canticle of Canticles, from the letter to the Romans, from the book of Revelation, etc. But it is absolutely certain that the antecedent is false; for if the testimonies were so clear concerning all the articles of the Creed, and all the Sacraments, all controversies would have ended. But since there are very serious controversies about each article of the Creed, and each one of the Sacraments, not only do Catholics disagree with heretics over these tatters, but also the heretics disagree among themselves.

The eighth argument. John Chrysostom in homily 3 on Lazarus, where he shows that the philosophers have spoken obscurely, goes on to say this: "But on the contrary the Apostles and Prophets made everything manifest, and the clear things they handed on they explained to all, like common teachers of the world, so that each person by himself could learn the things that were said just by reading them." Also in homily 3 on 2 Thess., he said: "Why is there any need for a preacher? All things are clear and open from the divine Scriptures; but because you are delicate hearers, looking for pleasure in your hearing, on this account you seek preachers."

I respond: Chrysostom, in order to counter the inactivity of many who could, if they so wished, read the Scriptures with great fruit, was accustomed to use those exaggerations. For in general in those places he says that the Scriptures are difficult. In homily 3 on Lazarus, before the words cited above, he says: "What advantage is there, if we do not understand the things contained in the books? In fact there is very much, and even if you do not understand some profound things there, nevertheless such reading produces great virtue." And further on he admits that, when he says the Scriptures are easy, he is speaking only about the histories, and similar things. He also says that even these things are not clear and easy for all. "Take the book," he said, "into your hands, read all the history, and what you understand commit to memory; things that are obscure and less evident review again and again. But if you are not able, after assiduous reading, to understand what is being said, then go to someone wiser, go to a teacher." And in that homily 3 on 2 Thess., after the quoted words, he adds: "Can you tell me what the obscurity is? Are they not histories? Is it not because you know what is clear, so that you can investigate the things that are obscure? There are a thousand histories in the Scriptures, tell me one of them; but if you do not, they are only words and a pretext." Likewise, in homily 10 on John he warns his listeners that, before they come to the lecture, they should read the text, and write down anything obscure, so they may get an explanation from the lecturer. Finally, in homily 44 on John he teaches very clearly that the Scriptures are obscure, as was said above.

The ninth argument. This is the difference between the Old and the New Testaments—that the Old Testament was a sealed book, as is said in Is. 29, while the New Testament is an open book, as is said in Rev. 5, for the slain Lamb opens the book. For the argument in this matter, at the death of the Lord the curtain of the temple was torn as recorded in Matt. 27:51; and it is confirmed by Jerome in chapter 44 of Ezekiel, where he explains those passages of Scripture on the difficulty and ease of Scripture itself.

I respond that the difference between the Old Testament and the New consists in this, that then not only the thoughts of the Scriptures, but also the mysteries of Christ were not understood, because everything was covered over with figures, and for this reason in Is. 29:11 it is said to be a sealed book, both for those who know how to read and for those who do not. But in the New Testament, because Christ fulfilled the figures and the prophecies, although many do not understand the thoughts of the Scriptures, still even peasants and women understand the mysteries of redemption. But that neither the Scriptures nor Jerome speak about the thought of Scripture is clear both from Origen in homily 12 on Exodus, where he says that it is still necessary that the Lamb of the tribe of Judah open for us the sealed books; and from Jerome himself, who in his letter to Paulinus on the monastic life says that still today the veil remains, not only on the face of Moses, but also on the face of the Evangelists and Apostles, if we consider the difficulty of the Scriptures, and therefore that we should pray with the Prophet:

"Open my eyes, and I will consider the wonders of your law" (Ps. 119:18).

The tenth argument is proper to Luther. The Fathers prove their own ideas from Scripture, but what is more known is not to be proved by what is less known. Therefore the Scriptures are clearer than the commentaries of the Fathers.

I respond: it is amazing why Luther, who so often rebukes the sophists, now does not hesitate to engage in sophistry. For, since the philosophers say that what is less known should be proved by what is more known, they are not talking about the knowledge of words, which consists in the clarity of thought, as we say that it is an idea, that is, an easier and clearer idea than a figurative one, but about the idea of the truth of the thing, which consists in this, that someone understands that what is said is true. Examples of this are motion and life. For if you look at the words, it is equally easy to understand this sentence "a man lives" and "a man is moved." But with regard to what concerns the knowledge of the truth of the matter, it is easier to know that a man is moved, than to know that he lives. Therefore, in this way the Fathers confirm their ideas with the testimony of the Scriptures, because it is more known that what is contained in Scripture is true, than what is had in the Fathers. Nevertheless the same Fathers explain the Scriptures with their own Commentaries, because the words of Scripture are more obscure than the words of the Fathers.

The eleventh argument. The Fathers of the first Church read the Scriptures without commentaries. And later all the other ancient Fathers did the same. So to what purpose do we follow this new way of the commentaries?

I respond: the contrary is true, and Luther offers no example, but we can cite many such examples. I say, therefore, that the first Fathers, who lived immediately after the Apostles, did not read commentaries, because none existed; but they could approach living commentaries, that is, the Apostles and their disciples, and they did not want to understand the Scriptures on the basis of their own ingenuity. Thus Papias gives testimony about himself in the last chapter of book 3 of Eusebius's *History*, and Clement of Alexandria in book 1 of his *Stromata*, when he mentions his teachers as disciples of the Apostles, and among them especially Panthenus. Then Justin, and Irenaeus, and others began to write commentaries on the divine books, as Jerome says in his book on illustrious men in the chapter on John; similarly the ancient Fathers after that began to write, as Ruffinus says about Basil and Gregory in book 2, chapter 9 of his *History*, and Jerome about himself in the preface to his commentary on Ephesians. The same thing could be shown about all the others, if it were necessary.

Chapter 3: A Question is Proposed About the Judge of Controversies, and at the Same Time There is an Examination of the Senses of the Scriptures

Since it has already been established that Scripture is obscure and needs an interpreter, that fact gives rise to another question: Whether the interpretation of Scripture should be sought from one visible and common judge, or should it be left to the choice of each individual? Surely this is a very grave question, and on it all the controversies depend in some way. Many have written about this question, but especially John Driedo in book 2, chapter 3 on ecclesiastical dogmas. John Cochlaeus in his book on the authority of Scripture and the Church: Cardinal Warmiensis in books 2 and 3 against the Prolegomena of Brentius, and Peter a Soto in the defense of his Confession against the same Prolegomena of Brentius (par. 2 and 3), and also Martin Peresius in his book on tradition (assertions 2, 3, 4, and 5); Michael Medina in book 7 on the right Faith in God, and Melchior Cano in book 2, chapters 6, 7, and 8, in his book on Theological Places.

Therefore, in order to understand what this question is all about, it is necessary to clarify a few points: the first one has to do with the meanings of Scripture. For it is something proper to the divine Scriptures, because they have God as their author, that often they contain two senses—the literal or historical, and the spiritual or mystical. The literal sense is that which the words immediately express; the spiritual is that which refers to something other than what the words express immediately; this distinction is deduced from the Apostle in 1 Cor. 10:11 where he says that everything happened to the Jews as a warning for our instruction. And the things said literally about the exodus of the Jews from Egypt, on passing through the sea, on the manna which came down in the desert, on the water that flowed from the rock—these things he accommodates spiritually to Christians. Jerome teaches in his comments on Rev. and on Ez. 2 that these two senses are signified by the book written on the inside and the outside.

Philo in his book on the theoretical life of suppliants, and Nazianzen in his letter to Nemesius compares the literal sense to the body and the spiritual sense to the soul. And just as the generated Word of God has an invisible divine nature and a visible human nature, so also the written word of God has an external and an internal sense. St. Gregory in book 21, chapter 1 in his *Magna Moralia* teaches that this is proper to the divine Scriptures alone.

Further, the literal sense is twofold: one simple, which consists in the property of the words, the other figurative, whereby the words are transferred from their natural meaning to something else. And there are as many kinds of this as there are different kinds of figures. Since the Lord says in John 10:16: "I have other sheep that are not of this fold," etc., that is the literal sense, but the figurative is that other persons besides the Jews must be brought into the Church. This is said directly in John 11:52 that he would gather into one the children of God who are scattered abroad. On these figures of speech see what Augustine says in book 3 on *Christian Doctrine*.

But the sense of Scripture is distinguished in three ways by more recent theologians: allegorical, tropological, and anagogical. They call the meaning allegorical, when the words of Scripture, besides the literal meaning, signify something in the New Testament, which pertains to Christ or to the Church, like Abraham who really and literally had two wives, one free and one a servant, and two sons. Isaac and Ishmael. It signified that God is the author of two Testaments, and the Father of two peoples, as the Apostle explains in Gal. 4. They call the meaning tropological, when the words or facts are used to signify something which pertains to morals. For example, Deut. 25:4 says, "You shall not muzzle an ox when it is treading out the grain," which is understood literally to concern real oxen, but spiritually it means that preachers should not be prevented from receiving support from the people, as the Apostle explains in 1 Cor. 9:9-12. They call the meaning anagogical, when the words or facts are used to signify eternal life. For example, Ps. 95:11 says: "Therefore I swore in my anger that they should not enter my rest." Literally this refers to the Promised Land, but spiritually it also refers to eternal life, as the Apostle explains in Heb. 4:3-11.

This distinction of the spiritual senses was not always observed by the ancient authors. For although they recognize, in what pertains to the reality, all of these meanings, nevertheless sometimes they call all of them allegories, like Basil at the beginning of homily 9 on Examination, and Augustine in chapter 3 in his work on the Creed. Moreover, Jerome, in his letter to Hedibias (question 12), by the word "tropological" understands also the allegorical, and then in his comments on Amos 4 by the word "allegorical" he understands what is tropological.

Among these meanings, the literal is found in every sentence, both of the Old and of the New Testament. And it is not improbable that sometimes several meanings are found in the same sentence, as St. Augustine teaches in many places, and especially in book 12, chapter 26 if his *Confessions*, in book 11, chapter 19 of *The City of God*, and in book 3, chapter 27 on *Christian Doctrine*. But the spiritual meaning is found in both Testaments. For no one doubts that the Old Testament has the allegorical, tropological, and anagogical senses. Many think the same thing about the New Testament and rightly so. For Augustine explains in an allegorical way, in his treatise 122 on John, the capture of the fish, when the net was torn (Luke 5:6), but in an anagogical way when the net was not torn (John 21:6). And similarly in treatise 124 on John, he explains allegorically what was said to Peter, "Follow me" (John 21:19), and anagogically what was said about John, "If it is my will that he remain," etc. (John 21:22). But the Lord explains tropologically his own humility, because of which he washed his disciples' feet (John 13:14f).

Although these cases do occur, still a spiritual sense is not found in every sense of Scripture, neither in the Old Testament nor in the New. For the expression, "You shall love Lord your God with all your heart," in Deut. 6:5 and Matt. 22:37, and similar precepts, have only one meaning, that is, a literal one, as Cassian rightly teaches in Collation 8, chapter 3. That being the case, there is agreement among us and our adversaries that effective arguments should be sought only from the literal sense. For it is certain that the sense which is derived immediately from the words is the sense of the Holy Spirit. But the mystical and spiritual senses are various, and although they edify when they are not against Faith and good morals, nevertheless it is not always certain that they are intended by the Holy Spirit. Therefore, St. Augustine in letter 48 to Vincent rightly ridicules the Donatists, who give a mystical explanation of these words: "Tell me where you pasture your flock, where you make it lie down at noon" (Cantic. 1:6), because they conclude from this that the Church of Christ has survived only in Africa. Also Jerome in his commentary on Matt. 13 says that the dogmas of the Faith cannot be effectively proved from the mystical meanings of Scripture.

But with regard to the literal sense, sometimes there can be doubts for two reasons. The first is the ambiguity of the words, such as is seen in Matt. 26:27, "Drink of it, all of you." That phrase "all of you" is ambiguous, if only those words are considered. For it is not known whether it signifies absolutely all men, or only all the faithful, or all the Apostles. The second and more serious doubt concerns the property of the words. For since the literal sense sometimes is (as we have said) simple, and sometimes figurative, it is doubtful in many places whether the true sense is simple or figurative. For regarding the words in Matt. 26:26, "This is my body," Catholics want them to be understood simply according to the property of the words, but the Zwinglians take them as the figure of metonymy. And for this reason at times some people fall into very grave errors. Origen is an example of this, who erred because what should be taken simply, he understood figuratively, as Jerome says in his letter to Pammachius on the errors of John of Jerusalem, where he says that Origen so allegorized the earthly Paradise that he removed its historical truth, since he understands angels for the trees, and the heavenly Virtues for the rivers, and he interprets the skin clothing of Adam and Eve as their human bodies, as if before their sin they were living without a body.

On the other hand, others have fallen into error, because they have taken something simply which should be understood figuratively, like Papias, and those who followed him—Justin, Irenaeus, Tertullian, Lactantius, and some others: they thought that what is said in Rev. 20 about the New Jerusalem, and the thousand years during which the saints will reign with Christ, will be fulfilled here on earth. Jerome refutes their error in the preface to his book on Isaiah 18, and on Ezekiel 36; Augustine does the same in book 20, chapter 7 of *The City of God.*

There is also agreement between us and our adversaries that the Scriptures must be understood in the same spirit in which they were made, that is, in the Holy Spirit. The Apostle Peter teaches this when he says in 2 Pet. 1:20-21: "First of all you must understand this, that no prophecy of Scripture is a matter of one's own interpretation, because no prophecy ever came by the impulse of man, but men moved by the Holy Spirit spoke from God." St. Peter proves there that the Scriptures should not be explained from one's own cleverness, but according to the direction of the Holy Spirit, because the Scriptures do not come from human genius, but from the inspiration of the Holy Spirit.

Therefore this whole question comes down to where the Spirit is. For we think that this Spirit, although he is often conferred on many individual persons, nevertheless is certainly found in the Church, that is, in a Council of the Bishops confirmed by the Sovereign Pontiff of the whole Church, or in the Sovereign Pontiff together with a council of the other Pastors. For we do not want to debate in this place concerning the Sovereign Pontiff and the Councils, whether the Pontiff alone can define something, and whether a Council alone can do it: we will treat this matter in its proper place. But here we wish to say in general that the judge of the true sense of Scripture and of all controversies is the Church, that is, the Pontiff with a Council, and about this all Catholics are in agreement; and it is stated expressly in session 4 of the Council of Trent.

But all the heretics of this time teach that the Holy Spirit is the interpreter of Scripture, and that he is not tied to the Bishops, or to any group of men, and therefore that each person should be the judge, either by following his own spirit if he has the gift of interpreting, or by following someone else whom he sees is endowed with this same gift. In the preface to his article on this matter, Luther clearly refers us to the spirit, which each person has, while he is carefully reading the Scriptures. And in article 115 which Cochlaeus gathered together from the works of Luther, he says the following: "This is a key point of the Gospels, since it has not been granted either to Councils or to any group of men to establish and to conclude what the Faith is; therefore I must say, Father, you have finished with the Councils, so now I have to make the judgment whether I can accept them or not. Why is that? Because you will not stand up for me and respond for me when I must die. And no one can judge false doctrine except the spiritual man. Therefore this matter is insane, that the Councils want to deduce and decree what must be believed, since often there is no man who can detect the divine Spirit even in a small way." He repeats the same idea in his assertions, articles 27, 28 and 29.

Philippus, in his chapter on the Church, seems indeed to attribute something to the Church: but really he leaves the whole judgment to each private person. "Who," he said, "will be the judge, when dissent arises over the meaning of Scripture, since then it is necessary to have a voice to put an end to the controversy? I respond—the word of God itself is the judge, and the confession of the true Church is added to it." That is what he says there. But further on, when he teaches that by the true Church he does not mean the Prelates of the Church, nor the major part of the faithful, but those few men who are familiar with the word of God: he covers everything with obscurity and he makes each person his own judge. For I cannot judge which is the true Church, unless I first judge which opinion is in agreement with the word of God: "There is," he said, "a difference between the judges of the Church and political judges. For in politics, either the Monarch alone pronounces something by his authority, or in a Senate the opinion of the majority prevails; but in the Church what prevails is the opinion agreeing with the word of God, and the confession of the pious, whether they are more or fewer than the impious." See more on this in the place in the notes of the Church.

Brentius teaches something similar in the *Confession of Wittenberg*, in the chapter on sacred Scripture and more extensively in the Prolegomena against Peter a Soto, where he says two things. First: "It is not allowed," he said, "in the matter of eternal salvation to so adhere to the opinion of another that we embrace it without our own judgment." Secondly he adds: "It pertains to each private person to judge about the doctrine of religion, and to distinguish what is true from what is false. But there is this difference between a private Person and a Prince, that just as a private person has the private power of judging and deciding, so the Prince has the public power of judging about the doctrine of religion." And he tries to prove these two points in almost the whole book, namely, that the secular Prince should force his subjects, even with the punishment of death, to embrace the Faith which he judges to be true. And at the same time he says that the subjects should follow their own judgment, not that of another, whomsoever he may be. And Brentius does not recognize how absurd and conflicting these views are, namely, that the Prince must command, and that the subjects must not obey. Nor has he realized that, if this opinion is true, Caesar would be acting rightly, and the other Catholic Princes of Germany, if they also force all Lutherans, with the threat of the punishment of death, to adopt the Catholic Faith.

John Calvin in book 4. chapter 9 § 8, 12, and 13 in his Institutes orders that the definitions of the Councils, even the General ones, are to be examined exactly in the light of the Scriptures. Therefore he makes individual men the judges in matters of faith, not only of the Fathers, but also of the Councils, and he does not allow for any common judgment of the Church. Finally, Martin Kemnitius, in his examination of session 4 of the Council of Trent, and all the other contemporary heretics, remove the authority of interpreting Scripture from the Councils of Bishops and confer it on the spirit of private individuals.

Chapter 4: Testimonies from the Old Testament are Cited for the Opinion of Catholics

Now the thought of Catholics is proved, first, by testimonies from the Old Testament. The first testimony is found in Ex. 18:13f, for there we read that, when the people began to be established as a kind of ecclesiastical Republic, Moses presided as the leader and head of that assembly, and he would respond to all doubts that arose concerning the law of the Lord, nor did he refer men to some revealing spirit. In the same place, when, according to the counsel of his father-in-law, he had constituted minor magistrates who would judge the people, he always reserved to himself doubts about religion. Actually, he did this so that we might understand that there should be one common tribunal from which all seek the interpretation of the divine law, and with which all simply agree.

This argument is wont to be evaded by certain authors who say: Moses was a political leader, not a Pontiff or Priest, since Aaron was the High Priest. And therefore from this passage it cannot be concluded that judgment about the matters of faith pertains to priests, but rather in a certain way it pertains to Kings. I respond: Moses was a priest, in fact a High Priest, and greater than Aaron, but he was not a priest in the ordinary sense with successors, for there could be only one like that and that was Aaron; but Moses was an extraordinary priest who had been constituted specially by God. Just as in the New Testament all the Apostles were not indeed greater than Peter, nor completely equal to him, but still in some sense they were equal to Peter in ecclesiastical power, as Cyprian says in his treatise on the simplicity of Prelates. However, there is this difference—that Peter was the ordinary Pastor of the whole Church, who alone was to have successors; the others were extraordinary Pastors who were not to have successors in their special powers. David bears witness to the fact that Moses was a priest, since he says in Ps. 99:6, "Moses and Aaron were among his priests. Samuel also was among those who called upon his name."

But, they say: Moses is said to be a priest, because he was a distinguished man, as we read in 2 Sam. 8:18 that the sons of David were priests. The contrary is true: because if in this place distinguished men were called priests, Samuel also, who was a distinguished man, would have been called a priest. But David did not do that, because he knew that Samuel was not a priest, but only a judge; for he did not descend from the family of Aaron, since Kohath was his cousin (1 Chron. 6:3). But it is clear from Ex. 28 and 29, where Moses exercises all the sacerdotal offices, that Moses really and truly was a Priest. That is so because he offers sacrifice, teaches, consecrates clothing, and what is even more important, he anoints and initiates Pontiffs and Priests. Therefore almost all the fathers teach that Moses was a priest in the proper sense. The same point is made by Philo in book 3 on the life of Moses, Dionysius in chapter 5 of the Church hierarchy, Gregory Nazianzen in his sermon in the presence of Gregory of Nyssa, Augustine on Ps. 99. Jerome in his book of Jovinian, where he also shows that Samuel was not a priest.

The second testimony is found in Deut. 17:8-12, where a general law is proclaimed: "If any case arises requiring decision between one kind of homicide and another, one kind of legal right and another or one kind of assault and another, any case within your towns which is too difficult for you, then you shall arise and go up to the place which the Lord your God will choose, and coming to the Levitical priests, and to the judge who is in office in those days, you shall consult them, and they shall declare to you the decision. Then you shall do according to what they declare to you from that place which the Lord shall choose; and you shall be careful to do according to all that they direct you; according to the instructions which they give you, and according to the decision which they pronounce to you, you shall do; you shall not turn aside from the verdict which they declare to you, either to the right or to the left. The man who acts presumptuously, by not obeying the priest who stands to minister there before the Lord your God, or the judge, that man shall die." Here also it is very clear that those in doubt are not referred to their own spirit, but to a living judge, that is, the High Priest.

But Brentius will object: that precept is conditional, because he adds: "You shall do according to what they declare to you from that place ... and you shall be careful to do all that they direct you according to his Law." For it seems to be concluded from this place that one must not abide by the judgment of the High Priest, unless he provides the testimony of the divine Law. I respond: that phrase, "all that they direct you," etc., is found only in the Vulgate edition, which Lutherans do not accept, and it is not a condition, but an assertion or promise: for he did not want to say, "Abide by the judgment of the priest, if he directs you according to the Law," for then men would be more doubtful and perplexed than they were before; and it would not have been necessary to go to the priest, if they could judge their own case by themselves on the basis of the Law. Indeed, then the priest would not have been the judge, but they themselves, since they would be the ones to judge the decision of the priest. Therefore it is not a condition, but a promise, for the Lord wants to make the people secure, when they accept the judgment of the priest; and this is what he does, since he affirms that they will be judged according to his Law.

Brentius objects a second time: he says in this place that those who have doubts are sent not only to the priest, but also to the judge who was a political leader. I respond that the word "judge" here can be understood as the High Priest. For in Hebrew it is, "You shall go to the priests and to the judge," as if he were to say, to the council of priests and their chief, the High Priest. In the second place I say: if we understand by the word "judge" a political leader, then here there would be distinct offices. For the definitive decision belongs to the priest, but the execution belongs to the judge in the case of the obstinate. "The man who acts presumptuously," he said, "by not obeying the priest and the decree of the judge shall die."

There is a third objection: here it is not a matter of religious doubts, but political. I respond: that is false. For the general law is about all the doubts, which arise because of the Law. Moreover, the occasion of this law was because of those who worship foreign gods, as is clear from the beginning of chapter 17 that it is contrary to religion to be serving foreign gods.

The third testimony is in Eccles. 12:11: "The sayings of the wise are like goads, and like nails firmly fixed are the collected sayings which are given by one Shepherd. My son, beware of anything beyond these." In this place Solomon is teaching that there should be no further inquiry, but only complete agreement, when a decision has been given by the supreme Shepherd, especially when the counsel of the wise is added to it. But if this is said about the priest of the Old Testament, how much more can it be said about the priest of the New Testament, who has received much greater promises from God?

The fourth testimony is in Haggai 2:11: "Thus says the Lord of hosts: Ask the priests about the law." And Malachi 2:7: "The lips of a priest should guard knowledge, and men should seek instruction from his mouth, for he is the messenger of the Lord of hosts." From these words we understand that it does not belong to individual men to judge about the decree of the Law of the Lord, but to the priest, who, since he is an angel, that is, a messenger of God, has the right officially to explain the law of God.

Finally, in 2 Chron. 19:10-11, the good King Jehoshaphat speaks thus to the Priests: "Whenever a case comes to you from your brethren who live in their cities, concerning bloodshed, law or commandment, statutes or ordinances, then you shall instruct them, that they may not incur guilt before the Lord and wrath may not come upon you and your brethren. Thus you shall do, and you will not incur guilt. And behold, Amariah the chief priest is over you in all matters of the Lord; and Zebadiah the son of Ishmael, the governor of the house of Judah, in all the king's matters." You can see here how clearly the King distinguishes the office of Priest from the office of King, and he attributes to the Priest alone judgment about doubts of the Law.

Chapter 5: The Same Point is Proved from the New Testament

Now from the New Testament. The first testimony is Matt. 16:19: "I will give you the keys to the kingdom of heaven," etc. For by those keys is understood not only the power of forgiving sins, but also to free men from all other chains and impediments, which, if they are not removed, one cannot enter into the kingdom of heaven. Since the promise is general, and it is not said, "whomever you loose," but "whatever you loose," so that we may understand that all difficulties can be solved by Peter and his successors, either by dispensing from the laws, or by forgiving sins and punishments, or by explaining dogmas and resolving controversies. We will say more about this in book 1 of our treatise on the Sovereign Pontiff.

Another testimony can be found in Matt. 18:17: "If he refuses to listen even to the Church, let him be to you as a Gentile and a tax collector." But in this place it should be noted that the Lord is talking about the injuries which one man suffers from another; but even more it is to be understood about the injuries which are inflicted on the whole Church, and on God, such as heresy. For he orders that the adulterer should be subjected to the judgment of the Church, and even more so the heretic. But it cannot happen that they be brought before the assembly of all the faithful: therefore the word "Church" here should be understood to mean the Prelate, as Chrysostom explains it, or (as others prefer) the assembly of Prelates. For just as a man does not speak or hear, except by his head, but still the whole man is said to speak and to hear, so also the Church through her Prelates hears and speaks. Therefore, if someone does not listen to the Church, that is, the Pastors of the Church, he should be like a Gentile or a tax collector; it follows that the final judgment belongs to the Pastors.

The third testimony is in Matt. 23:2: "The scribes and Pharisees sit on Moses' seat: so practice and observe whatever they tell you, but not what they do." Please note three things here. First, that in that whole chapter the Lord is rebuking the vices of the scribes and Pharisees, and that the weak could conclude therefrom that it is not necessary to believe Prelates who live an evil life. Therefore, at the beginning of the chapter he wants to teach clearly that, notwithstanding the evil life of some Prelates, their teaching must be followed. Secondly, observe with Cyprian in book 4, letter 9, that neither the Lord nor the Apostles, in all of Scripture, ever rebuke the Pontiffs and Priests of the Jews, by calling them Pontiffs and Priests, but only under the title of scribes and Pharisees; they do this lest they seem to blame the chair and the priesthood, and so that we may understand that honor is always due to the priesthood and pontificate, even if perhaps some person, who occupies the chair, is less worthy. From this we understand that contemporary heretics, who are found among Bishops and Priests, and especially in the highest place in the Church, have nothing in common with the mores of the Lord and the Apostles.

Thirdly, note that what the Lord says about the chair of Moses is to be understood *a fortiori* of the chair of Peter. For thus the ancients understood it, and especially Augustine in letter 165. "In the order of Bishops," he said, "which has existed from Peter until Anastasius, who now occupies the same chair, even if a traitor during that time had crept in, that would be no prejudice against the Church, and innocent Christians, to whom the provident Lord says about evil commanders: Do what they say, but do not do what they do."

The fourth testimony is in John 21:16: "Simon Peter, feed my sheep." Here also three points should be noted. First, what is said to Peter is said also to his successors: for Christ did not want to provide for his Church for 25 years only, but for as long as the world exists. Second, that word "feed" is to be understood especially about doctrine; for in this way rational sheep are fed. On this see Jer. 3:15: "I will give you shepherds after my own heart, who will feed you with knowledge and understanding." Third, the word "sheep" signifies all Christians, for anyone who does not want to be fed by Peter, is not one of Christ's sheep.

From this we conclude that it has been committed to Peter and his successors to teach all Christians. But this cannot be understood in a better way than this—that Peter and his successors have been commissioned to teach all what must be held regarding the doctrine of the faith. For if we understand it to be only about sermons, this precept will never be fulfilled, for the Pontiff cannot preach to all men, nor is it necessary, since there are men in each Church who do the preaching.

Also, if we understand this to be about commentaries on the sacred Writings, so that, whom the Pontiff cannot teach with words, he teaches by written commentaries, then we are reprehending several very holy Pontiffs, who did not do that. Therefore, the Lord is speaking about the special office of teaching the whole Church, by establishing what must be believed by all. But it is in this way that this text was understood by St. Jerome in his letter to Damasus on the word "Hypostasis," because he was seeking an explanation of a certain controversy concerning the Son: "From the Shepherd," he said, "I ask earnestly for the protection of a sheep."

The fifth testimony is in Luke 22:31: "I have prayed for you that your faith may not fail; and when you have turned again, strengthen your brethren." From this text St. Bernard in letter 90 to Innocent deduced that the Roman Pontiff, teaching *ex cathedra*, cannot err; and before him the same was said by Lucius I in letter 1 to the Bishops of Spain and France, Felix I in a letter to Benignus, Mark in a letter to Athanasius, Leo I in sermon 3 on his acceptance of the Pontificate, Leo IX in a letter to Peter, Patriarch of Antioch, Agatho in a letter to the Emperor Constantine in the Fourth Synod which was approved by the whole Council, Paschal II at the Roman Council, which is found in the Chronicle of the Abbot Urspergensis; to these I add, whether the heretics agree or not, Innocent III in the chapter *Majores* on Baptism and its effect. Therefore, if the Roman Pontiff cannot err when he is teaching *ex cathedra*, certainly his judgment must be followed, and he must be the supreme Judge.

The sixth testimony is in Acts 15:6ff. For we read there, when a serious question about the Faith had arisen, namely, whether the Law of Moses must be observed by the Gentile converts, that each person was not referred to his own spirit, but to the Council held in Jerusalem, over which Peter presided. We read that Peter, the first of all, spoke at the Council and then that James confirmed the thinking of Peter, and so the question was resolved with these words: "It has seemed good to the Holy Spirit and to us," etc. With these words they show that the decision of the Council, over which Peter presided, is the decision of the Holy Spirit. And in the same chapter we read that Paul, wherever he went, was wont to preach that the decree of that Council should be observed, that is, that they should accept it and not wish to pass judgment on the decree of the Council.

The seventh testimony is in the letter to the Galatians 2:1ff: "I went up again," said Paul, "with Barnabas ... and I laid before them (but privately before those who were of repute) the gospel which I preach among the Gentiles, lest somehow I should be running or had run in vain." But who those men were with whom he consulted, he explains later, saying that it was Peter, James, and John. In their explanation of this passage Tertullian in book 4 against Marcion, St. Jerome in letter 89 to Augustine, which is 11 among the letters of Augustine, and Augustine himself in book 28, chapter 4 against Faustus say clearly that the Church would not give credence to Paul unless his gospel was confirmed by Peter. Therefore it was Peter then, and so his successors now, who pass judgment on the doctrine of the Faith.

The eighth testimony is in 1 Cor. 12:8-10: "To one is given through the Spirit the utterance of wisdom, and to another the utterance of knowledge, to another the interpretation of tongues, to another prophecy," etc. Here it is said clearly that the spirit of interpreting the Scriptures is not given to all the faithful. Also, it is certain from 2 Pet. 1:20, "no prophecy of Scripture is a matter of one's own interpretation, that Scripture cannot be explained well without the spirit of interpretation." Therefore it is evidently deduced that no private person is the judge of the true meaning of Scripture. So what does the person do who does not have this spirit? In fact, who will be certain that he has this spirit, since we know that it is not given to all, and we do not know to whom it is given? Therefore, the conclusion is that we acknowledge the Church alone as the judge, about which there cannot be any doubt that she does have the Spirit of God, and that she teaches her children without error, since she is the pillar and foundation of truth. This is something that even Luther confesses in his book on the power of the Pope with these words (in spite of what he wrote elsewhere, since in an amazing way he was changeable and unstable): "Of no private man do we have certitude whether or not he has the revelation of the Father; but the Church is the one about whom it is not permitted to doubt." But the Church does not speak otherwise than through the mouth of her Pastors and doctors, and especially in a general Council of Bishops. Such a Council will have either the Sovereign Pontiff present and presiding, or his confirmation, and it must obtain his approbation.

But, they say, that man is certain that he has the spirit who asks for it. For it is written, "How much more will the heavenly Father give the Holy Spirit to those who ask him" (Luke 11:13);

and also James 1:5: "If any of you lacks wisdom, let him ask God, who gives to all men generously." I respond that here and in similar places the Lord is not talking about the spirit of interpretation, which is a certain freely given grace, but about the spirit of Faith, Hope and Charity, and the Wisdom necessary for salvation. For as St. Augustine teaches in tracts 73, 81 and 103 on John, prayer does not obtain infallibly except what is necessary or useful for salvation for the person who prays. Moreover, the gift of interpreting, like the gift of tongues and miracles, and the other gifts mentioned there, are not always helpful for the one who has them.

Therefore, just as we cannot always obtain the Spirit of speaking in tongues, or performing miracles, even though it is written: "the Holy Spirit will give good things to those who ask him," so also neither the spirit of interpretation. For otherwise it would come about that the whole body of the Church would be one member, that is, all would be eyes, all hands, etc., which is opposed to what the Apostle says in Rom. 12:4 and 1 Cor. 12:14ff. Furthermore, even if the Lord in those texts were speaking about the gift of interpreting, still it would not be certain that whoever asks for it receives it, because it is not certain whether or not he asks well. For it is written: "You ask and do not receive, because you ask wrongly" (James 4:3). Otherwise when Lutherans ask for that spirit, Anabaptists ask for it, Zwinglians ask for it, why is it that they receive spirits that are very different and fighting with each other, if that one and true Holy Spirit is given to all who ask for it?

The ninth testimony is in 1 John 4:1: "Beloved, do not believe every spirit, but test the spirits to see whether they are of God; for many false prophets have gone out into the world." The spirit of private men should be tested, whether it is of God: for many boast about having the Holy Spirit, who are moved by a spirit of giddiness and lies, as is said in 1 Kings 22, 2 Chron. 18, and Isaiah 19 and 29. Therefore a private spirit cannot be the judge. For how can he be a judge, since judgment must still be pass on him?

Therefore, if someone explains the words. "This is my body," by saying it means. "This signifies my body," because in this sense the spirit is revealing it to him. the matter is still not finished. For John warns us that we should test that spirit whether it is of God, lest perhaps is may be a spirit of giddiness.

But this cannot be proved from Scripture, as they claim, because in this place we can doubt about the meaning of Scripture itself. Therefore it must be proved from its conformity with the spirit of those concerning whom it is certain that they have the true spirit; but such persons are the Prelates lawfully assembled together in a Council. For we read in Acts 15:28, "It has seemed good to the Holy Spirit and to us." Now such is the Pontiff teaching *ex cathedra*, whom we have shown is always guided by the Holy Spirit, so that he cannot err. Such also were the Apostles and the first faithful, concerning whom it is certain that they had the Holy Spirit.

Calvin cannot deny this, because he argues in the same way in his *Institutes* 1, chapter 9 § 1 against Swenexfeldius, who wanted the spirit alone to be the judge, while repudiating the Scriptures. If that spirit were good, it would be the same as the spirit of the Apostles, and of the first faithful; but their spirit did not want to be the judge, while contemning the Scriptures. But in this way also we can argue against Calvin and other heretics: If their spirit were good, it would be the same as the spirit of the Apostles and the first faithful; but the spirit of the latter did not want to be judge, but it appealed to Peter and the Council, and it accepted their decision, as we showed above from Acts 15. Therefore their spirit, which establishes itself as judge, is not a good spirit. [...]

Chapter 9: The Same Point is Proved from Reason

It is proved finally by reason. God was not ignorant of the fact that many difficulties would arise in the Church concerning the Faith. Therefore he had to provide a judge for the Church. But that judge cannot be Scripture, nor a private revealing spirit, nor a secular prince: therefore it had to be an ecclesiastical official, either alone or certainly with a council and the consent of his fellow Bishops. And it is not, nor could it be imagined anything else, to which it seems this judgment could pertain. And first of all, it is clear that Scripture is not the judge, because it is subject to various meanings, nor can it say which interpretation is true. Moreover, in every well-founded and ordered Republic, the law and the judges are distinct things. For the law says what must be done, and the judge interprets the law, and he directs men according to it. Finally, there is a question about the interpretation of Scripture, since it cannot interpret itself.

But, they say, from a comparison of the various places the true meaning can be derived by anyone skilled in languages. But what is to be done, if many are skilled in languages, and they confer on the same texts among themselves, and nevertheless they are still not able to agree. Who then will be the judge? Certainly many Lutherans and many Zwinglians were skilled in languages, and they studied the Scriptures together with great effort, and nevertheless in the explanation of the sentence, "This is my Body," they were never able to agree. But the Zwinglians, a Lutheran will say, are blind, and therefore it is not surprising that they do not understand the very clear words of the Lord. But what happens, if a Zwinglian says that the Lutherans are blind—who will be the judge?

It is easily demonstrated that a revealing spirit cannot be the judge for each private individual. Since the spirit, which is in you, is neither seen nor heard by me, then a judge should be seen and heard by both litigating parties; for the contending parties are of such a nature, that is, both are bodily men. For if we were spirits, perhaps the judgment of a spirit would suffice. Furthermore, in a temporal Republic all have a true natural light of reason, according to which the law is established, and that suffices to explain it, and still, the private interpretation of the law is never handed over to the private judgment of each person. For if that were permitted, the Republic could not exist for very long. Therefore how much less should the interpretation of Scripture be turned over to the judgment of each person, since all do not have that true supernatural light, by which Scripture was formed and which is necessary in order to understand it correctly.

Moreover, a judge must have effective authority, otherwise his judgment will mean nothing; but private individuals do not have such authority. Also many are so crude and ignorant, as they themselves admit, that they could in no way pass judgment on questions of faith, but still they also can be saved; therefore it is not necessary for all to judge.

Finally, if the private revealing spirit were judge, the way to convert heretics would be precluded, and no controversies could ever be brought to an end. For there is no heretic who does not claim to have the spirit, and who does not place his spirit before the spirit of others. And as in 2 Chron. 18, when Micaiah, a prophet of the Lord, said that he was speaking in the name of the Lord, but the false prophets were moved by a lying spirit the false prophet Zedekiah said to him: "Which way did the Spirit of the Lord go from me to speak to you?" (v. 23). So if a Catholic would say "the Spirit has revealed this to me." the heretic would respond. "Which way did the Spirit," etc.

It will now be proved that a secular Prince is not the judge. For nothing can act beyond the power of its own causes. But the causes involved in secular ruling are human and natural. For the efficient cause is the choice of the people, while the end is the peace and temporal tranquility of the Republic: therefore the Prince as such does not have power or authority, except what is human; the people can give this to him and it is required in order to keep the peace. A sign of this is the fact that even without the Church there are true Kings, and temporal Princes; and without them there can be the true Church, as in the city of Rome during the first three centuries.

There is not obstacle to this in what is said in Rom. 13:1-2: "There is not authority except from God ... and he who resists the authorities resists what God has appointed." For the Apostle does not want to say that kingly power is from God immediately, but in a mediated way, because God placed the natural instinct in men to constitute a King for themselves. In the same way, human laws can be said to be from God, because they are the result of natural reason, which God implanted in the human mind when he created him. But the ecclesiastical governing power has divine and supernatural causes; for the efficient cause immediately is God, since the Pontiff does not have his authority from the Church, but from Christ, who said to him: "Feed my sheep" (John 21:17). And also: "I will give you the keys of the kingdom of heaven" (Matt. 16:19). But the final cause is eternal beatitude.

Therefore outside the Church a true Pontiff is not found, nor true Priests, nor without them can there be a Church. Hence Nazianzen in his sermon to the citizens struck with fear. Chrysostom in homily 4 on Isaiah, and Ambrose in chapter 2 of his book on the dignity of the priesthood say that a Bishop is as much greater than a king, as the spirit is to flesh, as the sky to the earth, as gold to lead. And for this reason also the pontificate and the priesthood pertain per se to the Church, but temporal rule pertains to her only accidentally. Therefore, since to define matters of Faith, and to interpret the divine Scriptures is an ecclesiastical and spiritual activity, for certain it does not pertain to the temporal Prince, but to the spiritual and ecclesiastical order.

INTRODUCTION TO WILLIAM WHITAKER'S *DISPUTATION ON HOLY SCRIPTURE*

Few today will recognize the name William Whitaker (1548–1595), yet one more casualty of our contemporary ignorance of the early modern era. During his own time, however, he was respected by both friend and foe. Reverend William Fitzgerald, who translated Whitaker's *Disputatio de Sacra Scriptura* into English, recounts the following:

> I have heard it confessed of English Papists them-
> selves, which have been in Italy with Bellarmine
> himself, that he procured the true portraiture and
> effigies of this *Whitaker* to be brought to him,
> which he kept in his study. For he privately ad-
> mired this man for his singular learning and inge-
> nuity; and being asked of some friends, Jesuits,
> why he would have the picture of that heretic in
> his presence? he would answer, *Quod quamvis
> haereticus erat et adversarius, erat tamen doctus adversari-
> us*: that, "although he was an heretic, and his ad-
> versary, ye he was a learned adversary."[1]

This is the more remarkable given the unsparing criticism which Whitaker poured forth upon the Jesuits in general, and Cardinal Bellarmine in particular.

---

[1] William Whitaker, *A Disputation on Holy Scripture*, translated and edited for The Parker Society by William Fitzgerald (Cambridge: Cambridge University Press, 1849), x.

We know little of Whitaker's early years, as a biography is yet to be attempted. But a few basic details are known. Whitaker was born in Lancashire, England in 1548, the same year the Holy Roman Emperor, Charles V, decreed the *Augsburg Interim*, sending several leading Protestant theologians to England for refuge, and also the year in which Cranmer began work on the *Book of Common Prayer* (which Whitaker would eventually translate into Greek).

After concluding his academic studies (he began his B.A. studies at Trinity College, Cambridge in 1568 and his M.A. in 1571), Whitaker was appointed to a number of influential posts. In 1578 he was installed as the Canon of Norwich Cathedral, and in 1580, Queen Elizabeth appointed him to the Regius Professorship of Divinity and to the chancellorship of St. Paul's, London. In 1595 he became a canon of Canterbury Cathedral.

While William Whitaker is often characterized as a puritan, the matter is not that simple. In a letter, Whitaker wrote the following about arch-puritan Thomas Cartwright: "I have read through a great part of that little book Cartwright recently wrote. If I should ever see anything more negligent and childish, I do not wish to live."[2]

He is chiefly known today for his role in the 1590s controversies over predestination that began in Cambridge and ultimately required the intervention of the Archbishop of Canterbury, John Whitgift to settle the dispute. The resulting *Lambeth Articles* of 1597 that Whitgift sought to promulgate (before the Queen put a stop to the whole proceeding) offered a pithy summary of Calvinistic doctrine and were based on an initial draft composed by Whitaker. Despite his many posts of authority and influence, and his voluminous writings, it appears that Whitaker died in relative poverty at the age of 47.

During his own life, Whitaker was best known as an untiring polemicist against Roman Catholic doctrine. If Bellarmine consid-

---

[2] Letter quoted in Richard Bancroft, *A Survey of the Pretended Holy Discipline* (London, 1593), 379.

ered Whitaker his worthiest opponent, Whitaker seems to have thought likewise of Bellarmine, singling him out in the Dedicatory Epistle of the *Disputation on Holy Scripture* as more learned and honest than all his predecessors. The *Disputation* appeared as a response to the first volume of Bellarmine's celebrated *Controversies of the Christian Faith*, excerpted above. Even though most of Whitaker's works are polemics against the Roman Catholic system, his works proved significant in the development of Protestant Orthodoxy, and he was highly esteemed by English theologians both conformist and Puritan over the following century.

The excerpt in this anthology is taken from Whitaker's *Disputation on Holy Scripture*. In this work, Whitaker defends the Protestant understanding of the Scriptures against the various arguments of Bellarmine. In the first chapter, Whitaker argues for what is today known as the Protestant Canon, in the second he argues for the authentic edition of Scriptures and against the supreme status of the Latin Vulgate. In the third chapter he contends that the Scriptures are authoritative because the Word inspired by God and thus require nothing else to ground their authority. In chapter 5, from which our excerpt is taken, he argues for the perspicuity of Scripture, discussing questions of who can interpret Scripture and how Scripture ought to be interpreted. In the final chapter, Whitaker argues that the Scriptures are perfect and thus do not need to be supplemented by sacred tradition.

In this work, Whitaker demonstrates a profound familiarity with the authors of the Early and Medieval Church, but he also shows himself familiar with the more current Roman Catholic literature. For instance, in the first chapter of this work, the reader may be startled to find Whitaker quoting the Catholic apologist Cajetan in support of his argument for the non-canonical status of the Apocrypha.[3]

The protestant commitment to the perspicuity of Scripture is often characterized as maintaining that all things in Scripture are

---

[3] See Whitaker, *Disputation*, 48.

perfectly clear, but this is hardly accurate. In this excerpt, Whitaker provides us with the classical Protestant understanding of perspicuity: that the Scriptures are sufficiently clear in declaring the key dogmas of the Christian faith. In order to make his case, Whitaker outlines and responds to five arguments from Bellarmine and then puts forward twelve arguments for the perspicuity of Scripture. Whitaker's lucid arguments in this work were to have a lasting legacy; indeed, some have gone so far as to argue that William Whitaker's *Disputation on Holy Scripture* was the single most significant influence upon the chapter on the Holy Scriptures of the *Westminster Confession of Faith*.[4]

Further Reading

For further reading, see Peter Lake, *Moderate Puritans in the Elizabethan Church* (Cambridge: Cambridge University Press, 1982), chs. 8–9; Mark Thompson, *A Clear and Present Word: The Clarity of Scripture* (Downers Grove, IL: IVP Academic, 2006).

---

[4] Garnet Howard Milne, *The Westminster Confession of Faith and the Cessation of Special Revelation* (Milton Keynes, UK: Paternoster, 2007), 52.

WILLIAM WHITAKER,
A DISPUTATION ON HOLY SCRIPTURE
AGAINST THE PAPISTS, ESPECIALLY
BELLARMINE AND STAPLETON (1588)[1]

The First Controversy: Question IV, Concerning the Perspicuity of Scripture

Chapter I: Of the State of the Question

IN COMMENCING to speak of this question, we must return to that foundation which was laid at the beginning. In John 5:39, Christ says, "Search the scriptures." The precept of Christ, therefore, is plain, declaring that the scriptures should be searched, whence the question arises whether those sacred scriptures, which we are commanded to search, are so full of obscurity and difficulty as to be unintelligible to us, or whether there be not rather a light and clearness and perspicuity in scripture so as to make it no useless task for the people to be engaged and occupied in their perusal. Here, therefore, we have to dispute concerning the nature of scripture. But, before coming to the argument, we must see what is the opinion of our adversaries upon this matter, and what is our own. As to our own opinion, the papists certainly either do not understand it, or if they do, treat us unfairly and slander us in an impudent manner. For we never said that everything in scripture is easy,

---

[1] Taken from William Fitzgerald, trans. and ed., *A Disputation on Holy Scripture Against the Papists, especially Bellarmine and Stapleton* (Cambridge: Cambridge University Press, 1849).

perspicuous, and plain; that there is nothing obscure, nothing difficult to be understood, but we confess openly that there are many
obscure and difficult passages of scripture, and yet these men object to us this, and affirm that we maintain the scriptures to be perfectly easy.

The council of Trent hath defined or expressly determined
nothing upon this matter. We must, therefore, investigate the opinion of our adversaries by the help of other writings of papists, so as
to be enabled to discover the true state of the controversy. Eckius,
the most insolent of popish writers, in his *Enchiridion*, writing of the
scripture, objects to us this opinion, that the scripture is so easy
that even the ignorant people may and ought to read it (*Loc. 14*).
His words are these: "The Lutherans contend that the sacred scriptures are clear, and accordingly laymen and doting old women treat
of them in a style of authority." Whence we understand that their
mind and opinion is that the people are to be kept from reading the
scriptures because they are so obscure as that they cannot be understood by laics, women, and the vulgar. We hold the contrary,
that the scriptures are not so difficult, but that they may be read
with advantage and ought to be read by the people. Hosius also, in
his third book of the authority of the church against Brentius, is
copious in proving and establishing the exceeding great obscurity
of the sacred writings. So the Censors of Cologne, against
Monhemius, write to precisely the same effect: for they say in their
preface that the difficulty of scripture "may be argument enough
that all are not to be indiscriminately admitted to the reading of it."
Hence they conclude that the unlearned are to be prohibited reading scripture, even the history of Christ's passion, in which they say
that there are so many doubtful points that even the learned can
hardly reconcile them. Thus they permit no part of scripture to the
people, not even that most sweet and easy narrative, altogether
worthy of our perusal and meditation, which contains the history
of the death of Christ. Andradius disputes largely upon the obscurity of scripture (*Orthodox. Explic.,* II). Lindanus, in his *Panoplia*, affirms of all scripture that which Peter said only of certain subjects

handled in Paul's Epistles: for he says that there are, throughout the whole body of scripture, many things "hard to be understood," and that such is the unanimous opinion of divines (III.6). Stapleton says that the church ought to interpret scripture on account of the difficulties which present themselves generally and in most places (X.2). The Rhemists, in their annotations upon 2 Pet. 3:16, say that the whole scripture is difficult, but especially the Epistles of Paul; whereas Peter, as shall appear hereafter, affirms neither: all that Peter observes is that there are some things in Paul's Epistles "hard to be understood, which the unlearned wrest, as they do the other scriptures, to their own destruction." What they subjoin out of Augustine, that of all things which Paul taught, nothing is more difficult than what he writes concerning the righteousness of faith, can by no means be conceded. For if Paul ever said anything plainly, he hath declared his mind upon this subject in a perspicuous discourse. The same Rhemists, in their marginal annotation upon Luke 6:1, attribute to us this opinion, "that all things are very easy." The Jesuit Bellarmine affirms that there are many obscurities in scripture, which we also concede, but when he determines the state of the question to be this, whether scripture be so plain of itself as to suffice without any interpretation for deciding and putting an end to all controversies of faith of its own self, he fights without an adversary; at least he hath no adversaries in us upon this point. Prateolus, in his *Elenchus Haereticorum*, says that it is the common article of all sectaries to affirm that the scriptures are clear of themselves and need no interpretation (XVII.20). Sixtus Senensis, in his *Bibliotheca*, objects to us this error: that we say that the whole scriptures are so clear and perspicuous of their own nature as to be capable of being understood by anyone, however illiterate, unless some external obstacle be interposed (VI, *Annot.* 151). Costerus the Jesuit, in his *Enchiridion of Controversies* lately published, confesses that many things in scripture are plain, but adds that many things are not of such a nature as to be intelligible to everybody without any trouble.

But they do us injustice, and openly preach falsehood concerning us, when they affirm us to say that all things in scripture are so plain that they may be understood by any unlearned person, and need no exposition or interpretation. Hence we see, both what they think, namely, that the scriptures are so obscure that they ought not to be read by the unlearned, and what they say, but falsely say that we think, that all things are plain in the scriptures and that they suffice without any interpretation to determine all controversies. Let us now see what our opinion really is. Luther, in his assertion of the articles condemned by Leo X, in the preface says that the scripture is its own most plain, easy, and certain interpreter, proving, judging, and illustrating all things. This is said by him most truly, if it be candidly understood. The same author, in his book of the *Slavery of the Will against the Diatribe of Erasmus*, writes almost in the beginning that in the scriptures there is nothing abstruse, nothing obscure, but that all things are plain. And because this may seem a paradox, he afterwards explains himself thus: he confesses that many places of scripture are obscure, that there are many words and sentences shrouded in difficulty, but he affirms nevertheless that no dogma is obscure, as, for instance, that God is one and three, that Christ hath suffered, and will reign forever, and so forth. All which is perfectly true, for although there is much obscurity in many words and passages, yet all the articles of faith are plain. Stapleton interprets these words of Luther as if he said that all the difficulty of scripture arose from ignorance of grammar and figures, and he objects to us Origen and Jerome, who certainly were exquisitely skilled in grammar and rhetoric, and yet confess themselves that they were ignorant of many things, and may have erred in many places (III.3). We answer that what he blames in Luther is most true, if it be rightly understood: for he who can always arrive at the grammatical sense of scripture, will, beyond all doubt, best explain and interpret the scriptures. But hitherto no one hath been able to do this everywhere and in all places. Certainly the grammatical meaning of scripture, as it is ever the best and truest, so is it sometimes the hardest to be found, so that it is no wonder that Origen and Jerome himself, although both of them most skill-ful grammarians, may have erred in the interpretation of scripture. Luther adds besides that the things themselves are manifest in scripture, and that therefore we need not be put to much trouble, if the words be sometimes in many places less manifest. His words are these: "The things themselves are in light; we need not care, therefore, though some signs of the things be in darkness." But some persons complain greatly of the obscurity of the things also, so that this distinction of Luther's between the things and the signs of the things may seem to be idle. Luther answers that this occurs, not from the obscurity and difficulty of the things themselves, but from our blindness and ignorance. And this he very properly con-firms by the testimony of Paul (2 Cor. 3:14, 15, 16), where Paul says that "the veil is placed upon the hearts of the Jews until this very day, which veil is done away in Christ," and from 2 Cor. 4:3, where the same apostle says, "If our gospel be hid, it is hid to them which are lost," and he illustrates the same thing by the similitude of the sun and the day, both of which, although very clear in them-selves, are invisible to the blind. "There is nothing," says he, "brighter than the sun and the day, but the blind man cannot even see the sun, and there are some also who flee the light." Stapleton endeavors to take this answer from him. He says that Luther, in this way, condemns all the fathers, and so all antiquity, of error and blindness. But I answer that Luther is speaking of things, that is, of the nature of the doctrine and of the articles of the Christian reli-gion, the truth of which (though not of all, yet of those which are necessary to salvation), it is manifest from their writings, was thor-oughly seen by the fathers. He is not speaking of the several words and passages wherein they might sometimes easily err, without, nevertheless, in the least incurring the blame of blindness on that account.

But Erasmus in his *Diatribe* contends that even some dogmas are obscure, as the doctrine of the Trinity, of the distinction of Per-sons, of sin against the Holy Ghost, and such like, and to this sense he tortures that passage which is contained in Rom. 9:33, where

Paul says that the "judgments of God are unsearchable, and his ways past finding out." Luther answers that these doctrines are indeed obscure in themselves, but that they are plain so far forth as they are proposed in scripture, if we will be content with that knowledge which God hath propounded and conceded to his church in the scripture, and not search into everything more curiously than becomes us. But as to the passage from Paul, he answers that indeed the things of God are obscure, but that the things of scripture are clear; that the judgments of God concerning the number of the elect, the day and hour of the judgment, and suchlike, are unknown and inscrutable, but that those things which God hath revealed in his word are by no means inscrutable to us; and that Paul in that place spoke of the things of God, not of the things of scripture. Furthermore, he says that the reason why so many dispute about the things of scripture is to be found in the perversity and depraved desires of men, especially the sophists and schoolmen, who, not content with the simplicity of scripture, have rendered everything obscure and intricate by their traps and devices, but that the scripture must not be falsely blamed on account of men's abuse of it. Luther uses another distinction also in that place. He says that the perspicuity or obscurity of scripture is either internal or external; the internal is that of the heart itself, the external is in the words. If we speak of the internal obscurity or perspicuity of scripture, he says that not even one jot is in this way clear in the scripture without the internal light of the Holy Spirit, for that all things in this view and respect are obscure to the fleshly understanding of men, according to that which is said in Ps. 14[:1]: "The fool hath said in his heart that there is no God." But if we understand the external clearness or obscurity of scripture, he says that all doctrines are in this way clear, and brought to light in the ministry of the word. And this distinction is very necessary, for although, in the external way, we perfectly hold all the doctrines of religion, we yet understand nothing internally to salvation, nor have learned any dogma aright, without the teaching of the Holy Spirit.

Assuredly, this is the difference between theology and philosophy, since it is only the external light of nature that is required to learn thoroughly the arts of philosophy, but to understand theology aright, there is need of the internal light of the Holy Spirit, because the things of faith are not subject to the teaching of mere human reason. We may, in a certain manner, be acquainted with the doctrines of scripture and obtain an historical faith by the ministry of the word, so as to know all the articles of faith and deem them to be true, and all without the inward light of the Spirit, as many impious men and devils do, but we cannot have the πληροφορία, that is, a certain, solid, and saving knowledge, without the Holy Spirit internally illuminating our minds. And this internal clearness it is which wholly flows from the Holy Ghost. Other arts serve our purpose when only externally understood, but this is of no avail unless understood internally. Meanwhile Luther was far from such madness as to say that there was nothing difficult in scripture, or that it did not need an interpretation. Yea, on the contrary, in the preface to his Commentary upon the Psalms, he acknowledges that there are many obscurities and difficulties in the scripture, which God hath left us, as if on purpose to keep us constantly scholars in the school of the Holy Spirit. And in the same place he affirms that a man must be impudent who would say that he understood even any one book thoroughly, and the same hath ever been the opinion of us all.

The state of the question, therefore, is not really such as the papists would have it appear, but our fundamental principles are these: first, that the scriptures are sufficiently clear to admit of their being read by the people and the unlearned with some fruit and utility; secondly, that all things necessary to salvation are propounded in plain words in the scriptures. Meanwhile, we concede that there are many obscure places, and that the scriptures need explication, and that on this account God's ministers are to be listened to when they expound the word of God, and the men best skilled in scripture are to be consulted. So far concerning the state of the question.

Chapter II: Why God Would Have Many Obscurities in the Scriptures

We should carefully bear in memory the preceding distinctions drawn by Luther, for they are sufficient to obviate almost all the arguments of the papists in this question. But before proceeding to their arguments, I have thought it proper to set forth the reasons on account of which God was willing that there should be so many things of considerable obscurity and difficulty in the scriptures. This contributes much to the better understanding of the matter upon which we treat. The fathers write excellently well upon this subject, as Clemens Alexandrinus, *Stromat.* VI.1, Augustine, *de Doct. Christ.* II, Gregory, *Homil. 6 in Ezekiel,* and others.

Now the causes are such as follow: First, God would have us to be constant in prayer, and hath scattered many obscurities up and down through the scriptures, in order that we should seek his help in interpreting them and discovering their true meaning.

Secondly, he wished thereby to excite our diligence in reading, meditating upon, searching and comparing the scriptures, for if everything had been plain, we should have been entirely slothful and negligent.

Thirdly, he designed to prevent our losing interest in them, for we are ready to grow weary of easy things: God, therefore, would have our interest kept up by difficulties.

Fourthly, God willed to have that truth, so sublime, so heavenly, sought and found with so much labor, the more esteemed by us on that account. For we generally despise and contemn whatever is easily acquired, near at hand, and costs small or no labor, according to the Greek proverb, επὶ θύρας τὴν ὑδρίαν [to break the pitcher upon the very door]. But those things which we find with great toil and much exertion, those, when once we have found them out, we esteem highly and consider their value proportionally greater.

Fifthly, God wished by this means to subdue our pride and arrogance, and to expose to us our ignorance. We are apt to think too honorably of ourselves, and to rate our genius and acuteness more highly than is fitting, and to promise ourselves too much from our science and knowledge.

Sixthly, God willed that the sacred mysteries of his word should be opened freely to pure and holy minds, not exposed to dogs and swine. Hence those things which are easy to holy persons appear so many parables to the profane. For the mysteries of scripture are like gems, which only he that knows them values, while the rest, like the cock in Aesop, despise them, and prefer the most worthless objects to what is most beautiful and excellent.

Seventhly, God designed to call off our minds from the pursuit of external things and our daily occupations, and transfer them to the study of the scriptures. Hence it is now necessary to give some time to their perusal and study, which we certainly should not bestow upon them, if we found everything plain and open.

Eighthly, God desired thus to accustom us to a certain internal purity and sanctity of thought and feeling. For they who bring with them profane minds to the reading of scripture, lose their trouble and oil: those only read with advantage, who bring with them pure and holy minds.

Ninthly, God willed that in his church some should be teachers, and some disciples; some more learned, to give instruction; others less skillful, to receive it, so as that the honor of the sacred scriptures and the divinely instituted ministry might in this manner be maintained. Such was the wisdom of the Holy Spirit, wherewith, as Augustine expresses it, he hath modified the scriptures so as to maintain their honor and consult our good (*De Doctrina Christ.* II.6). Other causes more besides these might be adduced, but it is not necessary to enumerate more.

Chapter III: Wherein the Arguments of the Papists are Obliviated

Let us come now to the arguments of our adversaries, which indeed might be omitted as neither injuring, nor even touching our cause, nor having any force against us whatsoever, for all that they prove is that there are some difficult passages in scripture, which we concede. Costerus, a papist, in his *Enchiridion* 1, mentions and sets forth some places full of obscurity and difficulties, as 1 Pet. 3:19, where Christ is said to have "preached to the spirits in prison, which were sometime disobedient in the days of Noah," and "What shall they do who are baptized for the dead, if the dead rise not at all?" (1 Cor. 15:29), "If any man's work be burned, he shall suffer loss; yet he himself shall be saved, yet so as by fire" (1 Cor. 3:15). He might verily have produced a thousand such passages, but in order to dispute pertinently against Luther and us, he ought to have shewn some doctrines or articles of faith not openly and plainly set forth in scripture. Bellarmine alleges five arguments in order to prove the scriptures to be obscure, which we acknowledge in some places to be true. But let us see of what sort these arguments are.

His first argument is taken from the authority of scripture, from which he cites some passages. In the first place he reasons thus: David was ignorant of many things, therefore much more we; consequently, the scriptures are obscure. Now that David was ignorant of many things, he proves from Psalm 119, where it is said, "Give me understanding, and I will search thy law," where also the psalmist entreats God "to teach him" his law, to "illuminate his eyes;" and in many places of that same Psalm he ingenuously confesses his ignorance of many things. To the same purpose he alleges what Jerome writes of David: "If so great a prophet confesses the darkness of ignorance, with what night of ignorance do you suppose that we, mere babes and hardly more than sucklings, are surrounded?" (To Paulinus, Ep. 13, *de Institit. Monachi*). From all which he concludes that the scriptures are obscure.

I answer, in the first place, these things do not touch the question. There is no one amongst us who does not confess with David that God is to be constantly besought to teach us his law, to illuminate our hearts, &c. Therefore the example of David is objected to us in vain. Who would believe that these men know what they are saying? Do we indeed affirm that the scripture is so plain that God needs not to be prayed to teach us his law, his will, and his word? No one was ever so impious and so mad. Therefore we ought continually to pray with David that God would give us understanding, that he would open our eyes, illuminate our minds, and teach us himself: otherwise we shall never understand anything aright. For it is not enough to know the words, the letter or the history, but a full persuasion is required. This it was that David sought that he might more and more make progress in true understanding and faith. Secondly, David speaks there not principally of the external understanding (for doubtless he knew the letter, and the grammatical and historical sense of most passages), but of that internal full assurance whereof we read Luke 1:1, in order to the obtaining of which we maintain that we must labor with continual prayers. Thus David was ignorant of some things, and did not perfectly penetrate the meaning of God and the mysteries of his word, which is plain from Jerome himself in that same place quoted by Bellarmine. For thus he subjoins: "Unless the whole of what is written be opened by him who hath the key of David, who openeth and no man shutteth, and shutteth and no man openeth, they can be unfolded by no other hand." The second passage of scripture which he objects is Luke 24:27, from which place he reasons thus: Christ interpreted the scriptures to his disciples, therefore the scriptures are not easy, but need an interpreter. I answer, in the first place, which of us ever took away the interpretation of scripture? Certainly, none of us, for we all readily confess that the scriptures need interpretation.

Secondly, those disciples were crushed and stricken at that time with a sort of amazement, and slow and unapt to understand anything, so that it is no wonder that they could not understand the scriptures without an interpretation. Thirdly, those who understand the grammatical sense of scripture, ought nevertheless to hear the exposition of scripture, to help them to a better understanding. This we never denied.

In the third place, he objects to us the case of the eunuch (Acts 8) whom he states to have been a pious man and studious of the scripture, and to prove this he cites the superfluous testimony of Jerome, from his epistle to Paulinus concerning the study of the scriptures. He, being asked by Philip if he understood what he was reading, replied, "How can I understand, unless some man declare it unto me?" Therefore, says Bellarmine, the scriptures need interpretation. I answer in the first place, we concede that many things in scripture are obscure and need interpretation, therefore this place concludes nothing against us. Secondly, although this eunuch was pious and very studious of scripture, he was yet unskillful and not much familiar with scripture, as is plain from his question, for he asked Philip whether the prophet spoke of himself, or of some other person. Now, we do not say that everything is immediately plain and easy in the scriptures so as to be intelligible to everyone, but we say that those things which at first seem obscure and difficult are afterwards rendered easy, if one be diligent in reading them and bring with him a pure and pious mind. Thirdly, as to Jerome, we say that he speaks of a certain higher understanding and illumination, as is manifest from his own words in that place. For thus he writes of that eunuch: "While he held the book, and conceived in thought, uttered with his tongue and sounded with his lips, the words of the Lord, he knew not him whom in the book he ignorantly worshipped. Philip comes, shews him Jesus, who lay concealed in the letter. O wonderful power of a teacher! In the same hour the eunuch believes, is baptized, and becomes faithful and holy, a master in place of a disciple."

In the fourth place, he objects to us the words of Peter which are contained in 2 Peter 3:16, where Peter says expressly that there are δυσνόητά τινα (some things hard to be understood) in Paul's epistles. And the Jesuit bids us observe that Peter does not say that there are some things hard to be understood merely by the unlearned and unstable, but simply and absolutely δυσνόητά (difficult), whence he wishes to infer that they are difficult to all, though especially to the unlearned. And to this purpose he alleges the testimony of Augustine, where he confesses that a certain place in Paul seems to him very difficult (*De fide et operibus*, 16).

I answer, first, we concede that some places are hard to be understood, therefore, this passage does not make against us. Secondly, Peter does not say that παντα (all things), but only τινα (some things) are hard to be understood. And what if some things be obscure? Yet it follows that the greatest part is plain and easy. Thirdly, Although Peter inveighs against the αμαθεῖς καὶ αστηρίκτους (the unlearned and unstable) who στρεβλοῦσι (wrest) the scriptures, he nevertheless does not debar them altogether from the reading of the scriptures.

Fourthly, Peter does not say that Paul's epistles are obscure, nay, not even that there are some obscurities in Paul's epistles, but only in those things concerning which he himself writes in his own. Now Peter speaks of the last judgment, and the destruction of the world, about which unlearned men had at that time many ridiculous fictions. That Peter is speaking of the subjects, not of the epistles of Paul, is manifest from the very words: for he does not say, εν αἷς (in the epistles), but εν οἷς (in the hard things), which plainly refers to the τοσοῦτος (of these things) immediately preceding. In these matters and articles of our faith we confess that there are many difficulties, as also in other mysteries of our religion.

The occasion of the mistake arose from the vulgate version, which renders *in quibus* (in this), which is ambiguous. Beza much more properly, in order to remove the ambiguity, translates it *inter quae* (among which). Peter, therefore, speaks not of the character of Paul's epistles.

But the Rhemists endeavor to overturn this reply, in which attempt they shew how stupid they are, while they desire to exhibit their acuteness. They say there is absolutely no difference between these two assertions: This author is difficult and obscure, and, There are many things difficult and obscure in this author. I answer, first, Peter does not say, as they would have him, that *all* or *many* but only *some things* in Paul's epistles are obscure: he narrows his expression as much as possible. Secondly, these two assertions are not equivalent: for an author may speak perspicuously and plainly of things most obscure and difficult. What is harder to be understood than that God made the world out of nothing, that God took flesh of a virgin, that God and man were one person, that this world shall be destroyed, and our bodies restored again to life after death, surpass our understanding? And yet concerning these the scriptures speak with the utmost clearness and explicitness. So much for Bellarmine's first argument.

His second argument is taken from the common consent of the ancient fathers, of whom he brings forward eight: Irenaeus, Origen, Ruffinus, Chrysostom, Ambrose, Jerome, Augustine, Gregory, all of which very learned fathers may be passed over by us, since they say absolutely nothing that makes against us. For they either say that there are some obscurities in scripture, or that without the internal light of the Spirit the scriptures cannot be rightly understood by us as they ought, both of which propositions we concede. However, let us return some reply, as briefly as we can, to each of the testimonies of these fathers. [...]

Bellarmine's third argument is founded upon necessary reasoning. In scripture, says he, we must consider two things, the things spoken, and the way in which they are spoken. Whichever we regard, there is the greatest difficulty. For firstly, the things are most difficult, namely, the divine mysteries which are delivered in the scriptures of the Trinity, the incarnation of Christ, and such like, and Bellarmine asks why metaphysics are more obscure and difficult than the other sciences, but because of their subject matter—because, that is, they treat of more obscure and difficult things? In the same way he concludes that the scriptures are hard and dark, because hard and dark subjects are treated of therein. I answer by observing that the subjects of scripture are indeed obscure, hidden, abstruse, and mysterious, yet not in themselves but to us. When I say, "in themselves," I do not mean to say it of the nature of the things themselves, as if the things were not all obscure (for I confess that they are obscure), but what I mean is that the subjects of scripture, as they are set forth and delivered in scripture, are not obscure. For example, that God is one in substance and three in persons, that God was made man and such like, although they be in themselves, if we regard the nature of the things themselves so obscure that they can by no means be perceived by us, yet they are proposed plainly in scripture, if we will be content with that knowledge of them which God hath chosen to impart to us. As to the fact that many have written with great acuteness and subtlety of these matters, I say that these subtleties are of no concern to the people, who can be saved without a knowledge of them. Yea, I say besides that some of them are impious and destructive to the very persons who invented them. Scripture would have us be contented with this plain, perspicuous, and simple doctrine, which it delivers. All difficulty therefore, if difficulty there be, in the things, is ours, and springs from ourselves. And so much of the obscurity of the things themselves.

Now as to the manner of expression, he proves the scriptures to be obscure by six reasons. The first reason is because there are many things in the scriptures which may seem at first sight contradictory and plainly repugnant to each other, such as these two places, Exod. 20:5, where God threatens that he "will visit the sins of the fathers upon the children, unto the third and fourth generation," and Ezekiel 18:20, where we read that the very soul which sinneth shall die, and that "the son shall not bear the iniquity of the father."

I answer: some things may seem contradictory in scripture to a man who does not consider them with sufficient attention, yet it is certain, nevertheless, that scripture is in perfect harmony with itself. God willed that some such shews of contradiction should occur in scripture that we might be so the more excited to diligence in reading, meditating upon, and collating the passages together, wherein whosoever shall use diligence, as Augustine formerly did in harmonizing the evangelists, will easily reconcile all those places which seem repugnant to each other. As to these passages, one readily perceives that they agree. For it is certain that God punishes men for their own, and not for other people's sins, as we are told

(Ezek. 18:20). Therefore, what is said of the punishment of parents being derived upon their posterity (Exod. 20:5) must needs be understood with this condition, if their posterity continue in their wickedness, for if they avoid their parents' sins they will not be subjected to their punishments.

The second reason to prove that the scriptures are obscure in their manner of expression is this: because many words in scripture are ambiguous, and many whole discourses also, as John 8:25: *Principium, qui et loquor vobis* [the beginning, who also speaks to you]. I answer: this is, indeed, ambiguous, and false, and utterly ridiculous, but only in the Vulgate version: for it should be translated, *quod loquor* [what I speak], not *qui loquor* [I who speak]. But in the Greek text all is easy; for the words are τὴν αρχὴν ο τι καὶ λαλῶ υμῖν [from the beginning, that which I also have been telling to you], that is, κατὰ τὴν αρχὴν [from the beginning]. Of which words this meaning is obvious enough: I am no other than what I have said that I was from the beginning.

The third reason is, because there are many imperfect speeches and sentences in scripture, as in Rom. 5:12, ὥσπερ occurs without anything to correspond to it, where the Jesuit says that the principal word is wanting. I answer that I cannot discover what word he means. I confess that there is a want of an apodosis, but the sentence is not so obscure as to be unintelligible, and the apostle seems afterwards to have subjoined the other member which corresponds to this.

The fourth reason is because there are in scripture many sentences put out of order, as Gen. 10:31, we find it written thus, "These are the children of Shem, according to their families and their tongues," but in chap. 11, at the very commencement, the whole earth is said to have been at that time of one lip and one tongue. I answer, first, that in every discourse, and especially in histories, some inversion of the order of time (ὕστερον πρότερον) is common. The rule of Ticonius given long ago was that some things are related in scripture by way of anticipation, so as to be told briefly before they occurred, in order to prepare and make more intelligible a fuller exposition of each circumstance in its proper place. And Augustine hath admirably explained that place in the following manner: "Although, therefore, these nations are said to have had their several languages, yet the historian returns back to that time when they all had but one language, and setting out from thence, he now explains what occurred to produce a diversity of languages" (*De Civit. Dei*, XVI.4). Secondly, it should not be translated, "The people was of one speech," but, "had been of one speech," and so indeed Tremellius most fittingly and correctly renders it so as to remove all ambiguity, to which version the Hebrew text is no way repugnant.

The fifth reason is because there are in the scriptures some phrases proper and peculiar to the Hebrew tongue, which are to us very hard to be understood, as Ps. 89:29, "like the days of heaven," as if there were day and night in heaven, or as if heaven lived by day and night like men. So Ps. 119:108: "My soul is always in my hand." I answer that there are, indeed, in the Hebrew, as in other tongues, certain idioms and phrases proper and peculiar to that language, yet such nevertheless as to be readily intelligible to those who are practiced in the scriptures, and such as express the meaning with a singular sort of emphasis and grace. For who is so dull as not to understand what such modes of speech as these denote "God spake by the hand of Jeremiah," or, "The word of the Lord came by the hand of Zechariah," that is, by the ministry of that prophet? So, "His throne is like the days of heaven," that is, shall endure perpetually like heaven itself, and, "my soul is in my hand," that is, is exposed to every danger.

The sixth reason why the scriptures are obscure in their mode of expression is this, because there are many tropes, many figures and schemes of rhetoric in scripture, as metaphors, ironies, metonymies, inversions, and such like. I answer and say that scripture is not obscured, but illustrated, by these tropes and figures. For even the rhetoricians themselves teach that tropes are to be employed for the purpose not of obscuring speech, but of lending to it ornament and light. Augustine writes thus upon this subject:

"No one doubts that things are more pleasantly understood by similitudes" (*de Doctr. Christ.* II.6). Chrysostom, upon Isaiah 8:7, treating of these words, "Behold the Lord will bring upon them the waters of the river, strong and many, the king of the Assyrians," &c., writes thus: "He hath in a metaphorical way used terms to express both the manners of a native prince and the power of a barbarian. This he does in order (as I have all along told you) to make his discourse more plain." And a little after: "Whenever scripture uses metaphors, it is wont to explain itself more clearly." In the same way Thomas Aquinas, in the first part of *Summ. Quaest. I*, Artic. 9, *respons. ad Arg. 2*: "Whence those things that in one place are spoken under metaphors, are expressed more clearly elsewhere." Therefore, although the scriptures are rendered more obscure in some places by metaphors, yet those metaphors are elsewhere explained so as to leave no obscurity in the discourse or sentence. So much for Bellarmine's third argument. [...]

Chapter IV: The Arguments of Our Writers Attacked by Bellarmine are Defended

Now follow the arguments upon our side. We shall use in this place those very arguments which Luther and Brentius formerly used against the papists, and to which our Jesuit endeavors to reply. They are nine in number, to which we will add three, and so this whole cause will be concluded in twelve arguments.

We have explained the state of the question above, and have shewn what the papists and we hold respectively. Our opinion is that the scriptures are not so difficult, but that those who read them attentively may receive from thence advantage and the greatest edification, even laymen, plebeians and the common mass of mankind. This we establish by the following arguments, whereof the first is taken from Deut. 30:11, where we read it thus written: "This commandment which I command thee this day is not hidden from thee, nor far from thee: it is not in heaven, that thou shouldest say, 'Who shall ascend for us into heaven, and take it for us, and tell it unto us that we may do it?' Neither is it beyond the sea, that thou shouldest say, 'Who shall pass over for us beyond the sea, and take it for us, and tell it unto us that we may do it?' But this word is very nigh thee, in thy mouth, and in thy heart, that thou mayest do it." From which words it is evident that the scriptures may be easily understood.

The Jesuit alleges a two-fold answer. First, he says that the ancients interpret this place, not of the facility of understanding the commandments of God, but of the facility of fulfilling them, and he brings Tertullian, *contra Marcion* IV, Origen, Ambrose, Chrysostom, *Comment. in 10 Rom.* as testimonies, and he says that thus this place makes against the Lutherans, who deny that the law of God can be fulfilled.

I answer, first, that it belongs to our purpose now to dispute of the meaning of this place and inquire how it is used by the apostle in the 10th chapter of the Romans. We have only to see whether it can be concluded from this place that the scripture is easy, which indeed is plain from the words themselves: first, because it says, that "the commandment is not hidden," next, because it says that there is no need that any one should "ascend into heaven and declare it unto us, or that we should pass over the sea" and seek it in foreign regions, whereby the sacred writer takes away the excuses which men are wont to make and concludes that this word is near, in the mouth and in the heart, therefore it was not unknown. Thus the meaning is that the will of God was so opened to them in the scriptures that they could not be ignorant of it or allege any excuse of ignorance. Secondly, if that be true which these fathers say, then that which we contend for must so much the rather be conceded. For if the commandments of God can be easily obeyed, then certainly they can more easily be understood. For it is much more easy to understand God's precepts than to fulfil them, and one cannot possibly do that which he does not understand. But the true meaning of the place is that the will of God is plainly revealed to us in the scriptures. Thirdly, the Lutherans truly deny that the law of God can be fulfilled by us, nor is it they only that deny this, but those very fathers also whom Bellarmine alleges, as shall appear afterwards when we come to that controversy.

The Jesuit's second answer (for he distrusts the former one) is this: that those words are to be understood of the facility of understanding the decalogue only, not the whole scripture, for that the decalogue may be easily understood, since the precepts of the decalogue are natural laws, and those Jews could easily know them who had heard them explained by Moses.

I answer: it is certain that Moses is there speaking of the whole will of God, which is declared in the whole of the word and scriptures, and so that this place relates to the entire scripture. For he carefully exhorts the people to walk in all the ways of the Lord, and keep all his precepts, ceremonies and judgments. And, in order that these might be the better understood, the monuments of scripture are delivered by Moses, as we find in Deut. 31: 9. But let us take what he gives. For if he concede the Decalogue to be plain and clear, it will follow that the historic and prophetic books are still more easy, which are, for the most part, a sort of commentary upon the Decalogue and contain in them a plainer and fuller exposition of its meaning. The Decalogue is everywhere repeated, inculcated, explained in the other books of scripture. Now no one will say that the text is more easy than the commentary. But that Moses does not speak only of the Decalogue is clear from the preceding verse and from Augustine, *Quaest. 54 in Deut.* and De Lyra upon the place, and Hieronymus *ab Oleastro*, a papist himself, who says, in his commentary on these words that Moses speaks of "the whole law," and then subjoins, "that we should be very grateful to God for making those things which are necessary to salvation easy, and reducing them to a small number," and in what sense he calls them easy, he shews before, where he says, "that the commandments of God are not difficult and hidden, but easy to be understood, said, and done." There is no reason why I should make any larger defense or discourse upon our first argument.

Our second argument is to this effect: in Ps. 19:9, the word of God is called clear, and Ps. 119:105, it is called a lamp to our feet and a light to our paths, and Proverbs 6:22, Solomon says, "The commandment is a lamp, and the law is light." From these and similar places it is evident that the word is not so obscure as to be unintelligible, but perspicuous and plain.

The Jesuit's answer to this argument is twofold. First, he says that this is to be understood of the Lord's precepts, not of the whole scripture. I answer: this is manifestly false, for in Ps. 119, the prophet David praises the whole word of God at great length, and prays of God that he may understand it all, not merely some part of it, and in Ps. 19, he speaks of those two things which manifest and declare God to us, and by which men attain to a knowledge of God, the creatures and the word of God, which latter is there described by him under many titles. For it is called the Law or Doctrine of the Lord, the Testimony of the Lord, the Statutes of the Lord, the Precepts of the Lord, the Fear of the Lord, by a metonymy, because it teaches the fear and reverence of the Lord, and this doctrine he declares to be sound and perfect, and to give wisdom to the simple. He therefore did not mean any part, but the whole scripture, the teacher of true and perfect wisdom.

Genebrard, upon Ps. 18, testifies that some interpret the place of the whole scripture, nor is he speaking of our writers, but either of his own or of ancient ones. Indeed, Jerome is plainly of that opinion, and Lyra and many others. Now the third place is likewise to be understood of the whole doctrine of scripture, which the wise prophet calls a lamp and a light. Secondly, the Jesuit says, that if these places be understood of the whole scripture, then the scripture is called clear and a lamp, not because it is easy to be understood, but because it illuminates men when it is understood. I answer, and affirm that it is therefore called a lamp, because it hath in itself a light and brightness wherewith it illuminates others, unless they be absolutely blind, or willfully turn away their eyes from this light. A candle is not kindled that it should be set under a bushel, but that it should shine on all who are in the house. The same is the case of the word of God. Ambrose, in his fourteenth discourse upon Ps. 118 writes thus upon this subject: "Our mouth is fed by the word, when we speak the commandments of the word of God: our inward eye also is fed by the light of the spiritual lamp, which shines before us in the night of this world, lest, as walking in darkness, we should stumble with uncertain steps, and be unable to find the true way." And Augustine, *Concio 23* in Ps. 118 hath these words: "The saying, 'Thy word is a lamp to my feet and a light to my paths, denotes the word which is contained in all the holy scriptures." This entirely overturns the Jesuit's first reply, wherein he determines that this place and others like it are not to be understood of the whole scripture, but only of the precepts of the Lord, for Augustine expressly expounds it of the whole scripture.

The comparison, therefore, of scripture to a lamp is to be understood to mean that we are thereby illuminated, who by nature are plunged in utter darkness, and see and understand nothing of what is pleasing to God. A lamp hath light in itself, whether men look upon that light or not, so also the scripture is clear and perspicuous, whether men be illuminated by it, or receive from it no light whatever. As to what Bellarmine says, that the scripture gives light when understood, it is most certain, for it can give no light otherwise. But we affirm that it may be understood by all who desire to know it, and bestow the pains they ought, even as a lamp may be seen by all who choose to open' their eyes. Then the scripture is called lucid, not only because it hath light in itself, but because it illuminates us, dispels the darkness of our minds, and brings us new light, which is what no lamps can do. For a lamp is beheld by those who have eyes, but to those who are blind no lamp shews light. But the scripture is so full of divine light as to dispel our blindness with its rays, and make us who before saw nothing in this light to see light. Therefore, Ps. 119:130, it is said to illuminate, or bring light to babes.

Our third argument is taken from Matthew 5:14, where Christ thus addresses his apostles: "Ye are the light of the world." Therefore, the apostolic doctrine, and consequently the scripture hath light in itself. So Brentius argues against Soto, and not ill. The Jesuit answers first that this is not spoken of the light of doctrine or of the scriptures, but is to be understood of the light of example and probity of life, and that therefore there is subjoined a little after, "Let your light so shine before men that they may see your good works," &c. I answer, and confess that these words may be understood of the light of conduct, but I say besides that they ought to be understood also of the light of doctrine. And this is manifest from the circumstance that the apostles are, in the same place, compared to salt, in respect of their doctrine and preaching. As the doctrine of the apostles was the salt of the world, so was it also the light of the world. And whereas the Jesuit objects the ensuing words, "Let your light so shine," &c., I say that those words also ought principally to be understood of the light of doctrine, inasmuch as doctrine is the principal work and fruit of an apostle. And so indeed by the fruit of heretics or false apostles (Matt. 7:20) their false doctrine and heretical preaching is signified. And in this manner some of the fathers also expound this place.

Secondly, the Jesuit admits that these words may also be understood of the preaching and doctrine of the apostles, but that this is there called light, as he before observed that the word was called a lamp, not because it is easily understood, but because, when understood, it illuminates the mind and instructs us upon the sublimest subjects. I answer that nothing can be more futile than this reply. As if forsooth the sun had no light in itself unless blind men could see it. For scripture in this matter is like the sun, because it illuminates with that light which it hath in itself all but those who are either blind, or do not choose to turn their eyes towards it. Hosius, however, gives another answer, in his third book against the Prolegomena of Brentius, namely, that the preaching of the apostles was plain and luminous, but that the scripture is not equally plain; that they preached plainly, but that their writings are more obscure. And he uses a comparison to illustrate this: for the orations of Demosthenes now written are much more difficult to be understood than when they were delivered, because many things in them are not now apparent which were then manifest, so as that it may be truly said that a great part of Demosthenes is lacking in the orations of Demosthenes, and the case is the same, he says, with the apostolic writings. Now, as to the solution of this argument, I wish to know in the first place, why the Jesuit, who doubtless had it before him, did not choose to make use of it? It is probable that the cardinal's reply seemed weak to that acute polemic, and that he therefore chose to go in quest of another. However, I answer thus: although the living voice of the apostles, when they preached, had more force in it to move the passions of men, nevertheless, in regard of the sum of evangelic doctrine, the same facility and perspicuity appears in their writings. For if the "word of prophecy" be like a lamp, that is, clear and plain, as Peter expressly affirms (2 Pet. 1:19; where he understands the writings, not the preaching of the prophets, as we shall afterwards prove) then certainly the apostolic word must needs be still clearer and more illustrious. And hence springs our next argument.

For thus we reason in the fourth place: it is written, 2 Pet. 1:19, "We have a more sure word of prophecy, whereunto ye do well that ye take heed, as to a lamp shining in a dark place, until the day dawn and the day-spring arise in your hearts." The prophetic scripture is like a lamp shining in a dark place, therefore, it is illustrious and clear. The Jesuit applies precisely the same answer which he used before, namely, that the words of the prophets are compared to a lamp, not because they are clear and plain and easy to be understood, but because then, when they are understood, they give us light and shew us the way to Christ, who is the sun of righteousness. I answer: it is nevertheless certain that scripture is compared to a lamp, because it hath light and clearness in it, which it also shews to men, unless they are either blind or turn away their eyes from it, as was said before. For as the sun is obscure to no one, nor a lamp when lit and set in the midst, save to the blind and those who shut their eyes, so also is the scripture.

Here also the Jesuit hath departed from Hosius' answer, and made use of another almost contrary to it, and far more futile. The prophetic word illuminates us, and leads to Christ, the sun of righteousness, and is therefore called a lamp, as if one used to kindle a lamp in order to look upon the sun. Hosius says that it is called a lamp, because there are many things in it clear, and because what were formerly shadows and enigmas are now declared by the gospel. What else is this but what we maintain: that there are many things in scripture so clear that any one may understand them. Although, indeed, the apostle said that the scripture was like a lamp, even then when those shadows were not entirely dispelled, for he mentions the prophetic word. The cunning Jesuit saw that our cause was confirmed by this answer, and therefore he devised another, that it is called a lamp because it illuminates if it be understood, although it be plain that it is called a lamp because it shines brightly and speaks perspicuously so as to be capable of being easily seen and understood, as if he were to say, it is not a lamp, unless you see it shining, whereas it is a lamp, and shines, whether you see it or will not see it. The apostle says that it shines *in a dark place*, therefore it dispels the shades. So the scripture dispels the darkness from our mind, by propounding a clear and luminous doctrine, which refutes our errors and shews to us the certain paths of truth.

Our fifth argument is taken from the words of the apostle (2 Cor. 4:3), which are these: "If our gospel be hid, it is hid to them that are lost." Therefore the gospel is plain and manifest, and, consequently, also the evangelic scripture, save only to those who, with a blind impulse, rush headlong upon their own destruction. The Jesuit answers that Paul in that place speaks not of the knowledge and understanding of scripture, but of the knowledge of Christ, and he says that this book was closed to the people of old, but is open to us.

I answer, and say in the first place that it is evident from the second verse of the same chapter that Paul speaks of the knowledge of scripture, and therefore of the whole doctrine of the gospel. For he says that he delivered to the Corinthians the gospel most sincerely, without any deceit or false coloring (μὴ δολοῦντες τὸν λόγον τοῦ Θεοῦ), and then presently follow these words: "If our gospel be hid, it is hid to them that are lost," as if he had said, our doctrine and preaching was so full and clear that none can fail to understand it, but those who choose to perish and have minds averse to God. Besides, if he confess that the knowledge of Christ is manifest in the scriptures, we desire no more, for this is as much as we require or contend for, that all things necessary to salvation may be easily known from scripture. For if we openly and easily know Christ from the scriptures, we certainly understand from the scriptures all things necessary to salvation. These men concede that Christ is openly set forth in the scriptures, from which admission we shall easily prove that the scriptures should be diligently read to the people, that they may understand Christ from the scriptures, since they who have obtained him, and learned him aright, want nothing for eternal salvation.

The fathers also interpret this place of the perspicuity of the doctrine itself. Chrysostom, in his 8th Homily upon these words, says that the apostles had nothing dark (συνεσκιασμένον) either in their life, or in their doctrine and preaching (εν τῷ κηρύγματι). Ambrose also understands these words of the whole gospel delivered by the apostles. So also Oecumenius, for he observes that it is as much as if the apostle had said: the fact that many believe not comes not from our fault, or from the obscurity of the gospel, but from this, that they are reprobate and unfaithful (Ουχ ημῶν ἔγκλημα ἡ ασαφείας τοῦ εὐαγγελίου, αλλὰ τῆς εκείνων απωλείας καὶ τυφλώσεως). Theophylact also says upon this place that the light and brilliancy of the gospel is such as to dazzle the eyes of the impious. Thomas Aquinas upon these words says that the cause why many understand it not is not in the gospel, but in the malice and incredulity of men. Likewise also Cajetan and Catharinus and other papists. Thus the confession of our adversaries confirms our cause that the evangelic scripture and doctrine is clear in itself, obscure or unknown to none but those who are not of the number of the faithful. Therefore the whole cause of obscurity or ignorance is not the difficulty of the things, but the blindness and incredulity of men.

Our sixth argument is as follows: the sum of the whole scripture, which consists in the precepts of the Decalogue, the Creed, the Lord's prayer and the sacraments, hath clear testimonies in the scriptures; therefore the scriptures are clear. The Jesuit puts in this conclusion: therefore the whole scripture is manifest, and denies the consequence. I reply, if by the whole scripture he understands every several passage of scripture, we frame no such argument, but if by the whole scripture he means the sum of doctrine necessary for any man's salvation, then we acknowledge the argument, and say that the whole is clear. As to what he subjoins, that if the articles of faith were clear in scripture then there would not be so many controversies about them, and hence collects that there are not such luminous testimonies to them in scripture, I answer that this is weak reasoning, because on these grounds the scriptures would have nothing whatever certain, plain, or evident. For there is nothing in scripture so plain that some men have not doubted it, as that God is Almighty, that he created heaven and earth, that Christ was born of the Virgin Mary, conceived of the Holy Ghost, and so forth: these are indeed plainly and openly set down in scripture, and yet there are controversies about them. Things therefore are not presently obscure, concerning which there are many controversies, because these so manifold disputes arise rather from the perversity and curiosity of the human mind, than from any real obscurity. The apostle says that the minds of infidels are blinded by the devil, lest they should see that brilliant light and acquiesce in it, which is most true of our adversaries.

Our seventh argument stands thus: there is this difference between the new and the old Testaments that the old Testament is like a book closed and sealed, as we find in Isaiah 29:11, but the new Testament is like a book opened, as we read (Rev. 5). We do not use this argument to prove that the whole scripture was obscure and unknown to the old Jewish people, but to shew that the knowledge of Christians is now much clearer than was formerly that of the Jews. The Jesuit answers by saying that this is true, not of the whole scripture, but only of the mysteries of our redemption which is wrought by Christ.

I answer, if he confess that the scripture is like a book opened, so far as the mysteries of our redemption are concerned, there is certainly no more that we need to demand, for from this admission it will follow immediately that all things necessary to salvation are plain in the scriptures, which is the foundation of our defense. Surely he was overcome and constrained by the force of truth to publish this open and ingenuous confession. But now, if the mysteries of our redemption are clear in the scriptures, why should it not be lawful for the people to read the scriptures and have them constantly in their hands, so as to recognize the goodness of Christ and understand the plan of their redemption and salvation? Jerome, in his *Commentary upon Ezekiel 44*, writes thus upon this subject: "Before the Savior assumed a human body and humbled himself to receive the form of a servant, the law and the prophets and the whole knowledge of scripture was closed up. Paradise was shut up. But after that he hung upon the cross, and said to the thief, 'To-day shalt thou be with me in Paradise,' immediately the veil of the temple was rent, and all things were set open, and, the covering being removed, we can say, 'We all with open face beholding the glory of the Lord are changed into the same image from glory to glory.'" As to what the same Jerome writes elsewhere (namely, in his *Epist. 13, de Instit. Monach. to Paulinus*) that a veil is placed not upon the face of Moses only, but of the apostles and evangelists also, he speaks there of the difficulty of believing without the Holy Spirit, but not of the difficulty of understanding, as is plain from that same place. Let it suffice to have said so much upon our seventh argument.

Our eighth argument is to this effect: the fathers proved their opinions out of the scriptures, therefore the scriptures are clearer than the writings and commentaries of the fathers, for no one proves what is unknown by what is still more unknown. Luther hath this argument in the *Preface of his Articles* condemned by Leo X. The Jesuit answers that the scriptures are indeed, in respect of their truth, clearer and more open than the writings of the fathers, but not in respect of the words. Which surely is a foolish answer, for to say that the scriptures are clearer than the fathers in respect of their truth is nothing more than saying that they are truer. But what sort of a distinction is this? If the truth of scripture be clearer, how can the words be more obscure? For it is from the words that the truth arises. If therefore he confess that the scriptures are plainer than the commentaries of the fathers, in respect of their truth, then he concedes that the truth is plainer in the scriptures than in the writings of any father, which is sufficient. And doubtless if we will compare the scripture with the writings of the fathers, we shall generally find greater obscurity and difficulty in the latter than in the former. There is no less perspicuity in the Gospel of John or in the Epistles of Paul than in Tertullian, in Irenaeus, in certain books of Origen and Jerome, and in some other writings of the fathers. But in all the schoolmen there is such obscurity as is nowhere found in scripture. "The words of scripture," says he, "are more obscure than the words of the fathers." Even if there were some obscurity in the words of scripture greater than in those of the fathers, it would not nevertheless be a just consequence that the scriptures were so obscure that they should not be read by the people. This should rather rouse men to an attentive reading than deter them from reading altogether. Besides, the scriptures speak of necessary things no less plainly than any fathers, or even much more plainly, because the Holy Spirit excels in all powers of expression. Where has Augustine or Chrysostom or any father written more plainly that Christ hath delivered men from their sins and from eternal punishment than the evangelists, than Paul, than Peter, than the rest of those whose ministry the Holy Ghost hath used in writing the scriptures? Surely all necessary things are so plainly set forth in the scripture that he who does not understand them in scripture will never be instructed by any commentaries of the fathers.

Now follows our ninth argument, which is this: formerly, in the earliest times of the church, there were no commentaries upon the scriptures extant, but the fathers read them without commentaries, and yet, even then, the scriptures were understood; therefore they are plain and easy in themselves. This is also an argument of Luther's. The Jesuit answers that the first fathers consulted the apostles themselves, and learned from them the sense of scripture, and afterwards wrote commentaries. And he shews out of Jerome that commentaries on the Apocalypse were published from the very first by Justin Martyr and Irenaeus.

I answer: it is certain that there was a time when the church both read and understood the scriptures without commentaries. For they can produce none before Origen, who published any commentaries upon the scriptures, and he lived two hundred years after Christ. Therefore the church was all that time without commentaries. As to his objection from Jerome's *catalogue*, article *Johannes*, that Justin and Irenaeus wrote commentaries on the Apocalypse, the statement is untrue. For Jerome does not affirm this, but only says that they interpreted the Apocalypse. Perhaps, therefore, they expounded some obscure places in the Apocalypse, but how correctly appears from the circumstance of their establishing the error of the Chiliasts by the authority of this book. But let us grant them to have written something upon this book: will it therefore follow that they published commentaries upon the whole scripture? By no means. Certainly the Apocalypse is a small book compared with the whole of scripture. Besides, the Jews before Christ had no commentaries on the prophets, and yet they understood them. The scriptures, therefore, are not so obscure as the papists wish them to appear. We confess, indeed, that we owe a deep debt of gratitude to those who have written learned commentaries, because by their means we understand scripture with increased facility; but yet that the scriptures may be understood without them is clear from the fact that they were understood before any commentaries were published, and if at the present day no commentaries remained, the scriptures would nevertheless be understood.

INTRODUCTION TO *THE CANONS OF DORT*

THE EARLY 17th century is generally considered to have marked the height of the process of confessionalization, a great sorting out in which the different doctrinal trajectories emerging from the Reformation defined themselves with greater precision and rigor—internally through catechesis and externally through polemics. Today, we often associate this process with a narrow dogmatism and intolerance that needlessly drove wedges between Christians of different persuasions and helped fragment the rich legacy of the Reformation. The poster child for such dogmatism is surely the great 1618-19 Synod of Dort in the Netherlands, which crystallized the so-called "Five Points of Calvinism," doctrines often considered intolerant and intolerable enough on their own, even without the harsh crackdown on Arminian opponents which accompanied and followed the Synod.

Yet there is of course a more favorable take on confessionalization, which sees it as a helpful and necessary endeavor to clarify the teaching of Scripture in the face of common confusions and to safeguard the pure preaching of the gospel against doctrines which would undermine it. To be sure, different Reformation churches (not to mention the Catholic Church) had differing ideas of what direction this clarification should take and what errors should be resisted, and thus confessions could tend to erect walls rather than bringing harmony. But during this period, there were many theologians, churchmen, and even Christian monarchs concerned about this tendency, and keen to use confessions as opportunities to resolve misunderstandings and build consensus. All of these different tendencies can be seen at work in the Synod of Dort and the Canons it produced.

Like most church conflicts of this period, the conflict which gave rise to the Synod was about much more than only doctrine. Since emerging in the 1580s from a successful war of rebellion against persecuting Catholic Spain, the Dutch Provinces and the Dutch Reformed church had a difficult question of identity to resolve, not unlike that which had generated the Puritan controversies in the Church of England: was this a Reformed church, which happened to be Dutch, or a Dutch church, which happened to be Reformed? That is, to what extent should the Protestant church in the Netherlands seek, like the Catholic Church before it, to be the Christian church for the whole people, relatively inclusive and tolerating a certain measure of theological fuzziness and moral laxity? And to what extent should it seek to be a consistently and rigorously Reformed church, excluding the doctrinally dubious and excommunicating the morally delinquent? As in England, the former policy suggested a closer cooperation of church and state authorities, and the latter policy implied a stricter separation of spheres and governments. The situation in the Netherlands was complicated by the lack of political clarity in the newborn republic, with power largely divided between the Advocate-General of Holland, Johan van Oldenbarnevelt (1547–1619), and Maurice of Nassau, the Prince of Orange (1567–1625).

These tensions remained largely in check until 1609, when a twelve-year truce with Spain allowed space for internal tensions to boil to the surface. That same year, Jacobus Arminius (1560–1609), the prestigious Professor of Theology at the University of Leiden, died. For several years Arminius had increasingly disagreed with some of the doctrines of predestination that had become standard in Calvinist Holland, particularly as articulated by his hardline Calvinist colleague Franciscus Gomarus (1563–1641). (Gomarus was a zealous advocate of the minority report of Calvinist theology known as supralapsarianism, which comes dangerously close to making God out to be the author of sin.) Although Arminius was relatively quiet about his doubts, Gomarus forced the issue, and after Arminius's death, many of his friends and supporters escalated the conflict by issuing a Remonstrance against certain features of Calvinistic orthodoxy in 1610. Most Dutch church leaders moved quickly to marginalize the Remonstrants (as they were soon called), but key political leaders, particularly van Oldenbarnevelt, championed their cause. Tensions between church and state, and between van Oldenbarnevelt and Maurice soon intensified the already-heated theological conflict, threatening to tear apart the young republic.

Although certainly imperfect, the resulting Synod that was called at Dort in 1618 proved a remarkable achievement given the highly-fraught situation. Delegates from Reformed churches around Europe were summoned to lend additional weight and scholarship, as well as much-needed outside perspective, on the conflict. Crucial among these was the British delegation, which included the gifted churchman George Carleton, Bishop of Llandaff, and later of Chichester (1559–1628), and the brilliant Cambridge theologian John Davenant, later Bishop of Salisbury (1572–1641). These carried instructions from King James VI and I (1566–1625) to do their utmost to ensure a peaceful and moderate resolution to the controversy, one that excluded genuine errors but not legitimate differences of opinion, and which would open the door to more comprehensive cooperation and reunion among the Protestant churches of Europe.

The British delegation largely succeeded in their mission, preventing the hardline party of Gomarus from using the Synod to define Calvinistic orthodoxy strictly along their own lines, and achieving a nuanced and irenic statement of the particularly disputed matter of the extent of the atonement. To be sure, all this was little comfort for the Remonstrant party in the immediate aftermath of the Synod; Arminian ministers were deprived of their pulpits, and van Oldenbarnevelt was beheaded for treason. But as an abiding theological statement of the central doctrines of grace for the Dutch church, and informally for all the Reformed churches, the Canons produced by the Synod proved an impressive and durable consensus document.

As you will soon find by reading on, the Canons do not, contrary to popular representation, include a statement of "Five Points of Calvinism" as we would normally recognize them. There are "five heads of doctrine" treated (the third and fourth together), but only the fifth lines up with the usual numbering of "TULIP." The first head more or less covers the "second point of Calvinism," unconditional election; the second head the third point, limited atonement (or, more accurately, particular redemption); the third and fourth heads the first and fourth points, total depravity and irresistible (or efficacious) grace; with the fifth covering perseverance of the saints. On each point, however, the Canons are considerably more moderate, nuanced, and judicious than usually represented, anticipating and avoiding many popular stereotypes and critiques of the five points. The tone throughout is more pastoral than scholastic. The concluding section is particularly instructive in this regard, going out of its way to condemn misrepresentations of Calvinistic teaching in the strongest terms. That the elect may live as they please and still be saved, that the damned can try as they might and still be rejected, that God is the author of sin, or that he reprobates just as unconditionally as he elects, all are teachings "which the Reformed Churches not only do not acknowledge, but even detest with their whole soul."

Here, as so often with the statements produced in the course of confessionalization, the attempt at resolving conflict did lead to further division in the course of time, but more through misrepresentation and misreading than through the words of the document itself.

Further Reading

For further reading, see S. Vandergugten, "The Arminian Controversy and the Synod of Dort," *The Clarion* 37.19–20 (September 1989); Aza Goudriaan and Fred van Lieburg, *Revisiting the Synod of Dort, 1618–1619* (Leiden: Brill, 2011); Anthony Milton, *The British Delegation and the Synod of Dort: 1618–1619* (Woodbridge, UK: The Boydell Press, 2005).

THE CANONS OF THE SYNOD OF DORDT[1]

First Head of Doctrine: Of Divine Predestination

Art. 1. AS ALL men have sinned in Adam, lie under the curse, and are obnoxious to eternal death, God would have done no injustice by leaving them all to perish, and delivering them over to condemnation on account of sin, according to the words of the Apostle (Rom. 3:19), 'that every mouth may be stopped, and all the world may become guilty before God;' (3:23) 'for all have sinned, and come short of the glory of God;' and (6:23), 'for the wages of sin is death.'

Art. 2. But 'in this the love of God was manifested, that he sent his only-begotten Son into the world,' 'that whosoever believeth on him should not perish, but have everlasting life' (1 John 4:9; John 3:16).

Art. 3. And that men may be brought to believe, God mercifully sends the messengers of these most joyful tidings to whom he

---

[1] Taken from Philip Schaff, ed., *Creeds of Christendom, Vol. 3: The Creeds of the Evangelical Protestant Churches,* (1877; Grand Rapids: Baker Book House, 1977). Schaff adds this note: [We append the English text of the Canons of Dort from the Constitution of the Reformed (formerly Reformed Dutch) Church in America, published in New York. It contains only the positive articles on the Five Points, and omits the Preface and Conclusion, the rejection of the opposite errors, and the Sentence against the Remonstrants. In this abridged form the Canons of Dort are still in force in said Church, together with the Belgic Confession and the Heidelberg Catechism, although the name Dutch (which had been first formally assumed in 1792) was dropped in 1867 from her ecclesiastical title, the Dutch language being now superseded by the English.]

will, and at what time he pleaseth, by whose ministry men are called to repentance and faith in Christ crucified. 'How then shall they call on him in whom they have not believed? And how shall they believe in him of whom they have not heard? And how shall they hear without a preacher? And how shall they preach, except they be sent?' (Rom. 10:14, 15).

Art. 4. The wrath of God abideth upon those who believe not this gospel, but such as receive it and embrace Jesus the Savior by a true and living faith are by him delivered from the wrath of God and from destruction and have the gift of eternal life conferred upon them.

Art. 5. The cause or guilt of this unbelief, as well as of all other sins is nowise in God, but in man himself, whereas faith in Jesus Christ, and salvation through him is the free gift of God, as it is written, 'By grace ye are saved through faith, and that not of yourselves: it is the gift of God' (Eph. 2:8); and, 'Unto you it is given in the behalf of Christ, not only to believe on him,' etc. (Phil. 1:29).

Art. 6. That some receive the gift of faith from God, and others do not receive it, proceeds from God's eternal decree. 'For known unto God are all his works from the beginning of the world' (Acts 15:18; Eph. 1:11). According to which decree he graciously softens the hearts of the elect, however obstinate, and inclines them to believe, while he leaves the non-elect in his just judgment to their own wickedness and obduracy. And herein is especially displayed the profound, the merciful, and at the same time the righteous discrimination between men, equally involved in ruin; or that decree of election and reprobation, revealed in the Word of God, which, though men of perverse, impure, and unstable minds wrest it to their own destruction, yet to holy and pious souls affords unspeakable consolation.

Art. 7. Election is the unchangeable purpose of God whereby, before the foundation of the world, he hath, out of mere grace, according to the sovereign good pleasure of his own will, chosen from the whole human race, which had fallen through their own

712

fault, from their primitive state of rectitude, into sin and destruction, a certain number of persons to redemption in Christ, whom he from eternity appointed the Mediator and head of the elect, and the foundation of salvation.

This elect number, though by nature neither better nor more deserving than others, but with them involved in one common misery, God hath decreed to give to Christ to be saved by him, and effectually to call and draw them to his communion by his Word and Spirit; to bestow upon them true faith, justification, and sanctification; and having powerfully preserved them in the fellowship of his Son, finally to glorify them for the demonstration of his mercy, and for the praise of the riches of his glorious grace, as it is written, 'According as he hath chosen us in him before the foundation of the world, that we should be holy and without blame before him in love; having predestinated us unto the adoption of children by Jesus Christ to himself, according to the good pleasure of his will, to the praise of the glory of his grace wherein he hath made us accepted in the Beloved' (Eph. 1:4–6). And elsewhere, 'Whom he did predestinate, them he also called; and whom he called, them he also justified; and whom he justified, them he also glorified' (Rom. 8:30).

Art. 8. There are not various decrees of election, but one and the same decree respecting all those who shall be saved both under the Old and New Testament, since the Scripture declares the good pleasure, purpose, and counsel of the divine will to be one, according to which he hath chosen us from eternity, both to grace and to glory, to salvation and the way of salvation, which he hath ordained that we should walk therein.

Art. 9. This election was not founded upon foreseen faith, and the obedience of faith, holiness, or any other good quality or disposition in man, as the prerequisite, cause, or condition on which it depended, but men are chosen to faith and to the obedience of faith, holiness, etc. Therefore election is the fountain of every saving good; from which proceed faith, holiness, and the other gifts of salvation, and finally eternal life itself, as its fruits and effects, according to that of the Apostle. 'He hath chosen us [not because we were, but] that we should be holy and without blame before him in love' (Eph. 1:4).

Art. 10. The good pleasure of God is the sole cause of this gracious election, which doth not consist herein that God, foreseeing all possible qualities of human actions, elected certain of these as a condition of salvation, but that he was pleased out of the common mass of sinners to adopt some certain persons as a peculiar people to himself, as it is written, 'For the children being not yet born, neither having done any good or evil,' etc.; 'it was said [namely, to Rebecca] the elder shall serve the younger; as it is written, Jacob have I loved, but Esau have I hated' (Rom. 9:11–13); and, 'As many as were ordained to eternal life believed' (Acts 8:48).

Art. 11. And as God himself is most wise, unchangeable, omniscient, and omnipotent, so the election made by him can neither be interrupted nor changed, recalled nor annulled; neither can the elect be cast away, nor their number diminished.

Art. 12. The elect in due time, though in various degrees and in different measures, attain the assurance of this their eternal and unchangeable election, not by inquisitively prying into the secret and deep things of God, but by observing in themselves, with a spiritual joy and holy pleasure the infallible fruits of election pointed out in the Word of God, such as a true faith in Christ, filial fear, a godly sorrow for sin, a hungering and thirsting after righteousness, etc.

Art. 13. The sense and certainty of this election afford to the children of God additional matter for daily humiliation before him, for adoring the depth of his mercies, and rendering grateful returns of ardent love to him who first manifested so great love towards them. The consideration of this doctrine of election is so far from encouraging remissness in the observance of the divine commands or from sinking men into carnal security that these, in the just judgment of God, are the usual effects of rash presumption or of idle and wanton trifling with the grace of election, in those who refuse to walk in the ways of the elect.

Art. 14. As the doctrine of divine election by the most wise counsel of God was declared by the Prophets, by Christ himself, and by the Apostles, and is clearly revealed in the Scriptures both of the Old and New Testament, so it is still to be published in due time and place in the Church of God, for which it was peculiarly designed, provided it be done with reverence, in the spirit of discretion and piety, for the glory of God's most holy name, and for enlivening and comforting his people, without vainly attempting to investigate the secret ways of the Most High.

Art. 15. What peculiarly tends to illustrate and recommend to us the eternal and unmerited grace of election is the express testimony of sacred Scripture, that not all, but some only, are elected, while others are passed by in the eternal decree, whom God, out of his sovereign, most just, irreprehensible and unchangeable good pleasure, hath decreed to leave in the common misery into which they have willfully plunged themselves, and not to bestow upon them saving faith and the grace of conversion, but permitting them in his just judgment to follow their own way; at last, for the declaration of his justice, to condemn and punish them forever, not only on account of their unbelief, but also for all their other sins. And this is the decree of reprobation which by no means makes God the author of sin (the very thought of which is blasphemy), but declares him to be an awful, irreprehensible, and righteous judge and avenger.

Art. 16. Those who do not yet experience a lively faith in Christ, an assured confidence of soul, peace of conscience, an earnest endeavor after filial obedience, and glorying in God through Christ, efficaciously wrought in them, and do nevertheless persist in the use of the means which God hath appointed for working these graces in us, ought not to be alarmed at the mention of reprobation, nor to rank themselves among the reprobate, but diligently to persevere in the use of means, and with ardent desires devoutly and humbly to wait for a season of richer grace. Much less cause have they to be terrified by the doctrine of reprobation, who, though they seriously desire to be turned to God, to please him only, and to be delivered from the body of death, cannot yet reach that measure of holiness and faith to which they aspire, since a merciful God has promised that he will not quench the smoking flax, nor break the bruised reed. But this doctrine is justly terrible to those who, regardless of God and of the Savior Jesus Christ, have wholly given themselves up to the cares of the world and the pleasures of the flesh, so long as they are not seriously converted to God.

Art. 17. Since we are to judge of the will of God from his Word, which testifies that the children of believers are holy, not by nature, but in virtue of the covenant of grace, in which they together with the parents are comprehended, godly parents have no reason to doubt of the election and salvation of their children whom it pleaseth God to call out of this life in their infancy.

Art. 18. To those who murmur at the free grace of election, and just severity of reprobation, we answer with the Apostle: 'Nay but, O man, who art thou that repliest against God?' (Rom. 9:20); and quote the language of our Savior: 'Is it not lawful for me to do what I will with mine own?' (Matt. 20:15). And therefore with holy adoration of these mysteries, we exclaim, in the words of the Apostle: 'O the depth of the riches both of the wisdom and knowledge of God! how unsearchable are his judgments, and his ways past finding out! For who hath known the mind of the Lord, or who hath been his counselor? or who hath first given to him, and it shall be recompensed unto him again? For of him, and through him, and to him are all things: to whom be glory forever. Amen' (Rom. 11:33–36).

Second Head of Doctrine: Of the Death of Christ, and the Redemption of Men thereby

Art. I. God is not only supremely merciful, but also supremely just. And his justice requires (as he hath revealed himself in his Word) that our sins committed against his infinite majesty should be punished, not only with temporal, but with eternal punishments, both in body and soul, which we cannot escape unless satisfaction be made to the justice of God.

Art. 2. Since, therefore, we are unable to make that satisfaction in our own persons, or to deliver ourselves from the wrath of God, he hath been pleased of his infinite mercy to give his only-begotten Son for our surety, who was made sin, and became a curse for us and in our stead that he might make satisfaction to divine justice on our behalf.

Art. 3. The death of the Son of God is the only and most perfect sacrifice and satisfaction for sin; is of infinite worth and value, abundantly sufficient to expiate the sins of the whole world.

Art. 4. This death derives its infinite value and dignity from these considerations, because the person who submitted to it was not only really man and perfectly holy, but also the only-begotten Son of God, of the same eternal and infinite essence with the Father and Holy Spirit, which qualifications were necessary to constitute him a Savior for us, and because it was attended with a sense of the wrath and curse of God due to us for sin.

Art. V. Moreover the promise of the gospel is that whosoever believeth in Christ crucified shall not perish, but have everlasting life. This promise, together with the command to repent and believe ought to be declared and published to all nations and to all persons promiscuously and without distinction, to whom God out of his good pleasure sends the gospel.

Art. 6. And, whereas many who are called by the gospel do not repent nor believe in Christ, but perish in unbelief, this is not owing to any defect or insufficiency in the sacrifice offered by Christ upon the cross, but is wholly to be imputed to themselves.

Art. 7. But as many as truly believe, and are delivered and saved from sin and destruction through the death of Christ, are indebted for this benefit solely to the grace of God given them in Christ from everlasting, and not to any merit of their own.

Art. 8. For this was the sovereign counsel and most gracious will and purpose of God the Father, that the quickening and saving efficacy of the most precious death of his Son should extend to all the elect, for bestowing upon them alone the gift of justifying faith, thereby to bring them infallibly to salvation, that is, it was the will of God that Christ by the blood of the cross, whereby he confirmed the new covenant, should effectually redeem out of every people, tribe, nation, and language, all those, and those only, who were from eternity chosen to salvation, and given to him by the Father; that he should confer upon them faith, which together with all the other saving gifts of the Holy Spirit he purchased for them by his death; should purge them from all sin, both original and actual, whether committed before or after believing; and having faithfully preserved them even to the end, should at last bring them free from every spot and blemish to the enjoyment of glory in his own presence forever.

Art. 9. This purpose proceeding from everlasting love towards the elect has from the beginning of the world to this day been powerfully accomplished, and will henceforward still continue to be accomplished, notwithstanding all the ineffectual opposition of the gates of hell, so that the elect in due time may be gathered together into one and that there never may be wanting a Church composed of believers, the foundation of which is laid in the blood of Christ, which may steadfastly love and faithfully serve him as their Savior, who, as a bridegroom for his bride, laid down his life for them upon the cross, and which may celebrate his praises here and through all eternity.

Third and Fourth Heads of Doctrine: Of the Corruption of Man, his Conversion to God, and the Manner thereof

Art. I. Man was originally formed after the image of God. His understanding was adorned with a true and saving knowledge of his Creator, and of spiritual things; his heart and will were upright, all his affections pure, and the whole Man was holy; but revolting from God by the instigation of the devil and abusing the freedom of his own will, he forfeited these excellent gifts, and on the contrary entailed on himself blindness of mind, horrible darkness, vanity, and perverseness of judgment, became wicked, rebellious, and obdurate in heart and will, and impure in [all] his affections.

Art. II. Man after the fall begat children in his own likeness. A corrupt stock produced a corrupt offspring. Hence all the posterity of Adam, Christ only excepted, have derived corruption from their original parent, not by imitation, as the Pelagians of old asserted, but by the propagation of a vicious nature [in consequence of a just judgment of God].

Art. 3. Therefore all men are conceived in sin, and are by nature children of wrath, incapable of any saving good, prone to evil, dead in sin, and in bondage thereto; and, without the regenerating grace of the Holy Spirit, they are neither able nor willing to return to God, to reform the depravity of their nature, nor to dispose themselves to reformation.

Art. 4. There remain, however, in man since the fall, the glimmerings of natural light, whereby he retains some knowledge of God, of natural things, and of the difference between good and evil, and discovers some regard for virtue, good order in society, and for maintaining an orderly external deportment. But so far is this light of nature from being sufficient to bring him to a saving knowledge of God, and to true conversion, that he is incapable of using it aright even in things natural and civil. Nay farther, this light, such as it is, man in various ways renders wholly polluted, and holds it [back] in unrighteousness, by doing which he becomes inexcusable before God.

Art. V. In the same light are we to consider the law of the decalogue, delivered by God to his peculiar people the Jews, by the hands of Moses. For though it discovers the greatness of sin, and more and more convinces man thereof, yet as it neither points out a remedy nor imparts strength to extricate him from misery, and thus being weak through the flesh, leaves the transgressor under the curse, man cannot by this law obtain saving grace.

Art. 6. What, therefore, neither the light of nature nor the law could do, that God performs by the operation of his Holy Spirit through the word or ministry of reconciliation, which is the glad tidings concerning the Messiah, by means whereof it hath pleased God to save such as believe, as well under the Old as under the New Testament.

Art. 7. This mystery of his will God discovered to but a small number under the Old Testament; under the New, he reveals himself to many, without any distinction of people. The cause of this dispensation is not to be ascribed to the superior worth of one nation above another, nor to their making a better use of the light of nature, but results wholly from the sovereign good pleasure and unmerited love of God. Hence they to whom so great and so gracious a blessing is communicated, above their desert, or rather notwithstanding their demerits, are bound to acknowledge it with humble and grateful hearts and with the Apostle to adore, not curiously to pry into the severity and justice of God's judgments displayed in others, to whom this grace is not given.

Art. 8. As many as are called by the gospel are unfeignedly called, for God hath most earnestly and truly declared in his Word what will be acceptable to him, namely, that all who are called should comply with the invitation. He, moreover, seriously promises eternal life and rest to as many as shall come to him, and believe on him.

Art. 9. It is not the fault of the gospel, nor of Christ offered therein, nor of God, who calls men by the gospel, and confers upon them various gifts, that those who are called by the ministry of the Word refuse to come and be converted. The fault lies in themselves; some of whom when called, regardless of their danger, reject the Word of life; others, though they receive it, suffer it not to make a lasting impression on their heart; therefore, their joy, arising only from a temporary faith, soon vanishes and they fall away; while others choke the seed of the Word by perplexing cares and the pleasures of this world, and produce no fruit. This our Savior teaches in the parable of the sower (Matt. 13).

Art. 10. But that others who are called by the gospel obey the call and are converted is not to be ascribed to the proper exercise of freewill, whereby one distinguishes himself above others equally furnished with grace sufficient for faith and conversion (as the proud heresy of Pelagius maintains), but it must be wholly ascribed to God, who, as he hath chosen his own from eternity in Christ, so he [calls them effectually in time] confers upon them faith and repentance, rescues them from the power of darkness and translates them into the kingdom of his own Son that they may show forth the praises of him who hath called them out of darkness into his marvelous light, and may glory not in themselves but in the Lord, according to the testimony of the Apostles in various places.

Art. 11. But when God accomplishes his good pleasure in the elect, or works in them true conversion, he not only causes the gospel to be externally preached to them and powerfully illuminates their minds by his Holy Spirit that they may rightly understand and discern the things of the Spirit of God, but by the efficacy of the same regenerating Spirit he pervades the inmost recesses of the man; he opens the closed and softens the hardened heart and circumcises that which was uncircumcised; infuses new qualities into the will, which, though heretofore dead, he quickens; from being evil, disobedient, and refractory, he renders it good, obedient, and pliable; actuates and strengthens it, that, like a good tree, it may bring forth the fruits of good actions.

Art. 12. And this is the regeneration so highly celebrated in Scripture and denominated a new creation: a resurrection from the dead, a making alive, which God works in us without our aid. But this is nowise effected merely by the external preaching of the gospel, by moral suasion, or such a mode of operation that, after God has performed his part, it still remains in the power of man to be regenerated or not, to be converted or to continue unconverted, but it is evidently a supernatural work, most powerful, and at the same time most delightful, astonishing, mysterious, and ineffable; not inferior in efficacy to creation or the resurrection from the dead, as the Scripture inspired by the author of this work declares, so that all in whose hearts God works in this marvelous manner are certainly, infallibly, and effectually regenerated, and do actually believe. Whereupon the will thus renewed is not only actuated and influenced by God, but, in consequence of this influence, becomes itself active. Wherefore, also, man is himself rightly said to believe and repent, by virtue of that grace received.

Art. 13. The manner of this operation cannot be fully comprehended by believers in this life. Notwithstanding which, they rest satisfied with knowing and experiencing that by this grace of God they are enabled to believe with the heart and to love their Savior.

Art. 14. Faith is therefore to be considered as the gift of God, not on account of its being offered by God to man, to be accepted or rejected at his pleasure, but because it is in reality conferred, breathed, and infused into him; nor even because God bestows the power or ability to believe, and then expects that man should, by the exercise of his own free will, consent to the terms of salvation, and actually believe in Christ; but because he who works in man both to will and to do, and indeed all things in all, produces both the will to believe and the act of believing also.

Art. 15. God is under no obligation to confer this grace upon any, for how can he be indebted to man, who had no previous gift to bestow as a foundation for such recompense? Nay, who has nothing of his own but sin and falsehood. He, therefore, who becomes the subject of this grace owes eternal gratitude to God, and gives him thanks forever. Whoever is not made partaker thereof is either altogether regardless of these spiritual gifts and satisfied with his own condition, or is in no apprehension of danger, and vainly boasts the possession of that which he has not. With respect to those who make an external profession of faith and live regular lives, we are bound, after the example of the Apostle, to judge and speak of them in the most favorable manner, for the secret recesses of the heart are unknown to us. And as to others, who have not yet been called, it is our duty to pray for them to God, who calleth those things which be not as though they were. But we are in no wise to conduct ourselves towards them with haughtiness, as if we had made ourselves to differ.

Art. 16. But as man by the fall did not cease to be a creature endowed with understanding and will, nor did sin, which pervaded the whole race of mankind, deprive him of the human nature, but brought upon him depravity and spiritual death, so also this grace of regeneration does not treat men as senseless stocks and blocks, nor take away their will and its properties, neither does violence thereto, but spiritually quickens, heals, corrects, and at the same time sweetly and powerfully bends it, that where carnal rebellion and resistance formerly prevailed a ready and sincere spiritual obedience begins to reign, in which the true and spiritual restoration and freedom of our will consist. Wherefore, unless the admirable Author of every good work wrought in us, man could have no hope of recovering from his fall by his own free will, by the abuse of which, in a state of innocence, he plunged himself into ruin.

Art. 17. As the almighty operation of God, whereby he prolongs and supports this our natural life, does not exclude, but requires the use of means, by which God of his infinite mercy and goodness hath chosen to exert his influence, so also the beforementioned supernatural operation of God, by which we are regenerated, in nowise excludes or subverts the use of the gospel, which the most wise God has ordained to be the seed of regeneration and food of the soul. Wherefore as the Apostles, and the teachers who succeeded them, piously instructed the people concerning this grace of God, to his glory and the abasement of all pride, and in the meantime, however, neglected not to keep them by the sacred precepts of the gospel, in the exercise of the Word, the sacraments and discipline, so even to this day be it far from either instructors or instructed to presume to tempt God in the Church by separating what he of his good pleasure hath most intimately joined together. For grace is conferred by means of admonitions, and the more readily we perform our duty, the more eminent usually is this blessing of God working in us, and the more directly is his work advanced, to whom alone all the glory, both of means and their saving fruit and efficacy, is forever due. Amen.

Fifth Head Of Doctrine: Of the Perseverance of the Saints

Art. I. Whom God calls, according to his purpose, to the communion of his Son our Lord Jesus Christ, and regenerates by the Holy Spirit, he delivers also from the dominion and slavery of sin in this life, though not altogether from the body of sin and from the infirmities of the flesh, so long as they continue in this world.

Art. II. Hence spring daily sins of infirmity, and hence spots adhere to the best works of the saints, which furnish them with constant matter for humiliation before God, and flying for refuge to Christ crucified; for mortifying the flesh more and more by the spirit of prayer and by holy exercises of piety; and for pressing forward to the goal of perfection, till being at length delivered from this body of death, they are brought to reign with the Lamb of God in heaven.

Art. 3. By reason of these remains of indwelling sin, and the temptations of sin and of the world, those who are converted could not persevere in a state of grace if left to their own strength. But God is faithful, who having conferred grace, mercifully confirms and powerfully preserves them therein, even to the end.

Art. 4. Although the weakness of the flesh cannot prevail against the power of God, who confirms and preserves true believers in a state of grace, yet converts are not always so influenced and actuated by the Spirit of God as not in some particular instances sinfully to deviate from the guidance of divine grace, so as to be seduced by and to comply with the lusts of the flesh; they must therefore be constant in watching and prayer that they be not led into temptation. When these are neglected, they are not only liable to be drawn into great and heinous sins by Satan, the world, and the flesh, but sometimes by the righteous permission of God actually fall into these evils. This the lamentable fall of David, Peter, and other saints described in Holy Scriptures, demonstrates.

Art. 5. By such enormous sins, however, they very highly offend God, incur a deadly guilt, grieve the Holy Spirit, interrupt the exercise of faith, very grievously wound their consciences, and sometimes lose the sense of God's favor, for a time, until on their returning into the right way by serious repentance, the light of God's fatherly countenance again shines upon them.

Art. 6. But God, who is rich in mercy, according to his unchangeable purpose of election, does not wholly withdraw the Holy Spirit from his own people, even in their melancholy falls; nor suffer them to proceed so far as to lose the grace of adoption and forfeit the state of justification, or to commit the sin unto death; nor does he permit them to be totally deserted, and to plunge themselves into everlasting destruction.

Art. 7. For in the first place, in these falls he preserves in them the incorruptible seed of regeneration from perishing or being totally lost; and again, by his Word and Spirit, he certainly and effectually renews them to repentance to a sincere and godly sorrow for their sins that they may seek and obtain remission in the blood of the Mediator; may again experience the favor of a reconciled God, through faith adore his mercies; and henceforward more diligently work out their own salvation with fear and trembling.

Art. 8. Thus, it is not in consequence of their own merits or strength, but of God's free mercy that they do not totally fall from faith and grace, nor continue and perish finally in their backslidings, which, with respect to themselves is not only possible, but would undoubtedly happen, but with respect to God, it is utterly impossible, since his counsel cannot be changed, nor his promise fail, neither can the call according to his purpose be revoked, nor the merit, intercession, and preservation of Christ be rendered ineffectual, nor the sealing of the Holy Spirit be frustrated or obliterated.

Art. 9. Of this preservation of the elect to salvation, and of their perseverance in the faith, true believers for themselves may and do obtain assurance according to the measure of their faith, whereby they arrive at the certain persuasion that they ever will continue true and living members of the Church, and that they experience forgiveness of sins, and will at last inherit eternal life.

Art. 10. This assurance, however, is not produced by any peculiar revelation contrary to, or independent of the Word of God, but springs from faith in God's promises, which he has most abundantly revealed in his Word for our comfort; from the testimony of the Holy Spirit, witnessing with our spirit that we are children and heirs of God (Rom. 8:16), and, lastly, from a serious and holy desire to preserve a good conscience and to perform good works. And if the elect of God were deprived of this solid comfort, that they shall finally obtain the victory, and of this infallible pledge or earnest of eternal glory, they would be of all men the most miserable.

Art. 11. The Scripture moreover testifies that believers in this life have to struggle with various carnal doubts and that under grievous temptations they are not always sensible of this full assurance of faith and certainty of persevering. But God, who is the Father of all consolation, does not suffer them to be tempted above that they are able, but will with the temptation also make a way to escape, that they may be able to bear it (1 Cor. 10:13), and by the Holy Spirit again inspires them with the comfortable assurance of persevering.

Art. 12. This certainty of perseverance, however, is so far from exciting in believers a spirit of pride, or of rendering them carnally secure that, on the contrary, it is the real source of humility, filial reverence, true piety, patience in every tribulation, fervent prayers, constancy in suffering and in confessing the truth, and of solid rejoicing in God, so that the consideration of this benefit should serve as an incentive to the serious and constant practice of gratitude and good works, as appears from the testimonies of Scripture and the examples of the saints.

Art. 13. Neither does renewed confidence of persevering produce licentiousness or a disregard to piety in those who are recovered from backsliding, but it renders them much more careful and solicitous to continue in the ways of the Lord, which he hath ordained that they who walk therein may maintain an assurance of persevering, lest by abusing his fatherly kindness, God should turn away his gracious countenance from them (to behold which is to the godly dearer than life, the withdrawing whereof is more bitter than death), and they in consequence thereof should fall into more grievous torments of conscience.

Art. 14. And as it hath pleased God by the preaching of the gospel to begin this work of grace in us, so he preserves, continues, and perfects it by the hearing and reading of his Word, by meditation thereon, and by the exhortations, threatenings, and promises thereof, as well as by the use of the Sacraments.

Art. 15. The carnal mind is unable to comprehend this doctrine of the perseverance of the saints, and the certainty thereof, which God hath most abundantly revealed in his Word, for the glory of his name and the consolation of pious souls, and which he impresses upon the hearts of the faithful. Satan abhors it; the world ridicules it; the ignorant and hypocrite abuse, and heretics oppose it. But the spouse of Christ hath always most tenderly loved and constantly defended it as an inestimable treasure, and God, against whom neither counsel nor strength can prevail, will dispose her to continue this conduct to the end. Now to this one God, Father, Son, and Holy Spirit be honor and glory forever. Amen.

Conclusion

And this is the perspicuous, simple, and ingenuous declaration of the orthodox doctrine respecting the five articles which have been controverted in the Belgic Churches, and the rejection of the errors with which they have for some time been troubled. This doctrine the Synod judges to be drawn from the Word of God and to be agreeable to the confession of the Reformed Churches. Whence it clearly appears that some, whom such conduct by no means be-

came, have violated all truth, equity, and charity, in wishing to persuade the public:

'That the doctrine of the Reformed Churches concerning
predestination, and the points annexed to it, by its own genius and.
necessary tendency, leads off the minds of men from all piety and
religion; that it is an opiate administered by the flesh and the devil;
and the stronghold of Satan, where he lies in wait for all, and from
which he wounds multitudes, and mortally strikes through many
with the darts both of despair and security; that it makes God the
author of sin, unjust, tyrannical, hypocritical; that it is nothing more
than an interpolated Stoicism, Manicheism, Libertinism, Turkism;
that it renders men carnally secure, since they are persuaded by it
that nothing can hinder the salvation of the elect, let them live as
they please; and, therefore, that they may safely perpetrate every
species of the most atrocious crimes; and that, if the reprobate
should even perform truly all the works of the saints, their obedience would not in the least contribute to their salvation; that the
same doctrine teaches that God, by a mere arbitrary act of his will,
without the least respect or view to any sin, has predestinated the
greatest part of the world to eternal damnation, and has created
them for this very purpose; that in the same manner in which the
election is the fountain and cause of faith and good works, reprobation is the cause of unbelief and impiety; that many children of
the faithful are torn, guiltless, from their mothers' breasts, and ty-
rannically plunged into hell; so that neither baptism nor the prayers
of the Church at their baptism can at all profit them' and many
other things of the same kind which the Reformed Churches not
only do not acknowledge, but even detest with their whole soul.

Wherefore, this Synod of Dort, in the name of the Lord,
conjures as many as piously call upon the name of our Savior Jesus
Christ to judge of the faith of the Reformed Churches, not from
the calumnies which on every side are heaped upon it, nor from the
private expressions of a few among ancient and modern teachers,
often dishonestly quoted, or corrupted and wrested to a meaning
quite foreign to their intention, but from the public confessions of

the Churches themselves, and from this declaration of the orthodox doctrine, confirmed by the unanimous consent of all and each
of the members of the whole Synod. Moreover, the Synod warns
calumniators themselves to consider the terrible judgment of God
which awaits them, for bearing false witness against the confessions
of so many Churches, for distressing the consciences of the weak,
and for laboring to render suspected the society of the truly faithful.

Finally, this Synod exhorts all their brethren in the gospel of
Christ to conduct themselves piously and religiously in handling
this doctrine, both in the universities and churches; to direct it, as
well in discourse as in writing, to the glory of the Divine name, to
holiness of life, and to the consolation of afflicted souls; to regulate, by the Scripture, according to the analogy of faith, not only
their sentiments, but also their language, and to abstain from all
those phrases which exceed the limits necessary to be observed in
ascertaining the genuine sense of the Holy Scriptures, and may furnish insolent sophists with a just pretext for violently assailing, or
even vilifying, the doctrine of the Reformed Churches.

May Jesus Christ, the Son of God, who, seated at the Father's right hand, gives gifts to men, sanctify us in the truth; bring
to the truth those who err; shut the mouths of the calumniators of
sound doctrine, and endue the faithful ministers of his Word with
the spirit of wisdom and discretion, that all their discourses may
tend to the glory of God, and the edification of those who hear
them. Amen.

That this is our faith and decision, we certify by subscribing
our names.

Here follow the names, not only of president, assistant president, and secretaries of the Synod, and of the professors of theology in the Dutch Churches, but of all the members who were deputed to the Synod as the Representatives of their respective
Churches; that is, of the Delegates from Great Britain, the Elec-
toral Palatinate, Hessia, Switzerland, Wetteraw, the Republic and
Church of Geneva, the Republic and Church of Bremen, the Re-

729

public and Church of Emden, the Duchy of Gelderland, and of
Zutphen, South Holland, North Holland, Zealand, the Province of
Utrecht, Friesland, Transisalania, the State of Groningen, and Om-
land, Drent, and the French Churches.

INDEX

WANT TO SUGGEST IMPROVEMENTS?

Given our desire to build on what we have begun here and to make this work as truthful, faithful, and useful as possible, we invite corrections and suggested improvements from all our readers (be they as small as a typo or as large as suggesting a different text selection that might profitably be substituted). If you desire to submit such a suggestion or correction, please email it to secretary@davenantinstitute.org and we will take it under consideration for inclusion in the next revised edition.

ABOUT THE DAVENANT INSTITUTE

The Davenant Institute supports the renewal of Christian wisdom for the contemporary church. It seeks to sponsor historical scholarship at the intersection of the church and academy, build networks of friendship and collaboration within the Reformed and evangelical world, and equip the saints with time-tested resources for faithful public witness.

We are a nonprofit organization supported by your tax-deductible gifts. Learn more about us, and donate, at www.davenantinstitute.org.